The Orthodox Christian Conspiracy

How Church Fathers Suppressed Original Gnostic Christianity

By Joseph P. Macchio
With Stephen Macchio

INFI(∞)ITY
PUBLISHING.COM

ISBN 0-7414-5516-1

Published by:
INFI∞ITY
PUBLISHING.COM
1094 New DeHaven Street, Suite 100
West Conshohocken, PA 19428-2713
Info@buybooksontheweb.com
www.buybooksontheweb.com
Toll-free (877) BUY BOOK
Local Phone (610) 941-9999
Fax (610) 941-9959

Printed in the United States of America
Published May 2010

Acknowledgments

I, Joseph, wish to express my heartfelt gratitude to my wife Maureen for encouraging and standing by me during the writing of this book. It is her love, which caused the seeds to sprout, grow, and yield the abundant harvest.

We offer special thanks to our mother, Kathleen, who first typed the manuscript and to Stephen Robbins Ph.D., who transferred the manuscript to computer and assisted in clarifying certain passages, editing others and offering invaluable suggestions and contributions.

We are and will always be sincerely grateful to Elizabeth Clare Prophet for her books, *The Lost Years of Jesus* and *The Lost Teachings of Jesus*, and for her inspiration, invaluable spiritual guidance and love. We are also indebted to Helena Blavatsky and the Theosophical Society.

We give special thanks to Stephan Hoeller for his brilliant analysis of Gnostic Theology; to Duncan Greenlees for his insightful commentaries on the Valentinian and Manichaean Gnosis; to Bently Layton for his invaluable commentaries on the great Gnostic teachers.

Finally, we wish to thank Elaine Pagels for her treatment of Christian Gnosis in her book *The Gnostic Gospels*, and Holger Kersten for his research into the life of Jesus in his book *Jesus Lived in India*. Our thanks to the many authors we quoted in this book and for their invaluable research.

We give our special thanks to our father, Joseph, for his daily prayers and for the strong spiritual foundation he laid for us, to our sister Mary for her humor and optimism, and to LaVerne for her invaluable assistance and patience in editing this work.

J.P.M.
S.M.M.

This book is dedicated to:

"The Lightbearers of the World"

Contents

Introduction   xiii

Chapter I The Lost and Hidden Years in the Life of Jesus   1
    The Hidden Years of Jesus   .   12
    The Secret Facts About the Crucifixion   18
    Did Jesus Spend His Heaven Doing Good on Earth?   27
    The Final Mahasamadhi   38

**Chapter II The Oldest Christian Sects, Communities,
and their Teachings--Part I**   42

The Gnostic Theology of St. Paul   42
    Christ as Archetypal Man   43
    Christ as Indwelling Presence   49
    St. Paul's Teaching on the Resurrection and Preexistence
    of Souls   50
    St. Paul's Teaching on Evil   57
    The Hidden Wisdom of St. Paul "Christ in You, the Hope
    of Glory"   61
    St. Paul's Teaching on the Vicarious Atonement   66

**Chapter III The Oldest Christian Sects, Communities,
and their Teachings--Part II**   72

Nazorean or Jewish Christianity   72
    The Nazoreans   72
    The Virgin Birth and the Sonship of Jesus   83
    Preexistence and Reincarnation in Early Christian
    Teachings   94
    The Qumran Essenes and the Nazorean-Christians   100
    The Fall of the Rebel Angels and the Watchers   105
    The Doctrine of Embodied Evil   105
    The Nephilim   116

Chapter IV Brief Scenario of Early Christian History   120
   Introduction   120

**Chapter V The Lost Christianity of the Original Sects
30 A.D.—120 A.D.**   129
   Christian Sects in Samaria   131
   The Seth Connection   132
   The School of Simon   135
   Menander and Satornilos   141
   Christian-Gnostic Sects on Evil   144
   The Ophite Christian Sect   147
   Lost Christianity's Most Suppressed Teaching:
   A Usurper Deity as the Cause of Evil   149
   The God Called "Man"   155
   Strategies of Light and Darkness   156
   The Origin of the Doctrine of Original Sin   163
   The Naassenes—Christ as Unveiler of the Mysteries   165
   Did Jesus Die on the Cross? The Docetists   173
   The Teaching of Cerinthus—A "Secret Doctrine"
   of Matthew?   185
   Carpocrates and the Secret Gospel of Mark   188

Chapter VI The Emergence of Orthodoxy   196
   The Misuse of the Old Testament—Clement of Rome   196
   Ignatius of Antioch—The Power Politics of Orthodoxy   203
   The Emergence of Creed   203
   Ignatius Attacks Sectarian Christian Communities   207
   Marcion Formulates the First New Testament Canon   214

Chapter VII The Great Schools of Christian Gnosis   227
   Basilides   227
   Basilides' Doctrine of Reincarnation   231
   Valentinus   235
   The Doctrine of the Three Natures   251
   The School of Valentinus   254
   Valentinian Literature—The Gospel of Truth   256

The Valentinian Sacraments   261
The Doctrine of the Resurrection   267

**Chapter VIII The Orthodox Movement Formulates
"Anti-Christian-Gnostic" Theology**   270
Justin Martyr   270
The Doctrine of the Incarnation of the Word   274
The Resurrection of the Body   285

**Chapter IX Irenaeus and the Formulation of Orthodox
Pseudo-Theology**   293
The Doctrine of Deity   300
The Doctrine of the Logos and Christ   303
The Doctrine of Salvation   305
Irenaeus Fabricates His Own Apostolic Succession   309
The Myth of the Orthodox Apostolic Succession   317
Tertullian   330
Cyprian of Carthage   337

**Chapter X Origin of Alexandria and The Golden Age of
Christian Theology**   340
The Catechetical School at Alexandria   340
Clement of Alexandria   343
Origen of Alexandria—The Synthesis of Christian
Orthodoxy and Christian Gnosis   346
The Theology of Origen   347
The Trinity   347
Origen on the Doctrine of Christ   348
Origen on the Fall of Souls   351
Origen on the Fallen Angels   353
Origen's Doctrine of Salvation   357
Origen and Reincarnation   358
The Golden Age of Christian Theology   361
The Attack on Origen   362

Chapter XI The Manichaean-Christian Revolution   370
The Universal Religion of Light   370

The Doctrine of Mani 376
The Conspiracy of Darkness 376
.The Realm of Light 377
The Original Purity of the Preexistent Soul 377
The Realm of Darkness 378
The Darkness Attacks the Light 380
The Soul Enters "Matter" 380
The Rescue of the Soul 384
The Judgment of the Archons and the Creation of
Physical Cosmos 385
The Archons Release Their Stolen Light 387
The Archons Entrap Souls in Material Bodies—"Adam
and Eve" 388
The Redemption of Adam and Eve 390
Mani's Doctrine of the Last Things 391
Comments on Christian-Gnostic and Manichaean-
Christian Anthropology 393
Manichaean-Christian Salvation—The Writings of Mani 398
The Character of Mani 401
The Controversy between Orthodox and Manichaean
Christianity 404
The Manichaean Concept of Christ 404

**Chapter XII The Arian Controversy and the Council
of Nicea** 417
Constantine Becomes Messiah 417
The Doctrine of Arius 420
The Council of Nicea 423
The Nicean Council's Secret Agenda? 428
Constantine Becomes the Messiah—The Dawn
of the Papacy 435
Aftermath of the Arian Controversy 442

Chapter XIII The Bondage of Orthodoxy 446
Augustine 446
Augustine Attacks the Manichaeans 449
The Theology of Augustine—The Theory of Original Sin 454

Augustine Denies Preexistence and the Law of Cause
and Effect   458
The Doctrine of Infant Damnation and the Eternality
of Hell   460
Augustine's Doctrine of the Soul   464
Free Will versus Human Bondage—The Donatist and
Pelagian Controversies   467
The Legacy of Augustine   473

Chapter XIV The Legacy of the Orthodox Conspiracy   478
The Triumph of Institutionalized Christianity   478
The Keys of the Kingdom and the Supremacy of Peter   488
The Destruction of the Mysteries—The Martyrdom of
Hypatia   495
The Debasement of Woman—Adam and Eve—
The Celibate Movement   497
The Emergence of the Vicarious Atonement Theory   514
The Hidden Gnostic Legacy   519
Conclusion   523

Epilogue What Is Christianity and Who Is Jesus?   525

Reference Notes   529
Chapter I   529
Chapter II   532
Chapter III   533
Chapter IV   536
Chapter V   537
Chapter VI   542
Chapter VII   544
Chapter VIII   547
Chapter IX   548
Chapter X   552
Chapter XI   554
Chapter XII   558
Chapter XIII   560
Chapter XIV   562

Introduction

If, throughout this book, it may seem to the reader that we are taking a sledgehammer to Christianity as a religion, we are doing so only with regard to the theological dogmas, man-made, that were constructed during the first five centuries in order to counteract and oppose innumerable ancient move-ments, schools and communities which taught what we con-sider to be original Christianity--that body of teaching which has been termed Christian Gnosis. Not one word in this book is written against the genuine teachings of Christ found in the New Testament and in other ancient texts. If we choose to regard Jesus not as God, but as Master, Adept and divine incarnation and as an example of what humanity may become, we hope we will not be taken to task. The most important theme of this book is that man has a "Christ Consciousness" and a divine spark which can be developed commensurate to that of Jesus. Through man-made dogma this teaching and others like it, including teachings on the mystery of "evil," have been suppressed.

Our research revealed that the original teachings of Christianity had to do with the preexistence and reincarnation of the soul and the fact that not only Jesus but everyone in his true nature is a "Son of God"; that we all have the potential within us to attain Christhood, as the ancient Christian Gnostics taught. Unfortunately, their teachings had been suppressed and banned by the orthodox church as heretical. We also came to the awareness that certain facts in the life of Jesus had been suppressed. After a decade of research and study, we decided to write this book and to put it all together as our personal view of the first four centuries of Christian history.

We are not suggesting that our readers, if they are Christians, abandon their faith or turn to other religions. If the Christian tradition is spiritually effective for them they should remain steadfast in it, since no matter what they believe in terms of dogma, their faith in and love for Jesus is real, as the love of Jesus for them is also real. Thus, our purpose is not to alienate Christians but to show that the religion they have chosen may be far deeper and more mystical than they had first suspected.

There are many Christians today who may welcome this book, if they are searching for the truths beyond doctrine and dogma and are willing to scale the uncharted heights and to begin probing the mysteries of Cosmos. We, like many others, have only glimpsed the surface.

Jesus said to his disciples, "Ye are the light of the world." He also said, "Ye are the salt of the earth." The salt of the earth is sprinkled everywhere. They are the leaven that leavens and brings out the best in Christianity and in any of the world's religions, and which defeats the false and misleading dogmas of those religions by what they do, who they are and what they stand for.

In the matter of the Christian religion, and as far back as the first century, those who saw themselves as "straight-thinking" (which is what the term "orthodox" means) believed it was their duty to remake and remold the doctrines of the oldest Christian sects and communities to fit a belief system which did not guarantee freedom of thought or, more im-portantly, the freedom of the individual to pursue God as he or she saw fit. The leaders of "orthodox Christianity" soon be-came mind-reformers and, convinced that they represented the original and pure stream of Christianity, eventually developed through voluminous writings and church councils a pseudo-theology which was passed off as authentic.

In this book we are attempting to view the development of Christian theology from the other side of the fence--from the point of view of those who taught and believed Christian doctrines vouchsafed to them (as they averred) from Christ and his apostles and which for the most part differed radically from the doctrines which later comprised "orthodox Christianity." In our view of the early history of Christianity, doctrines and beliefs that would today be considered "fundamental" to

Christianity did not exist in the first two centuries, not at least in the form we know them today. What we will be attempting to show is that as far back as we go, we do not find an "orthodox Christianity" or what is today regarded by the average Christian as the core of the Christian religion. Describing how this "orthodox Christianity" came to be developed is the purpose of this book. But simultaneously, then, we must describe the original fabric of belief from which orthodoxy was, as a caricature, extracted. If the most ancient doctrines of Christianity were not "orthodox," then what were they?

Why did it appear necessary that these teachings be destroyed? Simply put, the teachings of "Lost Christianity" contained the keys to the spiritual growth and regeneration of the human race–the keys that would enable humanity to have an equal share in the "Mind of Christ." These teachings contained the keys to the "Kingdom of Heaven"--a "Christ Consciousness" that was destined to become the inheritance of every man, woman and child. Anyone who applied these teachings could not be controlled, could not be a partaker in the "mass consciousness," would walk on the earth as a "Christ" knowing "Good" and "Evil" and would have the keys of "hell" and "death."

The reader may well ask why anyone would seek to prevent this magnificent resurrection of humanity. The modern need to ask this question is in good measure a function of the degree of the destruction of the original teachings. To give presently but a partial answer, we take as an example Jesus himself. He is called Saviour and Redeemer. His vision and mission were to "save" humanity from the burden of the sense of mortality and limitation, from the "human condition," to catapult mankind, as it were, into the divine life whereby a new world would dawn, a new age of enlightenment and peace which would spell an end to the old world. Did he not say, "The things that I do shall ye do also, and greater things than these shall ye do...." Jesus, everyone will readily admit, thought differently from the rest of mankind. He said God was his Father and he was one with God; he said he possessed "all power in heaven and in earth" and stated that those who became his disciples would follow him in the "regeneration." For this stance Jesus received the unmitigated wrath of the powers of Church and State. He was summarily tried and executed. Why? It is not at all difficult to conclude that Jesus was a serious threat to the authorities. They were convinced that his teachings would wrest authority from them--they then would be powerless to exert that authority. Jesus saw them for what they were; he starkly called them "vipers". He had a very definite and unmincingly expressed opinion about their origins and about the spiritual forces they represented: they were "tares in the wheat" sown by "the enemy" and, as he told them bluntly, "Ye are of your Father, the Devil." And he saw them for what they did--they tyrannized over the mind and soul of man, and they were in every race and nation. The only way they could be overcome was through the spiritual attainment of the individual disciple. The teachings of "lost Christianity" containing doctrines and keys leading to this spiritual attainment were part of the Gnosis (i.e., knowledge as divine revelation), the "secret doctrine" promulgated by the sects, schools, assemblies (i.e., churches) and communities we will be discussing. The "secret doctrine" was in part to be found in the writings of the New Testament (provided one possessed the keys to the interpretation of these writings) and in gospels, letters and treatises passed on from teacher to teacher, initiate to initiate, and through oral tradition. Portions of this doctrine were received through revelation to certain disciples during the first through third centuries. The early history of Christianity, as we are presenting it here, is the history of the suppression of this very doctrine. Not only did the "orthodox" suppress this doctrine, but they took mangled portions of this doctrine to formulate their own "Christian" theology, thus removing the heart from the doctrine, leaving but a corpse.

Not only do we find the suppression of teachings that were intended to liberate mankind, but we also find that certain facts in the life of Jesus were likewise suppressed. In this book we will attempt to uncover these facts. Those who formulated the dogmas of orthodoxy were careful to remove from the faithful the knowledge of the indwelling Spirit Spark which makes man intrinsically divine. They also removed the knowledge of "evil" and its causes. We will follow the teachings of the earliest Christian sects on these subjects.

And finally, we hope that by reading this book the adherents of Christianity and followers of Jesus will no longer abdicate their rights as sons and daughters of God to a power elite in the church, but will investigate and search for themselves the true, original doctrines of Christianity with open minds and hearts. We hope that this book will start them on their journey.

Joseph P Macchio
Stephen M. Macchio

Chapter I

The Lost and Hidden Years in the Life of Jesus

We are about to undertake a most exciting adventure, as detectives uncovering pieces of a long lost puzzle. Our invest–tigation of "Lost Christianity" necessarily will include texts hidden, suppressed, destroyed or otherwise ignored by those who very early on had aligned themselves with the orthodox movement within Christianity

We possess no autographs of the four gospels. The oldest, complete copy of the New Testament goes back to the fourth century. We have no detailed history of the events of the first century of Christianity. A number of scholars have concluded that the canonical gospels were edited and inter–polated, in many instances, for doctrinal reasons

Besides the four gospels, Acts and the epistles of St. Paul, numerous other gospels, epistles, revelation dialogues and tractates which are now lost were in circulation among Christian communities. Among these lost titles and in some cases partly lost titles are the following:

> The Gospel of Perfection
> The Gospel of Andrew
> The Gospel of Eve
> Gospel of Matthias
> Gospel of Appelles
> Gospel of Barnabas
> Gospel Harmony of Basilides
> Gospel of Cerinthus
> Gospel according to the Hebrews
> Gospel of the Ebionites
> Gospel of the Nazarens

Gospel of Mani [or Manes]
Gospel of the Twelve [Apostles]
Gospel according to Peter
Gospel of the Lord
Gospel of Lucius or Lucianus
Gospel of Life
The Legal Priesthood of Christ
Gospel of the Elkaisites
Gospel of Thaddeus
Gospel of Tatian, etc. <1>

This is only a small sampling of the lost, or more accurately, suppressed books. These writings surely contained further information regarding the life and teachings of Jesus.

But we are not completely in the dark. In 1894, Russian explorer Nicholas Notovitch published *The Unknown Life of Jesus Christ*.

The book contained Notovitch's translation of an ancient Tibetan Buddhist text, discovered at the Himis monastery in Ladak, which stated that Jesus travelled to India and Persia during the so called "lost years" between the ages of thirteen and twenty-nine. The fascinating details of the dis–covery and publication of this manuscript have been told by Elizabeth Clare Prophet in her book, *The Lost Years of Jesus*. In this best seller, Prophet presents overwhelming evidence toward proving the authenticity of this manuscript. The Tibetan text was also discovered by Swami Abhedananda, Nicolas Roerich, and others.

Quoting from Prophet's book, the story briefly is as follows: Jesus, known throughout the text as Issa:

...secretly left his father's house, departed Jerusalem and, with a caravan of merchants, traveled east in order to perfect himself in the "Divine Word" and to study the laws of the great Buddhas.

They say Issa was fourteen when he crossed the Sind, a region in present-day southeast Pakistan in the lower Indus

River valley, and established himself among the "Aryas"—no doubt a reference to the Aryans who migrated into the Indus valley beginning in the second millennium B.C. His fame spread and he was asked by the Jains to stay with them.

Instead, he went to Juggernaut where he was joyously received by the Brahmin priests who taught him to read and understand the Vedas, teach, heal, and perform exorcisms.

Issa spent six years studying and teaching at Juggernaut, Rajagriha, Benares, and other holy cities. He became embroiled in a conflict with the Brahmins and the Kshatriyas (the priestly and warrior castes) by teaching the holy scriptures to the lower castes—the Vaisyas (farmers and merchants) and the Sudras (the peasants and laborers). The Brahmins said that the Vaisyas were authorized to hear the Vedas read only during festivals and the Sudras not at all. They were not even allowed to look at them.

Rather than abide by their injunction, Issa preached against the Brahmins and Kshatriyas to the Vaisyas and Sudras. Aware of his denunciations, the priests and warriors plotted to put Issa to death.

Warned by the Sudras, Issa left Juggernaut by night and went to the foothills of the Himalayas in southern Nepal, birthplace five centuries earlier of the great Buddha Sakyamuni (a title of Gautama), born prince of the Sakya clan—literally, the same (muni) of the Sakya tribe.

After six years of study, Issa "had become a perfect expositor of the sacred writings." He then left the Himalayas and journeyed west, preaching against idolatry along the way, finally returning to Palestine at the age of twenty-nine. <2>

The Jesus presented in this text certainly revolutionizes our concept of Christ by presenting him, primarily, as a man who walked the path of Christhood and Godhood on earth rather than as a God who became man! Yet at the same time, Jesus or Issa was considered by the writers of those texts to be the incarnation of the "great Buddha" who became incarnate in a newborn infant. The "incarnation" of Buddha, according to

Eastern religions, had occurred in past ages and can occur again. Issa, according to the text, then, was not thought to be the "only Son of God" ever, but rather the only Son of God in incarnation at that time, and the most recent link in a long chain of Divine incarnations.

The Roman Catholic Church, apparently, has pos– session of the Tibetan manuscript. In his book, Notovitch writes,

"I may, however, add to what I have already said in my introduction, as to having learnt from him (a cardinal of the Roman Church) that The Unknown Life of Jesus Christ is no novelty to the Roman Church, that the Vatican Library possesses sixty-three complete or incomplete manuscripts in various Oriental languages referring to this matter, which have been brought to Rome by missionaries from India, China, Egypt and Arabia. <3>

The Roman Catholic Church had not seen fit to share this information with its adherents, the so-called laity. It is well known that the Apologists during the second century decided that all prior religions did not issue from the same God—that the so-called "Christian Religion," which was, in fact, being constructed at that time, had no connection with the past (except for the Old Testament) and that the founders of all prior religions were either deceived, ignorant or pawns of the "devil." Yet according to the Tibetan manuscript, Jesus himself studies the scriptures of India and Persia, sides with the lower classes, and challenges an entrenched priestcraft, the same priestcraft who later formulated the dogmas that came to compose what is called orthodox Christianity.

We ask, why would the Roman Church refuse to reveal its sixty three manuscripts of Jesus' journey to the East? The answers are to be found in the Tibetan texts.

According to the manuscript, Jesus' mission was:

...to show forth in the guise of humanity the means of self-identification with Divinity and of attaining to eternal felicity, And to demonstrate by example how man may attain moral purity and, by separating his soul from its mortal coil, the degree of perfection necessary to enter the kingdom of heaven, which is unchangeable and where happiness reigns eternal. <4>

The emphasis on this text is markedly different from our canonical gospels in that stress is placed on man's divine potential as opposed to Jesus' exclusive divinity. An even stronger statement is made concerning man's divinity when, according to the text, Jesus teaches that the Great Creator *"is the principle of the mysterious existence of man, in whom he has breathed a part of his Being."<5>* In man *"dwells a part of the Spirit of the Most High."<6>* Man is not a sinner, he contains a spark of God. We further read that the law of cause and effect, known in the East as the "law of karma," was taught by Jesus. Verse 23 of chapter 5 reads, *"Those who deprive their brethren of divine happiness shall be deprived of it themselves. The Brahmans and the Kshatriyas (the priest and warrior classes) shall become the Sudras (lower classes), and with the Sudras the Eternal shall dwell everlastingly."<7>* We are here face to face with a concept even stranger to today's Christian: the doctrine of past and future lives. It will be easily admitted that the only conceivable way in which the higher classes could become the lower classes, as stated in the text, is through the process of reincarnation.

It should be understood here that certain of these concepts are not in fact missing from the writings of the orthodox canon, but have become virtually invisible through a mindset which guarantees complete neglect. Consider this passage:

And His disciples asked Him, saying, "Why then do the scribes say that Elijah must come first?" Then Jesus answered and said unto them, "Elijah truly is coming first and will restore all things. But I say to you that Elijah has come already, and they did not know him but did to him whatever they wished. Likewise the Son of Man is also about to suffer at their hands." Then the disciples understood that He spoke to them of John the Baptist. (Matthew, 17: 10-13)

Jesus does not mince words here. He is not speaking of someone who comes simply in the "spirit" of Elijah. The embodied existence of Elijah and Jesus, the Son of Man, are completely equivalent—they did to Elijah physically what they are "likewise" about to do to Jesus. He is endorsing the concept straightforwardly that John the Baptist was Elijah re-embodied. (See also Mark 9: 11-13) But we shall have more on this and other passages in later chapters.

Jesus further teaches, *"You shall attain to supreme happiness, not only in purifying yourselves, but also in guiding others in the way that shall permit them to gain original perfection."<8>* We note that Jesus does not teach "original sin" as it has been passed down through orthodox channels, but rather he emphasizes "original perfection". Do we not also detect in Jesus' statement a doctrine of preexistence later taught by Origen of Alexandria but banned from the church for centuries? As in the canonical gospels, we see Jesus severely attacking entrenched evil in the persons of self-appointed teachers of the Zoroastrian priesthood:

19 "The spirit of evil dwells on the earth in the hearts of those men who turn aside the children of God from the strait path.

20 "Wherefore I say unto you, Beware of the day of judgment, for God will inflict a terrible chastisement upon all those who shall lead his children astray from the right path and have filled them with superstitions and prejudices;

21 "Those who have blinded them that see, conveyed contagion to the healthy, and taught the worship of the things that God has subordinated to man for his good and to aid him in his work.

22 "Your doctrine is therefore the fruit of your errors; for desiring to bring near to you the God of truth, you have created for yourselves false gods."<9>

We recall that Jesus was later to attack the Pharisees in a similar manner during his Palestinian mission as recorded in the gospels.

Upon his return to Palestine, Jesus preaches to the Israelites against temples made with human hands, then adds:

12 "Enter into your temple, into your heart. Illumine it with good thoughts and the patience and immovable confidence which you should have in your Father.

14 "For God has created you in his own likeness—innocent, with pure souls and hearts filled with goodness, destined not for the conception of evil schemes, but made to be sanctuaries of love and justice.

15 "Wherefore I say unto you, sully not your hearts, for the Supreme Being dwells therein eternally."<10>

The human heart as the repository of the Most High and the original innocence of man are two key teachings which have not passed down into orthodox mainline Christianity. We consider these teachings to be part of the vast body of teachings which we have termed "Lost Christianity." If this Tibetan text is an authentic presentation of Jesus' teaching, it is easy to see why it has been banned, perhaps for centuries. Had the average Christian been taught that the Supreme Deity dwells in his heart, he could not have abdicated his authority to the priestcraft who preach that man is a sinner. We shall later examine the creation of the doctrine of original sin and the suppression of the Christian-Gnostic doctrine of the divine spark within man as the key to man's spiritual liberation. We find the corroboration of this teaching in St. Paul's epistle to the Corinthians, "Know ye not that ye are the temple of God, and that the Spirit dwelleth in you?" This concept, as we shall see, has been suspiciously neglected by orthodox Christians.

Even in the canonical gospels themselves, disconcerting (to the orthodox) statements survive, covered with the usual neglect. Consider for example:

Then the Jews took up stones again to stone Him. Jesus answered them, "Many good works I have shown you from my Father. For which of these works do you stone me?" The Jews answered Him, saying, "For a good work we do not stone you, but for blasphemy, and because you, being a man, make yourself God." Jesus answered them, "Is it not written in your law, 'I said, "Ye are gods"'? "If he called them 'gods' to whom the word of God came (and the scripture cannot be broken), "do you say of Him whom the Father sanctified and sent into the world, 'You are blaspheming,' because I said, 'I am the Son of God?'" (John 10: 31-36)

Thus the whole weight of Jesus' argument is this: "I am making no claim which you yourselves cannot make by the authority of your own scriptures, in fact which you must make, since the scriptures cannot be broken." There is no other explanation for the effect of this argument, and silence reigns in orthodox literature on this passage so far as we are aware. It cannot be simply a verbal game-like trick to confuse his accusers, for Jesus implicitly endorses here the accuracy of the scriptural statement, a statement which references Moses' final denunciation of the Hebrews' abandonment of their true identity and its result:

I said, "Ye are gods," And all of you are children of the Most High, But ye shall die like men, and fall like one of the princes. (Psalm 82, vs. 6-7)

Jesus' hearers did attempt a refutation; their response was to take up stones. The Tibetan text also provides us with Jesus' teaching on women—also lost to generations. Chapter 12, verses 10-21 reads as follows:

10 "Listen, then, to what I say unto you: Respect woman, for she is the mother of the universe, and all the truth of divine creation lies in her.

11 "She is the basis of all that is good and beautiful, as she is also the germ of life and death. On her depends the whole existence of man, for she is his natural and moral support.

12 "She gives birth to you in the midst of suffering. By the sweat of her brow she rears you, and until her death you cause her the gravest anxieties. Bless her and worship her, for she is your one friend, your one support on earth.

13 "Respect her, uphold her. In acting thus you will win her love and her heart. You will find favor in the sight of God and many sins shall be forgiven you.

14 "In the same way, love your wives and respect them; for they will be mothers of tomorrow, and each later on the ancestress of a race.

15 "Be lenient towards women. Her love ennobles man, softens his hardened heart, tames the brute in him, and makes of him a lamb.

16 "The wife and the mother are the inappreciable treasures given unto you by God. They are the fairest ornaments in existence, and of them shall be born all the inhabitants of the world.

17 "Even as the God of armies separated of old the light from the darkness and the land from the waters, woman possesses the divine faculty of separating in a man good intentions from evil thoughts.

18 "Wherefore I say unto you, after God your best thoughts should belong to the women and the wives, woman being for you the temple wherein you will obtain the most easily perfect happiness.

19 "Imbue yourselves in this temple with moral strength. Here you will forget your sorrows and your failures, and you will recover the lost energy necessary to enable you to help your neighbor.

20 "Do not expose her to humiliation. In acting thus you would humiliate yourselves and lose the sentiment of love, without which nothing can exist here below.

21 "Protect you wife, in order that she may protect you and all your family. All that you do for your wife, your mother, for a widow or another woman in distress, you will have done to your God." <11>

According to the text, Jesus taught what may be termed the "liberation" of woman by equating her with the Mother of the Universe. It is well known that several Church Fathers, including Tertullian, Augustine, Jerome and Epiphanius taught the inherent evil of woman as a figure of lust, quite contrary to the teaching of Jesus as preserved in this text.

According to Swami Abhedananda's translation of the Himis Monastery scrolls, Chapter 4:

1 The Supreme God, Father of the Universe, out of great compassion for sinners, desired to appear on earth in human form.

2 That incarnation appeared as a soul separate from that Supreme Soul who has no beginning, no end, and is above all consequence.

3 [He] descended to show how a soul can unite with God and realize eternal bliss <12>

In verse 3 the entire mission of Jesus is succinctly stated! It is significant that there is no mention of a vicarious atonement as later taught in the orthodox church.

The first two verses describe the Eastern idea (Hindu and Buddhist) of the "avatar", understood as the descent of an enlightened being into incarnation. In previous lives of striving and service, the now enlightened one had gained his attainment. There is little question that Jesus was considered as such an one by the authors of this Tibetan text, and he may have been considered as such by his disciples. John, the apostle, may have been referring to the concept of the "avatar" when he wrote, "And the Word was made flesh and dwelt among us, and we beheld his glory, the glory as of the only-begotten son of the Father, full of grace and truth".

Verse 13 reads: ... *"At that time the desire was very strong in his [Jesus] mind to attain perfection through devotional service to God and that he should study religion with those who had attained enlightenment,"* that is, from the sages of the East.

Abhedananda's postscript at the end of the text states that the reverend lama related to him that the manuscript was compiled in Pali, three or four years after Jesus left his body, *"from descriptions of all those Tibetans who met him [Jesus] at that time, as well as from descriptions of the traders who, with their own eyes, witnessed his crucifixion by the king of his country."* <13>

This, of course, would make the Tibetan text far older than our canonical gospels. Russian explorer and artist Nicolas Roerich, who also wrote down legends of the life of Jesus in Tibet in his book *Altai-Himalaya* quotes Jesus as saying, *"I came to show human possibilities. What has been created by me, all men can create. And that which I am, all men will be. These gifts belong to all nations and all lands—for this is the bread and water of life."*<14>

The "universal divinity" of all mankind comes out quite strongly in these texts imbued as they are with the "Eastern" point of view. We may ask, "Are these the original teachings of Jesus?"

The question has often been asked, "Did Jesus teach reincarnation?" We have seen evidence already in the context of his comments on Elijah and John the Baptist. Roerich, in answer to this question, quotes another saying of Jesus, in *Altai-Himalaya*, as follows:

"Said Jesus of skilled singers: "Whence is their talent and their power? For in one short life they could not possibly accumulate a quality of voice and knowledge of harmony and of tone. Are these miracles? No, because all things take place

as a result of natural laws. Many thousands of years ago these people already molded their harmonies and their qualities. And they come again to learn still more from varied manifestations."<15>

Even conceding that a small portion of these texts and legends are accurate, what they portend for established ortho-dox Christianity is a total reversal of values and centuries of understanding or misunderstanding of Jesus and his teaching.

The Hidden Years of Jesus

As astounding as the "lost years" of Jesus may seem, there are also the so-called "hidden years" in the life of Jesus, after the crucifixion. The four gospels are, to be sure, vague and ambiguous regarding Jesus' life after the crucifixion and resurrection. According to Matthew 28:16-20, Jesus meets with his disciples an unspecified number of days after the res-urrection on a mount in Galilee. He proclaims, "I am with you always, even unto the end of the age." The gospel abruptly ends here. Nothing further is written of the fate of Jesus or his disciples.

Mark's gospel ends with the empty tomb, according to certain manuscripts. Later on, twelve verses were added, briefly summing up the "facts" of the resurrection and the ascension. Mark 16:19 reads, "So then, after the Lord had spoken unto them, he was received up into heaven, and sat on the right hand of God." This verse sounds curiously like a later orthodox interpolation, perhaps a creedal formula, and does not seem to bear the marks of historicity. Luke (24:50-51) writes that Jesus leads the eleven disciples out "as far as Bethany," presumably on the same day as the resurrection, whereupon he blesses them and is parted from them. Certain manuscripts add "And [was] carried up into heaven" and others do not. At best, the ending of Luke's gospel remains ambiguous.

John's gospel closes with Jesus and his disciples on the sea of Tiberius, and Jesus' exhortation to Peter, to "Follow thou me." (John 21:20-23) John then cryptically adds, "And there are also many other things which Jesus did, which, if they should be written, every one, I suppose that even the world itself could not contain the books that should be written. Amen." (John 21:25) There are no further statements as to what became of Jesus.

The Acts of the Apostles, written circa 75-85 A.D., supposedly by Luke, contains the most detail in the canonical New Testament regarding the fate of Jesus after the resurrection. Luke writes that Jesus remained with his disciples "Forty days speaking of the things pertaining to the Kingdom of God." (Acts 1:3) Unfortunately, Luke does not elaborate on these teachings. The story continues:

And when he had spoken these things, while they beheld, he was taken up, and a cloud received him out of their sight. And while they looked steadfastly toward heaven as he went up, behold, two men stood by them in white apparel; Who also said, Ye men of Galilee, why stand ye gazing up into heaven? This same Jesus who is taken up from you into heaven; shall so come in like manner as ye have seen him go into heaven. (Acts 1:9- 11)

The disciples then return to Jerusalem from the Mount of Olives where this scenario apparently took place.

The orthodox Fathers of Christianity had eventually transformed this scene into a dogma, known as the "Ascension". According to the dogma, Jesus bodily rose into the sky (heaven) and has remained there bodily ever since, the only one in history to ever have done so. Christian dogma also asserts that some time in the distant future, Jesus is destined to descend bodily from heaven to earth in a "Second Coming" at the "end of the world." The true facts, however, may be quite different!

During the sub-apostolic age, there were traditions of a long interval between Jesus' resurrection and his so-called ascension. The apocryphal Acts of the apostles are replete with innumerable instances of Jesus' appearances and disap—pearances after his alleged ascension recorded in Acts. Was Jesus really in heaven? Or did he spend his heaven doing good on earth?

Is it possible to interpret Jesus' "ascension" from the Mount of Olives as a levitation or disappearance, or most probably a "translation" of his being, thus enabling him to continue his mission in other areas or in secret among his disciples?

In his epistle to the Corinthians, St. Paul makes no mention of Jesus' "ascension," although he witnesses to Jesus' crucifixion, burial and resurrection. St. Paul writes that after his resurrection Jesus "was seen of above five hundred brethren at once...after that he was seen of James, then all of the apostles. And last of all he was seen by me also." (1 Cor. 15:6-8) Throughout Acts, Jesus is in constant communion with St. Paul as well as with Peter and other disciples. Could Jesus have returned from "heaven," shortly after his mysterious disap—pearance from the Mount of Olives?

One is left with the distinct impression that certain information regarding the facts in Jesus' life has been suppressed. Nevertheless, the "hidden life" of Jesus can be partly unveiled if one has enough courage to read the "con—demned" books of the Christian-Gnostics—those sects and communities of early Christians who claimed to have received the secret teaching of Jesus which he, apparently, taught for many years after the resurrection.

In the Apocryphon of James, one of the Christian-Gnostic manuscripts discovered at Nag Hammadi, Egypt, in 1945, James, a disciple of Jesus, writes a letter to another disciple enclosing a "secret book" in Hebrew letters. James begins to narrate a dialogue he had with Jesus. He writes that the "Saviour appeared, after he had departed from us while we gazed at him. And five hundred and fifty days after he rose from the dead, we said to him: "Have you gone and departed from us?" This statement is followed by a lengthy discourse and admonishments from Jesus to James and Peter. At the close of the book, Jesus says, "Now I have said my last word to you. I shall part from you. For a chariot of wind has taken me up, and from now on I shall strip myself in order that I may clothe myself." The two disciples apparently raise their consciousness to more exalted states, where they see and hear angelic hymns and praises. Later they are questioned by the other disciples as to what had occurred and they answered simply, "He has ascended." <16>

The Apocryphon of James, then, offers an amazing alternative to the traditional New Testament accounts. After Jesus' first "departure" (the "departure" mentioned by Luke in Acts), he is absent 550 days (teaching privately? traveling?) and then reappears only to announce another departure or ascension, presumed to be the final one. We may very well ask again, "How many comings and goings were there?" "How long was Jesus on earth after his resurrection?" "How are we to understand Jesus' description of his ascension as a 'chariot of wind,' and his reference to clothing himself"?

The Gnostic Gospel, Pistis Sophia (third century), no doubt originally suppressed by the Church Fathers, then virtually ignored by orthodox Christianity after its publication in 1896, (two years after the publication of Notovitch's Unknown Life) offers more astounding information on Jesus' "hidden" post-resurrection years.

The text begins,

"It came to pass, when Jesus had risen from the dead, that he passed eleven years discoursing with his disciples, and instructing them..." <17>

This matter-of-fact assertion concerning Jesus' years on earth on the part of the author or authors of Pistis Sophia once may have been common knowledge. As we have stated, there was a tradition of a long interval between Jesus' resurrection and "ascension." Both the Apocryphon of James and the Pistis Sophia are proof of it.

Obviously, this tradition has not been passed down into orthodox Christianity. Why? We would suggest that these "hidden" years of Jesus must have been suppressed by the creators of orthodox Christianity to suit their own ends. Whether these ends were conscious or subconscious, what the motives may have been, these are neither easy nor necessary to determine, for the fact is that it was done. One possible cause being simply a profound inner—even subconscious—rejection of the real message, and as we shall see, both Jesus and St. Paul were not reticent about the forces in this world that would be completely inimical to Jesus' teaching.

Another possible inner motive is power or control. If Jesus, after the resurrection, had given his disciples a teaching designed to liberate their souls and bestow spiritual power upon them, and through them to many believers, the agents of control in the churches would certainly have sought to prevent the propagation of this teaching.

Perhaps they considered that the only way to officially suppress Jesus' post-resurrection teaching was to first suppress Jesus' post-resurrection years. As long as Jesus was safely tucked away in heaven, he could never have revealed a "secret" teaching which certain Christian teachers claimed to possess. Whatever the inner springs, we shall see unfold the incon–testable fact of suppression.

According to the Sethian-Ophites, an ancient Christian sect, Jesus remained on earth for eighteen months after the resurrection, imparting great "mysteries" to his disciples, then was taken up into heaven.

Fortunately, all attempts to suppress Jesus' hidden years have not met with success. You can't fool all of the people all of the time—but you can try. Now and then we find a passage that has not been "deleted."

Orthodox Church Father Irenaeus, writing circa 180, states unequivocally that Jesus lived at least twenty or more years after the crucifixion:

He [Jesus] passed through every age; becoming an infant for infants...a child for children...a youth for youths...

So likewise, he was an old man for old men, that he might be a perfect master for all... sanctifying at the same time, the aged also, and becoming an example to them likewise. Then, at last, he came on to death itself...

...and on completing his thirtieth year, he suffered, being in fact, still a young man who had by no means attained to advanced age.

Now, that the first stage of early life embraces thirty years, and that this extends onward to the fortieth year, every one will admit, but from the fortieth and fiftieth year, a man begins to decline toward old age; which Our Lord possessed, while he still fulfilled the office of a teacher, even as the gospel and all the elders testify; those who were conversant in Asia, with John the disciple of the Lord, that John conveyed to them that information. And he (John) remained among them, up to the time of Trajan. Some of them, moreover, saw not only John, but the other apostles also, and heard the same account from them, and bear testimony to the statement.<18>

On the face of it, this is an extraordinary statement, one which has been ignored or overlooked for centuries. It is also extraordinary that this revelation comes from a Church Father who is respected in orthodox circles and who was instrumental in creating what later became known as "catholic" Christianity.

It is well known that in order to submerge unwanted history, one only has to ignore or deny that certain facts had ever occurred. Such might have been the case with Jesus' hidden years.

Ignatius, bishop of Antioch, writing to the Smyrnians in Asia Minor toward the close of the first century, insists upon the reality of Jesus physical resurrection from the dead. He writes, "But I know that even after his resurrection he was in the flesh; and I believe that he still is so."<19> Could Jesus still have been living in the flesh some fifty years after the crucifixion? The idea may not be as incredible as it sounds.

Before pursuing Jesus' "hidden years" after the cruci–fixion, it is necessary to cast some light on both the crucifixion and the resurrection.

The Secret Facts About the Crucifixion

It is an established "fact" that Jesus the Nazarene suffered crucifixion by the order of Pontius Pilate in the year 29 or 30 A.D., at age thirty three. For all intents and purposes, Jesus was pronounced dead and buried in the tomb of Joseph of Arimathea. However, historians and biblical scholars, since the nineteenth century, have sought to establish that Jesus may not have "died" on the cross, but somehow had survived the crucifixion.

If we accept as a possible scenario that Jesus may have journeyed to the East, learned and studied the laws pertaining to life and death, and eventually mastered a yogic science enabling him to "raise the dead" as we find in the New Testament, then Jesus' restoration of his own body becomes more readily comprehensible. It is certainly possible, then, that Jesus may have demonstrated his adeptship by surviving the crucifixion and reanimating his so-called "dead" body.

Author Holger Kersten in his book *Jesus Lived in India* attempts to prove that Jesus' body was not "dead" when placed in the tomb from the evidence of twenty-eight wounds (shown on the Shroud of Turin) that continued to bleed after Jesus' removal from the cross. This author also alleges that Jesus lost consciousness as the result of a drug given to him while yet on the cross, and once in the tomb, Jesus' wounds were healed by the use of herbs administered by Joseph of Arimathea, Nicodemus, and certain Essenes.[20] The author offers a large body of evidence in proof of this thesis, which we shall review in a later chapter.

Of course, orthodox Christianity (and its vested in–terests) is based on the concept of vicarious atonement by Jesus' death on the cross. If it could be shown that Jesus never

"died" on the cross, what would become of established Christi–
anity? Is the physical "death" of Jesus on a Roman cross really
as important as orthodoxy was later to make of it? Could the
one who uttered the words, "I AM the Resurrection and the
Life," have experienced death in all its supposed finality?

St. Paul's pronouncements concerning Jesus' "death"
have a mystical connotation. Jesus is said to have been a
propitiation for the remission of past sins, as well as effecting a
reconciliation between God and the believer. The initiate into
St. Paul's community is said to be buried with him [Jesus] by
baptism into death... so that the "body of sin might be
destroyed." Those who have been "planted together in the
likeness of his death," shall also be "in the likeness of his
resurrection." We will discuss St. Paul's concept of Jesus'
sacrificial "death" on the cross in our next chapter.

According to John's gospel, Jesus' death is interpreted
as an exaltation; "And I, if I be lifted up from the earth will
draw all men unto me. This he said, signifying what death he
should die." (John 12: 32-33) According to John, Jesus' death
is not a death at all but a prelude to his "glorification": "the
hour is come, that the Son of Man should be glorified. Verily,
verily I say unto you, except a grain of wheat fall into the
ground and die, it abideth alone; but if it die, it bringeth forth
much fruit." (John 12:24) Here Jesus likens his crucifixion and
"death" to a seed nurtured in the earth, and eventually
sprouting forth fruit.

It becomes obvious that Jesus suffered no ordinary
death, if "death" is the correct word to use. Perhaps Jesus'
death was in appearance only, as certain ancient Christian sects
observed.

According to the *Encyclopedia of Religion*, orthodox
theologians of the ancient church, including Irenaeus and
Origen, interpreted the death of Christ as a ransom paid to the
devil. Mark records Jesus as saying, "For even the Son of Man
came, not to be ministered unto but to minister, and to give his
life as a ransom for many." (Mark 10: 45) The ransom theory
states that Jesus permitted himself to become the victim of

death and the devil, by giving his life in place of that of mankind, and at the same time proving his supremacy over the powers of evil by his resurrection.<21> St. Paul also states that Jesus disarmed the evil powers by his cross.

From a brief examination of the above biblical pas—sages, Jesus' death and resurrection portended something far more significant than a mere physical death. This leads us into the realm of the mystical and symbolical.

Perhaps a clue to the crucifixion and resurrection can be found in a study of various Sun-Gods and "Christ figures" down through the centuries. We find no less than twelve mythical-historical personages before the advent of Christ, who are said to have suffered crucifixion/death and to have risen from the dead. Among them are:

Krishna
Wittoba
Osiris
Attis
Indra
Prometheus
Mithra
Dionysus
Hesus
Aesculapius
Adonis
Apollonius of Tyana

Several of these figures are said to have been crucified at the spring equinox and to have risen on the third day

Krishna is said to have died by the arrow of a hunter when seated under a tree, and is represented as having de—scended into the infernal regions, rising from the dead and ascending to heaven. <22>

Wittoba, one of the Hindu gods, is represented with holes pierced in the hands and arms outstretched in the form of a Roman cross (but not fastened). The figure is crowned with a

Parthian coronet, typical of all incarnations of Vishnu. The feet are also pierced. <23>

In *Anacalypsis* by Godfrey Higgins, the god Indra is described nailed to a cross with five wounds representing nail holes. <24>

In the oldest accounts of Prometheus, it is stated that this saviour was nailed to an upright beam of timber to which was affixed arms of wood. The cross was situated on Mt. Caucusus, near the Caspian Sea. The story of Prometheus' cru–cifixion, burial and resurrection was acted in pantomime in ancient Athens 500 years before Christ.

The Persian saviour, Mithra, had a death festival at the spring equinox. Like Jesus, Mithra is said to have risen from the dead accompanied by a joyous celebration when the following words were uttered by the priest, "Be of good cheer, sacred band of Initiates, your God has risen from the dead. His pains and sufferings shall be your salvation." There is also a significant passage in the Mithraic communion ritual (also a central rite in this teaching): "He who shall not eat of my body nor drink of my blood so that he may be one with me and I with him, shall not be saved."<25> Typical of the treatment of these correspondences by early Church Fathers is Tertullian's response when shown this passage. His reaction was that this must have been the devil, anticipating Jesus' words hundreds of years in advance, and attempting to create confusion. <26>

Osiris, the Saviour God of ancient Egypt, was murdered by his wicked brother, Set, and placed in a coffin which was cast into the Nile River. Osiris is resurrected by Isis and thence-forth reigns as king, descends into the underworld, and comes to judge all souls. <27>

Apollonius of Tyana, a miracle worker and con-temporary of Christ, is said to have undergone "ritual ini-tiation" in the Great Pyramid whereby he was "crucified", buried and rose again on the third day. <28>

The above accounts cannot be coincidental. They must, of necessity, have arisen from a primary source. Most scholars agree that the above accounts and rituals of crucifixion, death, burial and resurrection originated in the mystery religions of antiquity.<29> Many of these saviour figures were historical persons, some were legendary, but all enacted or experienced so-called death and resurrection, whether symbolic or actual, as a prescribed "initiation."

It is well known that the ancient mysteries of Greece, Persia, Egypt, India, or Syria enacted the stages through which a soul was to pass from its first spiritual awakening to its ultimate spiritual unfoldment. These stages or steps were known as "initiations," and the final stage or initiation resulted in the "apotheosis" or deification of the candidate. At this stage, the initiate was said to have merged with the Divine and, for all practical purposes, was said to be a God-Man.<30> Before this stage was attained, however, the initiate had to conquer death itself and the "crucifixion," death and burial were the means to this end, and resulted in the victory of the resurrection.

The ancient crucifixion mystery ritual has been preserved by theosophical writer A. Besant and is described as follows:

He [the initiate] was brought into the chamber of Initiations, and was stretched on the ground with his arms extended, sometimes on a cross of wood, sometimes merely on the stone floor, in the posture of a crucified man. He was then touched with the Thyrsus on the heart—the "spear" of the crucifixion—and, leaving the body, he passed into the worlds beyond, the body falling into a deep trance, the death of the crucified. The body was placed in a sarcophagus of stone, and there left, carefully guarded. Meanwhile the man himself was treading first the strange obscure regions called "the heart of the earth," and thereafter the heavenly mount, where he put on the perfected bliss body...In that he returned to the body of flesh, to reanimate it. The cross bearing that body, or the entranced and rigid body, if no cross had been used, was lifted out of the sarcophagus and placed on a sloping surface, facing the east, ready for the rising of the sun on the third day. At the *moment that the rays of the sun touched the face, the Christ, the perfected Initiate or Master, re-entered the body, glorifying it by the bliss body He was wearing, changing the body of flesh by the contact with the body of bliss, giving it new properties, new powers, new capacities, transmuting it into His own likeness. That was the Resurrection of the Christ, and thereafter the body of flesh itself was changed, and took on a new nature. (Brackets added) <31>*

The above "mystery ritual" has been attested to by several ancient writers, including Plutarch, Philostrates and others. It is indeed remarkable how the above scenario agrees with the gospel story of Jesus' crucifixion and resurrection: the cross, the spear, and the properties Jesus' body possessed after the resurrection. It is interesting to note that the initiate in the above ritual is not "dead" in the literal sense of the word, but rather in a trance and his body takes on the appearance of death. According to the crucifixion ritual, the initiate was often given a drink or draught which enabled him to lose consciousness, inducing a trance state in the initiate, and with the touch of the "thrysus", the subject departed the body. This ritual as the final test was administered in temples of initiation in Egypt and elsewhere in the ancient world.

Adherents of the ancient mystery religions, the esoteric doctrine of Israel, and no doubt, the secret doctrine of the Essenes and Nazoreans, believed in the existence of other "bodies" besides the physical body. One of these bodies, sometimes called the "etheric body," composed of more subtle matter, could be used by the soul for travel when absent from the physical body, either consciously or unconsciously. This navigation "outside the body" is mentioned by St. Paul in 2 Corinthians 12: 2-5:

I knew a man in Christ above fourteen years ago (whether in the body, I cannot tell; or whether out of the body, I cannot tell: God knoweth)—such an one caught up to the third heaven. And I knew such a man (whether in the body, or out of the body, I cannot tell: God knoweth): How he was caught up into paradise, and heard unspeakable words, which it is not lawful for a man to utter. Of such an one will I glory; yet of myself I will not glory, but in mine affirmities.

Most biblical scholars are of the opinion that St. Paul is relating his own "out of the body" experience. Could St. Paul have undergone the same "initiation" of traversing the higher heavenly realms in his "etheric body," perhaps in preparation for his own resurrection? At any rate, this passage gives evidence of the concept of the soul having the capacity to utilize another "body" other than the physical. We will later discuss St. Paul's teaching on the "celestial body," which bears a marked resemblance to the "perfected bliss body," mentioned in the crucifixion mystery ritual.

St. Paul may have experienced the inner crucifixion ritual himself as he consistently dwells on his own "death in Christ:" I am crucified with Christ: nevertheless I live; yet not I, but Christ liveth in me." (Gal 2:20) The piercing of the hands and feet are a mark that the initiate had undergone this "mystical death" of the old mortal self, only to be renewed as an unlimited divine being. We have seen that Wittoba and Indra both appeared with pierced hands and feet. St. Paul relates:

But God forbid that I should glory except in the cross of our Lord Jesus Christ, by whom the cosmos is crucified unto me, and I unto the cosmos... for I bear in my body the marks of the Lord Jesus. (Gal 6:14,17)

These "marks" (Greek: brands) may refer to what has been termed the stigmata, imprints on the hands and feet (either seen or unseen) showing that the initiate has passed through the "mystical crucifixion."

Comparing the crucifixion mystery ritual to the gospel scenario, we cannot escape the conclusion that Jesus, like those before him commemorated in the ancient mysteries, experienced a "mystical death", rather than a physical one; his body perhaps displaying all the appearances of physical death. Jesus would have departed from his body, while still on the cross, descending into the hell realms to preach to the rebellious souls confined there, then traversing heavenly realms, clothing himself in the "resurrection body", and finally entering again into his physical body while it reposed in the tomb, thereby resuscitating it. Jesus would then have lived out his remaining years in a "glorified body", yet still physical, bearing properties that would enable him to appear suddenly in a room without entering through the door and to change his appearance at will. We will have more to say concerning the subject of the crucifixion when we discuss the ancient Christian sect known as the Docetae or Illusionists.

By submitting himself to and passing the crucifixion initiation, Jesus followed the prescribed "path of initiation" to the unfoldment of his spiritual faculties, a path set down since antiquity and undoubtedly traversed by sages and saints in past ages.

One of these may have been King David, who, in Psalm 22 writes of an intense experience, which bears the marks of the "mystical crucifixion".

My God, my God, why hast Thou forsaken me? Why art Thou so far from helping me, and from the words of my roaring?... But I am a worm and no man; a reproach of men and despised by the people.... I am poured out like water, and all my bones are out of joint: my heart is like wax; it is melted within me.... For dogs have compassed me; the assembly of the wicked have enclosed me; They pierced my hands and my feet. I may count all my bones; They look and stare upon me. They part my garments among them, and cast lots upon my vesture. (Psalm 22: 1, 6, 14, 16-18)

In this moving passage, David vividly describes his soul being "crucified", experiencing a dark night of abandonment by God, an abandonment also experienced by Jesus while on the cross. We conclude that this abandonment is part and parcel of the "mystical crucifixion" and is a universal experience through which the initiate must pass. According to the gospels of Matthew and Mark, Jesus quotes Psalm 22 as if identifying with David's own experience. Jesus, like David, was enclosed by the "assembly of the wicked." David, although he did not experience a physical execution, yet remarks, "They pierced my hands and my feet." This verse must be viewed as the sign that David himself had undergone the "mystical death", and its accompanying physical and mental tribulations, as well as a prophecy of Jesus' own crucifixion.

Why did Jesus submit himself to a public execution while simultaneously experiencing the mystical crucifixion? We have briefly discussed the theory that Jesus allowed himself to be publicly "slain", as a price paid to the devil and his angels, to diffuse their evildoing toward mankind. We have also seen that, according to St. Paul, Jesus, by his cross, disarmed the evil powers and principalities by resuscitating his body and overcoming apparent death.

John's gospel may provide a clearer answer:

"For judgment I am come into the world... Now is the judgment of this world; now shall the Archon [Ruler] of this cosmos be cast out." (Jn 9:39, 12:31, brackets added)

From this statement, it would seem that Jesus, in his submission to a public execution, sealed the judgment upon the Ruler of the cosmos—a fallen angel or usurper god about whom we shall later speak. Many ancient Christian sects, as we shall also see, believed that Jesus' crucifixion (as a public execution) was instigated by evil powers, including Satan, and through their physical "slaying" of Jesus' body, their judgment (unbeknownst to them) was pronounced. Furthermore, the evil powers and fallen angels retain that judgment throughout all subsequent reincarnations until their cycle comes to a close.

Returning to the "hidden years" of Jesus, we have seen evidence which points to the fact that Jesus may have spent many years on earth prior to his final "departure" or ascension. Jesus would then have been able to walk the earth in a resurrected body, appearing to his disciples at will, perhaps instructing them in the mysteries of their own spiritual path, the mysteries of the universe and of the stages of "initiation" which Jesus had undergone and successfully passed.

The orthodox movement within Christianity, as we shall see, suppressed and submerged the knowledge that such a path exists, to the detriment of the followers of Christ for centuries. Certain Christian-Gnostic schools preserved the knowledge of this "initiatic path" and the knowledge of the "mystical death" of Jesus, as did the school of Alexandria headed first by Clement and then by Origen. In our discussion of the ancient schools of Christianity, we shall see how they interpreted the "death" of Jesus on the cross, misinterpreted by the orthodox Church.

Did Jesus Spend His Heaven Doing Good on Earth?

Returning to the idea of the Ascension, orthodox Christianity asserts that Jesus' physical body rose into heaven forty days after the resurrection, where he has remained tucked away ever since. We have reason to believe, however, that Jesus never really left the earth—at least not after forty days.

According to the third century text, Pistis Sophia, eleven years after his resurrection (Jesus would have been forty-four years old, if we assume he was thirty-three when crucified), Jesus is sitting together with his disciples on the Mount of Olives and:

It came to pass... there came forth behind him a great lightpower shining most exceedingly...And that light-power came down over Jesus and surrounded him entirely, while he was seated removed from his disciples, and he had shone most exceedingly, and there was no measure for the light which was on him... Then Jesus ascended and soared into the height, shining most exceedingly in an immeasurable light. And the disciples gazed after him and none of them spoke, until he had reached into heaven; but they all kept in deep silence. <32>

This passage then describes great agitation in the heavens three hours after Jesus' "Ascension". On the following day, at the "ninth hour" they see Jesus descend, "shining most exceedingly,...for he shone more [radiantly] than at the hour when he had ascended to the heavens." Jesus then draws "the glory of his light" into himself and joyously tells his disciples that from now on he will discourse with them on all the mysteries "from the Beginning right up to the Fulness", and will no longer speak to them in parables. Jesus also reveals to his disciples that the light-power which enfolded him was "my Light-vesture" which had been given to him in the beginning but which he had left behind during his earthly sojourn. Jesus then continues to discourse with his disciples. <33> According to the text, Jesus does not re-ascend or depart a second time. One is left with the impression in reading Pistis Sophia, that Jesus continued his mission on earth indefinitely after having received his "Light-vesture."

According to Pistis Sophia, then, the "Ascension" of Jesus eleven years after the resurrection was not permanent; he descended to earth the following day. This scenario of Jesus' ascending only to re-appear is, of course, curiously missing from orthodox tradition. Perhaps orthodox Church Fathers were unwilling to admit, as the above passage shows, that the "Second Coming" of Christ had already occurred on the day after the "Ascension!" (either forty days after the resurrection or eleven years later). Or that the "Second Coming" might very well have been Jesus' revelation of the "mysteries" to his disciples or his Revelation to John. Orthodox tradition opted for a "Second Coming" in a vague and distant future. And what was the orthodox believer to do in the meantime? Instead of partaking of the "mysteries" of the initiatic path trodden by Jesus and demonstrating the self-same spiritual unfoldment as Jesus had demonstrated (contained in the "lost" texts), the Christian believer for 2,000 years has been taught to gaze skyward hoping to catch a glimpse of Jesus' body descending from "heaven" in the "Second Coming." According to Pistis

Sophia and other texts, this scenario was not the intent of Jesus by any stretch of the imagination. The suppressed texts we will be reviewing make it clear that divine knowledge about themselves and the universe (Gnosis) leading to ultimate spiritual self-unfoldment and self-mastery was bestowed on Jesus' followers and that the "Second Coming" was the descent of the individual disciple's own Spiritual Self, called in ancient Christianity, the Anthropos or Heavenly Man, termed by St. Paul the "inward man" (Romans 7: 22) and by Peter "The hidden man of the heart." (1 Peter 3:4) The procrastination of Christ's coming toward a future which never arrives, instead of the assimilation of the Christ within by means of the "mysteries" has been the bane of orthodox Christianity.

The account of Jesus' "ascension" in Acts forty days after the resurrection when it was recorded that "a cloud received him out of their sight" may well have been a disappearance which occurred earlier than the "ascent" recorded in Pistis Sophia or in the Apocryphon of James.

We have seen that, according to Notovitch's Tibetan manuscript, Jesus was said to have studied in the East and in so doing, undoubtedly attained the siddhis or spiritual powers developed by the yogi or adept. Among these is the power to appear and disappear, and to materialize or dematerialize the body. Spiritual yogis and adepts have been known to materialize or magnetize "clouds" around themselves and then to dis-assemble the atoms composing their bodies, only to reassemble them in a different location. We consider Jesus to have been one of the greatest of the yogis who have ever walked the earth (no matter what orthodox Christianity has eventually made of him). We can define a true yogi as one who has attained union with God. Jesus repeatedly stated that he had become one with his Father and that "all power in heaven and in earth" had been bestowed upon him.

We have mentioned that Jesus' disappearance, as recorded in Acts and at the close of Luke's gospel, may have been a levitation of his form followed by a dematerialization, one of the yogic powers. This disappearance in a "cloud" may have signaled the close of his public ministry and the commencement of his secret or private ministry. With this demonstration Jesus may have departed Palestine, either temporarily or permanently, for other lands, thus continuing his mission and making new disciples. This departure would not necessarily have precluded Jesus' returning to teach his disciples in secret (on and off for 12 years) as attested by Pistis Sophia.

We would suggest, then, that Jesus' disappearance in a "cloud" was not his final disappearance or his final return to Spirit or the Heaven-world; neither was his departure or ascension as recorded in Pistis Sophia the final one.

Unfortunately, orthodox Christianity throughout the centuries has fostered a materialistic concept of the ascension of Christ. According to Eastern tradition, it is the soul's ecstatic union with God which is significant. Jesus, as the yogic master he certainly was, must have experienced this ecstatic union or samadhi continuously. Eastern tradition in fact routinely distinguishes two states of samadhi: sabikalpa samahdi, in which the devotee has attained the realization of his oneness with Spirit in meditation, but cannot maintain it except (staticly) in meditation, and nirbikalpa sahmadi, in which the devotee may move freely in the world without any loss of the absolute absorption in and identification with Spirit—an awareness of oneself as simply Spirit acting through a personality. <34> Such an individual, as the Eastern adepts demonstrated, becomes entrusted with complete power over matter, and we clearly have evidence in the gospels that Jesus had the ability to raise or accelerate the frequency of the matter composing his body, especially following the resurrection, when "all power in heaven and on earth" was given unto him.

The "ascension" episode in Pistis Sophia resulted in Jesus' receiving the "Light-vesture," as the text makes clear, after which he re-appeared and continued to discourse with his disciples. Mahayana Buddhist tradition teaches the existence of a body or vehicle known as the Sambhogakaya, the "Body of Bliss" (rapture or spiritual enjoyment). <35> This Body or vehicle of expression is attained by a Bodhisattva, whom we can define as one whose nature has become Wisdom. Perhaps the "Light-vesture" which enveloped Jesus was, in fact, the Sambhogakaya (Jesus' own Bliss Body) through which he was to manifest, enabling him to continue his mission as an enlightened Bodhisattva or perhaps a Buddha.

Jesus' disappearance (Luke—Acts; Apocryphon of James) and his subsequent receiving of the "Light-vesture" (Pistis Sophia) need not be construed as Jesus' final "ascension" or removal from the earth. There is nothing in these accounts to lead one to conclude that Jesus permanently left earth, either physically or spiritually. The phrases "carried up into heaven" or "ascended to heaven", may denote an acceleration of either soul or body or both into a higher spiritual frequency, a raising of consciousness, so to speak. Jesus' frequent appearances in the apocryphal Acts and his long life as attested to by Irenaeus, present evidence that Jesus' earthly mission was far longer than orthodox Christians are prepared to admit.

As we have stated, according to Kersten, Jesus survived the crucifixion, resuscitated his body, and after converting St. Paul, took refuge outside Damascus, at a place which, curiously, is still termed Mayuam-i-isa, "the place where Jesus [Isa] lived." The author states that Persian historian, Mr. Kawand, has cited sources claiming that Jesus lived not far from Damascus after the crucifixion. <36>

Persian sources also state, writes Kersten, that while living in Damascus, Jesus received a letter from the king of Nisbis, near Edessa, asking Jesus to come and cure him of an illness. Jesus, however, sent Thomas his apostle to heal the king. Later Jesus arrived with his retinue, but his stay eventually became dangerous.

Kersten also learned from an ethnologist who had spent years among the Kurdish tribes in Eastern Anatolia (Eastern Turkey) that Jesus resided in this area after the resurrection.<37> Jesus then is said to have moved northwest to the court of the King Andrapa in the extreme north of

Anatolia. Kersten then cites the apocryphal Acts of Thomas which tells the story of Thomas' missionary activity to the King Andrapa and to King Gundafor in Taxila, in modern-day Pakistan. Jesus makes appearances in both places, converses with Thomas and others including the king, who was converted to the teaching of Jesus and the apostle.

Other sources which Kersten does not cite, indicate that Jesus traveled westward to instruct congregations in France and England. <38>

According to the Acts of Peter, another text declared apocryphal, Peter is fleeing Rome at the outbreak of the persecution under Nero (circa 64 A.D.):

And as he went forth out of the city, he saw the Lord entering into Rome. And when he saw him, he said: Lord, whither goest Thou? And the Lord said unto him: I go into Rome to be crucified. And Peter said unto him: Lord, art thou (being) crucified again? He said unto him: Yea, Peter, I am being crucified again. And Peter came to himself: and having beheld the Lord ascending up into heaven, he returned to Rome, rejoicing and glorifying the Lord...<39>

What was Jesus doing walking into Rome some 30 years after he was reputed to have ascended into heaven? Did he for a time secretly remain among the faithful in Italy? We note that Peter doesn't seem at all surprised that Jesus is not in heaven, but simply asks, "Where are you going?" no doubt questioning Jesus' intention of going into Rome where there is danger. Peter, of course, was crucified, and Jesus, as the Master, was spiritually crucified with him. We also note Jesus' sudden departure through levitation and "disappearance", another of the yogic powers.

On the Appian Way, outside of Rome, there is a chapel commemorating this event. In the chapel the visitor is shown "footprints" of Jesus embedded in rock beneath an iron grating said to be on the exact spot where Jesus stood and discoursed with Peter. These "footprints" are said to be replicas of the originals which are supposedly in the possession of the Vatican, or, as one witness attested, "locked up somewhere." We need not remind the reader that a "spirit" from heaven does not ordinarily make footprints in stone. Unless, of course, the "spirit" is, in reality, a spiritual yogic Master and Adept of the stature of Jesus. It would not have been unusual for Jesus to transfer to and anchor in the earth the fires of the resurrection which permeated his body, thus leaving footprints for posterity. As we have said, there are numerous appearances of Jesus recorded in the suppressed apocryphal Acts, amply demonstrating that Jesus was alive and well on earth after his alleged "ascension."

Jesus also is said to have stayed in Persia, according to various sources cited by Kersten. Jesus appears to have been known under several names, including Issa and Yuz Asaf which Kersten states probably means "leader of the healed." There are said to be numerous place names bearing the names of either Issa or Yuz Asaf as far as Kashmir. <40>

Jesus, apparently, continued to move eastward and preached also in Afghanistan. In *Among the Dervishes,* author Michael Burke says that in Herat, in western Afghanistan, he encountered about a thousand Moslems who follow the teachings of "Issa, son of Maryam." The chief of these "Christians" named Abba Yahiyya or Father John, was able to recite to the author a succession of teachers through sixty generations back to "Issa, son of Mary, of Nazara, the Kashmiri." The author continues:

According to these people, Jesus escaped from the Cross, was hidden by friends, was helped to flee to India, where he had been before during his youth, and settled in Kashmir, where he is revered as an ancient teacher, Yuz Asaf. It is from this period of the supposed life of Jesus that these people claim to have got their message.

...The Abba lived on a farm and like all the 'Christians' says that their teacher stipulated that his followers should always have a worldly vocation. Jesus, according to this

community, was a carpenter and also a shepherd. He had the power to perform miracles... The 'Traditions of the Masih' (anointed one) is the holy book of the community. They do not believe in the New Testament; or rather, they say that these traditions are the New Testament, and that the Gospels which we have are partly true but generally written by people who did not understand the teachings of the Master. <41>

The author describes Abba Yahiyya as "a towering figure with the face of a saint," an erudite man who knows his own scriptures and the Jewish writings. Father Yahiyya considered the various sects of Christians known to us today, as heretics:

"My son," he said, in his softly accented Persian, "these people are reading and repeating a part of the story. They completely misunderstood the message. We have the story told us by the Master, and through Him we will be saved and made whole. Some of the events in that document which you call the Bible are true, but a great deal is made up or imagined or put in for less than worthy reasons. Issa lived for over thirty years after the materials you have were completed, and He told us what was true." <42>

The author continues:

Briefly, the doctrine is that Jesus was the Son of God because He had attained that rank through his goodness and sacrifices. Thus He was equal to a divine person. He came after John the Baptist, who himself had reached the highest degree of development possible at that time. John baptized with water, Jesus with spirit and fire. These were the three stages of understanding, which were taught by our Christians. There was a great deal of confusion at first, because I was talking about sacraments and being saved, while it took me some time to realize that Abba John's people regarded baptism, the Holy Ghost and the Kingdom of God to be three stages in a system of *human illumination. This is what they claim is the function of the Church: The preservation of and administration of these three "developments" for the worshippers. There is a ritual meal, like the Last Supper, but this is carried out once a week. Bread and wine are eaten, but as symbolic of the grosser and finer nutritions which are the experience of attainment of nearness to God. <43>*

In these astonishing passages, we get an insight into the "secret life" of Jesus and of a mission far greater and more extensive than Church Fathers of the first to fourth centuries were prepared to admit. From the above records, it appears that much is missing from Christianity, much has been suppressed, and many documents have been lost or destroyed. The above passage also confirms the ancient Nazorean-Ebionite belief that Jesus attained to the rank of Son of God, and was not God from all eternity.

According to various sources Kersten cites, Jesus under the name of Yuz Asaf, finally reached Kashmir, after having preached throughout Persia. In *The Mysteries of Kashmir,* author, Mohamand Yasin quotes Mulla Nadiri, the first Muslim historian of Kashmir, who stated that during the reign of Raja Gopadatta (49-109 A.D.), "Hazrat Yuz Asaf having come from the Holy Land to the holy valley [of Kashmir] proclaimed his prophethood."<44> Mulla Nadiri also writes that he saw "in a book of Hindus that this prophet (Yuz Asaf) was really Hazrat Issa (Jesus), Ruh-Allah (the Spirit of God)". <45>

Asiz Kashmiri, in his book, *Christ in Kashmir,* quotes a Persian history (Rausat-us-Safa, pages 130-135) by Mir Mohd. Khowand Shah, giving a vivid description of Jesus when he arrived in Nisbis or Nasaybia on the Turkish border near Syria, sometime after the resurrection:

Jesus was named the Messiah because he was a great traveler. He wore a woolen scarf on his head, and a woolen cloak on his body. He had a stick in his hand; he used to wander from country to country and city to city. At nightfall he *would stay where he was. He ate...vegetables...and went on his travel on foot. Journeying from his country, he arrived at Nasibain, which was at a distance of several hundred miles from his home. With him were a few of his disciples whom he sent into the city to preach. In the city, however, there were current wrong and unfounded rumors about Jesus and his mother. The Governor of the city, therefore, arrested the disciples and then summoned Jesus. Jesus miraculously healed some persons. The King of the territory of Nasibain, therefore, with all his armies and his people became a follower of his. <46>*

In this passage, we find a glimpse of Jesus almost in the guise of a wandering Eastern guru. We recall Jesus' statement in the canonical gospel of Matthew that he had been sent to the "lost sheep" of the house of Israel. Could not these "lost sheep" have been dispersed throughout the Near East even as far as India? The sources we have already quoted suggest that descendants of the children of Israel had established themselves throughout Asia Minor, many of them settling in Kashmir. We would also suggest that Jesus, in his role as the Avatara or divine incarnation of the age, certainly would not have confined his mission to Palestine alone. The mission of Jesus and his disciples was to "teach all nations."

Kersten quotes a remarkable passage in his book which we give here almost full length, describing a meeting between Shalivahan, the chief of the Sahkas, and Jesus sometime before 50 A.D. (as the Shalivahan reigned from 39 to 50 A.D.):

One day, Shalivahan...went into the Himalayas. There in the Land of the Hun (=Ladakh, a part of the Kushan empire), the powerful king saw a man sitting on a mountain, who seemed to promise auspiciousness. His skin was fair and he wore white garments. The king asked the holy man who he was. The other replied: "I am called a son of God, born of a virgin, minister of non-believers, relentlessly in search of truth." The king then asked him: "What is your religion?" The *other replied, "O great king, I come from a foreign country, where there is no longer truth and where evil knows no bounds. In the land of the non-believers, I appeared as the Messiah. But the demon Ihamasi of the barbarians (dasyu) manifested herself in a terrible form; I was delivered unto her in the manner of the non-believers and ended in Ihamasi's realm. O King, lend your ear to the religion that I brought unto non-believers: after the purification of the essence and the impure body and after seeking refuge in the prayers of the Naigama, man will pray to the Eternal. Through justice, truth, meditation and unity of spirit, man will find his way to Issa in the center of light. God, as firm as the sun, will finally unite the spirit of all wandering beings to himself. Thus, O King, Ihamasi will be destroyed; and the blissful image of Issa, the giver of happiness, will remain forever in the heart; and I was called Isa-Masih [Jesus Messiah]. <47>*

The above passage as quoted by Kersten is taken from the fifth century work, Bhavishyat Maha-Purana, Volume 9 verses 17-32.<48> It is difficult to refute the evidence that Shalivahan had a genuine encounter with Jesus, perhaps 10 to 15 years after the resurrection. Jesus' delineation of the religion he brought to the "non-believers" is noteworthy because it shows Jesus' own conception of what Christianity was to accomplish for man: nothing less than the unity of all humanity within the Being of God himself. Man's goal is to find his way to "Issa in the center of Light." Jesus here identifies himself with the spiritual heart of the sun—the son (sun) of God, which image is to remain in the heart of man. Jesus stresses purification, prayer and union with God.

To whom does Jesus refer when he speaks of "non-believers" at whose hands he suffered? We suggest that for the most part, Jesus is referring to the authorities in orthodox Judaism (Pharisees and the Sanhedrin) and in the Roman Empire (Pilate, Herod Antipas) who rejected him not only as Messiah but as the Avatara or divine incarnation of the age. The mass of the people for whom he labored in Palestine likewise did not rally to his defense when he was brought to trial, neither did they accept his Messiahship. Jesus' crucifixion at the hands of the rulers in Church and State, no doubt prompted him to remark that in the land where he labored, there is no truth and "evil knows no bounds." Jesus' reference to being delivered to the realm of the demon, may refer to his sojourn (while outside the body) into the realm of Hades where he is said to have preached to the rebellious spirits, as his body lay in the tomb. The demon Ihamasi, like Mara in the Buddhist scriptures, appears to be a female personification of evil, perhaps familiar to the king Jesus is addressing. The "Naigama," Kersten remarks, may indicate some holy scripture. <49>

From the above passage, it becomes plain that Jesus, rejected by the authorities and by the people at large in Palestine, chose to travel far and wide "in search of the truth" within the hearts of those to whom he was sent. These may not only have been the "lost sheep" of the house of Israel or the "ten lost tribes" in dispersion, but may also refer to those "elect" or "saints" or to those later designated as "the living unshakable race," the "seed of light," from above who would instantaneously respond to his person and his message.

The Final Mahasamadhi

According to the several accounts Kersten and others draw on, Jesus spent his final days in Kashmir, where he passed on, perhaps some fifty years after the resurrection. The tomb of Jesus at Srinagar in Kashmir exists to this day where it is generally called the tomb of the prophet Yuz Asaf, one of the names of Jesus. Kersten's book contains several photographs of the tomb, both in color and in black and white, which show, remarkably, a plaster cast of "footprints" carved into the stone, next to the gravestone. The footprints clearly show the scars of the crucifixion wounds in the feet. When the footprints were originally discovered by an archeologist, a certain professor Hassnain, a crucifix and rosary were found beside them. We refer the reader to Kersten's book for detailed descriptions and a diagram of Jesus' tomb in Kashmir. The evidence Kersten and others present is difficult to refute, especially in view of the fact that there are in existence "21 historical documents bearing witness to Jesus' stay in Kashmir."<50> These sources confirm that the prophet Yuz Asaf and Jesus were one and the same. Kersten writes:

An old manuscript describes the memorial as the grave of Isa Rooh-u-Ilah. Each year thousands of pious believers make pilgrimages to the tomb, not just the Moslems, but also Hindus, Buddhists, and Christians. The descendants of the old Israelites have remembered the true significance of the modest monument: they call the shrine "the tomb of Hazrat Isa Sahib", i.e., the tomb of the Lord (master) Jesus. <51>

The very fact that Jesus' tomb is visited by Moslems, Hindus, and Buddhists as well as Christians, shows us that Jesus is revered in the East as a universal Prophet and Teacher whose doctrines are considered applicable within the context of several religions. This also illustrates to us that the orthodox dogmas constructed by the councils of Western Christendom have no bearing on these Buddhist and Hindu devotees of Christ. It also shows us that Jesus is not considered by the Eastern devotee to be a "god" or God himself but is looked upon as one sent by God to fulfill a divine mission on earth.

The story of the final passing of Yuz Asaf/Jesus is quoted by Kersten from The Book of Balavhar and Budasof (pages 285-286) as follows:

And he [Jesus] reached Kashmir, which was the farthest region at which he ministered, and there his life ended. He left the world and bequeathed his inheritance to a certain disciple called Ababid who had served him. Everything that he did was perfect. And he admonished him and said to him, "I have found a worthy shrine and decorated it and brought in lamps for the dying. I have collected the flock with the true *face, which had been dispersed and to whom I was sent. And now I shall draw breath through my ascent from the world, by the separation of my soul from my body. Obey the commandments that were given to you, and do not deviate from the path of truth but keep firmly to it in gratitude. And may Ababid be the leader." He then commanded Ababid to level off the place for him; he stretched his legs out and lay down. Then, turning his head northwards and his face eastwards, he passed away. (Brackets added) <52>*

What strikes us about this passage is the way in which Jesus passed on—in full knowledge that his mission is completed and in full control of not only his faculties but of the manner in which he is to leave the body. Jesus' use of the breath to effect his transition demonstrates to us Jesus' adept-ship and mastery over his soul and body. The account shows that Jesus' passing was foreknown and was in accordance with the divine destiny.

This account is in fact entirely in accord with the Eastern tradition of Yogic attainment. In our own recent times two well known Indian teachers and adepts, Vivekananda (1863-1902) and Paramahansa Yogananda (1893-1952), demonstrated this mastery over the method of leaving the body; Yogananda before a gathering at the precise end of a talk at a large dinner banquet, <53> and Vivekananda in a more strikingly parallel fashion to the account given of Jesus:

At seven o'clock in the evening the bell rang for worship in the chapel. The Swami went to his room and told the disciple who attended him that none was to come to him until called for. He spent an hour in meditation and telling his beads, then called the disciple and asked him to open all the windows and fan his head. He lay down quietly on his bed and the attendant thought that he was either sleeping or meditating. At the end of an hour his hands trembled a little and he breathed once very deeply. There was silence for a minute or two, and again he breathed in the same manner. His eyes *became fixed in the centre of his eyebrows, his face assumed a divine expression, and eternal silence fell. "There was," said a brother disciple of the Swami, "a little blood in his nostrils, about his mouth, and in his eyes." According to the Yoga scriptures, the life-breath of an illumined yogi passes out through the opening on the top of the head, causing the blood to flow in the nostrils and the mouth. The great ecstasy took place at ten minutes past nine. Swami Vivekananda passed away at the age of thirty-nine years, five months, and twenty-four days, thus fulfilling his own prophecy: "I shall not live to be forty years old." <54>*

It is at or shortly after his passing that Jesus may have experienced the final mahasamadhi ("great" samadhi) or suspension of all earthly senses and the absorption into the Deity which has been termed the "Ascension" in the West. We suggest that the above description of Jesus' passing and ascent to heaven makes him no less divine than if his physical body floated up into heaven as orthodox Christianity would have us believe. The later conception of Jesus' Ascension was made to fit the orthodox dogma that Jesus was unique—a "god" totally unlike and removed from those he came to serve.

Jesus' passage from earthly life, however does not seem to have closed the door on his continued interaction with his disciples throughout the world. John, the beloved disciple, for example, is said to have received the Revelation of Jesus sometime during the close of the first century. And, as we shall see, "gnostic" Christians believed that Jesus' appearances and revelations continued on, well into the second century and beyond. We continue our survey of "Lost Christianity" in the next chapter.

Chapter II

The Oldest Christian Sects, Communities, and their Teachings—Part I

The Gnostic Theology of St. Paul

In this chapter we will review the oldest, most ancient teachings concerning Jesus, his life and mission, in order to gain some idea of what "original" Christianity was thought to have been.

We will not be discussing the four canonical gospels in this category since the earliest of the gospels, that of Mark, was written circa A.D. 65 or possibly after the Jewish revolt of A.D. 66. The gospels of Matthew, Luke, and John were composed A.D. 75-90. At present, we have no idea what the original gospels contained, as we possess no autographs, only edited copies primarily from the fourth century. The oldest copies were made circa A.D. 200.

The oldest documents in the New Testament are the letters of St. Paul. However, many scholars do not consider all the Pauline letters authentic. The so-called deutero-Pauline letters: 2 Thess, 1 and 2 Timothy, and Titus are thought to be written by the "school" of St. Paul. Certain of these letters contain a theology and point of view in marked opposition to St. Paul's·original letters.

The authentic Pauline letters were composed in the first century during the decade of the fifties. Therefore the epistles of St. Paul contain the oldest teaching in the New Testament. As we shall see, the teaching of St. Paul when examined closely bears little resemblance to the orthodox Christianity of today and yet St. Paul has been considered one of the pillars of Christendom for centuries. St. Paul did not base his teaching exclusively on the "tradition" of the Nazorean (Jerusalem) community but states unequivocally that his gospel was given to him "through a revelation of Jesus Christ." (Gal. 1:12) St. Paul's appeal to private revelation for the source of his gospel places him in the category of the "gnostic", that is, one who knows through divine insight or revelation. Ironically, several "gnostic" teachers, including Valentinus, pointed to St. Paul as the source of their teaching.

We will, therefore, attempt a partial analysis of St. Paul's theology, pointing out certain teachings or ideas which have been either ignored or misinterpreted but which are, nevertheless, firmly embedded in St. Paul's theological system. They are there for all to see. According to orthodox Christians, most, if not all, of the teachings which we have attributed to St. Paul would be considered "heretical." Why? Not only because they have been re-interpreted by orthodox fabricators from the close of the first century onward, but because the "gnostic" quality of St. Paul's theology became too uncomfortable for the early Church Fathers. We ask the reader to openly assess with an unbiased mind this analysis of St. Paul's teaching which we here offer for consideration.

Christ as Archetypal Man

St. Paul's theology appears to be based on the central idea of the Heavenly or "Cosmic" Christ. St. Paul knows Jesus not as a flesh and blood Master but as the resurrected Messiah who personifies what can be termed the Heavenly or "Archetypal Man." The teaching concerning the "Archetypal Man" has been ingeniously swept aside by the suppressors of St. Paul's doctrine, but had surfaced in the Christian-Gnostic schools (which looked to St. Paul as their teacher) under the term "Anthropos," which in Greek means the Man or Primal Man. In the gospels Jesus designated himself "Son of Man." We suggest that this phrase means the "Son of the Primal Man." Jesus, then, called himself the Son or image of the Archetypal or spiritual Adam. According to ancient Hebrew sources such as the Kabbalah, the esoteric doctrine of Israel, this divine Archetypal Man was known as Adam Kadmon. <1> We also find the term "Son of Man" in the books of Enoch, Daniel and throughout the New Testament, where it refers, esoterically, to the True, Ideal Man.

The Son of Man described in the Book of Enoch (3rd to 2nd century B.C.) is a pre-existent Messiah-figure who appears to be a divine personage bearing a divine "office". Enoch queries the angel in his vision of the Ancient of Days, asking who is the one whose "countenance resembled that of a man":

He answered and said to me, This is the Son of Man, to whom righteousness belongs; with whom righteousness has dwelt, and who will reveal all the treasures of that which is concealed; for the Lord of Spirits has chosen him; and his portion has surpassed all before the Lord of Spirits in everlasting uprightness...

[3] Before the sun and the signs were created, before the stars of heaven were formed, his name [the Son of Man] was invoked in the presence of the Lord of Spirits. A support shall he be for the righteous and the holy to lean upon, without falling; and he shall be the light of nations.

[4] He shall be the hope of those whose hearts are troubled. All, who dwell on earth, shall fall down and worship him; shall bless and glorify him, and sing praises to the name of The Lord of Spirits.

[5] Therefore the Elect and The Concealed One existed in his [The Lord of Spirits] presence, before the world was created, and forever.

[6] In his presence he existed, and has revealed to the saints and to the righteous the wisdom of the Lord of Spirits;... *(Brackets added.)<2>*

In Enoch this "Son of Man" is also termed the "Messiah" and the "Elect" who shall take command, be powerful upon earth and judge the kings and mighty men of the earth.

As we shall see, St. Paul understood Jesus as the pre-existent, divine Son of Man who had taken incarnation on earth. St. Paul, however, uses the term "Christ" and not "Son of Man." In the clear translation of The Jerusalem Bible, this divine figure descended to earth and became a man, as St. Paul describes:

His state was divine, yet he did not cling to his equality with God but emptied himself to assume the condition of a slave, and become as men are; and being as all men are; he was humbler yet, even to accepting death, death on a cross. But God raised him high and gave him the name which is above all other names so that all beings in the heavens, on earth and in the underworld, should bend the knee at the name of Jesus and that every tongue should acclaim Jesus Christ as Lord, to the glory of God the Father. (Phil. 2:6-11)

This teaching of St. Paul's is similar to the concept discussed in the Tibetan text which states that a portion of Buddha (Buddha-mind) or Brahma incarnated on earth in the soul of the infant Issa.

In his epistle to the Colossians, St. Paul further elaborates on his doctrine of the "Universal Christ", the Enochian Son of Man or Archetypal Man:

He [the Son] is the image of the unseen God and the first-born of all creation, for in him were created all things in heaven and on earth; everything visible and everything invisible, Thrones, Dominations, Sovereignties, Powers—all things were created through him and for him. Before anything was created, he existed, and he holds all things in unity. Now the Church is his body, he is its head. As he is the Beginning, he was first to be born from the dead, so that he should be first in every way because God wanted all perfection to be found in him and all things to be reconciled through him and for him, everything in heaven and on earth, when he made peace by his death on the cross. (Col. 1:15-18, Jerusalem Bible)

Where did St. Paul receive these ideas? According to Biblical scholar, Hugh J. Schonfield, St. Paul studied the "occultism of the Pharisees," and specialized in the "Lore of Creation."<3> St. Paul, of course, also claimed to have received his doctrine from Jesus himself.

Schonfield elaborates on the meaning of St. Paul's teaching as follows and helps to illumine the above passage:

The essential element in the teaching is that the visible universe conforms to a pattern or design, which represents the image of the Invisible God who, himself, has neither form nor substance. Man, the crown of creation, being made in the image of God, answers therefore completely to the original pattern, which thus may be conceived as a manlike figure. This primordial or Archetypal man, the "heavenly man" of Philo and the Adam Kadmon of the Jewish occultists, is the true image of God, the beginning of the creation and the Lord of it. Hence the first man on earth was given dominion over every living thing in it. <4>

Obviously, this concept of the Archetypal or heavenly Adam has been "lost" to modern Christianity. But who is this Archetypal Man? Schonfield continues:

We see man, therefore, as wearing physically the likeness of his spiritual Archetype, and that archetype is the expression of the nature of God....But for what purpose was man created? His creation must have had to do with the Messianic Plan, and the soul of Adam must have been knit with the soul of the ultimate Messiah (Christ). It was therefore to be deduced that the archetypal or heavenly man was also the pre-existing spiritual counterpart of the Messiah, the heavenly Spirit- Christ. <5>

Schonfield then equates the "heavenly man" with the Enochian Son of Man, as described above, and states that St. Paul "regards the heavenly Messiah as the sole Messiah, who by an act of temporary redemptive renunciation became the man Jesus... the firstborn of all creation...."<6>

If Schonfield's analysis is correct, as we believe it to be, the Jesus worshipped for centuries by orthodox Christians is not the Jesus of St. Paul but the Jesus constructed by Church Fathers and Church councils, e.g., the Council of Nicea. Schonfield adds:

Paul's Christ is not God, he is God's first creation, and there is no room for the trinitarian formula of the Athanasian Creed nor for its doctrine that the Son was "not made, nor created, but begotten." But inasmuch as the visible universe is the expression of the Invisible God, the Christ, as first-product, comprises the whole of that expression in himself. <7>

According to Schonfield's interpretation of St. Paul's theology, not only is Jesus not God but, is in fact, Man, in his original spiritual state! Schonfield continues:

Accepting with Paul the equation of the Messiah as the Adam Kadmon, it required that he should cast aside his glory and 'make himself small,' so as to atone for Adam's sin by the man Jesus and initiate the restoration of harmony between man and God, and between the visible universe and the Invisible God. By the resurrection, there was restored in Jesus the light-body which the first man had possessed and forfeited, and the re-expansion of his stature in a manner comparable to that of the first man before the Fall. Thus ennobled and reintegrated with the Adam Kadmon, Jesus was henceforth the Lord Jesus Christ. <8>

St. Paul therefore distinguishes between the Heavenly Christ and the earthly Jesus who was "made of the seed of David according to the flesh, and declared to be the Son of God with power according to the spirit of holiness by the resurrection from the dead." (Romans 1:3-4) It was through the resurrection that Jesus became the Son of God and thus restored man's true spiritual archetypal state.

...It is again evident that Paul did not think of Christ as God, only as being created in the image of God as the archetypal man and therefore having a godlike form....The heavenly Christ only took over when Jesus was raised from the dead and ascended to heaven.<9>

A thorough reading of St. Paul's epistles will confirm the relative accuracy of Schonfield's analysis of St. Paul's Christology, although Schonfield is of the opinion that St. Paul's theology differed radically from and was a distortion of the theology of the Jerusalem community. We however do not share this view.

It is impossible to construe from the above passages that St. Paul is referring solely to the historical Jesus, even in his resurrected state, as dwelling in the hearts of the faithful, especially in view of the fact that St. Paul continually uses the term, Perfect Man or inner man, and not Jesus Christ. It is clear that the Perfect Man is to be identified with the true or inner nature of man. This true or divine image has also been called the "Christ Self" or "higher Self" of each individual according to certain New Age teachings. Our analysis is corroborated by Father John Rossner, author of *In Search of the Primordial Tradition*:

The term "Bar Nasha" or "Son of Man" refers to the "divine human form." An archetype of the human creation itself, it is the perfect Cosmic blueprint for all human beings. This was equated by some ancient writers with the "Logos" or eternal "image of God" that was said to be in every man that comes into the world. <10>

In *The Myth of God Incarnate*, Frances Young, commenting on St. Paul's doctrine of the Son of God, writes:

This figure [the Son of God] is pre-existent not simply as a kind of divine being...but as the "man from heaven";...Indeed, he is the archetypal man and the archetypal Son of God in whom we become sons of God, fellow-heirs with Christ who will bear the image of the man of heaven. <11>

The heavenly Christ and the man Jesus having become one Lord Jesus Christ is a teaching which has been branded as heretical and "gnostic" by the orthodox fabricators of Christianity from the second century onwards. Christ as the divine Archetype whom the believer should follow and thus attain to his own spiritual inheritance which was lost at the time of the fall, has itself become a lost teaching. And yet, the orthodox, by reinterpreting St. Paul and superimposing second-and third-century theology upon St. Paul's Christology, have claimed him as their own.

Christ as Indwelling Presence

This Christ whom St. Paul preaches is also an indwelling presence, a presence not confined solely to Jesus. We cite the following examples: After St. Paul had submitted himself to the "mystical crucifixion," Christ, as an inner presence, dwelt in him: "I am crucified with Christ: nevertheless I live; yet not I, but Christ liveth in me." (Gal. 2:20) "And because ye are sons, God hath sent forth the Spirit of his Son into your hearts, crying, Abba, Father." (Gal. 4:6)St. Paul teaches that this indwelling Christ must be nurtured in the hearts of the faithful: *"My little children, of whom I travail in birth again until Christ be formed in you."* (Gal. 4:19, emphasis added.) St. Paul prays to the Father for the members of his community at Ephesus: "That he would grant you, according to the riches of his glory to be strengthened with might by his Spirit in the inner man; that Christ may dwell in your hearts by faith...And to know the love of Christ, which passeth knowledge, that ye might be filled with all the fullness of God." (Eph. 3:16, 17, 19)

The nurturing and development of this indwelling Christ as the Divine Spark in the hearts of St. Paul's disciples results in the believer's transformation into the Archetypal Man called by St. Paul an inner man, perfect man or new man: "Till we all come in unity of the faith, and of the gnosis of the Son of God, unto the perfect man, unto the measure of the stature of the fullness of Christ." (Eph. 4:13) "...Put on the new man which after God is created in righteousness and true holiness." (Eph. 4:24)

By accepting St. Paul's gospel, then, man is restored to his true estate: a preexistent spiritual being, as Jesus likewise was restored through the resurrection. How is this restoration to be accomplished? St. Paul answers: "And as we have borne the image of the earthly, we shall also bear the image of the heavenly." (1 Cor. 15:49) This restoration to the heavenly image or heavenly Man was to be accomplished by means of the "resurrection of the dead."

St. Paul's Teaching on the Resurrection and Preexistence of Souls

Did St. Paul teach the orthodox concept of the resurrection of the physical body from the graves on the last day? We can discover no evidence for this teaching in St. Paul's epistles, and yet this dogma has become a fundamental tenet of orthodox Christianity. St. Paul writes: "Now this I say, brethren, that *flesh and blood cannot inherit the kingdom of God;* neither doth corruption inherit incorruption." (1 Cor. 15:50, emphasis added.) "In a moment, in the twinkling of an eye, at the last trump; for the trumpet shall sound, and the dead shall be raised incorruptible, and we shall be changed. *For this corruptible must put on incorruption and this mortal must put on immortality.*" (1 Cor. 15:52-53, emphasis added.)

To arrive at a true interpretation of St. Paul's theology, we must ask, "Who are the dead?" Certain scholars have long contended that St. Paul utilizes the phraseology of the ancient mystery religions which were based on the scenarios of the dying and resurrected gods of the ancient world, and on the story of the soul's initiation into these mysteries through its mystical death and resurrection.<12> St. Paul's concepts are replete with Platonic, Kabbalistic and Jewish-gnostic references. In the mystical, gnostic phraseology of St. Paul, therefore, the "dead" are (1) those whose souls are confined to physical bodies and are in incarnation in the material universe (2) souls who are not quickened by the Spirit and who have been or are bound by sin and the sense of mortality, and who have forgotten their origins in the spiritual cosmos and (3) souls who through sin and neglect have caused the Divine Spark in the heart to be snuffed out, thus losing contact with their own inner "Christ Consciousness," and any hope for redemtion.<13> The "dead," then, are not those whose worm-eaten bodies are lying in graves and coffins as orthodox re-interpreters of St. Paul's teaching would lead us to believe. This teaching again is not to be found in the earliest letters of St. Paul or other early Christian documents.

Members of St. Paul's community asked him, "How are the dead raised?" In answer, St. Paul explains that the soul as a seed is sown in corruption, dishonor, and weakness, which he compares to the sowing of grain in the earth. Again, in St. Paul's mystery phraseology, the sowing of grain in the earth most likely refers to the fall of the soul, the loss of the Divine Spark and the descent of the soul into incarnation, where it is bound in the body, which St. Paul designates as both a psychic or soul-body and a physical body. This concept obviously presupposes a belief in preexistence. The soul is then destined to be raised in a pneumatic (Greek: spiritual) body. St. Paul carefully distinguishes between terrestrial and celestial bodies. It is evident from these passages in Corinthians that the soul is raised in a celestial body, and not in a resuscitated physical body: "The first [kind of] man is of the earth, earthy; the second man is the Lord from Heaven." (1 Cor. 15:47) Considering Schonfield's analysis of St. Paul's theology, the "Lord from heaven" can be no other than the Archetypal or Perfect Man, the image of the preexistent heavenly Christ which all men inwardly possess, and which has been called the "Christ Self." There is also no evidence in St. Paul's letters that this "resurrection of the dead" is to take place on the same day at the so-called end of the world, although St. Paul does teach the concept of a Last Day and Judgment upon the fallen angels and for those who are on the earth or in the underworld at that time. (Thess. 1:7:10; 2:1-12) Rather, we suggest that the resurrection is to be understood as the individual victory of each soul over death, corruption, and mortality when the process of incarnation and re-incarnation in the flesh is ended. This resurrection, St. Paul teaches, is not automatic, but comes as the result of spiritual striving, suffering, tribulation, and the rooting out of sin and the pull of the senses. The soul (the dead) is then raised "incorruptible" and changed: "So when this corruptible shall have put on incorruption, and this mortal shall have put on immortality, then shall be brought to pass the saying that is written, 'Death is swallowed up in victory.'" (1 Cor. 15:54)

We have suggested that St. Paul taught preexistence and reincarnation. This is not so impossible when we consider that, as Schonfield shows, St. Paul studied the occult (hidden) doctrine of the Pharisees. We shall later see that, according to Jewish historian Josephus, the Pharisees believed in and taught the pre-existence of souls. In Phil. 3:5, St. Paul admits that he is a Pharisee. Some form of reincarnation is almost always a corollary to the doctrine of preexistence, which teaches that all souls existed in a "spiritual" state before descending into bodies. Although we shall discuss reincarnation in a later chapter, it will suffice here to again quote Schonfield on the doctrines of the Pharisees, of whom St. Paul was one:

The Pharisaic faith included belief in angels and demons, the mapping of heavenly abodes...the mystery of the Archetypal Man, special creation and pre-existence, the Above and Below, the Messiah, transmigration of souls [reincarnation], revelation and divine intervention.... (Brackets added) <14>

St. Paul teaches that resurrection is made possible by faith in Jesus Christ and also by and through the personal crucifixion and personal resurrection of every believer. St. Paul himself is witness to this path: "That I may know him, and the power of his resurrection, and the fellowship of his sufferings, being made conformable unto his death, if by any means I might attain unto the resurrection of the dead. Not as though I had already attained, either were already perfect; but I follow after, if that I may apprehend that for which I am apprehended of Christ Jesus....I press toward the mark for the prize of the high calling of God in Christ Jesus." (Phil. 3:10-12, 14)

It is difficult to construe from this passage that St. Paul advocates simple belief in Jesus' historical crucifixion and resurrection and that, by virtue of this belief, the individual then is "saved" and "goes to heaven." Yet this teaching has been one of the roots of "Christian dogma" for centuries. On the contrary, the resurrection is apparently to be attained on an individual basis through rigorous striving.

Let us repeat that St. Paul's letters contain the oldest theology in the New Testament, being written prior to or during the decade of the fifties. As we shall see, they are decidedly "gnostic" in character. We shall also see that forms of "gnostic" Christianity seem to be the oldest forms of Christian teaching throughout the most ancient Christian communities.

We have earlier stated that St. Paul's concept of the descent (or sowing) of the soul in the earth (flesh) presupposes a belief in preexistence. In Ephesians, St. Paul clearly teaches the concept of preexistence in a manner in which the later Christian-Gnostics taught. "Blessed be the God and Father of our Lord Jesus Christ, *who have blessed us with all spiritual blessings in the heavenly places in Christ ....*" (Eph. 1:3, emphasis added.) Here St. Paul addresses the "saints" (holy ones), a sectarian term used by the Qumran Essenes to distinguish themselves from those who were not called or did not choose to keep God's covenant. The saints are the chosen remnant. The term is similar to the "elect" but different from the term "pneumatic" (spiritual) which St. Paul also utilizes. St. Paul also addresses a group called the "faithful" who are presumably to be distinguished from the "saints." St. Paul, therefore, designates his followers under various levels or degrees of spiritual initiation, as second century Christian-Gnostics taught.

Taking the above passage at face value, without centuries of reinterpretation, St. Paul seems to be saying that those who have been blessed did once exist in "heavenly places" before their sojourn on earth. He continues, "According as he [the Father] hath chosen us in him [Christ] before the foundation of the world, that we should be holy and without blame before him, in love..." (Eph. 1:4) Here St. Paul makes an even clearer statement: the saints and the faithful have been chosen before the world's foundation. They must then have preexisted with Christ before creation. This concept is not so unusual when we consider that the Pharisees taught preexistence and reincarnation. St. Paul continues: "Having predestinated us unto the adoption of sons by Jesus Christ himself, according to the good pleasure of his will..." (Eph. 1:5)

The chosen saints and faithful had a divine destiny to fulfill: they were to be adopted as sons by Jesus. This destiny was known by God before the saints became, as it were, pilgrims on earth, i.e., before they become incarnate on earth. This destiny was to be fulfilled coincident with the coming of Christ and in future epochs when the saints would still be upon earth: "That in the ages to come, he [the Father] might show the exceeding riches of his grace in his kindness toward us through Christ Jesus." (Eph. 2:7,)

· St. Paul explains that the faithful and embodied saints "in times past" walked according to the course of this cosmos and were "dead in sins." This statement undoubtedly refers to past epochs, and as we would suggest, past lives. The redemption of the saints which begins now may be fulfilled in future lives through the work of Christ: "For I reckon that the sufferings of this present time are not worthy to be compared with *the glory which shall be revealed in us.* For the earnest expectation of the creation waiteth for the manifestation of the Sons of God." (Rom. 8:18-19, emphasis added.)

It is evident to those not prejudiced by orthodox theology that St. Paul seems to be teaching preexistence, past and future lives, and a present and future glorious destiny for those who are able to win it, finally culminating in a future epoch when the sons of God will manifest on earth:

And we know that all things work together for good to them that love God, to them who are the called according to his purpose. For those whom he did foreknow, he also did predestinate to be conformed to the image of his Son, that he might be the firstborn among many brethren. Moreover, [those] whom he did predestinate, them he also called; and whom he called, them he also justified; and whom he justified, them he also glorified. (Rom. 8:28-30)

We have a clear statement of preexistence in verses 29 and 30: to be foreknown and predestined again presupposes that the souls to whom St. Paul addresses himself already existed in the heavenly realms before their descent to earth, in keeping with the occult doctrines of the Pharisees. St. Paul appears to be saying that those who were foreknown in the beginning were destined by God to be conformed to the Christic image and thus follow the firstborn one, Christ. These "predestinated" souls simply ratify and fulfill on earth the divine destiny bestowed on them by God in the beginning and are the "called." They are the "elect" because they "elected" to do God's will in a preexistent state. Nevertheless, in their sojourn on earth they have fallen into sin, have lost the way, have lost access to their inner "Christ" and have received "justification" through Christ. This "justifying" is brought about first through faith in Jesus as Christ and Lord whereby the "punishment" (karma) due to their transgressions (in past lives) is set aside or forgiven. As a corollary to this, faith in Jesus as Christ results in the restoration of the Divine Spark within the heart enabling the faithful to walk the initiatic path to reunion with God. Then the saints progress and become the "perfect" (i.e., initiated) by means of the "hidden wisdom" and gnosis taught by St. Paul. The "resurrection of the dead" is the final release from mortality and from the physical cosmos. We see that St. Paul's scheme of salvation is preeminently gnostic, based as it is on revelation and on the concept of the descent of the soul into matter and its eventual release or liberation therefrom. The agents of this resurrection are each one's indwelling Christ, the Archetypal Man, (expressed through the flame in the heart) and Jesus Christ, the firstborn from the dead.

Finally, it is worthwhile to reference the Epistle to the Hebrews in this context. Technically, Hebrews belongs to yet a third "partition" of St. Paul's writings: (1) Thessalonians, Titus and Timothy from the "school of St. Paul"; (2) the body of letters directly attributable to St. Paul; and (3) Hebrews, which is neither (1) nor (2), but is agreed upon by most scholars as almost certainly being written by someone other than St. Paul. Since a good many orthodox scholars routinely ignore this partition, two can play the same game. Thus consider what "St. Paul," i.e., the author of Hebrews, who would give his hearers "strong meat" but notes their inability to accept it, has to say on the figure of Melchizedek, "King of Salem," after whom Christ is a priest forever, to whom even Abraham gave tithe. Of Melchizedek, the author of Hebrews makes this significant statement: "Having neither father nor mother, nor beginning or end of days, but made like unto the Son of God." (Heb. 7:13) If this is not pre-existence, it is yet worse, for it is curiously equivalent to Jesus' statement, "Before Abraham was, I AM." Yet if the Jews took up stones against Jesus for making this statement, where are the stones of the orthodox for the author of Hebrews? Jesus, being the only Son of God in orthodox theology, should be the only one of whom this statement can be made. Again there is a loud silence.

St. Paul's Teaching on Evil

The letters of St. Paul reveal the knowledge of evil powers present in the cosmos. The origin and nature of these beings was later elaborated upon by certain Christian-Gnostic teachers who claimed St. Paul as the sole authority for their doctrine. To cite Ephesians 6:

Put on the whole armor of God, that ye may be able to stand against the wiles of the Devil. For we wrestle not against flesh and blood, but against principalities, against powers, against the archons of the darkness of this cosmos, against spiritual wickedness in the heavens.... Stand, therefore, having your loins girded about with truth, and having on the breastplate of righteousness,... Above all, taking the shield of faith with which ye shall be able to quench all the fiery darts of the evil one. And take the helmet of salvation, and sword of the Spirit which is the word of God. (Eph. 6: 11-12, 14, 16-17)

There is nothing preserved in the extant letters of St. Paul on the origin of these cosmic rulers of darkness. Perhaps this teaching was left to the "wisdom of God" spoken in a "mystery" by St. Paul to his initiates. Nevertheless, St. Paul must have been familiar with Apocalyptic Judaism such as is found in the Book of Enoch, which treats of the fall of the Watchers (angels or sons of God) from heaven. (Enoch 7-10) The well-known story of the fall of Lucifer, Satan and their angels from heaven, through pride, as described by Isaiah, must also have been known by St. Paul. (Isa. 14:12 f.)

From the above verses it is obvious that St. Paul is aware of cosmic forces of evil against whom the believer must arm himself. These archons (Greek: rulers) are not on earth, but "in the heavens" and are apparently engaged in a war against the faithful. Are they identical with the fallen angels of Apocalyptic Judaism as described in Enoch and Jubilees? Or can their origin be found in the writings of other sectarian

Jewish-Gnostic sects such as the Sethians, Samaritan and other Syrian gnostic texts?

In our discussion of Nazorean Christianity, we will comment on the "fall of the angels" as understood by the Essenes, Nazoreans and Jewish Gnostics.

St. Paul's teaching on the "archons of the darkness of this cosmos" can only be sufficiently illuminated in the light of subsequent Christian-Gnostic theology. We will later deal with the Christian-Gnostic systems and their teaching on evil. Suffice it to say that this teaching likewise has been suppressed by the creators of Christian orthodoxy.

Let us turn to other statements of St. Paul regarding the presence of "evil" in the universe:

And you, hath he quickened, who were the dead in trespasses and sins;

In which times past ye walked according to the Aeon of this cosmos, according to the Archon of the power of the air, the Spirit that now worketh in the children of disobedience; Among whom also we all had our manner of life in times past in the lusts of our flesh, fulfilling the desires of the flesh and of the mind.... (Eph. 2:1-3)

This distinct phraseology of St. Paul and the specific meaning of his words have been lost since the second century. They are virtually unknown to the average Christian today—and even to the average priest or minister.

It becomes obvious after several readings of this passage that the phrase "times past" cannot refer to the recent past, but to past epochs of history when the faithful and the saints were subject to the "Aeon of this cosmos," also called the "Archon." We turn to the second-century Christians to gain a greater understanding of these terms.

According to the Valentinian school of theology (which inherited its teaching from St. Paul), the Aeon of this cosmos refers to a usurper god, called the demiurge (Greek: artificer or fabricator).<15> The word "Aeon" has many meanings in

Greek, including age, space, or a spiritual being governing a vast space or dimension either in the heavens (Pleroma) or below.<16> Here it is used to refer to a spiritual being (Aeon), whom St. Paul also calls the "Archon of the power of the air." Archon is the Greek word for ruler, and "the power of the air" is identified with the devil by Valentinian theologians.<17> St. Paul therefore must be referring to the Ruler or usurper god who has had dominion over the physical cosmos (as opposed to the spiritual universe—called by St. Paul the Pleroma or fullness). This ruler, according to Valentinian theology, created the "devil" from the passion of grief which was transformed into the cosmic element of air. The "power of the air," then, is the devil who is the spirit working in the children of disobedience. <18> The element air has commonly been identified with the mind.

The "children of disobedience" are apparently a distinct group of individuals still under the dominion of the devil. The devil here may well be identical with Satan, known in Jewish lore as the one who was disobedient to the highest God. The Archon who rules the devil was known in the first and second century under many names, including Ildabaoth, Saclas (fool) or Sammael. This Archon is also referred to by St. Paul in 2 Corinthians 4: 3-4:

But if our gospel be hidden, it is hidden to them that are lost. In whom the god of this aeon hath blinded the minds of them who believe not, lest the light of the glorious gospel of Christ, who is the image of God, should shine unto them.

Those "lost" are blinded by the Archon whom St. Paul now refers to as "god." The word "Aeon" as used here must be translated as an "age," an exceedingly long period of time. The "lost" may be identical with the "children of disobedience," or they may refer to a separate group, known throughout the New Testament as the "ungodly" or "godless." They have not the capacity for belief since, as St. Paul states, their minds are blinded by the usurper god. Should the light of the gospel shine upon them, they may no longer be under the mental dominion of this "god." St. Paul's faithful and saints, apparently, in past ages have also lived according to the ways of the disobedient children, subject to rebellion, physical and mental desires, monitored and controlled perhaps by the Archon or god of this cosmos. In St. Paul's doctrine of salvation, Christ Jesus brought freedom from the dominion of this "god."

St. Paul preached liberation from the ordinances and legalities of the Mosaic code, which, he taught, were to be replaced by the redeeming work (crucifixion and resurrection) of Jesus. St. Paul also associated bondage to sin with the corrupt example of the same children of disobedience and their influence upon the faithful:

For this ye know, that no fornicator, nor unclean person, nor covetous man (who is an idolater) hath any inheritance in the Kingdom of Christ and of God.

Let no man deceive you with vain words; for because of these things cometh the wrath [judgment] of God upon the children of disobedience.

Be ye not, therefore, partakers with them.

For ye were once darkness, but now are ye light in the Lord [the Heavenly Man], walk as children of light."
(Eph. 5:5-8, brackets added)

The "children of disobedience" may be identical with the children of Satan (the devil). According to St. Paul, these are apparently on earth walking and living among the saints and faithful and have exerted a powerful influence on them, as we have said. In fact, one may speculate that the rebellious "children of disobedience" have continued to reincarnate along with the "children of light" and may very well be the originators of the decadence of late twentieth and twenty-first century civilization, for example, in the misuse of rhythm in rock and rap, abortion, drugs, child abuse, varieties of sexual depravity, and the manipulation of the economy. Could these disobedient children be the same ones referred to by Jesus in Matthew's gospel as "tares" or the "children of the wicked one"? (Matt. 13:38) What is their origin? According to Matthew, Jesus states that "the enemy that sowed them is the devil." The devil (Satan), then, is their father whose seed (offspring) they are. In our discussion of the fallen angels we shall see that Jesus confronts this wicked seed in the persons of the Pharisees.

St. Paul teaches, however, that Jesus triumphed over the archons and powers of the usurper god:

And you, being dead in your sins...hath he [Christ] made alive together with him, having forgiven you all trespasses,
Blotting out the handwriting of ordinances that was against us, which was contrary to us, and took it out of the way, nailing to his cross;
And, having exposed principalities and powers, he made a show of them openly, triumphing over them.... (Col. 2:13-15)

Christ, then, effectively blotted out the tyrannical ordinances of the usurper god and his powers against the faithful, while at the same time exposing them, revealing their origin and their powerlessness, by his triumph over "death" through the resurrection. Those called to redemption and resurrection may likewise triumph over the archons and powers.

The Hidden Wisdom of St. Paul "Christ in You, the Hope of Glory"

As we have previously stated, St. Paul taught a secret doctrine reserved for those whom he termed "the perfect," i.e., initiates. This doctrine may have related to the origin of man, the creation and to the origin of evil. Later Christian-Gnostic schools attest to this doctrine. St. Paul, in 1 Corinthians, affirms that his proclamation comes not in words of human wisdom:

> *However, we speak wisdom [Sophia] among them that are perfect; yet not the wisdom of this age [aeon], nor of the archons of this age, that come to naught;*
> *But we speak the wisdom of God in a mystery, even the hidden wisdom which God ordained before [in the presence of] the Aeons unto glory; which none of the archons of this age knew for had they known it, they would not have crucified the Lord of glory. (1 Cor. 6-8, brackets added)*

Again we must refer to later Christian-Gnostic theologians for the precise meaning of St. Paul's words. This passage is the most compelling proof that St. Paul did, in fact, teach a secret doctrine or hidden wisdom. St. Paul's "wisdom," as he states, does not derive from the archons (evil rulers) who strive to keep man in bondage through a deceptive wisdom, false teaching, or through legalism in religion.

St. Paul's "wisdom" comes from God, given in a "mystery," perhaps through myth, symbol or allegory; we are not told. This "wisdom" was ordained in the presence of the Aeons, a precise term meaning Divine Beings dwelling with the Father in the Pleroma (spiritual universe), who emanated from the Father before the physical cosmos was fashioned. This wisdom is also specifically ordained for the attainment of the faithful and the saints. The archons themselves do not know this wisdom which must, of necessity, have related to the purpose of Jesus' coming, his passion and resurrection, by which the archons were stripped of power over him. We should also note that in this passage Jesus is referred to as the "Lord of Glory," a term often used to describe the Heavenly or Archetypal Man.

According to scholar Elaine Pagels, the hidden wisdom of St. Paul related to "the secret mystery of Sophia," i.e., to the passion, fall, and restoration of Sophia (the world and universal Soul), the pattern for the passion, crucifixion and resurrection of Christ.<19>

Suffice it to say that the "wisdom teaching" of St. Paul had never been passed on to orthodox churches in the second century, much less to Christians today. Yet this teaching and its application may have been vital in attaining what St. Paul calls "the resurrection of the dead."

The Greek word "Aeons" used by St. Paul in this passage demonstrates that St. Paul seems to have accepted what has been called the "doctrine of emanations." Aeons, as we have said, were spiritual Beings of great magnitude who emanated from the One God who dwelt in the Pleroma (fullness). From a careful reading of St. Paul's theology, we have concluded that St. Paul taught that "Christ" was the highest (or one of the highest) of these Aeons or divine personages who, as we have seen, descended into or took incarnation in the body of the earthly Jesus.

This concept has been called "pneumatic Christology" by Adolph Harnack, author of *The History of Dogma*, who points out that this idea regarding Jesus' origin is found also in the epistle to the Hebrews and in the writings of John. Harnack defines it as follows: "Jesus was regarded as a heavenly spiritual being (the highest after God) who took flesh."[20] He writes further that St. Paul's theology begins with "the pre-existent Christ (the Man from Heaven) whose moral deed it was to assume the flesh in self-denying love, in order to break for all men the powers of nature and the doom of death."[21] Christ then is not God, but a Man from heaven.

This earliest of doctrines concerning Jesus carries us to the East and to the doctrine of the incarnating Buddhas and Bodhisattvas.

We have mentioned in the chapter concerning Jesus' travels in the East that Jesus was considered an incarnation of Buddha. A Bodhisattva, however, is a spiritual being whose very essence has become wisdom. St. Paul refers to Christ as the wisdom of God who, out of love for humanity, descends to earth as a Saviour to guide souls onto the path of righteousness, to bestow upon them salvation from suffering, sin, and ignorance. St. Paul's "Man from Heaven" is, no doubt, to be understood as such a Being who "emptied himself," by virtue of his incarnation in a body, but who appeared in a divine semblance after rising from the dead. Again, the Enochian "Son of Man" is a similar, if not identical, concept.

We return now to St. Paul's "hidden wisdom" and to what he considered to be the central mystery of his proclamation:

*Even the mystery which hath been hidden from ages and from generations, but now is made manifest to the saints, to whom God would make known what is the riches of the glory of this mystery among the Gentiles, which is **Christ in you, the hope of glory;** Whom we preach, warning every man, and teaching every man in all wisdom, that we may present every man perfect in Christ Jesus. (Col. 1:26-28, emphasis added)*

The indwelling Christ or element of Divinity as the hope of the Gentile faithful without which they, apparently, cannot be saved, was a hidden teaching. It constitutes the essence of the "mystery" for St. Paul. Why was this teaching hidden? Perhaps because, until the coming of Christ, the indwelling spirit or spark in the majority of mankind had been snuffed out due to misuse, sin or ignorance. Jesus, through the disciple's faith in him would restore that spark in his role as the incarnate Christ on earth. We believe this very restoration is what John refers to in his gospel: "But as many as received him, to them gave he the power to become the sons of God...." (John 1:12). A "son of God" is one who bears the Divine Flame in the heart and who has attained to a certain level of initiation.

We shall later see that those Christian sects and communities who emphasized salvation by "Christ in you" instead of by belief in the historical Jesus and in the church were branded as heretical.

In summary, and including some things upon which we haven't explicitly touched, the salient features of the Pauline theology are as follows:

(1) The heavenly Christ (Messiah), a divine Being, descends to earth, assumes a body and is born of woman, under the law of Moses, and is known as Jesus.

(2) Jesus is crucified and dies for the sins of Jews and Gentiles, which he takes upon himself, thus "justifying" them before God, freeing them from imminent judgment and from ancient Levitical ordinances which are now abrogated.

(3) By his resurrection from the dead, Jesus becomes the Son of God with power appearing in the semblance of divinity (as to St. Paul at his conversion) and eventually returns to the heavens, resuming his posture as the Spiritual Christ and the head of all sovereignties and powers.

(4) By faith in Jesus' life, death and resurrection, those called to follow Christ must follow him in his death and resurrection, be crucified and rise again in a celestial or pneumatic body at the close of their sojourn on earth.

(5) The faithful and saints who believe in Christ form a close-knit community (Greek: ecclesia) with Christ as its head and themselves as members, forming a mystical body.

(6) The faithful are at war with and must defend themselves against cosmic powers of evil or darkness among whom are the Archon or god of this aeon, the devil and his children of disobedience, and "the lost."

(7) Those who are called "the perfect" are initiated orally into a secret wisdom-teaching. These are the pneumatic (spiritual), while others are called psychic who are babes in Christ and are not spiritual. They receive a beginning or lesser teaching. The carnal or sensuous cannot receive or contain the teaching.

(8) St. Paul, as Apostle and minister, received his gospel from Jesus Christ through a revelation. Portions of St. Paul's gospel relating to Jesus' sojourn on earth were received from the apostles.

(9) The faithful and saints were predestined and fore-known by God for this salvation presumably in a preexistent state prior to their descent to earth and are known as the

"elect." They are destined to overcome sin, the carnal mind, death and corruption, and thus achieve immortality.

(10) The central mystery of St. Paul's doctrine is "Christ in you, the hope of glory," who leads the faithful to "the measure of the stature of the fullness (Pleroma) of Christ and to the Perfect Man."

St. Paul's Teaching on the Vicarious Atonement

In the chapter on the "hidden years" of Jesus, we discussed the "mystical crucifixion" of Christ as an ancient mystery ritual and as a stage in the initiatic path enacted in the mystery religions of the Near East. We have also touched on the idea that Jesus permitted himself to be publicly executed (simultaneously with his "mystical crucifixion") so that the judgment of the powers of evil could be pronounced. We will now discuss St. Paul's interpretation of Jesus' death as a "propitiation" for sin.

St. Paul, as will be readily admitted, was influenced in his interpretation of Jesus' death by the ancient Hebrew concept of the blood-sacrifice as an atonement for sin. St. Paul writes, "For we have all sinned and come short of the glory of God." (Rom. 3:23) If it is correct to attribute belief in the concept of preexistence and previous incarnations of the soul to the early Christians in the communities St. Paul founded and in the Nazorean-Jewish communities, we cannot escape the conclusion that "sin" or the "law of sin" had been operative among the Jews and Gentiles for centuries and millennia. The souls whom St. Paul addresses in his epistles would then be the same souls reincarnated who originally transgressed in ancient Israel and in previous ages through disobedience to God, who again were given over to the "sins of the flesh" in the so-called pagan world. The Lord's judgment for the collective sin of both Jews and Gentiles was thought of as being imminent and close at hand. This understanding no doubt prompted pious Jews such as the Essenes and the community at Qumran to band together and live a life of extreme purity as a possible expiation for this imminent judgment. It was believed that God's judgment, when it descended, could result in planetary war, planetary holocaust or both. The Covenanters of Qumran are known to have composed a "War Scroll" titled The War of the Sons of Light with the Sons of Darkness in anticipation of this war.

According to St. Paul, all have transgressed (in past lives and ages) and are "dead in sins," i.e., not quickened to their divine destiny or origin and are, as we have said, under the influence of the "children of disobedience," evil powers and rulers. St. Paul continues: "...Being justified freely by his grace through the redemption that is in Christ Jesus..." (Rom. 3:24)

As St. Paul seems to be saying, the entire planet is facing impending judgment for its evil deeds. Compensation must be paid. How is this to be accomplished? St. Paul answers, "Whatsoever a man sows, that shall he also reap." (Gal. 6:7) The debt or penalty for sin (what man has sown) must be paid (reaped) by every soul, both Israelite and Gentile. Those who incur the penalty must pay the penalty. However, explains St. Paul, God in his mercy and righteousness desired to bestow opportunity on both Jews and Gentiles and on the world as a whole by freely compensating (justifying) for the penalty or debt due to sin. The law of grace (mercy and opportunity) was made possible by the redemption (deliverance) offered by Jesus. According to the *Scofield Reference Bible*, redemption means "to deliver by paying a price." What was the price? Jesus' descent to earth, his obeying the Father's will, submitting himself to a voluntary crucifixion, undergoing "death," and triumphantly overcoming "death," thus becoming the mediator between God and man.

"[Christ Jesus] whom God hath sent forth to be a propitiation through faith in his blood, to declare his righteousness for the remission of sins that are past, through the forbearance of God;" (Rom 3:25) Scofield explains that "propitiation" is translated from the Greek, hilasterion, meaning "that which expiates" or the "gift which procures propitiation." The penalty or judgment due for sin is compensated or atoned for through Jesus' sacrifice. However, Christ's sacrifice is not brought to completion by his mere physical death, but by his "blood," which as the Book of Leviticus states is the very "life" [of Christ] understood both materially and spiritually. (Lev. 17:14)

How, then, should we understand St. Paul's view of Christ's death? The sacrifice of Christ includes not alone his death, but his voluntary incarnation in the flesh, his submitting to the initiation of the crucifixion, and his resurrection. The "death" of Christ Jesus, according to St. Paul, is Jesus' surrender of his life, soul and body to God's will in fulfillment of that will. The "life" or "blood" of Christ is not the life of a mere mortal, or even of a good man, but of the Son of God. Only the surrender and sacrifice of one who has become Son of God, as St. Paul teaches, will suffice to compensate or atone for the judgment due to sin, both personal and planetary.

Jesus' taking sin into himself, identifying with the effects of sin, and putting sin to death in himself (by his divine life or blood), results in the remission of sin or the "passing over of sins done formerly," as Scofield translates the phrase. Remission or forgiveness of the penalty due to sin, means that the penalty (planetary karma) is set aside so as to give opportunity (grace) to those called to accept the gift of Jesus (reigniting the Divine Spark) and to "put on the new man," who is, as we have said, the "Perfect Man" or Archetypal Man, resident within all humanity.

It is obvious, of course, that even after the death of Jesus on the cross, sin and evil continued in the world. The statement "Christ died for our sins" must not be construed (according to St. Paul's theology) to mean the obliterating of sin itself or the propensity to sin within the faithful, but, rather, the setting aside of the accumulated penalty/debt due to past sins. The debt which is set aside must one day be paid by every soul in future incarnations. Those who have attained to the resurrection in Christ will be in a position to balance that debt (negative karma). Those who attain to the stature of the fulness of Christ whereby they, in effect, become Christ will possess the wherewithal (the spirit of Christ) to balance that debt or negative karma. The ultimate result of the balancing or paying the debt is the "resurrection of the dead," which St. Paul understood to mean the soul's personal attainment of immortality, i.e., freedom and release from confinement in the flesh form, and from successive incarnations. The soul then inhabits a "celestial body." All this has been prefigured by Christ in his incarnation, crucifixion and resurrection. The pattern was set— the faithful must follow. St. Paul admonishes them to "work out your own salvation with fear and trembling." (Phil. 2:12) This "working out" of salvation would not have been possible if God's righteous judgment due for sin had not been set aside temporarily by Christ. As already stated, a planetary holocaust no doubt would have ensued as the Dead Sea sect anticipated. The "End of Days" and the descending judgment due for sin therefore were set aside by Jesus Christ. We may well ask, "How long has this penalty or judgment been set aside?"

The earliest Christians adhered to the concept of the "end of the age", mistranslated in the King James version as "the end of the world". The Greek word "aeon" has several meanings, one of which is "age." According to esoteric tradition, an age lasts approximately 2000 years. Jesus' prophecy of the destruction of Jerusalem and the future end of the age as recorded in the Synoptic Apocalypses (Matt. 24, Mark 13, and Luke 21) presents us with a scenario of the End of Days now postponed till the close of the age, i.e., 2000 years after Christ's coming. Certain Christians during the first centuries anticipated the "end of the age" to conclude in a thousand years after Christ's birth. Today, a number of Christian sects have also concluded that the closing decades of the twentieth century and the beginning of the twenty-first century mark the period for "the end of the age" prophesied by Christ. This is also the conclusion of many evangelistic Christians today.

As Jesus' sacrifice and resurrection set aside a planetary judgment/holocaust, so also was the personal judgment due to sins likewise set aside. Those called by St. Paul to a new life in

Christ, both Israelites and Gentiles, have had a certain percentage of their personal sins set aside to give them opportunity to progress from "glory unto glory." The initial requirement of those called and chosen is the profession of faith in Jesus as Christ and in his redemption on their behalf. As a corollary to this, those who are Jews need not practice the Mosaic code. They are not justified by works but by faith in Jesus' redemption on their behalf should they choose to accept it. Again, the setting aside of personal sin (forgiveness and justification) enables the believer to "put on" Christ and eventually to balance that personal sin by striving to attain to "the stature of the fulness of Christ." Only the fulness of "Christ in you," leading to the personal resurrection, can atone for personal sin.

Due to a covert or overt misinterpretation of the phrase "Christ died for our sins," and others similar to it throughout the New Testament, Christians today have been taught that mere belief in Jesus is sufficient to blot out their sins forever. Were this true, no sin or propensity to sin could have remained among the faithful the moment that Jesus bowed his head on the cross and "gave up the ghost." Sin would have been forever swept away from the earth and from the souls of humanity. To sin would have been impossible and humanity would have been immediately catapulted into heaven!

This of course has not been the case on earth. St. Paul's letters are indeed directed to those redeemed and forgiven by Christ, yet the propensity to sin remains. Why? St. Paul's teaching is clear: forgiveness is the setting aside of sins, (accumulated negative karma) committed in past lives in order to give the believer opportunity to balance those sins both in the present and in future lives. We find this teaching to be both implicit and explicit in St. Paul. His statement, "Whatsoever ye sow that shall ye also reap," corroborates this analysis.

Essentially, this was the theology of St. Paul, the oldest written theology in the New Testament. We shall see how, through the decades and centuries, portions of this theology (and others like it) were deemed heretical, effectively banned and replaced by a new or pseudotheology which eventually became the norm.

Many have also taken note that the closing decades of the 20th century marked a period of what can be described as an accelerated return of negative planetary karma (sin). According to the theology we are presenting, Jesus, by his attainment forestalled planetary judgment 2000 years ago. Mankind are now reaping what they have sown on a planetary scale. Unless this planetary karma be expiated, humanity cannot enter a new age of enlightenment and peace. Yet the new age begins with each of us nurturing and expanding the "Divine Spark" burning within the heart chakra, which St. Paul termed "Christ in you, the hope of glory"

Chapter III

The Oldest Christian Sects, Communities, and their Teachings—Part II

Nazorean or Jewish Christianity

The Nazoreans

It is generally considered by scholars that the oldest form of Christianity originated from the Jerusalem community subsequent to the feast of Pentecost, some fifty days after Jesus' resurrection.

The single complete "historical" record relating to the origin of the Jerusalem community is The Acts of the Apostles written circa 80-85 A.D. presumably by Luke, author of the canonical gospel. Acts was intended to be a history of the "early church"; unfortunately, the book offers no details on the theology of the Jerusalem community or the theology or preaching of any of the twelve apostles. The book is almost wholly concerned with the missionary activity of St. Paul and cites certain of St. Paul's speeches, which have the appearance of being "doctored" to suit the author's intentions.

We are concerned with the beliefs of those who founded this Jerusalem community, which is considered to be an example of "early Christianity" par excellence. Scholar Helmut Koester states that in the first year after Jesus' death the community in Jerusalem did not possess a unified theology or a firm organization. <1>

In Acts, however, an intriguing statement appears. St. Paul is accused of being a "ringleader" of the sect of Nazarenes. (Acts 24:5) The term "Nazarene" or "Nazorean" is considered by most scholars to refer to members of the early

Jerusalem community who were not initially designated Christians. According to Hugh Schonfield, Christians in Judea were designated "Nazoreans."<2> We must look then for the meaning of the term "Nazorean," or "Nazarene" as it is spelled in the Gospels.

On the surface, it would appear that the term "Nazorean" refers to a person from Nazareth, the village of Galilee where Jesus is reputed to have been raised as a child. A closer look at the word, however, shows that "Nazarene" could not have derived from the word Nazareth.

According to German theologian, Holger Kertsen, " *The Greek-German Dictionary on the Writings of the New Testament and other Early Christian Literature* (1963), openly admits that to find a connection between the actual word 'Nazarene' or 'Nazareth' is not possible."<3> Nazareth, a Galilean village, is not mentioned by Jewish historian Josephus. In the third century, an insignificant village, possibly En-Nazira, was designated as Nazareth and officially chosen as the village where Jesus was raised by his parents.

How do we account, then, for the designation "Nazareth" in the gospels? Simply put, Nazareth is a mistranslation. In all cases where Nazareth occurs, the term Nazarene should instead be translated. "Jesus the Nazarene" is the correct translation, not Jesus of Nazareth. In the gospel of Mark, considered to be the oldest of the canonical gospels, chapter 1 verse 9 should, in fact, be read: "And it came to pass that in those days, Jesus came from the Nazarenes of Galilee and was baptized by John in the Jordan," instead of "came from Nazareth of Galilee." Matthew, however, correctly designates Jesus as a Nazarene in chapter 2 vs. 23 in fulfillment of a prophecy. Schonfield reports:

The name borne by the earliest followers of Jesus was not Christians: they were called Nazoreans (Nazarenes), and Jesus himself was known as the Nazorean. It is now widely agreed that this is a sectarian term, of which the Hebrew is Notstrim, and is not connected directly with a place called

Nazareth or with the messianic Nezer (Branch) from the roots of Jesse. In the word-plays of the time these associations were made; but the name essentially relates to a community whose members regarded themselves as the 'maintainers' or 'preservers' of the true faith of Israel.... The same may be said of a pre-Christian sect of Nazarenes (Aramaic: Natsaraya) described by the Church Father Epiphanius <4>

If Jesus and the earliest "Christians" were, in fact, associated with the sect of Nazarenes which predated Jesus' own coming, we may ask, then, from where did the Nazoreans originate and what were their teachings? Why did copyists consistently translate "Nazarene" as "Nazareth"? What were they trying to hide? What "faith" were the Nazoreans trying to preserve, as Schonfield states? Would Jesus' association with the Nazarenes have become a source of embarrassment to the Church Fathers? Theologian Holger Kertsen adds more light on the subject:

*"The word "Nazarene" derives from the Aramaic word Nazar which means to keep watch, to observe, or to own. In a figurative sense, the word also means to vow or to bind oneself to serve God. Used as a noun, it means a diadem, the symbol for an anointed head. **Thus a Nazarene was a keeper or celebrant of the sacred rites.** The "Nazaria" were a branch of the Essenes (the Therapeutae or healers), and like the Ebionites, they were probably one of the first early Christian communities, all of which were referred to as "Nozari" in the Talmud. ...According to John M. Robertson, Samson was a Nazarite (Judges 13: 5-7), who would not allow his hair to be cut and who drank no wine—an ascetic existence. The non-ascetics gave themselves the name "Nazarenes", in order to distinguish themselves from the ascetic "Nazarites." (Emphasis added) <5>*

If Jesus were a keeper of the sacred rites or mysteries, these mysteries must have been a threat to the Temple in

Jerusalem, which considered itself "orthodox." If the Nazarenes were a branch or offshoot of the Essenes, this view would be understandable. The Essenes were considered an heretical sect or cult by the orthodox Temple, the Sanhedrin, the Sadducees, and the high priests. No doubt the Nazarenes were also considered as such. For Jesus to have originated from or been associated with a "cult" practicing unorthodox rites or mysteries would have been too much to bear for the architects of established Christianity. This association would have to be camouflaged.

Is there any evidence that Jesus did, in fact, practice secret rites? The discovery of a portion of the so-called secret gospel of Mark by Professor Morton Smith in 1958 shows Jesus as a practicing hierophant of the mysteries.<6> We cite a portion of the gospel, as preserved in a letter of Clement of Alexandria, following the scene wherein Jesus raises an unnamed youth (Lazarus?) from the dead:

And after six days Jesus told him [the youth] what to do and in the evening the youth comes to him wearing a linen cloth over his naked body. And he remained with him that night, for Jesus taught him the mystery of the kingdom of God. And thence, arising, he returned to the other side of the Jordan. <7>

According to this text then, Jesus practiced nocturnal initiations, imparting "the mystery" to the initiate. The "mystery" may have conferred knowledge or powers that would have threatened the vested interests in the Temple. The scene demonstrates vividly that Jesus' religion (if that is the proper appellation) did not depend on and most certainly was not a part of orthodox Judaism. Jesus and his followers were sectarians, practicing their own rites which they knew to be the "true Faith" of Israel.

Are there any records of the teaching of the pre-Christian Nazoreans? Theosophical writer, H.P. Blavatsky, discusses the practices and teachings of the Nazoreans from a source she mentions as Codex Nazareus, taken from Adolph Franck's *Kabbalah* of 1843. Blavatsky states that the Nazorean sect originated among the people of Galilee where Nazara, the present Nazareth, was built. *"It is in Nazara that the ancient Nazoria or Nazireates held their Mysteries of Life or Assemblies...which were but the secret mysteries of initiation....The oldest Nazarenes...were the descendants of the Scripture nazars...whose last prominent leader was John the Baptist."* <8> Jesus, as we know, was baptized by John the Baptist.

Jesus, writes Blavatsky, was the founder of the sect of new Nazars, and a follower of the Buddhist doctrine! <9> *"...The true, original Christianity, such as was preached by Jesus, is to be found only in those so-called Syrian heresies. Only from them can we extract any clear notions about what was primitive Christianity."* <10>

These Nazarenes apparently were baptized in the Jordan and could not be baptized elsewhere; they were circumcised and had to fast both before and after their baptism.<11> We recall that Jesus also fasted for forty days following his baptism. The Nazarenes were known for their long hair as was Samson, the Nazarite. The Holy Shroud, reputed by some to be the burial cloth of Jesus, likewise, in its depiction of the image of Jesus' body as it lay in the tomb, shows Jesus with very lengthy hair.

The Talmud, speaking of the Nazarenes, calls them a sect of physicians and wandering exorcists.<12> Jesus, of course, is described in the gospels as an exorcist who casts out demons at will—some of which, he states, only respond to prayer and fasting!

According to Blavatsky, the early Nazarenes were numbered among the gnostic sects and believed Jesus to be a prophet divinely overshadowed, sent for the salvation of nations, to recall them to the path of righteousness.<13> We quote the preface from the Codex Nazareus translated from W. Norberg regarding their teaching on Jesus, cited by Blavatsky:

The Divine mind is eternal... And it is pure light, and poured out through splendid and immense space (pleroma). It is the Genetrix of the Aeons [Spiritual Beings]. But one of them went to matter (chaos) stirring up confused movements; and by a certain portion of heavenly light, fashioned it, properly constituted for use and appearance, but the beginning of every evil. The Demiurge (of matter) claimed divine honor. Therefore Christus ("the anointed"), the prince of the Aeons (powers), was sent...who taking on the person of a most devout Jew, Iesu [Jesus], was to conquer him ; but who having laid it (the body) aside, departed on high." (Brackets added) <14>

If this Codex in any way exemplifies the teaching of the Nazarenes about Jesus (and thus possibly the earliest "Christian" sect), we are indeed treading on mysterious ground. In this short excerpt we find ideas later considered heretical. We also find terminology used by St. Paul (Aeons, pleroma) in his letters.

To review: the two outstanding concepts taught by the Nazarenes are (1) the existence of a hierarchy of spiritual beings, one of whom falls into matter, becomes a fashioner or creator of sorts, and claims honor for himself, and (2) the descent of the Christos, highest of the heavenly hierarchy, upon the man Jesus, who then overshadowed him. We find here the teaching on the fall and the very significant idea that the "Christ" is greater than Jesus and was not possessed by Jesus alone.

The Nazarenes apparently believed in a Supreme God, the ultimate Cause, Lord Mano or Primal Man, and a system of divine emanations. The pre-Christian Nazoreans possessed secret cosmogonies and cosmologies. They taught the existence of good and evil angels or Aeons. Their concept of "Christos" was a Primal Man (Lord Mano) much in the manner of the Enochian Son of Man. <15> They distinguish between the Heavenly Christ and the earthly Jesus.

The above teachings are certainly not orthodox mainline Judaism by any stretch of the imagination. And what is more, they are not orthodox Christian teachings. They are the doctrines of an esoteric sect. If the analysis of the term "Nazarene" is correct, we cannot escape the conclusion that the earliest form of Christianity was, in fact, a heresy by later orthodox standards!

We will now turn to the Acts of the Apostles—to Peter's first and second sermon after the feast of Pentecost, in our attempt to analyze the beliefs of the first Christians.

Ye men of Israel, hear these words: Jesus, the Nazarene, a man approved of God among you by miracles, wonders and signs which God did by him in the midst of you, as ye yourselves also know;

Him, being delivered by the determinate counsel and foreknowledge of God, ye have taken, and by wicked hands have crucified and slain;

Whom God hath raised up, having loosed the pains of death, because it was not possible that he should be held by it...

This Jesus hath God raised up, whereof we are all witnesses. Therefore, being by the right hand of God exalted...

Therefore, let all the house of Israel know assuredly, that God hath made the same Jesus, whom ye have crucified, both Lord and Christ. (Acts 2:22-24;32,33,36)

This speech purports to be Peter's original proclamation concerning Jesus, who is simply designated a Nazarene (sectarian) and a "man approved by God," who was crucified and subsequently "raised up" by the power of God. Peter also terms Jesus "Lord" and "Messiah" (Christ).

There is nothing in this proclamation to warrant the later theology that Jesus was "God of very God" from all eternity. This speech is therefore as significant for what it does not say, as for what it does say. Jesus is obviously considered an instrument of God, through whom God performed signs and wonders.

In Peter's second sermon after the healing of the lame man, he states:

The God of Abraham, of Issac, and of Jacob, the God of our fathers, hath glorified his Son, Jesus, whom ye delivered up and denied in the presence of Pilate, when he was determined to let him go.

*But ye denied **the Holy One** and **the Just**, and desired a murderer to be granted you; and killed the Prince of Life, whom God hath raised from the dead, of which we are witnesses. (Acts 3:13-15, emphasis added)*

Note the terms "Holy One" and "the Just", the meanings of which have been lost to later generations of Christians. Significantly, those titles are capitalized in the King James version.

We quote Schonfield for enlightenment on these terms:

The terms 'holy one' and 'just one' belong to the language of the Essene sects, some of whom followed a nazirite way of life.... The Prophet Samuel at Shiloh, whom Luke uses as an antetype of Jesus, was a lifelong nazirite. So was John the Baptist, whose parents are represented as blameless observers of the Law. <16>

We have previously noted that the pre-Christian Nazoreans were an offshoot of the Essenes. Could the so-called Jerusalem or "Jewish-Christians" have been Essenes who acknowledged Jesus as the "Just One" prophesied in the Essene scriptures?

The designation "Prince of Life" is also significant. In the Codex Nazareus, the Christ is called "the Prince of the Aeons" who descended upon the man Jesus. In Acts 7:52, Stephen, about to be stoned, says:

*Which of the prophets have not your fathers persecuted? And they have slain them who showed before of the coming of the **Just One**, of whom ye have been now the betrayers and murderers... (Emphasis added)*

When St. Paul recounts his conversion and healing by Ananias in Damascus, he quotes Ananias as saying, "The God of our Fathers hath chosen thee, that thou shouldst know his will, and see that Just One, and shouldst hear the voice of his mouth." (Acts 22:14)

Schonfield writes that the description of Ananias is of "a typical Essene," since he possesses the gift of healing and urges St. Paul to wash away his sins by baptism, again typical of the Essenes.

The Just One of whom Ananias speaks recalls the revered Teacher of Righteousness of the Qumran Essenes, who had been the leader of the Penitents of Israel, 'the students of the Law who came to Damascus.' It was in the land of Damascus that the Pentitents affirmed the New Covenant as prophesied by Jeremiah....We are meant to assume that Ananias of Damascus understood Jesus to be the expected Just One, and it is plain that the followers of Jesus did so. Obviously, they regarded the Messiah and the Just One as identical.... <17>

Was it merely accidental that Jesus confronted Saul on the way to Damascus? What is significant about Damascus? Holger Kersten speculates that after his resurrection, Jesus may have lived in the environs of Damascus where, he states, the Essene Order had their spiritual center. In Damascus, then, Jesus could enjoy the benefit of Essene protection. Around five kilometers outside Damascus there is a place that is still called Mayuam-i-isa, "The place where Jesus lived." The Persian historian, Mir Kawand, has cited several sources that claim Jesus lived and taught here after the crucifixion."<18>

If Jesus and his disciples were associated with the Essenes, why do we find no mention of the Essenes in the New Testament? Schonfield explains:

There is no reference to the Essenes in the Gospels or the Acts, and such references would be needless if the primitive Christians as Nazoreans came within the framework of what was commonly called Essenism, a generic term rather than the name of one particular sect. The followers of Jesus the Nazorean of Galilee simply established in Jerusalem a community of their 'Way', having a kinship as can be seen from the Acts with the communal 'Way of the Wilderness' followed by the various Essene groups bearing different names and having distinctive characteristics, but having also a family resemblance to one another. <19>

Primitive Nazorean "Christianity," then, may have differed from other Essene communities only insofar as they accepted Jesus as Messiah, or the Just One, as prophesied.

In examining the gospels, Acts, and other epistles, we find the following similarities in doctrine and practice between the various Essene communities, including Qumran and the Nazoreans or Jewish Christians in Jerusalem, and in communities founded by St. Paul and other apostles:

1. Sale of goods and property and the holding of all things in common.
2. Communal and sacred meal of bread and wine.
3. Close-knit brotherhood.
4. Promoters of a New Covenant or Testament.
5. Reject ion of animal sacrifice.
6. Initiates considered the chosen ones or the remnant calling themselves by various names, e.g, the saints, the elect, the poor (Ebionim), sons of light.
7. Use of the power of prophecy.
8. Use of parables or allegories.
9. Initiation by baptism.
10. Use of white garments and/or linen garments.
11. Practice of healing.
12. Use of apocalyptic literature.
13. Belief in preexistence and reincarnation.

14. Belief in final judgment for the wicked, i.e., fallen angels and their followers.
15. Belief in the establishment of the kingdom of God.
16. Taught the existence of fallen angels, Watchers (fallen beings on earth), Satan, the devil, archons, etc.
17. Taught existence of heavenly beings, Aeons, angels, etc.
18. Taught eternal bliss for the righteous.

We have seen that Nazorean Christians probably saw Jesus as a man approved and anointed by God to be the Messiah or the Just One, or that the Christ (the Prince of the Aeons) had descended into the man Jesus, as Codex Nazareus taught. We have further evidence of this latter teaching from Church Fathers in their writings on the Ebionites (from Ebionim, i.e., the poor) which were a further development of the original Nazorean community of Jerusalem. They were known as observers of the Law of Moses. According to biblical scholar Adolph Harnack, the name Ebionaei (as Irenaeus designated them) was given to the Christians in Jerusalem as early as the Apostolic age and the Jerusalem Christians applied this name to themselves. <20>

Unfortunately, no Jewish Christian (Nazorean) writings have been transmitted to us, even from the earliest period. <21> It is our contention that these documents have been suppressed by the orthodox movement. Harnack also reports that the names Ebionites and Nazarenes were used synonymously. <22>

The Ebionite-Nazoreans numbered among their members the family of Jesus, his brothers, sisters, cousins, and certain of his disciples, e.g., Peter, James (Jesus' brother), Jude and, at least initially, John. The later Ebionite-Nazoreans used at least two gospels not presently in our canon, variously labeled the Gospel of the Hebrews, the Gospel of the Nazarenes, and the Gospel of the Ebionites .

James, Jesus' brother, became the first leader of the Jerusalem community or church and was known as a Nazarite.

He was reputed to have worn long hair, like Jesus, drank no wine, abstained from flesh foods and wore linen garments. James was also designated "the Just," an exclusively Essene office. <23> In light of the above, it is quite reasonable to hold that, perhaps, the oldest Christian community was almost wholly composed of Essenes and Nazoreans. Their teaching, therefore, would have been wholly Essene or Nazorean.

The Virgin Birth and the Sonship of Jesus

The Ebionites are said to have believed that Jesus was the son of Joseph and Mary, and that he was begotten by Joseph in a natural manner. They rejected the virgin birth and taught that Jesus was anointed Messiah or Christ at his baptism, at which time he was uniquely inhabited by the Holy Spirit and thus made the Son of God. <24> According to Church Father Epiphanius, the Ebionites believed that Christ was not begotten of God but created as one of the archangels. <25> We would conclude that the Ebionites, among whom were Jesus' own relatives, knew more about Jesus, his origin and mission, than the Church Fathers of the fourth and fifth centuries, who, with one voice, opposed the Ebionites.

An excerpt from the Hebrew or Aramaic gospel used by the Ebionites reads:

When the people were baptized, Jesus also came to be baptized by John. And as he came up from the water, the heavens were opened, and he saw the Holy Spirit in the form of a dove descending and entering into him. And a voice from heaven said: Thou art my beloved Son, in thee I am well pleased... Today I have begotten thee. <26>

The crucial words, "Today I have begotten thee," suggest that Jesus was "begotten" by God at his baptism and was not previously thought of as "begotten" of God. Interestingly enough, the Epistle to the Hebrews in our canonical New Testament reproduces the phrase, "This day I have begotten thee," (Heb 1:5) as being bestowed by God upon Jesus. One is left with the impression from Hebrews that Jesus was "begotten" by God as an initiation or anointing—not by virtue of a miraculous birth. It is likewise significant that Luke 3:22, according to the text found in Codex Bezae CD and the old Latin version, has the phrase "This day I have begotten thee" in place of the more well known, "In thee I am well pleased." Could this have been the original reading? Could the Aramaic gospel used by the Ebionites be closer to the original than our canonical gospels?

This concept of Jesus becoming the Christ, receiving the Holy Spirit at baptism and not before, was later termed Adoptionism and subsequently labeled a heresy! The teaching embedded in Adoptionism is that Jesus was "adopted" by the Father at baptism and had not yet attained to his full Christhood prior to baptism. Now if Jesus were God or begotten of God from all eternity as the Church Fathers later attempted to prove, he certainly could not have been "adopted" by God at his baptism. This would make Jesus appear too human, thus conveying the notion that Jesus might have had to prepare himself to become the Son of God. To the architects of orthodox Christianity, these concepts would not do. Jesus must not be seen as following a path to God (lest others should follow after him and thus become like him?) but must of necessity always be God from all eternity, forever separate from all mankind.

The teaching that the Heavenly Christ or Christ Spirit descended upon Jesus and that the two became one was, no doubt, appalling to certain of the Church Fathers, such as Irenaeus, Tertullian, Jerome, Epiphanius, etc. Why? If the "Christ," Christ-Spirit or Holy Spirit were seen as separate from or greater than Jesus, then that same Christ-Spirit might also descend upon anyone who was worthy! Thus we would have the impossible situation of there being more than one Christ! This would never do, since from early on it was the policy of the orthodox movement in Christianity to make certain that there was only "one Lord Jesus Christ," as the

Creed affirmed, and that no one else could ever aspire to that title. We shall see later that certain Christian sects of a gnostic persuasion affirmed that a believer in Christ could become Christ and that it was possible to attain a level of Christhood commensurate with that of Jesus—taking seriously his words: "Behold, greater things than I do, ye shall do". These sects and their teachings were, of course, branded heretical.

In the words of no less an authority than Adolph Harnack: "...We must point out that in the Adoption Christology, the parallel between Jesus and all believers who have the Spirit and are Sons of God, stands out very clearly....But this was the very thing that endangered the whole view."<27> In the eyes of the Church Fathers, of course!

The Adoption Christology is clearly expressed in the Shepherd of Hermas, a first-century work originating from the community in Rome and considered inspired by several Church Fathers, including Origen. Harnack writes:

"The representatives of this Christology, who in the third century were declared to be heretics, expressly maintained that it was at one time the ruling Christology at Rome and had been handed down by the Apostles .... A closer investigation shows that the Adoption Christology must at one time have been very widespread, [and] that it continued here and there undisturbed up to the middle of the third century...." <28>

It is not surprising, then, that the gospels used by the Ebionites and Nazoreans were eventually suppressed, in that they stressed the innate humanity of Christ, as opposed to his divinity, and rejected the virginal conception of Jesus. Church Father Hippolytus, writing about 225 A.D., states: "And the Ebionites allege that they themselves, also, when in like manner they fulfill the law, are able to become Christs; for they assert that our Lord Himself was a man in like sense with all humanity." <29>

Obviously, the Ebionites could not have asserted that they were capable of becoming Christs had they believed in the virgin birth. Otherwise, they themselves would have to have been born from virgins without the agency of human fathers.

It is our contention that the virgin birth and/or virginal conception of Jesus could not have been a part of the oldest Christian teaching. Paul, John and Mark make no mention of it. It is merely implicit in Luke. Our canonical Matthew is the only source of this account. Several scholars have suggested that the virginal conception and birth in Matthew is a later Hellenistic or Jewish-Hellenic interpolation early in the second century.<30> Matthew attempted to prove through his gene—alogy that Jesus was a descendant of David and thus the rightful King of the Jews. This lineage could only be proven authentic if Joseph was the real father of Jesus. The original Matthew, then, could not have contained the virgin birth, as this sequence would have defeated the purpose for which the gospel was written.

The genealogical passage in the canonical King James version of Matthew Chapter 1 vs. 16 reads: "And Jacob begot Joseph, the husband of Mary, of whom [feminine gender] was born Jesus, who is called Christ." However, the Sinatic Syriac gives this reading: "And Jacob begat Joseph; Joseph to whom was betrothed the virgin Mary, was the father of Jesus who is called Christ." According to Emil Kraeling, author of the *Clarified New Testament*, the above reading is closest to what the received genealogy must have been. Kraeling writes:

It was characteristic of the second century Aramaic speaking Jewish Christians...that they held Joseph to be the father of Jesus. It is improbable that this was an innovation—it was obviously held by their predecessors in apostolic times. For Paul, too, Jesus was of the seed of David according to the flesh (Rom. 1:3). A genealogy obtained from the Jewish-Christian quarter could only have had for its point to prove the Davidic lineage of Jesus via Joseph....It is significant that there are several different manuscript readings for verse 16; the fact indicates that the passage has been much tampered with.<31>

Kraeling then cites the Sinaitic Syriac above as the most probable reading, although most scholars do not accept the Sinaitic Syriac as original.

What is the origin of the virginal conception? Many theologians have looked to Isaiah 7:14, "Behold, a virgin shall conceive and bear a son, and shall call his name Immanuel." This passage, of course, could be explained to mean that a woman who was a virgin conceived. Obviously, once she conceived, she is no longer a virgin. However, according to the reading discovered in the Isaiah scroll from Qumran, the original word used to describe the woman was "alma," correctly translated as "the young woman." When the Hebrew text of the Old Testament was translated into the Greek, known as the Septuagint, the word "alma" was translated into "parthenos," i.e., virgin.

At present, it is impossible to determine how or why the word was changed. It is also a point of contention as to whether or not the "young woman" could possibly refer to Mary. It would seem likely that the young girl was someone known to Isaiah and King Ahaz. Elizabeth Clare Prophet, discussing the Isaiah 7:14 prophecy of a child's birth, states:

While scholars do not agree on the identity of the child, at most it may refer to a Davidic prince who would deliver Judah from her enemies. What is really at issue in Isaiah 7:14 is not the manner of conception, nor the prophecy of the Messiah—messianism had not yet developed to the point of expecting a single future king—but rather the timing of the birth of the providential child vis-a-vis events in the Fertile Crescent. Thus, in the final analysis, neither the Hebrew nor Greek of Isaiah 7:14 refers to the virginal conception about which Matthew writes; nor was there anything in the Jewish understanding of the verse that would give rise either to the idea of conception through the Holy Spirit or to the Christian belief of the virginal conception of Jesus. <32>

In the *Clarified New Testament*, Kraeling contends that the idea of a supernatural pregnancy is in line with thought found in Hellenistic Judaism and evidently originated from that quarter:

There, too, a tendency existed to rule out human paternity in the births of a few great personages of early Hebrew history, such as Issac, Esau and Jacob, and Gershom, as shown by Philo Judaeus (De cherubim, 45-47). This in turn was, perhaps, a thought produced under the influence of the pagan belief that the life of a great man (cf. Heracles and Alexander the Great) should begin supernaturally. In ancient estimation, it required divine or semidivine procreation for a human being to do superhuman deeds (cf. Genesis 6:4). But the idea could also be applied to men of genius like Plato, who was allegedly begotten of Apollo and whose mother had no intercourse with her husband until after his birth. Christianity could not accept mythology, but the claim of a procreation of Jesus by the (as yet impersonal) Holy Spirit satisfied the ancient requirement and at the same time remained chaste and inoffensive. <33>

Could the tale of the virginal conception have been inserted into Matthew under the influence of the teaching of Philo of Alexandria (first century), who, in turn, absorbed so-called pagan or Greek influences? Or was Philo teaching a mystical doctrine relating to the activity of the Holy Spirit at birth?

It was believed in ancient times that great heroes were fathered by the gods. Perseus, Theseus, and Hercules were all sons of Zeus. Zeus was known to have cohabited with any number of women to produce sons. The Book of Enoch treats of the cohabitation of fallen angels or gods called Watchers with the "daughters of men" in order to produce mighty men or heroes. It seems probable, that, in order to make Jesus palatable to so-called pagan converts, his supernatural conception might have been considered a necessity to the interpolators or editors of Matthew's gospel.

It is also entirely plausible that Jesus' conception was made to correspond to the birth myths of Krishna, the Indian Avatar who lived several thousands of years before Christ. Holger Kersten writes that the oldest sources available state that Vishnu (the Second Person of the Hindu Trinity) appeared in the presence of the virgin Devanaki in the form of a man. Devanaki fell down in ecstasy and was overshadowed by the Spirit of God, who joined her in divine and majestic splendor. Devanaki then conceived a child. The event is prophesied in the Atharva-Veda: "Blessed are thou, Devanaki, among all women, welcome amid the holy Rishis. Thou hast been chosen for the work of salvation....He will come with a lightened crown and heaven and earth will be full of joy....Virgin and Mother, we greet you; Thou art the mother of us all, for thou wilt give birth to our Saviour. Thou shalt call him Krishna." <34>

The similarity between this passage and that found in Luke 1:26-34 (the angelic annunciation) is unmistakable. To be overshadowed by the Spirit of God or Holy Spirit, however, does not necessarily presuppose a virginal conception. Luke may not have had in mind a virginal conception but simply a sacred birth, brought about by the Holy Spirit's activity. Certain scholars concede that Mary's question to the Angel Gabriel is only partly authentic: "How shall these things be, seeing I know not a man?" Kraeling comments:

Mary now raises the innocent question of how she can become a mother, not (sexually) "knowing" a man. (cf. Genesis 4:1) The question is surprising if her marriage impends as verse 27 implies. An engaged maiden would naturally have construed this prediction as one that was to be fulfilled after her marriage. The remark is appropriate only if Mary is not betrothed. <35>

Mary, of course, was betrothed. The question then makes little sense. Archibald Robertson, in *The Origins of Christianity,* writes that Luke 1:34-35 is a "palpable interpolation," as is evident from Mary's "inept" question. Robertson also comments on the genealogies as follows:

Luke inserts early in his Gospel a genealogy (different from that of Matthew) tracing the descent of Jesus through Joseph. This is one more proof that the virgin birth was not originally in the Gospel. The genealogy has been feebly doctored by interpolating the words "as was supposed," in 3:23. As in Matthew, the whole genealogy is pointless unless Luke believed Jesus to be really the son of Joseph. <36>

Could Mary have become pregnant by Joseph during their betrothal? According to scholar William E. Phipps, as quoted by E. C. Prophet, this scenario would not have been unusual in the light of prevailing marriage customs:

Within a short time after the betrothal covenant was completed, the boy had the privilege and obligation of cohabitation with his spouse. In the case of the earliest tradition pertaining to Hebrew marriage customs, there appears to have been only a few days lapse between the betrothal transaction and the cohabitation....The Mishnah and the Talmud indicate that Palestinian Judaism showed considerable tolerance towards prenuptial unions in the era of the New Testament, and children conceived as a result were not stigmatized as illegitimate. <37>

According to Phipps, the Hebrews, prior to the birth of Jesus, assumed that God was active in the generation of each individual, that Yahweh creates when parents procreate. In the Bible, Eve exclaims: "I have gotten a man from the Lord". This was interpreted, says Phipps, by a Rabbi: "There are three partners in the production of a man: The Holy One, blessed be he, the father and the mother." The rabbinic theory of marital intercourse is thus summed up. <38>

In light of the above, there would be nothing incongruous in the notion that Mary could have conceived by Joseph, with the overshadowing of or through the agency of the Holy Spirit. Joseph, then, would have been the worthy instrument or vessel of the Holy Spirit in Jesus' conception. Perhaps this is the meaning of John's statement that the sons of God are born "not of blood, nor of the will of the flesh, nor of the will of man, but of God." (John 1:13) Jesus' office as Son of God, Son of Man, or avatar would in no way be compromised through a normal birth, since the Holy Spirit would have been active through Joseph. The Essenes and Nazoreans would naturally hold conception and birth to be a sacred ritual, especially if Mary and Joseph (assuming they were Essenes/Nazoreans) knew beforehand that Jesus was to be the Messiah as prophesied. They would have undergone stringent spiritual and physical purification to prepare for Jesus' birth. In teaching that Jesus was the son of Joseph and Mary, the early Nazorean-Jewish Christians may not have intended to undermine Jesus, as later Church Fathers believed.

In a remarkable text called The Gospel of the Holy Twelve, purportedly translated from Aramaic fragments discovered in an unnamed Buddhist monastery in Tibet by the Edenite Society, there is an angelic annunciation to Joseph on the same day that Mary received her annunciation. According to this gospel, the angel Gabriel declares to Mary that, "The Holy Spirit, even the Mother of Wisdom shall come upon Joseph." Mary is then admonished to abstain from animal flesh and strong drink and is told that the child shall be consecrated to the "All-Eternal" from the womb. The gospel then continues:

And in the same day, the angel Gabriel appeared unto Joseph while he was asleep, and said unto him: "Hail, Joseph, thou that are highly favored by God, for the Fatherhood of God is with thee this day. Blessed art thou among men and blessed be the fruit of thy loins." Joseph, his mind confused, *wondered at these words, but Gabriel said unto him: "Fear not, Joseph, thou son of David...For thou shalt beget a child, and thou shalt call his name Jesu-Maria, for he alone shall save his people from bondage to sin..." Thus Joseph, being raised from his sleep, did as Gabriel told him, and went in unto Mary, his espoused bride, and she conceived in her womb the holy one of God. <39>*

If the above text or any portion of it could be found to be authentic, the foundations of orthodox Christianity would be shaken indeed. The act of sexual intercourse between Joseph and Mary resulting in a sacred conception overshadowed by the Holy Spirit would topple the orthodox church's attitude on sex as sinful or degrading, or at least as a lesser vocation than the celibate state, and the dogma of original sin based on the alleged tainting of the male seed with sin would cease to have any influence. The single concept of Joseph as the father of Jesus would dignify man because it would demonstrate to all men that potentially they could give birth to a Christed being.

We contend that the concepts of the virginal conception and virgin birth of Jesus (as they continued to develop throughout the history of Christian dogma) have effectively removed Jesus into a far corner where he no longer becomes plausible as the great exemplar or pattern that one should follow. The concept of "becoming Christ" as the Ebionite-Nazoreans believed is no longer possible if Jesus had no human father. The only way, then, to "become Christ" is to be a product of a supernatural birth. Thus even the greatest of the saints and miracle workers of the Church are denied any acknowledgment as "other Christs."

· Perhaps the virgin birth concept is to be understood mythically and not literally. Students of comparative religion are well aware that numerous saviour figures, god-men or sun-gods in antiquity are reputed to have been born from virgins. Miraculous, supernatural and/or virgin births have been attributed to the following personages:

Gautama the Buddha
Sri Krishna
Horus, an Egyptian Saviour
Osiris, a god-man and Saviour
Mithra
Zoroaster
Attis
Orpheus
Adonis
Dionysus
Yu, a Chinese Saviour
Hercules
Asklepios
Pythagoras
Plato
Alexander the Great

Few would argue that all of the above figures had had literal virginal conceptions or births. Yet the virginal conception and/or birth are written of each. It is likewise astonishing that several of these figures, including Horus, Mithra, Adonis, and Dionysus, were said to have been born December 25, during winter solstice. Jesus' birth is also celebrated December 25 (although most scholars do not consider Jesus to have been born on this date).

Theosophical writer Annie Besant claims that the virgin birth concept has a purely astrological significance, when one understands what she terms the Solar Myth:

The Hero of the myth is usually represented as a God or Demi-God, and his life...must be outlined by the course of the Sun, as the shadow of the Logos. The part of the course lived out during the human life is that which falls between the winter solstice and the reaching of the zenith in summer. The Hero is born at the winter solstice, dies at the spring equinox and conquering death, rises into the mid-heaven. <40>

Besant explains that a divine personage (such as those listed above) is said to be an Ambassador of the Logos (or Word) personified as the sun. High initiates who are sent on special missions to incarnate among men as teachers or rulers would be designated by the symbol of the sun. Why then a virgin birth? The initiate or hero *"is always born at the winter solstice after the shortest day of the year, at the midnight of the 24th of December, when the sign Virgo (the Virgin) is rising above the horizon; to be born as this sign is rising, he is born always of a virgin, and she remains a virgin after she has given birth to the Sun-Child, as the Celestial Virgo remains unchanged and unsullied when the Sun comes forth from the heavens."* <41> Besant goes on to explain that the life of the "Sun-God" follows the prescribed "mystery ritual" of death, resurrection, and ascension. <42>

In attributing to Jesus a virgin birth, the intent, as we have said, might have been to conform Jesus to the various historical and semi-historical figures who preceded him and to identify Jesus as an ambassador of the Divine Word and as a Sun-God or Sun (Son) of God. In any event, the virginal conception and birth were obviously to be taken symbolically and mythically and not literally. It is an astrological symbol or sign of Divine appointment. Those who interpolated the gospels must have deemed it a necessity that Jesus be born literally of a virgin, in order, perhaps, to compete with heroes, Sun-gods and religious teachers of the past. How the symbolic virgin birth became an historical physical virgin birth is unknown. We contend that the physical virgin birth was not part of the original gospels of Matthew and Luke and that it is alien to Christianity.

Preexistence and Reincarnation in Early Christian Teachings

To return to the teachings of the Nazorean-Jewish Christians, it was stated that there were unmistakable similarities between the practices and beliefs of the Essenes and the earliest Nazorean-Jewish Christians. Besides the Jewish-Christian concept that Jesus was begotten by the Father and became the Christ at his baptism (Adoptionism), the earliest Nazorean-Christians must have accepted the doctrines of preexistence, reincarnation and the fallen angels. We shall examine the Old Testament, the Gospels, certain New Testament epistles, and the Dead Sea Scrolls on these subjects in order to determine whether they were part of the original Christian teaching.

We draw attention to certain passages of the Old Testament which are suggestive of preexistence and rein-carnation.

Psalm 90: 3-6 reads:

Thou turnest man to dust; and sayest, Return ye children of men. For a thousand years in thy sight are but as yesterday when it is past, and as a watch in the night. Thou carriest them away as with a flood; they are as asleep; in the morning they are like grass which groweth up. In the morning it flourisheth, and groweth up, in the evening it is cut down and withereth.

The law of death and rebirth is clearly expressed in this passage. Man's body turns to dust, yet he is given the com-mand to "return" (to embodiment). Man is carried away by the cyclic law of death; the soul can be said to be asleep in between its embodiments; but with a new birth, it is morning and man once again flourishes on the earth.

In Proverbs, reputed to have been written by King Solomon, the King, identifying himself with preexistent Wisdom, soliloquizes about his preexistence and his subse-quent sojourn on earth with the sons of men:

The Lord possessed me in the beginning of his way before his works of old. I was set up from everlasting, from the beginning, or ever the earth was. When there was no depths I was brought forth: While as yet he had not made the earth nor the field....When he prepared the heavens, I was there...When he appointed the foundations of the earth; then I was by him, as one brought up with him: and I was daily his delight, rejoicing always before him; rejoicing in the habitable part of his earth; and my delights were with the sons of men. (Proverbs 8:22-31)

Ezekiel 26:11-19 treats of an angelic being (cherub) who through pride was cast down into a mortal body, and at the time of prophet Ezekiel, lived as the King of Tyre. In this passage there are obvious references to preexistence and subsequent incarnation on earth, as the result of the Lord's judgment.

Ezekiel's vision of dry bones may also relate to the reincarnation of the redeemed house of Israel in a future epoch. Ezekiel sees a vision of dead dry bones being covered with muscle and flesh:

Then he [the Lord God] said unto me, Prophesy unto the wind, prophesy, son of man, and say to the wind, thus saith the Lord God: Come from the four winds, O breath, and breathe up these slain, that they may live. So I prophesied as he commanded, and the breath came into them, and they lived, and stood up upon their feet, an exceedingly great army...thus saith the Lord God: Behold, O my people, I will open your graves, and bring you into the land of Israel...And shall put my Spirit in you, and ye shall live, and I shall place you in your own land; (Ezekiel 37:9-10; 12-14)

This passage cannot refer to the orthodox dogma of the resurrection of the body (which had not yet been formulated) since the reborn house of Israel are to occupy their own land, presumably Palestine, and not heaven or paradise. We suggest that these words graphically illustrate the re-enfleshing (reincarnation) of the souls of the Israelites in their own land in the future when they will experience the signs of the new age or epoch.

Perhaps the most pointed illustration of preexistence and reincarnation in the Old Testament is to be found in Jeremiah 1:4-5.

The word of the Lord came unto me, saying; Before I formed thee in the womb I knew thee; and before thou comest forth out of the womb, I sanctified thee, and ordained thee a prophet unto the nations.

The most reasonable interpretation of this is that Jeremiah had served God in a previous life or lives and merited his being ordained a prophet. God knew the soul of Jeremiah well, before he embodied as the prophet.

And why, we may ask, did the two children of Issac and Rebekah (Jacob and Esau) struggle together in Rebakah's womb? Genesis 25: 22-23 reads:

And the children struggled together within her; and she said, If it be so, why am I thus? And she went to inquire of the Lord. And the Lord said unto her, Two nations are in the womb, and two manner of people shall be born of thee; and the one people shall be stronger than the other people; and the elder shall serve the younger.

We would postulate that the two children in Rebekah's womb were antagonists in previous existences, and both represented two distinct psychological types, or in New Testament phraseology the "children of the kingdom" (good seed) and the "children of the wicked one" (tares or weeds).

It is well known that various sects existed in Palestine prior to and during the time of Jesus, among them Pharisees, Sadducees, Nazoreans, Essenes, Rechabites, Dosithians, etc. Most, if not all of these sects (with the exception of the Sadducees) believed in preexistence and/or reincarnation. These beliefs were indigenous to the ancient world prior to and during the time of Christ.

Jewish historian Josephus (A.D. 37-100), in his *Wars of the Jews,* describes the religious doctrine of the Pharisees: "Every soul, they maintain, is imperishable, but the soul of the good alone passes into another body, while the souls of the wicked suffer eternal punishment."<43> Josephus maintains that the Pharisees were esteemed in the explication of their laws and were the most popular sect. In Phil. 3:5, St. Paul states that he belongs to the sect of the Pharisees. If, as Josephus states, the Pharisees maintained a belief in reincarnation, then, as was noted earlier, St. Paul also must have believed this doctrine. From this we must conclude that reincarnation was an accepted doctrine among the Jewish people. In the New Testament we find no condemnation of this doctrine by Jesus or his disciples, and rather, as we shall see, statements indicative of its implicit acceptance.

In Josephus' dissertation on the teachings and practices of the Essenes, we see that this sect was not solely confined to a monastic community near the Dead Sea; its members also dwelt in towns and villages. A certain order of Essenes was known to have accepted married life. The monastics at Qumran may have represented only one aspect of Essene life.

According to Josephus, the Essenes taught the pre-existence and incarnation of the soul:

"For their doctrine is this: that bodies are corruptible, and that the matter they are made of is not permanent; but that the souls are immortal, and continue forever; and that they come out of the most subtle air, and are united to their bodies as in prisons, into which they are drawn by a certain natural enticement; but that when they are set free from the bonds of flesh, they then, as released from a long bondage, rejoice and mount upward." <44>

The concept of the soul being drawn into a body presupposes the understanding of reincarnation. There is no question but that the Nazarenes (an offshoot of the Essenes) also affirmed this belief.

Josephus continues:

"There are also among them who undertake to foretell things to come by reading the holy books, and using several sorts of purifications, and being perpetually conversant in the discourses of the prophets and it is but seldom that they miss in their predictions." <45>

In the gospels, Jesus is represented as foretelling not only the destruction of Jerusalem, but the end of the age, as well as his own passion and resurrection. Jesus likewise is conversant with the prophetic books of the Old Testament, and apparently with apocalyptic texts such as Enoch. The term "Son of Man" is to be found in Enoch, as has been stated. Jesus assimilated this title and office to himself, and in general scholars have identified over one hundred references to Enoch (which, of course, is not in the orthodox set of "canonical" books) in the New Testament.<46> A number of fragments of Enoch have been discovered at Qumran in Cave IV.

One of the most eminent of Jewish theologians and philosophers, Philo of Alexandria (20 B.C.—A.D. 54), a contemporary of Christ, also taught preexistence and re-incarnation as follows: "The air is full of souls; those who are nearest to the earth descending to be tied to mortal bodies return to other bodies, desiring to live in them." (De Somniis 1:22) <47> In modern terminology, we might note, the term "air" or "subtle air" would be replaced by terms describing "planes of existence," higher frequencies of matter or other dimensions.

In another work Philo writes:

"The company of disembodied souls is distributed in various orders. The law of some is to enter mortal bodies and after certain prescribed periods be again set free. But those possessed of a diviner structure are absolved from all local bonds of earth." (De Gigantes, 2 et seq.) <48>

The influence of Philo upon Judaic thought is incalculable. Alexandria was one of the great centers of Jewish learning. The theology and philosophy of Judaism was raised to sublime heights by Philo. It is significant that such a respected teacher and philosopher so matter-of-factly mentions pre–existence and reincarnation. How then could it have been considered heretical? We conclude that reincarnation was commonly accepted in Israel both before and during Jesus' mission.

The Qumran Essenes and the Nazorean-Christians

Let us return to the Dead Sea Scrolls and compare the phraseology, terminology, concepts and ideas of the Qumran community with the early Nazorean-Christian community and the communities founded by St. Paul as evidenced in the New Testament. Below is a list of comparative examples from *The Dead Sea Scriptures*, edited by Theodore H. Gaster:

1. *The members of the Qumran community style themselves 'the elect' or 'the elect of God.' Compare Titus 1.1: 'Paul, a servant of God and an apostle of Jesus Christ, according to the faith of God's elect'; or I Peter 1.1: 'Peter, an apostle of Jesus Christ to the elect who are sojourners of the Dispersion.'*
2. *The truth of God as revealed in His law, is constantly called the Light. Compare John 1:7-9: '[John] came for witness, that he might bear witness of the light....There was the true light, which lighteth every man coming into the world'; John 8:12: 'I am the light of the world.'*
3. *The enlightened members of the community describe themselves as 'Sons of Light.' Compare John 12:36: 'While ye have the light, believe on the light, that ye may become sons of light.' Ephesians 5:8: 'Walk as children of light.'*
4. *In The Book of Hymns, the faithful frequently declare that they stand in the eternal congregation of God, hold direct converse with Him, and 'share the lot of the holy beings.'*

Compare Ephesians 2:19: 'Ye are no more strangers and sojourners, but ye are fellow citizens with the holy ones (i.e., saints), and of the household of God.'

5. [Gaster compares the use of the term 'remnant' among the Covenanters and among the Christians citing Romans 11:3-5.]

6. *The spiritual leader of the community is called 'teacher' or 'right-teacher.' In John 3:2, Jesus is hailed as the teacher sent by God—that is, the teacher who, it was held, could arise in the last days. So too, in John 16:13, the incarnate Spirit of Truth is described as one 'who shall guide you into all the truth,' and these words are an almost perfect translation of the term rendered 'right-teacher'; for Hebrew has only one expression for 'teacher' and 'guide.'*

7. *In The Manual of Discipline, it is said that, if the community abide by the prescribed rules, it will be a veritable 'temple of God, a true holy of holies.' Compare 1 Corinthians 3:16-17: 'Know ye not that ye are a temple of God and that the Spirit of God dwelleth in you? If any man defile the temple of God, him shall God destroy; for the temple of God is holy, which temple ye are.' (A similar sentiment may be found also in Ephesians 2:20-22.)*

8. *In the Manual of Discipline, there is a long passage describing the Two Ways, viz. of good and evil, light and darkness, which God sets before every man. The idea is indeed a commonplace of ancient Iranian and later Jewish thought, but it is interesting to note the development of the same basic imagery in the familiar picture of the wide and strait gates in Matthew 7:13f. and Luke 13:23f.*

9. *The Prophet that is to arise at the end of days, in accordance with the promise in Deuteronomy 18:18, was, as we have seen, a key figure in the religious doctrine of the Dead Sea Scrolls. Compare, then, Matthew 17:10f. and Mark 9.11f. where Jesus is asked whether Elijah should not have preceded his coming. Compare also John 6:14: 'Then those men, when they had seen the miracle that Jesus did, said, This is of a truth that prophet that should come into the world.' And note that*

Stephen, when arraigned before the council, quotes the very passage of Deuteronomy in evidence of the true character of Jesus (Acts 7:37).

10. The Manual of Discipline quotes the famous words of Isaiah (40:3), 'Prepare in the desert a highway,' in token of the fact that the final apocalyptic age is at hand. In John 1:23, the Baptist quotes exactly the same passage in exactly the same context.

11. The community is often styled 'God's plantation' (after Isaiah 60:21). So, in 1 Timothy 3:6, a novice is called 'neophyte,' literally one 'newly planted.'

12. The river (or lake) of fire graphically portrayed in Hymns as destined to burn up the wicked (cf. Daniel 7:10f.) finds its counterpart in Revelation 19:20.... <49>

It is difficult to avoid the conclusion that the Qumran Essenes and primitive Christians in Jerusalem were somehow inextricably linked together or that the Essenes had, in fact, become Nazorean-Christians. Gaster remarks that the realm of doctrine and ideas in the Dead Sea Scrolls, indeed, presents startling affinities to early Christianity. Gaster then adds:

No less arresting are certain parallels between the organization of the community and that of the primitive Church. It is significant, for instance, that some of the terms used to define its several constituent elements from the Old Testament possess in the Palestinian Aramaic dialect of the early Christians exactly the same quasi-technical sense as denoting parts of the ecclesiastical organization....In other words, the technical vocabulary of the early Palestinian Church seems to reproduce that used by The Dead Sea Covenanters to describe their own organization. <50>

If the early Nazorean-Christian community was or-ganized on the basis of the Essene Covenanters, and if they both are found to share parallel ideas and practices, we must conclude that ideas of preexistence and reincarnation were likewise shared by both, especially in view of the above statements of Josephus concerning the Essene's belief in pre-existence.

We cite now passages from the New Testament suggestive of preexistence and reincarnation:

When Jesus came into the coasts of Caesarea Philippi, he asked his disciples, saying, Whom do men say that I, the Son of Man, am? And they said, Some say that Thou art John the Baptist; some Elias; and others, Jeremiah or one of the prophets. (Matthew 16:13-14)

Surely the most reasonable way to interpret the above passage is to admit that the disciples were citing opinions of the populace regarding exactly who Jesus may have been in a past life. According to the prophecy of Malachai 4:5, the prophet Elijah (Elias) was expected to reincarnate in a future epoch: "Behold I will send you Elijah the prophet before the coming of the great and dreadful day of the Lord." Due to its significance, it is worth quoting again the conversation between Jesus and his disciples cited in Chapter 1:

And as they came down from the mountain, Jesus charged them saying, Tell the vision to no man, until the Son of Man be risen again from the dead. And his disciples asked him, saying, Why then say the scribes that Elias must first come? And Jesus answered and said unto them, Elias truly shall come first and restore all things; But I say unto you, that Elias is come already, and they knew him not, but have done unto him whatsoever they listed. Likewise shall also the Son of Man suffer of them. Then the disciples understood that he spake unto them of John the Baptist. (Matthew 17:9-13)

In this passage Jesus clearly reveals that, indeed, the Old Testament prophecy has been fulfilled. Elijah had returned, reborn as John the Baptist, and had been beheaded by Herod Antipas. Without the understanding of reincarnation, the passage has no clear meaning. In another passage, Jesus announces in no uncertain terms that Elijah had been reincarnated as John the Baptist:

> *Verily I say unto you, Among them that are born of woman, there hath not arisen a greater than John the Baptist...and if ye will receive it, this is Elias, which was for to come. He that hath ears to hear, let him hear. (Matthew 11:11, 14-15)*

Equally important is the much-quoted verse from John 9:1-3:

> *And as Jesus passed by, he saw a man who was blind from his birth. And his disciples asked him saying, Master, who did sin, this man or his parents, that he was born blind? Jesus answered, Neither hath this man sinned, nor his parents, but that the works of God should be made manifest in him.*

In asking their question, the disciples were obviously well aware that sins committed in a previous life would cause disease or illness to outcrop in a succeeding life as a compensation. Note that Jesus does not rebuke his disciples for accepting reincarnation, but simply tells them that the blindness was not for a specific sin committed by the man or because his parents owed him a debt of service (from a previous life), but rather that the man might grow in virtue as a result of a lesson gained by blindness and thus manifest the works of God in his life. The man, no doubt, learned his "karmic" lesson, for he was healed by Jesus. He became the instrument for the "works of God" manifested through the hand of Jesus.

An interesting passage occurs in the epistle of James 3:6: "And the tongue is a fire, a world of iniquity; so is the tongue among our members that it defileth the whole body, and setteth on fire the course of nature, and it is set on fire of hell." This warning on the wages of the misuse of the spoken word takes on greater significance according to the Catholic edition of the Revised Standard version. In place of the innocuous phrase "course of nature," which bears little or no meaning to the modern reader, the Revised Standard Version has the phrase "wheel of birth" in a footnote, as an alternate reading. The term "wheel of birth" is a distinctively well-known Buddhist term. James' meaning here becomes abundantly clear: the misuse of the tongue can result in the karma of successive births spent in paying the debt for that misuse. There is no other possible meaning that can be given to the phrase "wheel of birth." We recall that James, the brother of Jesus, was appointed head of the community at Jerusalem and that he bore the title "the Just," a definitive Essene term. We must again conclude that reincarnation must have been a tenet of early Christianity, and that early Christian beliefs, in turn, absorbed Eastern religious beliefs. This, of course, may have been due to Jesus' own journeys to the East both before and after the crucifixion, as we have seen.

The Fall of the Rebel Angels and the Watchers

The Doctrine of Embodied Evil

We cannot conclude a survey of Nazorean-Jewish Christianity without discussing a teaching which pervades the New Testament: the concept of the fallen angels. This teaching has, suspiciously, been virtually ignored for centuries. Ancient sects of Christians, whether Nazorean, Gnostic, Johaninne, Ebionite, Pauline or otherwise, all maintain a belief in the fallen angels, not exclusively as the denizens of a mythical, murky hell, but as the inhabitants of this earth, appearing no different from, for instance, one's next-door neighbor, yet distinguished by a distinct psychology.

In *The Forbidden Mysteries of Enoch*, [republished as *Fallen Angels and The Origins of Evil*], Elizabeth Clare Prophet writes of these fallen ones as follows:

...The embodied fallen angels, who are the main subject of Enoch's prophecy, have been from the beginning the spoilers of the dreams of God and man, on every hand turning the best efforts of the noblest hearts to a mockery of the Word incarnate and setting in motion the relentless spirals of degeneration and death in both Western and Eastern civilization. <51>

Other than the Bible, one of the oldest books to treat of the fallen ones is the Book of Enoch. Fragments of the text were found at Qumran, so it appears that the text was studied and read by the Essenes. Portions of this book tell the story of the fall of certain divine beings known as Watchers, their subsequent cohabitation with the "daughters of men," and their bringing forth of offspring known as "evil spirits" or "giants." These events were to have taken place in a remote time in the past prior to the flood of Noah. The book treats of Enoch, a messenger and prophet of the Lord, whose mission is to reveal, reprove and judge the Watchers as well as to prophesy of their eventual destruction and the salvation of the "elect."

According to the story, two hundred of these Watchers, goaded by their leader, Samayaza, bound themselves together by mutual oaths, descended upon Mt. Hermon, and through lust took wives for themselves from among the daughters of men. The Watchers taught them sorcery, incantations, cannibalism, murder, abortion. The daughters of men, in turn, conceived and brought forth giants who devoured everything produced by man and finally turned upon mankind to devour them. The giants injured beasts and reptiles and even turned against one another until an enormous quantity of blood was shed upon earth.

Azazyel, one of the Watchers, taught men to make war against one another until impiety increased, warfare raged on earth, fornication multiplied and "the world became altered."

Prophet, commenting on this portion of the story, remarks:

There, millennia ago, someone explained war not as a man-invented or God-sent plague, but as a vengeful act of a fallen angel barred from the planes of God's power. The implication is that man, through one form of manipulation or another, latched on to the war games of the fallen angels and allowed himself to commit genocide in defense of their archrivalries. <52>

When the men of earth cried out to God against these atrocities, the Archangels Michael, Gabriel, Raphael, Suryal and Uriel appeal to the Lord on behalf of the mankind of earth. The Lord then commands Raphael to bind Azazyel hand and foot. Gabriel is dispatched to destroy the offspring of the Watchers by inciting them to mutual destruction. Michael is sent to bind Samayaza and his wicked offspring for "seventy generations underneath the earth, even to the day of judgment". God then sends the flood to wipe out the evil giants, the children of the Watchers.

Unfortunately, in subsequent generations, the giants (or at least their genetic strain) return again to plague mankind. Giants are mentioned in the Old Testament under various names in the original Hebrew: Nephilim, Giborim, Anakim. The children of Israel encounter them during the conquest of Canaan. According to the Book of Judges, David, the shepherd boy, conquers Goliath, the giant, and later as the great Psalmist, he implores the Lord's protection against "the wicked and the ungodly," the names David apparently uses for the evil race of Watchers.

The existence of this evil race, known by various names, pervades the New Testament as well as the Old Testament. They are also called "children of the wicked one," "vipers," "workers of iniquity," "heathens" and "evildoers." According to Enochian prophecy, however, the Watchers will hold power over man until the fallen angels are finally judged. The judgment of the fallen angels, the Watchers and their offspring, the evil spirits, is the main theme of the Book of Enoch . The salvation of the righteous, the coming of the Son of Man, the eventual renovation of the earth are corollary themes. What is most significant about the text is its insistence on the presence of "evil spirits" on earth in physical bodies moving among mankind. We quote a portion of the text:

> *Now the giants, who have been born of spirit and of flesh, shall be called upon earth, evil spirits, and on earth shall be their habitation. Evil spirits shall proceed from their flesh, because they were created from above; from the holy Watchers was their beginning and primary foundation. Evil spirits shall they be upon earth, and the spirits of the wicked shall they be called. The habitation of the spirits of heaven shall be in heaven; but upon earth shall be the habitation of terrestrial spirits, who are born upon earth.* <53>

According to Enoch, then, the earth has been and still is host to embodied evil spirits, Watchers and fallen angels who are the cause of evil, war, hatred, genocide, abortion, moral degeneration, and the myriad atrocities which have been committed on earth since the beginning of time. Even the "Serpent" who seduced Eve was not a mere snake but one of the fallen Watchers whose name was Gadrel. Yekun, whose name means "rebel," likewise seduced all the sons of the "holy angels" and caused them to descend to earth, thus leading astray the offspring of men. Kesabel, another Watcher, induced the holy angels to "corrupt their bodies by generating mankind," a remarkable passage which demonstrates that angels, both good and evil, could either remain in heaven or descend to earth (presumably through incarnation) and live their lives as human beings, even procreating offspring.

Kayyade, another of the fallen Watchers, taught the children of men "the stroke of the embryo in the womb, to diminish it." Abortion, according to Enoch, was originally taught by the fallen angels to the women of earth, and it remains so to this day.

Enoch also points out that mankind were originally created to remain pure and righteous like the angels. Death would not have affected mankind if it were not for their corruption by the Watchers.

Like the Book of Revelation in the New Testament, Enoch prophesies concerning the final judgment of the Watchers. The judgment is to take place at a remote era in the future and is to be executed by the Son of Man. After the evil spirits and Watchers are destroyed by the flood of Noah, they return again by reincarnation, as we have said, to incite mankind to evil until their final judgment. Although Enoch does not directly state how the evil angels and evil spirits return to earth, the method is presumably through reincarnation, along with the righteous and children of God. This recalls Jesus' interpretation of his parable on the end of the age, "the tares among the wheat":

He answered, saying to them, He who sowed good seed is the Son of Man. The field is the world; the good seed are the sons of the kingdom; but the tares are the sons of evil. The enemy who sowed them is Satan; the harvest is the end of the age; and the reapers are the angels. Therefore, just as the tares are picked out and burned in the fire, so shall it be at the end of the age. (Matt. 13:37-40)

Jesus himself apparently believed in and accepted the reality of the embodied fallen ones, whom he designated as "tares" or weeds who are closely intertwined with the "sons of the kingdom" until, of course, they are separated at the end of the age, over 2000 years after his coming. The "sons of evil" can only refer to the race of evil spirits (the offspring of the original Watchers) who reincarnated, and were to continue to plague the earth in physical embodiment.

It appears that Jesus also saw himself as inheriting the mantle of the ancient prophet Enoch in his role as executor of judgment upon the fallen ones on earth. The prophet Enoch was given the "power of reproving the Watchers" and in chapters 93-99 of his book, Enoch pronounces "woes" upon the

Watchers for their sinful deeds. Jesus also pronounces "woes" upon the Pharisees of his day, in terms reminiscent of Enoch:

Woe unto you, Scribes and Pharisees, hypocrites! Because ye build the tombs of the prophets, and garnish the sepulchers of the righteous;
And say, If we had been in the days of our fathers, we would not have been partakers with them in the blood of the prophets.
Wherefore, ye are witnesses against yourselves, that ye are the sons of them who killed the prophets.
Fill up, then, the measure of your fathers.
Ye serpents, ye offspring of vipers, how can ye escape the condemnation of Gehenna? (Matt. 23:29-33)

In this amazing passage, Jesus actually accuses the Pharisees of being the murderers of the prophets by virtue of being the sons of those who murdered the prophets. On the surface, this may seem unjust, for how can a mere descendant be guilty of the acts of his or her ancestor? But could Jesus be referring to the Pharisees as offspring of the Watchers who may have been the ancestors of the Pharisees? Or could the term "sons" be used to mean the reincarnation of the very ones who killed the prophets in Old Testament times? Jesus' denunciation of the Pharisees as "serpents" and "offspring of vipers" would seem to answer the question. The term "viper" is another designation for the fallen angels. We have seen that in The Book of Enoch the "serpent" who seduced Eve was one of the fallen Watchers.

In Jesus' day, "Gehenna," mentioned in this passage, was a place outside the walls of Jerusalem where fire was kept burning for the incineration of refuse. In ancient times the Israelites would burn their children there under the behest of the god Moloch. Gehenna, then, was used by Jesus as a metaphor for the judgment and final dissolution of the offspring of the Watchers, namely, the very Pharisees who stood before him! According to Jesus' parable, the "sons of evil" are not to suffer eternal torment but are to be burned as weeds in the fire and consumed. The place of this consuming fire may well have been the so-called "lake of fire" mentioned in Revelation.

Even more startling, however, is Jesus' confrontation with the Pharisees as recorded in the gospel of John, chapter 8. In verses 23-26 Jesus declares to them, "Ye are from beneath; I am from above; ye are of this world; I am not of this world....I have many things to say and to judge of you."

Jesus seems to be designating the Pharisees as solely of the earth. According to Enoch, the Watchers who sought forgiveness from the Lord were told through Enoch that they were barred from heaven and could not re-ascend once they had fallen to such a low estate. In a previous Enochian passage we have quoted, "the evil spirits" were to remain on earth in flesh bodies and were designated "terrestrial spirits." Jesus also declares he is to "judge" the Pharisees. His attitude toward them leads us to believe that the Pharisees are not simply misguided, rigid, or hypocritical religious leaders, as we shall come to find out in the next passage.

Jesus continues to contend with the Pharisees as follows:

I speak that which I have seen with my Father, and ye do that which ye have seen with your Father.

They answered and said unto him, Abraham is our father.

Jesus said unto them, If ye were Abraham's children, ye would do the works of Abraham.

But now ye seek to kill me, a man that hath told you the truth, which I have heard of God; this did not Abraham.

Ye do the deeds of your father. Then said they to him, We are not born of fornication; we have one Father, even God.

Jesus said to them, If God were your Father, ye would love me; for I proceeded forth and came from God; neither came I of myself, but he sent me.

Why do ye not understand my speech? Even because ye cannot hear my word.

Ye are of your father, the devil, and the lusts of your father ye will do. He was a murderer from the beginning, and abode not in the truth, because there is no truth in him. When he speaketh the lie, he speaketh of his own; for he is a liar and the father of it . *(John 8:38-44, emphasis added)*

There is no clearer passage in the New Testament demonstrating Jesus' acceptance of the physical reality of the offspring of the fallen ones. It is difficult to explain why, since the fourth century, the doctrine of embodied evil has not been accepted by the orthodox church.

Jesus clearly designates the father of the Pharisees to be the "devil" and the Pharisees as the very offspring of the "devil," i.e., the product of intercourse between the Watchers and the daughters of men in ancient times. How could they be standing before Jesus thousands of years later? There is no logical explanation unless it be by means of reincarnation.

It is also interesting to note that Jesus accuses them of doing the "lusts" of their father. Jesus' specific use of the term "lust" would again ally the Pharisees with the Watchers who fell through lust for the daughters of men and moreover demonstrated a distinct lust for killing as well.

We can also note that the Pharisees seek to justify themselves before Jesus by declaring that they were not born of fornication. Was Jesus simply accusing all the Pharisees of being born out of wedlock? This would seem ludicrous, unless the Pharisees were specifically denying that they were the offspring of angel fornication, the unlawful sexual intercourse of the rebel Watchers with the same daughters of men. <54>

Although, in the above passage, Jesus does not name who the devil is, he may have used this term as a generic one. The "devil" is accused of being a murderer, a liar—characteristics which would well fit Samayaza or Asazel, the two foremost leaders of the band of Watchers. However, in the above quote, Jesus may also be referring to the fallen angel Satan or even to Lucifer, the fallen archangel.

The Book of Revelation, written toward the close of the first century by the apostle John, gives an alternate account of a fall which may have taken place before the fall of the Watchers, although it is not possible to conclusively prove this. <55> The passage reads as follows:

And there appeared another wonder in heaven; and, behold, a great red dragon, having seven heads and ten horns, and seven crowns upon his heads. And his tail drew the third part of the stars of heaven and did cast them to the earth;...And there was war in heaven; Michael and his angels fought against the dragon, and dragon fought and his angels, and prevailed not, neither was their place found any more in heaven. And the great dragon was cast out, that old serpent, called the Devil and Satan, who deceiveth the whole world; he was cast out into the earth, and his angels were cast out with him (Rev. 12:3-4, 7-9)

According to this passage, evil originates not on earth but in heaven, not through the fall of Adam and Eve, but through the dragon, presumably another generic term for, perhaps, a conglomerate of rebellious angels. We are told of a cosmic war between Michael the Archangel and the dragon with their respective angelic armies engaged in the battle. It is significant to our study of embodied evil that the dragon/serpent/devil and his angels are not cast into hell or hades but into the earth. We presume, then, that like the Watchers and their offspring, the giants, the dragon and his angels are also on earth ready to devour "the woman" and her offspring, as Revelation records.

In the above quote we are not told specifically who or what the dragon/devil is nor are we told what caused the dragon to cast the stars (angels) from heaven to earth, or why Michael was forced to fight the dragon. A passage from Isaiah, however, may afford us a clue:

12: How art thou fallen from heaven, O Lucifer, son of the morning! How art thou cut down to the ground that didst weaken the nations!

13: For thou hast said in thine heart, I will ascend to heaven, I will exalt my throne above the stars of God; I will sit also upon the Mount of the congregation, in the sides of the north.

14: I will ascend above the heights of the clouds, I will be like the Most High.

15: Yet thou shalt be brought down to Hades to the sides of the pit.

16: They that see thee shall narrowly look upon thee, and consider thee, saying, Is this the man who made the earth to tremble, who did shake kingdoms,

17: Who made the world like a wilderness, and destroyed its cities, who opened not the house of his prisoners? (Isaiah 13:12-17)

Ever since the early centuries of Christianity, this passage has been used to describe the fall of Lucifer, the rebellious Archangel. The quote demonstrates that pride was Lucifer's motive—the desire to surpass all of the angels (stars of God) and to be like the Most High God himself. But more importantly the passage shows that Lucifer fell from heaven to the earth as did the Watchers. According to verse 16, he became a man on earth, and a very powerful man at that—one who could shake kingdoms. According to Isaiah, then, Lucifer walked the earth in the flesh, even as an ancient king, such as Nebuchadnezzar, the king of Babylon, as Aphrahat, a fourth century Persian Christian theologian believed. <56>

An alternate account of the fall of Lucifer/Satan is given in the third century text the Gospel of Bartholomew. Satan informs Bartholomew that he was the first angel God created even before Michael and the other Archangels. When God created man, Michael worshipped the man because he was God's image:

And Michael said to me [Satan]: Worship the image of God which he has made in his own likeness:

But I said: "I am fire of fire. I was the first angel to be formed, and shall I worship clay and matter? And Michael said to me: Worship, lest God be angry with you." I answered: "God will not be angry with me, but I will set up my throne over against his throne, and shall be as he is." Then God was angry with me and cast me down, after he had commanded the windows of heaven to be opened.

"When I was thrown down, he asked the six hundred angels that stood under me whether they would worship Adam. They replied: "As we saw our leader do, we also will not worship him who is less than ourselves."

After Satan and his angels fall to the earth, they are put into a deep sleep. When Satan awakens, he decides how he will deceive Adam and Eve:

And I devised the following plan. I took a bowl in my hand, and scraped the sweat from my breast and my armpits, and washed myself in the spring of water from which the four rivers flow. And Eve drank of it, and desire came upon her. For if she had not drunk of that water, I should not have been able to deceive her. <57>

The above account is important in two respects: the motive behind Satan/Lucifer's challenge to Deity, and the fact that Lucifer/Satan is shown scraping the sweat from his body and taking a bath—clear evidence that the "devil" was not thought to be a vapory spirit inhabiting the murky realms of hell, but a physical man on earth capable of seducing Eve in more ways than one. We may also assume from this passage that the six hundred other angels who were cast to the earth were also inhabiting physical bodies like their counterparts, the fallen Watchers.

Just like the Book of Enoch, the Gospel of Bartholomew was declared apocryphal by the powers that be in the orthodox church, and therefore was banned from the canon of accepted scriptures. It seems as though the Church Fathers were forever wary about the doctrine of embodied evil. Occasionally, however, they overlooked certain books, some of which found their way into the New Testament.

The letter of Jude unabashedly mentions the "angels who kept not their first estate" and who gave themselves over to "fornication, going after strange flesh." It is difficult, indeed, for angels to accomplish this without bodies. Jude calls them "spots in your love feasts," "clouds without water," and "wandering stars, to whom is reserved the blackness of darkness forever." Jude then goes on to quote Enoch, almost word for word, describing the Lord who "cometh with ten thousand of his saints...to execute judgment upon...the ungodly," namely the fallen angels, who are described by Jude as murmurers and complainers whose mouths speak great swelling words, who are distinguished by their pride and sensuality. It is obvious that Jude is warning his congregation that the fallen angels have infiltrated the Christian communities, to beware of them, and to be alert to the signs by which they are recognized.
2 Peter also goes on about the fallen angels, using almost the exact phraseology of Jude, describing the "angels that sinned" as "beguiling unstable souls" who "cursed children" and are "servants of corruption." Apparently the apostles, like Jesus, were aware that the fallen angels in their midst were marked by a certain animal magnetism and a definite "psychology."

The Nephilim

The Essenes, Nazoreans, early Jewish-Christians, and Christian-Gnostics all believed in the presence of the fallen angels on earth. It is indeed astonishing that the Christian church in succeeding centuries was not heir to this vital teaching by which, as we believe, the existence and continuation of evil on earth is explained. In Revelation 12:3-9 we read that "evil" in the form of the "dragon" originated not on earth but in heaven. In Genesis 6:1-4 (Jerusalem Bible translation) the "sons of God, looking at the daughters of men saw they were pleasing, so they married as many as they chose." We have established that the "sons of God" were the Watchers who fell to earth from heaven and mated with them. The passage continues: "The Nephilim were on the earth at that time (and even afterward) when the sons of God resorted to the daughters of men, having children by them. These are heroes of days gone by, the famous men." Who, then, are the Nephilim? In *The Twelfth Planet*, Biblical scholar Zecharia Sitchin offers a vast body of evidence to the point that the Nephilim were an extraterrestrial race of an advanced evolution who originated from a planet called Nibiru/Marduk outside the solar system. Sitchin translates the Hebrew term "Nephilim" or "Nefilim" as "those who fell to earth." They came, he argues, nearly 450,000 years ago. From his study and translation of Sumerian tablets, Sitchin offers a well-documented thesis that the Nephilim "gods," whose names were Anu, Enki, Enlil, Ishtar, Ninurta, among others, were responsible for the creation of man, i.e., homo sapiens, through a process of advanced genetic engineering, to aid in what had become burdensome mining operations in Southern Africa. This event, according to the Sumerian chronology of the Nephilim, occurred approximately 200,000 years ago in Africa—a figure coincident with the current position of scientists who are arguing, based on crossracial studies of mitochondrial DNA and its natural mutation rate, that the human species originated from a single African "Eve" 200,000 years ago. The Sumerian creation account bears clear parallels to the account in Genesis—which is a later production and very possibly a condensed version of the Sumerian.

The Nephilim, Sitchin argues, were responsible for the origins of the city of Sumer and its culture—a culture that suddenly originated, post-flood, with no previously known history, from a dearth of any civilization on the planet, circa 4000 B.C. with the following achievements, any one of which would have to be considered a major human invention or development of vast proportion and consequence: medicine; a sun-centered astronomy with all the planets, which included facts re-discovered only in modern times, such as the asteroid belt and the existence of Pluto; mathematics; a body of laws and a judicial system; agriculture, including the science of hybrids; architecture to include sophisticated pyramids, arch-work, etc.; governmental structure with a hierarchy of officials; an alphabet and writing; art and sculpture; mining and metallurgy, including the creation of alloys. Someone brought all this knowledge suddenly to bear, and the Sumerians were quite explicit in acknowledging its source—the "gods."

The Nephilim "gods" were described by the Sumerians as lusty, capricious and constantly in a state of rivalry with one another. In fact, Sitchin shows that warfare itself originated among the "gods" who, in ancient times, taught the arts of war to their creation—"man." The Nephilim are said to have sponsored ancient kingship, especially in the Fertile Crescent where they initially landed. They are characterized by Sitchin as manipulative, warlike, not above mass murder and genocide to accomplish their ends. In short, the Nephilim bear a very close resemblance to the fallen angels and the Watchers, who are also said to have taught the arts of war to mankind. Could they be identical with the Nephilim? Genesis 6, however, makes a distinction between the "sons of God" (Watchers) and the Nephilim, who were already on earth when the Watchers fell. Could the "daughters of men" have been the product of Nephilim genetic engineering? Could the Nephilim have been the angels who were cast out of heaven as recorded in Revelation 12 and in the Gospel of Bartholomew? Is it possible that Anu, Enki, Enlil could have been rebellious angels who sought to rival God by their advanced scientific achievements on this and other planets, even competing with or mimicking God's creation by creating a race of their own?

As we have seen, the Old and New Testaments seem to make a clear distinction between two races, one of light and one of darkness. David writes of the "wicked" and the "ungodly." Jesus speaks of the "children of the wicked one." In the Old Testament, Joshua makes war on races of "giants"

(King James translation) who inhabit the land of Canaan (compared to whom the Israelites describe themselves as "grasshoppers"), and variously designated as Ghiborim, Anakim and Rephaim. Could these "giants" have been a super race sired by the Nephilim? St. Paul writes of "the archons (rulers) of the darkness of this cosmos." We will later examine Christian and pre-Christian Gnostic texts which describe the usurper deity, Ildabaoth and his archons, who create a kind of "man" by the light they have stolen from above. Christian-Gnostic theologians in the second century wrote of "hylic" (Greek: material) men who possessed no soul and who were doomed to extinction. Could these material men have been identical with the race of "homo sapiens" engineered by the Nephilim who were not created by God, hence did not possess a soul? Is the Gnostic usurper deity, Ildabaoth, to be identified with Lucifer, or, perhaps, a rival of Lucifer? Or could Ildabaoth, the chief Archon, be the Anu of the Sumerians, the chief god of the Nephilim pantheon?

We are in the midst of a vast body of ancient Christian teaching regarding the "mystery of evil" and of the fallen angels—a body of teaching truly ignored for 1,800 years by the leaders of Christendom. If the fallen angels/Nephilim are truly on earth as ancient Christian texts, both canonical and apocryphal, seem to be saying, would they not seek to suppress evidence that they, in fact, exist? Or if such evidence does exist, would they not seek to ignore or downplay its significance? We leave it to the reader to answer these questions.

Chapter IV

Brief Scenario of Early Christian History

Introduction

Contrary to popular opinion, we know very little concerning the true history of what has been called "Early Christianity." In fact, "Early Christianity," as an homogeneous, unified body of doctrine and practice, never really existed. In the New Testament alone there are contrasting and conflicting accounts of Jesus and his teaching. There is Pauline Christianity, Johannine Christianity, Nazorean-Essene-Jewish Christianity—each represented by certain books in the New Testament—to say nothing of the extracanonical accounts of Jesus' life and teaching, later judged apocryphal or heretical. For example, Jesus' words and teaching differ markedly when one compares the synoptic gospels with the gospel of John. The theology preached by St. Paul was not the same theology as preached by Peter. Nor did the communities founded by St. Paul receive the same doctrine as those founded by Peter. Each of the apostles founded communities which came to be identified, more or less, with that apostle. These communities became, as it were, colored by the apostle's own understanding, interpretation, and internalization of the doctrines received from Jesus. Not only were communities founded by the twelve apostles, but we read in the New Testament that seventy-two disciples were also sent by Jesus himself during his own lifetime for the purpose of spreading the teaching. This simple and somewhat overlooked fact of sheer numbers—twelve apostles, seventy-two disciples, at the least, each having a special claim to authority wherever he (or she) went due to his close association with Jesus—makes it not only probable, but certain, that a diversity of groups and communities were founded due to the very diversity of teachers. Certainly it is also possible that, from the beginning, there existed a diversity of teaching. These diversities, however, need not have been mutually exclusive. They might have been complementary. They certainly were not orthodox-Christian in the sense that we understand the term today.

It is well known that the earliest schism in the Christian communities was between Peter and St. Paul. According to *A History of Christianity* by Paul Johnson, the apostle Paul rescued Christianity from extinction. <1> Johnson writes that St. Paul was the first "fully to comprehend Jesus' system of theology, to grasp the magnitude of the changes it embodied, and the completeness of the break with Judaic law."<2> Johnson calls St. Paul's doctrine "cosmic and universalist."<3>

In contrast, Peter is represented as being a traditionalist. Peter's insistence on the implacability of the Mosaic code and its absolute importance in the scheme of salvation tended to confine the new religion to a sect within Essene-Nazorean Judaism, as opposed to a universal doctrine meant for people of all religions.

Johnson remarks that St. Paul did not believe in organization, but in the Spirit working through him and through others in the various communities. He did not want a fixed system with rules and prohibitions. He taught that the church's leaders should exercise authority through the gifts of the Spirit and not through office. According to St. Paul, the two noblest spiritual gifts were prophecy and teaching. Worship in his communities was unorganized and subject to no special control. There was no distinction between a clerical priestly class and a laity. <4>

In contrast, the Nazorean-Essene communities were marked by the inclusion of presbyters and bishops as authority figures within the community. These offices, as we have seen, were based upon the organization of Essene communities at Qumran, which in turn had their origin in the Old Testament. These offices were not necessarily bestowed as the result of the candidate "receiving the Spirit" or receiving the "gift of pro-phecy." The office of bishop became primarily administrative and organizational. This is not to say, however, that the bishop could not or did not "receive the Spirit".

From their inception, these two "types" of Christianity overlapped each other and mutually included one another. Johnson writes that "the Church expanded not as a uniform movement but as a collection of heterodoxies."<5> From the beginning, there were "numerous varieties of Christianity which had little in common, though they centered around belief in the resurrection."<6> There was nothing to warrant the notion that one type or variety of Christianity was any better or more "true" than the other. There was one tendency, however, or thread that ran through them all.
Johnson continues:

*Before the last half of the third century, it is inaccurate to speak of a dominant strain of Christianity...So far as we can judge, by the end of the first century, and virtually throughout the second, **the majority of Christians believed in varieties of Christian-gnosticism**.* (Emphasis added) <7>

In our examination of the theologies of St. Paul and of the Nazorean-Essene communities we have been made aware of certain teachings which have not passed into orthodox or "modern" Christianity, i.e., preexistence, reincarnation, the ex-istence of divine emanations, evil powers, etc., which have always been called "gnostic" or "esoteric." This strain, Johnson observes, was present in early heterodox Christianity. Ernst Wilhelm Benz, professor of history at the Phillips University of Marburg Germany, writes:

A tradition of esoteric Christianity has long existed alongside institutional Christianity. It traces its roots to the New Testament and the early church, which adopted many pre-Christian elements of the arcane disciplines.
The esoteric form of teaching and its related form of

community and liturgical practices represent an original form of religious experience, understanding and community life that has been present in Christianity from the beginning, that was able to find a connection with certain basic esoteric elements of Christian tradition and that had been suppressed or pushed aside in the course of the development of Christianity into an institutionalized church. <8>

We will attempt to reconstruct a possible "history" of primitive heterodox Christianity, paying special attention to those communities and sects which claimed to have received esoteric teaching from Jesus and his disciples, and who considered themselves to be primitive or original Christians. We shall later see that orthodox, institutionalized Christianity (as we now call it) emerged at a very early date, as a reaction to these so-called esoteric communities.

As we begin our scenario with a general overview, we must first understand that there were certain Christian communities toward the end of the first century that had received or were receiving their doctrines from a succession of teachers who studied under or had been trained by one or more of Jesus' disciples. These teachers, as distinguished from bishops, imparted what came to be known as the secret doctrine of Jesus. The evidence in the epistles of St. Paul points to the Pauline communities in Asia Minor as having received a "wisdom" imparted by St. Paul and by other teachers sent by him. A circle of communities founded by John, the disciple, originating in Syria and continuing in parts of Asia Minor, shows evidence of "gnostic" ideas.<9> Communities originating as a result of the work of the apostle Judas Thomas, called by some scholars the school of Thomas, in Syria, Mesopotamia and later in Egypt, also bear witness to an "esoteric" tradition or doctrine. The Gospel According to Thomas, the Acts of Thomas, and the Book of Thomas the Contender all point to this tradition.<10>

There were other communities, however, which received teaching and traditions from bishops, presbyters, deacons or elders. More often than not, these traditions were based on oral and written sources of what others had taught or observed from either the disciples or their successors. The office of overseer or bishop was oftentimes associated with a church or community basing its organization on Essene rules of administration similar to Qumran. Some of these bishops, no doubt, imparted Jesus' secret doctrine and others did not. As we have said, the office of bishop did not exist in the communities founded by St. Paul.

Until the end of the first century, it was impossible to distinguish between "orthodox" or "non-orthodox" Christianity, and "gnostic" or "non-gnostic" Christianity. Dogma and creed were, of course, unknown. Divergent interpretations of Jesus' life, teaching and mission existed. This was reflected in the diversity of "scripture" being written at the time, i.e., the close of the first century.

Scholar Bently Layton, discussing early Christian scriptures, states:

> *Early Christians lived in urban, and sometimes economically comfortable settings; a proportionally high number of them must have been able to read and write. Thus small collections of Christian writing quickly accumulated in one place or another; and it was in these writings that the inspired insights of interpreters and leaders of the religion were often set forth. These works served many different purposes and so were written in many literary forms, appropriate to their functions within the churches that used them. <11>*

The key words here are "inspired insights of interpreters and leaders," denoting that in the first to the mid-second century there was extensive creative freedom among various Christian communities, among teachers, writers, and theologians. Sometimes, explains Layton, if a group of early Christians agreed in recognizing the presence of inspired authority in a writing or collection of writings, the work usually rose to the status of scripture. In other cases new books were deliberately composed as scripture: <12>

Early Christian scriptures then sometimes presented messages or points of view that conflicted with one another. This is not surprising, for in the first three centuries, there was only sporadic coordination among the various Christian groups and certainly no centralized uniformity....

In fact, the lack of uniformity in ancient Christian scripture during the early period is very striking, and it points to a substantial diversity within the early Christian religion, probably going back to a time just after Jesus' death in about the year 30. Although it is historically correct to speak of early Christianity as one religion, it can also be described as a complex network of individual parties, groups, sects, or denominations. <13>

One of the reasons for this diversity, Layton continues, came from "the coexistence of essentially different theological opinions and traditions about the significance of Jesus, some of which seem to be as old as Christianity itself." <14>

We will later take note that a majority of these diverse scriptures and "different theological opinions and traditions" about Jesus never found their way into what later became known as mainstream or orthodox Christianity, yet these very traditions at one time composed the prevailing viewpoint of the vast majority of Christian sects and communities. Some prolonged and intense force had to be applied to this diversity of materials to build the orthodox monolith that dominated the landscape of thought for over one thousand years as the body of Catholic orthodox doctrine, only in fact to narrow yet further, in what was not in any way a return to original Christianity, but in the even more stark and narrowed architecture of Protestantism.

In the midst of this early diversity, then, a movement began among certain bishops toward the end of the first century, such as Ignatius of Antioch and Clement of Rome, which sought to monitor, label, systematize, amalgamate and finally control the doctrines being taught in the various churches and communities. This movement was to eventually result in the establishment of "orthodox" or institutionalized Christianity.

This early process of labeling or monitoring began when certain groups of Christians, communities or various teachers were singled out as being sectarian or "heretical" in their beliefs and practices. These groups, communities, or individuals eventually came to be called "gnostic" or "heretical". It is most surprising to find that the communities so labeled were the very ones who were imparting the esoteric doctrines of Jesus, St. Paul or one of the other disciples.

The word "heresy" derives from the Greek "haerens", which means an act of choosing; that is to say, originally a "heretic" was one who chose freely for himself in matters of belief or religion, whether or not that belief was opposed to a prevailing belief system. Eventually "heresy" meant a "school" or "sect", and terming the denomination "heretical" simply meant "sectarian," i.e., one who affiliates with a sect.

The early Christian movement, heterodox and diverse, was composed primarily of sects, groups, or schools. The word which is translated as "church" in the New Testament derives from the Greek "ecclesia" meaning "assembly." The ancient Christian movement was composed exclusively of assemblies (churches), groups, sects, and schools. The entire movement was, therefore, sectarian.

Toward the close of the first century, certain bishops started what may be called a "disinformation campaign," directed at those who were apparently teaching the esoteric doctrines of Jesus. The motive of these bishops remains highly questionable. This "campaign" reached its peak toward the middle of the second century, as will later be described.

Simultaneously, these same bishops initiated an equally aggressive campaign to "unify" the various churches and communities in an attempt to codify their teachings. Certain doctrines were singled out as being "sectarian," "heretical," and were subsequently labeled as incorrect, misleading or false.

What was the nature of the doctrines so labeled? Although we shall delve into this question in greater detail, suffice it to say that doctrines and teachings that resulted in a greater spiritual independence and creative freedom for the individual believer were singled out in almost all cases. On the other hand, teachings, doctrines and practices that led the individual Christian to depend on the bishops and the organized churches as the source of salvation were designated as "correct," or in later terminology, orthodox ("straight-thinking": Greek: ortho: straight, and doxos: opinion or thought). The systematized, codified doctrines with their accompanying rituals came to be known as "tradition." These traditions were based on the witnesses of past generations (either of disciples or their successors) and oral and written works such as the diverse gospels that were in circulation. They were not based on the individual's present mystical awareness or apprehension of God, nor on what was later termed the secret teaching of Jesus (likewise handed down). The handing down of this tradition became known as "apostolic succession," that is to say, a tradition based on successive witnesses of disciples in the past.

Architects of "orthodoxy" attempted to organize a "federation of churches," ruled by bishops. No such federation was intended by Jesus, or, for that matter, by St. Paul. We search the New Testament in vain to find a blueprint for such an organization as was later established and designated the "catholic" or universal church.

The end result of the establishment of this "federation" was, of course, greater spiritual and temporal power for the federation. Churches, communities and individuals who found themselves in disagreement with this federation and its tra- ditions were ostracized and categorized under various labels, i.e., gnostic, heretic, satanist, etc. In general, those who dis- agreed tended to believe that divine knowledge received from within, through insight or revelation, was superior to that received through faith in tradition. As a result of the controversy between the orthodox federation and the so-called Christian-Gnostics, dogmas and creeds were fabricated.

Eventually, Christian-Gnostics were forced to separate from the orthodox federation of bishops. The united federation branded itself the "one, true, catholic and apostolic church," by the end of the second century.

However, it was indeed ironic that the orthodox federation succeeded in copying and reproducing what the Christian-Gnostic sects taught as regarding the origin of their teaching.

By the end of the third century, the federation of bishops, calling itself the "Church," succeeded in permanently ousting the Gnostic-Christian sects, who themselves were the repositories of the original Christian teaching. The federation of "churches" was characterized by a marked distinction between clergy and laity—a distinction that Jesus would have abhorred and that St. Paul, likewise, would have disparaged.

These, then, were the general developments in a movement whose motive was power, pure and simple, and control over the minds and souls of men. Our inheritance from this movement is the loss of what was the original body of Jesus' teachings.

Chapter V

The Lost Christianity of the Original Sects

30 A.D.—120 A.D.

As we have earlier stated, it is generally agreed upon by scholars that the oldest Christian community was located at Jerusalem, established some time after Jesus' resurrection. We have examined the Nazorean community and have concluded that the doctrines taught by this earliest group of Christians would today be termed heretical.

Likewise, the communities founded by St. Paul are considered very ancient. Pauline Christianity, as we have seen, promulgated doctrines that would later be termed "gnostic." As far back as we go, we find a gnostic, heterodox Christianity, characterized by the following world view:

1. The whole world "lieth in wickedness" (1 John) and has come under the dominion of evil. This state of affairs is the direct result of a fall in the realm of the Aeons, angels, Watchers, and/or Nephilim, and their subsequent reincarnations on earth.

2. Humanity have been seduced by evil powers and have themselves fallen from a higher to a lower estate. The "elect" were predestined for glory, but due to the fall (allegorically explained as the fall of Adam and Eve), they have been corrupted by ignorance and sin.

3. A Redeemer is needed to rescue humanity from this plight. Jesus, the Saviour and Son of God, has redeemed humanity from corruption, ignorance and sin, through his life, sacrifice and resurrection and by means of his Doctrine (Gnosis), which

brings knowledge and wisdom and dispels ignorance. Belief in the Person of Jesus as Saviour and acceptance of his doctrine are the initial means to salvation/redemption, brought about by the restoration of the Divine Spark within the heart of the believer.

4. There exists a spiritual universe upon which the physical universe is patterned. The spiritual universe is the abode of innumerable divine emanations, all of whom have free will. Elect souls once found their abode in the heavenly state before their descent to earth and their "fall". On earth they still contain a portion of this divine spark which has its origin in the spiritual universe. Man is composed of Spirit, soul and body (see St. Paul). The destiny of man is to return to the spiritual realms (eternal life) by a process termed "the resurrection", demonstrated by Jesus.

Early heterodox Christianity was an attempt to elaborate on this essential cosmic world-view through varying interpretations, which naturally differed according to the religious and cultural backgrounds of the communities. The apostle, disciple or teacher who founded the community heavily influenced the way the teaching was presented and whatever doctrines were taught. For instance, a community of Jews or Essenes would receive a teaching colored by the background of Jewish Apocalyptic and Hebrew scriptures. A community of Greeks would naturally receive teachings influenced or explained by means of the Greek world-view and would be, in essence, Platonic or neo-Platonic in its conception of things. Communities in Asia Minor with oriental backgrounds would evidence strains of Hindu, Persian, Egyptian or Babylonian conceptions. They would be marked by teachings concerning reincarnation or the cosmic battle of Light and Darkness. It was the utter universalism of early heterodox Christianity which allowed these various interpretations and conceptions to be contained under the canopy called "Christianity" and to thrive. It was not until self-styled authorities attempted to reduce these rich theological interpretations to a creedal religion, largely based on the Old Testament world-view (exoterically understood), that Christianity became a closed system characterized by intolerance on the part of its leaders.

As we review the oldest of the Christian sects and communities, we shall often be treading on unfamiliar ground. Yet we must remember that the teachings we are about to review were considered to be authentically Christian by those who adhered to them.

Christian Sects in Samaria

One of the earliest of groups calling themselves "Christian" was later known as Dositheans. This ancient sect was founded by one Dositheus, said to be a disciple of John the Baptist. After the execution of the Baptist by Herod Antipas, Dositheus founded a group consisting of thirty disciples. Many, if not all, were said to be initiates of John and later of Jesus. The sect was founded in Samaria, where the Baptist was said to be buried. In the gospel of John, Jesus is said to have taught the Samaritans after his encounter with the woman at the well. We can, therefore, safely say that Samaria was host to a group founded by Jesus himself, and perhaps before Jesus, John's disciples had been previously established in Samaria.<1> This would place the foundation of this earliest of Christian sects well before that of the Jerusalem community and, perhaps, a decade before St. Paul founded his churches. Dositheus, Simon, his follower, and others in the sect were, therefore, con-temporaneous with the twelve disciples of Jesus. It is intriguing to speculate whether or not Dositheus could have been one of Jesus' seventy-two disciples sent out by him to spread the word.

According to G.R.S. Mead, the followers of Dositheus followed a mode of life "closely resembling that of the Essenes" and possessed their own secret volumes. <2> We have seen a connection between the Essene and Nazarene-

Ebionite Christians. We now see a connection between the Essenes and Dositheans. Scholar R. McL. Wilson has noted these references in "Simon, Dositheus and the Dead Sea Scrolls."<3> Dositheus is also said to have come from Arabia, traveled to Egypt and subsequently to Samaria. Jungian Gnostic scholar Stephan Hoeller claims that Jesus, Simon (a disciple of Dositheus) and Dositheus himself, whom Hoeller calls Doshtai, were all initiates of mysteries conferred by John the Baptist.<4> The nature of these mysteries is enshrouded in secrecy. We may possess a clue, however, to the teaching of Dositheus and his ancient sect. The Nag-Hammadi Library contains a text entitled The Three Steles [Tablets] of Seth and purportes to be a revelation to Dositheus.

The text begins:

The revelations of Dositheus about the Three Steles of Seth, the Father of the living and unshakable race which he (Dositheus) saw and understood. And after he had read them, he remembered them. And he gave them to the elect, just as they were inscribed there. <5>

The Seth Connection

This brings us to Seth, the son of Adam, whose memory and teaching was enshrined by the Sethians, a Christian-Gnostic sect. According to Jewish historian Josephus, Seth had left esoteric information for his posterity in the form of tablets on a high mountain.<6> This esoteric doctrine had been handed down to the "seed of Seth." This "seed," calling itself the "living and unshakable race," is the direct inheritor of this doctrine. Seth was considered to be the son of the Man (Adam) and thus was seen as a divine Archetypal man or Son of Man. The Sethian-Gnostics looked to Seth as their divine archetype, and this archetype was reproduced in Jesus.

Commenting on another Sethian-Gnostic gospel, called

the Gospel of the Egyptians, Stephan Hoeller writes:

The prototype of all Gnostic messengers of light according to this gospel is Seth, third son of Adam and Eve, who unlike the imperfect, contending brothers Cain and Abel had a clear knowledge of his own nature and of his connection with the imperishable realm and its celestial denizens. Seth is represented as the father of a race of enlightened, knowing humans who uphold the principles of Gnosis in every generation....The race of Seth may also be understood as a body of enlightened Gnostic adepts present in the world in every generation who possess a distinguished, luminous prehistory in their own right. <7>

There is no question that the earliest Christian sects, whether they were called Nazoreans, Christianoi or Dositheans, believed themselves to be an elect and chosen race with a decidedly "distinguished" prehistory. This is evident in the epistles of St. Paul, who repeatedly speaks of the "elect" and of the "saints" whom the Father foreknew in the beginning and who are the inheritors of the promise. These early Christian sects considered themselves enlightened through a superhuman knowledge bestowed upon them by Jesus. The Essenes, some of whom later joined the various Christian sects, also considered themselves as a chosen race who preserved in purity the teachings of Seth, Enoch, Abraham, Moses, etc.

According to Church Father Epiphanius, the Sethians believed Jesus to have been previously incarnated on earth as Seth. He writes:

Now, these Sethians proudly derive their ancestry from Seth, the son of Adam, and honor him and attribute to him whatever belongs to excellence and righteousness and the like. They do not stop short of calling him the Christ and insist that he was Jesus....

But the anointed (Christ) itself came as Jesus, a descendant of Seth by descent and by succession of peoples;

[the Christ] was shone forth in the world not through being born but in a mysterious way. **This was Seth himself,** *who both formerly and at that time—as the Christ—visited the human race, having been sent from above, from the Mother. (Emphasis added)* <8>

The doctrine of reincarnation, previously discussed, appears to have been accepted by this Christian sect, even with regard to Jesus himself, who, it was taught, had a previous life as Seth. We must remember that the Sethians, along with other early sects, believed themselves to be authentic Christians and the inheritors of a true body of teaching.

Scholars have been unable to trace the origins of the Sethian-Gnostic sect. In the Nag-Hammadi collection the Sethian-Gnostics are represented in several texts, among which are The Apocalypse of Adam, Zostrianos, The Gospel of the Egyptians, Allogenes, and Marsanes.

The Three Steles of Seth is a lofty meditation on the Son, the Mother and the Unknown Father, as received by Dositheus. Could Dositheus have been a founder or one of the founders of the Sethian Christian community? We have no proof. There is little doubt, however, that Dositheus and his followers envisioned themselves as "a body of enlightened Gnostic Adepts," whose mission was to spread the inner, esoteric doctrine of Jesus.

It also would appear that Seth may have been known under various names. According to author R. W. Morgan, the teachings of ancient Druidism in the British Isles were established by Seth, but under the name of Gwyddon Ganhebon. The teachings of the Druids were said to be brought to Britain by one Hu Gadarn, a contemporary of Abraham.<9>

The Arch-Druids were priest-adepts, and Druidism appears to have been a mystery religion complete with levels or stages of initiation. The preexistence of the soul was taught, its fall and descent into incarnation and its final resurrection from matter. These mysteries were vouchsafed to the Druids by none other than "Seth." Therefore this knowledge was believed to be a divine revelation. Amazingly enough, several historians assert that the Druids were the first converts to Christianity through the missionary work of Joseph of Arimathea in about 36 A.D.<10> As we will later note, the Druids believed in a trinity and prophesied concerning a coming saviour known as Hesus/Yesu. Due to the preaching of Joseph, St. Paul and others, the Druids accepted Jesus as Saviour, but needless to say, Druidic Christianity bore little resemblance to the orthodox Christianity of later centuries. We must therefore consider Druidic Christianity as among the earliest sects, again, with a decidedly "gnostic" emphasis.

The School of Simon

This school was founded by Simon, who, from all reports about him written in the first centuries of Christianity, was another Christian-Gnostic adept versed in the esoteric doctrine. Simon was later called Magus. This term, however, in its original sense, denoted an adept in the spiritual arts and a practitioner of astrology. Later the term was degraded into "magician" with the inevitable connotation of charlatan or trickster.

Simon is one of the most controversial figures in the history of early Christianity and one of the most defamed. Church Fathers Justin, Irenaeus and Hippolytus wrote against Simon, proclaiming him an arch-heretic. Simon figures in The Acts of the Apostles (Acts 8: 9-25) as a Samaritan and sorcerer who was baptized and converted by the apostle Philip and who later attempts to purchase from Peter the art of laying on of hands. Simon is duly rebuked by the righteous Peter and is, presumably, reconciled with the community of apostles after repenting of his deed.

According to Gnostic scholar Kurt Rudolph, this scenario in Acts does not do justice to the importance of Simon and reduces him to a mere charlatan. Rudolph also states that "the Christian reports about Simon are often either misunderstandings...or they are conscious misinterpretations and slanders to which already the title "Magus" seems to belong...." <11>

Simon also appears as a central character in the Pseudo-Clementine Homilies, written in the third century and attributed to Clement, bishop of Rome. In this work, Simon is cast as a dangerous rival of Peter. Stephan Hoeller comments on this most interesting relationship between Simon and Peter:

...Simon, both as a Samaritan and as a Gnostic, stood in opposition to the Jewish faction of the early Christians who were represented by Peter, sometimes known as the "apostle of the circumcision" in recognition of his attachment to Jewish customs. The legendry evolved by the Christian detractors of Simon has him engaged in a prolonged rivalry and contest of will with Peter, replete with duels involving miraculous powers and contests of what one today might call spiritual one-upmanship. Interestingly, both men are called Simon, and so Simon Peter, the Judaizing Christian apostle and Simon the Magician appear as two sides of the same or at least similar archetypal image. It has even been suggested (by the early scholar of Gnosticism W. Baur and his Tubingen school) that Simon Magus is but a disguise for the apostle Paul. Petrine, restrictive Christianity is thus contrasted with Pauline universal Christianity.... Could it be said that in the juxtaposition of Peter and Simon we find a symbolic confrontation of the sort of Christianity that subsequently became normative and orthodox, with the liberating and Gnostic Christianity that Jesus himself taught and that the Petrine church, under the influence of the Old Testament archetypal structure, came to deny? And it is certainly true that Pauline Christianity with its openness to the non-Jewish populace and its pluralistic view of the composition of the church was certainly nearer in spirit to the Simonian Gnosis than its more rigid counterpart. <12>

The remarks of Hoeller are both interesting and in-triguing, and we would fully agree with him. We have seen the rivalry between Peter and St. Paul and it has been suggested that Peter represented the orthodox, dogmatic Christianity and St. Paul, the Gnostic, universal Christianity. Could Simon Magus have really been a disguise for St. Paul?

Theosophical writer H.P. Blavatsky, discussing the characters and teachings of Peter and Paul, states:

In the eyes of Peter, Paul, who had humiliated him, and whom he felt so much his superior in "Greek learning" and philosophy, must have naturally appeared as a magician, a man polluted with the "Gnosis" with the "wisdom" of the Greek mysteries—hence, perhaps, "Simon the Magician." <13>

Blavatsky then states, in a footnote, that although Peter may have persecuted St. Paul under the name Simon Magus, this does not imply that there was no Simon Magus individually distinct from St. Paul. The name of Simon Magus may have become a generic name of abuse.

Our purpose is not to decide conclusively whether Simon Magus was a "true" or "false" teacher but to point out the rich heritage of early Christians—a heritage of teaching unfortunately lost to the modern Christian. What, then, were the teachings of the School of Simon and precisely when did Simon disseminate them? The orthodox Christian apologist Justin, who died in 167 A.D., states in his Apology that Simon worked and taught in Samaria in the time of the emperor Claudius (41-54 A.D.).<14> This would be coincident with the ministry of St. Paul. Simon's teaching then would be as old as, if not older than, St. Paul's.

Simon is said to have written several treatises, among them The Great Announcement, The Four Quarters of the World and The Sermons of the Refuter. According to G.R.S. Mead, Simon and his followers believed in the mystical Christ, that is, in Christ as an indwelling spiritual being, distinct from the physical Jesus. <15> Dositheus must have also taught this, since we have learned that Simon was a disciple of Dositheus.

Simon, moreover, was reputed to have studied in Egypt. Mead furthermore suggests that the title "Magus" establishes a link with Persia and the Magi, who were priests of the sacred fire and followers of Zoroaster. <16> We recall that, according to the Tibetan texts, Jesus himself studied the scriptures of Zoroaster while sojourning in Persia.

Simon's Great Announcement, as quoted by Church Father Hippolytus in the third century, begins:

Of the universal Aeons, there are two growths, without beginning or end, springing from one Root, which is the Power, Silence, invisible, inapprehensible. Of these, one appears from above, which is The Great Power, The Universal Mind, ordering all things, male; and the other from below, The Great Thought (or Conception), female, producing all things. <17>

We are in the presence of a very profound cosmology and are immediately confronted with a characteristic doctrine of innumerable early Christian sects—the concept of Deity as both male and female. We find this teaching concerning the Godhead to be one of the most ancient of teachings, carrying us back to the Vedas of India and to the Jewish mystical idea of the Shekinah as the feminine principle of Deity.

According to Simon, then, there is a fundamental polarity—Universal Mind as the male or positive force and its complement in the female or receptive mode, the Great Thought—which together produced all things. The male and female unite to manifest what is termed The Middle Space, without beginning or end, which is Air or Spirit, the second Father over all who sustains and nourishes all things and is himself a male-female power.

Simon also taught that the Logos was the Son or divine idea. He taught the existence of an ideal or spiritual universe within which were pairs of divine emanations or aeons, male and female. The world-soul represented the Thought or female aspect of the Logos. The cosmic or world-soul descended into the lower regions, into matter, and there generated angels and powers by whom the world was made. Thus we encounter the classic doctrine of the fall of the archetypal Soul as a feminine principle into matter and the material universe.

This Thought or feminine principle (the soul):

> ...*was made prisoner by the Powers and Angels that had been emanated by her. And she suffered every kind of indignity at their hands, to prevent her [from] reascending to her Father, even to being imprisoned in the human body and transmigrating into other...bodies, as from one vessel into another....So she, transmigrating from body to body, and thereby also continually undergoing indignity, last of all, even stood for hire in a brothel; and she was the "lost sheep."*
>
> *"Wherefore, also am I [Christ the Logos] come to take her away for the first time, and free her from her bonds; to make sure salvation to men by my Gnosis." (Brackets added)* <18>

Thus we have the fall of the soul, its subsequent re-incarnation and entrapment in matter and its redemption by Christ briefly outlined in the teaching of Simon. We find nothing in this teaching antithetical to the concepts upon which Pauline theology itself is based. Christ coming to save the lost soul from material or sensual entrapment—this is the very foundation of Christianity. We also find in St. Paul the teaching that the sovereignties or powers are hostile to the soul. We have learned that reincarnation is explicit in the Old and New Testaments, as it is in this system of Simon.

Like St. Paul, his contemporary, Simon abrogated the Mosaic code as binding upon every new Christian and considered the Old Testament revelation to be a preparatory one, and to have been brought to completion by the teaching of Christ.

In The Sermons of the Refuter, Simon subjects the Old Testament to criticism and reinterprets the Adam and Eve serpent myth in Genesis. This work, as well as The Four Quarters of the World, has been lost. <19>

From the above excerpt, Simon seems also to have taught the existence of "tyrannical creator angels" who have imposed restrictions on the world.

"Whereas freedom from restriction is the natural consequence of Gnosis," remarks Hoeller, *"the few fragments of Simon's writings available to us indicate that he was not concerned with freeing of the Jews from political oppression, but with the freeing of the souls of men and women from what today we would call psychological restrictions, such as one sidedness and narrowness of consciousness."* <20>

The liberation of the soul as the feminine or passive principle was used, apparently, by either Simon or his followers under the myth of Simon and Helen. G.R.S. Mead comments:

The main symbolism, which evolvers of the Simon-legend parodied into the myth of Simon and Helen, appears to have been sidereal; thus the Logos and his Thought, the World-Soul, were symbolized as the Sun (Simon) and Moon (Selene, Helen); so with the microcosm, Helen was the human soul fallen into matter and Simon the mind which brings about her redemption. Moreover, one of the systems appears to have attempted to interpret the Trojan Legend and myth of Helen in a spiritual and psychological fashion. <21>

According to Church Father Hippolytus (as quoted by Elaine Pagels), Simon claimed that each human being is a dwelling place, "and that in him dwells an infinite power...the root of the universe." Moreover, this power "exists in a latent condition in everyone, potentially, not actually." <22>

In this statement by Simon we have reached the crux of why this teaching was so condemned: precisely because it restores to man the infinite power of the universe itself. If man has the potential of an infinite power dwelling within him, he need not submit to authorities outside of himself to access that power. He need only learn how to tap this power for himself. Most importantly, external forces, be they temporal or spiritual, principality or power, are themselves rendered powerless before such an one. What power did Jewish authorities truly have before one who says with effect to the winds and waves, "Peace, be still!" other than that which he gave them? And we can safely assume that techniques for tapping this infinite power within were taught by Jesus and possibly by Simon, who was accused of making himself out to be "The Great Power of God." Jesus was likewise condemned for allegedly making himself God.

Thus, in this earliest Christian-Gnostic sect, we find the following outstanding teachings:

1. The concept of God as male and female, thus androgynous. 2. The concept of angels, hierarchies and divine emanations. 3. The descent of the soul from heaven, its entrapment and subsequent reincarnations. 4.The existence of tyrannical angels or powers. 5. The concept of an infinite power within man, the universal root—which exists as potential in all men.

We draw attention to these concepts because we believe them to be authentically Christian and to be characteristic of ancient Christian Gnosis. Further, we believe that these teachings, whether they were promulgated by Simon or not, were part of the secret or esoteric doctrines of Jesus and, of course, were duly suppressed or disfigured. At the close of the first century these teachings, wherever they were found, were condemned and replaced by an alternative theology. This process continued until the fifth century, unabated.

Menander and Satornilos

Menander was said to be a disciple of Simon and a native of Capparatea in Samaria. He taught at Antioch in Syria, as did Peter and Paul, and may have lived to 80 A.D. According to Mead, Menander handed down the general outlines of the Gnosis or secret doctrine of Jesus. He insisted on the distinction between the God over all and the creative powers or forces of nature. Wisdom, he taught, was to be attained "by the practical discipline of transcendental 'magic'." "Transcendental magic," Mead states, means that "the Gnosis was not to be attained by faith alone, but by a definite endeavor and conscious striving along the path of cosmological and psychological science."<24> This science, no doubt, was akin to the spiritual sciences of yoga and meditation. It must have included the purification and cleansing of the spiritual centers known in the East as "chakras". There is no reason to deny that the so-called secret doctrine of Jesus must have included such techniques, especially considering the evidence that Jesus studied in the East prior to his Palestinian mission. Mead further remarks that Menander taught the knowledge of the powers of nature and the method whereby they could be subjected to the purified human will.<25> This may very well refer to yogic science.

Detractors of Menander claimed that he designated himself as the Saviour. Mead, however, disagrees:

The claim of the Gnostics was that a man might so perfect himself that he becomes a conscious worker with the Logos; all those who did so, became 'Christs,' and as such were Saviours, but not in the sense of being the Logos himself. <26>

We cannot imagine any of the Church Fathers of the orthodox bent taking kindly to anyone labeling himself as a "Christ." Yet the Gospel of Thomas reports Jesus as saying, "He who will drink from my mouth will become like me. I myself shall become he, and the things that are hidden shall be revealed to him." The Gospel of Philip teaches a similar doctrine: "You saw the Spirit, you became Spirit. You saw Christ, you became Christ. You saw the father, you shall become the father." <27>

This identification with one's own indwelling Christ,

we recall, is the central mystery of St. Paul's theology—Christ in you, the hope of glory—and as we shall see, the chief cornerstone teaching of Christian-Gnostic sects.

Menander is said to have been opposed to the materialistic doctrine of the resurrection of the body. We can find no such doctrine promulgated in the earliest Christian sects— nor do we find it taught by St. Paul. However, before A.D. 80 this teaching must have been disseminated by certain communities, perhaps as a misinterpretation of St. Paul's theology on "the resurrection of the dead" in a celestial body.

Naturally, Menander's teaching concerning the resurrection was denounced by Justin, one of the fabricators of later orthodox Christianity. Justin, of course, flourished at a later date than Menander. One would assume that Menander, being a contemporary of the apostles, would have had access to a more authentic doctrine than Justin's, since he seems to have taught the esoteric doctrine of Jesus prior to Justin.

We turn now to Satornilos (sometimes called Saturninus), who also taught at Antioch in Syria toward the close of the first century. Satornilos is said to have been an ascetic who abstained from animal food.

Justin Martyr, writing between 150 and 160, mentions the followers of Satornilos as a very important body and claims that this Christian-Gnostic teacher had many adherents.<28> Satornilos also gives us one of the earliest descriptions of Christ as the gnostic Redeemer. <29>

Satornilos taught the existence of great intermediate hierarchies, some good and others evil. The World Saviour is said to have descended in the form of a man in order to bring about the defeat of the evil powers and to rescue all who have the light-spark within them.

Satornilos taught that the body of man was formed by inferior angels or builders, but that the Power above sent forth the light-spark into man. This early Christian community taught that the light-spark in man was the real man. Man, then, was divine by virtue of this light-spark from above .<30> Many of the adherents of Satornilos' teaching practiced celibacy as did certain of the Essenes. <31> We find a remarkable similarity to the teachings of St. Paul, especially with regard to the existence of powers of good and evil, and St. Paul's description of Christ, being in a Godlike form, yet taking the form of a servant to accomplish his mission. St. Paul taught that Christ came to disarm the powers and did so through his crucifixion and resurrection. Since St. Paul taught in Antioch, one wonders whether he influenced Satornilos or whether the latter was a recipient of St. Paul's "wisdom of God in a mystery."

Christian-Gnostic Sects on Evil

In the teaching of this early Christian sect, we again find instruction on the forces of evil which, as in the New Testament, seems to be a pervading theme of these ancient Christian sects.

According to Irenaeus in his volume, *Against Heresies,* the school of Satornilos taught that "two kinds of men were formed by the angels, the one wicked and the other good."<32> We have previously reviewed the teaching of the Nazorean community and certain New Testament books regarding the fallen angels, Watchers, etc., who took embodiment on earth and thus have wreaked havoc among mankind, literally altering civilization.

There is no reason to reject the New Testament or the early esoteric Christian schools concerning their teachings on the cause and continued presence of planetary evil. We suggest that this very teaching on evil, had it been accepted by Christians in the later centuries, would have removed much of the mystery as to why the people of earth have been unable to challenge evil successfully. We would further suggest that these very same forces of evil have seen to it that all references to the race of evil (whether they be fallen angels, archons, or Nephilim) have been either removed, suppressed or destroyed outright, and that one of the chief causes for the unmitigated suppression of Christian-Gnostic teachings is their fearless exposure of cosmic evil and its presence on earth. There is scarcely one text in the Nag Hammadi Library which does not treat of the origin and cause of evil. <33> In general, this evil is the result of either fallen, inferior or usurper deities, angels or rulers. It is very probable that the Christian-Gnostics believed that these powers not only inhabited certain of the planetary spheres but other frequencies, wavelengths or dimensions of matter not readily detectable by ordinary humans. Further, there is every reason to suspect that the schools of Christian-Gnostics were aware of the existence of beings navigating in not only the physical dimension but in other, more subtle frequencies. These beings were most often termed rulers or archons, and were created by or ruled by a chief Archon known by various names such as Ildabaoth, Sacklas, Satan, Sammael, etc. That these beings possessed the power of creating bodies, no doubt by genetic engineering is evident from the texts in question; that they believed themselves to be creators or "gods" is also evident.<34> As a result of their fallen state, they are hostile to humanity and attempt to prevent mankind from attaining to spiritual liberation.

Christian-Gnostics believed that knowledge of the existence of these beings is crucial to salvation. We also tend to accept the Gnostic viewpoint at face value, just as we would accept Jesus' statement to the Pharisees who stood before him: "Ye are of your father, the devil." (Jn. 8:44) That the angels were given the power to create bodies, is obvious from Jewish Apocalyptic text (Enoch, Jubilees) and Christian-Gnostic texts such as The Apocryphon of John and The Apocalypse of Adam. After their fall, the angels retained this knowledge and apparently continued to utilize it, much to the detriment of the race. Hence, we find the school of Satornilos teaching that the angels created "evil men". These, we believe, are the "wicked" repeatedly mentioned in the Old and New Testaments—those who are soulless and "fade away as grass", as the Psalmist wrote. Might not these be the ones whom Jesus refers to as the "children of the wicked one", in Matthew 13:38? That these mysteries were taught in the earliest Christian schools, there is little doubt. Furthermore, what meaning should we give to St. Paul's exhortation: " For it is not against human enemies that we have to struggle, but against the Sovereignties and the Powers who originate the darkness in this world, the spiritual army of evil in the heavens ." (Ephesians 6:12) Might not this "army" refer to extraterrestrial agencies or beings? As we have said, there is a rather close connection between this statement of St. Paul's and the Christian-Gnostic insistence on the influence and power of the heavenly archons or rulers. Hoeller elaborates on the teaching of Satornilos and Menander regarding these inferior powers as follows:

The authentic Godhead is an impersonal fullness, utterly transcendent and beyond the reach of the human mind in its present condition. This Godhead, referred to at times as the Unknown Father, emanated a portion of its own sublime essence, which became the created cosmos. It also emanated a number of angels and creative spirits, some of whom became estranged from their ultimate source and came to look upon themselves as autonomous rulers....The star-angels and other ruling spirits appear as tyrannical, limiting agencies in this Gnostic view. They are usurpers who lord it over humanity and creation in order to enhance their own self-importance and glory. It is incumbent upon the knower to realize this and to extricate himself from the grasp of these powers whenever possible. The existential predicament of human life lies in the uncomfortable dominance to which these lesser godlings subject the spirits of human beings, and from which only the experiential realization of Gnosis can extricate them. <35>

Orthodox Christianity, of course, has imputed all evil to human sin, namely, to those two unfortunate individuals who ate of a forbidden tree. This solution is not only frivolous but simplistic. Hoeller continues:

If...evil and imperfection exist in the world, they must be due at least in part to the activity of agencies who interpose *themselves between manifest existence and the Absolute and who do not partake of the perfection and goodness of the former....An imperfect world replete with every real evil must be the work of gods or a god partaking of the qualities of imperfection. Such was the judgment rendered by the Gnostics and before them of other sophisticated thinkers of the ancient world....The Sumero-Babylonian religious matrix that exercised a large influence on ancient Judaism squarely admitted that the gods were responsible for evil as well as for good. Enki and other Babylonian gods freely amused themselves by creating monsters and freaks and visiting humanity with evil conditions purely for their own divinely perverse amusement. <36>*

The early esoteric sects were not afraid to face the reality of evil and its origin. On the contrary, the early Christian schools were replete with such notions. There will be more to say concerning evil and its causes when we take up the further study of pristine Christianity through the second century.

The Ophite Christian Sect

The so-called Ophites were, at one time, an exceedingly widespread school and community of early Christians who took for their symbol the serpent, the emblem of wisdom. In certain schools of Hinduism, the serpent symbolized the power of the Goddess Kundalini, the white fire of the Mother aspect of God, locked at the base of the spine. When this energy rose up the spinal column, due to the aspirant's love and devotion as well as to certain meditative techniques, it took the form of an uncoiling serpent. And when the energy rose to the spiritual center at the top of the head, full illumination had been attained. The term "Ophis" in Greek is translated "serpent." So we can conclude that the Ophites saw the serpent as the sign of mystical illumination.

The Ophites, we learn, did not designate themselves as

such, but called themselves "knowers" or "gnostics" and considered themselves the only real Christians. On the face of it, we have no reason to doubt this statement or refute it.

According to Kurt Rudolph, the Ophites taught that the soul had to ascend through the demonic planetary spheres and cross the "barrier of evil" by traversing the "eternally chained gates of the Archons," addressing prayers to various divine beings, in order to be saved.<37> Could the Ophites have received the doctrine of St. Paul regarding "the spiritual army of evil in the heavens"? Did they prepare themselves through the science of invocation to wrestle against "sovereignties and powers" as St. Paul phrases it?

The Ophites, like the Essenes and Jewish gnostics, are said to have existed before the coming of Christ, and to have continued as a distinct group through the second century. As certain Essenes and pre-Christian Nazoreans may have embraced the teaching of Christ, there is evidence to suggest that this school also adopted and apparently taught the esoteric doctrine of Jesus and perhaps St. Paul.

In disseminating their teachings, the Ophites drew upon the books of the Old Testament, including the Prophetic books and the Book of Enoch. We recall that the Book of Enoch is quoted in the letter of Jude in the New Testament. The Ophties taught the doctrine of emanations, so hated by the Church Fathers, as the immanence of the Divine Light in all beings. In this view, man is not a creation of God but an emanation of God, that is to say, a man-ifestation of God. The Light in man is identical with the Light of God, which makes man worthy of God.

All beings, said the Ophites, emanated from One Source. Among the original emanations were the Primal Man (Archetypal Man), Sophia, or the feminine Wisdom and the Christos, the guide of all who proceed from God. The Christos, as the Light-emanation of God, is to be distinguished from the man Jesus, and is, essentially the Light or Divine Consciousness within all humanity.

The Ophites explained, allegorically and symbolically,

the descent or fall of the Soul. The Soul (Sophia-Achamoth) became entangled in matter and as a result of this defection, produced Ildabaoth, an inferior being, marked by pride and ambition, who formed the material worlds by stealing the light of the Mother. This being also created soulless men who, however, received a ray of Divine Light through the agency of Sophia, the feminine Wisdom that had not fallen into matter. To accomplish the redemption of man, the Christ, the Light-emanation of God, entered into the man Jesus at his baptism. Jesus, then, began his mission and the working of miracles.

The Ophites taught that Jesus was crucified at the instigation of Ildabaoth and his malignant powers. While Jesus hung on the cross, the Christos and Sophia departed from the body of Jesus, and he cried out, "My God, why hast thou forsaken me?" At his resurrection, Jesus was endowed with a body consisting of aether, the subtle plenum of energy from which matter is formed. The physical matter composing the body of Jesus thus returned to the elements.

Jesus sojourned on the earth communing with his disciples for eighteen months after he had risen. He received the true Gnosis from the Divine Mother Sophia and imparted it to his disciples who were capable of receiving it. According to this sect of Christians, redemption is accomplished when all the souls purified by the knowledge of Christ have been gathered together in the Light-Kingdom and when all of the stolen Light has been reabsorbed out of Ildabaoth's empire, into the Pleroma (the Spiritual Kingdom). <38>

The above account is extremely abbreviated and is, of course, taken from detailed accounts of Church Fathers Irenaeus and Hippolytus. We are unable to vouch for the accuracy of these reports, considering the hostility with which they are given.

Lost Christianity's Most Suppressed Teaching:
A Usurper Deity as the Cause of Evil

The existence of another "deity" besides the supreme

God was a point of contention between the earliest esoteric Christian sects and the leaders of what later became the orthodox movement. This so-called deity, of course, was considered to be a usurper, even mimicking the creation of Divine Archetypes in the Spiritual Kingdom by producing physical beings without souls. The character of Ildabaoth approximates both Lucifer and Satan in the Bible and in other apocalyptic texts, as well as other fallen angels mentioned in non-canonical texts, such as Sammael, Beliar or Belial.<39> In fact, Ildabaoth is also called Sammael in several texts. Just who or what Ildabaoth is remains a point of dispute among scholars. Michael Grant claims that Gnostic-Christian thought owes a great deal to Iranian teaching about Ahriman, the Evil Spirit in Zoroastrian theology and opponent of Ahura Mazda. It would appear, says Grant, that Ahriman is the prototype of Ildabaoth. According to Plutarch, Ahriman "resembles darkness and ignorance." In the Apocryphon of John, Ildabaoth is an ignorant god who is referred to as "the first archon of darkness". <40>

According to Bently Layton, Ildabaoth is the name for the chief ruler, i.e., Satan. His name means "begetter of Sabaoth." Since "Sabaoth" translates as armies or powers, Ildabaoth is, therefore, the god of armies. In the text Hypostatis of the Archons, Ildabaoth has a son, Sabaoth, who is beneficent and who rebels against his father, whom he considers to be inferior or evil. In the above text, Ildabaoth is also called Sakla, Aramaic for "fool", which traditionally is another name for Satan. Ildabaoth is also considered to be an enslaver of humanity. <41>

Ildabaoth also bears the title "craftsman" or "fabricator"—in Greek, Demiurgos or Demiurge—and was considered to be the craftsman of the lower material worlds, made as a replica or copy of the higher spiritual worlds. According to Hans Jonas, through the demiurge's "Law", as well as through cosmic fate, he exercises a despotic world rule aimed at enslaving man. Nevertheless, the texts are careful to point out that spiritual, Archetypal man is a "supra-cosmic deity above the demiurge who existed before the demiurge." <42> The parallel here is very strong to the Buddhist concept of the "law" of karma, which binds or enslaves man on the wheel of death and rebirth, and man's liberation through enlightenment and identification with the Samboghkaya or Christ, which stands free from this law.

How did Ildabaoth come to have such a flawed and inferior character? According to these texts, apparently used by the early Christian sects, a divine Aeon (Being) known as Sophia, through presumption, gave birth to a child— Ildabaoth—without the consent of her consort. We quote the account as given in the Apocryphon (Secret Book) of John:

She (Sophia) wanted to bring forth a likeness out of herself without the consent of the Spirit—he had not approved—and without her consort, and without his consideration...And because of the invincible power which is in her, her thought did not remain idle and something came out of her which was imperfect and different from her appearance, because she had created it without her consort. And it was dissimilar to the likeness of its mother for it had another form.

And when she saw (the consequences of) her desire, it changed into a form of a lion-faced serpent. And its eyes were like lightning fires which flash. She cast it away from her, outside that place, that no one of the immortal ones might see it, for she had created it in ignorance. And she surrounded it with a luminous cloud, and she placed a throne in the middle of the cloud that no one might see it except the Holy Spirit who is called the mother of the living. And she called his name Yaltabaoth.

This is the first archon who took a great power from his mother. And he removed himself from her and moved away from the places in which he was born. He became strong and created for himself other aeons with a flame of luminous fire which (still) exists now. And he joined with his arrogance which is in him and begot authorities for himself.

...And he placed seven kings— each corresponding to

the firmaments of heaven—over the seven heavens, and five over the depth of the abyss, that they may reign. And he shared his fire with them, but he did not send forth from the power of the light which he had taken from his mother, for he is ignorant darkness.

And when the light had mixed with the darkness, it caused the darkness to shine. And when the darkness had mixed with the light, it darkened the light, and it became neither light nor dark, but it became dim.

Now the archon who is weak has three names. The first name is Yaltabaoth, the second is Saklas, and the third is Sammael. And he is impious in his arrogance which is in him. For he said, "I am God and there is no other God beside me," for he is ignorant of his strength, the place from which he had come....

But Yaltabaoth had a multitude of faces more than all of them so he could put a face before all of them, according to his desire, when he is in the midst of seraphs. He shared his fire with them; therefore he became lord over them. Because of the power of the glory he possessed of his mother's light, he called himself God. And he did not obey the place from which he came. <43>

This astonishing account treats of the existence of an inferior god, who was begotten by an act of presumption and disobedience and whose very nature was the result of a breach of harmony in the spiritual realm, a flawed or unbalanced creation. The evil, darkness and rebellion were intermingled in the lower planes of the cosmos due to this false, counterfeit, inferior creation. As Jesus said, "If the light that is in thee be darkness, how great is that darkness."

The Christian sects who adhered to these teachings did not attribute evil or darkness solely to the rebellion of angels, but to an inferior creator, who like Lucifer and Satan, is arrogant and rebellious. These Christians seem to be saying that, in a universe of free will, Sophia made the choice to create unwisely, thus producing effects or "karmic" consequences that reverberated through the lower realms and became part of the cosmos itself. According to the above scenario, all is the result of cause and effect. By Sophia's presumptive and rash act of creation, she brought forth what might be termed a cosmic ego, a being with a God-complex, a Lucifer or lightbearer who not only has the power to create but who lords his authority over his creation.

Prior to the birth of Ildabaoth, the above text describes in detail the emanations of the spiritual Light-Kingdom known as the fullness or Pleroma. Among the hierarchies of this kingdom are innumerable Aeons, male and female, who all spring forth from the invisible, unnameable and ineffable Spirit or the One. The Divine Aeons include the Father-Mother, the Holy Spirit, the self-begotten Christ, the First Man, the seed of Seth and the souls of the saints. Thus, we have the superior creation of the Divine Images and Archetypes including preexistent souls, and an inferior creation fabricated through Light stolen from the spiritual planes or worlds resident in Sophia, the last of the Aeons.

The history of early Christianity and the eventual emergence of the orthodox church is a history of the attempted suppression of this "Lost Christianity" of the esoteric sects. Specifically, this struggle, in part, revolved around the insistence among the esoteric sects that evil resulted from the activities of a usurper god, and that the physical cosmos was an intermingling of both light and darkness due to the activities of this god. The exposure of the workings of the chief ruler and his archons enraged the Church Fathers, who at all costs sought to suppress this teaching. We can only guess why.
To continue the scenario:

And when he [Yaltabaoth] saw the creation which surrounds him and the multitude of the angels which had come forth from him, he said to them, "I am a jealous God, and there is no other God beside me." But by announcing this he indicated to the angels who attended him that there exists another God...

And when the mother [Sophia] recognized that the garment of darkness was imperfect, then she knew that her consort had not agreed with her. She repented with weeping. And the whole Pleroma heard the prayer of repentance and they praised on her behalf the invisible, virginal Spirit... And he consented; and when the invisible Spirit had consented, the holy Spirit poured over her from their whole pleroma. For it was not her consort who came to her, but he came to her through the pleroma in order that he might correct her deficiency. And she was taken up not to her own aeon but above her son, that she might be in the ninth until she has corrected her deficiency. (Brackets added) <44>

The fall, repentance and restoration of Sophia repeatedly utilized by these sects was a cosmic myth which many scholars have likened to the fall and redemption of the Universal Soul of humanity.<45> The so-called "deficiency" of Sophia was the production of the ego, proud and arrogant, who envisions itself as the sole deity.

However, are we to interpret this scenario as pre-cosmic history, allegory, or myth? Or all three? There are several versions of the Sophia Myth extant, not only from the Coptic Gnostic (Nag Hammadi) Library but also from the Christian-Gnostic Gospel Pistis Sophia, as well as accounts of Church Fathers such as Irenaeus.

Stephan Hoeller has interpreted the Sophia Myth as a psychological allegory. In describing the character of the inferior god, Ildabaoth, Hoeller writes:

We may thus initially define this being, Ildabaoth, the usurper god, as a symbol for primitive, undifferentiated psychic energy that constellates itself in a human ego. As soon as this energy has assumed an ego identity, it begins to create its own world. The ego comes forth from its larger psychic background, but soon turns it back upon its mother and arrogantly declares its independence from the unconscious mystery from whence it arose....The imperfect creator serves thus as a suitable metaphor for what depth psychologists call "the alienated ego." Defined by its own sense of selfhood, this psychic entity draws away from the wisdom (Sophia) contained in the unconscious and declares itself as a creator and ruler in its own right. He who could have become an angel of light becomes a dark tyrant.

The ultimate proof of the tyrant ego's arrogance is implicit in the statement of the Demiurge: "I am God and there is no other God beside me!" ...Sophia thus stands for the transpersonal, supernal matrix (from the Latin, mater, or mother), whereas Yaldabaoth represents the tyrannical ego, which is unwilling to acknowledge the existence of transcendence and thus of any limits that may be set to its power. <46>

The God Called "Man"

To continue the story:

And a voice came forth from the exalted aeon-heaven: "The man exists and the son of man." And the chief archon, Yaldabaoth, heard (it) and thought that the voice had come from its mother. And he did not know where it came. And he taught them (the archons), the holy perfect Mother-Father, the complete foreknowledge, the image of the invisible one who is the Father of the all (and) through whom everything came into being, the first Man. For he revealed his likeness in a human form. <47>

In the Christianity of these ancient sects, Archetypal Man is a Divine Being greater than the archons and their chief. This exalted view of True Man is unique to the esoteric Christianity of the original sects. We will find that the debasement or virtual elimination of the True Man was a product of the orthodox movement.

The above scenario is presented in an alternate fashion in the text entitled On the Origin of the World. After the chief ruler declares that he is God and no other exists apart from him, the text states that the ruler, by uttering this statement, sinned against all the immortal beings above Him:

> *Then when Pistis [Faith, the higher form of Sophia as the Divine Mother] saw the impiety of the chief ruler she was filled with anger. She was invisible. She said, "You are mistaken, Sammael," that is "blind god." "There is an immortal man of light who has been in existence before you and who will appear among your modelled forms; he will trample you to scorn just as potter's clay is pounded. And you will descend to your mother, the abyss, along with those that belong to you. For at the consummation of your works the entire defect that has become visible out of the truth will be abolished, and it will cease to be and will be like what has never been." (Brackets added) <48>*

St. Paul termed this "immortal man of light" the "new Man", the "Perfect Man" and the "inner Man." We recall that Jesus identified himself as the Son of the True Man who came, as he said, "for judgment". In John 12:31-32, Jesus proclaims: "Now is the judgment of this cosmos; so shall the archon of this cosmos be cast out. And I, if I be lifted up from the earth, will draw all men unto me."

The meaning of the above mysterious passage, with certain key Greek words transliterated into English, has been a source of controversy. Who is "the archon of this cosmos," translated as "prince of this world" in the King James version? In the light of suppressed Christian-Gnostic texts, the meaning of Jesus' words becomes perfectly apparent. The being referred to is the rebellious ruler who thought he was God—Ialdabaoth. Jesus' overt statement makes us wonder whether the story of the chief archon was considered by certain early Christian mystics to be an historical event—and not alone an allegory.

Strategies of Light and Darkness

After the revelation of the First Man to the archons and

the pronouncement of their impending judgment:

> *...The whole aeon of the chief archon trembled, and the foundation of the abyss shook. And of the waters which are above matter, the underside was illuminated by the appearance of his [the First Man's] image which had been revealed. And when all the authorities and the chief archon looked, they saw the whole region of the underside which was illuminated. And through the light they saw the form of the image in the water. And he [the chief Archon] said to the authorities which attend him, "Come let us create a man according to the image of God and according to our likeness, that his image may become a light for us." (Brackets added) <49>*

The Archon and powers then fashion a psychic man consisting of a soul-body (psychic-body), yet containing all the organs. Sophia, however, desired to retrieve the power which she had given to the chief Archon, and she petitioned the Mother-Father who, through the divine Aeons, advised the Archon to blow into the face of Adam "something of your spirit and his body will arise." Yaltabaoth then blew into Adam the power of Sophia, not knowing that he was endowing his creation with the divine spark. The psychic body of man gained strength and became luminous, provoking the jealousy of the archons since Adam's intelligence "was greater than that of those who had made him, and greater than that of the chief archon." In rage, the archons then hurl Adam into the lower region of all matter, presumably the physical realm. The Father-Mother God then sends Divine After-Thought, a Feminine Being, as a helper to Adam. Her role is to assist Adam and the whole creation *"by toiling with him and by restoring him to his fullness and by teaching him about the descent of his seed and by teaching him about the way of ascent, (which is) the way he came down."* This luminous After-Thought of the Father-Mother God, also called Life, is hidden in Adam so that the archons might not know her and that she "might be a correction of the deficiency of the mother."

Because of Adam's superior thinking, which he gained by virtue of the Spark of Life within him, the archons became further enraged, took counsel and mixed together elements of earth, water and fire and made for Adam a physical body. Within this body they injected the "ignorance of darkness and desire, and their counterfeit spirit." Adam, then, became a mortal man, encased in the tomb of the body, still bearing within him, however, the Light of Divinity.

As the story continues, the archons place Adam in their own paradise and bid him eat of their trees of godlessness, hate, deception and desire. The tree of knowledge, also in paradise, was hidden from Adam by the archons, so that Adam might not gain the knowledge of his divine origin. The chief Archon then brings a forgetfulness over Adam, in order that he might extract the light of the Divine Mother within him—"But the Epinoia [AfterThought] of the light cannot be grasped." This failing, the Archon makes another creature "in the form of a woman", according to the likeness of the Divine Mother which the Archon had seen in the higher realms.

The moment Adam awoke and saw the woman as his counterpart beside him, "the luminous Epinoia [AfterThought] appeared, and she lifted the veil which lay over his mind". Jesus, who is narrating the course of events to his disciple John, states that the Epinoia is none other than "our sister Sophia" who came down to correct her deficiency, and thus illumine Adam. Jesus then appears in the form of an eagle on the tree of knowledge "that I might teach them and awaken them out of the depth of sleep".

Adam and Eve, thus illumined, withdraw from the chief Archon, who, in anger, curses his earth, and casts Adam and Eve out of paradise. Yaldabaoth then gazes at Eve and recognizes that the light of the Divine Mother has appeared also in her. When "the foreknowledge of the All" noticed that the chief Archon thus gazed at Eve with lust for the light, she sent emissaries who snatched the divine Life out of Eve, presumably to protect her light.

The Archon then seduces Eve and by sexual intercourse begets in her two sons, one righteous and the other unrighteous, later called Cain and Abel. The text then adds, *"Now up to the present day sexual intercourse continued due to the chief Archon. And he planted sexual desire in her who belongs to Adam, and he produced through intercourse the copies of the bodies, and he inspired them with his counterfeit spirit."*

Adam, however, by now recognizes the "likeness of his own foreknowledge" and begets a son with Eve whom he calls Seth. Because of Adam's recognition of his divine origin, this child bears the likeness of the "Son of Man" or son of the Immortal First Man, one of the Divine Aeons. The text makes it clear that the strategy of the Divine Mother is to prepare dwelling places in the world for the seed of light in the Pleroma, the "aeons which will come down" and take incarnation on earth. This strategy is a counterweight to the strategy of the archons to people the earth with their godless reproduction of bodies without the divine spark, injected with lust and their counterfeit spirit. The means by which this was accomplished was, no doubt, through genetic engineering and cloning. Jesus then describes the mission of the race of light who will incarnate on earth from the Pleroma, in answer to John's query as to whether or not all the souls of light who take incarnation will be safely brought into the "pure light." He replies:

Those on whom the Spirit of life will descend...will be saved and become perfect and be worthy of the greatness and be purified in that place from all wickedness and the involvements in evil. Then they have no other care than the incorruption alone, to which they direct their attention from here on, without anger or envy or jealousy or desire and greed of anything. They are not affected by anything except the state of being in the flesh alone, which they bear while looking expectantly for the time when they will be met by the receivers (of the body). Such then are worthy of the imperishable, eternal life and the calling. For they endure everything and bear up *under everything, that they may finish the good fight and inherit eternal life. <50>*

The chief Archon, in turn, planned to bring a flood upon the earth. As a countermove, "the light of the fore-knowledge" informed Noah, who proclaimed it to the sons of men. When the flood was unleashed, Noah and "many other people from the immovable race" went into a secret place and hid themselves in a "luminous cloud." This portion of the text shows that the race from the Pleroma had already taken in-carnation on earth.

Still undaunted, the chief Archon made another plan—he sent his angels to the daughters of men to cohabitate with them and raise offspring, apparently with the intention of pol-luting the race. At first they were unsuccessful. The archons then came with an alternate plan:

"They created a counterfeit spirit, who resembles the Spirit who had descended, so as to pollute the souls through it. And the angels changed in their likeness into the likeness of their (the daughters of men) mates, filling them with the spirit of darkness, which they had mixed for them, and with evil." *<51>*

This strategy appeared to have corrupted the race of men; the people were led astray with many deceptions. They died "not having found the truth and without knowing the God of truth." The whole creation thus became enslaved, due to the presence of a race polluted with evil. We might add here that it is likely that even the race of light may have become partially or totally corrupt.

In the midst of this apparently hopeless state of affairs, the Divine Mother had yet another plan. She, the perfect Fore-thought (Pronoia), changed herself into her own seed, i.e., her own spiritual posterity! She entered into the midst of the prison of the body, she became incarnate in the body of each in-dividual on earth who originated from the light and declared:

*"He who hears, let him get up from the deep sleep."
And he wept and shed tears. Bitter tears he wiped from himself
and he said, "Who is it that calls my name, and where has this
hope come to me, while I am in the chains of the prison?" And
I said, "I am the thinking of the virginal spirit, who raised you
up to the honored place. Arise and remember that it is you who
hearkened, and follow your root, which is I, the merciful one,
and guard yourself against the angels of power and the demons
of chaos and all those who ensnare you, and beware of the
deep sleep and the enclosure of the inside of Hades." <52>*

The individual is then raised up and sealed and thus
comes to know his or her origin and the fact that, in reality, the
Divine Mother has so identified herself with the creation that it
is she who thinks within them and who ultimately saves them.

It is easy to see, from even a cursory reading of this
astonishing text, why it and others like it had become so abhorrent to the Church Fathers. They obviously were not willing
to accept the scenario of the strategies of evil or the possible
reality of the archons. Yet thousands of ancient Christians saw
themselves as "knowers" or gnostics who came to earth to reveal, expose and judge the race of evil proliferated on earth by
the archons. Were these "knowers" a threat to the Church
Fathers?

We find parallels in the Apocryphon of John to the
Book of Enoch and the Book of Jubilees, both of which treat of
the corruption of the race by the Watchers.

The orthodox Jew and Christian believed that God
created a material man as a somewhat limited physical creature.
Both Jewish and Christian-Gnostics saw it otherwise. The
dense genetically engineered body was a device of the archons
to trap the light. The Christian-Gnostics asked, Would God, the
Father, chain man to this kind of a body if man is made in
God's image? If God is a Spirit, man also must be spiritual and
not physical. God, they said, could not be responsible for
creating man as a limited physical creature subject to desires,

temptations and moral failings. This must be the work of another deity who opposes the highest God, and who engineered bodies or vehicles as a counterfeit to the light bodies created by God (Elohim) The early Christians clearly had a rich structure of teaching on the origin, existence and nature of dark forces. Yet our contemporaries are not without experiences that would lead to the same conclusions, with the unfortunate lack, however, of the orthodox-dismantled framework of the early Christians which could have interpreted these things. Witness an out-of-body experience described by an author of books on this phenomenon, Robert A. Monroe:

The same impersonal probing, the same power, from the same angle. However this time I received the firm impression that I was inextricably bound by loyalty to this intelligence force, always had been, and that I had a job to perform here on earth. The job was not necessarily to my liking, but I was assigned to it. The impression was that I was manning a "pumping station," that it was a dirty ordinary job but it was mine and I was stuck with it, and nothing, absolutely nothing could alter the situation....I got the impression of huge pipes, so ancient they were covered with undergrowth and rust. Something like oil was passing through them, but it was much higher in energy than oil, and vitally needed and valuable elsewhere (assumption: not on this material planet). This has been going on for aeons of time, and there were other force groups here, taking out the same material on a highly competitive basis, and the material was convertible at some distant point or civilization for something very valuable to entities far above my ability to understand....

I mentally (orally also?) asked who they were, and received an answer that I could not translate or understand. Then I felt them beginning to leave, and I asked for some actual indication that they had been there, but was rewarded only with paternal amusement. Then they seemed to soar up into the sky, while I called after them, pleading. Then I was sure that their mentality and intelligence were far beyond my *understanding. It is an impersonal, cold intelligence, with none of the emotions of love or compassion which we respect so much.... <53>*

The Church Father Epiphanius describes the Gnostic teaching on the reason for the archons' vested interest in the entrapment of the soul and their requirement for light or "dew from above"— perhaps the "something like oil" described by Monroe: "They say the soul is the food of the Archons and Powers without which they cannot live, because she is of the dew from above and gives them strength." <54>

There are also parallels here to the Sumerian texts which describe the creation of mankind as primitive workers by the "gods." The Sumerians also believed that the "gods" unleashed the flood upon the earth (or at least deliberately failed to warn mankind of its coming). It appears that Christian-Gnostics of every persuasion saw parallels between the chief Archon and his powers and the Sumerian god, Anu, and the Sumerian-Babylonian pantheon. It is also significant to our study that we mention here the two creation accounts in Genesis. Genesis, chapter 1 treats of the spiritual creation of man—man made male and female in the image and likeness of God by the plural Elohim. Chapter 2 deals with the physical creation of Adam and Eve (by the now singular Yahweh), who are made to till the land as servants of the "Lord." There are close parallels in the second chapter of Genesis to the Sumerian creation accounts and to the creation of physical man in the Christian-Gnostic texts.

The Origin of the Doctrine of Original Sin

We may also find the origin of the later distorted doctrine of "original sin" in the Apocryphon of John. As we recall, the text states that lustful sexual intercourse originated with the seduction of Eve by the chief Archon, Yaldabaoth. The genetically engineered body was a counterfeit creation of the archons, who transmitted sexual lust to Eve through their counterfeit spirit. The "original sin," therefore, was the sin of the chief Archon and his angels, who attempted to establish the reproduction of their bodies through physical sexual intercourse. Yet, as we have seen, Adam was able to produce a Son of Man—namely Seth— by his own awareness of the light within him. The subsequent birth of the seed of light who descended from the Pleroma thwarted the plan of the archons— a race of light from above could propagate itself on earth through the very bodies created by the archons themselves and even through sexual intercourse.

We would suggest that the doctrine of original sin, the earliest trace of which, as a developed doctrine, can be found in Irenaeus and Tertullian, may have been appropriated from the above text or others similar to it. The Church Fathers, however, especially Augustine, refused to acknowledge the presence of the divine spark and the Divine Mother in the bodies of the race being propagated by sexual intercourse. They refused to accept that the race of light was taking incarnation on earth from the Spiritual Realms. The Church Fathers readily admitted that sexual desire or lust may have been or was being transmitted to the race through intercourse, but they neglected to tell their congregations that this lust did not ultimately derive from the children of God but was injected into the body, by genetic manipulation through the archons and through evil angelic intercourse. The seed of light were still able to propagate pure souls of light and not souls and bodies tainted with "original sin," as the Apocryphon of John states. The Church Fathers, therefore, imputed the original sin of the archons/fallen angels/Watchers to the average Christian believer who felt tainted by the alleged "impurity" of sexual intercourse while all along he or she was not responsible for that sin and had not originated it.

By condemning preexistence and reincarnation, the Church Fathers effectively banned the idea that the spiritual posterity from above were taking earthly incarnation. Why was this idea banned? The answer may be found in an illuminating text discovered at Nag Hammadi entitled On the Origin of the

World. The excerpt treats of the incarnation of "blessed beings" or souls from the heavenly realms:

Whenever they [souls of light] appear in the world of perdition, immediately and first of all, they reveal the pattern of imperishability as a condemnation of the rulers and their forces. Thus when the blessed beings appeared in forms modelled by authorities, they were envied. And out of envy the authorities mixed their seed with them, in hopes of polluting them. They could not....

So when all the perfect appeared in the forms modelled by the rulers and when they revealed the incomparable truth, they put to shame all the wisdom of the gods. And their fate was found to be a condemnation. And their force dried up. Their lordship was dissolved. (Brackets added) <55>

In the above passage we can plainly see that the presence of the seed of light on earth is a judgment to the rulers/archons and will eventually spell an end to their authority on earth. Could the posterity of light fulfill their purpose on earth if they were not told of their point of origin? If they had no awareness of the continuity of existence prior to their earth life or of their spiritual potential, how could they effect change in the world? If they were born with original sin, where would their self-esteem be? If they had no mission from the spiritual realms, how could they fulfill it? To answer these questions honestly would be to lift the veil on an ancient conspiracy of suppression. We will leave our readers to ponder on and answer these questions during the course of this work.

The Naassenes—Christ as Unveiler of the Mysteries

We continue our examination of the ancient sects of "Lost Christianity" with the Naassenes. The title "Naassene" recalls to us the sect of the Essenes. Could the Naassenes have had some connection with the Essenes? Could the former have been an offshoot of the latter? It is certainly possible.

Like the Ophites, the Naassenes were a school of Christianity, not a church in the way we understand the term today. The word "Naas" means "serpent," and again like the Ophites, the serpent was understood to be the emblem for wisdom. We recall that the term "wisdom" as used by St. Paul, for instance, refers to the mystery teaching, the secret doctrine of Jesus. The Naassenes, perhaps, preserved a teaching lost to Christianity for centuries.

This Christian school is said to have possessed many books, some of which have been lost, or more likely, destroyed by the budding orthodox movement: The Gospel of Perfection, Gospel of Eve, Questions of Mary, The Gospel of Phillip, The Gospel According to Thomas, and The Gospel According to the Egyptians. <56> The last three titles are, fortunately, to be found among the Nag Hammadi collections of Christian-Gnostic texts. We cannot, however, be sure that the texts used by the Naassenes are identical with the documents discovered at Nag Hammadi.

According to a report by the third-century Church Father Hippolytus, the Naassenes received their doctrines and traditions from James, the brother of Jesus, through one called Mariamne. <57> James, as we have seen, was a leader of the original Nazorean community established at Jerusalem, even before St. Paul founded his communities throughout the Gentile world. James, therefore, may have been privy to a secret doctrine of Jesus. The collection of texts discovered at Nag Hammadi include a number of texts bearing the name of James: The Apocryphon of James, The First Apocalypse of James and The Second Apocalypse of James.

According to the Apocryphon of James, which we have earlier quoted, Jesus appears to his disciples 550 days after the resurrection to give them his final admonishment and exhortations. The text also mentions at least two "secret books," one vouchsafed to James and the other to both James and Peter. The disciples are also portrayed as writing down in books what the Saviour said to them, "whether in secret or openly." We, therefore, see a tradition of secret teaching embedded in the

Apocryphon of James. This makes us wonder whether these texts had any connection to the Naassenes, since, as they tell us, their traditions derived from James, Jesus' brother.

Hippolytus also reveals that all members of the Naassenes were initiated into "the mysteries of the Great Mother."<58> The veneration of the Mother Goddess, as is well known, permeated ancient civilization. Jesus' own attitude toward woman was of a most lofty character and, no doubt, could have been derived from the Mysteries. (Cf. Chapter I.)

The mysteries of Eleusis in Greece, established centuries before Christianity, concerned themselves in part with the worship of the Goddess Demeter, symbolical of the plentitude of the earth. Isis and Cybele, further representations of the Great Mother, bestowed their mysteries upon initiates. These mysteries were concerned with the true nature of man, his origin and destiny, the nature and structure of the universe, and man's place in it. The ancient sects of Christianity, so universal in scope, repeatedly taught of the nature of God as Mother—both male and female. This subject of the femininity of the Deity is covered in detail by Elaine Pagels in her popular book, *The Gnostic Gospels*, chapter 3, "God the Father/God the Mother." She concludes that by the year 200, virtually every mention of feminine imagery for God disappeared from orthodox Christian tradition as a result of the controversy between the esoteric Christian sects (called Gnostic) and the emerging orthodox movement. <59>

According to the Naassenes, then, Jesus came to earth precisely to reveal the mysteries. This sect has preserved a "Hymn of Jesus," illustrating the purpose of his mission, quoted by Hippolytus in the Philosophumena, V. 10, 2.

See, Father, how, pursued by evil, the soul is wandering far from thy Spirit over the earth. She tries to flee from hateful chaos; she knows not how to emerge from it. To that end, Father, send me! I will descend, bearing the seals. I will pass through all the aeons; I will unveil every mystery; I will denounce the appearances of the gods and, under the name of

Gnosis, I will transmit the secrets of the holy way. <60>

There are several key concepts embedded in this passage. The first one is the plight of the soul on earth, in the grip of evil and unable to extricate herself. The soul cannot save herself. Jesus asks to be sent to earth to unveil the mysteries—those very mysteries that are vital to the soul's salvation, and without which the soul could not hope to be saved. We get an understanding of the causes of the soul's plight—the presence of the forces of chaos and the "gods" whom Jesus denounces. These "gods" are the fallen angels, archons, Nephilim, etc., who see to it that the soul cannot rise. The "secrets" of the way out for the soul must be transmitted through Gnosis, the revelation of Divine Knowledge.

Innumerable Christian sects proclaimed that they possessed the "secrets". Yet where are these "secrets" today? And are they being taught today by the Christian churches? The emerging movement in early Christianity known as orthodoxy saw to it that these mysteries were either suppressed or destroyed. We can gain some insight into the nature of some of the "secrets" in examining the teachings of the early sects of Christian Gnosis.

The Naassenes, for example, are said to have taught reincarnation—the periodic return of the soul to earth from which, until purified, it is finally freed from the shackles of earth. We can conclude that these teachings had to include, as an absolutely essential key, methods of purifying the soul such that it could eventually be free. The Naassenes taught the preexistence of the soul and elaborated on the causes of the soul's descent to earth. Another characteristic of ancient Christianity which the Naassenes likewise taught is the presence of the primeval spirit-spark in the body of man and woman, which constitutes the true Man. According to this sect, the resurrection is the release and expansion of the Spirit-Man buried in the tomb of the body. (See St. Paul's "inner man," "perfect man.") The soul then inhabits the higher dimensions of the heaven-world and is no longer subject to rebirth. As quoted by the Naassenes, this pure spiritual man "is the virgin with child, who conceives and brings forth a son, which is neither psychic, animal, or fleshy, but a blessed aeon of aeons."<61>

This concept shows us that the Naassenes believed that man in his true state can bring forth divinity, can give birth to a divine son. Divinity is within, not without. The mysteries Jesus brought were undoubtedly designed to demonstrate how to bring forth the hidden innate divinity of man. Recall Jesus' statement in Luke: "Behold, the Kingdom of God is within you." This "you," we should note, that the Kingdom is "within" cannot be merely the physical body—it could not contain such a Kingdom. It is consciousness, to which the spatial terms "internal/external," "within/without," are only metaphors.

In Pistis Sophia, an ancient gospel suppressed for over a thousand years and ignored by the orthodox churches even after its publication in the last century, Jesus, after his resurrection, elaborates on the mysteries and how necessary it is that his disciples not only receive these mysteries, but impart them to others.

For this cause have I said unto you aforetime: "Seek, that ye may find. I have, therefore, said unto you: Ye are to seek after the mysteries of the Light, which purify the body of matter and make it into refined light exceedingly purified.

Amen I say unto you...I have torn myself asunder and brought unto them all the mysteries of the Light, that I may purify them...else would no soul of the total race of men have been saved, and they would not be able to inherit the Kingdom of the Light, if I had not brought unto them the purifying mysteries.

...For this cause, therefore, herald to the whole race of men saying: Cease not to seek day and night, until ye find the purifying mysteries which will purify you...so that ye will go on high and inherit the light of my Kingdom.;>

According to this text, the purpose of receiving the mysteries is clear: that men may purify themselves to enter the

Kingdom of the Light. Without these mysteries, no hope of purification is possible!

Jesus admonishes his disciples to make thirty specific renunciations before they (or those to whom they speak) can be worthy to receive the mysteries. Among those things which must be renounced are: pride, craftiness, avarice, cursing, robbery, slander, sloth, adultery, atheism, and doctrines of error. To replace these qualities, the initiate must be loving-unto-men, gentle, merciful, must love God, be righteous, and should minister unto the poor, sick and distressed. The renunciation of negative qualities and the inculcation of positive ones is only the prerequisite to receiving the higher teachings, the mysteries known as "the forgiveness of sins":

> *Unto such, therefore, who have renounced in this renunciation, give the mysteries of the Light **and hide them not from them at all**, even though they are sinners and they have been in all the sins and all the iniquities of the world, all of which I have recounted unto you, in order that they turn and repent and be in the submission which I have just recounted unto you. Give unto them the mysteries of the Light-Kingdom and hide them not from them at all; for it is because of sinfulness that I have brought the mysteries into the world, that I may forgive all their sins which they have committed from the beginning on. For this cause have I said unto you aforetime: "I am not come to call the righteous." Now, therefore, I have brought the mysteries that [their] sins may be forgiven for every one and they may be received into the Light-Kingdom. For the mysteries are the gift of the First Mystery, that he may wipe out the sins and iniquities of all sinners. (Emphasis added) <63>*

Then follows a lengthy conversation, in the form of a dialogue, among Jesus and certain disciples concerning what occurs to different types of souls who go out of the body at death. Details about reincarnation are elaborated upon—some souls return to bodies that are deformed due to their sins, other souls receive purified bodies, some go to lower regions in various purgatorial states awaiting rebirth, and some souls go to the Light-Kingdom. Various after-death states are described by Jesus in detail. How and why souls enter bodies to be reborn is also discussed. In Pistis Sophia, then, we find absolute proof that the doctrine of reincarnation was taught by Jesus. Jesus' own post resurrection experiences in various planes or dimensions of the universe from the highest to the lowest are also detailed during the course of this fascinating and instructive gospel. The keys to the liberation and ascension of the soul are revealed by Jesus, as well as the pitfalls, not the least of which is the "counterfeiting spirit." This "spirit", the counterfeit self or dark side of man, is under the dominion of the "rulers of the Fate", those fallen, prideful or rebellious rulers who retard the spiritual evolution of man:

And the inner power stirreth the soul to seek after the region of the Light and the whole Godhead; and the counterfeiting spirit leadeth away the soul and compelleth it continually to do all its lawless deeds, all its mischiefs and all its sin and is persistently allotted to the soul and is hostile to it....

Now, therefore, this is in fact the foe of the soul, and this compelleth it until it doeth all sins. <64>

According to this text, the soul cannot overcome the counterfeiting spirit unless and until it receives the "mysteries of the baptisms." Jesus continues:

Now, therefore, he who shall receive the mysteries of the baptisms, then the mystery of them becometh a great, exceedingly violent, wise fire and it burneth up the sins and entereth into the soul secretly and consumeth all the sins which the counterfeiting spirit hath made fast on to it. <65>

The text then describes how the hostile spirit is burned by fire, transmuted, and how the sin is separated off from the soul and consumed. The receiving of this fire was a part of the mysteries conveyed by Jesus to his disciples.

Among the mysteries bestowed upon the disciples who prepare themselves is a certain power of the spoken word. The soul, in order to break the bonds and seals of the "counterfeit spirit" and the evil rulers who are bound to the souls, must utter "the mystery of the undoing of the seals and of all the bonds of the counterfeiting spirit."

And when the soul uttereth the mystery of the undoing of the seals, straightway the counterfeiting spirit undoeth itself and ceaseth to be assigned to the soul. And in that moment the soul uttereth a mystery and restraineth the counterfeiting spirit and the destiny...

...And it [the soul] uttereth the mystery and releaseth the counterfeiting spirit to the rulers of the Fate to the region in which it was bound to it.

And in that moment it [the soul] becometh entirely wings of light, and penetrateth all the regions of the rulers and all the orders of the Light, until it reacheth the region of its Kingdom up to which it hath received mysteries. (Brackets added) <66>

As we peruse this gospel of a lost Christianity, we appear to be in the midst of a vast spiritual science, and of a knowledge intricate and variegated, and utterly important to the freedom of the soul. But orthodox Christianity has been stripped of it all! All is unfortunately lost to the modern Christian.

We find echoes of a science of the spoken word, the uttering of which removes or restrains the evil self, the "karmic record" or "destiny" of the individual. These spiritual sciences and techniques, we may believe, were not all revealed to the faithful. According to Pistis Sophia, the mysteries are given to those who make themselves worthy. There are levels and degrees of teaching apparently corresponding to the levels and degrees of the regions or planes of existence. With each mystery given, the disciple is given dominion over each respective plane and its inhabitants.

After describing and enacting a ritual and offering with his disciples for the forgiveness of sins, Jesus says:

This is the manner and way and this is the mystery which ye are to perform for the men who have faith in you, in whom is no deceit and who hearken unto you in all good works. And their sins and their iniquities will be blotted out up to the day on which ye have performed for them this mystery. But hide this mystery and give it not to all men, but unto him who shall do all the things which I have said unto you in my commandments. <67>

It is noteworthy that the text makes no mention of Jesus' vicarious death on the cross as being instrumental in the forgiveness of sins. Sins are either forgiven (set aside) or blotted out through the "mystery of baptism" and by the ritual of the "baptism of fire." This brings us to the teachings of the Docetae, an ancient Christian sect which denied the reality of Jesus' "atoning" death.

Did Jesus Die on the Cross?

The Docetists

The sect of the Docetae, one of the most widespread schools and communities of early Christians, was apparently influenced by Hindu and Buddhist thought. There is nothing unusual in this, since, according to Notovitch's Tibetan text, Jesus sojourned in India and Tibet. We recall the evidence provided by Kersten and others, that Jesus spent his remaining years travelling throughout the Near East, finally ending his days in Kashmir.

Upon his return to Palestine, after his initial journey to the East, Jesus may have promulgated the Hindu doctrine of the illusoriness of matter and the reality of Spirit. His disciples may have also taught these doctrines, both during Jesus' Palestinian mission and after he had departed Palestine. We cannot escape the conclusion that, if Jesus lived many years after his resurrection, as Irenaeus attests, he may well have founded circles of disciples to whom he imparted the more subtle and transcendent doctrines of the East.

Among these doctrines, as we have said, is the concept of the non-reality of matter and the material universe when compared with the Spirit and the spiritual universe—a "non-reality" to which the student of modern physics might easily resonate The Docetae in Greek translates as "the illusionists,"<68> and this group was imbued with the Hindu notion that the created universe was "maya" or a "dream" spun out of the thought of God (Brahma).

The Docetae, apparently, made a distinction between Christ Jesus as a spiritual being and Jesus as a bodily being. Although the Docetae taught that the Divine Aeon Jesus withdrew his glory into himself and incarnated in a body, Jesus as a Divine Being was far more significant to them than Jesus as a flesh and blood being. This concept recalls to us the words of St. Paul, who taught that the heavenly Christ "made himself of no reputation" and was born on earth as a man. The Docetae were concerned to demonstrate that Jesus transcended matter and the physical body and was himself not subject to matter. This transcending of the body was demonstrated preeminently by Jesus at his resurrection. St. Paul similarly taught that Jesus was designated "Son of God with power" at his resurrection, and as we previously noted, St. Paul was more concerned with Christ as a resurrected heavenly being than with the earthly Jesus. We find, then, points of similarity between the Jesus of St. Paul and the Jesus of the Docetae.

The Docetae accepted and taught the doctrine of preexistence and reincarnation as did the Nazoreans, Ebionites and other innumerable Christian sects, including the Pauline communities. They taught that all souls were originally "breathed out" from the Divine Aeons above, but were seized upon by darkness and succumbed to the delusion of matter and the material senses. Matter, though real, hides and dulls the greater reality of Spirit.

This greatly misunderstood Christian sect, later so defamed by the Church Fathers, applied this spiritual understanding to Christ and specifically related it to his "death." Jesus, so they taught, came to set souls free from the cycle of rebirth and thus from the delusions of the senses in the physical body. To prepare for this mission, Jesus, at his baptism, became possessed of a "spiritual body." This is probably a reference to an "initiation" of sorts which occurred at the baptism when the Father pronounced the words, "Thou art my beloved Son, this day I have begotten thee!" We recall that this statement was once found in the now lost Gospel of the Hebrews. At his baptism, then, Jesus was begotten by the Father as a "spiritual being," and this "spiritual body" was said to be a copy of his physical body. Jesus, however, was at no time made subject to the delusion of the body throughout his mission.

The sect taught that the world-ruler, known in John's gospel as the "Prince [Archon] of this world" determined to condemn Jesus to death, since Jesus taught souls how to escape from the cycles of rebirth and thus from the power of the world-fabricator who seeks to sustain the illusion of matter, from life to life. The world-ruler, moreover, only succeeded in condemning and crucifying the body of Jesus to so-called death, but the true spiritual Christ triumphed over the powers and authorities of the world-ruler specifically by his resurrection. Jesus as a physical being then suffered, but the true Christ as a spiritual being was not subject to death. At his resurrection, so the Docetists taught, Jesus "stripped off" [transmuted] his physical body and put on his spiritual body of perfection. Jesus, as Christ, then, did not die on the cross, and as Christ, could not be said to have experienced death.

This, briefly, was the theology of the Docetae. The only death they would admit to would be, perhaps, the death of sin and limitation. Spirit is the victor over matter, and matter or the body can be transcended by Spirit. Jesus came to earth to overcome death and the senses, not to succumb to them. So taught the Docetae.

Congruent with the doctrine of the "illusion" of or basic nonreality of matter, came the understanding that Jesus had both the ability and the adeptship to leave his body while on the cross and thus not experience suffering. It was in this sense, also, that the Docetae taught that Jesus' crucifixion and death were only an appearance and that he only seemed to suffer.

One finds this outlook concerning Jesus' sufferings in certain texts preserved in the Nag Hammadi Library, showing that this concept was widespread in early Christianity and certainly not confined to the Docetae specifically. We reiterate that during the first two centuries of Christianity, there was no fixed doctrine regarding the crucifixion of Jesus, nor was there a definitive interpretation of it.

We quote the Second Treatise of the Great Seth, which claims to be a revelation of Jesus Christ concerning, among other things, his passion and "death":

...And I was in the mouths of lions...I did not succumb to them as they had planned. But I was not afflicted at all... And I did not die in reality but in appearance, lest I be put to shame by them....I was about to succumb to fear, and I (suffered) according to their sight and thought...For my death which they think happened, (happened) to them in their error and blindness, since they nailed their man unto their death...But in doing these things, they condemn themselves. Yes, they saw me; they punished me. It was another, their father, who drank the gall and the vinegar; it was not I....It was another upon whom they placed the crown of thorns. But I was rejoicing in the height over all the wealth of the archons and the offspring of their error, of their empty glory. And I was laughing at their ignorance. And I subjected all their powers. <69>

St. Paul taught that Jesus "disarmed the [evil] powers" and put them to naught, through his crucifixion and resurrection. How did Jesus accomplish this? Did he, in fact, actually succumb to death as the orthodox church later taught?

Or did he escape death and torture, at least to a certain degree? Was Jesus' so-called death in reality a "mystical death," as we have explained, and not a literal death? Did he die in appearance only?

The intricate details involving the subject of Christ's crucifixion are not to be found in the New Testament. The statements made throughout the New Testament, that Jesus died, have never been fully explained. If, in fact, Jesus did disarm the evil powers and put to naught the principalities and archons, as St. Paul avers, may he not have accomplished this by escaping their condemnation, yet allowing them to believe that he was dead, when, in reality, he was not? Could the judgment of the powers have been fulfilled because they dared to "slay" the body of Jesus? The above passage makes clear that the judgment and condemnation heaped upon Jesus was actually turned back upon those who attempted to put him to death. Could this have been the manner in which Christ "subjected" the powers and their instruments in the world?

In answer, we ask: Why should a literal, physical interpretation of the crucifixion of Christ prevail over all others? If various sects of Christianity taught varying theological interpretations of it, would one sect or community possess or be given exclusive right to be the sole interpreter of what actually occurred? Even the disciples saw the crucifixion in different ways, as we shall see.

If Jesus were the Master and Adept that he is made out to be in the New Testament and apocryphal texts, possessing unusual spiritual powers, could he not have had the power to depart the body while on the cross, thus turning the tables on his self-styled enemies?

In the Apocalypse of Peter, the apostle Peter sees a vision of Jesus, who tells him that, "...This one into whose hands and feet they drive nails is his fleshy part, which is the substitute, being put to shame," but "what they released was my incorporeal body....I am the intellectual Spirit filled with radiant light." <70>

From what we can gather, the Christians who used these

texts believed in the existence of not just one body but of other bodies, more spiritual, apparently existing in congruency, and which had the ability to separate from one another. Jesus, being the divine Redeemer, could navigate in his "incorporeal body" at will. St. Paul taught much the same concept when he wrote that there are natural (psychic) bodies and spiritual (pneumatic) bodies, and that one body differs from another in glory.

In one of the most intriguing texts, still extant, The Acts of John, the disciple John is given a vision and understanding of the cross and crucifixion from none other than Jesus himself. In this section, John describes the events following Jesus' arrest in the Garden of Gethsemane:

And we were like men amazed or fast asleep, and we fled this way and that. And so I saw him suffer, and did not wait by his suffering, but fled to the Mount of Olives and wept at what had come to pass. And when he was hung upon the cross on Friday, at the sixth hour of the day there came a darkness over the whole earth. And my Lord stood in the middle of the cave and gave light to it and said, "John, for the people below in Jerusalem I am being crucified and pierced with lances...But to you I am speaking, and listen to what I speak...And when he had said this he showed me a cross of light firmly fixed, and around the cross a great crowd, which had no single form; and in the cross was one form and the same likeness. And I saw the Lord himself above the cross, having no shape but only a kind of voice...which said to me, "John, there must be one man to hear those things from me; for I need one who is ready to hear. This cross of light is sometimes called Logos by me for your sakes, sometimes Mind, sometimes Jesus, sometimes Christ, sometimes a Door, sometimes a Way, sometimes Bread, sometimes Seed, sometimes Spirit, sometimes Life, sometimes Truth, sometimes Faith, sometimes Grace; and so it is called for men's sake....

This cross then is that which has united all things by the Word and which has separated off what is transitory and inferior, which has compacted all things into one. But this is not that wooden cross which you shall see when you go down from here; nor am I the man who is on the cross, I whom now you do not see but only hear my voice...

So then I have suffered none of those things which they will say of me; even that suffering which I showed to you and to the rest in my dance [a ritualistic dance Jesus performed with his disciples after the Last Supper], I will that it be called a mystery. For what you are, that I have shown to you, as you see; but what I am is known to me alone, and no one else. Let me have what is mine; what is yours you must see through me; but me you must see truly—not that which I am, as I said, but that which you, as my kinsman, are able to know. You hear that I suffered, yet I suffered not; and that I suffered not, yet I did suffer; and that I was pierced, yet I was not wounded; that I was hanged, yet I was not hanged; that blood flowed from me, yet it did not flow, and, in a word, that which they say of me, I did not endure, but what they do not say, those things I did suffer. Now what these are, I secretly show you; for I know that you will understand. You must know me then, as the torment of the Logos, the piercing of the Logos, the blood of the Logos. And so I speak discarding the manhood. The first then that you must know is the Logos, then you shall know the Lord; and thirdly the Man, and what he has suffered."

When he had said these things to me, and others which I know not how to say as he wills, he was taken up, without any of the multitudes seeing him. And going down I laughed at them all, since he had told me what they had said about him; and I held this one thing fast in my mind, that the Lord had performed everything as a symbol and a dispensation for the conversion and salvation of man. (Brackets added) <71>

We will not attempt to interpret the full meaning of this passage, except to say that this portion of the text attempts to explain the passion and crucifixion of Christ on many levels, symbolically and allegorically. The Cross of Light replaces the wooden Roman cross. The inner, spiritual and cosmic initiation of the crucifixion is far more significant to the writer of this text than the mere physical execution of Jesus by the Roman authorities. The cross, from ancient times, has always symbolized the meeting of heaven and earth, of God and man. The disciple John, in the text, is taken up to a higher level of awareness (the "cave" of the heart) where he receives Jesus' words on the higher, spiritual meaning of the cross. We should consider the above passage to be the most sublime yet enigmatic sequence relating to the passion of Christ extant.

Duncan Greenlees, commenting on this passage, names the above text a "precious relic of an early Johannine mystic school" and remarks:

The apparent bodily sufferings of Jesus have no reality; the actual pains of the Christ are beyond imagination—the strain of uplifting all mankind. The Cross changes every measure we have known, inverts all our values, and turns the lowly into the transcendentally high. Only by embracing this Cross can man enter the Kingdom of eternal Life, for it alone leads from the pit, like Jacob's ladder, to the skies....

...The reality can never be told another—each can see his own experience in the radiant mirror of the Saviour's soul. Suffering there is, yes; but it is not what men can see or think about. Nails, thorns, spear gave no real pain to God; the real agony was the laboring to give birth to souls, to lift them from the depths. It is the Word, the salvific Will of God, that really suffers.... <72>

This mystical insight into the passion of Christ was reduced by orthodox Christianity into a literal, dogmatic death of the physical Jesus, emphasizing the physical shedding of his blood, and nothing more.

Returning to our question, did Jesus die on the cross?, we would remark here that, in examining the previous passages, the "death" Jesus is supposed to have suffered would certainly have been in the eye of the beholder.

Holger Kersten, in his book, *Jesus Lived in India*, carefully analyzes the Holy Shroud and concludes that Jesus could not have been clinically dead when taken down from the cross.

Even more cogent evidence can be seen in the blood stains visible on the linen. One can clearly distinguish between two different types of bleeding on the shroud; blood that had dried up after it had flowed during Jesus' crucifixion, and fresh blood that left the body after Jesus had been laid down on the shroud in a horizontal position!
...Corpses just do not bleed! In Jesus's case, there were a total of twenty-eight wounds that continued to bleed even after his removal from the cross. It can be regarded as a fact that Jesus could not possibly have been dead when his body was laid in the sepulchre.... <73>

Kersten also concludes that the alleged vinegar given to Jesus on the cross was, in fact, a narcotic drink, prepared from the herb Asclepias acida, also known as the Haoma drink or soma drink, and used as a sacred drink in India:

The holy soma drink of India enabled anyone familiar with the drug to appear dead for several days, and to awake afterwards in an elated state that lasts a few days. In such a state of religious ecstasy, a higher consciousness could speak forth, expressing newly acquired powers of vision. <74>

The author contends that Jesus received this drink while on the cross from those sympathetic to him—the centurion, Joseph of Arimathea, Nicodemus and especially certain Essenes versed in the herbal arts. Kersten quotes John's gospel, chapter 19:

The reason for Jesus' apparent death can be found in a few verses before, verses 29 and 30: "Now there was set a vessel full of vinegar: and they filled a sponge with vinegar, and put upon it hysop, and put in into his mouth. When Jesus therefore had received the vinegar, he said It is finished: and he bowed his head, and gave up the ghost." <75>

Kersten states that the drink administered to Jesus tasted as sour as vinegar, as does Asclepias acida. But vinegar would have had the effect of stimulation (which was its somewhat Romanly sadistic purpose for being there), whereas the opposite took place. Jesus cries out with a loud voice (which would have been impossible in a state of asphyxiation and near exhaustion), then gives up the ghost and apparently "dies".

This apparent death is a comatose state resembling deep sleep, where all the signs of life such as respiration, heart beat and pulse are no longer noticeable. <76>

Jesus was then taken down from the cross by Joseph of Arimathea (who received permission from Pilate) and Nicodemus, and placed in Joseph's own tomb. Jesus was interred with a mixture of myrrh and aloes, which is still regarded as very effective medication in treating open wounds. Naturally, Nicodemus would not have administered one hundred pounds of myrrh and aloes (as the gospel states) to a corpse. Kersten remarks:

If one assumes that Joseph of Arimathea and Nicodemus were secret lay members of the Essene Order, it is logical that they would have been well suited for the task of treating Jesus' wounds and helping the healing process. As experienced healers, the Essenes were familiar with exotic drugs and remarkable methods of treatment....Heat has a therapeutic effect in the process of healing; heat could have been produced by the aloe and myrrh....<77>

Kersten continues:

Jesus was of course considerably weakened by the torture that he had been forced to undergo. Nonetheless, the loss of blood had been relatively little: all indications on the shroud point to a loss of less than one litre of blood. Surgical *experiments with corpses have shown that being nailed to the cross destroys neither major blood vessels nor any bones. The nail was driven between eight wrist bones, pushing them slightly apart. The perforation of the feet took place at the second metatarsal specium, only causing wounds to the flesh. After the larger wounds had been sown up, the injured man would have needed absolute peace and quiet, and this could have been insured by the narcotic drink. <78>*

Kersten concludes with the resurrection scenario as follows:

Three days later, a few women dared to approach the tomb. The Gospel of Saint Mark mentioned Mary Magdalene, Mary the mother of Jacob, and Salome, bearing balsam for the body of Jesus. In the Gospel of Saint Matthew, only two women came to the tomb, and in Saint John's Gospel, it is only Mary Magdalene. But there is agreement in all four of the Gospels that the tomb was empty, save for one or more men in white robes. These "angels" could have simply been members of the Essene Order, who always wore white. The Essenes were evidently the only people who had been let in on the entire mystery. Even the disciples seem to have been completely ignorant of the events when they later met their Master....

This period of the events following the resurrection is fraught with so many contradictions that it is impossible to ascertain its exact length. Three days were said to have elapsed between crucifixion and Jesus' reappearance, but three is a mystical number which had played a role in earlier resurrection myths. Perhaps Jesus was treated longer, and only later began to show himself gradually to his followers. At any rate the encounters seem to have been short and secret. Obviously Jesus could not appear in public, for he would have been immediately rearrested (although the injuries, or his miraculous recovery, or even his sheer divine normality, do seem to have altered his appearance; this made it difficult for his acquaintances to recognize him). <79>

We should note again that Jesus' "death" appears to have been no ordinary death but an initiation—a crucifixion ritual—that Jesus permitted to be "publicly" performed. The crucifixion may very well have been a ritual of the Essenes carried out to perfection in Jesus, with the assistance of the Essenes, as Kersten states. We would tend to attribute Jesus' altered appearance to the sheer radiation of light/energy flowing through him—perhaps a divine source of energy little understood, which he clearly manifested already in the transfiguration as his real state. This would explain Jesus' puzzling words to Mary Magdalene when she encountered him on resurrection morning: "Touch me not, for I have not yet ascended to my Father," as well as his altered appearance to the disciples on the road to Emmaus.

To review and summarize these findings:

1) Jesus may have intermittently left his body while on the cross. He would then have been functioning in a spiritual (etheric) body.

2) Jesus, as the Christ or Logos, may have suffered spiritually far more than physically.

3) The soul of Jesus while on the cross may have experienced what in mystical theology has been called the "Dark Night of the Spirit," a severe test whereby the soul is cut off from God (its Divine Self) and must spiritually maintain itself without the assistance of God for a certain period of time. This is illustrated when Jesus uttered the cry while on the cross, "My God, my God, why hast thou forsaken me?"

4) When Jesus "gave up the ghost," he departed the body, traversed the heavenly and lower realms, and three days later reentered the body as it rested in the tomb, reanimated it and transformed it into a "glorified" body. Herbs were administered to Jesus' body as it lay in the tomb, thus securing the healing process. This scenario closely followes the myth of the dying and resurrected gods of antiquity. Although Kersten contends that Jesus lost consciousness and did not experience

an actual death, we are of the opinion that Jesus may very well have experienced "clinical" death, whereby the Divine Spark was withdrawn from his body. Jesus, then, as the ultimate initiation, would have had to call back the flame to his body, and re-enter it, thus physically proving the continuity of consciousness over death. For, esoterically, the definition of death is the withdrawal of the Divine Spark from the body temple.

We can conclude from the various texts quoted above, including the gospels, that the purpose of the crucifixion was to overcome death, not to succumb to it and to pass the initiation of the Dark Night of the Spirit. The resurrection was the mark that Jesus had successfully passed this test, thus demonstrating dominion over death itself, and for the remainder of his years Jesus would then move throughout the earth in a God-conscious state, and in a body permeated with the spiritual fires of the resurrection.

Jesus, as earlier stated, may have permitted his body to be tortured and "slain" so that the "forces of darkness," in outplaying their hand, would bring upon themselves the judgement for their actions in slaying the Messiah and at the same time would be "disarmed" by the power of the resurrection.

The Teaching of Cerinthus—A "Secret Doctrine" of Matthew?

We now move from the doctrine of the Naassenes and Docetists to that of Cerinthus, who taught during the close of the first century in Asia Minor. Cerinthus was said to have been trained in the Egyptian discipline and to have been a contemporary of John, the disciple of Jesus. Cerinthus' doctrine, therefore, is one of the oldest of Christian teachings and would have been contemporaneous with the writing of the gospels of Luke and John.

This Christian school taught that Jesus was the son of Joseph and Mary, and denied that he was born in a supernatural or miraculous manner. As with the Nazoreans, Paul and John, there is no mention of a virginal conception or virgin birth. According to Cerinthus, Jesus became the Christ or "anointed one" at his baptism when "the Father in the form of a dove" descended upon him, whereupon Jesus began to prophesy and accomplish mighty works. This teaching coincides with the oldest Nazorean-Jewish conception of Jesus, who, as was stated, became the Christ, but was not born the Christ. We recall that this idea became known as the heresy of "Adoptionism."

Jesus, according to Cerinthus, taught about the Father who was unknown to the Jews, the Jews having worshipped either a lesser god or a lesser image and conception of God. We saw a parallel to this teaching in John's gospel when Jesus says to the Pharisees, "Ye neither know me, nor my Father, if ye had known me, ye should have known my Father also....I speak that which I have seen with my Father, and ye do that which ye have seen with your father." (John 8:15, 38) Jesus clearly distinguished between two fathers; Jesus' Father, a different Personage, is not known by the Jews. Is John referring here to the lesser deity, known as the demiurge?

Cerinthus likewise taught that the Christ left the man Jesus while he hung on the cross. Again we are faced with one of the oldest conceptions of the crucifixion: the Christ as the spiritual man departs the physical body and is in no way bound to it. This idea may also refer to the Dark Night of the Spirit—the severing of the soul temporarily from its connection to God.

Cerinthus is known to have taught the idea of Chiliasm: the doctrine that Christ at his Second Coming will establish an earthly kingdom to endure a thousand years. This doctrine was also taught by the Ebionites, Hebrew Christians who apparently adapted the Judaic and Messianic concept of an earthly kingdom ruled by the Messiah.

According to G.R.S. Mead, Cerinthus used a collection of sayings of Jesus by Matthew written in Hebrew, not, however, connected with our canonical Matthew.<80> This may very well have been the so-called Gospel of the Hebrews, used by Nazorean-Jewish Christians and by the Ebionites.

Church Father Jerome, writing at the beginning of the fifth century, mentions a gospel written by Matthew in Hebrew and used by the Nazarenes who lived in Berea, a city in Syria. The gospel was also used by the Ebionites, and Jerome apparently translated it into Greek. In his Commentary on Matthew, he states that the Hebrew gospel by Matthew "is by most esteemed the authentic Gospel of Matthew" and gives brief excerpts from it, none of which are to be found in our canonical Greek Matthew. <81> Jerome also asserts that Origen, the greatest of the Church Fathers, often used this gospel. Could Cerinthus and his school have been in contact with the authentic Gospel of Matthew, now lost to us? And if the Hebrew gospel was deemed authentic, why does Jerome insist on using our canonical Matthew, apparently a later edited version?

This is not all. Jerome seems to have been in contact with a "secret doctrine" of Jesus written by Matthew found in the library at Caesarea, which, as H.P. Blavatsky states, may have been identical to the Hebrew gospel. We quote Blavatsky from her magnum opus, *Isis Unveiled*:

That the apostles had received a "secret doctrine" from Jesus, and that he himself taught one, is evident from the following words of Jerome, who confessed it in an unguarded moment. Writing to the Bishops Chromatius and Heliodorus, he complains that "a difficult work is enjoined, since this translation has been commanded me by you Felicities, which St. Matthew himself, the Apostle and Evangelist, DID NOT WISH TO BE OPENLY WRITTEN. For if it had not been SECRET, he (Matthew) would have added to the evangel that which he gave forth was his; but he made up this book sealed up in Hebrew characters, which he put forth even in such a way that the book, written in Hebrew letters and by the hand of himself, might be possessed by the men most religious, who also, in the course of time, received it from those who preceded them. But this very book they never gave to any one to be transcribed, and its text they related some one way and some another...."

He [Jerome] admits, himself, that the book which he authenticates as being written by the hand of Matthew; a book which, notwithstanding that he translated it twice, was nearly unintelligible to him, for it was arcane or a secret. Nevertheless Jerome coolly sets down every commentary upon it, except his own, as heretical. More than that, Jerome knew that this original Gospel of Matthew was the expounder of the only true doctrine of Christ, and that it was the work of an evangelist who had been the friend and companion of Jesus. He knew that if of the two gospels, the Hebrew in question and the Greek belonging to our present Scripture, one was spurious, hence heretical, it was not that of the Nazarenes; and yet, knowing all this, Jerome becomes more zealous than ever in his persecutions of the "Heretics." Why? Because to accept it was equivalent to reading the death-sentence of the established Church. The Gospel according to the Hebrews was but too well known to have been the only one accepted for four centuries by the Jewish Christians, the Nazarenes and the Ebionites. (Brackets added) <82>

The remarks above are intriguing, to say the least. Was the persecution of Cerinthus and his followers due to the fact that his school of Christianity possessed the original teaching of Matthew, which might have contradicted orthodox Christianity then being formulated? Again, we are face to face with the suppression of an "original Christianity" now lost.

Carpocrates and the Secret Gospel of Mark

One of the more controversial of early Christian schools was that of Carpocrates, who was accused by Irenaeus and others, including Clement of Alexandria, of teaching sexual promiscuity. The basis of this charge was that Carpocrates apparently taught that man experiences every kind of sin in his long circuit of past lives before attaining spiritual freedom. It may also have been true that the followers of Carpocrates entertained liberal ideas concerning sex. In an age when certain Christian communities looked upon sex as sinful, this school promulgated the opposite viewpoint: sex was natural. We can well see why this school was deemed heretical.

We should be more concerned, however, with the ideas of Carpocrates concerning Jesus. Carpocrates taught his doctrine at Alexandria circa 117-138 A.D. and was the head of a Christian school. Its adherents called themselves "gnostics."

As in the earliest Christian communities, this school considered Jesus to have been born as other men were and to have been the son of Joseph and Mary. They taught that Jesus' soul, being strong and pure, remembered its conversation with the ineffable Father. This statement is itself astonishing for it shows that Jesus' claim to divinity was based upon his own soul's remembrance of its origin, not because he was God from all eternity or because of a miraculous or supernatural birth.

The Carpocratians also taught that the Father clothed Jesus with powers which enabled him to escape from the dominion of the evil rulers of the world, pass through all their "spheres" and, being freed from each, finally ascend to the Father. The doctrine of the dominance of evil powers disarmed by Jesus appears again.

If one were to ask a member of this school the question, "How did Jesus overcome?", he would answer that Jesus' sole claim to divinity was that he triumphed over human passions, conquered himself and thus became the Saviour of others. The logical corollary to this, of course, is that anyone who thus so conquers can also attain to a degree of spirituality commensurate with that of Jesus. This is precisely what this Christian school taught. They averred that all souls who rise above the constraints of the world rulers may receive similar powers and perform like wonders as did Jesus. It was possible that individuals could even reach higher degrees of illumination than Jesus reached. Nevertheless, these higher degrees of illumination are not won in a single lifetime, but rather, as this school taught, the soul has to pass through every kind of existence and activity during its cycles of rebirth.

The sect established a branch in Rome circa 130 A.D., under a woman named Marcellina—another reason for the sect's condemnation, especially in an age when women were not generally given authority as spiritual teachers. The Carpocratians apparently revered many great teachers, such as Pythagoras and Plato, collected statues of them and, so we are told, possessed a portrait of Jesus, who was equally revered alongside other teachers. <83>

The sect made use of a "secret Gospel of Mark", excerpts of which are preserved in Greek in a fragment from a letter of Clement of Alexandria, a Church Father who wrote at the close of the second century. In this letter (discovered by Scholar Morton Smith at Mar Sarba Monastery in Palestine in 1958), Clement denounces the Carpocratians for their libertine ways and readily admits that this sect possessed the "secret gospel," proof again that a secret doctrine was being taught in certain sects and communities. Quoting Clement's letter:

As for Mark, during Peter's stay in Rome, he wrote an account of the Lord's doings, not however, declaring all of them, nor yet hinting at secret ones, but selecting what he thought most useful for increasing the faith of those who were being instructed. But when Peter died a martyr, Mark came over to Alexandria, bringing both his own notes and those of Peter, from which he transferred to his former book the things suitable to whatever makes for progress toward knowledge. Thus he composed a more spiritual Gospel for the use of those who were being perfected. Nevertheless, he yet did not divulge the things not to be uttered, nor did he write down the hierophantic teaching of the Lord, but to the stories already written he added yet others and, moreover, brought in certain sayings of which he knew the interpretation would as a mystagogue, lead the hearers into the innermost sanctuary hidden by seven [veils]. Thus, on sum, he prearranged matters, neither grudgingly nor incautiously, in my opinion, and dying, he left his composition to the church in Alexandria, where it *even yet is most carefully guarded, being read only to those who are being initiated into the great mysteries. <84>*

There is no question that Mark was in possession of and taught a "secret doctrine" which not only the Alexandrian Church but also the Carpocratians inherited. Morton Smith believes that Carpocratian "Gnosticism" appears to have been "a Platonizing development of the primitive secret doctrine and a practice of Jesus himself."<85> Smith also observes that Egypt was the place where the secret, expanded gospel of Mark originated, and concludes that the material used in the secret text may have been drawn from "an older Aramaic Gospel, a source used also by canonical Mark and by John."<86> The Greek text of secret Mark, continues Smith, was derived from this source, by a translation that was made after the canonical Mark had been written. <87>

The term "hierophantic" used by Clement in the above passage designates Jesus as a "hierophant" or expositor of the sacred mysteries—mysteries that have not passed down to the orthodox Christianity of subsequent centuries.

We recall that the "secret" portion of Mark's gospel contained a variant of what appears to be the resurrection of Lazarus (although Lazarus is not named in the "secret gospel"). After Jesus raises the unnamed "youth" from the tomb, the gospel adds:

But the youth, looking upon him [Jesus], loved him and began to beseech him that he might be with him. And going out of the tomb they came into the house of the youth, for he was rich. And after six days Jesus told him what to do and in the evening the youth comes to him, wearing a linen cloth over [his] naked [body]. And he remained with him that night, for Jesus taught him the mystery of the kingdom of God. And thence, arising, he returned to the other side of the Jordan. (Brackets added) <88>

Jesus is here pictured as a "hierophant" imparting the

"mystery" during a nocturnal initiation. What was the nature of the mystery? It appears from the above passage that the mystery was bestowed from the Master to the disciple in secret and by word of mouth. Was the "mystery of the kingdom" ever written down? Were the Carpocratians privy to this "mystery"? Could the "mystery" have transmitted power to the recipient, thus making the recipient a threat to the already established powers in church and state? Did the Carpocratian Christians, in fact, receive powers enabling them to perform seemingly miraculous feats as Jesus did? Is this why they were so condemned? Irenaeus writes that Carpocrates himself claimed to be able to dominate the "angels" and to use them for "magical operations."<89> And what is worse, the Carpocratians denied the resurrection of the body. Is this why the alleged "Aramaic gospel" was suppressed?

It should be understood that the impartation of the mystery of the kingdom of God can be very real, very experiential, when transmitted in the master/disciple or guru/chela (student) relationship of spiritual tradition. The early Christians, as the passage quoted shows, give every evidence of accepting and carrying on this tradition, with Jesus as their exemplar. To give the reader an idea of how real and concrete this experience can be, and simultaneously why these things were (1) likely to be kept secret, (2) limited to the few who had prepared themselves, and (3) difficult to transmit in written form in the first place, we might note here the description which the well-known Indian mystic Paramahansa Yogananda gave of his own experience with his guru— this after a fruitless trip to the Himalayas to seek enlightenment:

"...Poor boy, mountains cannot give you what you want." Master spoke caressingly, comfortingly. His calm gaze was unfathomable. "Your heart's desire shall be fulfilled."

Sri Yukteswar seldom indulged in riddles; I was bewildered. He struck gently on my chest above the heart.

My body became immovably rooted; breath was drawn out of my lungs as if by some huge magnet. Soul and mind instantly lost their physical bondage and streamed out like a fluid piercing light from my every pore. The flesh was as though dead; yet in my intense awareness I knew that never before had I been fully alive. My sense of identity was no longer narrowly confined to a body but embraced the circumambient atoms. People on distant streets seemed to be moving gently over my own remote periphery. The roots of plants and trees appeared through a dim transparency of soil; I discerned the inward flow of their sap.

The whole vicinity lay bare before me. My ordinary frontal vision was now changed to a vast spherical sight, simultaneously all-perceptive. Through the back of my head I saw men strolling far down Rai Ghat Lane...

All objects within my panoramic gaze trembled and vibrated like quick motion pictures. My body, Master's, the pillared courtyard, the furniture and floor, the trees and sunshine, occasionally became violently agitated, until all melted down into a luminescent sea; even as sugar crystals, thrown into a glass of water, dissolve after being shaken. The unifying light alternated with materializations of form, the metamorphoses revealing the law of cause and effect in creation.

An oceanic joy broke upon calm endless shores of my soul. The Spirit of God, I realized, is exhaustless Bliss; His body is countless tissues of light.... <90>

This is a contemporary experience of the impartation of a "mystery."

Let us now review the basic concepts and teachings of the oldest sects and schools comprising what we have termed "Lost Christianity" and which comprised primitive or original Christianity. We find that most, if not all, of the earliest heterodox Christian sects and communities taught the following:

1. A "Doctrine of Emanations" from one Eternal Source, or the idea that all individuals have their origin in the Eternal and all partake, in their inmost being, in the eternal.

2. The preexistence of souls in a spiritual state who subsequently fell into matter and became clothed with bodies. Some still retained a Divine Spark within, this spark being the means of salvation. Many lost the Divine Spark and were in need of redemption.

3. Redemption/Salvation through Knowledge, Wisdom or Gnosis revealed and imparted by Jesus, the Saviour, who descended from the Heavenly Realms to earth. The means and method by which this "incarnation" took place varied from sect to sect.

4. A distinction between the earthly Jesus and the Heavenly Christ (the Higher Self), although both Jesus and Christ had become one, hence the title Jesus Christ. The earthly Jesus was considered to be the natural son of Joseph and Mary.

5. The concept of a Divine Feminine of whatever name and of God as partaking of attributes of both Male and Female. A portion of the divine feminine was responsible for the fashioning of the lower realms of matter.

6. The existence of a "secret doctrine" or mystery teaching imparted by Jesus to his disciples.

7. The crucifixion of Jesus as an event interpreted on various levels: literal, symbolical and allegorical. The "death" of Jesus was only in appearance as the "spiritual Christ" could not be subject to death.

8. The existence of evil powers, rulers, inferior or fallen angels, ruled over by a chief archon known by various names and who was instrumental in fashioning the lower worlds of matter. These beings have enslaved humanity but Christ triumphed over them and all those who follow Christ will likewise do so.

9. Since their descent into matter, souls have been subject to reincarnation, due to the weight of sin, matter and ignorance. Christ brought liberating Gnosis (knowledge) of man's true origin and demonstrated a way out of rebirth known as "the resurrection of the dead." Christ, as Saviour, possesses the power to restore the soul to its true nature by reigniting the Divine Spark within the heart. This was the "atonement," not a blood sacrifice of a Son to an otherwise implacable God for an

"original sin."

10. A system of "initiation" whereby the esoteric doctrine of Jesus by degrees was imparted to all who made themselves worthy.

Although there were divergences among the various sects and schools, there was room for creative freedom and individual interpretation. The earliest Christianity was diverse yet all inclusive. The believer, no matter what his religion, could embrace Christianity in the form that best suited him. Since there was a preponderance of sects and schools, this was not difficult. Christ remained the center and cornerstone of the new religion, and the believer could accept Christ as he or she was able to perceive him. The Jew, the Greek, the Persian, the Egyptian, the Hindu could accept Christ and yet not discard his own religion and the concepts most dear to him. We have seen evidence of the universalism of early Christianity in our examination of these sects. We see threads of many differing religious concepts among the teachings we have just reviewed. An examination of the Christian texts from the Nag Hammadi Library will bear this out. Scholars have detected Platonic, Babylonian, Essene and Jewish-Gnostic influences in these diverse texts. Yet they all comprise what was once known as Christianity. We contend that "Lost Christianity" was the most universal of faiths, eclectic and syncretistic in nature. We also contend that Jesus himself was universal in his view. If we accept the evidence of Jesus' sojourn in the East, his study of teachings of the Buddhas and sages in India, the religion he taught must have been universal and capable of being applied in the context of any religion. Unfortunately, it was not to remain so. We continue our survey.

Chapter VI

The Emergence of Orthodoxy

The Misuse of the Old Testament—Clement of Rome

Coincident with the universalism of the early Christian sects, schools and communities, there began to emerge a narrow view of Christianity from circles of bishops, primarily having their origin and background in Judaism. The term bishop, meaning "overseer," harks back to the formalism of the Essene hierarchy in the Qumran monastic community. It also recalls to us the Levitical or Aaronic priesthood from Old Testament times, who were understood to be intercessors between God and man. This concept of the necessity of a mediating priesthood comes out of the Old Testament, its social/religious structure, which, in turn, was influenced by the concept of priesthood in Sumer, Babylon and Persia, who were mediators between God or the "gods" and man.

In the authentic letters of St. Paul, we find no mention of a priesthood or of bishops. St. Paul names teachers, apostles, ministers and prophets. The Pauline communities had no formal hierarchy; positions of authority appear to have been fluid. If a member was moved to prophesy, he would do so. Many teachers are designated by St. Paul, all having authority to teach the Gospel of Christ.

We search the four gospels in vain to find a concept of a mediating priesthood. In fact, in the Epistle to the Hebrews, Jesus alone is termed high priest and mediator. The term "priest" or "mediator" is not bestowed on anyone else in the New Testament. Nor is the term "bishop" or overseer used in the gospels. In the Epistles to Timothy and Titus (the Pastoral Epistles), considered by most scholars to be pseudo-Pauline letters and perhaps composed by a school of writers calling themselves "Pauline," the term "bishop" is mentioned. These letters, however, are thought to have been written at the close of the first or beginning of the second century. According to scholar Helmut Koester, the Pastoral Epistles were composed circa 120-160 A.D., and differ in many respects from the other letters in the Pauline corpus.<1> They also betray an unusual (for St. Paul) emphasis on ecclesiastical organization.

The Pastorals may very well have originated in circles surrounding Clement of Rome, who was bishop circa 90-100 A.D. Clement is said to have been a disciple of Peter. I Clement was written to the church at Corinth and addressed a so-called rebellion that took place against "church leaders." Clement admonishes and warns the instigators of the sedition to repent, recalling incidents of rebellion from the Old Testament and threatening divine wrath and judgment upon those who rebelled. In the course of the letter, Clement compares the so-called rebels with the "wicked" mentioned in the Old Testament.

This lengthy letter is permeated with Old Testament references and quotations. In fact, its entire tone comes out of the Old Testament and not the New. After a careful reading of this letter, one is left with the impression that he is back in Old Testament times, that there has been no spiritual progress of a people. It is as if Christ had never come. Even taking into consideration the purpose for which the letter is written, its emphasis seems restrictive and narrow. Addressing the "rebellious" members, Clement writes:

So they who were of no renown, lifted up themselves against the honorable; those of no reputation, against those who were in respect; the foolish against the wise; the young men against the aged.

Therefore righteousness and peace are departed from you, because everyone hath forsaken the fear of God; and is grown blind in his faith; nor walketh by the rule of God's commandments, nor liveth as is fitting in Christ;

But everyone follows his own wicked lusts: having taken up an unjust and wicked envy, by which death first entered the world. <2>

Clement exhorts those whom he addresses to be humble, repent and to live by the rules. He admonishes obedience and submission to authority:

Let us consider those who fight under our earthly governors: How orderly, how readily, and with what exact obedience they perform those things that are commanded them...

But everyone in his respective rank does what is commanded him by the King, and those who have the authority over him.

They who are great cannot subsist without those that are little, nor the little without the great. <3>

Clement appears to be justifying the conditions for subservience to authority—it is convenient that there be the "great" and the "little," else how can authority be administered? Clement's concept of man, in general, is no less elevating:

But what can a mortal man do? Or what strength is there in him that is made out of dust?....Shall a man be pure before the Lord? Shall he be blameless in his works? Behold he trusteth not in his servants; and his angels he chargeth with folly.

Yes, the heaven is not clean in his sight, how much less they that dwell in houses of clay; of which also we ourselves are made?

He smote them as a moth; and from morning even unto evening they endure not....<4>

We are in the midst of clay, dust and mortality (throw in a few moths and some worms for good measure), and a concept of man that we might call "reactionary". Even the heavens are not clean, much less man himself. Gone are the references to the "elect" and the "saints" and the freedom from sin and judgment offered by Jesus. We are a long way from the idea of man as originating in the heavenly realms with the dignity of God bestowed on him. We are even farther from archetypal Perfect Man. There are no references to the divine spark within. The accent is on fear and judgment, which, as we shall see, is the earmark of Christian orthodoxy, as it remains to this day.

Clement explains that offerings and services must be performed at appointed seasons, at predetermined times and hours. In Clement's conception of Christianity, all is ordered and rigid. Speaking of such offerings, Clement adds:

And therefore he has ordained by his supreme will and authority, both where and by what persons, they are to be performed....

They therefore who make their offerings at the appointed seasons, are happy and accepted, because that obeying the commandments of the Lord, they are free from sin...

For the chief-priest has his proper services; and to the priests their proper place is appointed; and to the Levites appertain their proper ministries; and the layman is confined within the bounds of what is commended to laymen.

Let everyone of you therefore, brethren, bless God in his proper station, with a good conscience, and with all gravity, not exceeding the rule of his service that is appointed to him.

The daily sacrifices are not offered everywhere; nor the peace offerings, nor the sacrifices appointed for sins and transgressions; but only at Jerusalem; nor in any place there, but only at the altar before the temple; that which is offered being first diligently examined by the high priest and the other minister we before mentioned.

They therefore who do anything which is not agreeable to His Will are punished with death. *(Emphasis added)* <5>

What we are witnessing in this letter is an attempt by Clement, and perhaps by others in the Roman church and in other churches, to engraft the entire Old Testament dispensation onto Christianity. The religion founded by Jesus in fulfillment (a finishing) of the Old Testament becomes, in Clement's view, merely an offshoot, a sect within ancient Mosaic Judaism. Christians are subject to the innumerable laws and regulations of the Mosaic Law. They are even threatened with death if they do anything disagreeable to God's will. Clement's concept of God recalls to us the character of Ildabaoth, the usurper deity, who opposed the highest God and who became the enslaver of humanity. St. Paul's view of Christianity as an abrogation of the Mosaic covenant is set aside here. The believer is once again in bondage to the law, not freed from the law and justified by Christ as St. Paul taught. At this point it should be said that by the "Mosaic Law" is not necessarily meant the Ten Commandments and other sound moral precepts found in the Old Testament, but the regulations and rituals meant for the children of Israel during the time of Moses, and which were being imposed on Christians in the first century who were supposed to be functioning under the dispensation of grace and mercy, brought by Jesus.

It is our conclusion that Clement's Christianity must have had its origin in the rigid formalism of Petrine Christianity and in a return to the Old Testament way of life. And what's more, as we shall see, these communities with their emphasis on a strict hierarchy patterned after the Old Testament priesthood were the very ones to insist on a unified federation of churches in opposition to those sects and churches that stressed a fluid structure, freedom from the Old Testament priesthood and the creativity of their adherents.

Commenting on Clement's letter, biblical scholar Elaine Pagels remarks:

This letter marks a dramatic moment in the history of Christianity. For the first time, we find here an argument for dividing the Christian community between "the clergy" and "the laity." The church is to be organized in terms of a strict order of superiors and subordinates....

Many historians are puzzled by this letter. What, they ask, was the basis for the dispute in Corinth? What religious issues were at stake? The letter does not tell us directly. But this does not mean that the author ignores such issues. I suggest that he makes his own point—his religious point— entirely clear: he intended to establish the Corinthian church on the model of the divine authority. As God reigns in heaven as Master, Lord, commander, judge, and king, so on earth he delegates his rule to members of the church hierarchy....

Clement may simply be stating what Roman Christianity took for granted—and what Christians outside of Rome, in the early second century, were coming to accept. The chief advocates of this theory, not surprisingly, were the bishops themselves. <6>

The position of this work couldn't be more in line with Pagels. The theory of God's power invested in a church hierarchy of all-powerful bishops remains just that—a theory. Outside of the Old Testament religious structure, the concept of all-powerful ruling priests and bishops is essentially, in our view, foreign to true Christianity. We would also question the authority of Clement to reorganize the church in Corinth along the lines of the Roman church. The Corinthian church, possibly founded by St. Paul himself, would have been based on freedom from Old Testament religiosity, its rules and regulations. St. Paul repeatedly warned against those who would enslave this faithful to the bondage of the old law. Although Clement mentions St. Paul highly in his letters, he demonstrates no familiarity with St. Paul's theology—no understanding of St. Paul's universal viewpoint. Clement, in reality, ignores St. Paul, and his attempt to reorganize the Corinthian church along Old Testament lines might have been seen by some Christians as a betrayal of St. Paul. In fact, a scenario for the supposed "rebellion" can be proposed and it is simply this:

In the normal desire for organization and structure in a group, which must be recognized as necessary and useful when held in balance, there emerged a leadership structure in Corinth that had become increasingly rigid, authoritarian, domineering, proud of its position, and forgetful of the fundamental equality, spiritual origins and possible inner spiritual greatness of each individual in the community. As this attitude grew and the Spirit waned, there was less and less prophecy, fewer visions, fewer communications with "beings of light," fewer reminders of the spiritual status of each one. The atmosphere created moved increasingly away from the original flame and spirit of the beginnings of the community and toward a dead-letter authoritarianism and ritualism. This was increasingly recognized as a violation of the original spirit of St. Paul and of the early teachings, and a cause was taken up by the younger members as well as older members not in leadership positions, demanding either a change of leadership or a change in attitude and approach (thus the youth against the aged, those of no renown, the "little," etc.). One can only sympathetically imagine the ice-water effect of Clement's letter upon this sincere and concerned group. We would contend then that in viewing this letter, we are at, or close to, the root of orthodox Christianity—that movement characterized by suppression and misuse of power—that would eventually result in the extermination of a tremendous body of Christian teaching.

Clement closes his letter with these words:

Do ye therefore who laid the first foundation of this sedition, submit yourselves unto your priests; and be instructed unto repentance, bending the knees of your hearts.

Learn to be subject, laying aside all proud and arrogant boasting of your tongues. For it is better for you to be found little, and approved, in the sheepfold of Christ, than to seem to yourselves better than others, and be cast out of his fold. <7>

We cannot help but conclude that Clement is using the unfortunate incident of "rebellion" within the Corinthian church to justify total submission to the priests' and bishops' authority— "Let us do evil that good may come."

We move on to another step in the politics—yes, politics—of orthodoxy: the letters of Ignatius of Antioch.

Ignatius of Antioch—The Power Politics of Orthodoxy

The Emergence of Creed

Only a generation after Clement, the oppressive measures of the orthodox movement took another stride due to the influence of Ignatius, bishop of Antioch, in Syria, during the first decade of the second century. In the brief scenario of early Christian history, we spoke of the attempt by certain Christian bishops and leaders to form a federation of churches as a political bastion of power against those who were thought to be teaching "blasphemous" and "dangerous" doctrines—dangerous, of course, to the power of the bishops. We shall trace this development in the letters of Ignatius.

Ignatius writes to the Ephesians, another of St. Paul's communities:

It is therefore fitting that you should by all means glorify Jesus Christ, who hath glorified you; that by a uniform obedience ye may be perfectly joined together, in the same mind, and in the same judgment: and may all speak the same things concerning everything.

And that being subject to your bishop, and the presbytery [elders], ye may be wholly thoroughly sanctified. (Brackets added) <8>

We trace here the beginnings of uniformity and conformity which was to characterize these communities which adhered to the federation of churches. We see it emerging in the first decade of the second century. Freedom of thought and speech is discouraged. Subjection to the bishops and elders is a way toward sanctification, not subjection to God or to Jesus' teaching. Note the absence of references to the mystery teaching of Jesus, the Gnosis, and the idea of the "elect" as the sons of God.

Ignatius continues:

For even Jesus Christ, our inseparable life, is sent by the will of the Father; as the bishops, appointed unto the utmost bounds of the earth, are by the will of Jesus Christ.

Wherefore it will become you to run together according to the will of your bishop, as also ye do. <9>

In Ignatius' mind, the will of God is the will of the bishop. Ignatius then warns that it is a mark of pride not to come together in the same place and pray:

Let us take heed therefore, that we do not set ourselves against the bishop that we may be subject to God....It is therefore evident that we ought to look upon the bishop, even as we would look upon the Lord himself. <10>

The above concept—the bishop as God—would, no doubt, be considered alien to St. Paul and most probably to the apostles themselves. The concept of those having spiritual authority through attainment, through inward spiritual development and knowledge—the basis for the authority of a "guru" in Eastern tradition and the basis of the authority of Jesus, St. Paul and the early teachers—is lost here. In its place is simple hierarchical succession.

Also in this letter, we trace one of the earliest attempts at consolidation of belief as a creedal formula—one of the marks of orthodoxy:

For our God Jesus Christ was according to the dispensation of God, conceived in the womb of Mary, of the seed of David, by the Holy Ghost; <11>

We have previously seen that the doctrine of the

virginal conception and/or Virgin Birth of Jesus could not have been a part of the earliest Christian communities. In fact, the so-called Virgin Birth was entirely unknown throughout most of the first century. Ignatius, however, gives us a clever argument as to why the Virgin Birth was unknown to the first generation of Christians:

Now the virginity of Mary, and he who was born of her, was kept in secret from the Prince of this world; ... <12>

Why now is a good time for the Prince to know is a mystery! In any case, we can conclude that by the time of Ignatius' writing (first decade of the second century) the doctrine of Mary's Virginity had already been interpolated, perhaps, in the gospel of Matthew and thus was being promulgated in certain communities. We might also add that by the second century, the theology of St. Paul had been slowly eroded even in the communities he himself had founded. We recall that St. Paul, in his epistles, knows nothing of the Virgin Birth.

Along with the above concept, we see a progressive movement toward the deification of Jesus in Ignatius' letters. Ignatius remarks that Jesus was "God himself appearing in the form of a man," a statement not found in the gospels or epistles of St. Paul.<13> In the creedal formula quoted above, Ignatius addresses Jesus as "Our God Jesus Christ."

But it is in Ignatius' insistence on the supreme power of the bishop and in a structured church hierarchy that this letter takes on a significance for our theme—the institutionalization of Christianity as a power base for the bishops and the means by which uniformity of belief is forced upon the believer. To the Magnesians, Ignatius writes:

*I exhort you that ye study to do all things in a divine concord: Your bishop presiding in the place of God; your presbyters in the place of the council of the apostles; and your deacons—entrusted with the ministry of Jesus Christ...**neither*** *do ye anything without your bishops and presbyters: neither endeavor to let anything appear rational to yourselves apart;* (Emphasis added) <14>

If the bishop is God, in effect, there can be no dissension. Freedom of thought and conscience can have no place here—for what devout Christian, in his right mind, would set himself up against God? Further, in the injunction against all self-generated rational thought, we see the concrete foundation laid here for a structure of mind imprisoning both "laity" and "clergy" alike. This structure would only begin to crack one thousand years later in events such as the struggle of Abelard with St. Bernard—Abelard as an exponent of the "new" science of rhetoric—rational analysis applied to doctrine—and thus a movement to restore the dignity of the mind of man, and Bernard, still in the tradition of Ignatius, distrusting reason and demanding guidance by faith and faith alone.

According, then, to Ignatius' clever argument, the "laity" are powerless to act without the bishops and elders. The average Christian, in fact, is not entrusted with the ministry of Jesus—only the elders and the deacons are. What has become of St. Paul's concepts of the Christian believer as a "joint heir with Christ," the "elect" of God, and of the "high calling of God in Christ Jesus" accessible to all? "Now are ye the sons of God," writes the apostle John addressing the believer in Christ. The members of the churches addressed by Ignatius are not even permitted to exercise their rational faculty, the very power of reasoning itself, apart from the bishops and presbyters, much less acknowledge their divine sonship and joint-heirship with Christ. The common Christian, rather than exalting the common Light of Christ and the Mind of Christ within all, is asked to relinquish his individualism in Christ to a "group mind" presided over by the bishop and other officers, to surrender freedom of belief to a "mass consciousness" held together by creed and dogma. The "oneness" advocated by St. Paul ("one body, one spirit") as the mystical body of Christ, finds no place in Ignatius' brand of Christianity. Nor is there found any place for the "Mind, which was in Christ Jesus," which St. Paul urged all to put on. St. Paul preaches the Fatherhood of God and the brotherhood of man in Christ. Ignatius preaches the Fatherhood of bishop over the brotherhood of man—a totalitarian form of religion, supported by three key ideas: the deity of Jesus, the deity of the bishop and the relative insignificance of the individual Christian.

*...Let us reverence the deacons as Jesus Christ; and the bishop as the father; and the presbyters as the Sanhedrin of God, and college of the Apostles. **Without these there is no church** .... (Emphasis added) <15>*

What Ignatius is saying here is not difficult to discern: the individual Christian who is not a bishop, deacon or elder is of no account. The union of "ordinary" believers in Christ does not make a church. There is nothing in the individual believer that could compose a body called the church. God is accessible to mankind through the hierarchy of the church and is not accessible to the individual.

We suggest that this insidious doctrine is the root of orthodoxy—the cutting off of man from God promulgated by the teaching that man is unworthy and has nothing within him that resonates with God—and a far cry from the Christian sects and communities we have been examining, which exalted man as a manifestation of God, as an emanation of God, bearing a Divine Spark.

Ignatius Attacks Sectarian Christian Communities

Advocates of the orthodox federation of churches, in order to accomplish their ends, must necessarily alienate their competitors—those who think independently or differently from themselves, and as a consequence, threaten their power base. One of the earliest attempts to alienate fellow Christians from other bodies of Christians occurs in Ignatius' letters. He writes to the Trallians:

> *For they that are heretics, confound together the doctrine of Jesus Christ, with their own poison: whilst they seem worthy of belief.... <16>*

We recall that "heretic" in Greek translates as "sectarian," one who chooses. A sectarian, as understood during and after the time of Christ, is an adherent of a particular school of thought or school of religion. We remember that both Jesus and St. Paul were said to have been Nazarenes, a sect antithetical to orthodox Judaism. One would conclude from this that Jesus himself must have advocated freedom of conscience and chose to disagree with prevailing orthodox opinions in matters of religion. Witness his ongoing contention with the Pharisees and chief priests throughout his ministry, and his insistence on the sanctity and freedom of the individual over against mass conformism and control preached by the Pharisees and others among the priesthood. We quote Jesus' conversation with the Persian priests as published in Notovitch's Tibetan texts:

> *"But", said the priests, "how could a people live according to the rules of justice if it had no preceptors?"*
> *Then Issa [Jesus] answered, "So long as the people had no priests, the natural law governed them, and they preserved the candor of their souls....*
> *"The spirit of evil dwells on the earth in the hearts of those men who turn aside the children of God from the strait path. (Brackets added) <17>*

The justification for imposing rigid rules and regulations upon the average Christian by the clergy was, of course, to keep the believer in line, to be certain that the faithful live according to the commandments, the so-called "rules of justice." But Jesus' retort is disarming: left alone the natural law will govern them. There is no need of priests.

People were led astray from the path by men in whom the "spirit of evil dwells." Then those same men sought to impose restrictions upon those whom they purposely led astray. No doubt, another justification for control and suppression.

It is well known that innumerable Christian churches, schools and communities in the first and early second centuries had no hierarchy who imposed codes of behavior and belief. It is against these that Ignatius writes:

Wherefore guard yourselves against such persons. And that you will do if you are not puffed up; but continue inseparable from Jesus Christ our God, and from your bishop, and from the commands of the Apostles.

He that is within the altar is pure; but he that is without, that is, that does anything without the bishop, the presbyters, and deacons is not pure in his conscience. <18>

Apparently there were many Christians who were doing things without the bishop, presbyters and deacons. There were Christian prophets and teachers whose continued eminence is shown in the Didache, a first century document. <19> The Didache mentions traveling teachers whose object was to "increase righteousness and knowledge of the Lord." A proven prophet could also celebrate the Eucharist. <20> There were different interpretations of the faith even among churches and communities that fell within the bounds of an emerging orthodoxy, as represented by Clement of Rome and Ignatius of Antioch, during the sub-apostolic period, roughly 66-135 A.D. <21> According to W.H.C. Frend, "alternative interpretations" of Christianity were emerging sometimes as a response to assertions of Christian orthodoxies whenever the new religion was taking root, as we are witnessing in Ignatius' writings. <22> We have reviewed some of these alternative views earlier and noted that they are older or at least contemporaneous with Ignatius.

According to Elaine Pagels:

Ignatius knew that he was appealing to a still emerging and fragile institutional system. What concerned Ignatius especially was that this system had not yet won the allegiance of all who counted themselves among the believers. Nor was there as yet, among the Christian groups scattered throughout the Roman world, a single central organization. Christians in different provinces—and even in neighboring communities— demonstrated great diversity, from the wandering ascetics of Asia Minor to the settled "house churches" that were becoming established in Asian and Greek cities. <23>

The brand of Christianity, in doctrine and liturgy, that Ignatius sought to impose upon the churches, therefore, was certainly not "normative" for the period of time we are discussing. Ignatius had no other choice but to resort to the creedal formula as did Clement to hammer his doctrine into the ears of his hearers and nail his structure over the alternative conception:

Stop your ears therefore, as often as any one shall speak contrary to Jesus Christ; who was of the race of David, of the Virgin Mary.

Who was truly born and did eat and drink; was truly persecuted under Pontius Pilate; was truly crucified and died; both those in heaven and on earth being spectators of it.

Who was also truly raised from the dead by his Father, after the same manner as he will also raise us up who believe in him by Christ Jesus; without whom we have no true life. <24>

It is as if Ignatius is trying to convince himself of the truth of these events in Christ's life by repeating them. For Ignatius the reality of Jesus Christ is to be sought in the physical, historical events of his life. To profess belief in these historical events is the heart of Ignatius' Christianity and the foundation of what has been termed orthodoxy. There is no attempt by Ignatius to interpret or to expand upon the significance of these events in Jesus' life. What did these events mean to the individual believer? Ignatius is not concerned, and, as we shall see, many orthodox writers were content to allow their congregations to believe in the historical reality of these events, as the essence of their faith, and very little else. It would require a profound psychology of mind to explain the mechanics that resulted in this position. It holds, it seems, the sense of a peaceful simplicity, a rest or inertia, the simple peace of the static mind content in a musing on the past and history, as opposed to the activity and dynamic nature of the early Christian mind we have seen with its restless striving towards an ever greater identity in God, its recognition of multiform forces of evil arrayed in action against this striving, its vision of evolving illuminations. In its emphasis on static historicity, then, the emergence of orthodoxy in the various churches and communities was the emergence of the religion **about** Jesus rather than the religion **of** Jesus.

In the above passage, Ignatius takes great pains to prove that Jesus was a flesh and blood being, with a flesh and blood body, who experienced certain events in time. According to many other Christian sects and communities, Jesus' physical experience of these events was the least significant. Nor could one readily apprehend on the surface the inner meaning or spiritual truths behind these physical historical events in Christ's life.

Ignatius must convince his hearers that Jesus was a physical being who ate and drank and finally died, and in this statement he is obviously attacking those Christians who viewed Jesus as a spiritual or semi-spiritual being. Ignatius continues:

But if, as some who are atheists, that is to say infidels, pretend; that he only seemed to suffer; (They themselves only seeming to exist) why then am I bound? Why do I desire to fight with beasts? ...
Therefore do I die in vain....
Flee therefore these evil spirits which bring forth

deadly fruits; of which anyone eat he shall presently die. <25>

Ignatius wrote this passage as he was on his way to martyrdom. His zeal for suffering was no doubt strengthened by his belief in the reality of Jesus' own sufferings. Nevertheless, Ignatius derides the concept of docetism which we previously discussed – the doctrine of the basic non-reality of matter. Certain sects and schools of Christians also had differing views regarding the nature of Christ's body and the nature of his incarnation. Some adhered to the Hindu concept of Christ as a materialized divine spirit; others taught that the matter composing Christ's body was of an ethereal substance, especially after the resurrection when Jesus was known to have changed his form so that even his close disciples were unable to recognize him. On the other hand, many Christians who adhered to esoteric and gnostic sects also believed that Christ was born, suffered and died, as Elaine Pagels has shown. "Yet", writes Pagels, "all [of the Gnostic sources she quotes] are concerned to show how, in his incarnation, Christ transcended human nature so that he could prevail over death by his divine power".<26> Some sects saw Christ as a spiritual Redeemer taking on the appearance of flesh but who neither ate nor drank, hence, Ignatius' reference to Jesus' eating and drinking. Although there is overwhelming evidence in the New Testament as to the physicality of Jesus' body, we are also reminded of the Transfiguration sequence when Jesus' raiment became dazzling and the disciples saw him in his spiritual state. Did Jesus seek to demonstrate to his disciples that Spirit and Matter are closely related and are two polarities of one Ultimate Reality? Or that his body—and theirs—were not as material as they had believed? Although the Gospels state that Jesus ate and drank with his disciples after the resurrection, he also passed through doors and appeared in their midst. These events as recorded led some Christians to think and to conclude that Jesus may have been more spiritual than material, or that he possessed the power to control or transform matter. It was these considerations and more that gave rise to the so-called docetism.

The Christians whom Ignatius labels atheists and infidels who purvey poisonous doctrine may well have had access to the more advanced Christian doctrines or themselves have been initiates of St. Paul's "Wisdom." These "heretics" may have thought very deeply about the nature of Christ, and as a result they may have reached certain conclusions, theological or otherwise. Ignatius, however, will not allow for private individual apprehension of Christ or diversity of doctrine. Those who come together without the bishop, who teach doctrines contrary to Ignatius' opinion, are labeled and alienated. Those who refuse to conform to the federation of churches in thought and doctrine are ousted.

Wheresoever the bishop shall appear, there let the people also be; as where Jesus Christ is, there is the Catholic Church.
...he that honors the bishop, shall be honored of God. But he that does anything without his knowledge ministers to the devil. <27>

The battle lines had been drawn! Ignatius' insistence, however, upon a universal (catholic) church, homogeneous in doctrine and presided over by a bishop, was, as noted, not the norm. Helmut Koester writes:

Ignatius calls himself "Bishop of Antioch" and presupposes that each of the churches to which he writes is headed by a bishop. This makes Ignatius the first witness for a rather novel concept of church order in which each congregation had one single leader who, at least according to Ignatius' thought about this office, is equipped with considerable powers. To what degree this new structure was a reality at this time is unknown. ***There are no earlier testimonies to the institution of the monarchial episcopate, and the assumption of appointments of bishops by apostles of the first generation is clearly a later fiction.*** *(Emphasis added)* <28>

Could Ignatius have been the architect or one of the architects of the so-called monarchial episcopate? And why does Ignatius insist upon the importance of the bishop? According to Koester, Ignatius urges the churches to stand together "in the unanimity of faith under the leadership of their bishop" for only one reason:

"Ignatius is convinced that the problem of heresy can only be solved in this way....This is a new method in the fight against heresy. The one local congregation is strengthened, held together through its regular worship services, mutual love and obedience to its bishop." <29>

Ignatius, then, is arming himself for the battle—a battle against the early Christian sects, churches and schools we have been examining. The consequences of this battle were the production of the New Testament canon, the fabrication of the orthodox "apostolic succession" and an "anti-Gnostic" set of dogmas which would eventually become the authoritative Christian theology, begun in earnest by Irenaeus toward the close of the second century.

Marcion Formulates the First New Testament Canon

The slowly emerging united federation of "orthodox" churches utilized a three-pronged attack to discredit and suppress what we have termed "Lost Christianity." We have reviewed a portion of the writings of Clement of Rome and Ignatius of Antioch as representative of the orthodox movement. They have urged a unity of doctrine, obedience to authority and a world view firmly rooted in the Old Testament. In addition to this, the leaders of the orthodox movement used as their three-pronged attack (1) the New Testament Canon, (2) "orthodox" apostolic succession, and (3) anti-Gnostic dogmas, evolved to discredit ancient Christianity.

Biblical scholars universally concede that there existed

no canon of the New Testament during the first and early decades of the second century. Scholars are also in agreement that the turning point in the promulgation of a canon of the New Testament was the teaching of Marcion, who was considered to be an arch-heretic by every subsequent Church Father. Before we discuss the teaching of Marcion, we would like to review the prevailing developments in the orthodox movement.

In the writings of Clement and Ignatius we have witnessed the emergence of a restrictive and narrow concept of Christianity based on the Old Testament Mosaic world-view and on the Mosaic code. Clement's statements to the congregation in Corinth threatening them with death is reminiscent of the Mosaic code where infractions of the law were punished with such severity. According to Clement, Ignatius and Polycarp, the bishop is the mediator between God and man much in the same manner as the Levitical priesthood functions in the Old Testament. Freedom from the Mosaic code and its endless regulations as preached by St. Paul had been abandoned in this concept of Christianity. Instead, the clergy takes the place of the Levites and enforces its brand of Christianity upon the faithful.

Orthodox churches, therefore, in the early decades of the second century, based their authority firmly on the Old Testament, which was declared exclusively to be a prophecy of the coming of Jesus Christ. The Old Testament prophecies, so they taught, were fulfilled in Christ and in no other. The sufferings and triumphs of the "Son of Man" or the "Suffering Servant" of Isaiah were not viewed as archetypal of the path of the initiate in all ages but were interpreted as referring solely to Jesus. The Christian-Gnostic concept of the "elect" or "unshakable race" who were to fulfill all prophecies and thus triumph over the oppressors of humanity, was judged heretical. Those who saw themselves as part of the orthodox movement taught that Jesus alone was worthy of fulfilling all prophecy. None could follow in his footsteps. None could share his mission, much less fulfill the same mission.

In addition, among the orthodox, the Old Testament was used exclusively as "proof" of the Messiahship and divinity of Jesus. The epistle of Barnabas, which allegorizes the Old Testament, attempts to prove that the Hebrew scriptures prefigured the coming of Christ in minutest detail. For example, when Moses invited the Hebrews into the land flowing with milk and honey, Barnabas writes, "It is as if it had been said, put your trust in Jesus who shall be manifested to you in the flesh."<30> The red heifer of Numbers "is Jesus Christ."<31> The scapegoat who was accursed, abused and driven into the wilderness is a type of Jesus who became a scapegoat for the sins of mankind. <32>

By the beginning of the second century, it was taught by orthodox reinterpreters that the Old Testament predicted the coming of Christ as an historical figure alone, the exclusive Jewish Messiah, and not as the coming of a Divine Archetype. These passages were then used as "proof texts" of Jesus' Messiahship by the orthodox Church Fathers, and thus utilized in "proving" Jesus the Son of God. This "proof" was not sought after through the Holy Spirit as in Pauline Christianity, nor through the inner vision of the gnostic or the mystic, but through an elaborate interpretation of the Hebrew Scriptures. This process was continued by Justin toward the middle of the second century. Whereas it cannot be denied that Jesus was the fulfillment of Old Testament prophecy, or that he was the promised Messiah, Christian-Gnostics of every persuasion taught that initiates who followed Christ would themselves walk the path of the "Suffering Servant," moving from the "Man of Sorrows," bearing with Jesus the karma/sin of the world, to the final experience of their personal resurrection, becoming "messiahs" to the world, thus likewise fulfilling prophecy.

Simultaneously, early orthodox writers began to reject all other Scriptures, except the Old Testament, as false. Prophecies contained in the Persian and Buddhist Scriptures and in the Sibylline Oracles regarding the coming of a Divine figure who would be a Saviour of the world were rejected. <33> We

recall that according to Notovitch's Tibetan text, Jesus was considered to be a Buddha, an enlightened one, destined to save the world through wisdom and compassion and to reform the abuses which had crept into religion. The Hindus saw him as the incarnation of Brahma, or of Vishnu, one who, like Krishna, taught a religion of love.

Among the purveyors of restrictive Christianity of the orthodox kind, Jesus was ultimately rejected as a universal avatar and as a herald of a universal faith. An avatar, from the Sanskrit, Avatara, refers to a Divine Being who descends from the heaven-world as a Saviour or Redeemer. The teaching of the Avatar transcends all creeds, doctrine, dogma and race. The Avatar himself is considered the way of salvation in that he has the power to place a believer in contact with God. The orthodox fabricators of Christianity viewed Jesus only in the light of the Messiah of Israel expected by the Jews. According to the texts and the evidence we have reviewed, Jesus' public Palestinian mission lasted but three years. His years of sojourn in the East, both before and after the crucifixion, covered much longer periods. It is probable that Jesus' mission was much greater than that of Messiah to Israel alone, and the religion he preached appears to have been much broader and all-inclusive than a form of Judaism based only upon the Hebrew Scriptures.

Increasingly, the bishops began subjecting Christians to a literal concept of an angry, vengeful Deity, as is allegedly portrayed in the Old Testament. The faithful were threatened by coercion and force by these same bishops, who used or misused passages from the Old Testament wherein God is depicted as wrathful. We clearly see these influences in Clement's letters, and subsequently, in the writings of Irenaeus and Tertullian.

Against this background, we can now look at Marcion, who was considered by every self-respecting Church Father as an arch-heretic. Since none of his writings are extant, we must depend upon the works of the Church Fathers to determine the nature of his thought. Marcion was born shortly after the year 100 A.D. in the province of Pontus, in the northern part of Asia

Minor. He grew up in a Christian home and was educated in the church. Between the years 135 and 138, he came to Rome and joined the Christian church there. The tradition of the followers of Marcion states that he departed from Rome about 144. Church Father Tertullian claims that Marcion was excommunicated for his beliefs. Sometime between 135 and 144, Marcion began expounding his views of Christianity, which led directly to his clash with the church authorities in Rome. We suggest that Marcion, no doubt, witnessed the abuses of the Christian bishops as they attempted to utilize and misuse the Old Testament to interpret and expound upon Christianity, in many instances taking power upon themselves as expositors of truth and intermediaries between God and man, mimicking the Levitical priesthood. As a result of these abuses, Marcion is said to have attempted to divorce the religion of Jesus from its dependence upon the Old Testament. In Marcion's eyes, the religion Jesus taught could stand on its own. Like St. Paul before him, whose disciple he claimed to be, Marcion rejected the necessity of the Old Testament and the Mosaic law as binding on the Christian believer, no doubt because he saw how the Old Testament was being abused. He likewise rejected a religion based on coercion and force and the promulgation of a concept of Deity as vengeful and wrathful.

Orthodox Church Fathers since the second century accused Marcion of teaching the existence of two Gods, one "Just" and the other "Good." The Father whom Jesus revealed, and who was hitherto unknown, was not the God worshipped by the Jews, nor was Jesus the Jewish Messiah. The God Jesus revealed was a God of love, not vengeance, and the religion Jesus preached was a religion of universal love. It is worth noting again, in this context, our previous discussion of Cerinthus and his similar teaching, based on Jesus' straightforward statement to the Jews: "Ye neither know me, nor my Father...."

Tertullian, Hippolytus and other Church Fathers, as well as Biblical scholars today, conclude that Marcion took the gospel of Luke, deleted all Jewish references and passed it off as the true "gospel" of St. Paul because of his antipathy to the so-called Jewish God. Nineteenth century scholars and Biblical critics, however, are more favorably disposed toward Marcion. They viewed him as an early philologist and critic of the texts which later became the New Testament. Marcion did not recognize any other gospel besides the one gospel he had access to and, perhaps, had brought with him to Rome from Asia Minor. This gospel appeared to be an earlier rescension of our canonical Luke, greatly abbreviated. Could Marcion's gospel, which he claimed as the true Pauline gospel, have been a source for Luke's gospel?

According to Charles B. Waite, a nineteenth century Biblical scholar, who, with other critics, attempted to reconstruct Marcion's gospel, when Luke is compared with the gospel used by Marcion, Marcion's, in its word construction and brevity, appears to be the older of the two:

> *The Gospel of Marcion is more simple and natural, not only in the mode of expression, but in the order of arrangement....At the same time, the fact that nearly every word of Marcion is in Luke, besides much additional matter, is strongly suggestive of the theory that the author of Luke had before him, besides other material, the Gospel of Marcion entire. On the supposition that Marcion was last written, it is difficult to conceive why he should have excluded so large a portion of the Gospel of Luke, especially as it is now conceded that it was not done for dogmatic purposes. On the other hand, if Luke was written last, the accumulations were in accordance with the spirit of the age, and the practice of the times. Besides, it was necessary to have a gospel different from that of Marcion, who was a heretic. There is no satisfactory evidence that Marcion had seen either of the canonical gospels, or had even heard of them. <34>*

Marcion also recognized ten Epistles of St. Paul as authentic, although he admitted that these had been interpolated by those who were bent on fostering a Judaic, Old Testament

Christianity. They were: Galatians, 1 and 2 Corinthians, Romans, 1 and 2 Thessalonians, Ephesians, Colossians, Philippians, Philemon. He called these Pauline epistles "The Apostolicon." Marcion's "gospel" and these ten epistles were the sole New Testament Scriptures he would recognize as authoritative. The Old Testament, the only Scripture recognized by the emerging orthodox churches, Marcion summarily rejected because, as we contend, it was being misused as an excuse to tyrannize over the faithful.

Marcion also wrote a work which he titled "Antitheses" in which he compared the idea of God as depicted in the Old Testament with Jesus' concept of God as revealed in the gospel he possessed. Marcion demonstrated that Jesus' idea of God as a loving Father was in sharp contrast to the ancient Hebrew idea of God or to the bishops' interpretation of the Hebrew God. He then concluded that the Christian Religion was or ought to have been an entirely distinct revelation with no ties to the Old Testament.

Needless to say, Marcion's view, when made known to the bishops and elders of the Roman church, caused great controversy. Marcion may have been expelled as a result of his attempt to reform the church along the lines of a Pauline church, i.e., a universal religion. Marcion was then forced to found churches of his own which spread rapidly over the Graeco-Roman world, *"in which brotherly equality, freedom from all ceremonies, and strict evangelical discipline were to rule....Marcion, like St. Paul, felt that the religious value of a statutory law with commandments and ceremonies, was very different from that of a uniform law of love."* <35>

Was Marcion, however so far wrong as the orthodox Church Fathers considered him to be? According to H.P. Blavatsky:

If in his [Marcion's] sincere desire to establish a purely spiritual religion, a universal religion based on unadulterated truth, he found it necessary to make of Christianity an entirely new and separate system from that of Judaism, did not Marcion *have the words of Christ for his authority? "No man putteth a piece of new cloth into an old garment...for the rent is made worse....Neither do men put new wine into old bottles, else the bottles break, and the wine runneth out, and the bottles perish; but they put new wine into new bottles, and both are preserved." <36>*

It is generally conceded by scholars that there were two broad parties in the primitive church, each consisting of a variety of churches, schools and sects. One "party" considered Christianity as a continuation of the Mosaic law, a narrow sect within Judaism, and the other "party" viewed Christianity as a new system, applicable to all, and supplanting the Mosaic law by a universal dispensation of grace. In the first century, these two "parties" were represented by Peter and Paul respectively, and in the second century by Ignatius, Irenaeus, Tertullian and Justin; and by Cerdo, Marcion and other Christian-Gnostic teachers, respectively.

According to his detractors, as we have stated, Marcion is said to have rejected the so-called "creator God" as depicted in the Old Testament, which they deemed blasphemous. On the surface this would appear to be true—unless, of course, Marcion was in contact with knowledge regarding the so-called tyrant angels or archons who were said to masquerade as lawgivers and rulers over humanity, as certain Christian sects believed. Had the writers or editors of the Old Testament been influenced by Sumerian or Babylonian concepts of God or of the "gods?" What was the origin of animal sacrifice, for instance, or of the concept that man was created to be a tiller of the soil, as found in Genesis? Could God really have demanded animal sacrifice?

Christian-Gnostics interpreted Genesis in a manner radically different from the prevailing orthodox Jewish and orthodox Christian exegesis. According to them, the "god" who created the bodies of Adam and Eve was the tyrant deity Ildabaoth or Sammael, the fallen angel. Adam and Eve were, in essence, spiritual beings but the "creator god" attempted to capture their "light" by creating bodies for them composed of dense matter. The Apocalypse of Adam, a decidedly Jewish-Gnostic text of the first or second century, purports to be a revelation of Adam to his son, Seth:

> *When god [the archon, Ildabaoth/Sakla] had created me out of the earth along with Eve, your mother, I went about with her in a glory which she had seen in the Aeon from which she came forth. She taught me a word of Knowledge of the eternal God. And we resembled the great eternal angels, for we were higher than the god who had created us and the powers with him, whom we did not know.*
>
> *The god, the ruler of the aeons and the powers, divided us in wrath. Then we became two aeons. And the glory of our hearts left us, me and your mother, Eve, along with the first knowledge that breathed within us. And it (the glory) fled from us; ....After those days the eternal knowledge of the God of truth withdrew from me and your mother Eve. Since that time we learned about dead things, like men. Then we recognized the god who had created us. For we were not strangers to his powers. And we served him in fear and slavery. (Brackets added) <37>*

Could Marcion have come in contact with this text or other texts similar to it? Could he have rejected the so-called "god" of Genesis 2 on the grounds that he was an inferior or fallen deity as both Jewish and Christian-Gnostics taught? Or could he have had access to Sumerian and Babylonian texts detailing the creation of the body of man?

We have previously reviewed the work of Zechariah Sitchin, and we recall that, according to Sitchin's analysis of the Sumerian tablets, the "gods" whom he termed "Nephilim" or "those who were cast down" created men and women as "primitive workers" by utilizing an advanced science of genetic engineering. As has been noted, there exists marked similarities between creation accounts in Genesis and in the Sumerian tablets. Could the Sumerian accounts have influenced the author of Genesis? Is it possible that, to a certain extent, the depiction of deity in certain passages of the Old Testament may have been influenced by the Sumerian concept of the "gods" as vengeful or capricious?

Marcion may have believed that the Mosaic code as it has been enforced in orthodox Judaism and in Christianity had been interpenetrated with the "laws" of fallen angels, a "god" or "gods" of inferior species, perhaps the very ones who defected from the heavenly ranks. Could this have been the real reason for his rejection of the Old Testament?

Hoeller sheds some light on the Christian-Gnostic conception of the Old Testament "law":

The old law is the law of collective psychology influenced by the dark unconscious tyranny of humanity's guilt-ridden unconscious. The new law recognized by the Gnostic, but often obscured by later so-called orthodoxy, is the law of individuation [wholeness and integration] with its attendant freedoms and responsibilities....

Sooner or later we all must come to the kind of Gnosis that inspires us to turn from the blandishments and threats, the carrot and the stick of the tyrant angels. Masquerading as religious law, customs of society, political and economic ideology, and many other manifestations, the designs of the tyrant angels keep us enmeshed in a condition of collective thralldom, lacking choice and individuation....

Externally imposed dogma thus meets and conspires with guilt, anger, and greed arising from the shadow side of the personality. (Brackets added) <38>

It is certainly possible or even probable that Marcion in his time may have reached the same conclusions as Hoeller regarding the modus-operandi of the tyrant angels. Marcion's motive may also have been to free the present-day Christian from codes and laws meant for a lesser developed humanity in Old Testament times who were consciously or subconsciously rebellious but who were currently being redeemed from that rebellion by Christ and his Gospel of Love. Or Marcion may have become aware of an ancient "Christian Conspiracy" as Walter Nigg, author of *The Heretics,* declares:

...Marcion concluded that a great conspiracy against the truth must have taken place very early in the history of Christianity. Even the twelve Apostles had not understood Jesus correctly, and afterward the Christian fellowships had been infiltrated by those men whom Paul denounced as false apostles and false brethren. These must have falsified the entire Gospel, acting as instruments of the evil powers who were seeking to destroy the revealed truth. According to Marcion, this carefully concealed event was the most fateful in the history of Christianity, for it turned everything into its opposite. <39>

Perhaps we shall never come to know the real purposes of Marcion, but we should not summarily reject Marcion's conception of Christianity on the grounds that he was or is a "heretic."

Marcion's conclusions with regard to the Old Testament were only a part of his view of Christianity. Certain other teachings promulgated by Marcion, likewise, did not set him in good stead with the architects of orthodox Christianity. For instance, Marcion is said to have rejected the doctrine of the resurrection of the body, then being developed in certain circles of orthodoxy. According to Martin Larsen, Marcion taught that matter is an inferior essence, and since the body is composed of matter, it can never be immortal. At the resurrection, only the spiritual portion of the elect will ascend to the celestial realms. In this teaching, Marcion seems to have followed the teaching of St. Paul, that flesh and blood cannot inherit the kingdom of God.<40> Marcion also viewed Christ as the Son of the Supreme God, not the son of the "deity" whom the Jews worshiped.

For the above views, Marcion received the condemnation of Church Fathers who aligned themselves with the orthodox movement. One of these was Tertullian, who wrote *Against Marcion* in 207 A.D. Marcion taught that God would never use fear as a force to compel obedience. Man, said Marcion, has an essential desire to do good. Christ did not die for sinful mankind as a vicarious atonement, but rather he came as a guide and teacher for the Elect, and as a redeemer who freed man from the bondage of the so-called lesser deity and his tyrant angels. Tertullian, on the other hand, taught that God should be feared, that human nature is corrupt<41> and that the physical body is raised in the resurrection, not the soul only, as Marcion and other ancient Christian sects taught. In a perusal of the early Christian sects, we seek in vain, as already noted, for a doctrine of the resurrection of the body as it was later taught in orthodox circles. It is our contention that Irenaeus and Tertullian, in order to counteract the popularity of the Marcionite church, evolved doctrines in opposition to Marcion, not because these doctrines were necessarily sound or essentially true, but because they formed a bulwark against the followers of Marcion.

As a result of Marcion's break with the orthodox community in Rome, the earliest New Testament canon was developed consisting of Marcion's Gospel, now lost, and ten of St. Paul's epistles. The Marcionite movement was, likewise, the earliest exclusively Christian church, not connected in any way with Judaism or the Hebrew Scriptures—a Christianity as a distinct religion open to all who would accept it.

It is not the intention here to judge the theological correctness of Marcion's decision or of his teaching, but to point out that Marcion's movement was the impetus that gave rise to the "Catholic Church." We quote from Martin Larsen:

He [Marcion] was not hated and maligned because he selected and edited the sacred books; it was because the Church he established was in competition with the Catholic and because he sought to create a limited communion which could never become the state....Marcion forced the Catholics to develop a definitive New Testament canon; to establish an empire-wide organization and discipline; and to evolve an orthodox dogma opposed to his. Thus he actually furnished an enormous impetus to the development of the universal Church. (Brackets added) <42>

Chapter VII

The Great Schools of Christian Gnosis

Basilides

During the time that Marcion flourished and when the orthodox movement was beginning to arm itself against the ancient sects of Christianity, two schools of Christian Gnosis developed in Alexandria and Rome respectively, that of Basilides and Valentinus. The history of orthodoxy after Ignatius of Antioch was primarily the history of the conflict between the orthodox dogmatists, with their weapons of orthodox apostolicity, creed and canon, and the schools of Christian Gnosis.

Basilides, one of the earliest of Christian teachers and philosophers, taught at Alexandria circa 120-130. He claimed to be a disciple of Glaucias, who was said to have been the interpreter of the apostle Peter. Basilides and his followers also stated that they received teachings given in secret to Matthias by Jesus after his resurrection. We note that Matthias, according to Acts, was appointed an apostle in place of Judas after Jesus' resurrection and before the feast of Pentecost. (Acts 1: 23-26) The school of Basilides appears to be based, therefore, upon apostolic doctrine. Basilides is said to have written a gospel which may have contained his commentaries on Jesus' sayings, titled "The Gospel of Basilides." Basilides also wrote twenty-four books of commentaries on the gospel which have since become lost or, more probably, suppressed. We do not know whether these "gospels" were the canonical gospels known to us today or other, lost gospels. The so-called commentaries of Basilides were the first to be written on the gospels from the hand of a Christian teacher. G.R.S. Mead suggests that Basilides' commentaries aimed at explaining Jesus' public sayings and parables by the light of a secret gospel or tradition.<1> Basilides is also known to have quoted from the letters of St. Paul.

Mead states that according to the Gnosis of Basilides, the Saviour was understood as the perfected spiritual Man within the animal man or soul. Man was looked upon by this Christian school as the crown of the world-process of evolution, and the perfected man, the Christ, was viewed as the crown of manhood and therefore the manifestation of Deity. <2> All men, therefore, could hope to achieve the ultimate crown of Christhood. Scholar Kurt Rudolph encapsulates Basilides' theological system briefly as follows:

The ineffable "non-existent" [unmanifest] God brought forth without volition a "world-seed" (similar to a world-egg) out of which everything that exists proceeds according to a predestined order (as out of a grain of mustard-seed), namely in an upward movement, for the seed is apparently "beneath, "...while God is "above. " The emanation takes place in three "sonships": the first, the lightest, speeds at once to God, the second, the coarser, can only get there with the help of the Holy Spirit, while the third sonship has to remain beneath and needs purification and salvation (it corresponds to the "soul," i.e., the physical world element)....Salvation consists of the leading back to the divine elements which, in the form of the third sonship, are still in the lower world....The "gospel" (which here stands for the heavenly Christ) travels like a ray of light through the intermediate worlds instructing them, until it reaches our world where it enlightens Jesus. His fate follows outwardly (bodily) the course of the gospels, but he initiates by means of a "separation of the species" the eschatological "restoration of all things, " in leading back the third sonship that was left behind into the spiritual world above the cosmos. When this has happened, mercy overtakes the "creation, "..."so that everything remains according to its nature and nothing rebels against its nature. " <3>

We view here a vast panorama of evolution, the separation of the universe into three elements, corresponding to the Spirit, mind and soul-body—or spirit, soul and body as St. Paul teaches. All three elements are restored to the ultimate principle of absolute, unmanifested Spirit. Jesus enacted in himself this cosmic and individual spiritual marriage, so to speak, this process of purification, "which brought unto men the Gnosis or perfection of consciousness." <4>

And it was thus through him [Christ] that the third sonship was purified, the sonship left behind in the state of mixture [or impurity] for the purpose of helping and being helped, and it passed upwards through all of these purified principles unto the blessed Sonship above. (Brackets added) <5>

The "Sonship above" is, obviously, Spirit and the spiritual cosmos, beyond manifestation into which souls are assumed.

Basilides, therefore, also taught the familiar doctrine of "emanations" so abhorred by the Church Fathers. It appears, from the above passage, that he also taught a concept of spiritual/material evolution from a seed, or the idea that creation, rather than being the work of an anthropomorphic God existing outside the universe who creates out of nothing, is, in fact, unfolded or evoluted out of a seed bearing an intrinsic blueprint or pattern, which is brought forth, according to cyclic law, from unmanifested, ineffable Being. All that springs forth from the seed, as in nature, is programmed according to prior causes and effects, and the three sonships evolve according to prior "karmic" causes or the universal law of necessity.

The above conception of Basilides is a preeminently theosophical and universal understanding of creation. We also note its similarity to Platonic and Oriental ideas as well as ideas found in the Kabbalah. According to Irenaeus, Basilides "asserted that God, the uncreated eternal Father, first brought forth Nous or Mind; and Mind, the Logos, Word; this in turn, Phronesis, Intelligence; whence came forth Sophia, Wisdom, and Dynamis, Strength." <6>

Basilides also taught the concept of a Demiurge, called the Great Ruler, who with his angels was responsible for the creation of worlds and all that is material. This fabricator was inferior to the Supreme, unmanifested Deity. This is likewise a Platonic notion: the ineffable Deity does not create; creation being the work of Demiorgos, collectively—the creators of the material cosmos. In this conception, however, the creators are not malevolent beings. The term "Elohim" in Hebrew refers to the creators of the worlds, as "Elohim" is a plural noun meaning "Gods." Elohim in ancient Israel were understood to be Divine Emanations or Divine Hierarchies of creative Intelligences. The term Elohim is translated in Genesis as "God," whereas it should read, "In the beginning Elohim [the Gods] created the heavens and the earth." Although Elohim refers to an indefinite number of beings, the later Church Fathers, to counteract the doctrine of emanations, taught that Elohim really referred to the Trinity in one God. The Trinity as we know it in Christian dogma, wasn't developed until the fourth century at the Council of Nicea. "Elohim," therefore, was translated as "God", and all references to a hierarchy of beings were suppressed.

The school of Basilides taught that the eternal Father, beholding the corruption of mankind, sent into the world his Firstborn, Nous [Mind], of which Jesus was a manifestation. The Nous appeared in the form of Jesus and wrought miracles. The Nous or Divine Mind is not corporeal and cannot perish or die. The followers of Basilides identified this Nous with Christ and were accused of teaching that Christ did not die and that his death was an illusion. The most that could be said, regarding the death of Jesus, was that the gross or material elements of his body or form perished or dissolved as the case may be: "Whoso therefore maintains," writes Irenaeus, quoting the teaching of Basilides, "that Christ has died is still the bondmen of Ignorance, but whoso denies the same, he is a freeman, and hath understood the purpose of the Father."<7>

Basilides therefore rejected the blood sacrifice of Jesus as a vicarious atonement—he would neither impute death to Jesus the man or to the Christ, the Divine Mind who appeared in him. Again we are faced with the dangerous (to the orthodox) doctrine that the Christ or Divine Mind was not necessarily confined to the man Jesus, but was rather the first universal divine emanation of the eternal Father. The Basilideans reverenced the Christ not in Jesus alone but as the Divine Mind which could be appropriated by all men after sufficient purification of the "sinful" nature—the same Mind that St. Paul referred to as "that Mind that was in Christ Jesus."

Basilides' Doctrine of Reincarnation

This brings us to a discussion of Basilides' ethics. According to Clement of Alexandria, a somewhat orthodox Church Father and contemporary of Basilides who also lived and taught in Alexandria, Basilides taught the doctrine of reincarnation. Scholar Bently Layton writes:

Basilides accepts the Platonist and Pythagorean doctrine of reincarnation of souls and believes that each soul retains its identity from one incarnation to the next, at least to the extent that in a subsequent life it will pay for its sins of a previous one. Souls therefore survive the series of bodies that they inhabit and "transcend" them, being permanent and therefore "alien" to the corruptible realm of bodies and matter. <8>

We gain an insight to Basilides' thought from fragments of his writings preserved by Clement. Basilides apparently taught that there is no injustice in the universe and that the cause of suffering can be traced back to sins committed in previous lives, as the above passage shows.

We recognize in this doctrine the oldest teaching concerning the causes of suffering, i.e., "sinful" thoughts, words and deeds come full circle and are experienced by the soul as "punishment" but in reality, are lessons for the soul, thus aiding and making possible the soul's redemption. We have previously reviewed the teaching on reincarnation and have discovered that the most ancient sects and communities of Christians and non-Christians alike were agreeable to this doctrine, among them the Nazorean-Jewish Christians, the Essenes, the philosophic Jews of the school of Philo, the Hasidim, the Pharisees, the Platonists, as well as the innumerable Christian-Gnostic schools in the first and early second centuries.

Imbedded in the doctrine of reincarnation is the obvious denial of the resurrection of the physical body at the so-called end of the world; since the soul has put on many bodies and by its very nature, Basilides taught, transcends the body which it no longer needs. At the individual resurrection, the soul is resurrected, but clothed with a finer celestial body. As St. Paul taught: flesh and blood cannot inherit the kingdom of God.

Basilides also elaborated on the situation, so frequently encountered in life, of "good" people—such as newborn babies, martyrs, and exceptional people who never committed sinful acts—experiencing apparently undeserved suffering. Apart from his contention that these sufferings were for specific sins committed in previous lives (although not remembered by the soul in its outer, waking consciousness), suffering also might be caused by sinful desires, sinful or evil inclinations, that is, the capacity for sin, still resident in the soul until the final purification takes place and it ascends on high. In Eastern terminology this tendency to sin is related to the "karmic record," so-called, meaning the subconscious record of past misdeeds existing as potential sin and which may at any time bear fruit as suffering, i.e., karmic recompense. Basilides therefore affirmed that Providence is both all-powerful and good, and that God does not cause suffering but merely allows that suffering to come upon the soul for its education and redemption.<9>

After the death of Basilides, his son Isidore headed the

school and continued to teach. Clement of Alexandria has preserved for us the teaching which analyzes the animal nature of man or the body of desire:

The Basilideans are accustomed to give the name of appendages [or accretions] to the passions. These essences, they say, have a certain substantial existence, and are attached to the rational soul owing to a certain turmoil and primitive confusion. On to this nucleus, other bastard and alien natures of the essence grow, such as those of the wolf, ape, lion, goat, etc. And when the peculiar qualities of such natures appear round the soul, they cause the desires of the soul to become like the special natures of these animals, for they imitate the actions of those whose characteristics they bear. And not only do human souls thus intimately associate themselves with the impulses and impressions of irrational animals, but they even imitate the movements and beauties of plants because they likewise bear the characteristics of plants appended to them. Nay, there are also certain characteristics [of minerals] shown by habits, such as hardness of adamant. (Brackets added) <10>

Psychologists today are only beginning to recognize the existence of certain forces and forcefields, entities and such, which may be connected to man's animal nature. Jesus was known to have exorcised these "alien natures" from the form and consciousness of a number of individuals as recorded in the gospels. Could the above text on the "appendages" have preserved a teaching traceable to Jesus or one of his apostles, such as Peter or Matthias, as the Basilideans claimed? Could the existence of "entities" occupying, perhaps, a different dimension, be the cause or one of the primary causes of sinful habits? Could the Basilideans be teaching that human thoughts and feelings take on specific animal forms, which then have a life of their own so long as the individual sustains the consciousness which these forms represent? These questions, no doubt, were answered in the school of Basilides, which leads us to believe that the doctrine of Basilides was not based on abstract theology, but on psychological, scientific and religious truths.

In his book, On An Appended Soul, Isidore writes:

Were I to persuade anyone that the real soul is not a unit but that the passions of the wicked are occasioned by the compulsion of the appended natures, no common excuse then would the worthless of mankind have for saying, "I was compelled, I was carried away, I did it without wishing to do so, I acted unwillingly"; whereas it was the man himself who led his desire towards evil, and refused to battle with the constraints of the appendages. Our duty is to show ourselves rulers over the inferior creation within us, gaining the mastery by means of our rational principle. <11>

An important key to spiritual attainment is embedded within this teaching. For how can the Christian battle the so-called appendages (which may be subconscious or conscious desires with a "life-force" all their own) if he is not taught that they, in fact, exist? Basilides was accused by Clement of Alexandria, of teaching the reincarnation of the soul into animal bodies. This may have been a misinterpretation of the above passage, which states that the desires of the soul become like the animal natures and that human nature imitates the impulses of animals. In other words, the animal nature of man is akin to the impulses of animals when the soul allows herself to be carried away by animal impulses and does nothing to correct them. Unfortunately, we find no mention of this teaching in any other writings of the second and third century, which leads to the belief that this teaching, like so many others, has become a part of the enormous body of doctrine we have termed "Lost Christianity."

G.R.S. Mead writes that one of the greatest festivals of Basilides' school was the celebration of the Baptism of Jesus on the fifteenth day of the Egyptian month, Tybi (January 6 or 10). It was on this date that the Father, in the likeness of a dove, came upon Jesus, so they taught. <12> We may assume from this statement that the followers of Basilides believed that Jesus became the Christ at Baptism, and not at birth. This was noted as the position of the most ancient Christian communities: the Nazorean-Jewish or Ebionite community. We may then assume that the Basilideans taught that Jesus, the man, became the Christ through a prescribed period of "initiation" or testing—a doctrine hateful to the later Church Fathers because it was viewed (erroneously) as a denial of the intrinsic divinity of Christ.

Valentinus

From the middle of the second century to the year 200 may have been the richest period in the history of Christianity. During these years we see the flowering of many Christian schools and "study groups" even within so-called orthodox communities. A majority of these schools saw Christianity as a universal religion, a religion which naturally included aspects of other religions, not as an artificially contrived system, but as an eclectic unit comprising the quintessence of many of these same religions. Christianity, then, was understood to include the essence of the highest revelations of past ages distilled by Jesus, the Saviour, into an all-embracing faith; yet a faith based on knowledge, insight, revelation and mystical experience. These Christian-Gnostic schools represented what we may term a revolution in Christianity—a Gnostic revolution complete with revelation dialogues and a vast science of Being promulgated on a scale never before attempted. It was truly an era of progressive revelation for those who continued to receive the "testimony" of Jesus Christ.

The school of Valentinus was one of the greatest, if not the greatest, of these early Christian schools prior to the time of Origen, and the movement marked the spread of Christian Gnosis throughout the Roman Empire. The Valentinian movement began with one of the most gifted of the early Christian teachers, Valentinus. Although our knowledge of Valentinus' life is very meager, scholar Bently Layton gives the best historical introduction to Valentinus and his school in his book, *The Gnostic Scriptures*. We will be drawing primarily from this source. Valentinus (ca 100-175 A.D.) was born in the Egyptian Delta at Phrebonis. He was educated in Alexandria, the capital of Hellenistic culture. Valentinus may have even met Basilides, who was also teaching there, and, writes Layton, may have been influenced by him. Valentinus must have become acquainted with Greek philosophy, as his writings show a familiarity with Platonism and the work of Philo, who interpreted the Hebrew Scriptures allegorically according to Hellenistic Jewish interpretations of the Bible. <13>

According to Layton, Valentinus began his career as a teacher at Alexandria sometime between 117-138 A.D., and may have written and published there during the course of his teaching career. Valentinus' followers later reported that he claimed to have received lessons in Christian teaching from Theudas, who had been a pupil of St. Paul. <14> The teaching of Valentinus, then, like Basilides, was based on apostolic succession, and the followers of Valentinus stated that the "hidden wisdom" of St. Paul was the origin of their teaching and their interpretation of St. Paul's letters. The Valentinians claimed that St.Paul communicated his pneumatic [spiritual] teaching to Theudas, which in turn was passed on to Valentinus, who transmitted it to his own initiated disciples. St. Paul, then, was looked upon as the source of their own esoteric tradition. <15>

Sometime between A.D. 136-140, states Layton, Valentinus migrated to Rome, where he assumed a role in ecclesiastical affairs. In Rome he may have become familiar with a gnostic sect, if he had not already done so in Alexandria. Layton remarks that central to Valentinus' Christianity is mysticism, "an acceptance of salvation through gnosis (acquaintance) of the Saviour, the self, and god, whose most brilliant exposition is found in his sermon, The Gospel of Truth." <16> Layton remarks that Valentinus' mystical approach to salvation was a major revision of gnostic tradition and supposes that

Valentinus might have known The Gospel According to Thomas or similar works. <17> Writing of this period in Valentinus' life, Layton states:

Once at Rome, Valentinus began to play an active role in the affairs of the Roman Church as teacher and leader. It is even reported that he expected to be chosen bishop of Rome, on the grounds of his outstanding talent and literary ability (Greek was at this time the language spoken by Christians living in Rome). If this was his hope, it was dashed and had it not been, the whole future of Roman Christianity might have been unimaginably altered.

Although Valentinus played a public role in the teaching and worship of the Christian community, he and his students also met privately. Apparently they accepted a shared, traditional Roman formulation of correct belief, but by a means of allegorical interpretation they discovered also a "deeper" meaning within it, which was partly expressed in the form of Valentinus' version of the gnostic myth....Valentinus was a successful and productive teacher, for the next generation of the Valentinian movement was populated by important exegetes and writers, who continued in the trail Valentinus had blazed.

The Roman Christian community at mid second century was noteworthy for the great variety of its theologians and for their acrimonious debates with one another. Valentinus was the subject of a bitter series of attacks, in which he was lumped together with many different sects and past figures in Christianity. However, it is not clear that this opposition ever caused him to leave Rome, as later church fathers claimed in retrospect. In any case, Valentinus' public Roman career probably ended around A.D. 165, and his death is shrouded in silence. <18>

Layton further writes that "Valentinus' genius and Greek eloquence were publicly acknowledged by even his bitterest enemies. It is not surprising, then, to find an astonishing range and variety in his literary remains—so astonishing, in fact, that some critics even doubt they can have been written by one and the same author." <19>

It is well known that Valentinus composed sermons, hymns, psalms, myths, letters and poems, all of a decidedly mystical bent. He also taught and expounded upon a cosmological-psychological myth in which he explained the origins of the spiritual and material universes, the fall of the feminine principle and its restoration by Christ.

Before we peruse the cosmic myth of Valentinus through his disciple, Ptolemy, we will quote excerpts from Valentinus' own writings to gain an insight into the doctrines of this remarkable Christian school:

From the very beginning you have been immortal, and you are children of eternal life—such life as the Aeons enjoy; yet you would have death shared among you that you might spend it and use it up, so that death might die in you and through you. For inasmuch as ye dissolve the world and are not yourselves annihilated, you are lords over all creation and destruction. <20>

The first concept that strikes us in this passage is the obvious belief Valentinus shares with other Christians concerning the preexistence of the soul. Those whom he addresses, presumably Christians, have been immortal from the beginning—they transcend the body—and are children of eternal life. This lofty concept of man's origin, sadly, has been lost to Christianity. Ever since the time of Augustine, Christians have been taught to believe that they have had no divine preexistence, but are the mortal children of Adam stained with "original sin." Valentinus asserts that the eternal life Christians enjoy is the life the Aeons—the celestial hierarchy of spiritual beings—themselves enjoy. Valentinus is apparently teaching a doctrine of the resurrection for he asserts that "death" is being dissolved in, through and among these "children of eternal life." The fallen world-system is dissolved by each one, but the individual remains unscathed. The victorious Christians who conquer death (as a force and vibration) are "lords over all creation and destruction." The mortal/death consciousness is spent and used up, enabling the Christian to say with St. Paul, "O death, where is thy sting? O grave, where is thy victory?" (1 Corinthians 15: 55) We interpret this as a possible teaching on the resurrection of the individual Christian not after death but during life, so that the individual emerges as a lord over all creation. Such a sublime teaching concerning the mission of the follower of Christ has not passed into later Christian doctrine, but it finds an early expression here.

From a letter of Valentinus, we find the following:

One alone is Good, whose free utterance is His manifestation through His Son; it is by Him alone that the heart can become pure, only when every evil essence has been expelled out of it. Now its purity is prevented by the many essences which take up their abode in it, for each of them accomplishes its own deeds, outraging it in divers fashions with unseemly lusts.... Thus it is with the heart so long as it has no care taken of it, ever unclean and the abode of many demons....But when the alone Good Father hath regard unto the heart, it is sanctified and shines with light; and he who possesses such a heart, is so blessed that "he shall see God." <21>

Here we see a doctrine reminiscent of Basilides: the evil essences or entities which may take up their abode in the heart and the necessity of purification of the heart from these essences. The potential of the heart as the abode of the Father whereby it is sanctified and shines with light recalls to us also the words of Jesus as preserved in the Tibetan text: "Wherefore I say unto you, sully not your hearts, for the Supreme Being dwells therein eternally." The possibility of man possessing such a pure heart and thereby enabling him to "see" God is an ever-present reality held out to the Valentinian Christian. It is obvious that Valentinus is not referring to the heart as a physical organ, per se, but to the spiritual center of cognition existing as a counterpart to the physical heart. This teaching is clearly found in the Kabbalah, the compendium of the esoteric tradition of Israel originally transmitted orally, and Valentinus may have absorbed it in Alexandria as a result of his familiarity with Philo, the Jewish mystic-philosopher. In the Kabbalah, Tifereth, one of the ten Sefiroth or Divine Emanations, is the chest of Adam Kadmon, the Archetypal, Primordial Man, and houses Understanding, or Binah, the heart. <22>

Another excerpt states:

Many of these things which are written in the public volumes are found written in the church of God. For those teachings which are shared are the words which proceed from the heart, the law written in the heart. This is the People of the Beloved who are loved by and love Him. <23>

Commenting on this passage, Mead adds that the "public volumes" mentioned by Valentinus included not only the works of the philosophers and the Jewish scriptures but also the scriptures of all other religions as well as the Christian documents in general circulation. <24>

Who are the people of the Beloved? And to whom is Valentinus addressing himself? Mead answers the question for us:

The Self within the heart, the seed of the divine, the pneumatic light-spark, the dweller in light, the inner man, was the eternal pilgrim incarnated in Matter; those who had this alive and conscious within them were the spiritual or pneumatic. To such Valentinus is speaking. <25>

This is the focal point of Valentinus' teaching summarized by Robert M. Grant:

For Gnostics know that they were originally spiritual beings who have come to live in souls and bodies; they once dwelt in the spiritual world above but have been made to fall *into this world of sense and sin. Now, thanks to their Self-Knowledge, they are hastening back above, having been redeemed from this world below. We were born into it, but now we are reborn into the spiritual world....The Gnostic is a Gnostic because he knows, by revelation, who his true self is. Other religions are in varying measure God-centered. The Gnostic is self centered. He is concerned with mythological details about the origin of the universe and of mankind, but only because they express and illuminate his understanding of himself. <26>*

From the writings of Church Father Hippolytus, Grant quotes Monoimus, a Christian-Gnostic, on the subject of Self-knowledge:

Abandon the search for God and the creation and other matters of a similar sort. Look for him by taking yourself as the starting point. Learn who it is who within you makes everything his own and says, "My god, my mind, my thought, my soul, my body." Learn the sources of sorrow, joy, love, hate. Learn how it happens that one watches without willing, becomes angry without willing, rests without willing, loves without willing. If you carefully investigate these matters you will find him in yourself. <27>

To answer these questions, Valentinus and his followers propounded a vast cosmological/psychological myth on the origin and destiny of the spiritual and material universes and the fall and restoration of the universal feminine principle or universal soul. This panoramic myth undergirded their allegorical interpretations of scripture, and a form of this myth may have been received from the apostle Paul through Theudas. The purpose of this myth was to expound on the nature and process of redemption. Irenaeus quotes the followers of Valentinus, of the school of Marcus, on the redemption:

These hold that the knowledge of unspeakable

Greatness is itself perfect redemption. For since both defect and passion flowed from ignorance, the substance of what was formed is destroyed by Gnosis; and therefore Gnosis is the redemption of the inner man. This, however, is not of a corporeal nature, for the body is corruptible; nor is it animal, since the animal soul is the fruit of defect, and is, as it were, a lodging to the spirit. The redemption must therefore be of a spiritual nature; for they affirm that the inner and spiritual man is redeemed by means of Gnosis, and that they, having acquired the Gnosis of all things, stand thenceforth in need of nothing else. This, then, is the true redemption. <28>

This analysis of redemption by the Valentinian school bears a marked resemblance to St. Paul's teaching on the "inner man," the "perfect man" or the "Archetypal Man." This "inner man" is released and given full expression through the redemptive process. The redemption is spiritual, and the body which is raised is celestial, as St. Paul taught, and not physical. The oldest Christian sects knew nothing of the resurrection of the body.

We will review the myth of Valentinus from an interpretive commentary given by Duncan Greenlees in his book, *The Gospel of the Gnostics*, taken from the accounts of Irenaeus and Hippolytus. The Myth of the Soul begins as follows:

...At the first there was only the One, reposing for endless eternities in solitude and silence, wrapped in the one thought of infinite Mind...then...the Absolute One became as it were Two-in-One; Silence became pregnant with Thought, and so became active as Creative Mind, passive as immutable Truth. Once begun the process followed itself; Mind was expressed as Word or Speech, the "Logos," and Truth was realized as Life— for what lives is the only reality. The perfect expression of God's Word is in the Ideal Man, while His Life is manifested in the community of the Elect, the Knowers, His Church. These eight whom we have named are the Divine

Ogdoad, from whom all come and in whom all subsist. <29>

The secret doctrine of Christianity taught the origin of the spiritual universe through the process of emanation—or the outflow of Divine Aeons from the boundless Depth and Silence. An "Aeon" in this context signifies a "spiritual being governing a vast space," plane or cycle of evolution. <30>
We therefore have the first eight Aeons:

[Depth, Silence] —> [Mind, Truth] —> [Word, Life] —> [Archetypal Man, Community (Church)]

These give rise to and subsist within the Pleroma or spiritual universe, known also as the entirety. The Aeons emanate in pairs, male and female, as Twin Rays of the Divine:

Now other Aeons, eternal Beings, differentiate off from this Primal Root of Being.... The Word and the Life put forth ten other Aeons... While the Man also, along with the Church emanated twelve Aeons, (the last of which were) Willed and Wisdom [Sophia]. These are the thirty Aeons... This the unseen and spiritual Fullness [Pleroma]....<31>
Now it is only the Divine Mind, closest to God's Self, which can realize Him or share His nature; being Good like the Father Himself, This Mind longs to share its infinite wealth with Heaven's other Powers; but the incomprehensibility of God, beyond all word and thought, veiled in impenetrable Silence, made this impossible. <32>
The youngest of these Powers, [Sophia or Wisdom], the human Soul...was not content to be in ignorance of her all glorious Father; out of love and yearning for Him, and that restless curiosity which is man's saving grace, she plunged into the fathomless Deep to seek him out. But there is a limit beyond which none can pass, for the finite soul cannot know or grasp the Infinite; it must first change its whole nature and be made Divine. Realizing then the futility of her effort, the Soul dropped her desire—which at once became a "shapeless

being," an "abortion," as St. Paul calls it. In her shame and misery, the Soul tried to abandon her "child" [her lower desire] and to struggle back to her heavenly place, but could not; she then prayed for help..., and thus was purified of her foolish transgression and restored to union with God's Will— though still in misery outside His Kingdom of Perfection. (Brackets added) <33>

The Valentinian school attempted to explain the fall of the Soul, as feminine principle, by analyzing and delineating the inner motives or psychological causes within the Soul that gave rise to the fall, through the myth of Sophia. The motives and passions of the Sophia are the motives of the collective universal Soul within all beings. The fall is a pre-cosmic event and not solely the result of the disobedience of two ancestors named Adam and Eve, whose alleged "sin" was passed on to later generations.

Commenting further on the fall of Sophia, Greenlees remarks in a footnote:

Her sin, or error, was to try to fathom God's infinity without the cooperation of His Will; it was a sacrilege, like that of a layman entering the Holy of Holies. Hippolytus (6:25) tells us how she wanted to emulate the Father by producing without a consort, whereas all the other Aeons paired off; this savors of pride.... <34>

Presumption, misplaced desire, pride and a breach of the Divine Harmony are the causes of Sophia's fall, and the consequences of the fall are the passions of Ignorance, Grief, Fear and Consternation. From these passions later arose the universe apart from the Divine Fullness, which subsequently coagulated into the physical world or cosmos. According to orthodox Christianity, the world, in its present state, with all of its incongruities, natural disasters and cataclysms, was created by God, imperfect as it is. To continue:

To help Wisdom [Sophia/Soul] God sent Christ and the Holy Spirit, who taught her in the whole of creation how unattainable God is and how true Peace can be found. Then all the eternal Powers [Aeons] joined together to produce the Perfect Man, flower of all Divinity, Jesus, the universal Saviour; and at the same time they produced his younger brethren, the Angels, to help restore the human Soul to her lost heritage. (Brackets added) <35>

Meanwhile the Soul [the lower soul or Desire of Sophia] cut off from its Divine Source, has become deformed and darkened, being robbed of all its light....The Redeemer [Archetypal Saviour] comes to her and overshadows her with the mystic Cross, discerning right from left (wrong), and things celestial and things infernal. So she becomes the Soul in proper form, though still lacking the Gnosis which will finally restore her to the heights. Christ leaves her with the ideal, so that she may strive for this, and for lesser things, worldly and unworldly. (Brackets added) <36>

Her Higher Self or Mother, Wisdom above, then implored Christ to save her from these troubles. Christ then sent forth the Saviour with his comrades, his Angels. Seeing him in all his brilliance, the lower soul took strength from Him. The Saviour then shaped her form according to Gnosis, healed her passions and separated them from her. He then changed her passions (Ignorance, Grief, Fear and Consternation) into incorporeal matter which later became compounds and bodies. <37>

The Saviour, therefore, becomes the creator of incorporeal matter and, in effect, the creator of the invisible universe of incorporeal matter, yet still outside the Pleroma.

Now Ahamoth [the lower soul] coming outside passion and joyfully taking up the contemplation of the Angels with him, and having yearned after them, was impregnated with fruits like the image, a spiritual progeny.... (Brackets added) <38>

The lower soul possessed the image of Christ, not in the inner spirit but in the soul. She however:

...undertook to shape the psychic being which arose out of the conversion....So first of all she fashioned from the psychic substance the Father and King of all...for she shaped everything according to Him, unconsciously moved by the Mother.... <39>

"The Father and King of all" was designated the Demiurge by the school of Ptolemy. Commenting on the inner, psychological aspects of this portion of the myth, Greenlees remarks: "Her [the lower soul's] longing then shapes her like the Redeemer, so far as the lower personal self is concerned, and on that Image she builds a splendid Personality, essentially human, yet inspired with almost divine power. The Personality becomes the Demiurgic Ruler and Maker of worlds."<40>

We are at a crucial point of our story: the lower soul builds to itself a personality or ego which believes itself to be autonomous and independent. The Demiurge then, as suggested previously, is a mythological metaphor for the Cosmic Ego, and Sophia, both higher and lower, is a metaphor for the Cosmic Soul.

Then he [the Demiurge] became the Father and God of those outside the Fullness, being Maker of all things, both psychic and material. For, having parted the two mingled substances and made from incorporeals a body; he fashioned both the heavenly and earthly things... For he built seven heavens, over which is the Creator (Himself)... Now the Creator imagined he was building these things by himself, but he made them while Ahamoth was emanating... Thus he did not know throughout the forms [prototypes, models] of what he made, or the Mother herself, but imagined himself to be all. The cause of this fancy of his became the Mother, willing thus to lead him on (as) head and source of her substance and lord of the whole work... For which reason he, being too weak to know any spiritual beings, thought himself alone to be God... Having indeed created the world, he had also made the earthly man—not indeed from this dry mud, but from the unseen essence, taking of liquified and poured matter and into this he breathed the psychic [human soul, personality]....

But the embryo of the Mother of the Seed, Ahamoth...even the Creator himself did not know, and it was placed in him unawares without his Knowledge, so that having been sown by him in the Soul and in his material body...it might become fit to receive the Perfect. So then the Spiritual Man, sown altogether in the implanting of him by Wisdom with ineffable forethought, escaped the Creator's notice, for as he did not know the Mother, so too (he knew not) her Seed. (Brackets added) <41>

Greenlees comments as follows on the meaning and interpretation of this portion of Valentinus' myth:

This delusion prevails in the human mind. Sharing the Father's creative powers, it fashions worlds and every kind of creature—each different for every individual—and believes itself the real God and Source of all....The Soul divorced from its real Root...sees the world of its own desires and fears, not the eternal Reality, being misled by the "Mother" of humanity, the impulsive urge for knowledge. It is this Demiurge, this Fashioner, who made the man we see, body and living soul, though he knows little of the realities that eternally lie behind these manifesting forms. And so the "psychic" man or ordinary man is dark to the truth until this day; to enlighten him, Jesus the messenger put on a body like his own in seeming and came down to live in his company. <42>

Valentinus' disciple Ptolemy, who originated the myth in the form we possess it, gives us remarkable insight into what Jungian psychologists designate as "depth-psychology." Man's soul and ego are divorced from ultimate Reality. Fears and terrors proceed from our own psyche and, as Jungian scholar Stephan Hoeller writes, "in turn evolve into tyrants and tormenting demiurges of our authentic being."<43> The tragedy of human existence is that the ego sees itself as God and has, in fact, created its own universe:

> *The imperfect creator serves thus as a suitable metaphor for what depth psychologists call "the alienated ego." Defined by its own sense of selfhood, this psychic entity draws away from the wisdom (Sophia) contained in the unconscious and declares itself as a creator and ruler in its own right. He who could have become an angel of light becomes a dark tyrant. <44>*

The Valentinian Gnostics seem to be saying that the real enemy is not merely outside of ourselves lurking in the cosmos in the personages of the chief Archon and his powers, but within us as the alienated ego. Once the ego submits to and allows itself to be influenced by the Soul and the Christ, it passes into the region of the Midst, where dwells the Mother of Wisdom, according to the Valentinian myth. In the scenario given to us by Ptolemy, the ego (the Demiurge) accepts Christ and thus ascends to its rightful place, while the soul (Sophia) ascends into the Pleroma. If the ego does not accept Christ, it is doomed to destruction, as we see in other Gnostic texts. Ptolemy writes:

> *Now the end will be when all the spiritual has been shaped and perfected by Gnosis, that is, the Spiritual Men who have the perfect knowledge about God and Ahamoth, and those are initiated in mysteries... And soon as all the seed is perfected... The Mother is to pass from the region of the Midst and enter within the Fullness and receive her Spouse, the Saviour... Now this is the "Bridegroom" and the "Bride," and "Bridechamber" is the whole Fullness.*
> *Then the Spiritual, having put away the souls and become intuitional spirits, entering without force and invisibly*

within the Fullness, will be assigned as Brides to the Angels around the Saviour. Now the Creator, he too, will pass into the region of Wisdom, the Mother, that is, into the Midst, while the souls of the righteous will also take rest in the region of the Midst, for nothing psychic finds place within (the) Fullness.

And when (all) this has so happened, the fire lurking in the world bursts out and flares up and, destroying all matter, will with it be spent away and come to exist no more. <45>

Greenlees then encapsulates the eschatological meaning of Ptolemy's grandiose cosmic myth. He begins:

Jesus took from the world such as could benefit by his use, so he had no body of gross physical matter—which of itself is senseless, dead, incapable of light. <46>

The Valentinians were wont to teach that Jesus incarnated in and made use of what they termed either the "psychic" body or a "pneumatic" body, that is, a body composed of matter of a higher frequency. The body of Jesus, so they taught, was not composed of dense matter, in order that, in his work as the Saviour, Jesus could contain and dispense the Light element to souls. Jesus' body, therefore, was full of Light, which enabled him to appear and disappear at will, especially after the resurrection. The Valentinians, however, taught that from the beginning of his mission, even at his birth, Christ's body was of a higher order of matter. This doctrine, as we have seen, came to be designated "docetism" in various forms and was labeled a heresy by Church Fathers, who, in their standard inability to make distinctions, saw in this doctrine an attack against Jesus' physical incarnation in the flesh. The Valentinians were not denying Christ's incarnation, but they were denying that Jesus took to himself a dense body of material substance that could not have been a chalice or vehicle to contain the essence of Light. Nevertheless, the Valentinians were careful to point out that Jesus' body appeared to be as dense or physical as any other body. This demonstrates beyond doubt that the Valentinian Christians knew and taught that there are an infinitude of gradations of "physical" matter and that one body differeth from another body in glory, as St. Paul taught. Again we find that the Church Fathers associated with the orthodox movement had little or no knowledge of the spiritual-material laws of the universe as disseminated by Christian-Gnostics and continued to slander doctrines they either would not or could not understand. Yet Jesus' disappearances at will, his walks on water, his transfiguration, should have given them at least some pause to question whether they truly understood the "matter" of Jesus' body. Considering the state of modern physics, no one even today, save the ignorant, would be willing to say we understand what matter is. Some room for question had to be allowed, but not in the minds of the Church Fathers.

Greenlees continues:

So he [Jesus] taught men the Gnosis, that their immature souls born into fleshly bodies might mature, shake off the carnal burden, and leap away into eternal Light. It is knowledge that liberates, for all actions devoid of real knowledge only chain the soul deeper in this lower world. When every individual human soul has been enlightened, freed from attachment to the flesh and its concerns, Wisdom, the composite Human Soul, ascends from this middle state of conflict into the perfect Fullness of God's life and becomes the Spouse of Jesus, Flower of all the Aeons. This is the "Mystical Marriage, "...the ultimate human destiny, shared spiritually by every individual human soul when matured—until which time the merely righteous, uninitiated by God's grace, tread the long paths of rebirth in the lower worlds until they became able to receive the Gnosis. (Brackets added) <48>

The ultimate goal of Christianity, as understood and taught by the Valentinian Christian, is the ascension of the soul into God, the Divine Fullness. The souls who ascend to the Pleroma experience the marriage to their "Higher Selves" in the persons of the Angels who surround the Saviour. The spiritual or mystical marriage is attained by the spiritual or "pneumatic," while the righteous, also called the "psychic," (who have an emotional-mental-soul awareness) reincarnate until they also receive the Gnosis and thus become "spiritual." The "spiritual marriage" of the soul to one's own Divine Presence takes place in the heart chamber, also called the "bride chamber" by the Christian-Gnostics.

The Doctrine of the Three Natures

The Valentinian Christian understood that the Christian message as received by the elect (the pneumatic) differed from the message as received and comprehended by the "called," or the psychic, according to the individual's level or degree of spiritual unfoldment. The "hylic" or purely material man could not receive the message as he or she was incapable of understanding it and had not even the soul-awareness that the psychic had. The Christian doctrines as promulgated by the schools of Basilides and Valentinus attracted the "pneumatic"—those who were searching for a higher revelation of the Christian message, who were apparently initiated into the "mythos" of the Valentinian School. The "psychic" Christian, on the other hand, had no desire to probe the inner mystery of Christianity. He was concerned primarily with belief in Jesus as an historical Saviour and with salvation through good works and ethical living as opposed to salvation by Gnosis or infused knowledge and revelation. The psychic receives the message of Christ through faith; the pneumatic through Gnosis or insight. The psychic worships the "image" of God in the person of the Demiurge, the Creator of the lower worlds; the pneumatic worships the Father in Spirit and Truth. The psychic Christian experiences salvation as the result of a free will choice to either accept or reject Christ; the pneumatic "elect" experience salvation as a gift from God, the Father, through no choice of their own, as Jesus declared to his disciples, "You have not chosen me, I have chosen you." This is not to say that the pneumatic have never made a choice in the past, but in the present they experience salvation as an election bestowed upon them by virtue of the pneumatic "seed" or light-spark deposited in them from the Pleroma or Divine Fullness, which is dominant in their lives.

The Church Fathers of the second and third centuries, such as Irenaeus, Hippolytus and Clement, accused the Valentinians of teaching determinism and of denying free will. According to scholar Elaine Pagels, the Church Fathers fundamentally misunderstood the doctrine of not only Valentinus but also of his followers Heracleon, Theodotus and Ptolemy who, says Pagels, developed a theology of election and grace based on the teachings of Paul and John which they explicated in their scriptural exegesis.<49> The Valentinians were accused of denying that the psychics or ordinary Christians could ever enter the Pleroma or Divine Fullness, and of considering themselves as a spiritual elite. However, declares Pagels, the Valentinians actually taught that the pneumatic, psychic and hylic elements exist in all individuals; that in some persons, the pneumatic (spiritual) seed is predominant and in others, the psychic (soul) predominates; whereas in the hylic, the material is dominant. She further shows that on the evidence from Theodotus and Heracleon, teachers of the Valentinian school, the psychic element of being does not and cannot enter the Pleroma—only the pneumatic or spiritual element does. In other words, even the "psychic garments" of the pneumatic elect do not enter the Pleroma since that which is solely spiritual enters there.<50> The three levels of humanity, therefore, taught by the Valentinian school were meant to describe three types of humanity at different stages of unfoldment, according to which element predominates. Some will be assumed into the Pleroma at the end of this present life; others will be saved only at the end of the age; and still others will continue to reincarnate, etc. The purely material or hylic were considered to be "sons of the devil by nature," and therefore could not be saved.<51> The Valentinians and other Christian-Gnostics, as we have seen, taught the existence of embodied evil in the persons of evil angels, powers, archons and the "seed of the wicked" or offspring of these fallen beings. The hylic person may also have been created a soulless being of pure matter by the archons themselves or generated by Lucifer/Satan, et al. This doctrine along with the doctrine of emanations and the election theology of the Valentinians was, as a matter of course, condemned as heresy despite all evidence of its ancient origin as an authentic teaching of Jesus.

In reviewing Ptolemy's "myth of the soul," we are struck by the remarkable insight the followers of Valentinus possessed with regard to the nature of soul and consciousness. The schools of Valentinus were schools of mystical psychology. The Valentinian Christian was initiated into the mysteries of the Self and the Self as God. The Valentinians diagrammed the very nature of Being itself as described in their cosmic myth on the origin and nature of Being. We may illustrate their teaching on consciousness as in Figure 1.

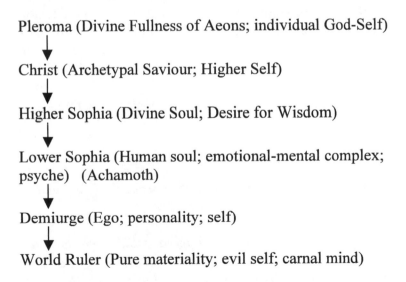

Pleroma (Divine Fullness of Aeons; individual God-Self)
↓
Christ (Archetypal Saviour; Higher Self)
↓
Higher Sophia (Divine Soul; Desire for Wisdom)
↓
Lower Sophia (Human soul; emotional-mental complex; psyche)   (Achamoth)
↓
Demiurge (Ego; personality; self)
↓
World Ruler (Pure materiality; evil self; carnal mind)

Figure 1. The Valentinian Schema of Being

The teachings of the Valentinian schools were designed to illumine the minds and hearts of Christians by revealing to them the origin and descent of the Divine Effulgence from a spiritual/psychological perspective. Valentinian Christians were made to understand that levels and spheres of being exist within themselves from the highest to the lowest, from the spiritual to the material, and that a breach in the Divine harmony through misplaced desire was responsible for the evolution of lower frequencies of consciousness, resulting in the material cosmos. The Christian is able, however, to reverse the process and ascend from materiality to spirituality by virtue of the divine spark or seed within. This process, called Redemption, signaled both the restoration of the individual and the cosmos back to the original spiritual universe.

We find no hell-fire damnation, no coercion, no threatening of death, no doctrine of original sin in the teachings of Valentinian Christianity and in other Christian-Gnostic sects and schools. Yet evil, existing both in the individual and in the cosmos, was seen for what it is and dealt with in extraordinary candor by these most enlightened Christians. Unlike the orthodox, the Christian-Gnostics of Valentinian persuasion were not obsessed with sin and its punishment, but with ignorance and its causes. The remedy was not personal salvation from sin but the enlightenment of the self which banishes ignorance. These doctrines were taught by an ever-widening circle of teachers associated with the Valentinian school.

The School of Valentinus

Bently Layton writes that after Valentinus arrived in Rome:

· *...His followers blossomed into a brilliant international school of theologians and biblical commentators. Their activity began while Valentinus was still alive. Like their master, the first and second generation of Valentinians aspired to raise Christian theology to the level of pagan philosophical studies...*

Thus the Valentinian movement had the character of a philosophical school, or network of schools, rather than a *distinct religious sect. Because of its brilliant efflorescence, the number of second and third-century Valentinians still known by name is remarkably large.... <52>*

By the mid-third century, two branches of the school had developed—the Western or "Italic" branch and the Eastern branch. Ostensibly these two branches differed over the precise nature of Jesus' incarnation. Layton explains that the Western branch held that Jesus had been born with a body of "animate" or soul/psychic essence to which the Holy Spirit later united at Jesus' baptism. The Eastern branch held that Jesus was conceived by the Holy Spirit and born with a body of spiritual essence.<53> The teachers of the Valentinian movement did not feel the need to homogenize their doctrines or to present them to their initiates in the form of creedal statements. There was no attempt to construct a dogma to be accepted on faith. This very notion was alien to Valentinian teachers. Diversity of doctrine was not discouraged and this, of course, enraged Irenaeus and others, who accused the Valentinians of coming up with new doctrines every day. The two branches of Valentinus' school were, therefore, complementary and not antagonistic to one another. Antagonism among theologians is a phenomenon to be found exclusively in orthodox circles down through the centuries.

The Italic school had been founded in the second century by Ptolemy and Heracleon. It has been noted that Ptolemy authored "The Myth of the Soul" as we have it today. Unfortunately, the only complete version we possess is from the pen of Irenaeus, who detested Valentinians. Heracleon was the author of the earliest Christian allegorical exegesis of scripture in his commentary on the gospel of John, which Origen attempted to refute, in part. Origen, as we shall see, based much of his theology on the doctrines of the Valentinian school, which resulted in his being included among the "heretics." Other teachers of the Italic school were Secundus, Alexander, Flora, Florinus and Theotimus. <54>

The teachers of the Eastern branch, centered mainly in

Alexandria, were Axionicus of Antioch, Kolorbasos, Mark, Theodotus, Ambrose and Candidus, the last two flourishing in the third century. <55>

Layton states that Valentinian Christianity spread to all parts of the Roman world. He designates Gaul (Southern France), Rome, Asia Minor, Syria, Egypt, Carthage and Mesopotamia as containing Valentinian congregations.<56> The Valentinian movement lasted until the seventh century.

The movement and its teachers were opposed by Justin Martyr, Irenaeus, Tertullian, Hippolytus, Clement of Alexandria, Origen (in part), John Chrysostom, Ambrose of Milan and, of course, Constantine, who legislated against the Valentinians in 326, forbidding them to hold meetings. <57>

By the middle of the second century, the attack against the Valentinian school began initially with Justin Martyr, one of the earliest orthodox Fathers, who attempted to alienate the Valentinians from the greater church at large. The attack against the Valentinian school was taken up in earnest by Irenaeus (A.D. 130-200) in his work *Against Heresies*, written about 180 A.D. Layton notes that when *Against Heresies* was written, "the work was also the occasion for a precedent-setting discussion of what the ordinary Christian ought to believe, and an early assertion of the idea that this formulation of ordinary Christian beliefs had been handed down uncontaminated by a chain of teachers stretching back to the apostles."<58> We shall show in the next chapter that Irenaeus' strategy was to establish a derogatory image of the Valentinians by subjecting their sublime esoteric teachings to mockery and by accusing them of absurdities and sorceries. We consider it a supreme tragedy that the average Christian has not been exposed to such a body of authentic Christian teaching as is represented by the Valentinian school.

Valentinian Literature—The Gospel of Truth

Unfortunately, we possess no systematized body of doctrine from the Valentinian school as we have, for instance, from the pen of Origen. Many of their works have never survived the heresy-bashing Church Fathers. We possess none of the complete scriptural interpretations of Ptolemy, Heracleon or Basilides, which were trend-setting allegorical exegeses.

Outside of Ptolemy's cosmic myth preserved by Irenaeus, we possess Ptolemy's Letter to Flora, which elaborates on the theme that the Highest ineffable Deity, the Father, is not the creator or craftsman of the world. The letter is important in many respects, not the least of which is its assertion that the teaching it contains is apostolic tradition received by succession, a declaration which subsequent Church Fathers refused to consider or take seriously.

Other works attributed to the Valentinian school found in the Nag Hammadi Library are: The Treatise on the Resurrection, The Gospel of Philip and The Gospel of Truth. The latter work is considered by several scholars, including Bently Layton, to have been composed by Valentinus himself. <59> Layton writes that the Gospel of Truth is "one of the most brilliantly crafted works of ancient Christian literature" and "the earliest surviving sermon on Christian mysticism."<60> The main themes of the "gospel" are the search for the Father and the deliverance of those in ignorance through the teaching and work of Jesus, who revealed the truth about the Father and thus banished ignorance through knowledge. The underlying conception of the work is the return of the totality of creation to the unity of the Father. Speaking of the mission and work of Jesus, the gospel proclaims:

When he [Jesus] had appeared instructing them about the Father, the incomprehensible one, when he had breathed into them what is in the thought [of the Father], doing his will, when many had received the light, they turned to him... For he came by means of fleshly form, while nothing blocked his course because incorruptibility is irresistible. Since he, again, spoke new things, still speaking about what is in the heart of the Father, having brought forth the flawless word.

When light had spoken through his mouth, as well as his voice which gave birth to life, he gave them thought and understanding and mercy and salvation and the powerful Spirit from the infiniteness and the sweetness of the Father....He became a way for those who were gone astray and knowledge for those who were ignorant, a discovery for those who were searching, and a support for those who were wavering, immaculateness for those who were defiled. (Brackets added) <61>

We can think of no more lofty description of the mission of Jesus in all ancient Christian literature, with the possible exception of the Gospel of John. And this sublime work has been withheld from the Christian world for centuries. Why? Perhaps because the "Lost Christianity" of Valentinus restores to man and woman their rightful place in the world, as expositors of light and truth and as children of the Father from whence they sprang. This idea, as we have said, is anathema to the orthodox—as it threatens their power base.

The gospel addresses those to whom the revelation of Jesus is given:

But those who are to receive teaching [are] the living who are inscribed in the book of the living. It is about themselves that they receive instruction, receiving it from the Father, turning again to him... Those whose names he knew in advance were called at the end, so that one who has knowledge is the one whose name the Father has uttered.... Therefore if one has knowledge, he is from above. If he is called, he hears, he answers, and he turns to him who is calling him, and ascends to him. And he knows in what manner he is called. Having knowledge, he does the will of the one who called him, he wishes to be pleasing to him, he receives rest. <62>

We note here the basic difference between orthodox Christianity and Gnostic-Christianity: the former emphasizes the sinfulness of humanity and the ultimate deity of Jesus, who is worshipped as a god; the latter emphasizes the innate divinity of humanity and their resemblance to the Father and to Jesus at the very core of their beings. As we read above, those who receive the teaching receive instruction about themselves, that is, their origin in the Father, for they are "from above" and possess this knowledge or gnosis innately.

Rather than emphasize this unique mission of Jesus (although his mission was considered unique) the Christian of Valentinian persuasion chose to emphasize his or her own mission on the Father's behalf—a mission identical to that of Jesus:

> *Say, then, from the heart that you are the perfect day and **in you dwells the light that does not fail** . Speak of the truth with those who search for it and (of) knowledge to those who have committed sin in their error, make firm the foot of those who have stumbled and stretch out your hands to those who are ill. Feed those who are hungry and give repose to those who are weary, and raise up those who wish to rise, and awaken those who sleep. For you are the understanding that is drawn forth... **So you, do the will of the Father, for you are from him** ....The children of the Father are his fragrance, for they are from the grace of his countenance. (Emphasis added.) <63>*

The significance of these passages lies in the concept that the Christian is worthy to fulfill the self-same mission of Jesus by virtue of the light within him—a light which he possessed before the foundation of the cosmos, as did the Christ. The gospel thus addresses the Christian initiates:

> *...They themselves are the truth, and the Father is within them and they are in the Father, being perfect, being undivided in the truly Good One, being in no way deficient in anything, but they are set at rest, refreshed in the Spirit. And they will heed their root....This is the place of the blessed....They are the ones who appear in truth, since they*

exist in true and eternal life and speak of the light which is perfect and filled with the seed of the Father, and which is in his heart and in the pleroma....And his children are perfect and worthy of his name, for he is in the Father: it is children of this kind that he loves. <64>

We can readily appreciate that those Christians who were proclaiming that they are in the Father and the Father is in them, as Jesus himself declares, were a threat to the emerging orthodox clergy in the second century and beyond. These Christian initiates did not stop with simple faith in Jesus, but went on to greater spiritual attainment, declaring their immortality and their intimacy with the Father. We note that the initiates so addressed have themselves become the truth, as Jesus did. We are witnessing in this gospel the full flowering of mystical experience within the hearts, minds and souls of numerous Christians whom Valentinus is addressing. Those who reach the ultimate stage of union with the Father, as Christ did, can revolutionize the world and transform it into the Kingdom of God prophesied by Jesus. The forces of totalitarianism in both Church and State, then as now, would not have it so. We would contend that, from the evidence of the extant texts, the Valentinian movement may have produced a vast body of Christian mystics who had begun to wield tremendous spiritual power by actually putting into practice and demonstrating the works that Jesus himself demonstrated. These works were not being demonstrated en masse by the bishops of the emerging orthodox movement, nor were they attaining as a group the heights of mystical union to which Valentinians had attained. The only recourse left to the bishops was to label Valentinus a heretic, and his disciples and his movement as a heresy. The gradual "spiritualization" of the body of Christians due to the teachings of the various Christian-Gnostic schools reached a peak apparently around the close of the second century, precisely when Irenaeus began his attack. Thereafter, Christians who attained to the "mystical union" were far and few between, as the keys to attainment were gradually removed and otherwise suppressed.

The Valentinian Sacraments

Having discussed The Gospel of Truth, we now briefly turn to another writing of Valentinus himself preserved by Hippolytus in his *Philosophumena:*

All things depending in spirit I see;
All things supported in spirit I perceive;
Flesh from soul depending;
Soul by air supported;
Air from ether hanging —
Fruits borne of the deep —
Babe born of the womb. <65>

The above passage clearly demonstrates Valentinus' knowledge of planes or dimensions of reality. The universe is not composed of merely matter (bodies) and Spirit, but is a gradation of frequencies or waves down from Spirit to flesh or bodies. All manifestation, then, according to Valentinus, is an emanation or outflowing from Spirit to matter (flesh); therefore, all is connected ultimately to Spirit; in fact, the essence of all things is spiritual. We have, therefore, the following:

Spirit
ether
air
soul
flesh

Valentinus designates five gradations, each becoming denser and more concrete, but having its origins in Spirit, which Valentinus also terms the Deep. The universe, consisting of the five waves or frequencies, is "borne" or evoluted from the Deep and these become the "fruits" of the Deep. The "fruit" contains in itself the seed or pattern of its existence and is not a creation from an outside source. The manifested universe is as a "babe born of the womb," the womb being the pre-cosmic Depth, and the babe or child individually is likewise the fruit of the Spirit/Depth containing within the five elements of Being—from Spirit to flesh. Man, therefore, as the fruit of the womb, is designed to unfold these five seeds or "bodies" and resolve back to Spirit, which is his true essence.

This is the core of the doctrine of emanations, perhaps the most ancient understanding of creation found in Hinduism, the Kabbalah and in Plato, which was once part and parcel of Christianity, preserved by the Valentinians as a secret doctrine. This doctrine was replaced by the doctrine of "creationism," which alleges that the universe (and all therein) is the work of a personal "God" existing outside the universe who causes the universe to be created from nothing. Man is a creature and the handiwork of this God, but has no real connection to him—he does not emanate or flow out from God, he is created by God as a potter would mold clay, and he remains, in essence, forever separate from the Creator. The orthodox church, of course, proclaimed that since man is, in fact, by nature separate from God, the church is the divine intermediary between God and man and can connect man to God through the sacraments administered by the hierarchy of the church. For the orthodox church to have accepted the doctrine of emanations, it would have had to admit that man's origin is in Spirit and not in matter, and that man possesses, or did possess, an innate seed or spark of Spirit which, if allowed to become the dominating force of his life, would lead him back to Spirit without the institution of the church or its clerics. Man, in other words, possesses in himself the seed of salvation which, taught the Christian-Gnostics, is a product of the Fullness.

The doctrines, techniques and sacraments of the Valentinian school were designed to reawaken this spark, to release it, and thus to assist the soul's journey back to the Father. The Valentinian sacraments were not in themselves salvation but were an assistance to salvation, whereas, in the later orthodox church, the sacraments were, in fact, salvation, and without them one could not hope to be saved.

According the Stephan Hoeller, The Gospel of Philip, which scholars consider to be a product of Valentinian Christianity, "is primarily a manual of Gnostic sacramental theology, in other words, an account of the Gnostic mysteries." <66> The Gospel of Philip states:

The Lord worked all things as a mystery; a baptism and an anointing and a eucharist and a redeeming and a bride-chamber. <67>

Two of these sacraments, redemption and bride-chamber, have never, so far as we know, been administered in the orthodox church, whether Roman or Greek. For the Christians of the Valentinian persuasion, these sacraments were mysteries and initiations and not mere rituals, as they later became in the orthodox movement. According to Hoeller, the sacrament of redemption and bride-chamber were "changed by the mainstream Church into the much more mundane sacraments of penance and matrimony." <68>

The baptism bestowed by the Valentinian community was understood to be a higher form of the sacrament than that used by orthodox communities. The orthodox administered a "psychic baptism," designed for people *"whose consciousness was lodged in the mind-emotion complex and who were not ready to enter the realm of spirit. A higher form of baptism was known as 'pneumatic baptism,' indicating that when administered in this fashion, the baptismal rite no longer merely served the purpose of purifying the soul, but rather put the personality in touch with the higher, or spiritual self."* <69>

Anointing is the next initiatory sacrament and, remarks Hoeller, as water is used to wash, oil was employed to seal. <70>

In this sacrament, the initiate was anointed with oil:

Oil, when ignited, burns and is thus associated with the element of fire, whereas baptism is associated with water.

These two elements have traditionally been regarded by the ancients as the primary polarity, which when conjoined produce wholeness. <71>

After baptism and anointing, declares Hoeller, the Gnostic-Christian is prepared to partake of the Eucharist. <72> Speaking of the Eucharist, The Gospel of Philip states:

The cup of prayer contains wine and water, since it is appointed as the type of the blood for which thanks is given. And it is full of the holy spirit, and it belongs to the wholly perfect man. When we drink this, we shall receive for ourselves the perfect man. <73>

The "perfect man," as we have shown, is the indwelling Archetypal man, the living Christos within, who is assimilated by the initiate and into which he is transformed. In the Valentinian initiation, two supreme sacraments follow: redemption and bride-chamber. <74> Hoeller continues:

In a heroic act of renunciation and commitment called "redemption," the Gnostic initiate becomes free of the compelling attachments to this world and its rulers. The Gospel of Philip gives us only minor details concerning this mystery, but the anti-Gnostic church father Irenaeus repeats certain statements that were ritually uttered by those who have received this sacrament: "I am established, I am redeemed, and I redeem my soul from this aeon, and from all that comes from it, in the name of IAO, who redeemed his soul unto the redemption of Christ, the living one." And the people present respond: "Peace be with all on whom this name reposes." The author then states that the initiate is subsequently anointed with the oil of the balsam tree, which is the sweet savor that transcends all terrestrial things. <75>

The sacrament of the bride chamber is the final initiation in the Valentinian church and, remarks Hoeller, "is the decisive event in the reunion of the divisions of the human being." <76> Hoeller explains that on earth the individual possesses a body, soul and spirit in the state of "imperfect association."<77> This division is "rendered perfect by the experience of the bride chamber," <78> and is described by Valentinus as "the marriage of the human spirit to an angel of the Redeemer who resides in the heaven world of this earth."<79> We suggest that this "angel" is the higher Self of the individual coexisting with the individual, but on a higher dimension of reality, and to whom the initiate is "married." This experience has been termed the mystical or spiritual marriage by Christians down through the centuries. We find its most ancient Christian expression in the writings of the Valentinian school, but it was later described in detail by mystics such as St. Teresa of Avila and St. John of the Cross. It should be recognized that the orthodox church has always held such individuals and their writings at arm's length, never truly incorporating their statement of experience (i.e., Gnosis) and teachings into the standard body of Church doctrine or discussion—this the natural legacy of the original attack by the Church Fathers.

The sacrament of the bride-chamber was also instrumental in uniting the opposing polarities of masculine and feminine within the initiate, thus rendering him or her spiritually and psychologically androgynous, that is, by reuniting the basic elements of male and female into a complete whole. According to Valentinian theology as recorded in the Gospel of Philip, the separation of masculine and feminine within the individual was the cause of death.<80> Christ came to take away the separation and reunite the two, thus revealing to the initiate the key to integration of the self, as well as the key to the reuniting of the divine pairs which emanated from the Pleroma. As the Gospel of Philip expresses it:

If the woman had not separated from the man, she should not die with the man. His separation became the beginning of death. Because of this Christ came to repair the separation which was from the beginning and again unite the two, and to give life to those who died as a result of the separation and unite them. But the woman is united to her husband in the bridal chamber. Indeed those who have been united in the bridal chamber will no longer be separated....

When Eve was still in Adam death did not exist. When she was separated from him death came into being. If he enters again and attains his former self, death will be no more. <81>

We have come across several of these concepts in Ptolemy's "Myth of the Soul," e.g., the spiritual marriage of Sophia to Christ in the Pleroma. In Valentinian esoteric parlance, the woman symbolizes the soul or feminine polarity of being and the man, the Spirit or masculine polarity. Both must be integrated if the initiate is to achieve wholeness in God. Through the fall, the soul separated from the Spirit, and this event was allegorized in the story of Adam and Eve. The sacrament of the bride chamber was the initiation whereby this wholeness or marriage was effected, and this union took place in the "secret chamber of the heart" where Christ and the soul unite in marriage, as it has been described by mystics down through the centuries. This experience apparently took place on earth, not in heaven, as the gospel records, and while yet on earth the initiate transcended time and space as a result of this transforming sacrament:

But the mysteries of that marriage are perfected rather in the day and the light. Neither that day nor its light ever sets. If anyone becomes a son of the bridal chamber, he will receive the light. If anyone does not receive it while he is here, he will not be able to receive it in the other place. He who will receive that light will not be seen, nor can he be detained. And none shall be able to torment a person like this even while he dwells in the world.... The world has become the eternal realm, for the eternal realm is fullness for him. <82>

In this state of mystical union and spiritual integration,

the initiate dwells in heaven while yet walking the earth. This was the hope and experience held out to the Valentinian Christian, who would prepare himself or herself by first partaking of the secret doctrines offered by the Valentinian school and then by becoming initiated by degrees through the five sacraments.

The Doctrine of the Resurrection

In order to understand the teachings of the Valentinian School on the resurrection, we must review the basic components of the individual according to the Valentinians: the spiritual or pneumatic element (the divine spark) or true Self, destined to reunite with the Father; the psychic or soul element, which either reincarnates or is sublimated and absorbed into the true Self; and the physical or material, which is destined to perish.

Ordinary Christians who did not receive the higher teaching believed in and looked forward to a resurrection of their dead bodies at the end of the age or world. This teaching was fostered and promoted by the orthodox bishops in order to counteract or suppress, if possible, the doctrine of preexistence and reincarnation. Those Christians who received and accepted this doctrine were termed "psychic" by the Valentinians because their understanding was at the level of the soul or psyche rather than at the level of the spirit. To these Christians, their hope of immortality was to come back to life in their same bodies, now fully and physically restored on the so-called "Last Day."

As Bently Layton explains, the Valentinian teachers did not believe that the identical physical body, once buried, was capable of preservation; nor did they believe the soul element and pneumatic element capable of "death."<83> To the Valentinian and to other Christian-Gnostics, resurrection was a process whereby the soul casts off her mind-emotional complex (her "psychic garments") and ascends or is assimilated into the true Self or pneumatic element and discards the dense material body. The hope of resurrection was to transcend material existence and the material cosmos and thus return to the Pleroma or spiritual universe, the true home of all beings. The Valentinians did not anticipate a restored earthly kingdom, at least not on the same level of dense physicality. The true "earth" and all that it contains was part of the Archetypal universe and existed in its true nature within the Pleroma. Therefore, the restoration of the dead physical body was to them meaningless.

The ordinary Christian who did not have access to the esoteric doctrine of Jesus believed that Christ's death referred to his biological death, from which he came back to life in a revivified physical body. The Valentinian Christians believed that Jesus died only in appearance and that his resurrection was a demonstration of the process of "spiritualization" whereby they too, would transcend earthly life and ascend to the Father. For them, resurrection was a quickening of the entire being by the awakened pneumatic element, that is, the Divine Spark. This started the process of assimilation unto the Father while the initiate was still on earth. The Treatise on the Resurrection, a tractate by an anonymous Valentinian initiate, describes it as follows:

> Now the Son of God...was Son of Man. He embraced them both, possessing the humanity and the divinity, so that on the one hand he might vanquish death through his being Son of God, and that on the other hand through the Son of Man the restoration of the Pleroma might occur; because he was originally from above, a seed of the Truth, before this structure (of the cosmos) had come into being.... The Saviour swallowed up death...for he put aside the world which is perishing. He transformed [himself] into an imperishable Aeon and raised himself up, having swallowed the visible by the invisible, and he gave us the way of our immortality. <84>

The Valentinian Christian believed that he, too, was capable of transforming himself into an "imperishable Aeon," that is, into an immortal spiritual being. How? Because he saw himself as "originally from above" and "a seed of truth" like Christ, before his sojourn in the physical cosmos. The allegorical fall, suffering and restoration of the Aeon Sophia prefigured the Valentinian Christian's own suffering and restoration. Jesus' descent to earth, his suffering and resurrection were archetypal patterns for all to follow and recapitulated the suffering of the soul of humanity on earth within the illusory realm of matter. For the Valentinian, however, the resurrection begins here and now, once the initiate sets his feet on the spiritual path and begins to partake of and assimilate the Gnosis, thus purifying himself and raising himself to a higher level of being through transmutation. Those initiates who failed to attain to the resurrected state at the end of their present life on earth were subject to reincarnation or future lives in which they would continue to pursue the resurrection. Many, however, would reincarnate till the end of the aeon or age and would attain the resurrection at that time. The emphasis, however, in the Valentinian School, was not on a future resurrection, but, as we have said, on attaining it as a living experience, here and now. As the Treatise phrases it:

It [the resurrection] is the revelation of what is, and the transformation of things, and a transition into newness. For imperishability [descends] upon the perishable; the light flows down upon darkness, swallowing it up; and the Pleroma fills up the deficiency....

Therefore, do not think in part...nor live in conformity with this flesh for the sake of unanimity, but flee from the divisions and the fetters, and already you have the resurrection...These things I have received from the generosity of my Lord, Jesus Christ. <85>

Chapter VIII

The Orthodox Movement Formulates
"Anti-Christian-Gnostic" Theology

Justin Martyr

Justin (100-165 A.D.), who falls within the realm of orthodox Christianity, was one of the earliest writers to alienate the Valentinian school of Christianity. According to Bently Layton, Justin's attempt was virtually ineffective, <1> yet Justin began a movement, later brought to completion by Irenaeus: the fabrication of orthodox dogma—a dogma which was still fluid even up to the third century.

Justin is known as an apologist. He, with several others, such as Aristides, Quadratus and Athenagoras, argued the truth of Christian religion before pagans, Jews and the Roman Emperor himself. The word "apology," from the Greek Apologia, is a written defense or justification of what appears to be incorrect by the other party.

Justin wrote *Against Marcion* in 150 A.D., condemning the teaching of Marcion, whose views we have previously examined. Although this work is lost to us, we may conclude that Justin argued in favor of retaining the Old Testament as the necessary Scripture to interpret or understand Christianity. In Justin's other works, *Dialogue with Trypho and Apology* 1 and 2, he sought to defend Christianity against the Marcionites, Valentinians and other Christian-Gnostics, as well as the Jews. Justin, like the Christian-Gnostics before him, appealed to apostolic tradition for the source of his interpretation of Christianity, which, as we shall see, was firmly rooted in his narrow interpretation of orthodox Judaism.

According to W.H.C. Frend, during the time of Justin

the Roman Church was beginning to emerge as an authoritative center of Christianity and had become a magnet for Christians of every persuasion. Cerdo, Marcion and Valentinus represented the "unorthodox" and Polycarp, Justin and Hegesippus, the "orthodox." Frend remarks that Rome was not conspicuously orthodox at first, since both Marcion and Valentinus were well received, and Valentinus was nearly elected bishop; Rome maintained "a certain elasticity in outlook as late as 150 A.D."<2> The above statement leads us to conclude that Christianity was, as noted already, not a unified system of belief even from early times, as the Apologists and Irenaeus sought to prove. In Rome herself, later the center of "orthodoxy," beliefs and interpretations of the Christian message were still varied or fluid. By the year 200, however, this was no longer true. Adolph Harnack remarks that the ancient baptismal confession was eventually transformed into what he calls the "rule of faith." The shortest formula defined the Christian faith as belief in the Father, Son and Spirit and appears to have been universally current in Christendom about the year 150. A fixed creedal formula which every candidate for baptism had to confess was also possessed by the Roman Church by about 140. <3> Outside of this simple creed that we find in the writings of Clement of Rome and Ignatius of Antioch, which professed a belief in Jesus Christ as Son of God who was crucified, died and was resurrected, there was no set doctrine or interpretation of doctrine. The first writers to affirm an apostolic tradition and an interpretation of Christianity based on a secret or esoteric transmission from the apostles were the Christian-Gnostics of the various schools, sects and communities we have been reviewing.

What then was sound doctrine? And what was the content of tradition? asks Harnack:

There is no doubt that Justin in opposition to those whom he viewed as pseudo-Christians, insisted on the absolute necessity of acknowledging certain definite traditional facts and made this recognition the standard of orthodoxy. To all *appearances it was he who began the great literary struggle for the expulsion of heterodoxy...but judging from those writings of his that have been preserved to us, it seems very unlikely that he was already successful in finding a fixed standard for determining orthodox Christianity! <4>*

In other words, a standard Christian doctrine was undetermined by 180 A.D. and even after! If this be true, how could Justin's Christianity or Irenaeus' be any more sound or true than the Christianity of the Ophites, Basilides, Valentinus or Ptolemy? It is well known that the Valentinians accepted the Roman creed which was supposed to have originated with the Apostles. However, Harnack remarks that "it is not demonstrated that any creed emanated from the Apostles, nor that the churches they founded always preserved their teaching in its original form." <5> He adds further that "...at this period the Alexandrian Church neither possessed a baptismal confession similar to that of Rome, nor understood by 'regular fidei' [rule of faith] and synonymous expressions a collection of beliefs fixed in some fashion and derived from the apostles." <6>

In regard to the New Testament, by the year 150, the main body of Christendom, writes Harnack, had no collection of gospels and epistles possessing equal authority with the Old Testament. <7> We do learn from Justin that the Gospels and the Old Testament were read in public worship.<8> There were also innumerable texts which circulated at this time, some of which have surfaced in the Nag Hammadi Library, and others, such as apocryphal Acts and the Apocalypses, which have been extant for centuries. Justin, therefore, began what might be called a consolidation process by which an authoritative federation of churches was constructed and a "sound" or orthodox doctrine formulated. This doctrine, we contend, was not the original doctrine of Jesus.

In his writings Justin attempts to prove that his brand of Christianity is a rational series of truths "revealed by the prophets in the Holy Scriptures, and summarized in Christ, which in their unity represent the divine wisdom, and the recognition of which leads to virtue and eternal life." <9> In this quote, we have one of the roots of orthodoxy—truth is only to be found in the written scriptures, and to recognize this written truth leads to eternal life. In other words, truth is not made known to each individual through insight, experience, prophecy or through the indwelling Christ, as St. Paul teaches, but through the written word as handed down and interpreted by only certain individuals who claim themselves as orthodox. Such a state of mind recalls Jesus' statement to the Pharisees: "Search the scriptures, for in them ye *think* ye have eternal life."(John 5:39, emphasis added)

Justin, therefore, argues that Jesus is the Son of God exclusively, by virtue of his having fulfilled Old Testament prophecy. There is no other way for a Christian, pagan, or Jew to recognize Christ except through the Old Testament, according to Justin. This recognition does not come about through Gnosis or through the purified heart as with the Christian-Gnostics, but through rationally understanding the Old Testament and its pre-figuration of Christ.

Justin claimed that all the events before Christ's appearance on earth as recorded in the Old Testament had led up to the incarnation of Christ, which was the final act of God's self-revelation. <10> While the Christian-Gnostics were pro—ducing revelation dialogues and mystical tractates, and no doubt, receiving visions and prophecies, Justin was proclaiming an end of prophecy and revelation! This doctrine effectively puts an end to what is termed progressive revelation—that is, the possibility that God or Christ can commune with each individual and reveal, perhaps, hitherto unknown truths. Thus Justin places his human limit on God and the continuing revelation of and guidance by the Divine in the world.

In his works Justin proclaims himself a former pupil of Plato and Socrates and admits that these philosophers have glimpsed the truth. But Justin claims that his version of Christianity is superior to all other religions and philosophers. Justin was troubled by the marked similarity in the rites and doctrines of the mystery religions of antiquity which professed belief in a series of Saviour figures, who, as we noted earlier, were born (usually on December 24), died, were resurrected and eventually ascended into heaven. He noted the similarities between the rituals of the followers of Mithras, the Mithraic mysteries and the Christian baptism and Eucharist. He remarked on the fact that the God-men of antiquity were usually born of virgins and that Jupiter, among others, had fathered a number of sons—thus, there were many "sons of God." However, writes Justin, these figures were fictional and Jesus Christ is not—he really was born of a virgin in a supernatural manner (instead of by Jupiter, it was through the Holy Spirit). On a wondrous presumption that Justin held forth, all these other figures were false and their legends were inspired by demons, who put forth these myths in order to counteract and preempt the advent of Christ. The entire pagan religious world view, the mystery religions (including the Eleusinian mysteries), the teachings of Pythagoras and the Persian Scriptures were all summarily rejected as false. Where it could be harmonized with Justin's Christianity and the Old Testament, the philosophy of Plato was accepted as prefiguring the coming of Christ. However, taught Justin, even Plato plagiarized his doctrine from Moses! As is common to orthodox writers, we find a narrowness of vision in Justin, an inability to accept truth wherever it is found, especially when we compare him to the Christian-Gnostics such as Basilides and Valentinus, who have a universal yet totally Christian outlook.

The Doctrine of the Incarnation of the Word

With regard to Christ, Justin taught that the Logos appeared in Christ and was, in fact, Christ Himself. This Logos or Reason was possibly active through many of the great philosophers in the past, but in Christ alone was the Logos incarnated. According to Justin, this incarnation of the Logos had never occurred before Christ nor will it ever occur again. In

Christ the Logos or Divine Reason appeared bodily—the same Reason/Logos who created and arranged the world took human form in order to draw the whole of humanity to itself.<11> Justin was asking his readers to believe that the Logos Himself had taken form quantitatively in Jesus Christ and in no one else. Let us review the implications of this doctrine which Justin claims to be unique to Christianity, or, at least, to Justin's view of Christianity. We shall see that Justin's doctrine of the Incarnation is not only traceable to the ancient Hindu Scriptures, but is a distortion of the authentic doctrine of the Incarnation as found in these scriptures.

The germ of the Logos doctrine, as disseminated in the West, had been originally propounded in 500 B.C. by Heraclitus of Ephesus who taught that all things come to pass through this Divine Word or Reason. Stoics and Platonists conceived the Logos to be the Mind of God reflected or immanent in the intelligibility, rationality, order and harmony of the universe.<12> The Jewish philosopher, Philo of Alexandria, synthesized Jewish and Greek concepts of the Logos as the image of God's Mind in creation, in the law and in man's reason. Philo also taught that the Logos was the head of numerous logoi and an intermediary between God and Man. Valentinus taught that the Logos was one of the emanations of the Supreme Deity. In the gospel of John, the Logos is one with God, and in fact, is God and it is through the Logos that all things came into being. John, however, carries the Logos doctrine further when he writes that "The Logos was made flesh and dwelt among us; and we beheld his glory, the glory as of the only Begotten of the Father, full of grace and truth." (John 1:14)

To find the roots of John's doctrine, we must not only go back to Greek philosophy, but look further into the Vedas. John states, "In the beginning was the Word and the Word was with God and the Word was God." The Veda states:

Prajapatir vag idam asit, In the beginning was Brahman, Tsya vag dritiya asit... with whom was Vak or the Word...

Vag vai paranam Brahma. and the Word is Brahman. <13>

Vak or Word was understood by the ancient Hindus to be the Sound which brought all things into existence-the Sound or Word-the primordial emanation of God expressing and clothing the creative Thought. Astonishingly, we see a marked similarity between John's opening verses and that of the Vedas. Between 500 to 100 B.C., the doctrines of Hinduism were given their most exalted form in the Upanishads, which gave rise to the Brahmanic religion. We find the oldest doctrine of the Trinity embedded in ancient Brahmanism—the triad of Brahma as the Creator, Vishnu as the Preserver, and Shiva as the Destroyer. These correspond to the later Western Christian conception of Father, Son and Holy Spirit evolved by the Church Fathers. In the Bhagavad Gita, circa 500 B.C. to 250 B.C., we find, perhaps, the earliest doctrine of the divine incarnation. In this text the figure of Krishna is considered to be an incarnation of Vishnu, the Son of God, the second Person of the Hindu Trinity. Krishna was the eighth incarnation of Vishnu and it was understood that the Son of God, Vishnu, would incarnate himself on earth a number of times in every age and epoch for the salvation of humanity. Gautama Buddha was later understood by the Hindus to be the ninth incarnation of Vishnu; and according to the Tibetan text published by Nicholas Notovitch, Jesus was believed to be yet another incarnation of Vishnu by the Hindus. The similarities between the Hindu doctrine of the incarnation and John's doctrine as set forth in the opening statement of his gospel are unmistakable. In the gospel for example, Vishnu would be termed "The Only Begotten Son," which refers to the Universal Logos, the pre-cosmic Word or Vak. The earliest formulation of the doctrine of the Incarnation is thus proclaimed by Krishna, the avatar of the Son of God, Vishnu, who states that he is an embodiment of God:

The foolish, unacquainted with my Supreme Nature despise me in this human form, while men of great minds, *enlightened by the Divine principle within them, acknowledge me as incorruptible and before all things, and serve me with undivided hearts... I am not recognized by all because concealed by the supernatural power which is in me... I existed before Vaivasvata and Manu. I am the Most High God, the Creator of the World, the Eternal Purusha. And although in my own nature I am exempt from liability to birth or death, and am Lord of all created things, yet as often as in the world virtue is enfeebled, and vice and injustice prevail so often do I become manifest and am revealed from age to age, to save the just, to destroy the guilty, and to reassure the faltering steps of virtue. He who acknowledgeth me as even so, doth not on quitting this mortal frame enter into another, for he entereth into me; and many who have trusted in me have already entered into me, being purified by the power of wisdom. I help those who walk in my path, even as they serve me. <14>*

In the above passage we find the root of many of the doctrines of Christianity, some of which are expressed similarly in John's gospel. Jesus, like Krishna, promises eternal life to all who believe in him and states that he will abide in his disciples. Jesus declares that he existed before Abraham, as Krishna declared he existed before Vaivasvata. Amazingly, we also find the core of what later became the "heresy" of Docetism. Krishna avers that in his nature he is not subject to birth or death, yet he manifests on earth from age to age, as we saw early Christian sects claiming that Jesus' birth and death were illusory. These Christians understood that Christ as a divine incarnation, in his true nature, could not be subject to the change of birth and death except in appearance only, while in his human nature, Christ experienced all things, including birth and death.

We also find this ancient Hindu doctrine of the incarnation of Vishnu in the statement of St. Paul who writes that Christ, being in a Godlike form, emptied himself, took the form of a servant and was made in the likeness of men (Phil 2: 6-8). St.Paul also writes in Colossians, that God the Son [Vishnu] is the image of the invisible God [Brahman] the first born of every creature—"For by Him [Vishnu/Christ/Logos] were all created, that are in earth, visible and invisible... all things were created by Him and for Him; and he is before all things, and by Him all things consist... For it pleased the Father [Brahma] that in Him should all the Fulness dwell (Colossians 1: 15-19). In the Bhagavad Gita passage, Krishna, speaking as the Incarnation of God, declares that he is the Creator of the world. St. Paul also asserts the same for Christ whom he declares to be the world Creator when he writes "All things were created by Him." It is obvious that St. Paul sees Christ as the Hindus saw Krishna; and in comparison, we might say that Christ is Vishnu and Jesus is Krishna. As Krishna was the incarnation of Vishnu, so Jesus is the incarnation of Christ—the Son of God, namely Vishnu.

According to the Tibetan text discovered at Himis Monastery, we noted that Jesus was said to be the incarnation of the Buddha. Notovitch writes of his conversation with a Buddhist Lama regarding Jesus. The Lama remarks:

We also respect the one whom you recognize as the Son of the One God—not that we see in him an only Son, but a perfect being, elect from among all. The spirit of the Buddha was indeed incarnate in the sacred person of Issa [Jesus], who...has spread knowledge of our great and true religion throughout the world...

Issa is a great prophet, one of the first after the twenty-two Buddhas. He is greater than any one of all the Dalai Lamas, for he constitutes part of the spirituality of Our Lord [Gautama Buddha]. It is he who has brought back within the pale of religion the souls of the frivolous, and who has allowed each human being to distinguish between good and evil. His name and his acts are recorded in our sacred writings... (Brackets added) <15>

Another Lama who converses with Notovitch explains to him the doctrine of divine incarnation from a Buddhist point of view:

> *The great Buddha, Soul of the Universe, is the incarnation of Brahma. He remains almost always in passivity, preserving within himself all things from the beginning of time, and his breath vivifies the world. Having abandoned man to his own resources, he yet at certain epochs comes forth from his inertia taking upon himself a human form to save his creatures from irremediable ruin...* <16>

The Lama goes on to relate how there were twenty incarnations of the great Buddha, the last two being Gautama and Jesus. Of Jesus he says:

> *Nearly two thousand years ago the perfect being, again breaking through his state of inaction, became incarnate in the newborn infant of a poor family. It was his will that a child in simple words should enlighten the ignorant as to life eternal— by his own example, bringing men back to the ways of truth in setting before them the paths most surely leading to the attainment of moral purity...* <17>

According to the Tibetan text itself, the incarnation of Jesus took place in the following manner:

1. At this time came the moment when the All-merciful Judge elected to become incarnate in a human being.

2. And the Eternal Spirit, dwelling in a state of complete inaction and of supreme beatitude, awoke and detached itself for an indefinite period of time from the Eternal Being.

3. So as to show forth in the guise of humanity the means of self-identification with Divinity and of attaining to eternal felicity...

5. Soon after, a marvelous child was born in the land of Israel,

God himself speaking by the mouth of this infant of the frailty of the body and the grandeur of the soul. <18>

In another translation by Swami Abhedananda of the same or perhaps similar text, the process is again described:

1. The Supreme God, the Father of the Universe, out of great compassion for sinners, desired to appear on earth in human form.

2. That Incarnation appeared as a soul separate from that Supreme Soul who has no beginning, no end, and is above all consequence.

3. [He] descended to show how a soul can unite with God and realize eternal bliss.

4. And assumed a human form to demonstrate in his own life how a mortal can achieve righteousness and separate the soul from the mortal body in order to gain immortality and proceed to that heaven of the Father of the Universe, where there exists eternal bliss. <19>

It is clear that the above texts are describing the birth of what has been called an avatara. The term avatar derives from a compound of two Sanskrit words: ava meaning "down," and tri meaning to "cross over." Ava-tri thus means to "pass down" or to "descend." <20> An Avatara, therefore, is the descent of a ray or portion of a Celestial Being or Buddha into the unborn child who is to become the manifestation or incarnation of that Divine Being. <21> This is precisely what is stated by the Lama in regard to Jesus: "the spirit of Buddha was incarnate in the sacred person of Jesus," that is, a celestial energy or the psycho-spiritual part of the Buddha passed down into Mary's womb at or during conception. According to Theosophical writer G. de Puruker, "At the appropriate time, the Buddha projects his own soul and inspirits the growing embryo with the spiritual fire of his own soul...and thus is formed the union of the divinity above, the buddhic soul-splendor, and the pure body—and this union is an avatara." <22> According to this understanding, Jesus was, therefore, the vehicle or manifestation of a Celestial Buddha who transmitted part of his essence to Jesus. The final linking of the Celestial Buddha above to the pure form of Jesus below, apparently occurred at the Baptism. We have seen that several ancient Christian sects, including the Ebionites, Ophites and the Basilideans believed that the "Christ" or "Holy Spirit" descended upon Jesus at the Baptism and that Jesus began his mission in Palestine at that time. The "Christ" as used here may well be a term describing the descent of the Celestial Buddha into the form of Jesus. According to the Lamas, this Buddha was Gautama who, 500 years before Jesus, had entered Nirvana; or the Celestial Buddha who manifested himself in Jesus may have been the Buddha Maitreya—the Coming One. In the gospels, especially that of John, Jesus frequently states that he and his Father are one and that "he who has seen me has seen my Father also." There are many such similar statements uttered by Jesus which would lead one to conclude that Jesus was the incarnation of a Divine Being, a Buddha of Compassion, who fused his being with that of Jesus. Theosophists and other esoteric schools such as The Summit Lighthouse, have taught that the Buddha Maitreya dwelt in the form of Jesus, and was indeed, the Guru (Father) of Jesus, and that Jesus was the messenger of Maitreya.

The same teaching is found in modern times, for example in the relationship of the great Indian saint Ramakrishna and his disciple, Vivekanada, whose yogic death was described in Chapter 2. Ramakrishna once had related how he won Vivekananda's presence on earth:

Absorbed, one day, in samahdi, Ramakrishna had found that his mind was soaring high, going beyond the physical universe of the sun, moon, and stars, and passing into the subtle region of ideas. As it continued to ascend...it crossed the *luminous barrier separating the phenomenal universe from the Absolute, entering finally the transcendental realm. There Ramakrishna saw seven venerable sages absorbed in meditation. These, he thought, must have surpassed even the gods and goddesses in wisdom and holiness, and as he was admiring their unique spirituality he saw a portion of the undifferentiated Absolute become congealed, as it were, and take the form of a Divine Child. Clambering upon the lap of one of the sages and gently clasping his neck with His soft arms, the Child whispered something in his ear, and at this magic touch the sage awoke from meditation. He fixed his half-open eyes upon the wondrous Child, who said in great joy: "I am going down to earth. Won't you come with me?" With a benign look the sage expressed assent and returned into deep spiritual ecstasy. Ramakrishna was amazed to observe that a tiny portion of the sage, however, descended to earth, taking the form of light, which struck the house in Calcutta where Narendra's [Vivekananda's] family lived, and when he saw Narendra for the first time, he at once recognized him as the incarnation of the sage. <23>*

In the doctrine of the Avatara, we may also find the root of the later distorted dogmas of the virginal conception and the Incarnation. The Avatara doctrine states that the Buddha invigorates the human seed which will produce the child-body of a hereditary pure type.<24> A portion of the Self of the Buddha is in fact, part and parcel of the avatara to be born— there is no real separation.

One more point should be made regarding the Avatara doctrine. It is explicitly stated that the emergence of an avatara is a cyclic event. It has occurred in past ages and will occur again. The oldest proponents of this doctrine from the Brahmins to the Buddhists to the Christian-Gnostics have declared that the Divine Word [Logos] whether it be that of Christos, Vishnu, Gautama Buddha, or Maitreya can and does incarnate periodically for the benefit and salvation of humanity.

We recall the teaching of Justin to the effect that the

incarnation of the Logos in Jesus never occurred before in history nor will it ever occur again. And here we find the point of demarcation between the ancient doctrine of the incarnation and the new orthodox pseudo-Christian dogma as it was emerging from the pen of Justin. We also recognize the core of the exclusively orthodox idea of Jesus as the only Son of God, a concept which became the trademark of orthodoxy and effectively cut off other possible incarnations of the Deity, at least in the eyes of Christians. And yet the oldest doctrine of the Divine Incarnation found in Hinduism and Buddhism centuries before Christianity affirms successive divine in-carnations. Justin, however, through his Apologies, severs his ties to these religions which contain the prototypes of his dogmas in favor of the new and exclusive religion of Christianity. But to do so, Justin, whether consciously or un-consciously, borrows from Hinduism, Buddhism, Plato, Philo, and the Christian-Gnostics, while simultaneously attempting to disprove them all! We observe this same pattern in the writings of many, if not all, of the subsequent Church Fathers.

Justin argues that the Logos whole and entire, quan-titatively embodied as Jesus and presents his doctrine as a totally unique revelation. But can the finite contain the Infinite? No, but the Infinite can focus, can act through the finite. If we recall the verse in John's gospel, it states: "We beheld his glory, the glory *as of* the Only-Begotten Son of the Father, full of grace and truth."(John 1:14) That is to say, the glory of Jesus in the flesh was like the Only-Begotten Son, the Universal Logos, and that in Jesus the Logos was qualitatively incarnated. Jesus Christ was, therefore, of the same nature as the Logos and that Divine Nature was capable of acting in and through other holy men who purified themselves accordingly. Justin, however, would have it that the Logos never had nor could ever again embody fully as it had in Jesus. Christian-Gnostics of every persuasion, in contradistinction to Justin, taught that man possessed within him the potential to become the embodiment of the Logos.

We have previously seen how the concepts of preexistence and reincarnation were widespread in the ancient world and were accepted by the Greeks, Jews and early Christian sects and communities. In his *Dialogue with Trypho*, Justin describes his conversion to Christianity. During the course of a conversation with a Stoic philosopher, Justin found himself refuting the doctrine of transmigration or reincarnation on the grounds that the soul doesn't remember its past lives, nor does it recall that it is being punished by or for its sins through transmigration. <25> This philosopher, with whom Justin argued, claimed himself a convert to Christianity— obviously a Christianity of the narrow, orthodox persuasion. Justin followed suit and affirmed that the entire truth is to be found only in the Old Testament and its fulfillment in Christ. He summarily rejected reincarnation as defined in Pythagorean and Platonic doctrines. He seems, however, to have accepted a form of pre-existence.

We find no trace in Justin's writings of an under-standing of the theology of St. Paul or in a personal resur-rection of the believer in Christ. According to Justin, the gen-eral resurrection will take place at the end of the world. Christ and his angels will suddenly appear on the clouds of heaven, to be followed by the resurrection in which the souls of men and women would be reunited with bodies that perished at death. <26> Furthermore, Christ with all Christians (of Justin's per-suasion) will establish an earthly kingdom in a rebuilt Jerusalem.

The doctrine of the resurrection of the body at the end of the world may have had its origin in the misunderstanding of Jewish Apocalyptic texts which appears to have been derived from ideas current in Zoroastrian eschatology (the doctrine of the Last Things). The oldest Christian documents we possess, the letters of St.Paul, deny a bodily resurrection but affirm a resurrection in a celestial body, which St. Paul calls the pneu-matic body. The debate regarding the nature of the resurrection was intense in the mid-second century among various Christian-Gnostic sects and schools and emergent orthodox churches. The Ophites, Marcion, Basilides, and Valentinus were the great enemies of Justin. Their Christian theology was developed decades before Justin's and not one of them taught the resurrection of the physical body at the end of the world. Justin, however, insists on a Creator who has the power to newly create physical bodies at the end of the world. In his writings, Justin reveals no knowledge of the types of bodies designated in the ancient world as etheric, pneumatic, or aerial. We find no real understanding of St. Paul's doctrine on the hylic (material) body, the psychic/soul body, and the pneumatic (spiritual) body, in the works of Justin.

The Resurrection of the Body

We look, then, for the origin of the orthodox doctrine of the resurrection of the body. We must first distinguish between (1) the resurrection at the end of the age or world, and (2) the resurrection of each individual which commences while he is yet on earth and continues after death.

The oldest account of the general resurrection of the body at the end of the age may be found in the texts of Apocalyptic Judaism. The Book of Enoch, third to second century B.C., records the "end times" as follows:

In those days shall the earth deliver up from her womb, and hell deliver up from hers, that which it has received; and destruction shall restore that which it owes.

He shall select the righteous and holy from among them; for the day of their salvation has approached...

Their countenance shall be bright with joy; for in those days shall the Elect One be exalted. The earth shall rejoice; the righteous shall inhabit it, and the elect possess it. <27>

The concept of the renovation of the earth is quite clear in this passage; the righteous are to inherit the earth, but the passage says nothing about the resurrection of the physical bodies from graves. Another Enochian passage runs:

The saints and the elect have risen from the earth, have left off to depress their countenances, and have been clothed with the garment of life. That garment of life is with the Lord of Spirits, in whose presence your garment shall not wax old, nor shall your glory diminish. <28>

The "garment of life" mentioned in Enoch probably does not refer to resurrected physical bodies, but may refer to ethereal or transformed bodies, or perhaps to the "wedding garment" referred to by Jesus.

In the Old Testament Book of Daniel 12: 2-3, we find a passage that may have been taken by literalists in Judaism and Christianity to mean the resurrection of physical bodies at the end-times:

Many of those who sleep in the dust of the earth will awake; some to everlasting life; some to shame and everlasting contempt.

And the wise shall shine like the brightness of the firmament; those who turn many to righteousness, like the stars forever and ever.

Are we to take literally the verse "those who sleep in the dust of the earth" and insist that this refers to the ashes of decayed bodies? More likely this verse is referring to those who sleep in ignorance, sin or mortality. Moreover, if their bodies are to "shine," they cannot be mortal, physical bodies, but ethereal or spiritual bodies.

In early Christianity a distinction was made between the personal resurrection which could occur at the close of any given life, yet could commence during that life, and the general resurrection at the end of the age or ages, in which all humanity would somehow be involved and by which they would find themselves transformed. It was taught by certain sects that the personal, individual resurrection was attained by the Christian at the close of a series of embodiments and represented the culmination of those embodiments—the resurrection therefore spelled an end to reincarnation. Man, the last Adam, as St. Paul wrote, becomes a "quickening spirit" through the resurrection. In reviewing St. Paul's doctrine of the resurrection, we find that his metaphorical, gnostic phraseology has been literally interpreted by less-than-knowledgeable, though zealous Church Fathers such as Justin and Tertullian. In 1 Corinthians 15: 50-53, St. Paul writes:

Now this I say brethren, that flesh and blood cannot inherit the kingdom of God; neither doth corruption inherit incorruption.

Behold, I show you a mystery; we shall not all sleep, but we shall be changed.

In a moment, in the twinkling of an eye, at the last trump; for the trumpet shall sound, and the dead shall be raised incorruptible, and we shall be changed.

For this corruptible must put on incorruption; and this mortal must put on immortality.

The key points in the above passage are that flesh and blood do not inherit the kingdom of God and that the resurrection is a process of transmutation and change, whereby the corruptible body becomes incorrupt. Therefore it can no longer be a physical body as we know it. The term "dead" is again a mystical phrase, and St. Paul is apparently using mystery language. The "dead" are those unawakened, still in a body of flesh, still sojourning in the physical cosmos, but who, on the instant, are changed in soul and body by Light swallowing up the darkness. There is nothing in the above verses to warrant the belief that this scenario must take place at the end of the world. St. Paul certainly does not say so. The resurrection process may take place in the above manner during the life of the initiate, at the moment of death or after death for those who have attained it.

Some have cited I Thess. 4:14-17 to defend a doctrine of the general, mechanical resurrection of the body at the end of the age. The passage reads:

For if we believe that Jesus died and rose again, even so them also who sleep in Jesus will God bring with him.

For this we say unto you by the word of the Lord, that we who are alive and remain unto the coming of the Lord shall not precede them who are asleep.

For the Lord himself shall descend from heaven with a shout, with the voice of the archangel and with the trump of God; and the dead in Christ shall rise first;

Then we who are alive and remain shall be caught up together with them in the clouds, to meet the Lord in the air; and so shall we ever be with the Lord.

Again we must interpret these verses in the context of ideas and language in use at the time, keeping in mind St. Paul's mystical, "gnostic" orientation. Those who "sleep in Jesus," we would suggest, are disciples of Jesus who have passed on and are inhabiting various levels of the heaven-world. We recall that the esoteric doctrine of the Pharisees taught the existence of at least seven heavens. These souls who have passed on would not be subject to reincarnation and are ready for the "resurrection," and "ascension", i.e., their final assimilation unto the God-Source (where, however, they retain their divine individuality). "We who are alive" (i.e., those living on earth in this future epoch) refers, no doubt, to the reincarnation of the same souls St. Paul is addressing. When the "Lord" descends from heaven, those who are in the heaven-world ("the dead in Christ") shall "rise," i.e., ascend unto God first. This "rising", we suggest, refers to the soul's union with its Divine Nature. Those on earth are likewise prepared to take their final "ascension" and are "caught up together with them in the clouds to meet the Lord in the air," where they remain forever in what we may term the "ascended state." This entire scenario obviously refers to a "mass ascension" of the righteous in this future age (though neither automatic, mechanical, nor applying generally to everyone regardless of the attainment of the soul). However, it is not possible to discern from this passage whether those still on earth at this time rise with translated or transfigured bodies or whether their souls depart their bodies and are clothed in "ethereal" or "aerial" bodies. This event is apparently coincidental with the descent of a future avatar ("Lord") which may refer to Jesus or to a future Buddha. The word "air" used in vs. 17, no doubt refers to one of the subtle planes of matter which were understood to compose the heaven-world. We find nothing in this passage which explicitly states that dead bodies shall rise from graves and be reconstructed. We would propose that from the tone of these verses, those who will be experiencing resurrection in this future age have previously prepared themselves through lifetimes of striving to this precise cycle in time where they are destined to "ascend" to God (as Jesus previously ascended) as the final culmination of their sojourn on earth. Therefore, the resurrection comes to those who have made themselves ready through personal attainment, and in the above scenario, perhaps thousands or millions have so prepared themselves.

Once the Church Fathers, beginning with Justin, continuing with Irenaeus, Tertullian and ending with Augustine, decided to refute the universal doctrine of reincarnation and the personal resurrection as a spiritual initiation for which the Christian initiate prepares over lifetimes, then the doctrine of the general resurrection at the end of the age had to be substituted as the only resurrection possible. But this doctrine is certainly a dilemma. If the resurrection is a personal initiation; if it was demonstrated by Jesus as one of the initiatic steps in life, then it is a spiritual attainment. And for those who have not attained it, at the "last day," how will one now suddenly merit this attainment? If the resurrection is not a personal attainment, then we have, at the last day, some form of spiritual socialism on a vast scale—the granting of a singular spiritual initiation to mankind in general for actions described by even less than the lowest common denominator. One need merely follow the mechanistic rules of orthodoxy to be granted this and avoid (after being granted this) being sent to eternal fire.

The other half of the dilemma of this doctrine is simply this: If "flesh and blood" cannot inherit, what possible reason can there be for the physical body to be reassembled, re-"mattered," or whatever it would take to accomplish re-establishing the physical form, all just to immediately trans-mute it to a state beyond "flesh and blood?" And from a simple matter of physics, what is it that is being reconstituted? The ensemble of atoms and electrons that compose the body are always in dynamic flux, constantly in change. The set that was there at one time in one's history are long gone. The set that comprises "me" now may be part of many other people on the "last day." Why should we be so worried about reconstructing what is a mirage, a pure function of a particular scale of time and space, a particular view of the mysterious "present?" This is surely the "flesh and blood" consciousness. Why not simply let the soul be directly clothed in a celestial form? The fundamental problem here is that the orthodox have identified themselves with the body. But what is "you" is not the body. The body is not the "you" the kingdom of heaven is within. This realization is truly for the "fundamentalist" in the spiritual life. In the final analysis this doctrine of the general res-urrection is severely problematic and distinctly non-spiritual, and it is little wonder it is not found in the earliest Christian teachings.

Through the work of Justin, then, we find the refutation of the following previously taught Christian teachings of the original Christian sects:

1) The truth of Christianity can be apprehended through personal gnosis, insight, experience and inner vision and through the secret doctrine of Christ. Prophecy is ongoing and progressive.
2) Truth, as a thread, runs through all the scriptures of all religions.
3) Qualitatively, men have the potential to become incar-nations of the Logos, to become "Christs" through the divine spark within.

4) The Logos has incarnated in the flesh through past epochs of history and will continue to do so. Jesus was a singular incarnation of the Logos.
5) The soul resurrects in a celestial or spiritual body at the culmination of its cycle of incarnations. The resurrection is the result of personal attainment.

In place of these doctrines, Justin substituted the following pseudo-doctrines:

1) The truth of Christianity is found in the written revealed word of the Old Testament and through the gospels. The fulfillment of Old Testament prophecy began and ended with Christ. There is no secret doctrine and no ongoing revelation.
2) Truth in its entirety is to be found in the Hebrew Scriptures alone. All other religions must be rejected.
3) Men do not have the potential to become incarnations of the Logos; however, their rational faculty is a part of the Logos.
4) The Logos has incarnated quantitatively in the flesh in Jesus Christ once in history.
5) All souls automatically resurrect at the end of the world in physical bodies resuscitated from the graves. There is only one life on earth. There is no reincarnation.

In Justin, we have witnessed a process, born in some strange arrogance, both curious and sad, engaged in generally by the Church Fathers. The Christian teachings, as we have seen, existed within a vast context of thought, doctrines, spiritual and philosophical tradition—an extensive framework of ideas within which Jesus, as well as any other man of his age, or any age, must work and communicate with his fellow men. A Justin, in a sad operation of narrowing, of constriction of vision, cut and scalped this context and framework away from the teachings of Christ, lifting out a deformed caricature of the original, a caricature now strewn with contradictions, unexplainable elements, and back pedaling to merely metaphoric understandings everywhere one turns. The position on the end of revelation is contradicted instantly within Revelation itself: the seventh angel is coming with his little book of the Everlasting Gospel—but how can this be and how can he be recognized if revelation has ceased? The teaching on the resurrection dissolves into incoherency on closer examination. Jesus' statements on Elias as John the Baptist remain forever enigmatic, explainable only by contortion—as metaphor. His "Ye are gods" argument must be ignored. St. Paul's teaching on the putting on of the "Mind which was in Christ Jesus" must be interpreted now as metaphorical. John's "Now are we the Sons of God," is now—metaphorical—the orthodox brand of adoptionism—oh yes, he means "adopted" sons. Hebrews' Melchizedek, "having neither beginning nor end of days, but made like unto the Son of God," is persona non grata. And on. And on. Such is the legacy of Justin and his pseudo-doctrines.

We now move on to Irenaeus, who formulated his "anti-gnostic" theology—a theology which eventually became normative for Christians through the next centuries.

Chapter IX

Irenaeus and the Formulation of Orthodox Pseudo-Theology

Before we begin a discussion of Irenaeus' theology we must ask, "What prompted Irenaeus to formulate a theology in opposition to other Christian doctrines?" In order to answer that question we must remember that those Christians who were later termed "Valentinians" were at one time members of the "church" at large. Their teachings were an esoteric exegesis of the doctrines of Christianity and not a rival religion. There is no doubt, however, that Irenaeus saw the Valentinian Christians and other Christian sects who presented a system of initiation as rivals and as competing with the authority of the bishops. Irenaeus, of course, was bishop of Lyons, France and thus his power base was seriously threatened. We recall that the Valentinian Christians derived their doctrines from an esoteric teaching of the apostle Paul, through Theudas. They referred to themselves as pneumatikoi (spiritual) and teleioi (the "perfect" or initiated, from the Greek: telos—end or completion) in accordance with terms used by St. Paul for his initiates. Layton states that the term "Valentinians" must have been coined by their enemies to imply that they followed not Christ but Valentinus.<1> He also asserts that this term began to appear about A.D. 160 in pamphlets attacking the followers of Valentinus and other theologians of the time.<2> We regard the use of these pamphlets as an early "disinformation" campaign directed against fellow Christians to discredit their teaching, and in all likelihood based in gross ignorance of the actual teaching. The result of this campaign was the establishment of orthodox theology which is with us to the present day—a theology which, then as now, denies freedom of religion and creative expression in matters of religion. Irenaeus' campaign was likewise an attack on individual progressive revelation, which incidentally, began, as far as Christianity is concerned, with the apostles Paul, John and Mary Magdalen who all claimed private revelations from Jesus Christ.

Bently Layton very well describes the situation in which Christian schools found themselves prior to 160 A.D.:

In this period Christian theological schools, whatever tradition they taught, normally had a loose and ill-defined relation to local Christian congregations and bishops. Their meetings, which were open to qualified students, would be held in private quarters under the direction of a scholar, as a supplement to the regular church life of worship and service....

The structure of the Valentinian movement is a typical, early instance of this pattern. The spectrum of its theological and mythical speculation was held together not only by academic tradition, but also by the members' allegiance to ordinary Christian congregations. Followers of Valentinus read and interpreted the same scripture that most Christians read today...presumably in service attended by other kinds of Christians as well; they accepted the usual sacraments of the second century church...and referred to the same kind of creed, or rule of faith, as what in retrospect seems to have been proto-orthodox Christianity....

...By the year 200 it was still possible for a follower of Valentinus to hold the ecclesiastical rank of presbyter in the church at Rome. The writings of the Valentinian school were not simply dismissed out of hand by all opponents, but were sometimes taken as a topic of serious discussion, especially by Clement of Alexandria (A.D. ca. 150—ca. 215) and Origen (A.D. ca. 185—ca. 254).

For a long time, then, the Valentinian movement remained firmly within the church at large, causing their opponents to call them bitterly "wolves in sheep's *clothing."<3>*

The "church at large" did not mean what it does today. As yet, circa 160-180 A.D. (when the attack on sectarian Christians began) there was no uniform theology or interpretation of Christianity and no normative dogma. The attempt to formulate a dogma was begun by Justin and continued in earnest by Irenaeus circa 180 A.D. in his book *Against Heresies*. With this work Irenaeus set a precedent in discussing what ordinary Christians ought to believe; even more unique was his assertion that Christian teaching from Christ down through the apostles remained unbroken and uncontaminated to Irenaeus' time.<4> No scholar today accepts such an assertion nor is there a shred of proof. Discussing the diversity of early Christianity (which Irenaeus paints as uniform), Elaine Pagels writes of her search to discover this original "simplicity":

...But during the first and second centuries, Christians scattered throughout the world, from Rome to Asia, Africa, Egypt and Gaul, read and revered quite different traditions, and various groups of Christians perceived Jesus and his message very differently....

What I did not find in the process of this research was what I had started out to find—a "golden age" of purer and simpler early Christianity. What I discovered instead is that the "real Christianity"—so far as historical investigation can disclose it—was not monolithic, or the province of one party or another, but included a variety of voices, and an extraordinary range of viewpoints....From a strictly historical point of view, then, there is no single "real Christianity."<5>

Yet this "golden age" of Christianity is precisely what Irenaeus sets out to prove, all in the name of apostolic tradition, which tradition his so-called enemies also claimed for themselves. In our review of these various traditions, we have singled out the following as representing the earliest forms of Christianity:

1) Pauline
2) Nazorean—Ebionite—Petrine
3) Samaritan (e.g., Simon, Menander, Satornilos)
4) Johannine
5) Ophite/Naassene
6) Cerinthian
7) Carpocratian
8) Clementine (i.e., of Rome)
9) Ignatian (i.e., of Antioch)
10) Basilidean
11) Marcionite
12) Valentinian
13) Justinian
14) Irenaean, circa 180 A.D.

     The first eight types of Christianity are all encompassed within the first century. The remaining comprise the foremost types throughout the second century. Orthodox dogmatic theology did not begin to take root until Irenaeus. The canon of "accepted" books began to be formulated as reaction to Marcion, circa 144-150, but did not achieve any degree of finality until 200 or even a decade or two later. We find, therefore, that the earliest Christianity was not orthodox and bears little resemblance to the so-called fundamental Christianity of today.

     Irenaeus' purpose was to alienate all Christian sectarians including Valentinians, whom he lumps in with all the rest. He had to prove uniformity in the midst of diversity—and, as a result, had to construct uniform doctrines to combat sectarian diversity and varying traditions, even if they claimed to be apostolic. Part of his strategy was to establish a derogatory image of those Christians and to deride their doctrines by accusing them of blasphemy, sorcery and debauchery. In *Against Heresies*, we find the worst kind of religious prejudice and a vituperative hatred not uncommon among orthodox Church Fathers of the school of Irenaeus,

Tertullian, Epiphanius and Augustine. Irenaeus and others were not above rewriting history to suit their ends, all in the name of Christ and his church. Irenaeus makes no attempt to understand the doctrines of his fellow Christians, whom he views as his worst enemies. Freedom of religion and freedom to worship as one sees fit are unknown commodities to Irenaeus and those who follow him. Respect for another's beliefs is also unknown to Irenaeus while, ironically, the so-called pagan philosophers of the second century included everyone, or almost everyone, in their breadth of vision. The Stoics, Neo-Pythagoreans, Platonists and Christian-Gnostics were far more Christ-like than Irenaeus and his followers.

There is no doubt, as we have said, that Irenaeus felt threatened by the Valentinian Christians and other Christian sects who presented a system of initiation into the Christian mysteries, as against rules, tradition, dogma and sacraments. Elaine Pagels has clearly shown that the motives of Irenaeus and later orthodox Church Fathers were primarily social and political, not necessarily theological.<6> She is careful to point out that any doctrine which would tend to restore spiritual power or knowledge to the individual was also condemned by these self-styled religious authorities. The sacramental initiatic system of, for example, the Valentinian school was so designed, as we have seen, to put the initiate in contact with his divine spark or higher Self, thus eventually freeing him from outwardly-imposed religious rules and regulations. Valentinian Christians, therefore, could no longer be controlled from without. This would tend to lessen the influence of the bishop and hence his power—based not on spiritual attainment—over the individual. The primary tactic of the bishops was to appeal to morals, ethics and discipline, as Pagels also shows.

We have seen how Clement of Rome and Ignatius of Antioch sought to impose by force the Old Testament Mosaic code upon Christians in their sphere of influence. This process had been continuing in proto-orthodox communities up until the time of Irenaeus, and certain churches were becoming institutionalized and more rigid. But writes Pagels:

...Some Christians resisted that process. For while certain bishops, including, for example, Irenaeus of Lyons, attempted to formulate community morals and to enforce discipline by teaching, penalizing, or expelling those who, for whatever reason, dissented, some, no doubt, resented these intrusions upon their behavior. Others, although they accepted the ethical basis of Christian teaching, regarded conformity, whether in doctrine or in discipline, as something that only beginners needed to take seriously. Some ardent Christians wanted to recover the sense of spiritual transformation that they found in Jesus' message. For these Christians conversion meant more than accepting baptism and following a new set of moral rules derived from Jesus' teaching. Becoming a Christian meant discovering one's spiritual nature—discovering, as one teacher put it, who we are, and what we have become; where we were...whither we are hastening; from what we are being released; what birth is, and what is rebirth [Theodotus].

Many Christians striving for a higher level of spiritual consciousness had no quarrel with what the bishops taught....But some Christians objected to being told what to think and how to behave. Although they agreed that the first step toward becoming a Christian was to accept the faith and receive baptism from the bishop, these Christians wanted to go further. They yearned to become spiritually "mature," to go beyond such elementary instruction toward higher levels of understanding. And this awareness they called gnosis, which means "knowledge" or "insight." To achieve gnosis, these Christians said, they no longer needed the bishop or the clergy.
<7>

To no longer need the bishop or clergy would spell an end to the power of the bishops and their proposed confederation of churches as a bastion for that power. Irenaeus was acutely aware of this and he had no recourse but to discredit and defame his fellow Christians who wanted to grow spiritually.

The imposition of moral rules was not effective in and of itself. Irenaeus, as we have said, had to construct a new theology and pass this off as an unchanged apostolic tradition to counterattack the claims of fellow Christians. Irenaeus, however, not only attacked the Christian-Gnostics but also borrowed from their techniques. As Harnack remarks, "Little as we can understand modern orthodox theology from a historical point of view...we can just as little understand the theology of Irenaeus without taking into account the schools of Valentinus and Marcion."<8>

The Christian-Gnostics, of course, were the first theologians of the first century, as Harnack states.<9> The earliest Christian commentaries we possess are from the pen of Gnostic-Christians of the Ophite school and the Valentinian school, such as Theodotus, Ptolemy and Heracleon. The earliest collection of what later became the New Testament books also originated among sectarian, not orthodox, Christians prior to Irenaeus. Harnack writes:

*Undoubtedly sacred writings were selected according to the principle of apostolic origin. This is proved by the inclusion of the Pauline Epistles in the collections of books. There is evidence of such having been made by the Naassenes, Peratae, Valentinians, Marcion, Tatian, and the Gnostic Justin. The collection of the Valentinians and the Canon of Tatian must have really coincided with the main parts of the later Ecclesiastical Canon.... If it should even be proved that Basilides...and Valentinus himself regarded the Gospels only as authoritative yet the full idea of the Canon lies already in the fact of their making these the foundation and interpreting them allegorically ....But finally we must refer to the fact that it was the highest concern of the Gnostics to furnish the historical proof of the Apostolic origin of their doctrine by an exact reference to the links of the tradition....From this it further follows that **the Gnostics may have compiled their Canon**

*

solely according to the principle of Apostolic origin. (Emphasis added) <10>

The New Testament canon, scriptural interpretation, theology, apostolic tradition, etc., all were used by the Christian sectarians whom Irenaeus opposes decades before Irenaeus. We ask, "Whose Christianity is the oldest?" Yet the writers of Christian history for centuries have claimed that Irenaeus was defending a pure apostolic tradition against the intrusions of the so-called heretics, whereas, in fact, they and their theology preceded Irenaeus.

Let us now delineate the main dogmas of Irenaeus, which, with little variation, remain the Christian orthodox theology of today, and show what prior Christian-Gnostic doctrines Irenaeus' dogmas were designed to oppose.

The Doctrine of Deity

Irenaeus forcibly condemns the ancient universal doctrine of Emanations which was taught by most of the early Christian sects. Part of this doctrine was the understanding of the Higher and Lower Deity, i.e., God as Unmanifest and as Manifest. God was universally conceived by numerous sects and schools in the ancient world as a Supreme, Unknown, ineffable Father-Mother who unfolds from within a series of hierarchical Beings, the lowest of which are directly involved in the creation of the material cosmos. These Beings were known collectively as the Demiurge, or craftsman. In the Old Testament, as noted, they are known as Elohim, a plural noun meaning "Gods," and are the creator Deities and symbolize God as Creator. In later Apocalyptic Judaism, the revelations given to the patriarchs and prophets were believed to have originated from Angels or one of the Elohim.<11> Some of these hierarchical Beings had transgressed and had fallen to a lower estate where they remained hostile to mankind. However, they retained their creative abilities and later came to be associated with various planets over which they governed.<12>

These hierarchical angelic powers were thought to be both beneficent and hostile depending on whether they had fallen or not. According to the emanationist doctrine, then, the Supreme, ineffable Deity does not create the cosmos; creation is the work of the Creator Deity or Deities who emanated from the Supreme God.

Irenaeus, in his theology, and for the first time in history, decided to overturn this doctrine which, as we have seen, lay at the root of Zoroastrianism, esoteric Buddhism, Platonism, the Kabbalah, Apocalyptic Judaism, and early Christianity. He replaced it with the doctrine that the unmanifest, unknown Supreme God and the Creator are one and the same, and that there is no emanative principle in God, and no Hierarchy of Beings which proceeded forth from Him.<13> Irenaeus also argues against the existence of a spiritual universe (Pleroma or Fullness) in which subsisted the Aeons, arguing that this concept represents the Deity as a composite, i.e., finite and conditioned.<14> Irenaeus also fails to understand emanations as personifications of divine qualities, arguing that emanations make God a differentiated Being and not One.

However, it was taught by the Christian-Gnostics that although God is One, he can be multiplied or differentiated infinitely and still remain One, and that multiplication of Himself is the universe, both spiritually and physically. As $1 \times 1 \times 1 = 1$, so God x God x God always equals God. This is the very symbology of the fragmentation of the host in the communion ritual, undoubtedly lost on Irenaeus even as he participated.

Irenaeus argues that the Supreme God as envisioned by the Christian-Gnostics does not possess the ability to create, which is, he says, inconceivable.<15> But according to the Valentinians and those who preceded them, emanation from the Supreme God is creation, not out of nothing but out of the Root of Being—the same Supreme God. We do not demand that God sit down and construct a mouse to qualify as a creator. There is no less creation in this doctrine of emanation than in our modern concept of the evolution of the universe from the infinitely dense originating point of the "Big Bang" into multiple life-forms over time.

Irenaeus, therefore, concludes that the Demiurge or Creator God is the Supreme God, and that there is no God higher than the Demiurge—an opinion surely appreciated by the Demiurge. Moreover, he asserts that the Mosaic Law and the New Testament both were received from this one God, not through the "dispensation of Angels," as Stephen, the martyr, proclaims in Acts. In ancient Judaism, it was understood that the law and the prophets were given to mankind through intermediary beings, Archangelic powers, who, like transformers, stepped down the will of the Supreme Father. In one blow, Irenaeus overthrows the concepts of the Spiritual Hierarchy, the spiritual, psychic and material universes, in favor of a God who creates a physical cosmos out of nothing at a point in time for no apparent reason. The Christian-Gnostics, on the other hand, conceived the spiritual/material universe as emanating from the Depth and Silence of Infinite Be-ness according to the cyclic law of evolution. This concept is far more scientific than that conceived of by Irenaeus, who offers us a supernatural god who, one fine morning, decides to create a universe. This concept of Deity, unfortunately, has remained as the foremost idea of God in the West.

Irenaeus was likewise horrified over the notion, promulgated by various Christian sects, of an inferior, usurper or fallen deity who is hostile to mankind and to the Supreme God. We have noted that this teaching may have ultimately derived from the idea of Ahriman, the Evil Spirit, in the Persian Scriptures, who is depicted as creating a rival universe and an evil hierarchy to counteract the universe of Ahura Mazda, the Good God, and his spiritual hierarchy. In Zoroastrian theology, the universe is a battleground for the forces of Light and Darkness, and this teaching passed down into Apocalyptic and Gnostic Judaism and ended up as part of the Essene/Nazorean tradition. The earliest Christian sects and schools knew and taught these traditions, as we have seen, and the letters of St. Paul are witness to this knowledge of the "god of this aeon," as well as Jesus himself, who speaks of the "archon of this cosmos."

Although Irenaeus readily accepted the doctrine of the fallen angels or Watchers who corrupted the earth as described in Enoch and Jubilees, he and other Church Fathers who followed could not bring themselves to accept or face the possibility that a rival god or gods existed in the universe, and that this god or gods possessed the power to create. Therefore, he chose to denigrate and ridicule the concept of the usurper god, refusing to reveal what had been a vital doctrine of early Christianity.

The Doctrine of the Logos and Christ

Irenaeus argues that the Logos is Jesus Christ, who is both the Son of God and, in some mysterious way, God Himself. But Irenaeus' Christology remains ambiguous and incomplete. Harnack states:

Irenaeus expressly refused to investigate what the divine element in Christ is, and why another deity stands alongside the Godhead of the Father. He does not admit the distinction of a Word existing in God and one coming forth from him, and opposes not only the ideas of emanation in general, but also the opinion that the Logos issued forth at a definite point in time. Nor will Irenaeus allow the designation "Logos" to be interpreted in the sense of the Logos being the inward reason or the spoken Word of God. God is a simple essence and always remains in the same state. <16>

What we receive, therefore, in the theology of Irenaeus are mere husks. The whys and wherefores of his system of belief are not elucidated. Irenaeus was at a loss to explain the existence of the Logos because he had already rejected the doctrine of emanations, and the Logos is none other than an emanation of the Supreme God, as the Valentinians taught before him. The school of Valentinus taught that the earthly

Jesus was the vehicle for the Aeon Christ and that in Jesus was found "the Pleroma of the Godhead bodily," to quote St. Paul. That is, the Divine Emanations existing in the Pleroma were within Jesus, who was understood to be the fruit of the Pleroma. This is similar to the Eastern doctrine of the Avatara. Irenaeus summarily rejects this theology in favor of the concept that the Son/Logos/Christ who always existed with the Father descended to earth, was born of a virgin, died, was resurrected and ascended to heaven in order to redeem mankind. How this was accomplished, or why there existed a Son/Logos/Christ to begin with, is not explained. Who, then, is the Logos? Irenaeus does not answer satisfactorily, except to say that the function of Christ was to reveal the Father, to redeem mankind, and that the Son is the "hand" of God (a self-conscious hand?). Irenaeus also argues that Christ is "truly God and truly man," and was truly in the flesh, but does not explain how this occurred, except to assert that " the same person who created the world, was born, suffered and ascended."<17> Christ/Jesus is not only the redeemer but the Creator of the universe, as well as being the Son, who, incidentally, also appeared to the prophets in the Old Testament, including Moses, then at a future date decided to come to earth. The inconsistencies in which Irenaeus had involved himself, through this theology, are all too obvious. Once Irenaeus had determined to reject the doctrine of emanations, the Aeons, and the hierarchy of angelic powers, he had no recourse but to resort to a preposterous dogma— the creator of the universe was born in the body of a virgin, quantitatively! Note that Irenaeus does not explain the incarnation of the Logos/Christ as a fragment of divinity which, like a ray, descended to earth and appeared in or as a man, but that Gòd, whole and entire, descended to earth and appeared as the Son. If we examine this doctrine closely, we find that Irenaeus is, in fact, teaching that God cannot and does not multiply himself in and through man [as an e-man-ation] but in order to communicate with man, has to come to earth physically. Why? Because, says Irenaeus, man is created by God as a physical being and not a spiritual being. Man, therefore, has no intrinsic connection to God, no divine spark from the spiritual realms through which God can communicate. Man was created as a finite being and therefore separate from God. Man does not preexist with God, in Irenaeus' view.

In examining Irenaeus' doctrine we must draw the conclusion that he is, in actuality, denying that God individualizes or multiplies himself in and as his creation. In other words, he denies that the one God, whether manifesting as Father, Son, or Holy Spirit, is able to differentiate Himself in the creation and in man, ad infinitum, and still remain as One. Jesus, according to Irenaeus, was God, the creator and Redeemer who came to earth to save men, not a man who became God because he was of the same essence as God (as all men are) and thus became the Saviour of all men, by virtue of his becoming the chalice of Divinity or vehicle of Divinity. The underlying, ancient Christian doctrine, here explicitly discarded by Irenaeus, is that man originated in Spirit, by virtue of the divine spark or flame within him. This spark (so taught the sectarian Christians) the periodic Saviours of the world, from Krishna to Christ, are able to re-kindle in those in whom it had gone out.

The Doctrine of Salvation

According to Adolph Harnack, Irenaeus' views, with regard to the destination of man, his original state, the fall, and sin, etc., again led him into inconsistencies because of the "heterogeneous" nature of his theology.<18> He then adds, "But those very contradictions were never eliminated from the Church's doctrinal system of succeeding centuries and did not admit of being removed...."<19> We will follow Harnack's review of Irenaeus' system.

To begin with, Irenaeus argues that everything created is imperfect, [corruptible] from the very fact of its having had a beginning. Man is included in this original imperfection since he also had a beginning.<20> God was capable of bestowing perfection on man from the beginning, but man was unable to retain it. For Irenaeus, perfection or incorruptibility consists in the contemplation of God and is conditioned on man's voluntary obedience. Perfection, in Irenaeus' system, was never an original state with man but could only be the future destiny of man. Goodness, therefore, is not inherent in man.

According to this system, Irenaeus would be forced to admit that God created imperfectly and therefore was Himself imperfect. He, of course, does not admit this, so he never adequately solved the problem of corruption in the cosmos. We recall that the Christian-Gnostics solved the same problem of corruptibility in the universe by their teaching on: (1) the precosmic fall of Sophia [the soul]; (2) the original perfection of man as the Divine Archetype who preexisted the material cosmos and who emanated from the Pleroma by the will of the Father; (3) the intrusions of rebellious powers (archons) and a usurper deity who were instrumental in the creation of mortal or bodily man, and/or the creation of the dense material universe by a demiurgic power as a consequence of Sophia's Fall; (4) the infusing of a Divine Spark by Sophia (in her aspect as the Divine Mother) in corruptible man, which made him, in essence, superior to the inferior, fallen demiurgic powers and intrinsically divine, therefore akin to the Supreme Father.

According to Irenaeus, however, man had no spiritual preexistence. God created Adam and Eve as perfect mortal beings, possessed of both soul and body in the beginning. Man, therefore, was originally a bodily creature and not a spiritual creature, whereas the Christian-Gnostics taught that man was bound in a body as the result of a fall in consciousness and through the work of the malevolent archons, who sought to limit man's spiritual faculties through the body. Irenaeus' "God" chains man to a body from the moment of creation for no apparent reason. Men, therefore, have no inherent divine essence and their future immortality can only be achieved by obedience to God, not by virtue of their intrinsic worth. Irenaeus will admit of no fall into matter by one of the divine emanations or by the souls of men, as in the Sophia myth. Irenaeus argues that man became imperfect almost immediately after the creation by disobeying God, hence he never really possessed a kinship with God. After the fall in Eden, man became subject to decay and death, and moreover, this death was transmitted to Adam's whole posterity. All men who have been born since Adam have, therefore, been born subject to death. Since in Irenaeus' theology there is no spiritual pre-existence and no reincarnation, man has no choice but to inherit Adam's state of corruption. In other words, all mankind born after Adam inherit the taint of sin and mortality through no fault of their own. We find here the earliest traces of the dogma of original sin, later taught by Tertullian and Augustine.

What does this theological system tell us about the "God" of Irenaeus? We can conclude that Irenaeus' God is both unjust, tyrannical and lacking in foresight. He condemns the entire race of humanity to death through no fault of their own. Unwittingly, Irenaeus has transformed his beneficent Creator-God into a malevolent demiurge, although he repeatedly asserts that God is "good."

Irenaeus justifies the actions of his "God" by affirming that man's disobedience in Eden was conducive to his development. <21> By the fall, man learned how to freely choose to obey God's commands. Further, through the fall, man was obliged to learn that "goodness and life do not belong to him by nature as they do to God."<22> The fall was intended by God "as a means of leading men to attain to the perfection to which they were destined."<23> We need not go any further to perceive the startling implications of this doctrine: God willed the fall and purposely created man as a bodily creature, hence subject to failure. It was further sufficient for this God that one pair and one pair alone fell—and that's it—his plan has the excuse to be set in motion. Every man who was henceforth born on this earth is, in essence, estranged from God and doomed to death. The ramifications of this dogma, as it penetrated the collective psyche of humanity through the centuries, certainly had to have been profoundly disturbing and deeply widespread. It could well account for the emergence of the "dark ages," (spiritually and historically) wherein man saw himself as a lowly, subservient creature dependent on the whims of an awful, tyrannical Deity and His long-suffering Son, who were both proclaimed as Good and Merciful—and who were approached only through their Middleman, the church of—you guessed it—Irenaeus.

In order to save man from this degrading situation, Jesus Christ descended to earth as "true God and true man." Christ was the first and only man to realize in his person the destiny of humanity: the Spirit of God became united with his soul and accustomed itself to dwell in men.<24> Jesus Christ undid the sin and fall of Adam through his life, death and resurrection. How did Christ save man? By calling upon man to freely obey God's commandments whereby man can be rendered capable of receiving incorruptibility. <25> Spirituality, in Irenaeus' view, is only a matter of obeying regulations and commandments. There is no Gnosis, no divine spark to be released within man—no self-knowledge as knowledge of God. How, then, does man realize in himself God's image? Irenaeus answers that "Jesus Christ is the realization of our possession of God's image."<26> In other words, man can only realize God by beholding Jesus Christ, his life, death and resurrection, and not through himself. Man is intrinsically incapable of living the life that Christ lived. By accepting Christ's redemption dispensed through Irenaeus' church and theology, the believer is united to Christ and his church, reconciled to God and saved. Irenaeus, therefore, argued that man is, in fact, deified through Christ only in a future state of resurrection on the last day, when his body would rise from the grave and be reunited with his soul. A chasm, therefore, separates man from Christ, in Irenaeus' view. Salvation lies outside of man, not within him. And the gospel was mistranslated—the Kingdom of Heaven is not within you.

In this theology, with its resultant emphasis on simple observance of regulations and the simple acceptance of the fact of Christ, we see now why the pattern of the Church has always been this: a mass of "laity" content to observe the prescribed Sundays, holydays and rules of the Church; another mass of "laity" discontent and inwardly rebellious without knowing why; and the third case, the saint, the individual seeking real knowledge, the direct experience of God, who has always been the exception. The saints have arisen in spite of the Church and its theology, which is in reality antagonistic to the idea of the saint. In fact, within the Church the saint, the mystic and mysticism appear as and are felt as uncomfortable anomalies, seldom discussed, almost disturbing events to the Church, a phenomenon not truly necessary given its fundamental mechanistic spiritual methodology of simply following rules, and therefore, in fact, ambiguous, and sometimes just plain dangerous.

In the theology of Irenaeus as presented here, we have what essentially became the theology of Christendom over the following centuries. It was further developed by Tertullian, Cyprian and Augustine, with disastrous consequences for the Christian believer, as we shall see.

Irenaeus Fabricates His Own Apostolic Succession

In *Against Heresies*, Irenaeus seeks to convince his readers that his theology represents the identical teaching of the apostles Peter and Paul which had been handed down uncontaminated and preserved in its purest state by the Church of Rome. Nothing, of course, could be farther from the truth. This original "theology," of course, was known and explicated by none other than Irenaeus. Quoting Irenaeus:

Because of its great antiquity, it is with this Church [at Rome], in which tradition from the apostles has always been preserved by the faithful everywhere, that every church, consisting of the faithful who are from everywhere, must conform....For it is necessary that every church should agree with this church, on account to its pre-eminent authority. <27>

Great antiquity? Surely a self-serving exaggeration. You would think he's writing in 1180 here, not 180 A.D. We're talking barely the distance of the American Civil War from today. Is this just a cover for his hidden agenda? And what of the "great antiquity" of the Christian community in Glastonbury, England, founded in A.D. 36 by Joseph of Arimathea? In any case, we hope it has been sufficiently shown that the earliest Christianity, even in Rome, was diverse, heterogeneous, and contained doctrines that most, if not all, Christians today would consider "heretical."

Irenaeus bases his theology and his supposed apostolic succession on written documents: the Old Testament and the four gospels, which he claims are the only authentic gospels. How does Irenaeus arrive at the number four? There are four winds, four ends of the earth, he says, so there must be only four gospels. No one today takes Irenaeus seriously, especially in view of the extensive collection of "other gospels" found at Nag Hammadi in Egypt, bearing the names of various apostles, which, if not written by these apostles, may have been transmitted through them, or may represent authentic teaching deriving from circles surrounding them. To list a few:

The Apocryphon of John
The Gospel of Thomas
The Gospel of Phillip
The Book of Thomas the Contender
The Apocalypse of Paul
The First Apocalypse of James
The Acts of Peter and the Twelve Apostles
Apocalypse of Peter
Letter of Peter to Phillip
The Gospel of Mary
The Acts of Peter.

This is in addition to the list of "lost" works noted in Chapter I.

Ironically, all these texts were produced by authentic Christians (if not by the apostles themselves) who affirmed the apostolic origin of these decidedly "gnostic" doctrines. In *The*

Gnostic Dialogue, Pheme Perkins writes that at least half of the dialogue-type texts discovered at Nag Hammadi "appeal to a common apostolic tradition. Therefore, one must conclude that the Gnostic position on apostolic tradition is much closer to the general second-century view than is sometimes admitted." <28>

Nevertheless, the apostolic tradition itself was not stable, based as it was upon diversified oral traditions. Throughout the second century various Christian communities were moving in the direction of seeking a textual or written form of apostolic tradition. Marcion, we noted, was the first Christian teacher to develop a New Testament canon consisting of one gospel which he knew to be authentic and the Pauline Epistles, while the earliest exegeses of St. Paul's letters were from Christian-Gnostics. Irenaeus desperately needed a uniform body of teaching in a written form to combat other Christians. Perkins remarks that Irenaeus:

...seems to have been the first to realize the potential of such a canon as a way of embodying and stabilizing the tradition....After all, the Gnostics considered the same sayings and Pauline letters to be authoritative, as did orthodox Christians. Irenaeus responds to Gnostic claims that the apostolic tradition itself is Gnostic by inventing a counter-genealogy for Gnosticism and by treating the Gospels and Acts as an authoritative historical record of the actions and preaching of the Apostles. <29>

According to Helmut Koester, the New Testament canon as we know it "was essentially created by Irenaeus."<30> Naturally, texts which were being circulated in communities and schools opposed to Irenaeus' brand of orthodox Christianity would not have been included . For nearly 2,000 years, the vast body of Christians worldwide have been deprived of these texts, which represent a large percentage of ancient Christian thought virtually ignored for centuries, some desperately buried in an earthen jar near Nag Hammadi to escape the wholesale destruction of texts that was to come—released by this doctrine and this truth-despising attitude of Irenaeus.

Christian-Gnostic schools and communities, however, did not accept any written text as binding and authoritative, yet innumerable and diverse texts circulated among them. What then was the Christian-Gnostic attitude toward written authoritative tradition? Perkins remarks:

These Gnostic writings reflect the liturgy, teaching, preaching and polemic of their respective communities. But they never claim to do more than to embody true tradition. They never claim to be the textually authoritative source of reflection, authority or even contact with the divine. The revelation about which they speak may put an individual in touch with the truth about God, about cosmos, about himself or herself, or about salvation, but that truth is not definitively embodied in any inspired text. Gnostic interpretation is still the hermeneutic [interpretation] of an oral tradition. It does not provide the formalized interpretation of a text that would sponsor a systematized and rational account of Christian theology such as that proposed by Irenaeus....<31>

We are again at the root of another aspect of orthodoxy rampant in the Christian world today, and that is the notion that all revealed truth, whole and entire, is to be found in a written text (namely, the Bible), is embodied in that text, and further, that there is only one true interpretation of the same text.

This notion Irenaeus successfully popularized because the Christian-Gnostic schools did not counterattack with an authoritative canon of their own, for, to them, revelation was progressive and ongoing and could not be limited to a few scriptures, and also because they were in contact with an esoteric tradition, apparently not handed down among the circles in which Irenaeus moved. This is made clear by Pheme Perkins in her discussion of the Christian-Gnostic text known as the Apocryphon of James, which, she writes, is "very much concerned with written transmission," as is Irenaeus.<32> This text, she points out, contradicts Irenaeus' picture of an authoritative, public, uniform written tradition handed down from apostolic times. She discusses the Apocryphon of James as follows:

> *Its opening scene may well be a Gnostic version of the creation of that very canon to which the orthodox are beginning to appeal. The disciples are sitting around and individually recording what the Saviour has said to the group as a whole and to each one privately....Thus there is no unified, completely public apostolic tradition such as Irenaeus claims. Each account is a mixture of the public and private teaching of Jesus. Irenaeus had also claimed that the apostles transmitted their teaching to all simply and ungrudgingly (Adv. Haer 111, 14, 12). The concluding interaction between James and the apostles contradicts this picture. At first, the apostles accept the revelation given to James and Peter. That acceptance might be said to authenticate the "apostolic" claims of the gnosis. But then they all, including Peter, refuse to wait in Jerusalem, to enlighten the Gnostic race for whom the teaching was intended. James is forced to send them away because of their resentment. Thus,* **an imperfect and impartial revelation came to be spread abroad as apostolic tradition** *(DB 1 16, 3-11). Apocry Jas has given narrative authority to the picture of the New Testament which underlies Irenaeus' list of objections. Its* **narrative shows that New Testament writings are individual, mixed with error, not authoritative and out of touch with the tradition which the Saviour wished to be passed on to all his beloved followers.** *(Emphasis added)* <33>

Irenaeus, naturally, refuses to accept the existence of an esoteric tradition, yet we know that this tradition did exist, as is witnessed by statements made by Clement of Alexandria, a contemporary of Irenaeus, and representative of the orthodox school in Alexandria. Clement, we recall, admits the existence of a secret gospel of Mark and writes of initiation into the Christian mysteries. He declares that the "Gnostic" is a spiritually mature Christian who had received this higher knowledge. Yet Clement also relies on the apostolic doctrine which is in many ways remarkably different from that of Irenaeus.

We may ask, what apostolic tradition is Irenaeus familiar with? According to the above text it is the "imperfect and partial revelation" that eventually became the public and apostolic doctrine. We are of the opinion, however, that even this partial doctrine was misrepresented by Irenaeus who, it is likely, fabricated his own pseudo-apostolic doctrine to combat the schools of Christian-Gnosis and declared it to be authentic.

Prior to and during the lifetime of Irenaeus, the oral traditions of the various communities and schools had a greater claim to authority than the written tradition. This is attested to by Papias, bishop of Hieropolis in Asia Minor, who flourished in the first decades of the second century. Papias made it his life's work to collect the oral traditions from the elders and those who accompanied the original apostles. Papias, apparently, did not put much credence into written traditions. He says, "If ever any man came who had been a follower of the elders, I would inquire about the sayings of the elders. For I did not consider I got so much profit from the contents of books as from the utterances of a living and abiding voice."<34> Yet Irenaeus' sole proof for the authenticity of his apostolic tradition is the four written Gospels, which were at that time not universally received in the churches.

Papias wrote five books called *An Exposition of the Oracles of the Lord,* according to fourth century church historian Eusebius, who cited Irenaeus for this information.<35> Naturally, this book has been lost, for it apparently contained sayings, traditions and stories unlike anything found in the New Testament. Eusebius records that Papias had set down unwritten traditions and "some strange parables and instructions of the Saviour, and some other things of a fabulous nature."<36> What these traditions were we can only guess, but they must have bordered on "heresy" if Papias' books are now lost. They certainly were not included in

Irenaeus' "apostolic tradition."

Concerning the written gospels, Papias asserts that Matthew put together the "oracles of the Lord in the Hebrew language, and each one interpreted them as best he could."<37> Of course, there is no extant Hebrew or Aramaic gospel of Matthew, we posses only the Greek canonical Matthew. What became of the original Hebrew/Aramaic Matthew? Papias' statement leads one to conclude that the "oracles" (revelations) of the Lord were arcane or hidden, since he states that the Lord's sayings needed to be "interpreted." Papias also cites a story of a woman accused of many sins before the Lord, "which was to be found in the Gospel of the Hebrews."<38> It is well known that the "Gospel of the Hebrews" was later declared heretical and by no means canonical. According to historian Paul Johnson, in Papias' day knowledge of the authorship of the canonical gospels and the manner in which they were composed is "confused."<39> "At this stage," he writes, "the oral tradition was still preferable to the written one."<40>

How reliable then are our canonical gospels? While they do contain much regarding the life and sayings of Jesus, there is also a great deal of information which has obviously been eliminated for, no doubt, doctrinal reasons. Some of these traditions surfaced in the Christian-Gnostic texts and in oral tradition.

Commenting on the gospels, Johnson remarks, "All the documents [earliest Christian sources/gospels] have a long pre-history before they reached written form...their evaluation was a source of acute puzzlement to thoughtful Christians even in the earliest decades of the second century and probably before." <41> Johnson writes that oral accounts continued to circulate long after the earliest written gospels appeared in 60-80 A.D. The gospels, he adds, were still attaining written form well into the second century.<42> "They [the canonical documents] are products of the early church and they are tainted in the sense that they reflect ecclesiastical controversy as well as evangelistic motivation...."<43> Johnson writes that the origins of the canonical gospels are "complex" and their reliability "variable."<44> Mark's gospel, he adds, "was much altered and interpolated during the earliest period," and in the Book of Acts, "the evangelical speeches he [Luke] produces are to some extent reconstructions, inspired by appropriate passages in the Septuagint...." <45>

Helmut Koester writes that the oldest copies of the New Testament documents (that are now extant) were made circa 200 C.E., except for a fragment of John's gospel written in the first half of the second century. <46> He says:

We also find deliberate corrections of NT texts. After these writings obtained canonical recognition, such corrections were often made on the basis of a comparison with other manuscripts....Parallel texts of the gospels were often assimilated to each other....Dogmatic motifs also caused corrections....Finally, there are a number of additions to the original text." <47>

Most scholars agree that our present gospels were based on prior literary sources, of which the gospels were compilations. Koester remarks that the gospels rely on "sayings books" and "collections of miracle stories" as sources. To these may be added a collection of "apocalyptic sayings" and "a written form of the Passion narrative."<48> When or by whom these "sources" were woven into our canonical gospels is unknown. Most scholars today do not accept that the present four gospels are actually the work, verbatim, of the four evangelists. And yet, ironically, an entire religion is based upon these documents, which are considered absolutely authoritative by most Christians today. Numerous rival gospels circulated by the middle of the second century, all of them reputed to be memoirs of apostles or their associates. Which of these "gospels" were authentic, or were they all, to some extent, authentic? According to Irenaeus, only four (in honor of the four corners of the flat earth) were authentic. This is, of course, absurd.

In *Against Heresies*, Irenaeus takes great pains to authenticate the canonical documents as the sole source of authority for the Christian teachings. But, to quote Paul Johnson, what Irenaeus says about the authorship and emergence of the canonical writing "is, in part, manifest nonsense," and adds that Irenaeus "knew no more about the origins of the gospels than we do; rather less, in fact." <49>

And so we are left with John's statement:

And there are also many other things that Jesus did, which if they were written down one by one, I suppose that even the world itself could not contain the books that could be written. Amen. (John 21: 25)

Four is such a curious number.

The Myth of the Orthodox Apostolic Succession

Irenaeus seeks to authenticate his brand of orthodox Christianity, as we have said, by appealing to an unbroken apostolic succession—from apostles to bishops. But where did Irenaeus and those who preceded him, such as Ignatius of Antioch, derive this idea of anointed successors? Johnson believes that the idea of a consecration of a successor *"was first developed by the gnostics who listed teachers, and their teachers, going back to Jesus and transmitting sacred knowledge....During the second century this gnostic device was adopted by orthodox Christianity. Indeed, to some extent it was systematized, about 180, by an orthodox writer from the East, Hegesippus."* <50>

Ironically, the "apostolic succession"—the fountainhead of orthodoxy—may very well turn out to be "gnostic"! The succession list in Figure 2 used by the Christian-Gnostics serves to illustrate

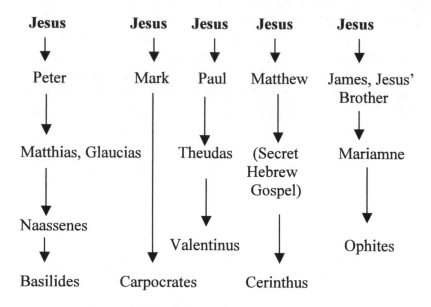

Figure 2. The Schemas of Gnostic Succession

Ignatius of Antioch, Hegesippus and Irenaeus had a ready-made formula at their disposal—the succession lists of Christian-Gnostics—with which to fabricate the so-called monarchial episcopate. We have seen that Clement of Rome and Ignatius of Antioch were among the earliest bishops to establish the idea of the monarchial episcopate in order to bestow authority upon the particular brand of Christianity they were encouraging among the faithful. But as we have previously shown, many communities and churches did not accept such an all-powerful episcopate.

We turn then to Hegesippus. Paul Johnson states:

His [Hegesippus'] writings are lost, but according to Eusebius [fourth-century bishop and church historian] he travelled round collecting evidence about the succession in various Churches and he wrote a huge tome in which he presented the undistorted tradition of the apostolic preaching in simplest form....He thus linked the 'correct' tradition and *succession with order and unanimity. Early teachers were identified and then transformed into a series of monarchial bishops. There was no conscious falsification, since by the second half of the second century it was assumed there had always been such bishops; all that was necessary was to prod peoples' memories to get the details, then the list could be tidied up. Hence the longer and more impressive the list, the later is the date of compilation and the less its accuracy. Eusebius, however, presents the lists as evidence that orthodoxy had a continuous tradition from the earliest times in all the great episcopal sees and that all heretical movements were subsequent aberrations from the mainline of Christianity. (Brackets added) <51>*

Johnson's analysis of the establishment of succession lists is particularly illuminating. Hegesippus, of course, was attempting to promote the orthodox party line as against the esoteric, gnostic heterogeneous tradition, which was, as we have seen, more valid than the strictly orthodox. The lists had to be gathered to prove a uniform tradition in the fierce battle against the Christian schools and communities of Gnosis. We see in the above passage that Hegesippus, according to Johnson, identified "teachers" and then transformed them into bishops, based on the assumption that there were always bishops. This state of affairs was certainly not the case. We know that Eusebius was a front for Constantine's totalitarian state religion, and, as is well known, the all-consuming desire of the Emperor was to establish a uniform body of doctrine which could be authenticated as a solid replacement for the old Roman State religion. But the movement toward apostolic orthodox tradition began with Irenaeus.

Archibald Robertson, in *The Origins of Christianity*, further illumines this period of Christian history, as follows:

...From the end of the first century the democratic organization of the primitive churches depicted in the Teaching of the Twelve Apostles gradually gave place to government

*by irremovable elders or "bishops" claiming to derive their office by succession from the first apostles. By the middle of the second century the necessity of presenting a united front to disrupters of one kind or another, as well as to the imperial government was leading to a further step in centralization. Of the committee of elders who ran each particular church, one was coming to be regarded as the bishop, par excellence, with unlimited power to discipline and in the last resort to expel undesirable or insubordinate members. The new episcopate, like the older presbytery, claimed apostolic authority, **though the New Testament may be searched in vain for evidence of its existence.** (Emphasis added) <52>*

We have clearly seen these developments in our review of the writings of Clement of Rome and Ignatius of Antioch. According to Robertson, a committee gave place to a single bishop. How and why we are not told, but it is safe to assume that centralization of authority with its inevitable concentration of power is the root cause and motive. The churches, then, moved from democratic to totalitarian rule.

Robertson continues, writing of Hegesippus:

*The **myth** of primitive episcopacy was further bolstered by the industry of Hegesippus, a converted Jew who came to Rome about 160 and **with slender historical warrant** compiled lists of supposed bishops from apostolic times to his own day. (Emphasis added) <53>*

Robertson further on adds that Irenaeus was the first writer to single out the church of Rome as a model to which all churches and the faithful should conform. <54> Why Rome? Because, says Irenaeus, the church at Rome was founded by the apostles Peter and Paul, who likewise taught the same orthodox tradition that Irenacus is teaching. However, as scholars are well aware, Peter and Paul did not agree with one another as to the nature of Christianity. Their doctrines differed in many essentials, and each apostle preached a separate school of doctrine, particularly, as we have seen, on the role of Mosaic law. Irenaeus may have chosen Rome as the model of "original" Christianity because he already knew that both Marcion and Valentinus had clashed with the church authorities in Rome between 140 and 160 A.D. The bishop of Rome at that time may have been sympathetic to the cause of the new orthodox movement, bolstered by Irenaeus. Robertson states that Irenaeus "forsakes history to follow the romance of Hegesippus" in devising his orthodox succession lists originating in Rome.<55> Robertson later remarks that Irenaeus' story, that Peter and Paul founded the church at Rome, is "irreconcilable with either the Pauline Epistles or the Acts of the Apostles." <56>

Why does Irenaeus choose to follow the historic "romance" of Hegesippus? It seems as though Irenaeus and Hegesippus were of like mind—they both detested the Christian-Gnostics, their esoteric tradition and their apostolic succession of teachers. Hegesippus wrote five books opposing the teachings of the ancient Christians whom he terms "gnostics," according to Eusebius in his *Ecclesiastical History*. Hegesippus traced these "gnostic" teachings back to an alleged Jewish ancestry of Jesus' time via certain groups of Jewish Christians. But, as we have observed, so called "Jewish" Christianity of the Nazorean-Ebionite variety was one of the most ancient and, perhaps, authentic forms of Christianity in Palestine, which asserted that Jesus was a man imbued with the Christ Spirit. This idea would naturally clash with the theology Irenaeus was attempting to promote: Jesus as preexistent God from all eternity who later descended to earth. No doubt Irenaeus considered that a Jesus who was God eternally would be a much more effective focal point for a centralized church authority to revolve around than a man who merely became God-like, as the Jewish Christians taught.

Irenaeus had chosen the church at Rome as the model of his Christian orthodoxy. But what of the other churches in Egypt and Syria who may have had traditions just as old as or older than the traditions of the church at Rome? What was the nature of the Christianity these churches taught? Did these churches maintain a universal, orthodox tradition?

To shed some light on these questions, we turn again to Paul Johnson's revealing *History of Christianity*:

> *Looking behind the lists [of bishops in various cities as compiled by Hegesippus, then Eusebius] however, a different picture emerges. In Edessa, on the edge of the Syrian desert, **the proofs of the early establishment of Christianity were forgeries,** almost certainly manufactured under Bishop Kune, the first orthodox bishop, and actually a contemporary of Eusebius [fourth century]. Christianity seems to have been brought to that area by **Marcionites**, about 150, and later flourished in various non-orthodox forms, including Manichean [third century]. **Different texts of the N.T. varying in important essentials, were in use. Thus orthodoxy did not arrive until the last decades of the third century.** (Emphasis added, brackets added) <57>*

So much for Hegesippus' "undistorted apostolic tradition" from earliest times, upon which Irenaeus based his Christianity and upon which our present Christianity is based. Johnson continues:

> *Equally, the first Christian groups in Egypt were heterodox by later standards. They came into existence about the beginning of the first century and were Christian-Gnostics. There, put in writing about this time, was the 'gospel of the Egyptians,' in Coptic, later declared heretical. Very recent discoveries in the Upper Nile Valley suggest that gnosticism was also the dominant form of Christianity in Upper Egypt at this time. And in Alexandria in lower Egypt there was a Jewish-Christian community using the 'gospel of the Hebrews,' also later declared heretical. <58>*

Considering the nature of Christianity in Egypt, we may well ask, who brought Christianity into Egypt? According to

Dr. William Stewart McBirnie, author of *The Search for The Twelve Apostles*, at least three of Jesus' original apostles were responsible for bringing Christianity to Egypt: Bartholomew, Matthew, and Simon the Zealot. <59> We conclude then that these three apostles must have taught a form of what was later designated Christian Gnosis, not orthodox Christianity. If the earliest Christians in Egypt used the "Gospel of the Egyptians" and "The Gospel of the Hebrews," their Christianity was decidedly not orthodox. Yet Irenaeus seeks to prove the orthodox nature of Christianity (along with Hegesippus) in all the churches.

To digress slightly for a moment, let us briefly look at the content of the Gospel of the Egyptians which was discovered at Nag Hammadi. Scholar Stephan Hoeller describes the "gospel" as follows:

This scripture distinguishes itself from many other treatises of its kind by the fact that it is not only a mythical or cosmological narrative but also a liturgical text or initiatory liturgy, which undoubtedly was intended to serve as a ritual of admission into some profound mystery of Gnosis. It is divided into three parts: (1) a description of the incorruptible realm of the high Fullness; (2) an account of the mythic history of Gnostic humanity, as personified by Seth and his descendants; and (3) an initiation text, which may merit being called a document of ecstasy because it appears to be based on the experience of ecstatic initiation undergone by a Gnostic visionary. <60>

There is no proof, of course, that the "Gospel of the Egyptians" discovered at Nag Hammadi is the same gospel used by these early Christians. Nevertheless, it points to the fact that the earliest Christianity in Egypt seems not to have been orthodox. On the contrary, the early Christians in Egypt might well be termed Sethians, who, from all reports, were an exceedingly mystical sect. We are reminded that the Sethians believed Jesus to be the reincarnation of Seth, the great patriarch of ancient times. They thus taught the doctrine of reincarnation.

The apostle Matthew is also mentioned by McBirnie as bringing Christianity to Egypt, and according to Johnson, the Christians there used "the gospel of the Hebrews." We recall that Eusebius and Jerome admit that the Hebrew gospel, later declared heretical, was the authentic gospel of Matthew, which, according to Papias, needed to be interpreted. So much for the "orthodoxy" of early Christianity in Egypt.

In Edessa, on the border of Syria, orthodox Christianity was not established until the third century, as Johnson states. We recall that Judas Thomas, Jesus' alleged "twin," travelled to and taught in Edessa and was acquainted with the king, Agbar. According to Holger Kersten, Jesus himself had journeyed to Edessa after the resurrection. The accounts of Thomas' work in Edessa are preserved in The Acts of Thomas, later declared heretical. The apostle Thomas is also connected with two other decidedly unorthodox gospels: The Gospel of Thomas and The Book of Thomas the Contender. So much for the "orthodoxy" of early Christianity in Syria.

We turn now to the city of Antioch in Syria, one of the oldest centers of Christianity, and to other localities, in our search for an orthodox apostolic succession:

*Even in Antioch, where both Peter and Paul had been active, there seems to have been confusion until the end of the second century. Antioch harbored a multitude of esoteric religious cults....Some early Christians there seem to have used an heretical text, called the "gospel of Peter." **The apostolic succession may have been lost completely.** (Emphasis added) <61>*

According to H.P. Blavatsky, Peter represented a school which she terms "the Christian Kabalists of the Jewish Tanaim school," opposed to St.Paul, who represented "the Christian Kabbalists of the Platonic Gnosis."<62> Both, however, taught an esoteric Christianity in many ways remote from today's

Christian orthodoxy.

The lost Gospel of Peter used by Christians in Antioch is mentioned by Serapion, bishop of Antioch in 190 A.D. Origen, likewise, mentioned this gospel in his writings in about 253 A.D. Justin Martyr writing circa 150 A.D., refers to the "memoirs of Peter"—very likely the lost gospel. In the small fragment that remains, in which the crucifixion and resurrection scenes are described, we note twenty-nine variations of fact between the Gospel of Peter and the four canonical gospels. These are listed by the editor of *The Lost Books of the Bible*:

1. Herod was the one who gave the order for the execution [instead of Pilate].

2. Joseph [of Arimathea] was a friend of Pilate.

3. In the darkness [after the crucifixion] many went about with lamps and fell down.

4. Our Lord's cry of "my power, my power, and etc." [instead of "my God, my God," why hast thou forsaken me]

5. The account of how the disciples had to hide because they were searched for as malefactors anxious to burn the temple.

6. The name of the centurion who kept watch at the tomb was Petronius.

The above work also quotes a learned theologian, Rev. W.H. Stanton, to the effect that the Gospel of Peter "once held a place of honor, comparable to that assigned the Four Gospels, perhaps even higher than some of them...." <63>

There is no doubt that Irenaeus knew that the Gospel of Peter was used by Christians in Antioch, yet he and other Church Fathers after him refused to acknowledge it as canonical. No less an authority than Helmut Koester writes:

In a number of instances The Gospel of Peter contains features that can be traced back to a stage in the development of the passion narrative and the story of the empty tomb which is older than that known by the canonical gospels....Its basis must be an older text under the authority of Peter which was independent of the canonical gospels. <64>

Koester also remarks that in a number of places it appears that the author of canonical Matthew has altered information found in a more reliable, natural form in the Gospel of Peter. <65>

Peter, it will be remembered, has often been identified with an Ebionite-Nazorean-Essene type of Christianity. *The Clementine Homilies*, circa 300 A.D., purports to represent the school and teaching of Peter. In this text, Peter is depicted as vying with "Simon Magus," alias Paul, the Apostle. Nevertheless, we gain some insight into the Christology which may have been taught by Peter. Martin Larson, discussing the *Homilies*, states that Jesus, according to the preaching of Peter, was considered to be a Teacher and Prophet and not a God. He was considered a Son of God only in the same sense that we all are. Encapsulating the theology of the *Homilies*, Larson writes, "Christ, then, was a divine power which dwelt in Jesus from the time of his baptism until his death; and differs only in degree from the spirit which is in all of us." <66>

Could this have been the teaching of Peter? If so, we can see why this theology was suppressed in favor of the doctrines of Irenaeus and Tertullian: the concept of Jesus as "God of very God."

We return now to Johnson's remarks on the orthodox apostolic succession lists:

When Eusebius' chief source for his episcopal lists, Julius Africanus, tried to compile one for Antioch, he found only six names to cover the same spell of time as twelve in Rome and ten in Alexandria. Orthodoxy in Antioch really dates *from the episcopate of Ignatius in the late second century who had to free himself as well as his diocese from the local gnostic tradition and who imported orthodox clergy from elsewhere to help the process. We have evidence that the same sort of process was repeated in Western Asia Minor, in Thessalonica, and in Crete. Indeed, wherever evidence exists, it indicates that the process of achieving uniformity, thereby making orthodoxy meaningful, began only towards the end of the second century, and was far from complete by the end of the third. <67>*

It appears from the above remarks that the entire orthodox apostolic succession is, in the main, a fabrication. And, interestingly enough, the process began during the episcopate of Irenaeus, who was the cornerstone of orthodoxy, both theologically and politically.

The apparent fabrication of succession lists spread even to Alexandria. Johnson states:

Orthodoxy [in Alexandria] was not established until the time of Bishop Demetrius, 189-231, who set up a number of other sees and manufactured a genealogical tree for his own Bishopric of Alexandria, which traces the foundation through ten mythical predecessors back to Mark and so to Peter and Jesus. Orthodoxy was merely one of several forms of Christianity during the third century, and may not have become dominant until Eusebius' time. (Brackets added) <68>

If Johnson's analysis of the process by which the "apostolic tradition" was established is correct, then Christian orthodoxy stands to lose any credibility. The sources above quoted are in agreement that wherever one turns, the earliest type of Christianity was "gnostic" in content, not orthodox.

Turning to the church of Rome, Harnack points out that the "theory" that the office of the bishop confers on them the apostolic heritage of truth,

"...must have been current in the Roman church before the time when Irenaeus wrote; for the list of Roman bishops, which we find in Irenaeus and which he obtained from Rome, must itself be considered as a result of that dogmatic theory. **The first half of the list must have been concocted,** *as there were no monarchial bishops in the strict sense in the first century....* " (Emphasis added) <69>

Yet Irenaeus claims an unbroken tradition handed down from bishop to bishop back to Peter and Paul. Furthermore, Irenaeus claims that the only authority for Christianity is to be found in the tradition of Rome and its bishops, for "outside the church, there is no salvation." We trust we have sufficiently proven that Christianity at Rome was likewise diverse, as it was throughout the churches of the Roman Empire. We recall that Harnack stated that the earliest Christology in Rome was later termed Adoptionism, which taught that Jesus became the Christ fully at his baptism, and had been designated a heresy. So much for the "pure orthodoxy" of the church at Rome.

We close this section on Irenaeus by reiterating the one premise which is at the root of Irenaeus' orthodox system: the individual Christian cannot trust his own testimony as to the nature of Christianity or the nature of Christ. Only the apostles' testimony can be trusted in written, accepted, canonical texts. Religion, to Irenaeus, is not a matter of an individual's personal communion with God or Christ; it is a matter of an individual's accepting someone else's (namely, the apostles') testimony of truth and believing it. This, to Irenaeus, is the church—the worldwide union of believers in a written tradition delivered through the bishops. Such is the nature of mainline orthodox Christianity today.

We may well ask, "Who, then, possesses the authority in the church?" This question is answered succinctly, writes Pagels, by Valentinus and his followers: Whoever comes into direct, personal contact with the "living One."<70> The Valentinian and other esoteric Christian sects were not about to surrender their personal union with God in favor of an outer federation and its written traditions. Nevertheless, the power and the force of orthodoxy as it spread throughout the Roman world could not be withstood by the various Christian-Gnostic schools and communities, although they made a valiant effort.

However, by the year 200, as Pagels declares, "The battle lines had been drawn: both orthodox and gnostic Christians claimed to represent the true church and accused one another of being outsiders, false brethren, and hypocrites."<71> Pagels remarks that orthodox Christians in the late second century established "objective criteria" for church membership. She writes:

Whoever confessed the creed, accepted the ritual of baptism, participated in worship, and obeyed the clergy was accepted as a fellow Christian. Seeking to unify the diverse churches scattered throughout the world into a single network, the bishops eliminated qualitative criteria for church membership. <72>

The various Christian-Gnostics and their leaders would not surrender their freedom and their right to pursue their spiritual search—their quest for the ultimate truth. They would not obey a clergy whom they considered to be inferior in their depth of understanding of the mysteries of Christianity. The Christian-Gnostic sects, schools and their adherents were in a state of fluidity, which is ever the earmark of those who are spiritually mature enough to receive progressive revelation. They could not be bound by creeds, rules or dogmas. For the Christian-Gnostics, the church was the union of all souls who are seeking God, i.e., the experience of God. For the orthodox, the church is the union of individuals who happen to confess the creed and obey the bishops who tell them what to believe.

Although we possess the writings of the Church Fathers against the Christian-Gnostics, which are, indeed, voluminous, we do not possess similar writings of the Christian-Gnostic sects against the orthodox. However, the text known as the Apocalypse of Peter, preserved in the Nag

Hammadi Library, is the closest we come to a statement by a Christian-Gnostic group in its battle against the orthodox. The text is quoting a prophecy of Jesus delivered to Peter:

And there shall be others who are outside our number who name themselves bishops and also deacons, as if they have received their authority from God. They bend themselves under the judgment of the leaders. Those people are dry canals. <73>

This statement encapsulates the attitude many Christian sects harbored toward the emerging federation of orthodox churches of the early decades of the third century. It was during this period that the various ancient Christian sects were first coming into disrepute, due to the ceaseless outpouring of writings against them which had begun at the middle of the second century and would continue unabated through the middle of the third century. Justin Martyr, Hegesippus, Irenaeus, Tertullian and Hippolytus had all written volumes against the Christian-Gnostics. The sects of ancient Christianity could not hold up to such a barrage. Fortunately, many of the tenets of the Christian-Gnostics were taught by Clement and Origen, although both, being Church Fathers, chose to side with orthodoxy against the Christian-Gnostic sects.

Tertullian

Orthodoxy took a turn for the worse with the writing of Tertullian, who passionately hated the Christian-Gnostics. Tertullian added fuel to the fire Irenaeus had started and further consolidated orthodox dogma. In the writings of Tertullian, as later with Augustine, the original Christianity has all but disappeared.

Tertullian, writing about 190, carried the concept of the resurrection of the body to absurd lengths. He opted for a literal bodily resurrection at the "end of the world," and, of course, denied the reincarnation of the soul. He writes that in the resurrection, on the last day, what is raised is "this flesh, suffused with blood, built up with bones, interwoven with nerves, entwined with veins, (a flesh) which was born, and dies, undoubtedly human."<74> Pagels writes that Tertullian expects the idea of Christ's sufferings, death and resurrection to shock his readers. "He insists that it must be believed, because 'it is absurd.'" <75> Tertullian continues by saying that anyone who denies the resurrection in the flesh is a heretic. <76>

Tertullian's theology of the bodily resurrection is grossly material. Yet it is precisely this doctrine that is blindly believed in by the majority of those who call themselves Christians, to include the so-called fundamentalist movement. The "fundamentals," unfortunately, are the fundamentals of the orthodox dogmatic theology developed by such minds as Irenaeus, Ignatius, et al. They have naught to do with original primitive Christianity. All Christians today, given the new facts that are coming to light, must decide whether it is Irenaeus, Tertullian, etc. who they accept as their teachers, or the true teaching of Christ—the inner Christ of each and the original teachings of Christ Jesus.

The ancient Christian doctrine of successive reincarnations from which the soul was finally released through the resurrection is likewise denied by Tertullian as Irenaeus denied it before him. In *On the Soul*, Chapters 28-35, Tertullian devotes several pages to refuting reincarnation for the following reasons: reincarnation doesn't account for the increase in the world's population; there is no remembrance of past lives; man does not return to animal forms. Tertullian regarded a devotee of truth of the stature of Pythagoras as a deceitful fabricator of stories when he claimed to remember former lives. <77>

The above arguments, to this day, are the classic ones used against reincarnation. What Tertullian does not know and apparently cared less about researching so as to find the truth is this: souls reincarnate according to cyclic law—not all souls are on earth in embodiment at the same time. Some inhabit other planes of being in the matter universe until they embody, and are released to earth in cycles—some groups of souls embody together in a certain epoch, while other groups are held back. These doctrines were taught as part of the Christian mysteries and were disseminated by Origen of Alexandria. The Christian-Gnostic gospel *Pistis Sophia* is proof of this.

Tertullian may not have remembered past lives but others certainly have, both Christians and non-Christians alike. However, it is a matter of attainment and readiness of the soul. The memory of former lives may become a terrible burden on the psyche— especially among those who have suffered severe traumatic experiences in the past. On the opposite side of the coin, the ego may not be sufficiently mature to remember a former life of great achievement or position. It is the mercy of God that allows the veil of forgetfulness to descend upon memory, for there are many reasons why past life memories could interfere with the task at hand in this life. As Christ said, "Sufficient unto the day is the evil thereof." The outer memory and mind, then, in most cases, is not aware of the past-life records and memories which are below the threshold of consciousness, hence subconscious. If Tertullian took the trouble to study the laws governing reincarnation, as they were undoubtedly taught by Christian initiates, he might never, acting truly responsibly, have refuted the doctrine. Further, the concept that men reincarnate in animal forms may be a misunderstanding of the doctrine of Basilides, earlier discussed, likening lower thoughts and feelings to psychic "appendages" which take on animal forms (presumably in the aura). This "transmigration" doctrine is not truly a doctrine of reincarnation.

The doctrine of reincarnation affirms the Goodness of the Supreme God, who does not visit evil upon humanity through whimsy or through an equally mysterious "Will." The evils that befall the race of humanity are self-generated and are the working out of the law of cause and effect; they are allowed by God for the edification of the soul. "Whatsoever ye sow that shall ye reap." To condemn this doctrine is to enforce belief in an unjust, tyrannical God who arbitrarily strikes one person down with a dreaded disease, allows another to live "happily ever after," allows babies to be born blind, others to be born as geniuses, all for no discernible reason. We shall return to this problem and doctrine, however, when we take up the theology of Origen.

Tertullian, on the other hand, justifies his doctrine of the bodily resurrection by affirming that the Creator who allegedly produced everything out of nothing can certainly restore the very same flesh that had been buried. Tertullian's God has no respect for Natural Law, nor is he, apparently, the originator of Natural Law. Tertullian's theology is superstitious, not enlightened.

Irenaeus and Tertullian seem to have been the originators of the doctrine, already noted, of "creationism." This doctrine, later formally approved by the Roman church, teaches that God originally created the universe and man out of nothing, and that he is the immediate Creator of every newborn soul at the moment of conception.<78> The soul is not a divine emanation, but simply a separate creation by God out of "nothing." "Nothing" as used by Irenaeus and Tertullian does not mean the Unknown or Unmanifest Deity, as in the Hindu Brahman or the Kabbalistic Ein Soph, but simply "nothingness" in its literal sense—whatever that is—for no philosophy subsequently has ever been able to make sense of this notion—a notion just tossed out there by Tertullian for Scholastics and philosophers to puzzle upon for a couple millennia. No philosophical or theosophical school in the ancient world, including the Christian-Gnostics ever taught this doctrine. It was new and totally fabricated by Irenaeus and Tertullian, and it denies that creation is an emanation from the unmanifest to the manifest. The preexistence of souls is, of course, rejected also.

In his doctrine of the resurrection of the dead, Tertullian again betrays a grossly materialistic bent. Tertullian argues that the word "dead" relates to the dead body at the end of the world. This again is a fabrication in doctrine without precedent. The earliest Christian sects along with St. Paul taught that the word "dead" referred to the soul fallen into matter, the sleeping or unawakened soul "dead" in its sins, from which state the soul needed to be resurrected. Tertullian, of course, will have none of this. For him the soul doesn't fall into death, the body does—therefore, the body is the only subject of resurrection because it is the only thing subject to death. Tertullian had obviously never read the Biblical statement: "The soul that sinneth it shall die." (Ezk. 18:4,20) Why did Tertullian insist on the body, instead of the soul, as the subject of resurrection? Once Tertullian denied the pre-cosmic fall of the soul into matter, he had to make the body resurrect, because for him the soul had never fallen into matter. For Tertullian to accept the pre-cosmic fall of the soul would be to accept the soul's preexistence and this, Tertullian, like Irenaeus, refused to do, for to do so would be to concede to the "heretics." We find that Tertullian's Christianity is material, literal, and legalistic. Tertullian sees scripture as a legal document to be interpreted literally, not allegorically as the Christian-Gnostics were doing.

Despite attempts to refute the oldest forms of Christianity that we have been discussing, Gnostic-Christian sects were strong and widespread by the year 200, and were not yet defeated by the writings of the Church Fathers of the orthodox federation. Their only recourse was the appeal to absolute authority. Martin Larson remarks:

The Church [orthodox] soon found that it could not defeat the heretics by reason, moral persuasion or scriptural authority. Some other weapon soon became imperative; and this was found in the indivisible authority of the apostolic Church, descending through the bishops from generation to generation and in their exclusive right to administer sacraments and interpret the scriptures. (Brackets added) <79>

We have already noted how the orthodox episcopacy

was essentially a fraud and how it was based on the Christian-Gnostics' own succession of teachers, the oldest and most authentic apostolic succession. With the writings of Irenaeus and Tertullian, however, the cause of the orthodox movement made great strides, primarily through the misuse of power. Tertullian himself admits that the most prudent and faithful church members go over to the "heretics," or in other words, the sectarian Christian-Gnostics. Tertullian's formula to defeat the Christian-Gnostics is to oppose them by:

...not admitting them to any discussion of the Scriptures...nor must controversy be admitted on points in which victory will either be impossible or uncertain....As they are heretics, they cannot be Christians; and they have acquired no right to the Christian Scriptures. <80>

Tertullian declares that truth "is all doctrine which agrees with the apostolic churches," which they "received from the apostles, the apostles from Christ, and Christ from God." <81> Thus, in effect, no Christian can approach Christ to receive the truth nor can he appeal to the divine spark within to access the truth. This, of course, is precisely what the Christian-Gnostics were doing.

Irenaeus and Tertullian had no recourse but to use slander against these enlightened Christians. The label of "heretic" as a term of abuse and alienation was freely used by Irenaeus and Tertullian in their ceaseless battle against the Christian-Gnostics, so much so that all subsequent Church Fathers continually use this libelous term to alienate and slander those who do not agree with them. This tactic has continued almost unabated throughout Christian history and is still used today by certain Christians when they come in contact with those who do not agree with their brand of theology.

Tertullian is an example of an early Christian fundamentalist who refuses to allow others to believe in the religion of their choice. He not only despised his fellow Christians of the Gnostic persuasion, but also preached a hatred of all philosophy, a hatred of Pythagoras and Plato and their teachings, i.e., a hatred of the mind. Tertullian's Christianity was a Christianity of fire and brimstone, of a tyrannical God and a frightening last judgment. He preached a God of fear who compelled his poor creatures to obey him lest they be damned to hell. Unfortunately, this type of Christianity is typical of the Church at Carthage, and Tertullian found worthy successors in Cyprian and Augustine.

Ironically, although Tertullian labeled the Christian-Gnostics "a camp of rebels," he, himself, later rebelled and abandoned the church at Carthage to join the Montanist sect—also known as the Church of New Prophecy—certainly causing him to lose his canonization and "sainthood" from the Church. Perhaps non-St. Tertullian's untempered zeal became even too much for Tertullian to stomach. Whatever the case may be, Tertullian concluded that the so-called catholic church had been too rigid and lifeless, at least in Carthage, or perhaps Tertullian needed to channel his over excessive zeal elsewhere.

Before we leave Tertullian, we should point out that we find strong traces of the doctrine of original sin in his writings, more so than in any other theologian of his day. We find no developed doctrine of original sin prior to 200 A.D. as it was later understood and interpreted in the orthodox church in later decades and centuries.

Tertullian taught that every man on earth received the fallen image or sinful state from Adam, who had disobeyed God in the Garden of Eden by eating the forbidden fruit. At birth, every soul automatically inherits this deficiency. This sin is a congenital defect, according to Tertullian and Irenaeus before him, and is not the result of a freewill descent into matter or into duality since souls have no preexistence. Nor did this "original sin" result from the attempt of the evil archons to entrap the light of spiritual man in dense physical bodies through subjecting them to ignorance, lust and sin. According to Tertullian, all men are born in sin through no fault of their own since they have no previous existence. The "God" of Tertullian, therefore, like the "God" of Irenaeus, is unjust and tyrannical and in his character he again approximates the usurper deity, Ildabaoth. Unfortunately, this is the "God" of orthodoxy—the "God" most Christians were taught to believe in, especially from the fourth and fifth centuries onward, thanks to the writings of many Church Fathers.

By the early decades of the third century, the Christian-Gnostics fell more and more into disrepute. As early as 175 A.D., the orthodox federation of churches possessed its complete canon, further bolstered and tightened by Irenaeus. Larson remarks:

This [canon] consisted of many diverse documents, which are full of discrepancies and express a variety of viewpoints. In the face of these facts, Justin Martyr laid down the rule which was to become the dogma of Catholic as well as of Protestant Christianity: "no scripture contradicts another." (Brackets added) <82>

Hence, the so-called "gnostic gospels" could never be and never were a part of the canonical New Testament, since they, more often than not, contradicted the dogmas of the orthodox.

Cyprian of Carthage

The orthodox movement consolidated its authority further as a result of the theories of Cyprian of Carthage (A.D. 200-256), who elaborated on the ecclesiastical doctrine of Tertullian. Cyprian went further than Irenaeus and Tertullian in promoting the power of the orthodox clergy. He explained why "heresies" had arisen:

God's priest is not obeyed....The church is founded upon the bishops, and every act of the church is controlled by these same rulers. <83>

Whoever is separated from the church is joined to an adulteress...nor can he who forsakes the church of Christ attain to the rewards of Christ. <84>

Whoever...has not maintained...ecclesiastical unity has lost even what he previously had been. <85>

We can clearly see here what tremendous strides the orthodox federation of churches had taken in its drive for centralization of authority. And strides in arrogance. However did Cyprian attain such authority to make these statements? We are now assuming complete authority over the destiny of the soul. So now to be separated from the "church" as it was being fabricated by the various bishops is a fate worse than death.

According to Martin Larson, in the third century Roman bishops began insisting that the entire apostolic authority had been transmitted through Peter to the Roman See, a single church, and that the Roman bishop was preeminent. <86>

Cyprian acknowledged the Roman See as the "source" of episcopacy. But he was careful to point out that:

Other apostles were also the same as with Peter, endowed with an equal partnership both of honor and of power, but the beginning proceeds from unity so that the church of Christ may be shown to be one. <87>

Summarizing Cyprian's views on the church, W.C. Frend writes:

The church was an institution led by bishops who were the successors of the apostles and to whom absolute obedience was due. While accepting much of Tertullian's escha-tology...Cyprian grafted onto this a logical scheme of church government based on his understanding of the unity of God. God was one, and hence his church must be one and each community must have one leader, the bishop, maintaining peace and unity with his colleagues....The church was an all-pervading unity in its theology, organization and sacrament. <88>

Hopefully we have demonstrated that there was no all-pervading unity of theology, organization and sacrament even from the first century, and all such appearances of unity were being speedily concocted by the bishops. The theology, organization and sacraments of the Christian-Gnostic sects and communities differed from their orthodox counterparts and were as ancient, if not more ancient, hence more authentic and expressive of true Christianity. We will not belabor the point further, except to repeat that the drive for consolidation and the emphasis on obedience to the bishop had behind them (as motive) the **extermination** of the Christian-Gnostics, their teachings, their mysteries and their apostolic succession.

Chapter X

Origen of Alexandria and The Golden Age of Christian Theology

The Catechetical School at Alexandria

The development of Christian orthodoxy took a dif–ferent course in Alexandria. According to tradition, the ancient "church" at Alexandria was founded by Mark, the author of the gospel, sometime in the second half of the first century.<1> Outside of our canonical gospel, we possess no records or texts describing the theology of Mark. However, we have previously noted that Mark may have been the author of a "secret gospel" containing more advanced teaching for those being initiated into the Christian mysteries. We have also noted that excerpts from the "secret gospel" contain passages portraying Jesus as a hierophant of the mysteries. Thus we see that from the very beginning in Alexandria a "secret doctrine" was being taught to those who made themselves worthy.

Prior to and during the establishment of a Christian community in Alexandria, numerous mystery religions and sectarian groups flourished which taught the ancient mysteries and which were initiatic in nature. Alexandria was host to Philo, one of the greatest Jewish philosophers and a con–temporary of Christ, who taught that the philosophy of Pythagoras and Plato could be found in the Hebrew Scriptures, which he interpreted allegorically. Philo also asserted that the teaching of Moses was the more ancient theology and could be reconciled with the Platonic philosophy. Philo taught the preexistence of souls, reincarnation, and elaborated upon a "Logos theology" in which he declared that all men were, in effect, incarnations of the Logos, whom he termed "logoi."

Thus the intrinsic divinity of man was taught by Philo.

The famous Neo-Platonic School was also founded in Alexandria by Ammonius Saccas, probably toward the close of the second century.<2> The school was founded to restore the Platonic philosophy and theology. According to M.P. Hall, the aristocratic intellectuals of Alexandria recognized Ammonius as an outstanding thinker and conferred upon him the title "divinely taught." <3> Ammonius apparently taught a mystical theology and philosophy which had as its object the soul's ultimate union with the Divine. Ammonius numbered among his disciples Origen, the greatest of the Church Fathers, and Plotinus, who brought the Neo-Platonic School to its full flowering. Ammonius is said to have died between 240 and 245 A.D.

Before the establishment of both the Neo-Platonic School and the Christian Catechetical School, however, the Christian-Gnostic schools of Carpocrates, Basilides, Isidore, Valentinus and Heracleon flourished. The earliest of these schools, that of Carpocrates and Basilides, are dated circa 117 A.D. Gnostic Christianity is, therefore, the earliest form of Christianity that can be traced in Alexandria. According to W.H.C. Frend, between 130 and 180, Basilides, Valentinus, and Heracleon dominated Christian intellectual life in Alexandria, and:

...were among the pioneers of an authentic Gentile Christianity, a religion that had a place for all knowledge and experience, scriptural and pagan alike, in a scheme of salvation centered on a divine figure, Christ. It was a fantastic hope, but the last of human endeavors to fuse all knowledge into a single pattern of truth....Even their opponents held the Gnostic leaders in high regard....

Alexandrian Gnostics laid the foundation of much that became the Alexandrian school of theology in the next two centuries. Christian Platonism [of Clement and Origen] was indebted to a half century of Gnostic preparation.

...The Gnostics also brought a sense of progression in

religion, from ignorance and irrationality to knowledge and understanding, and in this they anticipated Clement of Alexandria and, above all, Origen. (Brackets added) <4>

The Alexandrian school of Christian proto-orthodox theology was founded circa 175 A.D. by Pantaenus, who is said to have been a converted Stoic philosopher. <5> According to Eusebius, Pantaenus eventually journeyed to India as a herald of Christ, where he found a previously established Christian community using the Gospel of Matthew in Hebrew/Aramaic. <6> This gospel, we can be assured, was not our present canonical Greek Matthew, and the Christian community Pantaenus discovered may have been an ancient Ebionite-Nazorean community of a decidedly Jewish-Gnostic character. The Hebrew Matthew, which was written in secret code, as Jerome states, was reputed to be the original Matthew. The theology and mysteries contained in this gospel have never been divulged. This Christian community in India may have been originally founded by Jesus himself and his disciple, Judas Thomas, who is said to have brought Christianity to India. The Apostle Matthew is reputed to have labored in Persia, which was on the direct trade route from Antioch in Syria to India. Thus Matthew's gospel may have found its way to India if Matthew himself had been in Persia.<7> We recall that Jesus was present in various parts of Persia and India prior to his three-year Palestinian ministry and also after the resurrection. Thus an "esoteric" form of Christianity may have flourished there, and Pantaenus may have come in contact with it.

Pantaenus taught a "philosophical" interpretation of Christianity but related it to traditional biblical teaching. <8> Thus, the foundation of the Catechetical School was biblically oriented and did not share in the so-called oriental doctrines of the Christian-Gnostics. We possess, however, no record of the theology of Pantaenus. He passed on the leadership of the Catechetical School to Clement, who remained its head from 190 to 203 A.D. Pantaenus, then, left for India never to return.

It is interesting to speculate what became of Pantaenus. Perhaps, like Jesus, he returned to Kashmir or to the remote fastnesses of the Himalayas, where Jesus himself had journeyed.

Clement of Alexandria

We possess several writings from the hand of Clement, namely *Miscellanies* and *Excerpts from Theodotus*, a Christian-Gnostic teacher. In the Christianity of Clement, we begin to see the intertwining of orthodoxy and Christian Gnosticism, and we note again the prejudice against the schools of Gnosis. In the hands of Clement, the school at Alexandria maintained a combative edge. It attempted to compete with and rival the school of Philo, the Neo- Platonic school, and the schools of Christian Gnosis. Beginning with Clement, the byword of the school seems to have been, "If you can't lick 'em, join 'em." Thus the Catechetical School conceded to Platonic philosophy and to the Christian-Gnostics, claiming to be against both, yet borrowing from these schools as its theology developed. From A.D. 189-232, the school came under the control of the stringently orthodox bishop Demetrius, with whom Origen later quarreled. The oppressive strains of orthodoxy made themselves felt even in this school, perhaps the most sublime exponent of Christian proto-orthodox theology. We will briefly touch on the teachings of Clement, noting the similarities and dissimilarities with the prevailing Gnostic Christianity.

There is no doubt that Clement was in contact with and received from Pantaenus a secret esoteric Christian tradition, which he claims had been "derived directly from the holy Apostles Peter, James, John and Paul."<9> Clement writes further:

The Lord...allowed us to communicate of those divine Mysteries, and of that holy light, to those who are able to receive them....The Mysteries are delivered mystically, that what is spoken may be in the mouth of the speaker; rather not

in his voice, but in his understanding.... <10>
...It is requisite, therefore, to hide in a Mystery the
wisdom spoken, which the Son of God taught. <11>

Clement taught that the Christian progresses from simple faith to knowledge or Gnosis. The Gnosis:

...imparted and revealed by the Son of God, is
wisdom.... And the Gnosis itself is that which has descended by
transmission to a few, having been imparted unwritten by the
Apostles. <12>

Clement gives a long exposition on the life of the mature Christian, whom he calls the Gnostic, the deeply learned, initiated Christian. The Gnostic should and must avail himself of branches of learning as a preparatory exercise prior to his initiation into the Mysteries: "He who is conversant with all kinds of wisdom will be preeminently a Gnostic." <13> According to Clement, the scriptures of both Old and New Testaments contain allegories and symbols intended to stimulate inquiry. The Gnostic must seek to mine these hidden truths for himself. Thus, like the Christian-Gnostics before him, Clement interpreted Scripture allegorically but in a manner different from the Gnostics.

Clement rejected the claims of the Christian-Gnostic teachers that they also possessed an esoteric teaching of Jesus handed down from the apostles. Clement's catechetical esoteric tradition, so he declared, was alone authentic and represented the tradition of the "church." Thus the Catechetical School and the Christian-Gnostic Schools both claimed authenticity.

Clement viewed God as absolutely transcendent, but he could be known by man through his Son or Logos. For Clement "the Trinity consisted of a hierarchy of three graded Beings and on that concept—derived from Platonism—depended much of the remainder of this theological teaching." <14>

Clement rejected the ancient doctrine of emanations, the concept of a Demiurge or creator-God, and the Christian-

Gnostic teaching on a usurper deity who took part in the creation of matter. Clement denied that evil is or could be a positive force in the universe, and thus he rejected outright the existence of lesser gods or archons who intruded themselves between God and man. The world was created by God and was "good." Matter and the material world, according to Clement, was not the result of a precosmic or cosmic fall. For Clement, there were no pairs of graded beings called Aeons, no Pleroma. There were no hylic (material), psychic or pneumatic men by nature, as he (incorrectly) claimed the Christian-Gnostics taught. Clement accused his opponents of teaching determinism and of denying man's free will by their categorizing of mankind into these three essential types.

Clement probably taught the doctrine of the pre-existence of souls, as his pupil Origen later did, but he seems to have rejected the doctrine of reincarnation taught by the Christian-Gnostics and most other religions of the ancient world. His statements, such as we have them, are ambivalent regarding preexistence. We know that Clement attacked Basilides and Valentinus on their doctrine of reincarnation. Yet because of the overwhelming popularity of the Christian-Gnostic sects, schools and teachers, Clement was forced to admit that they taught much truth but had erroneous opinions. The Christian-Gnostics of course, would be the first to deny this, since they attributed their "opinions" to an authentic esoteric apostolic tradition.

Again, unlike the Christian-Gnostics, Clement viewed the Old Testament, especially the five books of Moses, as superior to the philosophy of Pythagoras and Plato. The Christian-Gnostics, universalists that they were, saw truth wherever it was found. Not so, Clement. The Old and New Testaments were the highest and only source of truth. In this, Clement shares the opinion of Justin Martyr and other Apologists. Nevertheless, Clement is miles ahead of Irenaeus and Tertullian in his breadth of understanding, although, as W.C. Frend notes, Clement was not a systematic thinker, and he never evolved a theological system. <15> This tremendous task was left to Origen, the greatest and most controversial of the Church Fathers.

Origen of Alexandria—The Synthesis of Christian Orthodoxy and Christian Gnosis

The great Origen (185-253 A.D.) eventually succeeded Clement as the head of the Catechetical School when the latter departed Alexandria during the persecution of the Emperor Severus. Origen himself narrowly escaped death when his own father, Leonidas, was martyred. Thus, at the age of 18, Origen found himself head of the school. Origen found increasing success as a teacher, and he is said to have worked day and night with the crowds that came to hear him—both "orthodox" Christians and Gnostic-Christians alike. <16>

Although Origen placed himself in the orthodox camp and defended the "orthodox" tradition against various Christian-Gnostic schools and sects, the theology he eventually evolved seemed more "gnostic" than orthodox, and even during his lifetime, Origen was accused of teaching "heretical" doctrines, as the Christian-Gnostics were.

In 215, Origen visited Caesarea in Palestine. He was asked by the bishops of Jerusalem and Caesarea to lecture on the scriptures. Demetrius, patriarch of Alexandria, objected, since Origen had not been ordained.<17> Origen was ordered back to Alexandria, and he obeyed.<18> For the next 12 to 15 years, G.W. Butterworth writes, Origen began the literary work which would establish his fame in the church. <19>

Between 219 and 230 at Alexandria, Origen wrote *On First Principles*, "a comprehensive investigation of Christian doctrine on a scale never before attempted."<20> Origen then was invited to Greece and on the way was ordained presbyter by the bishops of Jerusalem and Caesarea. This action caused the final break with Demetrius, who called a synod of Egyptian bishops. The decision was that Origen was forbidden to teach at Alexandria, and he was soon afterwards excommunicated.

The sentence, however, had little effect outside Egypt. Origen became an honored teacher of the church, working out of the city of Caesarea in Palestine from 231 through the rest of his life. <21> From 231 to his death, Origen produced a vast body of works, including scriptural commentaries on both the Old and the New Testaments. In 250, when the persecution of the Emperor Decius broke out, Origen was imprisoned at Tyre and subjected to torture. He was released in 251 but succumbed two years later. He died at Tyre in 253. <22> The theology evolved by Origen was the final and greatest attempt to revive the secret, esoteric doctrine of Jesus—or, at least, a great portion of the doctrine. It was also the first attempt in the orthodox church to systematize a theology on so vast a scale. Although Origen defended orthodoxy, he included in his system the wisdom of the Neo-Platonists and the Christian-Gnostics. His theology thus became a perfect synthesis of "orthodox" and "gnostic", and comes closest to reviving the "Lost Christianity" of the original sects, communities and schools, at a time when the Christian-Gnostics were falling into disrepute.

The Theology of Origen

The Trinity

Origen was the first Church Father to develop an actual doctrine of the Trinity—a doctrine that was to eventually produce controversies in the church for the following three centuries. For Origen, the Father, Son and Holy Spirit possess a unity and harmony of will and are One. The Father is absolute and immutable as in the unmanifest first principle of the gnostic schools. The Son, declared Origen, is subordinate to the Father and was created by the Father. Origen identifies the Son with absolute Wisdom of the Logos. The Son, he says, is eternally generated and is the mediator between the Father and the divine powers created by him.

The Holy Spirit was the primary Being created by the

Son or Word. This act was then followed by the creation of spiritual beings or rational souls. The rational souls or beings thus preexisted their bodies and even the creation of the material cosmos. All beings are subordinated to God the Father from the beginning. The Son thus mediates between God's absolute Oneness and this multiplicity of beings.

Origen rejected the Christian-Gnostic concept of the Aeons who emanated from the Supreme, unknown Father and who subsisted in the Pleroma or spiritual universe. In place of emanation, Origen substituted his doctrine of the "eternal generation of the Son." In place of Aeons, Origen substituted the rational spirits or minds created (not emanated) by the Father, through his Wisdom, the Son/Logos. Thus, Origen preserved the idea of emanation while conceding to the orthodox concept of creation as against emanation. Origen's theology, however, leaves us with preexisting minds dwelling in a spiritual universe, a Christian-Gnostic teaching he was unable or unwilling to refute. Thus, the first complete theological system in orthodox theology includes the doctrine of the preexistence of souls, so abhorrent to the later Church Fathers.

Origen on the Doctrine of Christ

Origen makes a clear distinction between the Divine Wisdom or Logos and Jesus, the man, much in the same manner as the Nazoreans, Ophites and Valentinians. In an age when Church Fathers were debating whether or not Jesus Christ preexisted, Origen gives us the astounding but rational doctrine that **the soul of Jesus preexisted along with all other souls and the nature of Jesus' soul was the same as all other souls**. This doctrine, so simple and so lucid, was to produce thunderous reverberations of "blasphemy" down through the ages. And yet Origen taught nothing more than the ancient doctrine of the preexistence of all beings, which as recently as the time of Irenaeus (circa 180) had begun to come under attack.

How, then, did the soul of Jesus in his preexistent state become one with the Logos? Origen writes in *On First Principles:*

It cannot be doubted that the nature of his [Christ's] soul was the same as that of all souls; otherwise it could not be called a soul, if it were not truly one. But since the ability to choose good or evil is within the immediate reach of all, this soul which belongs to Christ so chose to love righteousness as to cling to it unchangeably and inseparably in accordance with the immensity of its love. (Brackets added) <23>

The soul of Christ, then, chose to cling to virtue and thus remained one with the Logos. When did the freewill choice occur?

That soul [of Jesus] clinging to God from the beginning of the creation and ever after in a union inseparable and indissoluble, as being the soul of the wisdom and word of God and of the truth and the true light, and receiving him wholly, and itself entering into his light and splendor, was made with him in a preeminent degree one spirit. (Brackets added) <24>

The soul of Christ, since the beginning, never separated from the Wisdom of God, which Origen terms the Only Begotten Son. Therefore, the soul of Jesus was called the Son of God and later descended into flesh. Origen continues:

This soul, then, acting as a medium between God and the flesh (for it was not possible for the nature of God to mingle with a body apart from some medium), there is born, as we said, the God-man, the medium being that existence to whose nature it was not contrary to assume a body.... <25>
It is therefore right that this soul, either because it was wholly in the Son of God or because it received the Son of God wholly into itself, should itself be called, along with that flesh

which it has taken, the Son of God and the power of God, Christ and the wisdom of God....

It was on this account also that the man became Christ, for **he obtained this lot by reason of his goodness** *....It was appropriate that he who had never been separated from the Only begotten should be called by the name of the Only-begotten and glorified together with him. (Emphasis added)* <24>

The soul of the preexistent Jesus, one with the Only-begotten Son, clung to this union unchangeably:

...The result being that by firmness of purpose, immensity of affection and an inextinguishable warmth of love all susceptibility to change or alteration was destroyed, and what formerly depended upon the will was by the influence of long custom changed into nature.... <27>

What Origen is saying is that the preexistent soul of Jesus, by a freewill choice and through love, clung to the Only-Begotten Son, the Wisdom of God, and thus became forever and unchangeably merged with this Son in an unalterable union. It is clear that Origen did not consider the soul of Jesus part of the Godhead or God from all eternity, but rather as one of the rational souls created by God. The soul of Christ chose to love and identify with the Second Person of the Trinity and thus became inseparable from that Son qualitatively and, in effect, became the embodiment or incarnation of the Son. Thus Jesus preserved the continuity of his existence as a spiritual being from the beginning, whereas others, due to the fall, did not preserve the knowledge of their spiritual origin.

The logical deduction to be made from Origen's doctrine is that any preexistent rational soul who, in the beginning, likewise chose to cling in love to the Son of God would have experienced the selfsame unchangeable union as did the soul of Christ, and thus become the wisdom and power of God, that is, the Son of God Himself. We can also conclude from Origen's doctrine that there is no basic intrinsic difference between Jesus Christ and any other soul on earth except in the degree of holiness and oneness with God attained.

The ramifications of this doctrine were felt down the centuries and eventually resulted in two dissimilar schools of thought, both looking to Origen as the father of their doctrine. We will discuss these in the context of the Arian controversy (Chapter 12).

The above teaching of Origen, in essence, attacked the growing tendency among the orthodox confederation to deify Jesus and proclaim him God and God from all eternity. It is easy to see why Origen, who himself attacked the "heretics," later became identified with them and received, even in his own lifetime, the condemnation of the "Church." Origen's doctrine of the inherent divinity of man was too dangerous to go unnoticed—too much a threat to the orthodox confederation and, worst of all, too "gnostic." The idea that Jesus' soul is the same as all other souls is a hard pill to swallow, for it could mean the dissolution of the institutionalized church and the crumbling of its power base—the authority of the bishops. We would argue that the doctrine of Origen on Christ is the most sublime Christology in the early church and perhaps the closest to the original doctrine of Jesus.

Origen on the Fall of Souls

We have said that according to Origen's view of creation, God, through his Son, created spiritual intelligent beings in the beginning. These beings, whom Origen terms "minds," were good, not by nature but through the beneficence of their Creator. Therefore, says Origen, these rational minds were subject to change and alteration. <28> Further, these minds were given free will by their Creator. Origen explains:

For the Creator granted to the minds created by him the power of free and voluntary movement, in order that the good that was in them might become their own, since it was *preserved by their own free will; but sloth and weariness of taking trouble to preserve the good, coupled with a disregard and neglect of better things, began the process of withdrawal from the good. Now to withdraw from the good is nothing else than to be immersed in evil; for it is certain that to be evil means to be lacking in good. <29>*

The fall of these minds, therefore, had its origin in sloth, weariness and neglect. Origen does not tell us how many of these minds began to "withdraw from the good." In Origen's view, their goodness had to be won or preserved as a result of their self-effort until absolute goodness became part of their nature. We can conclude that Jesus, in Origen's opinion, was one of these spiritual intelligences who did not withdraw from the good, but, as we have said, remained steadfast and clung to the good. Continuing his delineation of the Fall, Origen teaches that when the minds or rational intelligences withdrew from the good, their love of God "cooled." Origen thus describes the origin of the term "soul" as being related to the cooling of love toward God:

...We must ask whether perhaps even the word soul, which in Greek is psyche, was not formed from psychesthai, with the idea of growing cold after having been in a diviner and better state...because the soul seems to have grown cold by the loss of its first natural and divine warmth.... <30>
...All these considerations seem to show that when the mind departed from its original condition and dignity it became or was termed a soul, and if ever it is restored and corrected it returns to the condition being a mind. <31>

In his chapter on "Loss or Falling Away," Origen explains that the fall necessitated the use of bodies of various levels of density. He writes:

All rational creatures who are incorporeal and invisible, if they become negligent, gradually sink to a lower *level and take for themselves bodies suitable to the regions into which they descend; that is to say, first ethereal bodies, and then aereal. And when they reach the neighborhood of the earth they are enclosed in grosser bodies, and last of all are tied to human flesh. <32>*

We distinguish in this passage four types of bodies: ethereal, aereal, gross, and fleshly. This doctrine of the descent of the soul into four lower bodies is preeminently Platonic and has much in common with the doctrines of the various schools of Christian-Gnosis we have been examining. We recall that Valentinus designated four gradations of matter with Spirit as the point of origin. The Valentinians taught that matter and the material cosmos came to be as a consequence of the fall. In the case of Valentinus' allegory, this fall was of one of the Aeons, Sophia, which produced a chain of events—the demiurge's creation of matter and souls. For Origen, the rational minds fell away through negligence and thus became souls who were forced to incarnate in bodies as a consequence. The idea is the same: a preexistent, precosmic fall. We see, therefore, the clear rationality of Origen's system. Unlike Irenaeus, Tertullian and others who declare that God created matter and the material world for a physical creature called man, Origen teaches that God created matter to accommodate the fallen souls so that they could be restored to their spiritual state. The density level of the body that the soul inhabits is directly related to the degree of the fall in each soul. In Origen's universe, all is the result of self-effort and free choice and is pervaded by the justice of God.

Origen on the Fallen Angels

Tied to his doctrine on the fall of souls is Origen's teaching on the fall of angels and other heavenly powers whom the Christian-Gnostic sects termed archons or rulers. Origen writes:

...Before the ages, minds were all pure...offering service to God and keeping his commandments. But the devil, who was one of them, since he possessed free will, desired to resist God, and God drove them away. With him revolted all the other powers. Some sinned deeply and became daemons, others less and became angels; others still less and became archangels; and thus each in turn received the reward for his individual sin. But there remained some souls who had not sinned so very greatly as to become daemons, nor on the other hand so very lightly as to become angels. God therefore made the present world and bound the soul to the body as a punishment. <33>

Origen teaches that souls who incarnated in bodies on this earth occupy a midway position between daemons and angels. God, says Origen, did not create daemons, men or angels out of whimsy, for he is no "respecter of persons." The lot of daemons, men and angels is the result of the degree of their falling away from God. The term "sin" as used here by Origen must not be interpreted as an outright malicious act in reference to the angels' fall but as an imperceptible (at first) movement away from the exalted state of being minds or intelligences. Origen continues:

...For if this were not so, and souls had no preexistence, why do we find some newborn babes to be blind, when they have committed no sin, while others are born with no defect at all? But it is clear that certain sins existed before souls, and as a result of these sins each soul receives a recompense in proportion to its deserts. They are sent forth from God as a punishment, that they might undergo on earth a first judgment. That is why the body is called a frame, because the soul is enclosed within it. <34>

What is known in the East as the "law of karma" is here described at least to an approximation by Origen. Souls find themselves in bodies here on earth because of "sins" committed before they were born in bodies. Thus, the law of cause and effect holds sway in Origen's system. Again, we find a similarity to the doctrines of Origen's predecessors, Basilides and Valentinus.

Origen further teaches the controversial doctrine that Lucifer and the various fallen angels, whom he designates as "opposing powers," have also taken their abode on this earth and walk the earth in flesh bodies. As an example, Origen shows that the "Prince of Tyre" mentioned in Ezekiel 28: 11-19, is in fact a fallen angel or adverse power who was assigned to govern the city of Tyre.<35> Likewise, Origen shows that Lucifer/Satan was once of the light and was cast out of heaven and fell to "this earthly place." (Isaiah 14: 12-22) According to Isaiah, whom Origen quotes extensively, Lucifer appears to have been incarnated on earth as a great king who destroyed cities and received the judgment of God, who calls him "thou most wicked seed." Origen concludes with the following words:

All this shows that no one is stainless by essence or by nature, nor is any one polluted essentially. Consequently it lies with us and with our own actions whether we are to be blessed and holy, or whether through sloth and negligence we are to turn away from blessedness into wickedness and loss; the final result of which is, that when too much progress, if I may use the word, has been made in wickedness, a man may descend to such a state...as to be changed into what is called an opposing power. <36>

It is readily apparent from the above passage that Origen drew no clear-cut line of demarcation between men, angels and demons. Men may become angels or demons and demons may become men or angels. Origen also clearly shows that men, angels or demons may, at one time or another, inhabit flesh bodies. Here are two excerpts of Origen's teachings from the writings of Jerome:

Once again a beginning arises from the end and an end

from the beginning, and all things are so changed that one who is now a man may in another world become a daemon, while a daemon, if he lives negligently, may be bound to a grosser body, that is, may become a man. <37>

...The daemons themselves and rulers of the darkness in any world or worlds, if they desire to turn to better things, become men and so revert to their original condition, in order that being disciplined by the punishments and torments which they endure for a long or short period while in the bodies of men they may in time reach the exalted rank of angels. It follows logically from this that any rational creature can develop out of any other, not once or suddenly but over and over again; that we may become angels or, if we live carelessly, daemons, and on the other hand daemons, if they desire to possess virtue, may attain the dignity of angels. <38>

In his *Commentary on John*, Origen remarks that John the Baptist was, in fact, an embodied angel who had previously lived on earth as the prophet Elijah. The above passages are not found in the fourth century translation of *On First Principles* by Rufinus; the ideas embedded in these passages are given in a much-watered-down version, presumably to "soften" the "heretical" doctrines of Origen. As the editor of *On First Principles* states, "No opinion of Origen was so vehemently opposed as this one." <39>

From even a cursory reading of Origen's doctrine, it becomes obvious that we are in the midst of the Christian mysteries, which Origen is revealing to those who are ready. Never before had the secret doctrine of Jesus been revealed to so many, and, as a result, Origen earned the wrath of later Church Fathers, who themselves were not privy to the mysteries and who ultimately condemned Origen as a "heretic."

The ramifications of Origen's doctrine on men, angels and daemons cannot be overestimated. The presence of embodied daemons and fallen angels on earth who must work out their "karma" is an important key to the problem and continuance of evil on planet earth. Yet Origen offers no closed system. There is hope and salvation for all creatures, even for the devil, says Origen, if he should so choose to repent.

Origen's Doctrine of Salvation

What strikes us most about Origen's soteriology (doctrine of salvation) is the absence of any developed doctrine on the vicarious atonement although Origen reverences the cross and the "mystery" of the cross as the way of salvation. The blood-sacrifice of Jesus as the only cause of the soul's salvation is, however, neglected for all practical purposes. In this area, Origen is close to the ancient Christian-Gnostics, who saw Gnosis as necessary for salvation, not Jesus' death on the cross.

For Origen, the path to salvation begins with faith in Christ, (in the "rule of faith" as preserved by the "church") proceeds to the attainment of Wisdom or Gnosis and ends with sanctification. Each individual may choose to participate in Christ in his character of Wisdom and Gnosis and advance by degrees of perfection until he is sanctified by the Holy Spirit, made purer and holier until all stains of pollution and ignorance are purged and removed.<40> Man, then, says Origen, makes such a great advance in holiness and purity that he becomes worthy of God and receives from God the power to exist forever and to endure for eternity. <41> All created spirits, at the final consummation, would return then to: "that unity and perfection which was theirs at the beginning." Origen, therefore, envisioned the final restoration of all things. The ultimate perfection which will be conferred on man, however, is always in proportion to man's merits. Man can attain God-like perfection and must eventually live in the same condition as God lives. <42>

Origen did not interpret the resurrection of the body in its literal, material sense. There are numerous passages in *On First Principles* which clearly demonstrate that Origen believed that in the resurrection, grosser bodies would be discarded or would be etherealized into garments of the lightest and most tenuous nature conceivable.<43> Origen taught that our bodies, both earthly and psychic, contain a vital life principle as a seed from which would be refashioned the spiritual or pneumatic body of the resurrection. In this, he followed certain of the Christian-Gnostic sects and also St. Paul, whom he quotes frequently on the resurrection. The phraseology of hylic, psychic and pneumatic, used by the Valentinian schools, is also utilized by Origen following St. Paul's usage.

We find no doctrine in Origen of the eternal damnation of the soul in hell, nor do we find a doctrine of original sin as taught by Irenaeus and Tertullian. For Origen, the "original sin" is the movement of each soul, by free will, away from God, farther and farther until it is forced to assume a body. Origen preaches a God of infinite compassion and infinite justice, not the tyrant deity of Irenaeus and Tertullian and later, Augustine. The story of Adam and Eve is considered by Origen to be an allegory of the fall of the soul and is not interpreted by him in a literal sense.

Origen and Reincarnation

Scholars have disputed whether or not Origen accepted reincarnation; in certain passages, they aver, he seems to accept it, in others he appears to reject it. We are of the opinion that Origen did teach reincarnation, as we shall see. In his chapter on "Resurrection and Judgment" from *On First Principles*, Origen concludes that the wicked, instead of receiving bright and glorious bodies at the resurrection, may be clothed in "murky and black bodies" as befitting their state of consciousness of darkness and ignorance. He then adds a passage, apparently edited out of Rufinus' fourth-century translation, but preserved by Jerome:

...Perhaps, however, the "gloom and darkness" should be taken to mean this coarse and earthly body, through which at the end of the world each man that must pass into another

*world will receive **the beginnings of a fresh birth**. (Emphasis added)* <44>

Jerome comments on this excerpt as follows: "In so speaking he clearly supports the doctrine of transmigration taught by Pythagoras and Plato." The above excerpt, with Jerome's comment, is one of the clearest expressions of re-incarnation, although in the context given, Origen is referring to reincarnation on another world after the end of the age. Nevertheless, the "dark" individual so named had a previous earth life in the body before this world's end. After the end of this world, if there is sufficient "evil" within him, he would merit a new birth, albeit on another world. We note that at least two bodily lives are mentioned. Another passage which strikes us as suggestive of reincarnation is the following:

Whole nations of souls are stored away somewhere in a realm of their own, with an existence comparable to our bodily life, but in consequence of the fineness and nobility of their nature they are carried round with the whirl of the universe....There the representations of evil and of virtue are set before them; and so long as a soul continues to abide in the good it has no experience of union with a body. But by some inclination towards evil these souls lose their wings and come into bodies.... <45>

The above passage was reproduced by Gregory of Nyssa and is not found in Rufinus' fourth century translation of Origen's work. Besides the fact that this vision has the distinct flavor of a "gnosis" or revelation given to Origen, it is clear from this passage that Origen believed that souls preexist and subsequently enter into bodies. If so, one can ask, what other mechanism is left to allow the soul to ascend back to its orig-inal state but repeated embodiments which wean the soul by hard experience from its inclination towards evil? This would seem a logical consequence of Origen's statements above.

Commenting on the Old Testament story of Jacob and

Esau, Origen wrote that Jacob supplanted his brother Esau in the womb because "by reason of his merits in some previous life, Jacob had deserved to be loved by God to such an extent as to be worthy of being preferred to his brother."<46> In this passage, it is not easy to discern whether Origen is referring to another bodily life or previous incarnation of Jacob or to a life in another realm or world prior to his bodily incarnation on earth. It is clear, however, that Origen taught a type of re-incarnation doctrine. According to Geddes MacGregor, Origen "understands reincarnation to mean multiple embodiments within a single age."<47> However, he seems to have rejected the notion of endless successive reincarnations on earth (transmigration) as taught by the Hindus or as Pythagoras is alleged to have taught. The reason for this is that Origen taught and believed that the resurrection as demonstrated by Jesus, and when attained by the enlightened Christian, brought an end to life in the body and to future rebirths. The soul was capable of progressing upward to an almost infinite measure of spiritual perfection, "gradually and by degrees, during the lapse of infinite and immeasurable ages." <48> If the soul retrogressed, however, it could again fall into a body, perhaps in a future epoch or age, and this could occur many times.

So also with the earth—one earth will pass away and another will take its place, more refined and more perfect. Origen envisioned an endless succession of worlds and ages all following one another and coming into existence according to merits and demerits. In Origen's universe, nothing happens by chance or is predestined. All is the result of freedom of choice and movement.

Origen's understanding of man is just as lofty as the Christian-Gnostics envisioned. Man is created by God as a spiritual being, but one who must prove his goodness so that such goodness becomes natural, not accidental, thus enabling man to share and partake in the Divine Nature. Man, therefore, is capable of becoming as God.

The Golden Age of Christian Theology

The theology of Origen is all-encompassing and universal in scope. It can be considered the representative of the highest Christian Gnosis and the greatest systematized exposition of Christian theology yet advanced. It is ironic that although Origen opposed certain ideas of the Gnostic sectarian Christians such as the concept of a demiurge (Creator-God) considered as inferior to the Supreme God, pairs of Aeons or emanations and the allegorical works such as we find in Valentinus' cosmic myth, he actually popularized key Gnostic doctrines on the soul's preexistence, the fall and descent of the soul into matter, the resurrection of the soul in a celestial or heavenly body, Gnosis as the way of the soul's salvation, and the ultimate restoration into divine unity. The Christology of Origen is significant for its complexity and because it endeavors to give an adequate conception of Christ's humanity, that is, "the moral freedom pertaining to him as a creature." <49> Origen clearly taught that Christ earned his place as the incarnation of the Logos through choice and self-effort, not because he was God from all eternity. For the Christian-Gnostics, Christ is an emanation of the Pleroma; for Origen, he is one of the created spirits. The doctrines are similar, though not exact.

Harnack also asserts that Origen's eschatology or doctrine of the Last Things is more akin to the Valentinian Gnostics. Origen's doctrine, however, is permeated by his concept of free will, and he rejected what he felt to be deterministic tendencies in certain schools of Gnosis.

Prior to Origen, as we have seen, there were diverse views regarding the nature of Christ among the earliest sects of Christians. Some, such as the Ebionites, are said to have denied Jesus' preexistence while others asserted his preexistence. Harnack, we noted, distinguishes between the Adoption Christology and the Pneumatic Christology in the early church. Orthodox Christians and Gnostic-Christians each had differing views of the nature of Christianity. We have endeavored to prove that the earliest Christianity was, indeed, gnostic, however diverse. The great work of Origen was to unify the ancient doctrines of Christianity, as Harnack points out: "Origen...contrived to reconcile contradictions and thus acknowledged, outdid, reconciled and united both the theses of the Gnostics and those of orthodox Christians."<50> Origen, therefore, was the great synthesizer who, as we have said, inadvertently popularized the doctrines of the Christian-Gnostics, based as they were on the secret teaching of Jesus, and evolved them into the soundest, most rational theological system yet attempted. In the works of Origen the Christian world finally had a unified theology and doctrine it could call its own.

From the death of Origen to the close of the third century, the theology of Origen gradually replaced that of the Gnostic-Christian sects and schools. Up until the fourth century, Origen had numerous followers and disciples and, as a result, his theology and doctrines were considered to be the standard on which all other expositions were to be based. Christian theology had truly entered its Golden Age as the works of Origen penetrated the minds and hearts of learned Christians everywhere. Yet this "Golden Age" was soon to enter a period of decline. The same reactionary forces which had attempted to destroy the Christian-Gnostics were at work to destroy Origen.

The Attack on Origen

G.W. Butterworth, in his introduction to *On First Principles*, states that the first serious attack against Origen was made by Methodius, bishop of Patara in Lycia, in the early years of the fourth century. He is said to have written vigorously against Origen and his followers with regard to the eternity of creation, the preexistence of souls and the spiritual nature of the resurrection body. <51>

During the Arian controversy, the followers of Arius

found support in the works of Origen for their doctrine of the Son as subordinate to the Father. The opposing party, led by Athanasius, also claimed to find support for their doctrine in the works of Origen. Thus, from the early fourth century, Origen's theology was a subject of controversy.

Epiphanius (315-403), bishop of Salamis in Cyprus, renewed the attack against Origen towards the close of the fourth century. In two of his works he includes Origen among the heretics on the same grounds as Methodius and others, notes Butterworth, dealing with the Son's relationship to the Father.<52> Origen was charged with making the Son a creature, thus subordinating him to the Father, at a time when the trend toward the deification of Jesus, begun with the Nicene Council (325 A.D.), could not be stopped.

Epiphanius went so far as to travel throughout Palestine preaching against Origen, "to extirpate, if possible, from the minds of all who were well-disposed towards the great theologian, every trace of what he considered to be pestilent heresies." <53> We are now entering the times when the word "heresy" was taking on the full charge of its ultimately dreaded connotations—to include grave personal consequences. As is well known, Epiphanius was a vicious heresy hunter who wrote against the Christian-Gnostic schools, sects and their teachings. His writings reveal a hatred and vituperation of his fellow Christians that one ought to consider alarming in a bishop. Epiphanius, true to form, gave a sermon at the Church of the Resurrection, at the invitation of the bishop of Jerusalem, which was an attack against "Origenism." Among those who heard Epiphanius' diatribe was Jerome (342-420), who considered himself an "admirer" of Origen and his teaching. But, as we shall see, with a friend like Jerome, Origen needed no enemies. According to Butterworth, Jerome had begun to translate Origen's *Homilies*, and he used Origen's commentary on *Ephesians* in composing his own commentary on the same epistle. Jerome's preface speaks of Origen in the highest possible terms. <54> When Epiphanius also attacked the bishop of Jerusalem for sympathizing with Origen, Jerome became alarmed, for "he was sensitive to the least imputation of heresy."<55> Jerome, as a result, sided with Epiphanius, disassociated himself from the bishop of Jerusalem and turned against Origen. This caused a breach between Jerome and his friend Rufinus, who supported Origen. Rufinus later published a *Defense of Origen*, written by Pamphilius, the martyr. Eusebius of Caesarea, the Church historian, also translated Origen's *On First Principles*. Unfortunately, Rufinus shows timidity in translating the more controversial of Origen's teachings, such as those passages concerning the possibility of reincarnation, the nature of the resurrection body and the teaching on the embodiment of both good and evil angels on the earth. Rufinus either omits whole passages or softens them considerably. It is clear that, although Rufinus admired Origen and purported to defend him, he was apparently embarrassed by certain of Origen's doctrines.

After the initial breach between Jerome and Rufinus, they both became reconciled, only to split again. A controversy then ensued between Rufinus and Jerome over the doctrines of Origen, and Rufinus wrote his own *Defense of Origen.* Jerome then composed his own counter *Defense.* Butterworth remarks that Jerome's "own anxiety is to clear himself from any suspicion of heresy." <56> In his defense, Jerome refuses to admit that if Origen was a "heretic," he (Jerome) made a mistake in including Origen's opinions in his work.<57> If Jerome disagreed with Origen, he should never have included Origen's teaching in his works. Jerome then wrote a second *Defense* of his position in answer to a letter from Rufinus, wherein the latter threatened to publish "other facts" which, he states, would have destroyed Jerome's reputation forever.<58> In his last *Defense*, Jerome writes, "We were zealous in our praise of Origen; let us be equally zealous in condemning him now that he is condemned by the whole world." <59>

There is no question that Jerome betrayed Origen and in so doing suppressed one of the greatest Christian theologies the world had yet seen. Jerome had an opportunity to promulgate Origen's doctrine and thus defend the authentic

Christian mysteries, perhaps save them from obscuration, but he had not the character to defend Origen. He took the low road of compromise and betrayal, thus, in effect, bringing about the universal rejection of Origen through various synods and councils in the centuries ahead. In approximately 400, a council in Jerusalem condemned Origen's writings. In 401, the council at Cyprus did likewise.

The systematic condemnation of Origen began with Theophilus, who became bishop of Alexandria in 385, and who had once been another "supporter" of Origen. He convoked a council at Alexandria in 400 which condemned "Origenism" and continued his campaign against Origen, calling him the "hydra of heresies" and persecuting Origen's adherents.<60> Once the tide turned against Origen, as against the Christian-Gnostics, it could not be abated. Like a signal to the pack, the feeding frenzy had begun. In 494 the Roman Council condemned Origen and his work. Even Augustine, whom many consider to be the greatest theologian in the West, condemned both the doctrine of the soul's preexistence, as well as Origen himself.

According to Geddes MacGregor, Origen's opponents succeeded in getting Emperor Justinian to write a letter to the Patriarch of Constantinople, naming Origen as one of the heretics. <61> Justinian, therefore, convoked a synod at Constantinople in 543 and issued an edict setting forth a list of errors in doctrine attributed to Origen and attempted to refute them. The edict, however, divided East (Constantinople) and the West (Rome) further, instead of uniting them as was the intent of Justinian. Pope Vigilius at Rome initially opposed the edict, then upon arriving at Constantinople, seat of Justinius' imperial government, reversed his decision and issued a document which likewise condemned the writings anathematized (cursed) by Justinian. Origen, however, still had supporters among bishops in Gaul and Northern Africa who criticized the Pope's documents, notes MacGregor. Vigilius withdrew his document in 550 A.D. <62>

The anchorite monks near Jerusalem, continues

MacGregor, also became divided over Origen and finally broke into two groups: the Isochrists and the Protoctists. The Isochrists "held that eventually all human beings would become equal to Christ." <63> This doctrine is no doubt close to, if not identical with, Origen's idea that all created spirits could attain the fullness of Christhood, should they so choose. The Protoctists denied this, as well as repudiating the doctrine of the soul's preexistence. The latter group joined forces with the opponents of Origen. <64>

The Emperor Justinian eventually convened a council of the whole church on May 5, 553 A.D., known as the fifth Ecumenical Council or the Second Council of Constantinople. MacGregor remarks that 165 bishops signed the acts of the Council at its final meeting on June 2, but he remarks that not more than six bishops could have been from the West. <65> The Council, then, most certainly could not have been "ecumenical." Because Western bishops were not adequately represented, among other reasons, Pope Vigilius refused to attend. Justinian had Vigilius arrested and appointed Pelagius as the new Pope. Pelagius had previously convinced Justinian to issue the edict condemning Origen in 543. Since Justinian had no real power to appoint a Pope, it is a real question how the decision of the Council could be binding upon the Christian believer. The question is a significant one, for it was at this Council that the preexistence of the soul and its subsequent reincarnation was, or was supposed to have been, universally condemned. Justinian issued fifteen anathemas against the teachings of Origen. Especially condemned were teachings on the preexistence of souls, as noted, the fall of angels into the bodies of men (angel incarnation), and the general doctrine that spiritual intelligences had descended into bodies, at first subtle, then gross, as a result of sins committed in previous existences. Most of Origen's teaching on angels becoming men and demons and vice versa was likewise condemned.

Elizabeth Prophet comments on the authenticity of the council's decision as follows:

Because there exists today no manuscript documenting any papal approval whatsoever of the council's fifteen anathemas against Origen, some scholars deny that Origen's condemnation at this council was ever formalized through ratification by the Holy See.

But experts agree that in essence and in practice, Justinian and the bishops of Rome, Alexandria, Antioch, and Jerusalem condemned Origen's teaching on certain points and proclaimed it heretical—even if it did lack the signature of the Vicar of Christ. <66>

What matters is that, as Prophet adds, for Catholic Christians the preexistence of souls and reincarnation "became a nonsubject, more than forgotten—dead by neglect". <67>

The condemnation and neglect of the vital doctrines of preexistence, karma and reincarnation was a terrible tragedy for Christendom, and removed the understanding that all inequities and apparent injustices of life are the effects of prior causes in previous lifetimes, and that the seeds of sin in one life bear fruit in another according to the law of compensation. This law (taught by the Apostles, ancient Christians, Gnostics and by Origen) states that God is not the cause of injustice on earth. The inequities of life are the working out of "karma," whereby the soul reaps what it has previously sown. In the modern debate on abortion, for example, this understanding would imply that abortion directly denies a soul the opportunity to work out its karma, thus becoming a karma-making act for those responsible—a reason now lost to the Church's teaching on the issue. There is little doubt that the law of karma was the original teaching of Jesus and his apostles.

The Council's condemnation of Origen's teaching on the incarnation of evil angels likewise removed a vital key to the understanding of why evil continues to maintain so tenacious a hold on planet earth. Here Origen agreed with the Book of Enoch, which, as noted, taught the incarnation of the Watchers and their offspring on earth. We might speculate that perhaps the fallen angels themselves, moving among mankind, saw to it that all references to their race were removed. For if humanity knew of their existence and their tactics, they long ago would have exposed their deeds, thus rendering them powerless to act. The very viciousness of the attack on Origen prompts the question: From what source within his opponents did such intensity of hatred for and prolonged determination to destroy his doctrine arise? We take note that the Christian-Gnostic teaching on the evil archons, which we can trace back to St. Paul, was also conveniently removed from Christianity. We leave it to the reader to determine his or her own conclusions on this subject.

The doctrine of Origen, we see, restored the dignity of man and preserved the concept of free will. Origen offered wisdom and illumination and clarified for all time many obscure points of scripture. For Origen, all scriptures, both Old and New Testaments, were written on three levels corresponding to the body, soul and spirit. Origen's scriptural theology was therefore interpreted from these three levels—the allegorical or symbolical being the highest level, the literal or historical being the lowest level.

The general developments in theology after Origen's death and continuing for two centuries were toward a narrow, dogmatic interpretation of the Christian message. Origen's doctrine produced bitter controversies which themselves produced schisms in the church. Some of the most renowned Church Fathers in the two centuries following Origen—such as Gregory of Nyssa, Basil, Gregory Nazianzen, John Chrysostom, Athanasius, Jerome, Ambrose and Augustine—could not fully grasp the subtleties of Origen's theology, especially with regard to the Trinity. They were either not willing to or not capable of making the distinction between the Logos and Jesus. Although some of the Church Fathers, such as Gregory of Nyssa, claimed to admire or respect Origen, not one of the above Fathers was willing to accept preexistence or reincarnation in any form. Nor were they willing to accept the concept of angelic incarnation. As a result, the foremost theologians of each century, through their writings, not only deposed Origen from his place as the eminent theologian, but moved the mass of the Christian faithful further away from ancient and authentic Christianity. In examining the theologies of the Church Fathers after Origen, we find them to be gradually more intellectual, more codified, more speculative and more dogmatic. The ancient Christianity of the original sects was all but buried, and the Christian mysteries were all but suppressed.

The power of the bishops increased rapidly during the next two centuries after Origen. Power plays between and among bishops, churches and communities became commonplace. The church as a whole paid dearly for its condemnation of the Christian-Gnostics and Origen. Prior to the accession of Constantine, the church suffered persecutions during the reigns of Decius, Diocletian and Maximin. It refused to accept the rational theology of Origen. It was splintered into innumerable factions, each claiming to have the true theology and the true interpretation of the nature of Christ. The church, then, as a consequence, fell prey to Constantine, who finally turned Christianity into a state religion backed and controlled by the Emperor. Christians were now free to worship the Roman god, Jesus Christ, and his Messiah, Constantine. We will pursue these developments in a later chapter.

Chapter XI

The Manichaean-Christian Revolution

The Universal Religion of Light

While the "catholic" church was beset from within by Trinitarian controversy and schisms, besieged by religious factions and undergoing imperial persecution, an obscure prophet arose in the ancient land of Mesopotamia who was to exert a tremendous and lasting influence on all of Christendom. Just when the Church Fathers had subdued (or so they thought) the last vestiges of the heretical Gnosis, a new Gnostic revolution was brewing in the East. Just when Origen's grand Christian synthesis was falling into disfavor among the dogmatic architects of orthodoxy, a new yet ancient universal religion of truth was being promulgated which rapidly spread throughout the four corners of the Roman Empire. A new messenger of Light was heralding the Religion of Light, and yet another veil covering the mystery of the universe was being lifted and new mysteries were being revealed. What made the orthodox Church Fathers to tremble was that this universal theosophy proclaimed itself as the true, original Christianity, implemented by progressive revelation and carried forward by one who called himself, like St. Paul, an apostle of Jesus Christ—the prophet Mani.

Mani was born on April 14, 216, in the southern region of Mesopotamia (Iraq) in the vicinity of Seleucia-Ctesiphan on the Tigris River. <1> Mani's parents were of noble Persian descent, and his father Pattak had early on joined a Christian-Gnostic Baptist sect. At an early age Mani joined this sect founded by the prophet Elkesai in about 100 A.D. in Syria. The sect was almost wholly concerned with ablutions and the purification of the body and had an affinity with the ancient Nazoreans, the sect with which Jesus was identified.

When Mani was 12 years old, in 228 or 229, he received his first revelation, transmitted from the Highest God to an angel whom Mani calls "the twin," his companion or perhaps his "higher Self." This heavenly being or divine counterpart assured Mani of his constant help and protection; his message was as follows: "Forsake this congregation! Thou art not of its followers. The guidance of morals, the restraint of appetites, these are thy tasks. Yet because of thy youth, the time is not come to stand forth openly." <2>

According to Coptic texts, Mani also received complete knowledge at this time but yet was unable to act upon it. According to Mani's own words:

...This Living Paraclete came down and spoke to me [for the first time]. He revealed to me the hidden mystery, hidden from the ages, and the generations of Man: The mystery of the Deep and The High: The mystery of the Contest, the War, and the Great War, these he revealed unto me....Thus did the Paraclete disclose to me all that has been and all that will be. <3>

In the above passage, Mani associates his Twin with the Paraclete or the Holy Ghost. This is in agreement with what Western sources say concerning Mani: that he described himself as the Paraclete (or representative of the Paraclete) predicted by Jesus in John's gospel. <4>

Mani then left the baptist sect and spent the next 12 years in apparent obscurity. Scholars conjecture that Mani may have prepared for his coming mission by studying sacred literature. Duncan Greenlees writes that Mani was well informed of Christian doctrine, was familiar with the gospels of Matthew, John and Luke, and the epistles of Paul, and further showed a knowledge of the so-called apocryphal Acts of the Apostles by Leucius Charinus, who was said to be a disciple of John. <5>

In 240 A.D., when Mani was 24 years old, he received a final call from the angel, his celestial twin:

Peace unto thee, Mani, from me and from the Lord who sent me to thee and who has selected thee for his apostleship. He bids thee now to call the peoples to the truth and to proclaim from him the good message of the truth and to dedicate thyself to this task. The time is now come for thee to stand openly and to preach thy teaching. <6>

Thus, while the Church Fathers were hammering out their dogmas and "rational" arguments forbidding further revelations from above, Mani was receiving the most explosive revelation to date on the nature of existence and the purpose of the universe.

This was the beginning of Mani's public mission, and his first act as "Messenger of the Light" was to proclaim his revelation to his father and other members of his family and to convert them.

We next find Mani traveling to India, probably to what is now Pakistan, as he himself attests: "At the close of King Ardashir's years I set out to preach. I sailed to the land of the Indians. I preached to them the hope of life and I chose there a good selection." <7> Mani dwelt in India a little over a year, returned to Persia, then went on to Mesopotamia. During this time, King Ardashir died and his son Shapur succeeded him. Mani is said to have miraculously converted the King's brother by showing him a vision of the "paradise of Light." <8>

Mani's missionary activity now began in earnest throughout Babylonia, Media and Parthia. Mani eventually established a favorable relationship with King Shapur and was received by the new monarch in three successive audiences. <9> This was due to his having converted the King's brother Peroz, in whom Mani had found a powerful patron.

George Widengren tells us that Shapur "was deeply impressed by Mani's message and agreed to allow him to proclaim his teaching freely throughout the empire". <10> In fact, Mani accompanied King Shapur on his military campaigns during the days of the Roman Emperor Valerian. Thus, "there existed a special bond of obedience and loyalty between Shapur and Mani." <11> In the Kephalaia, quoted by Widengren, Mani writes in his own words: "King Shapur was solicitous on my behalf and wrote letters for me to all magnates in the following terms: 'Befriend and defend him, that none shall transgress or trespass against him.'" <12>

For a period of ten years Mani enjoyed the favor of the king, although the religion Mani taught never became the state religion. The King commanded his Zoroastrian "court chaplain" Karter, later Mani's archenemy, to reorganize the occupied provinces in Asia Minor according to the Iranian Fire-cult. <13> The Zoroastrian state church and its priesthood were so powerful and so firmly entrenched that the king never supplanted the old religion with Mani's new synthesis, which would have united the two theologies, Zoroastrian and Christian, into one grand universal religion and theosophic system. It was also, no doubt, meant to replace the narrow orthodox Christian creed which spurned every other religion as false. Although Shapur's personal sympathies lay with Mani, Mani's vision of a universal religion was to remain unfulfilled.

During his period of association with the King, Mani took extensive missionary journeys to various parts of the empire, founding new communities wherever he went, and sending his disciples east and west. One of Mani's disciples, Addai, founded monasteries, wrote books and "made of wisdom a weapon," preaching as far as Alexandria. <14> Mani himself wrote numerous books, letters and personal recollections, none of which have survived. We possess only fragments. In these letters Mani introduces himself at all times as, "Mani, Apostle of Jesus Christ." The religion of Mani, during this fruitful decade, spread into Egypt, Asia Minor, Mesopotamia, Persia, Afghanistan and parts of India. King Shapur died in April of 273 A.D. and was succeeded by his son Hormizd I, who was also favorably disposed toward Mani. Unfortunately Hormizd died after a reign of one year and was followed by his brother Bahram I, who reigned from 274 to 277. Mani, who at that time was preaching in the lower Tigris area, was commanded by the new King not to visit the realm Mani was intending to convert. Mani was ordered to return to the palace and present himself to the King. The powerful priesthood led by Karter had gained ascendancy and no doubt turned the king against Mani. A Parthian fragment quoted by Widengren states that Karter took counsel with the "royal vassals," and "envy and wiles were in their hearts." <15> The Magi submitted a bill of impeachment against Mani accusing him of teaching against the "law," i.e., the recognized Zoroastrian faith administered by the Magi. There is little doubt that Mani and his teaching were a threat to established Zoroastrianism—a threat to the power base enjoyed by the Magians, as Jesus was a threat to the priests of Judaism, and earlier to the Brahmins, and as the Christian-Gnostics were a threat to the bishops of the orthodox Christian Church.

When Mani entered the city (Belapat), the Magi accused him to the city authorities, who followed Mani to the court of the King. During the trial of Mani, the Magi and later the King are depicted as being enraged against Mani. This is more understandable when we realize that Mani was a healer and miracle-worker, who, like Jesus, his Lord, received the power to cast out demons and raise the dead. The Magi accused Mani of being a false teacher who led men astray, and an enemy of the state. Thus began the passion of Mani:

[The King] wrathfully said to [Mani]: 'Who bade thee do these things, or who art thou? Thou doest deeds that harm all men; who hast sent thee? For whom are thy preachings?...

Mani then answered:

Know, O King, that I am the servant of the God of Light, who has sent me in order to choose the Church out of a world which has fallen into many sins. It is God who has sent me to call thee, thou being a man, to the law of Life, and to teach thee the perfect commandments of Christ....Ask all the men about me. I have no human master and teacher from whom I have learned this wisdom....From God was sent to me a message that I should preach this in your kingdom, for this whole world has wandered into error and got into a bye-path; it has willfully fallen away from the Wisdom of God the Lord of All....For the proof of everything I bring is obvious; all that I teach existed in the first generations; but it is the custom that the Way of Truth is now and then revealed, and now and then conceals itself again.

Angered, the King replied:

How comes it that God reveals this to you, while the same God has not revealed it also to us, even though we are still the lords of the whole land?...Thou are a man of insignificance, unfit for God to give this unutterable favour and gift?

Mani answers:

Those who are of God do not seek after gold and the world's possessions; it is God who has the power to reveal His Truth to the one he chooses out of the crowd of all his creatures. It is God who teaches whom he will, and gives to him the Gift that surpasses all gifts, as a seal that he is a Prophet, the true Man of God in his deeds and his words. (Brackets added) <16>

The furious King then sentences him to death but first fetters him with chains on his feet, neck and back. Mani is kept in prison for 26 days, admonishing his disciples and communing with God. Finally, on February 26, A.D. 277, Mani, worn out by fasting and torture, ascended, in his soul, to the Father. He was sixty years of age. The vengeful King then proceeded to mistreat the body of Mani; his corpse was cut up and his head stuck over the gate of the city. After Mani's death a fierce persecution arose against Mani's disciples and all followers of the religion. Nevertheless, the Religion of Light spread in the following two decades over the entire face of the Roman Empire, finally threatening the "stability" of orthodox Christianity. Later in this chapter we will discuss the controversy between Manichaean and orthodox Christianity.

The Doctrine of Mani

The Conspiracy of Darkness

The religion of Mani was based on the backdrop of a pre-cosmic war between the Light and the Darkness. As a consequence of this War the elements of Light and Darkness became intermingled, giving rise to the creation of the physical cosmos. The purpose of existence, understood individually and cosmically, is to separate and redeem the Light from the Darkness.

Mani seems to have been vouchsafed a personal vision of the universe; a vision which he was commanded to share with all who would listen. In so doing he exposed a conspiracy of Darkness that threatened the vested interests in Church and State. His unveiling of "evil" as a positive force in the universe, as opposed to evil as "an absence of good," provoked persecution and vilification upon himself and his followers. Yet for every element of Darkness, Mani provided a counterpoint of Light, and in the end, Light is victorious.

Mani proclaimed that before the creation of the physical/material cosmos, there were two distinct realms: the Realm of Light, unbounded on three sides, spread North, East and West, and the realm of Darkness, which bordered the Light Realm on the South. These realms were also designated as two distinct natures, sources or principles.

Mani does not elaborate upon or attempt to explain the origin of these realms, except to affirm that they can be equated with two principles. The "Evil principle" is chaotic, destructive and warlike, and the "Good principle" is harmonious, peaceful and beautiful. Mani, therefore, would attribute no evil to the "Good principle." In Mani's theology God never was nor ever could be the cause of evil either directly or indirectly

The Realm of Light

God, whom Mani terms "the Father of Greatness," rules in the Realm of Light, which is described as a veritable universe of Light consisting of the spiritual or Light-counterparts of what later became the material cosmos. Thus, the Light-Realm is the Archetypal universe "consisting of the light of the earth and the light of the spheres."<17> Light is described by Mani as the substance of the Divine Being, and the entire Realm of Light is at once the body of the Godhead inhabited by numerous hierarchical beings. Surrounding God are his five glories who dwell with Him: Mind, Knowledge, Reason, Memory and Will. These are said to be parallel to the five aspects of the human soul.<18> The eternal God is also surrounded by twelve maidens described as angels with harps and lutes. There follows a description of the various Aeons. As a divine emanation or "evolution" from the Father, the Mother of Life is understood to be the first manifestation of God. Other Aeons who inhabit the Light-Realm are: the Friend of Lights; the Great Builder (Architect); the Living Spirit; the Holder (Custodian) of Splendour; the King of Honor; the Light-Adam; the King of Glory; Atlas the Supporter; the Third Messenger; the Archetypal or spiritual Sun and Moon; the Great Mind or Column of Glory; the Light Maiden; Jesus, the Archetypal Saviour; and the Primal Man and his five sons. <19> The latter have been equated with the ideal Souls of all humanity.

The Original Purity of the Preexistent Soul

Mani held that the Soul preexisted the material cosmos and in fact was of the same essence as the First or Primal Man. A Manichaean scripture reads as follows:

Now the Soul in men is part of the Light....<20> You shall see the Great of Glories [the Father] from whom every Soul has come forth in the beginning, and they shall also return to the Light and ascend to it in the end....O Soul, where art thou from? Thou art from on high, thou art a stranger to the world....<21> My holy Father [the Soul utters], let me see Thy Likeness that I saw before the universe was created.... (Brackets added) <22>

Far from teaching the debasement of man, as the Church Fathers accused him of teaching (in their own self-projection), Mani taught that the real man is the Soul, the Original Man, and that man's true home is the Land of Light, another descriptive term used for the Light-Realm. The system of Mani is pervaded by a sense of mission, as we shall later see, for the Soul came forth from the Father for the purpose of redeeming the cosmos. In contrast to the doctrine of original sin, propounded by Irenaeus, Tertullian and later by Augustine, Mani teaches the doctrine of the Soul's original purity prior to its descent into matter.

The Realm of Darkness

In marked opposition to the Light-Realm, Mani describes the Realm of Darkness as agitated, chaotic, possessing a lunar landscape of deep gulfs, abysses and pits. <23> In Manichaeism, the Darkness is sometimes termed "Matter," although not the matter of which this earth is composed. The matter of Darkness is more accurately termed "absolute dense matter." The Dark Realm consists of sub-worlds of smoke, fire, wind and water, each under its own ruler or archon in the form of an animal. The chief Archon of the Realm of Darkness, called the Prince or King of Darkness, rules with the Sons of Darkness over numerous demons whose chief characteristics are lust, concupiscence and desire. The Realm of Darkness is described by Mani as the exact antithesis of the Realm of Light.

Again, Mani does not reveal the origin of this realm. We may speculate, in accordance with Zoroastrian and Jewish Apocalyptic texts, that the inhabitants of the Realm of Darkness were rebels against the Light and perhaps were confined to this realm as a punishment for their rebellion. Mani, however, does not say.

Perhaps the Realm of Darkness was considered by the Manichaeans to be of unknown origin. Astronomers and physicists are speculating today about the origins of black holes, parallel universes and dark matter. Like Mani's Realm of Darkness black holes are thought to be absolutely dense. Was Mani the recipient of a Gnosis concerning the existence of invisible universes, realms or worlds occupying other octaves or frequencies of spirit and matter from the darkest and most dense or "evil" up to a universe of absolute Light where dwells the "Father of Greatness"?

Throughout the ages, humanity has wondered about the mystery of evil. Mani reveals quite logically that evil originates from a realm of evil which existed prior to and beyond the physical cosmos. Could this be a realm not yet dreamed of by scientists but known by visionaries down through the ages? We cannot dismiss, out of hand, Mani's vision any more than we can dismiss the vision of Zarathustra, or Enoch, or Jesus, or St. Paul, or Valentinus, or Origen regarding the origins of "Good" and "Evil." Perhaps these visionaries each unveiled a part of the truth, a part of the mystery.

Mani was the most persecuted, reviled and hated of all religious leaders. We can only conclude that his teachings on "evil" were, in fact, most threatening to Evil itself, acting through the powers that be in this world who perhaps wished to keep certain "secrets" regarding the nature of evil from the masses. It is a simple application of the law of action and reaction. The principles of physics are but a reflection of the laws of the spiritual sphere, and this is a principle that must be contemplated in the context of the actions we have seen taken against Christian-Gnostic teachings throughout this work. Thus it must be considered that the greater the light of truth released, the greater the reaction against it by its counterforce, the force of darkness. The intensity of reaction can be considered a gauge of the truth released. Did Evil and its embodied elements in fact feel the thrust, the action of Mani's teaching? Did they feel threatened? Their actions gave every indication that they did. Let us leave this question to the reader again to draw his or her own conclusions, as we continue to explore Mani's cosmological system.

The Darkness Attacks the Light

According to Mani, what precipitated the eventual creation of the physical cosmos was the attack of the Darkness and its inhabitants against the Light.

We recall that the Realm of Darkness bordered the Realm of Light to the south. After many ages, the Darkness became more and more disorderly and kept emanating many powers. As the Race of Darkness rose up, it gazed at the Light and desired, through lust, to possess it, to mingle with it and to occupy the Realm of Light, thus dispossessing God. <24> The King of Darkness, his five Sons, and the entire Race of Darkness determined to war against the Light-Realm, to seize and to blend their darkness with the Light.

The Soul Enters "Matter"

The Father of Greatness, seeing what was about to happen, considered that he would not send his five glories to fight the war (since the Realm of Light was a peaceful realm) but instead declared, "I myself will go out and see to this revolt." <25> God then devised a plan against the Darkness—a plan which would act as a bait for the force of Darkness while diminishing its ferocity by pervading the Darkness with Light. God's plan therefore was:

...To send...towards Matter [Darkness] a certain Power which is called the Soul, which should wholly permeate it. Now the Soul in men is part of the Light while the Body is of Darkness and Matter's handiwork...and there are these names of the Soul: Mind, Thought, Intention, Consideration, Reason...having taken a certain portion of the Light, He sent it out as a sort of bait and fishhook for Matter—a Power of the Good, not yet sensible Light but an emanation of God. (Brackets added) <26>

To accomplish this task, the Father of Greatness:

...called forth the Mother of Life, and (then) the Mother of Life evoked the First Man; then the First Man called forth his five Sons, like a man who puts on armor for war. Before him went out an Angel called Nahashbet, holding a crown of victory in his hand. So the First Man spread the Light in front of him. <27>

The First Man or Primal Man, as we have said, has been equated with the Archetypal Man. According to the "Gospel" of Mani, this man is the "Perfect Man" alluded to by St. Paul in his epistles and is, in fact, the "ideal of all humanity, manifesting God before the beginning of the worlds." <28> The First Man and his five Sons exist within the Souls of all humanity and, in a sense, are those Souls. The original Image of the First Man then is the pattern for all humanity. Jesus designated himself as the Son of Man—the Son (image) of the First Man, the Divine Man.

When the King of Darkness saw the First Man and his Sons and the Light emanating from them, he said, "What I was seeking from afar I have found nearby." <29> The Darkness, gazing at the Power sent forth, longed for it and became infatuated with it. Evil still continued to advance toward the Light in order to mingle with it and thus, through the power of Light, to sustain its (Evil's) own nature.

A supreme act of Self-sacrifice was now accomplished by the First Man and his five sons in order to diminish and eventually cause the dissolving of the Darkness:

The First Man gave himself and his five Sons in the five Elements as food for the five Sons of Darkness, just as a man who has an enemy mixes deadly poison in a cake and gives it to him. Then warring on him in return, the Rulers of Darkness...snatched from the Light, swallowed what had been sent, devoured from his panoply what was the Soul and distributed it to their own Powers. When they had eaten these, the intelligence of the five Bright Gods [the five Sons] was taken from them, and they were like the man bitten by a mad dog or a snake, because of the venom of the Sons of Darkness. (Brackets added) <30>

Here we come across a concept fundamental to Christianity: that of the "Lamb slain from the foundation of the world (cosmos)," as it is expressed in Rev. 13:8. The archetypal idea presented here is that the Son of Man/Son of God sacrifices himself and allows himself to be slain by the powers of Darkness, to accomplish the judgment and eventual dissolution of the Darkness. The light (blood) of the Lamb (Rev. 5:9, 7:14) is for the nourishment of the Sons of Light while at the same time, it is a poison for the Sons of Darkness. Jesus, in his role as Son of the First Man, reenacted the sacrifice of Archetypal Man when he permitted himself to be captured, crucified and slain by the powers of evil. The Book of Revelation is careful to point out that this process of "slaying" or self-sacrifice has been going on since the origin of the physical cosmos.

In Mani's sublime vision, God the Father sends a portion of himself, his Divine Image or Son, as a sacrifice for the salvation and redemption of the Light. In so doing the Souls of spiritual humanity are likewise sharing in the sacrifice, as they are one with the essence of the First Man—the Lamb—and have likewise sacrificed themselves.

So in this way...was the Soul mixed with Matter [Darkness], one unlike thing with an(other) unlike, and in the mixing the Soul has come to feel with Matter, and has been fettered and, as it were, snared in a sort of trap. (Brackets added) <31>

The fall and plight of the Soul is expressed beautifully in another Manichaean scripture:

(The Soul says:) "I am the Father's love, being the Robe clothing thee; I was a Prince wearing a crown among the kings; I knew not how to fight, belonging to the City of Gods. From the time that the Hated One cast an eye on my kingdom, I left my Fathers resting, I came and gave myself to death for them. I armed myself...and I fought. Thou didst agree with me at that time, saying: 'If victorious thou shalt receive thy garland!' I conquered in the first battle, (but) yet another struggle arose for me. I put on error and oblivion; I forgot my being and race and kinsfolk, not knowing the door of the place of prayer to Him and of invoking Him—I became an enemy to my Father, I was made to drink the cup of madness, I was made to rebel against my own Self. The Powers and Authorities entered. They armed themselves against me. <32>

The above passage also clearly states that the Soul preexisted in a divine state in the Kingdom of the Father, the Archetypal spiritual universe, before descending to battle with the forces of Darkness. The Soul's sojourn in the matter universe is imbued with mission: to be the very incarnation (Robe) of the Father's self-sacrificing love. As a result of the Soul's battle with Darkness, the now fallen Soul became a divine victim, lost the memory of its origin and became rebellious toward the Father, having imbibed the poison of the madness of the Dark Ones.

The Rescue of the Soul

The Gospel continues:

Then the First Man was cruelly afflicted down there by the Darkness. When the First Man came to his senses, he put up seven times a prayer to the Father of Greatness, and the Father heard when he prayed. God therefore pitied him and called for the Second Evocation, the Friend of Lights; and the Friend of Lights evoked the Great Builder; and the Great Builder called forth the Living Spirit—another Power emanated from Himself.

Then the Living Spirit called his five Sons; The Holder of Splendour from his Intelligence, the Great King of Honour from his Knowledge, the Diamond [Adamas] of Light from his Reason, the King of Glory from his Thought, and the Supporter from his Deliberation; these came to the Region of Darkness and found the First Man absorbed by the Darkness, he and his Sons.

Thereupon the Living Spirit called with a (loud) voice, and the Living Spirit's voice resembled a sharp sword swift as the lightning; and it became another God and revealed the form of the First Man. Then it said to him, "Peace to thee, O good one among the wicked, light amidst the darkness, god dwelling among wild beasts who know not their honour!" The First Man answered him saying, "Come in peace, bringing the merchandise [merits] of calm and peace!" He also said to him, "How are our Fathers, the Sons of Light, faring in their City?" The Caller said to him, "They are prospering."; and coming down he gave him a right hand and led him up out of the Darkness.

The Caller and the Answerer united and went up towards the Mother of Life and the Living Spirit; and the Living Spirit put on the Caller, while the Mother of Life put on the Answerer, her beloved Son, and they went down to the Earth of Darkness to the place of the First Man and his Sons. (Brackets added) <33>

Thus, by the agency of various members of the spiritual hierarchy, the Archetypal Man/Soul is rescued from the Darkness and united with the Divine Mother in the Kingdom of Light. Then commences the formation of the physical cosmos in order to separate the elements of Light and Darkness.

The Judgment of the Archons and the Creation of Physical Cosmos

Although the First Man was rescued, the light elements still remained in the throes of Darkness. Thus the "self" or "soul" of the First Man continued fettered and defiled and needed to be liberated and brought back to the Light Realm. This task was performed by the Living Spirit,<34> who called forth his Sons to kill and to flay the Rulers of Darkness and to deliver them to the Mother of the Living. <35> She then spread out the heavens with their "skins" and formed ten heavens; the archons' "bodies" were flung to the Region of Darkness and eight earths were constructed from these "bodies." Then the Living Spirit created the Universe by first descending to the Darkness and leading the Rulers up and fastening (crucifying) them in the heavens or firmament. The Living Spirit, then, commences the work of liberation: the particles of light that had not been befouled he purified and thus formed the Sun and moon as two vessels of Light. Light particles that had been partially mixed with Darkness he transformed into stars. To rescue Light elements (souls) that had been almost wholly sullied with Darkness, the Father of Greatness called forth the Third Messenger, who then prepared the mechanism for the saving of the Souls: a "machine" with twelve "waterwheels," i.e., the twelve Virgins or Virtues, corresponding to the twelve signs of the zodiac, expressing consecutive stages of spiritual growth within twelve dimensions or attributes of God's Being.

Greenlees expounds on the meaning of the formation of the physical cosmos as follows:

To rescue Soul bound up in Matter [Darkness], this

very Matter itself had to be fashioned into a universe subject to law; this very obedience imposed upon its evil qualities of disorder—"crucifying the demons" and binding them to a form molded of their own very nature—enabled God to overcome the rebelliousness inherent in every form of Evil. So the Divine manifestations of Mind each took over the control of a part of the vast universe, and the luminaries—Sun and Moon and Stars being themselves formed from Light—were devised as means to attract the Light-Spark held in dark Matter, to draw it up to its eternal Source, and so to free it from the entangling impurity. (Brackets added) <36>

The Third Messenger, therefore:

...revealed the first steps up the Path of Righteousness, the twelve great virtues symbolized and conferred by the Zodiacal signs after conquest of the opposite evils innate in them. While the rotating universe pursues its ceaseless course, the practice of these virtues gradually refines and elevates the Soul towards the endless Light of perfection. <37>

The cosmic wheel, therefore, the twelve signs of the zodiac, draws up the particles of light or souls to the Moon and to the Sun (understood in their archetypal nature). We quote again from the Gospel:

When the Moon, then, has handed over the freight of Souls to the Aeons [Divine Beings] of the Father, they remain there in the Column of Glory [visible in the Milky Way] which is called the 'Perfect Man'...it is a pillar of light because loaded with the Souls that are being purified. Now the Moon...first receives the radiant Souls from Matter, and then deposits (them) in the Light, and it does this continuously; this is the way in which the Souls are saved. So the Sun began to purify the Light which was mixed with the demons of Heat, and the Moon began to purify the Light mixed with the demons of Cold, that (Light) rises up in the 'Column of Praise' with the *hymns and worships, the good deeds and kind words which are sent up. (Brackets added) <38>*

Thus there are expressed here profound spiritual laws determining the rising of spiritual light in fact generated by "righteous" thought and action into higher spheres of being. Mani and his followers, however, received the condemnation of the Church Fathers for his "pagan" manner of expressing the mechanism of salvation by the use of the heavenly bodies and luminaries. Again, the Church Fathers interpreted Mani's doctrine literally and failed to appropriate the spiritual sense of his teachings. For the Sun and Moon have, from ancient times, represented stages or levels of spiritual unfoldment or evolution and stations that souls progress through on their way to Absolute Light. In Mani's concept, the entire universe is involved with the separation of Light from Darkness, which is the very process of salvation.

The Archons Release Their Stolen Light

As a consequence of the archons' devouring or assimilating the Light of the five Sons of the Primal Man, much Light was still entangled in the archons who themselves were fastened in the firmament, i.e., controlled by the laws of the material cosmos. In order to release this Light, the Third Messenger revealed his male and female forms to the male and female archons. At the sight of the beauty of the Messenger, the archons were filled with sexual lust for the Light and, as a result, began to emit the Light of the five Sons which they had stolen. This escaping Light is received by the angels and transported to the Moon and the Sun to the Realm of Light or Spiritual Source. However, as the archons released their Light, they also released their Dark substance or "sin." The substance of "sin", mingled with the Light, was separated out by the Messenger; the darkness or sin fell back upon the archons, who rejected it. Consequently the rest of the mingled Light and darkness fell upon the earth where it eventually produced plants, trees and grain. That which fell upon the sea (the plane of desire) became a female monster, who was slain by a divine being known as the "Diamond of Light." <39>

The Archons Entrap Souls in Material Bodies—"Adam and Eve"

We now arrive at that portion of Mani's doctrine which provoked the unmitigated wrath of the Church Fathers, as did the doctrines of the Christian-Gnostics over a century earlier: the creation/procreation of material man by the evil archons. Mani's exposè of the strategies of Darkness or Evil in its attempt to counteract the strategies of Light engendered both fear and unrelenting anger in his self-styled enemies, namely the orthodox clergy. In an age when the Church Fathers were seeking to suppress and conceal all evidence regarding the existence of the archons, demons, giants, fallen angels and other manifestations of evil, Mani was revealing the conspiracy of Darkness to his followers, for he taught nothing less than the counterfeit creation of mankind (a kind of man) by evil creative powers.

The scenario begins when Ashaqlun or Saklas, the Son of the King of Darkness, declares to the daughters of Darkness: "Come, give me some of the Light we have taken; it is I who will make for you a form like what you have seen which is the First Man." <40> We note the similarity to the previously quoted text The Apocryphon of John (2nd century) wherein Iladobaoth determines to create a material man as a copy of the spiritual man.

...moved by jealously, Matter made man out of itself by mixing with the whole of the Power, having also something of the Soul (in him). However the form did much to let Man gain somewhat more of the Divine Power than other mortal living things, for he is an image of the Divine Power. <41>

The King of Darkness, then:

...conceived anew a wicked plan in his poisoned heart: he then ordered Saklas and Nebroel [the female demon] to imitate Pure Spirit and Excellent Mother....They formed the body of Man and there imprisoned the Light Natures to imitate the Macrocosm. So then the flesh body, with the corrupt evil Greed and Lust, was the faithful image point by point, though smaller, of the heavens and the earths.... There was not a single formation of the universe they did not reproduce. (Brackets added) <42>

Then Nebroel and Ashaqlun [Saklas] united together and she conceived from him and bore a son whom she called "Adam"; she conceived again, and bore a daughter whom she called "Eve".... (Brackets added) <43>

Now whereas Adam was created beastlike, Eve was lifeless and motionless; but the male virgin whom they call Daughter of the Light and named Ioel gave Eve a share of Life and Light. Next Eve freed Adam from bestiality.... <44>

Thus, in this account, "Adam and Eve," representative of a certain race of souls of Light, took incarnation as the progeny of the rebellious archons in order to counteract the strategies of darkness and eventually to redeem and purify the bodies (from greed and lust carried in the genes) which they would propagate from generation to generation. Mani, like the Christian-Gnostics before him, viewed the archons as the originators of lustful sexual intercourse. Although Mani has been recorded as teaching that propagation is a device used by the archons to keep souls forever chained to bodies, it is also true that in Mani's "church" the "hearers" were not forbidden to marry. The Elect alone were celibate. Like the Buddha before him, Mani was concerned with the problem of untoward desire, which keeps the soul bound to the body and to seemingly endless successive reincarnations. And yet souls of Light, taking incarnation in these bodies, could themselves purify the act of sex, which the archons had injected with lust. It also becomes quite obvious that the two archons/demons mentioned in the above text are embodied and not vapory "spirits," as it would be impossible to propagate through sexual intercourse. The "Adamic race" had a mission to redeem future generations from the pollutions of the archons through whom corruption entered the race of humanity. But first "Adam and Eve" must themselves be redeemed.

The Redemption of Adam and Eve

Continuing our survey:

>So they both [Adam and Eve] asked for the Redeemer, and the Mother of Life and the First Man and the Spirit of Life (decided) to send to that "first child," one who should free him and save him, show him the Knowledge and Righteousness, and rescue him from the demons. Being kindly and pitiful....the Good Father sent from his bosom....His beloved Son...into the heart of the earth and into its lowest parts...for the saving of the Soul.... (Brackets added) <45>
>
>Jesus the Radiant approached Adam the Innocent, and awoke him from the sleep of death, so that he might be rescued from the Great Spirit [the Great Demon]....So he woke him, took hold of him and shook him....Then he warned him against Eve, showed him her reproach, and forbade him to touch her; he drove away from him the Seducer and bound the Great Queen [Greed—the female Archon] far from him. Thereupon Adam examined himself and realized whence (he came); and Jesus showed him the Fathers on high and his own Self in everything....
>
>· Then Jesus raised him and made him taste of the Tree of Life; and thereupon Adam looked and wept, he mightily lifted up his voice like a raging lion saying: "Woe, woe to the maker of my body, and to the binder of my Soul, and to the Rebels who have enslaved me." (Brackets added) <46>

This scenario is the archetypal pattern of Christian-Gnostic salvation: redemption from ignorance perpetrated by the archons through their attempt to bind men permanently to a genetically and otherwise manipulated physical matrix, an envelope of matter and consciousness tainted with rebellion and the lust of the archons. It is these desires, Mani taught, that enslave man, not mere physical matter alone. Thus Mani's rationale for the fallen state of humanity unveils a far greater and more complex scenario than the simplistic orthodox dogma that two individuals named Adam and Eve, in a one-time, God-given, all-or-none test for the whole of humanity, ate of forbidden fruit after being tempted by a talking serpent.

We can also note the very significant fact that Jesus in his preexistent state, prior to his descent into incarnation, is the instrument of Adam's redemption, the Saviour, par excellence. We find this scene curiously missing from the orthodox accounts of the fall. Thus, for Mani, Jesus' saving mission is far more ancient than his single incarnation in Palestine. This is nearly identical to St. Paul's teaching regarding Jesus, who, he writes, existed in a "Godlike" form before his mission on earth.(Phil.2:6-8)

As Adam and Eve were awakened and saved by the Redeemer, so all souls in this world must be awakened to their true origin and made aware of the Great Rebellion, the mingling of Light and Darkness, and the purpose of the Cosmos: to free the Light-Souls from darkness and matter. The instruments of this ultimate freedom and salvation are Jesus, the Saviour, the Hierarchies of Light, and the Light Mind, present in all spiritual beings and in the soul of Light.

Mani's Doctrine of the Last Things

The process of the liberation of the Light concludes when all the particles of Light are reassembled in the Light-Realm. The final eschatalogical event is the dissolving of dense matter and darkness, and thus the "world" as we know it ends, for all has been assimilated into the World of Light. This event will be heralded by a series of catastrophic scenarios similar to the synoptic apocalypses in the New Testament (Mark 13,

Matthew 24, Luke 21), and to the Jewish apocalyptic texts. Widengren mentions a Turkish Manichaean fragment which describes a "False Mithra" (in Christian terminology the Anti-Christ) who will appear in the last days mounted on a bull and whose token is war. <47> When the liberation of the Light has been nearly fulfilled the great war will break out, as Lieu observes, since by that time what remains on earth will be primarily Matter, dominated by sin and strife. <48> The other side of the coin of this "war" concerns the simultaneous triumph of the church of righteousness. Widengren encapsulates Manichaean eschatology as follows:

The scattered congregation would come together again, the church would be restored, the endangered scriptures saved, and Manichaeism's victory be complete. "The new generation will come and take firm possession of its estate." (Homilies, p. 28, 7-8) The Great King will come and assume dominion, for the new generation will do him homage. The last judgment will follow, when the souls will assemble in front of the throne, his bema. The Good will be separated from the Evil, the sheep from the goats....

Jesus...would reign on earth a short time. Then Christ and the elect together with the cosmic tutelary gods will leave the world and return to the realm of light. A last process of purification takes place. Those particles of light that it is still possible to rescue will be collected to form an "ultimate statue"...which will be raised to heaven like a cosmic pillar of light. Hereupon the terrestrial globe itself will be annihilated. The damned and the demons, the world of matter and darkness, will be thrown together in a shapeless clod, bolos, which will be sunk in the deeps of a moat of cosmic extent that will then be covered with a gigantic rock.

With these grandiose cosmic visions Mani ended his account of the world's course and thus came to the close of the "Third Epoch." The First Epoch embraced the state of the universe prior to the blending of the light and darkness; the Second Epoch was concerned with the period of that blending;

the Third Epoch signified the sundering of the blended elements. This doctrine of the Three Epochs is together with the Two Principles Manichaeism's main dogma. <49>

According to Manichaean-Christian doctrine, the "annihilation" of the earth refers to the process whereby the dense material globe is "raised" to its "etheric" counterpart, its true form and likeness as it existed in the universe of Light. This "annihilation" is made possible by the burning of a "Great Fire" (for a period of 1,468 "years") and the entire universe of matter is transmuted into the higher realms. Thus, the universe moves from the manifest to the (to our senses) unmanifest. We note the absence in this eschatology of an eternal hell as taught by the orthodox clergy. Darkness/Evil is rendered inactive, and a universe of Light prevails forever.

Comments on Christian-Gnostic and Manichaean-Christian Anthropology

The reader may find the idea of the "creation" of the physical or material man by the evil powers to be repugnant or perhaps even ludicrous. The reader may query, "Is not man made in the image of God?" To answer this question, we must remember that man is a spiritual being first and foremost, and in his true nature he is spiritual, not material—the image of the invisible God. The Divine Nature and soul of man are of God. The true Man is not to be found in the body, nor can we circumscribe man by his body alone. We recall Jesus' statement regarding men's true nature, "Ye are gods," i.e., spiritual beings. Once we have established that man is primarily spiritual, we can easily conclude that the appearance of man's body, of whatsoever shape, form or origin, does not and cannot define who man really and intrinsically is.

This dichotomy between spiritual and the physical we have previously reviewed in the first two chapters of Genesis: the spiritual creation of man in the first, and the physical creation of man in the second. St. Paul, we recall, writes of the

Adam of flesh, of the earth, earthy and the second Adam, the "Lord from Heaven." This duality of man's nature and its causes is a pervading theme of ancient Christianity as it was in ancient Judaism and Zoroastrianism. If man is created spiritually in God's image, why is he mortal and doomed to so-called death? The modern-day average Christian would answer that man became "mortal" after the fall in Eden. Yet, according to orthodox Christianity, the "fall" of man occurred in only two individuals: Adam and Eve. What of the rest of humanity? They had no free-will choice to fall or not to fall. They were born fallen from the womb, subject to mortality, since, according to the orthodox viewpoint, there is no preexistence.

But the ancient Christians answered differently. All souls were given free choice to fall or not to fall, and in lowering the frequency of their consciousness they became vulnerable to the machinations of the fallen ones of whatever species. The teachings of ancient Christianity, as we have seen, unveiled a "conspiracy of darkness" among hierarchies of rebellious beings who sought to compete with and usurp the authority of hierarchies of Light, and to seduce the souls and spirits evolving in various dimensions of the spiritual/material universe. For according to the law of spiritual evolution, all beings must come to the point of decision where the choice is given them to take what is known in esoteric parlance as the "right-handed path" or "left-handed path." In the former, the choice is made to serve all sentient beings as the expression of the One Life. In the latter, the choice is made to serve and aggrandize the self as the ego, now conceived as a "being" separate from and greater than the One Life. Hence we find the origin of duality as a self-made choice according to the texts we have perused. This "left-handed" decision with its attendant defection and rebellion took place on a grand scale at some point in the distant past, perhaps millions of years ago. We have seen this clearly in the Book of Revelation (Chapter 12), and in the Christian-Gnostic and Manichaean texts. As a corollary to this defection, the fallen hierarchies sought to imitate the spiritual creation by capturing the spiritual beings in dense bodies which they fabricated by various means, not excluding genetic engineering. Thus, in order to sustain themselves, the rebellious powers needed the "light" or energy of the heavenly realms of which the souls created by God were composed. The souls then became the "food" of the archons, without which they would perish. This interference in and manipulation of humanity's spiritual evolution as one of the causes of duality and mortality in man was clearly taught by the ancient Christian initiates of various schools and communities and was apparently known by Jesus. The creation of physical, material man by the archons, and what might be considered subsequent "nth derivative" creations of "homo sapiens" by the Nephilim and the propagation of an ungodly race by the Watchers, thus rendered man subject to not only the laws of mortality but to inbred emotions of rebellion and lust and animal-like behavior that could only be eradicated by "spiritual surgery" as it were, by man's submission to the path of initiation whereby he is restored to his original, inner Divine Nature. The initial means to this restoration or redemption was provided by the Avatars, such as Jesus, who either had never become subject to the seductions of the fallen ones or who had found their way out of the fallen condition by aeons of spiritual striving and evolution. If humanity lost the Divine Spark or if some had never had it, they could gain it by acceptance of the Saviour as the Archetype of the true man—an acceptance which now would be the symbol of that to which they would begin to strive. This, we believe, is the meaning of the statement in John's gospel, "But as many as received him [Jesus], to them gave he the power to become the sons of God, even to them that believe on his name: which were born, not of blood, nor of the will of the flesh, nor of the will of man, but of God." (John 1:12-13) To have been "born" or physically created through "blood" and the "will of the flesh" or the "will of man" relates to the genetic material in the bodies worn by humanity for aeons, which originated not from a Divine Source but from the evil or lesser "creators," whether we consider them to be advanced scientists ("gods") or self-proclaimed rulers (archons) who sought to make or remake the race of mankind in their own image. No matter how or by whom humanity's physical, corrupt human nature had arisen, humanity could receive the power to become the "Sons of God," as they were formerly in their preexistent state, through the person and teaching of Jesus. This was the key behind the distorted doctrine of "original sin," which, as it was developed in the church, ignored the true spiritual nature of man, which existed before the body. Are we to blame the woes of humanity on these fallen powers? Not necessarily. According to Origen, all in the universe is the result of cause and effect, or the working of karma. If the souls or created spirits had preserved their first love and had not grown "cold" as Origen expresses it, thus descending to a lower estate, they would not have been subject to the bodily entrapments and seductions of the fallen powers. Yet once they had so fallen, the Father in his Infinite Wisdom accommodated the souls in their fallen levels of consciousness by the creation of various realms or frequencies of matter in and through which the souls would evolve to work out their "karma" and thus again gain access to the spiritual realms and their lost first estate.

According to Mani, however, the plight of the soul is due to 1) its being sent by the Father into the realm of darkness/matter to dissolve the darkness and thus redeem not only itself but the entire universe, and 2) the soul's voluntary act of descent into matter for the judgment of the archons. Thus, in Origen's system, the souls fall because of a defect in their nature; in Mani's system, the souls "fall" of their own free will or the Father's will, to redeem the cosmos. We suggest that these two cosmologies are not antagonistic but complementary and that there are souls presently in incarnation for both these reasons.

We again ask the question, were mankind or at least the bodies of mankind created by God or the fallen powers? If we closely examine the teaching of ancient Christianity, the answer seems to be that the bodies of humanity were created or formed by both: by God (Elohim) as vehicles of self-expression in the material cosmos and by the fallen powers in imitation of God's creation. And what of the soulless beings created by genetic engineering, cloning, or by other means? This is simply answered by the understanding that all beings, whatever their origin, have the potential to receive the divine spark, and thus become spiritual beings.

In the final analysis, what is significant about man is not his body but his Divine Nature, his soul and his mind, which bears an affinity to the Divine Mind. The body of man, no matter what its origin, is, in reality, a chimera on the screen of life as matter itself resolves into Spirit. And as we have seen in the Christian-Gnostic and Manichaean texts, souls who take incarnation in dense bodies of whatever source, can redeem and "resurrect" those bodies, i.e., the matter of those bodies can become spiritualized. And thus a divine race of Sons of God was destined to replace the corrupt "human" race. Let us close this section with passages from St. Paul, illustrative of man's glorious destiny:

So when this corruptible shall have put on incorruption and this mortal shall have put on immortality, then shall be brought to pass the saying that is written, Death is swallowed up in victory! (1 Cor. 15:54)

For I reckon that the sufferings of this present time are not worthy to be compared with the glory which shall be revealed in us.

For the earnest expectation of the creature waiteth for the manifestation of the Sons of God....

Because the creature itself also shall be delivered from the bondage of corruption into the glorious liberty of the children of God.

For we know that the whole creation groaneth and travaileth in pain together until now.

And not only they, but ourselves also, who have the first fruits of the Spirit, even we ourselves, waiting for the adoption, that is the redemption of our body. (Rom. 8: 18-19, 21-23)

In this second passage, St. Paul writes somewhat mysteriously of the "creature" which, in the light of all we have reviewed, we understand to mean the counterfeit bodies, the genetically engineered man, the mechanized man; in short, all within man that is not of Divine Origin—the creation of the archons/demons. Yet, within this "creature" lies the potential to become the Son of God. St. Paul expects the "redemption" of the body. From what must the body be redeemed if not from the genetic "tares" sown among the "wheat" of man's higher nature? (As illustration, see Jesus' parable of the tares and the wheat.) Such were the "mysteries" of redemption unveiled by Mani and others before him who had access to the secret doctrine.

Manichaean-Christian Salvation—The Writings of Mani

From the beginning Mani divided his followers into the elect and the hearers. The elect were called, if they chose to accept the call, to live a life solely for the redemption of their souls. Thus they were celibate, and vegetarian, and practiced strict purity of thought and speech. It was taught that they were not subject to reincarnation. The hearers led a normal domestic life and provided for the elect. The basic teaching undergirding the Manichaean way of life was respect for the presence of Light elements in all of nature and, as a corollary, a rejection of the darkness which likewise permeated nature and the soul of man. This life of a Manichaean Christian initiate was to consciously liberate the Light in himself and the world, thus contributing to the alchemy of cosmic salvation.

The Manichaean Christians practiced Baptism, Bema Feast and Communion. The Bema Feast (Bema: throne or the focus of Mani's presence) was a celebration of the passion and death of their founder Mani. The Communion was in commemoration of Jesus' bestowing upon Adam the fruit of the tree of life. The Manichaean practiced the giving of hymns, prayers and chants for the purpose of releasing the soul from bondage. By practicing the codes and the way of life recommended by Mani, the initiate could free his soul from reincarnation and ascend back to the Source of Life, the Heavenly Realm from whence it had descended. By fasting, prayer and service to one's fellowman, and by following the precepts of Mani, the initiate won the "Robe of Glory" or "wedding garment"—the soul must wear this "vesture of Light" in order to ascend back to the Light Realm and to the Father. If the soul has not kept the precepts of the holy religion and is not worthy of the "Robe of Glory," it returns to the world and continues to reincarnate until a future age when, purified and made white, the soul then ascends. We quote a Manichaean scripture which beautifully expresses the joy of the soul who has won its spiritual victory by faithfulness to the Religion of Light:

I rejoice, I rejoice for eternity of eternities! I worship Thee, O Father of the Lights, and I bless you, O Aeons of Joy, and my brothers and sisters from whom I have been far away and have found again once more! I have become a holy Bride in the peaceful Bridechambers of the Light; I have received the gifts of the victory. <50>

I have left the garment [dense physical body] on the earth. I have put upon me the immortal robe....O Saints, rejoice with me, for I have returned again to my beginning, the Path of Light has stretched for me right up to my First City, it has victoriously given me unto the Lands of the Angels, and they have escorted me to my Kingdom....The gates of the skies have opened before me through the rays of my Saviour and his glorious Light-image. Christ my Bridegroom has welcomed me to his bridechamber, (and) I have rested with him in the land of the Immortals....O my end which has had (so) happy an issue! O my everlasting possession. <51>

Before closing this chapter, we should briefly discuss the writings of Mani, only fragments of which have survived. These works were considered to be the "canon" of Manichaean Christians: <52>

1) Sahbuhragan or Shapur-aquan was written in Persian expressly for King Shapur I in about A.D. 242, by Mani himself. This was the first publication in which Mani initially revealed his doctrine and contained Mani's cosmology. In it Mani wrote an account of his birth, calling and Prophethood.

2) The Living Gospel or The Great Gospel written in Syriac in 22 chapters. We know very little of the content of this book except that it was said to contain all truth and was written with illustrations. We possess a fragment of its alleged opening words: "I Mani, the Messenger of Jesus the Friend, in the love of the Father, of the Glorious One..." To this work seem to have belonged several surviving fragments on the Crucifixion and Resurrection.

3) The Treasure of Life dealt with, among other subjects, the condition of the dwellers in the Realm of Light, and the so-called "Seduction of the Archons." This work consisted of seven books and dealt with anthropology, psychology and a detailed interpretation of man as microcosm.

4) The Pragmateia, i.e., "what ought to be done." This book is said to have contained the "commandments" and rules for entering into religion, precepts for the "Elect" governing clothing, diet, fasts, rituals, the liturgy of hymns and psalms to be sung at home and in the churches.

5) The Book of Mysteries in eighteen chapters was written to refute the false doctrines of the established sects and creeds in the world, including the sect of Bardesain or Bardesan. The book evidently dealt with the esoteric life of Jesus. The nature of Soul and Body was defined, and this work clearly taught reincarnation. A portion of the book was in the form of a dialogue between Jesus and his apostles.

6) The Book of the Giants contained stories of the fall of angels

and Watchers of primeval times, of their offspring the "giants" and heroes. Two characters appear in this work, Sam and Nariman, dragon-killers. Both Seth and Enoch are mentioned in this work and are said to be "Messengers" of God.

7) The Book of Letters was a collection of Mani's letters about which we know very little, except to say that Mani dealt with doctrinal points and organizational problems, much in the manner of St. Paul's epistles.

There are numerous pieces of non-canonical literature extant, such as the recently discovered *Cologne Mani Codex*. We, of course, possess voluminous tracts and writings from Church Fathers, Popes and Muslims refuting Mani's doctrine and quoting from Mani's works. It would take an entire volume to properly discuss and delineate the doctrines of this Christian movement, despised and misunderstood for centuries. Yet we can do nothing less than take "Manichaeism" at face value and accept it as a legitimate body of Christian teachings, as another "gnostic" revelation worthy of our study and assimilation. Only then can we rightly discern the nature of early Christianity.

The Character of Mani

In analyzing Manichaeism or what we have chosen to term Manichaean Christianity, George Widengren argues that Mani, in fact, founded "a completely new religion"<53> comprised of earlier creeds and doctrines. We would agree with this, except for the fact that Mani seems not to have gathered past religious teachings and sewn them together to form a patchwork quilt of new ideas he then called a religion. Like St. Paul, Mani received his message as a revelation, and because of this, as Widengren states, he was the last of the great Gnostics. What Mani founded was a universal Christian theosophy, far ahead of its time, a universal religion and church destined to replace the warring creeds of the day, yet thoroughly imbued with the essence of true mystical Christianity.

We may even say that Mani, before Mohammed, was the last of the great prophets. Widengren reflects on the personality of Mani and the effect his character had on the times:

> *A vivid sense of mission sounded through all Mani's words. He proclaimed his teaching with natural authority....Astonishing too was his vigor and versatility. He intervened at all points, teaching, consoling, admonishing, bringing order. He was one of the most tremendous church founders and religious organizers the world has ever seen. In his own lifetime his faith stretched from the west of the Roman Empire to India, from the borders of China to Arabia....The facts cited do suggest the founder of this religion to have been a quite extraordinary personality who was brought low only by external forces.... <54>*
> *His personality was out of the ordinary in a way that is directly attractive to us. The brisk and successful missionary, shrewdly and methodically building up his propaganda, is as intelligible to us as the careful organizer who lays down both a firm and supple structure for his church....*
> *There were nevertheless other aspects of his character, aspects that have since ancient times been hallmarks of Middle Eastern religious leaders. He was a miracle-worker in the classic style. Above this he was a physician capable of driving out the demons possessing the sick and thus healing them....Mani himself evidently could command levitation at will....He apparently claimed to have ascended to heaven and there to have received the divine revelation in the shape of a book.... <55>*
> *Mani's artistic and literary endowment was surprisingly varied. He was a complete master of all the different branches of Oriental literature. Not only was he lyrical and epic, but so vivid in his description of the struggle between the world of light and that of darkness that he could almost be called a dramatist....His sermons too were admirably contrived. In unpretentious, simple language he showed the ordinary man the situation of the material world. He employed*

all the symbols, similes and allegories of the Gnostic language to give his preaching life and colour.... His capacity to hold his listeners must have been very striking....

Without pedantry, he preached with great vivacity, in a way that everybody could understand....

But Mani was a great ritualist who developed a special type of divine service in which the word of God as shaped by the Master was at the centre. His hymns and psalms gave the lead to the rich deployment of sacred poetry that so markedly distinguished his religion....His zealous efforts to enlist art in the service of religion reached from the sacred writings to the rich costumes of the officiating priests and the embellishment of the holy precincts. Ahead of his time, he grasped how to blend word and picture. <56>

From Chapter Seven, "Manichaean Art," Widengren discusses Mani as artist:

Mani had an aesthetic turn of nature. He loved music and painting, the former to such a degree that his followers, according to Augustine (De Moribus Manichaeorum 11, v. 16), ascribed music to divine origin....Mani dispatched scribes and illuminators together with his missionaries. According to his own testimony, the pictures illustrating his writings were to complete educated people's instruction whilst rendering the message easier to understand for others....

That he was himself a practicing artist is unanimously attested by all Oriental sources....He says: 'For the Apostles all, my Brothers, who before me came, [did not write down] their wisdom, as I wrote mine, [nor did] they paint their wisdom in pictures, as [I did paint] mine.' <57>

Widengren concludes by referring to Mani as an "eclectic-syncretic theosophist" who propounded not a religious philosophical system but "a divine revelation":

He should, however, be judged for what he was and

wanted to be: the bearer of divine revelation and the Apostle of Light. <58>

The Controversy between Orthodox and Manichaean Christianity

The Manichaean Concept of Christ

By the close of Mani's life, the teachings of the revolutionary religion he founded reached the Jordan in Palestine. Thomas, one of Mani's disciples, preached the doctrines in Judea, as well as Syria and Egypt. From Egypt, the religion spread to Northern Africa and Spain, from Syria via Asia Minor to Greece, Illyria, Italy and Gaul. Manichaeism suffered persecution as a result of the edicts of the Emperor Diocletian circa 297, but far worse was the persecution emanating from the orthodox Christian church, which had aligned itself with the Roman State. By 312 A.D. the religion was firmly established in Rome as a powerful rival of orthodox Christianity. What so incensed the orthodox clergy against the expositors of the doctrines of Mani was that its adherents were preaching what they considered to be original Christianity as carried forward by Paul the Apostle, and as restored and renewed by Mani, as the representative of the Paraclete. Why the necessity for renewal? Manichaean Christians taught that by the close of the third century, the original doctrines of Christ had been destroyed by dogmas alien to Christianity and by church leaders who continued to keep Christianity bound to Judaism, or at least orthodox Judaism, through their enforcing of the Old Testament upon Christians of whatever persuasion and from whatever background. Manichaean Christians, on the other hand, claimed that what they taught was a universal theosophic religion, all-inclusive, and that this religion was not only Christian but contained revelations as received by Mani, the Apostle of Christ, and these revelations were deemed authentic. Added to this was Mani's exposure of the "conspiracy of Darkness" in the cosmos and in the world and his resuscitation of certain banned texts such as the Book of Enoch. Mani produced his work, The Book of the Giants, which further expounded upon the infiltration of "embodied evil" on the planet. What further paralyzed the bishops with fear was the Manichaean viewpoint that the Christian church itself had been subject to this infiltration and that very early on the doctrines of Jesus had been purposely changed and distorted. So convincing was the doctrine of Mani that during the Council of Nicea (325 A.D.) Constantine besought a certain Musonian to report to him on Manichaean doctrine so as to choose between it and orthodox Christianity as a replacement for the Roman State religion. <59> This was not to be, however, and throughout the fourth century, both Church Fathers and orthodox Christian emperors fulminated against Manichaean Christianity, determined to destroy it.

The epitome of this controversy was soon to be seen in the debate between Augustine and the Manichaean bishop, Faustus. Prior to the debate runs a history of severe persecution against the Manichaeans by some of the most well-known and respected Church Fathers such as Basil of Caesarea, Gregory of Nyssa, Epiphanius, Ambrose of Milan, John Chrysostom and Cyril of Jerusalem.

In his ongoing debate with Augustine carried out through the written word, Faustus attacked the Christian Bible, which by the fourth century had become a "sacred cow" to the Church Fathers and, of course, the sole "proof" of the "truth" of their dogmas. Faustus argued that the Bible (which by that time had become the "official Bible," ordered and published by Constantine) is filled with contradictions and forgeries. He wrote to Augustine:

But what escape from this difficulty can there be for you, since you condemn the use of reason, which is the prerogative of human nature. By examining everything we determine which scriptures contain Christ's actual words... your predecessors have made many interpolations in the words of our Lord, which thus appear under His name, while they disagree with His doctrine. Besides...the writings are not the production of Christ and His apostles, but a compilation of rumors and beliefs, made long after their departure, by some obscure semi-Jews, not in harmony even with one another, and published by them under the name of the apostles, or of those considered the followers of the apostles, so as to give the appearance of apostolic authority to all these blunders and falsehoods. <60>

Faustus further adds that the gospels must "be tested to find whether they are true and genuine; for the enemy who comes by night has corrupted almost every passage by sowing tares among the wheat." <61> Faustus, of course, was destroying the very foundation upon which the orthodox church had built its edifice. In this view, Manichaeism was pre-eminently gnostic, as it looked to insight and revelation for the truth and not to the written word which so easily can become corrupted. Regarding the authenticity of the gospels, biblical criticism over the past century has come to much the same conclusion as Faustus: the Bible as it presently stands is not completely accurate. For example, the sayings of Jesus as recorded by Mark, when compared with the same sayings as written by Matthew and Luke, demonstrate reworking and re-editing to conform with the authors' viewpoint.

Faustus also rejected the doctrine of the Incarnation as it was being taught by orthodox Catholic Christians. Faustus pointed out that the birth sequences in Matthew and Luke are contradictory, as are the genealogies in these two gospels. Faustus rejected the virginal conception and birth and the perpetual virginity of Mary. He writes:

It is not in accordance with the laws of nature that a virgin should bring forth, and still less that she should still be a virgin after bringing forth.... <62>

...To begin with calling Jesus the Son of David, and then to go on to tell of His being born of Mary before the consummation of her marriage with Joseph, is pure madness.

<63>

We can well understand why the Manichaean Christians were so hated by the Church Fathers: the doctrines of Mani threatened to topple the orthodox Church.

Another thorn in the side of the Church Fathers was the Manichaeans' rejection of the Old Testament as necessary and binding upon the Christian. Faustus viewed the Old Testament, with the exception of the Ten Commandments, as binding upon the Jews alone and that the Levitical laws of the Old Testament had been brought to completion by Christ and had ended. In what is probably a somewhat extreme position, Faustus claimed he found no prophecies regarding the coming and subsequent mission of Jesus in the Old Testament. He claimed that the Old Testament prophecies concerned the coming of a Jewish Messiah only who was to establish a physical kingdom on earth in opposition to the Roman government. Christ, he taught, came to establish a spiritual kingdom, not an earthly one, and was not the kind of Messiah the Jews expected; he points out that Jesus was rejected by the Jewish authorities as their Messiah. Faustus argued that Christians from a non-Jewish background should not be forced to accept the Old Testament. He further argued that the prophecies of Christ's coming in the so-called pagan Sibylline Books, in the writings of Hermes Trismegistus and in the Orphic prophecies were more relevant to Christ than the Old Testament prophecies and were better suited to "Gentile Christians." The Manichaeans also found prophecies of Christ's coming in the Zoroastrian scriptures. Why were these attitudes so threatening to the Church Fathers? Precisely because the Church Fathers had determined to undermine the truths of other religions which they felt could not co-exist with what they termed "Christianity." Their attempt to found the "Christian Religion" as an exclusive church under which they had full control over the mind of men was being undermined by the Manichaeans such as Faustus, who saw the universality of the religion of Christ. Although the Manichaeans have been accused of denigrating the Old Testament prophets, Faustus and other Manichaean teachers actually believed that Enoch, Seth, Noah, Abraham, Shem, Enosh, Nikotheas (a gnostic teacher) were true messengers of the Light and had received special revelations and commandments from angels that were worthy of observance.

What most infuriated orthodox Church Fathers, however, were Mani's doctrines concerning Christ. Mani used the term "Christ," "Son of God" and "Jesus" in various ways, which the Church Fathers were unable to or refused to understand. Mani has been accused of teaching that Jesus was never born, never died and never had a "body." If we examine Mani's doctrine closely we shall find that Mani taught about "Christ" under three different aspects, as follows:

1) **Jesus of Light/Jesus Splendor or the Light-Mind:** This aspect referred to the Divine Mind or Nous (Greek: mind). This Mind is the Source from which emanate all the great religious leaders; the Nous is the father of all apostles and messengers and was active in the historical Jesus, who, with others, such as Zoroaster, Buddha, St. Paul and Mani, were earthly instruments or embodiments of this Divine Intelligence. This aspect also referred to Jesus as the preexistent Son of God, the Divine Archetype, before his descent to earth as the historical Jesus, the Nazarene; Mani also referred to the Jesus of Light as the Jesus after his ascension on "High." This "Jesus" was also the "guardian angel" of Mani, his divine twin. The primary role of the Jesus of Light was as supreme revealer to and the awakener of the soul. The Jesus of Light, being an aspect of the Divine Mind, was never really born, never suffered or died. The Jesus of Light is birthless, deathless and eternal, the "before Abraham was, I AM," and contains the "All." It was this "Jesus" who awakened Adam and revealed to him his origin, as we have seen. We quote from a Manichaean scripture the words of the Jesus of Light addressed to the soul who is prepared to ascend into the Light:

I AM thy Higher Mind, a security and seal; thou art my

body, a garment I have put on in order to terrify the Powers, while I myself am thy Light, the original Effulgence....I shall show thee the Father, eternally the Sovereign, and lead thee up in pure raiment before Him....I Am thy Light, thy beginningless Illumination. <64>

In the Manichaean view, as the above clearly shows, there is no difference between the Light-Mind in Jesus and the Light-Mind of the individual believer or disciple of Christ. In another Manichaean scripture we read:

The Light-Mind, who is the Awakener of those who sleep...is the Father of all the Messengers...the Physician of the Souls, he is the Light-Mind and this is the "New Man." <65>

The Light-Mind or Divine Intelligence therefore is fundamentally identical to the Jesus of Light and is the Redeemer of all sentient beings.

2) **The historical Jesus:** This figure refers primarily to Jesus as an historical personage in time, the Jesus who was born, lived, and "died." It also refers to the incarnation on earth of the Jesus of Light to fulfill his mission in Palestine. We quote the Manichaean scriptures as follows:

The Son of God...was thrown into a womb; he who is in the "All," in whom the "All" exists! For he was led from world to world, from age to age...he came down to the substance of the flesh, the vesture of humanity...he went about in all the land, he took a man's likeness, the raiment of a slave. He came for all the sheep of His flock, because he knew there was no other to rescue them. He had come without a body <66> yet his apostles declared of him that he took a boy's form, an aspect like us men; he came down and manifested in the world in the sect of the Jews.... <67>

We find in this passage a very intriguing sentence: "For he

was led from world to world, from age to age." Like Origen, the Manichaeans taught that Jesus, like all souls, had previously incarnated on other worlds in past ages, according to the law of cyclic evolution, and on this planet had previous incarnations. We recall that certain Gnostic-Christians believed Jesus to have been previously incarnated as the patriarch Seth. The phrase "age to age" also translates as "aeon to aeon," which would then be understood as Jesus' passage from the divine pleromic heights to the earthly plane or dwelling where he assumed a body. This agrees with St. Paul's statement noted earlier that Jesus, being in a Godlike form, took upon himself the form of a servant (Phil 2: 6-8). The reference in the above passage to Jesus' taking a boy's form relates to similar passages from The Acts of John and the Acts of Thomas, apocryphal texts which demonstrate that Jesus had the ability to change his form at will. Both these texts and others like them were banned by the orthodox church.

Another passage from the scriptures of the Manichaeans treats of the Passion of Christ. Manichaeans were accused of denying both Christ's Passion and the reality of the incarnation. In light of the above and the passage below, this accusation is false and misleading. To quote:

Then the Jews seized the Son of God, judged him lawlessly in an Assembly and unrighteously condemned him, although he had no sin. They raised him upon the wood of the cross. They crucified him on the cross together with robbers; they took him down from the cross and laid him in the tomb; but after three days he rose from the dead. He came to his disciples and appeared to them, he clothed them with power and breathed his holy Spirit into them, he sent them out into all the world to preach the Greatness, while he in his part raised himself up to the Height. <68>

The above passage applies to the historical Jesus, not the "Jesus of Light/Light-Mind," which has no birth nor death. The orthodox Church Fathers, in their ignorance or willful refusal to discern the truth of Mani's teaching, steadfastly confused one with the other, refusing to make this simple distinction, and condemned the Manichaeans for denying the sufferings of Christ. The Manichaeans were also known to have studied the so-called Hymn of Jesus, extant in The Acts of John, which we have previously quoted and in which Jesus states: "Amen, I was crucified; Amen, again I was not crucified!...Amen, I suffered; Amen, again I did not suffer!" Duncan Greenlees, editor of *The Gospel of Mani,* writes:

To the ignorant it seems a paradox; those with any kind of spiritual experience will understand the truth can be expressed in no other way—the most dreadful path is at times exquisite bliss. <69>

3) The Suffering Jesus/Jesus Patibilis: This aspect of Christ relates to the archetypal suffering of the Soul of Humanity, crucified in the realm of matter—on the matter cross formed by its beam of space and its transverse beam of time; in the words of Faustus, the "Suffering Jesus" refers to "the mystic nailing to the cross, emblematic of the wounds of the Soul in its passion." <70> The "Suffering Jesus" is eternally suspended on the mystical Cross of Light and is eternally "the life and salvation of Man." <71> Moreover, this mystical crucifixion is present in every tree, hcrb, fruit, vegetable, stone, and in soil. <72>

George Widengren explains:

...The sparks of eternal light were not confined to human souls but...the amount of light gone astray and not recovered was distributed throughout nature.... <73>

The "suffering" of the Light-Mind confined and scattered as Light particles throughout the material universe is beautifully expressed as follows:

The strangers with whom I mixed, me they know not;

they tasted my sweetness, they desired to keep me with them.

I am life to them, but they were death to me; I bore up beneath them, they wore me as a garment upon them.

I am in everything, I bear the skies, I am the foundation, I support the earths, I am the Light that shines forth, that gives joy to souls.

I am the life of the world: I am the milk that is in all trees: I am the sweet water that is beneath the sons of matter. <74>

We cannot think of a more exquisite way to explain the immanence of the Divine Light throughout all creation, spurned by some, ignored by others, crucified in those who misuse it. This is the "Suffering Jesus": the archetypal passion of the Light of the Soul in all nature.

Augustine, of course, in what appears to be another example of his ignorance of mystical teachings, accuses the Manichaeans of teaching "many Christs" without under–standing the esoteric and subtle nature of their universal view of Christ under three aspects. He writes:

Again, tell us how many Christs you say there are? Is there one whom you call the suffering one whom the earth conceives and brings forth by the power of the Holy Spirit, and another crucified by the Jews under Pontius Pilate, and a third who is divided between the sun and the moon? <75>

We note the sarcasm in Augustine's question. It is not the tone of a seeker attempting to penetrate the profound mysteries of Manichaean Christianity.

Several Catholic bishops, popes and emperors were instrumental in waging war against Manichaean Christianity. They targeted Manichaeans especially for their doctrines on Evil, reincarnation, the nature of God and of Christ. Emperors Honorius and Theodosius II maintained a secret service to fer-ret out and persecute Manichaeans. Augustine and Bishop

Porphyry were active in their persecution in the first half of the fourth century. Rabbula, Bishop of Edessa, was tireless in his campaigns against various Christian sects such as the Marcionites, the followers of Bardaisan, and the Manichaeans. An edict of Emperor Valentinian I in 372 called for the confiscation of houses and dwelling places of Manichaeans. Samuel Lieu, author of *Manichaeism*, writes that the Manichaeans in the city of Rome became a source of concern to the papacy as early as the pontificate of Miltiades (311-14). <76> He writes that from the end of the fourth century onwards, popes played an active part in suppressing Manichaeans and other so-called heretics. Popes Siricius (184-99) and Anastasius (399-401) both issued decrees against Manichaeans. Pope Leo I (440-461) ordered Manichaeans in 445 to be arrested and subjected to penalties. Lieu states that adherence to the sect was declared a public crime.
He elaborates:

In one of his sermons Leo urged the faithful to inform on the hiding places of the Manichaeans to their priests for to inform on such enemies of God was not only an act of piety but also a means of grace in the last judgment. He also wrote to the bishops of Italy urging them to be extra vigilant for Manichaean infiltration and a copy of the edict of 445 was also sent to them as a pastoral letter.... According to Prosper of Acquitaine, he [Leo] also dragged many of them out of their hiding places and compelled them to abjure their error in public. He also confiscated a large number of their books which he ordered to be burnt. <77>

Lieu adds that Prosper of Acquitaine considered Leo's zeal "divinely inspired". Pope Leo I has been known to Catholics for centuries as Saint Leo the Great!
Both detection and expulsion of Manichaeans, Lieu continues, occur regularly in accounts of fifth century popes. <78> Under Gelasius (492-496) Manichaeans discovered in Rome were deported and their books burnt before the doors of

the Basilica of St. Mary. Pope Symmachus (498-514) ferreted out Manichaeans, sent them into exile and burned their books and images before the Basilica of Constantine (somehow ironically appropriate). <79> Pope Hormisdas (514-523) subjected Manichaeans to investigation under torture in addition to exiling them and burning their books.

In 527 in Constantinople (Byzantium) Justinian and his Co-Emperor Justin I forbade Manichaeans to appear anywhere "as they defiled anything that came into contact with them. If they were caught in the company of others they would be subjected to capital punishment." <80> According to Lieu, Justinian put many Manichaeans to death, and due to such remorseless persecution the Manichaean sect became extinct in Byzantium in the course of the sixth century. <81> Lieu writes that "the refutation of Manichaean dualism also became a standard form of rhetorical training for the theologians." Byzantine theologians such as John of Caesarea, John of Damascus, Photius and John the Orthodox all wrote anti-Manichaean works. Lieu observes that these refutations are not based on first-hand knowledge of Manichaean works (not that it would have made any difference) and they display "a lack of interest in the genuine teaching of Manichaeism." <82>

To conclude this chapter, we would like to quote from various hymns and prayers of Manichaean Christians still extant and leave it to the reader to decide whether the adherents of the Manichaean religion were, in fact, "enemies of God" as the "saintly" Pope Leo averred.

The Bride is the Church, the Bridegroom is the Light-Mind; the Bride is the Soul, (and) Jesus is the Bridegroom! If he rises in us, we too shall live in Him;...if we believe in him, we shall transcend death and come to Life. <83>

My holy Father, let me see Thy Likeness that I saw before the universe was created, before the Darkness dared to stir up envy against the Aeons. On that *occasion did I become a stranger to my Kingdom: I have cut its root and have come up victoriously on high. <84>*

O eternal Victor, I call to Thee; hear my cry, Compassionate! Let thy Members cleanse me, and wash me, Thou, in Thy holy waters and make me spotless, even as I (really) am! Lo, the time has drawn near that I should return to my homes! Thou are the Way, Thou art indeed the Gate of eternal Life, O Son of God, my Saviour.... <85>

O Light-Mind, the Sun of my heart that gives my Soul the things of the Light, Thou are my witness, that I have no comfort save in Thee! <86>

Jesus, my Light whom I have loved, take me in to Thee! I have trusted to the knowledge of Thy Hope which called me to Thee, take me up to Thy homes, Jesus, my Spouse!...I have become divine again as I was at first....I have set myself to please Thee to the end! Make even me worthy of Thy holy bridechambers.... <87>

How great a lover of men Thou art, O Jesus, the First Rose of the Father! How gentle Thou art, my true Bridegroom! Glory to Thee, O Christ of the Bridechambers of the Light. <88>

God, God, God! Lovely is God, God, God! God, my God! I dived to the depth of the Abyss wishing to comprehend Thy depth!...Who can comprehend Thee, and who is able to understand Thee, my Lord? What light shall I find and compare it with Thy fragrance? Where is there a gracious Mother to compare with my Mother, Love? Where a kind Father to compare with my Father, Christ?...

My Mind has not ceased thinking of Thy wonders;
        My Thought has not swerved from searching Thy secrets;

*My Insight has not moved from aspiring in Thy
mysteries;*

*Nor has my Counsel swerved from seeking after Thy
marvels;*

*My Intention have I set up desiring to comprehend
Thee, my Lord.*

*I have tasted a sweet taste; I have found no sweeter
than the Word of Truth!*

*I have tasted a sweet taste; I have found no sweeter
than the Name of God!*

*I have tasted a sweet taste: I have found no sweeter
than Christ! Taste and realize that the Lord is sweet.* <89>

*"Be yourselves Refiners and Saviours for your Soul which
abides in every place, that you may lead it to the dwelling of
the Fathers of the Light."* Mani <90>

Chapter XII

The Arian Controversy and the Council of Nicea

Constantine Becomes Messiah

From the death of Origen to the accession of Constantine was a period of tremendous growth for the orthodox church, as well as a period of great persecution under Diocletian, Galerius and Maximin from 303 to 312. In 313, a year after the accession of Constantine, Christianity, such as it was, became the state religion. In 313, Constantine promulgated the Edict of Milan forbidding persecution of monotheistic religions in the Roman Empire. On the surface this would appear to have been a great boon to the church. But as we shall see, although the edict allowed Christians to practice their faith openly, the politics of the Roman Empire slowly assimilated themselves into the church and thus was formulated a totalitarian religion known as Roman Catholicism.

At this juncture, however, the church was vulnerable due to the continuing controversy over the Trinity and the nature of Christ. As was earlier stated, the orthodox tendency within the churches and communities was toward the absolute deification of Jesus. Yet, as we have seen, from earliest times Jesus was looked upon not as God but as 1) a man anointed by the Father/Holy Spirit at his baptism who was looked upon as a prophet and Messiah and who, after his crucifixion, rose again according to the scriptures, thus proving his Messiahship; and 2) a preexistent divine being who took incarnation on earth, was crucified and rose again, and thus became Christ and Redeemer. The former concept of Jesus was held by the Nazorean Jewish Christians, the Ebionites, Cerinthians and others. The latter concept of Jesus was held by St. Paul and innumerable Christian-Gnostic sects with much variation. The Apostle John was the first to identify Jesus with the Logos or Word who became flesh for the salvation of mankind. Certain sects and schools also differentiated between the Aeon Christ and the man Jesus. In this conception, the man Jesus was usually understood to be the instrument of the former. Prior to Origen, the most common understanding of Christ in proto-orthodox circles was that he was the "image of God," and the first born of every creature, not the eternal God himself. The movement toward absolute deification of Jesus was undertaken by Church Fathers who, in order to disprove the Christian-Gnostics, formulated new doctrines on the nature of Christ. We have seen that Ignatius of Antioch and Irenaeus, among others, began to identify Jesus as Son of God with the meaning that he was the same as God, i.e., he existed for eternity and was part of the Deity himself. However, it was well known that in the ancient mystery religions antedating Christianity, the term "Son of God" was used to designate the initiate who had received the highest mysteries and who had the final revelation—that revelation being the initiate's realization of his own Divine Self.

As we have seen, it was Origen who synthesized these conceptions of Christ into a viable system when he taught that since all souls preexisted and were created by God the Father as spiritual beings, Jesus was no different in essence from any other soul, except for the fact that he chose to cling to the Wisdom of God (The Word and Son) from the very beginning and thus, in effect, became one with that Eternal Wisdom. Origen, therefore, differentiates between the soul of Jesus and the second Person of the Trinity, the Son, yet he acknowledges that Jesus is the Wisdom and Word of God by virtue of his indissoluble union with the Word.

We see, then, that the first and earliest complete Christological formula within the church, that of Origen, fell short of making Jesus the absolute eternal Deity. Later Church Fathers either could not or refused to make a distinction between the preexistent soul of Jesus and the Son-Wisdom-Word with which he united. The danger of this doctrine and primary reason why it could not remain as an official doctrine of the church was its obvious implication that any soul at any time could likewise choose to identify itself with the Son or Word and thus progress toward a divine state of union with the Deity. The power and authority of the clergy would thus be threatened—for only spiritual attainment would fit one for any sort of true authority. Union with the Deity was the primary goal of the mystery religions prevalent before and during the early centuries of Christianity as it was with the original Christian-Gnostic sects. Therefore, these mystery religions and Gnostics had to be destroyed.

From time to time, various theologians sought to promote in various ways the doctrine that Jesus was a man who merged with the Logos-Word, either in the beginning of creation or at some later time. We have seen that Origen was eventually judged a "heretic" for promoting such a concept.

Paul of Samosata, bishop of Antioch (260-272) taught (as had others before him) that the Father, Son and Holy Spirit were not three persons but three modes of activity within the Godhead. This became known as the Monarchian concept, and its purpose was to preserve the absolute unity of God as against the idea of emanation which (it was taught) tended to promote polytheism. Monarchianists refused to consider God under the aspect of "Persons" for fear that these persons would become "Gods" and there was supposed to be only one God. It is probable that the Monarchian doctrine originated in circles where Judaistic Christianity prevailed, which advocated a strict and absolute monotheism.

With regard to Christ, Paul of Samosota taught that Jesus was a man who, at his baptism, became one with the Logos. The Logos-Word-Son is the second mode or aspect of the Deity, an impersonal power which had also manifested itself in Moses and the prophets. Jesus, therefore, became more and more like God by virtue of his perfect and sinless life, and when baptized functioned as Saviour and Redeemer. The virgin Mary, taught Paul, did not give birth to the Logos but to a man whose destiny it was to merge with the Logos. Paul, therefore, promoted the doctrine of the indwelling Logos within Jesus, but denied that Jesus was the eternal God. <1> Paul argued that Jesus, the man, was not consubstantial (of the same essence) as the Father, Son and Holy Spirit, and, he argued, to do this was to promote ditheism or the doctrine of two Gods. <2> Paul's doctrine was similar to what we have earlier seen described as "Adoptionism."

A synod was held at Antioch in 264 and formally condemned Paul's teaching as a heresy. Paul, however, was not easily defeated, and a third synod was convened in 268 during which Paul was excommunicated. Four years later he was driven from the church. <3> It is ironic indeed that the most ancient Christian conception of Christ, which Paul revived, was now, two centuries later, considered a heresy.

The Doctrine of Arius

The teaching of Paul of Samosata was reinstituted, along with variations, in the first decades of the fourth century, first by Lucian of Antioch and then by his follower Arius, circa 320. Arius was a presbyter of the church at Alexandria and presided over an independent parish within the city. Alexander had become bishop of Alexandria in 312, and during the course of a sermon, Alexander proceeded to explain the so-called "mystery" of the Trinity. He affirmed that the Son was equal to the Father and of the same substance as the Father who begot him. Arius took offense at this teaching and proceeded to controvert Alexander. He began to promulgate the view, taught by Paul the Apostle, that the Son was the firstborn of the Father, was created by the Father and thus was a creature, although the first and highest creature. Arius logically deduced that if the Son was begotten by the Father, there must have been a time when the Son did not exist, that is, before his creation by the Father. <4> The Son, therefore, had a beginning.

Arius taught his doctrine in the churches and in general assemblies. Eventually, Arius declared his position openly to bishop Alexander while the latter tried to convince Arius of his error. When Arius would not be silenced, Alexander wrote long letters to several bishops in various cities. One of these letters, written to Bishop Alexander in Constantinople, is noteworthy for its insights into what was really the underlying doctrine of Arius. Alexander first accuses Arius and the Arians of reviling what he terms "the religious doctrines of the apostles," and of conspiring against Christ. It becomes obvious from Alexander's letter, as we shall see, that Arius and his school were attempting, in vain, to preserve the humanity of Christ over against his divinity and deification. Alexander writes:

> *...they deny his divinity, and declare him to be on a level with other men. They collect all those passages which allude to the incarnation of our Saviour, and to his having humbled himself for our salvation, and bring them forward as corroborative of their own impious assertion; while they evade all those which declare his divinity, and the glory he possesses with the Father.* <5>

Alexander, at length, goes on to assert what Arius taught:

> *...(the son) must have had a beginning; and that when he was created he was made like all other men that have ever been born. God, they say, created all things, and they include the Son of God in the number of creatures, both rational and irrational....They...affirm that he (the Son) is by nature liable to change,..... 'We are also able,' say these evil-minded individuals, 'to become like him, the sons of God' ....They likewise assert that he was not elevated (as Son) because he had by nature any qualifications superior to those of the other sons of God; for God, say they, has not any son by nature....They consider that he was elected because, though mutable by nature, he was vigilant and zealous in avoiding evil. They add that if Paul and Peter had made similar efforts, their filiation [sonship] would in no respects have differed from his.*

(Brackets added) <6>

Arius and his followers had committed the unforgivable sin of declaring that they were sons of God and that they bore in themselves the image of the Son, and that the Son himself was no different, in essence, than themselves. This was essentially the doctrine of Origen, as we have seen, and of St. Paul, who taught that Christ was the firstborn of every creature, who dwelt in every creature as their "hope of glory." The Arians also taught, as did Origen just 50 years earlier, that the Son was chosen not by superiority of nature but by virtue of his self-effort. And we recall the words of St. John in his epistle: "Beloved, now are we the sons of God...." (1 John 3:2).

This, then, was the crux of Arius' doctrine and the reason why his teaching could not prevail in the Christian world; the hatred of Arius was not due to the supposed inaccuracy of his metaphysical conceptions on the Trinity but for what his doctrine implied: all men could become the sons of God, as Jesus had, and all could share his sonship with the Father.

In his letter, Bishop Alexander either refuses to acknowledge or avoids the remainder of Arius' teaching on the Logos. According to Alexander, Arius blasphemed against the Trinity by degrading the Son to creature status. Arius, however, did not teach the identity of the Son with the Logos or Word. Alexander failed to distinguish between the Son and Word in delineating Arius' doctrine. Unfortunately, we possess only fragments of Arius' work "The Banquet," in which he described his doctrine both in prose and poetry. Athanasius, the archenemy of Arius and the Arians, later quoted Arius' teaching from the above work as follows:

When God wished to create us, He first created a being which He called the Logos, Sophia, and the Son, who should create us as an instrument. There are two Sophias: one is in God (i.e., endiathetos), by which even the Son was made. It is only by sharing the nature of this inner Sophia of God that *the Son was also called Wisdom. So, also, besides the Son, there is another Logos—he who is God; as the Son participates in the Logos, He also is by grace called Logos and Son. God is ineffable, and nothing (therefore not even the Son) is equal to or like Him, or of the same glory. <7>*

For centuries, Arius has been accused of teaching that the Second Person of the Trinity was a created being, when in reality, he taught that the Logos-Word was, in fact, the Second Person by whom the Son was made and in whom the Son participates. The Son, therefore, in Arius' view, was the supreme Archetype of all created beings who was adopted by God. Arius perhaps occasionally interchanged the names of Logos, Son and Wisdom, thus adding to the confusion. We may, however, diagram Arius' teaching as in figure 3.

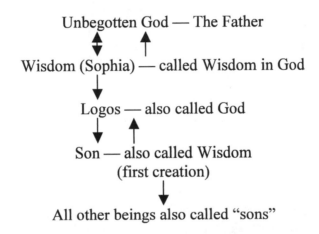

Figure 3. The Arian Schema of Being

The above doctrine, as diagrammed, appears to be similar to the ancient Christian-Gnostic doctrine of emanations. Arius, however, would not use the term "emanations" as this smacked too much of the heretical doctrines of the Christian-Gnostics. The term "creation" was used by the school of Arius.

The Council of Nicea

From the moment Arius and his followers began disseminating their doctrines, no distinction was made by their enemies between the Wisdom-in-God, the Logos and the Son. We possess no complete explanatory doctrine from the pen of Arius. The letter of Arius still extant concerns itself only with his teaching on the Son. We have no doubt that this letter was edited by later hands and that others like it were destroyed by the orthodox party at the Council of Nicea.

The controversy over the teachings of Arius continued unabated and threatened to split the Christian world in two. This, of course, was seen by Constantine as a threat, not only to the unity of his Empire but to the unity of the one-world religion he sought to impose upon the empire. The party opposed to Arius, which we may call the Alexandrian orthodox party, later headed by Athanasius, affirmed that the Logos-Word disguised himself and assumed a body, but had, in fact, been God for all eternity. The Arians taught that the highest creature, the Son (as opposed to the Logos) incarnated on earth (yet participated in the Logos who was God). For the orthodox, the Son, whom they identified solely with Jesus, was the eternal God in the flesh.

Prior to the outbreak of the Arian controversy, Constantine, as we have said, issued the Edict of Toleration at Milan in 313. By 325, however, the date of the famed Council of Nicea, Constantine rescinded the edict and made orthodox Christianity, such as it was, the only state religion. By the period of the Arian controversy, Constantine's sole purpose was to establish an homogeneous imperial religion with himself as its head.

When it came to the attention of Constantine that this controversy among the bishops might threaten the unity of his empire, he sent Hosius, bishop of Cordova, to Alexandria with letters in hopes of reconciling the disputants. <8> When this failed, Constantine summoned an ecumenical council at Nicea, in modern-day Turkey, to which over 250 were commanded to attend. Ironically, Pope Sylvester, the bishop of Rome, was unable to attend due to his advanced age, but he sent two presbyters to the council as his representatives. Sylvester, as will be seen later, was none other than a front for Constantine. Among those who attended were Eusebius of Nicomedia who supported the Arians, and Athanasius, a deacon of the Alexandrian church and right hand man to Bishop Alexander, the enemy of Arius. Athanasius, in less than a year, succeeded Alexander as bishop and continued to fight against the Arian party for the next forty years. <9> Arius and his followers, of course, were also in attendance as was Eusebius of Caesarea, a supporter of orthodoxy, who later rewrote Christian history his way and from the perspective of Constantinian imperial Christianity.

We are told that, for a short time previous to the general council, the disputants engaged in contests of logic with various opponents. When many began to gather and observe these disputations with interest, a simple man of unsophis-ticated understanding stood out from the crowd and rebuked the contestants, telling them that Christ did not teach the art of dialectic but simplicity of mind, which should be preserved by faith and good works. <10>

On the opening day of the council, Constantine entered in the guise of an absolute monarch glittering with jewels, purple and gold. The Emperor gave a solemn address, then allowed the various debaters to speak by turns. Eusebius of Caesarea records that "some began to impeach their nearest associates, while others, in reply, preferred complaints against the accusers themselves." <11> An intense controversy then ensued, Constantine listening to both parties and finally at-tempting to produce a conformity of opinion from all the bishops, who eventually acquiesced to what Constantine con-sidered "sound doctrine." Several bishops who sided with Arius drew up a declaration of their creed and presented it to the council. Rather than recognize it or attempt to reason among themselves, the bishops tore the creed to pieces, de-claring it to be spurious and false. The uproar was so great against Arius that all the bishops, except two supporters of Arius, stood up and excommunicated Arius. <12> The Arian creed, prior to being presented to the council, was signed by eighteen bishops. They also turned and condemned Arius, who disappeared before the close of the council. Arius' book, "The Banquet," from which we quoted above, was burned on the spot. <13> A confession of faith was then drawn up by unanimous consent and signed by all the bishops at the order of Constantine. All those who signed the creed, affirming that Jesus Christ was "Very God of Very God" and "of one substance with the Father by whom all things were made," were invited to stay on as Constantine's guests in honor of his twentieth anniversary as Emperor. All those who refused to sign the creed were threatened by the Emperor with banishment. Naturally, all signed. However, Eusebius of Nicomedia, Maris of Chalcedon and Theognis of Nicea afterwards regretted having put their signatures to the Nicene formula, as they so stated in a letter to Constantine written by Eusebius of Nicomedia: "We committed an impious act, O Prince, by subscribing to a blasphemy from fear of you."<14> It is indeed sad that the creed of faith professed by millions of Christians since the fourth century was born amidst this sorry scene and was at one time considered blasphemous by not only three bishops mentioned above but by hundreds of others who either openly or secretly sided with Arius. We quote the earliest draft of the creed known to us today and the one which was agreed upon at the council:

We believe in one God, the Father Almighty, the Maker of all things, visible and invisible. And in one Lord Jesus Christ, the Son of God, the only begotten of the Father; he is begotten, that is to say, he is of the substance of God, God of God, Light of Light, very God of very God, begotten and not made, being of one substance with the Father; by whom all things, both in heaven and on earth, were made. Who for us men, and for our salvation, came down from heaven, and took our nature, and became man; he suffered and rose again the *third day; he ascended into heaven, and will come to judge the living and the dead. And we believe in the Holy Ghost. The holy catholic and apostolical church condemns all those who say that there was a period in which the Son of God did not exist; that before he was begotten, he had no existence; that he was called out of nothing into being; that he is of a different substance from the Father; and that he is susceptible of variation or of change. <15>*

Jesus, then, for all time was declared to have been God for all eternity. Forever after there would always be a chasm separating humanity from Jesus Christ, who was deified beyond recognition as a result of the council's decision. The key Greek word used in the creed was homoousios, meaning that Jesus was "of one substance with" the Father; he was not created by God but was "very God of very God." The subtle distinction that Arius had made between the Son (as the Archetypal firstborn of God) and the Word-Logos who was "God from God" was either cleverly ignored or suppressed outright. The bishops who sided with Arius knew that they had blasphemed by placing the man Jesus, whom they knew to have been created by God, on the same level with the eternal God—the unmanifest and absolute Deity. As Origen gave the Son of God free will to choose to cling to the Wisdom-Logos and thus become the Logos, so the council condemned the teaching that the Son was susceptible to variation and change. Jesus Christ, therefore, according to the Nicene Fathers, did not choose to cling to the Logos and thus become one with him— he was himself the Logos for all eternity. The council concluded that Jesus, in effect, had no free will to choose or not to choose. The implication of the Nicene doctrine is that Jesus as God the Logos, God Himself, simply assumed a human nature and body (or the semblance of humanity) for the purpose of saving mankind. He himself did not need to follow a path to attainment, nor did he have to strive for union with God. Jesus then was not really man—he was the eternal God in the appearance of man. We recall that no Christian school or theology, either Christian-Gnostic or proto-orthodox, had ever taught such a doctrine regarding Jesus prior to the Nicene Council. The above formula also makes it unnecessary for each individual to follow Jesus. There is no purpose in seeking to experience the "initiations" that Jesus experienced. The esoteric gnostic doctrines of Jesus which taught man how to attain to Jesus' level of spiritual knowledge and power are now become superfluous. Jesus is no longer the mediator between God and man—bridging the gap between God and man and bringing man into a closer union with the Father; he is now God Himself—a full-fledged remote Deity. The Christian is therefore bereft of a mediator—an advocate before the Father—in the person of Jesus. The hierarchy of the church—the very bishops who supported the creed—have now insinuated themselves subtly between God and the aspiring Christian, who was taught not to think for himself but to simply acquiesce in favor of the greater knowledge of the bishops. Thus an entirely new theology would be developed out of the Nicene Creed—a theology far removed from the original doctrines of Jesus and his apostles. The new theology evolved from the Nicene formula promoted a passivity on the part of the average Christian. According to the creed, Jesus is God and he has already accomplished the salvation of every believer. The believer need only accept the creed, partake of the sacraments, obey the bishops and the decisions of the councils in order to be saved. He need not go through his own crucifixion and resurrection as Paul the Apostle taught and demonstrated. He need not become one with the Father as the Christian-Gnostic taught. The Nicene Creed prepared the way for the ultimate abdication by the faithful of their own nature as sons of God—that sonship that Arius ånd his followers were attempting to uphold in vain. The Nicene Creed prepared the soil into which was planted the new doctrine of original sin by Augustine in the following century, thus contributing to the final debasement of humanity.

The Nicean Council's Secret Agenda?

From even a cursory glance at the Nicene Creed, it is easy to see similarities to the ancient Hindu doctrine of the Incarnation discussed in the chapter on Justin Martyr (Chapter VI.) Krishna, we noted, was considered to be the incarnation of Vishnu, whose function was analogous to the Second Person of the Christian Trinity, namely the Word-Logos. In the Bhagavad-Gita, Krishna is depicted as the supreme Person-ification of Brahman—the Unmanifested Deity whose essence permeates all things. Krishna, therefore, describes himself in innumerable passages as the personality of Brahman made manifest in the flesh:

I am the birthless, the deathless,
Lord of all that breathes....

When goodness grows weak,
When evil increases,
I make myself a body.

In every age I come back
To deliver the holy,

To destroy the sin of the sinner,
To establish righteousness....

I am the birth of this cosmos:
Its dissolution also.
I am He who causes:
No other beside me
Upon me, those worlds are held
Like pearls strung on a thread.

I am the essence of the waters
The shining of the sun and moon:
OM in all the Vedas,

The Word that is God....

...The man of discrimination
I see as my very Self....

My devotees dwell
Within me always:
I also show forth
And am seen within them.
To love is to know me,
My innermost nature,

The truth that I am:
Through this knowledge he enters
At once to my Being
.

...He who worships me
With unfaltering love
Transcends these gunas.
He becomes fit
To reach union with Brahman.

For I am Brahman
Within this body,
Life immortal
That shall not perish:
I am the Truth
And the Joy forever. <16>

It would appear that the Church Fathers had a ready-made Incarnate God in Krishna as the model for their God Jesus Christ. Yet what they failed to include was the teaching so prominent in the Gita that the Self of Krishna is the same as the Self of every man and that Brahman resides within man in the innermost chamber of the heart as the Atman—the in-dwelling Divinity. This doctrine, as we have seen, was prom-inent in the teachings of the Christian-Gnostics. Krishna and his interlocutor, the warrior Arjuna, are thus of the same essence:

Know this Atman
Unborn, undying,
Never ceasing,
Never beginning,
Deathless, birthless,
Unchanging for ever.
How can it die
The death of the body?

...You and I, Arjuna,
Have lived many lives.
I remember them all:
You do not remember. <17>

The Nicene Creed, on the other hand, states nothing about man's intrinsic oneness with God or Christ. Jesus is proclaimed "Very God of Very God"—a deity to be worshipped but not a deity to be assimilated as in the teaching of the Gita.

Strangely enough we find in the teaching of the ancient Druids of Britain a Deity known variously as Yesu, Esus and Hesus. This Deity was understood as the personification of God as Saviour. It was believed and taught that Yesu would descend to earth sometime in the future as the Saviour of mankind. <18> Ironically, the Hebrew Joshua when spoken in Aramaic becomes Yeshu or Yeshua. The Druidic Yesu was considered to be a personage of a Trinity: Beli was the Creator; Taran, the controlling providence of the present; and Yesu was the coming Saviour. <19> The Druidic Trinity was depicted as three golden rays of light and this sign became the emblem of the Druids. The Druids were prominent in Britain for centuries before the advent of Jesus, and not only in Britain, but throughout Western Europe. It was, in fact, the dominant religious teaching with origins deep in the pre-Homeric past, with clear affinities to the Vedas and the Brahmins. Indeed, an extremely strong case has been recently made that the mystery teachings veiled in the Iliad and the Odyssey—those works so vastly respected in the ancient world—were, in fact, popularized, coded versions of Druidic initiatic teachings. <20>

Joseph of Arimathea, the uncle of Mary, had a thriving business in the tin trade with the Britons of Cornwall and is reputed to have taken the boy Jesus to Britain on one of his frequent journeys. <21> Other traditions state that Jesus himself built the first chapel—a mud wattle hut in the area today known as Glastonbury. Is it possible that Jesus may have studied with the Druids and been initiated into their mysteries? The Druidic mysteries taught the preexistence of the soul, its subsequent descent into matter and its reincarnation until, by the attainment of knowledge, the soul was free of rebirth. We would suggest that the Druids, either through Jesus himself or later through Joseph of Arimathea sometime after the resurrection, accepted Jesus as the coming Saviour—Yesu—whose very name was identical to their Deity.

According to certain historians, the Christian community in Britain and around Glastonbury, as noted in Chapter V, was founded in A.D. 35 or 36 by Joseph of Arimathea, who had traveled to Britain with twelve companions, as did St. Paul several years later. <22> Their first converts were Druids and the earliest Christians in Britain were designated "Culdees." They lived like monks, taught a secret doctrine of spiritual initiation and were decidedly unorthodox in their beliefs, holding to the concepts of preexistence, reincarnation and resurrection in a glorified body. The universe was considered to be the Body of God, and "matter was created and systematized by the Creator's pronouncing his own name." <23> Nature was understood to be the action of God through the medium of matter. Many of the teachings of the Druidic Christians were continued from the traditions of the Druidic priests, and the later "initiatic school" founded by Merlin and King Arthur appears to be a continuation in the sixth century of Druidic Christianity, Merlin himself being a Christian Druidic adept. The Culdee church, later identified with "Keltic Christianity," remained inimical to the pretentions of the Roman church and "papacy." And, what is more, their doctrine of Christ was Arian, in that they rejected the Deity of Jesus, yet reverenced him as the incarnation of Hesus or Yesu, the promised saviour prophesied by the Druid priests for millenia. Druidic Christianity, therefore, was older than the Roman church, being founded approximately five years later than the Jerusalem community.

The God Esus-Hesus-Yesu was known also to the Celts and Gauls, was associated with a tree and was depicted as a woodsman. <24> Sacrifices were made to him, and he appears to have been also associated with a rite of crucifixion—the tree being a substitute for the cross. It is intriguing that in one of Peter's first sermons in Acts, he accuses the Jews of slaying Jesus and hanging him on a tree. (Acts 5:30) Did the ancient Druids and/or Celts practice an initiatic crucifixion ritual as did the mystery religions of the Near East? How widespread was the worship of Hesus?

According to Professor Hilton Hotema, in his "Forward" to the publication of the *History of the First Council of Nice* originally published in 1925 by Dean Dudley, there was, in fact, a hidden agenda at the Council of Nicea. Hotema claims that the two chief Gods of the day were the Hindu Krishna and the Druidic God Hesus. <25> The two Deities were represented by two factions at the Council, who each proclaimed that its God was the oldest and only true God. The strife between the two factions, says Hotema, had grown so serious that "vigorous action was necessary to establish a more peaceful religious state." We quote in full from Hotema's "Forward."

The burning question which the Nicean Council was called to settle, was whether the Hindu Krishna should be worshipped accordingly, or whether they should be united and molded into one God.

Constantine first tried to settle the argument by proposing the adoption of both Gods. This policy failed, and the arguments of the bishops finally became so hostile between the two factions, that Constantine summoned the leading bishops of the sects to meet in council at Nicea and consider the matter.

Constantine was wise enough to have the council convene at Nicea, in the Roman province of Bythnia, in Asia Minor, so the people of Rome would have no knowledge of its real purpose. It is said that the Council convened in May and ended in August 325. But others say the struggle was so fierce in that Christian Council that it extended into September....

Sabinus, bishop of Heraclea, in a letter to a friend, stated that with the exception of Constantine and Eusebius of Caesarea, the 300 bishops who finally voted in favor of Constantine's scheme to unite the names of the two chief Gods were "a set of illiterate, simple men who understood nothing much," to quote his words.

And it was these ignorant prelates, subject to all kinds of motives, to fear of being branded heretics, their desire to agree with the Emperor and win his favor, anxiety to close the angry proceedings, that finally, by their votes, decided under duress that the world should accept and receive the name of the New God who would lead the new Religious System known as Christianity. <26>

Hotema further claims that the above facts were suppressed, but were brought to light 200 years after the council by one Eunomius, a leader of the party of Arius:

The facts presented by Eunomius explained the manner in which the Roman State Church was founded in the fourth century, and how its God, Jesus Christ was invented.

The Church could not allow the damaging revelations of Eunomius to be even remotely known. So by "holy decree" the powerful priesthood of Rome took steps to destroy forever all traces of the proceedings of the Nicean Council contained in his writings, and also the writings of all Christians who attempted to refute his charges. <27>

Although we cannot authenticate Hotema's statement concerning the council's hidden agenda, we should not dismiss outright the possibility of a controversy of this sort in finally establishing the "personage" of Jesus Christ, especially one that would conform to Constantine's idea of a powerful God to rule his Church-state. Considering the long-standing dominance and widespread power of the Druidic teachers and their mystery religion, extending from at least Homeric times and beyond and covering the whole of Europe, but especially Britain, Gaul, Germany, this element is a possibility that would perhaps merit research. It is difficult to conceive of this powerful religion and its influence simply disappearing. Admittedly, however, even in the eastern reaches of the Empire, the extent of any attraction to the concept of Krishna would appear offhand to have been very small, and Hotema's scenario tends to obscure what was a very real and intense historical controversy at Nicea, namely that over Arius. Nevertheless, stranger things have proven possible in the history of men.

Constantine Becomes the Messiah—The Dawn of the Papacy

According to popular tradition, Constantine had a vision of a luminous cross suspended in the heavens bearing the inscription: In Hoc Signo Vinces—By this sign you will conquer. He then, depending upon the historical authority consulted, either had his forces paint this sign on their shields or made this his standard, and went forth to engage Maxentius in battle at the Milvian Bridge in A.D. 312. As a result, Maxentius was killed and Constantine became sole ruler of the Roman world. Popular legend, no doubt fostered by the Roman church, also presents Constantine as a devout convert to Christianity and the first Christian emperor who finally declared Christianity to be the sole true religion. Constantine has become, therefore, somewhat of a saint in Roman and Greek Orthodox Christian circles.

The true facts, however, are quite different. According to Ian Wilson, Constantine did not appear to have been "recognizably Christian" before his victory over Maxentius.<28> Six years before the fateful Battle of the Milvian Bridge, states Wilson, Constantine had hundreds of Frankish rebel prisoners torn to pieces in an arena. <29> While Galerius supervised the burning of Christian texts and the mutilation of those who refused to sacrifice to pagan gods, Constantine stood by "without apparent qualms," <30> and after Constantine's victory the triumphal arch commemorating it was adorned with pagan symbols. Wilson continues:

A commemorative medallion struck by Constantine in 313 A.D. portrays him as Invictus Constantius alongside the image of Sol Invictus, the god of a pagan cult imported from Syria a few decades earlier by the Emperor Aurelian. Even eleven years after winning the battle at the Milvian Bridge, Constantine murdered his already vanquished rival, Licinius, former Emperor in the East; he then killed his wife, by having her boiled alive in her bath, and his own son—hardly the action of a true follower of Jesus. <31>

Whatever the truth behind Constantine's alleged vision, the facts bear out the conclusion that the Emperor's "conversion" was none other than a political maneuver to unify the empire. Constantine, like so many before and after him, appears to have been an opportunist—especially in regard to Christianity. The Christianity of Constantine was, in reality, an amalgamation of prevailing religious cults such as the Mithraic, the Orphic, the worship of Apollo, and the ever-popular sun-god, Sol Invictus, the invincible Sun. Wilson shows that in the West, Christians had begun representing Jesus as Apollo or Orpheus. Wilson states that "a third century mosaic from the Mausoleum of the Julii underneath present-day St. Peter's in Rome actually portrays Jesus as Sol Invictus, driving the horses of the sun's chariot." <32>

It could be stated, in favor of Constantine, that the

Emperor was tolerant enough in allowing these various religious cults to flourish and that, perhaps, he saw the unity behind all religions. A closer look behind our spiritually perceptive tyrant, however, would not confirm this view. Subsequent to the Nicean Council, Constantine ordered the books of Arius to be burned and "a reign of terror," as Wilson phrases it, was proclaimed for all those who did not conform to the "new, official 'Christian line.'" <33> Constantine's edict declares:

> Understand by this present statute, Novations, Valentinians, Marcionites, Paulinians...with what a tissue of lies and vanities, with what destructive and venomous errors, your doctrines are inextricably woven! We give you warning....Let none of you presume, from this time forward, to be deprived of all the houses in which you have been accustomed to meet...and that these should be handed over immediately to the catholic church. <34>

So much for Constantine's much-heralded religious toleration and so much for the freedom of the individual to pursue the religion of his choice. Constantine's benevolence in matters of religion did not extend to those Christian sects and groups who stood independent of totalitarian Roman Catholicism and who considered themselves to be the repositories of authentic Christian teaching, such as the Valentinians. The ascension of Constantine's Christian state religion marked the submergence of the sects and churches promulgating the esoteric doctrine of Jesus. Constantine's Christ was no longer recognizable as Jesus the Messiah, prophet, teacher, guru, avatara or Gnostic revealer. The personality of Jesus was all but obscured and overshadowed by Constantine himself who, for all intents and purposes, became the Messiah of the Christian world to whom even the bishop of Rome became subservient.

In *The Messianic Legacy*, authors Baigent, Leigh and Lincoln discuss the concept of Constantine as Messiah—a title the Emperor arrogated to himself based upon the priest-king idea found in the Old Testament and in certain conceptions of the Messiah as warrior-king:

It is difficult to imagine, for example, the Church acknowledging a secular ruler as a "fully-fledged" priest-king in the traditional biblical sense. And yet that, precisely is what the early Church did with the Emperor Constantine. In fact, it did more. Not only did it concur with Constantine's presentation of himself as Messiah, it also concurred with his presentation of himself as a specifically warlike Messiah—a man who implemented God's will with the sword and whose triumphs bore testimony to God's favour. In other words, the Church recognized Constantine as successfully achieving what Jesus had signally failed to do. <35>

In short, Constantine, in collusion with the bishops who supported him, effectively usurped the office of Messiah—an office previously reserved only for Jesus. Constantine, not Jesus, became the embodied Messiah, Saviour and head of the Church.

In 314, Miltiades, bishop of Rome, died. A month later, Constantine assembled all Christians and publicly appointed Sylvester as successor to Miltiades. Sylvestor became the first bishop of Rome to be crowned like a temporal prince, all under the auspices of Constantine. The Emperor donated the Lateran Palace to the Roman bishop, thus enabling the bishop of Rome, later to be called "pope", to consolidate his authority and establish supremacy over the churches of Antioch, Alexandria, Jerusalem and elsewhere. Previous to the reign of Constantine, the bishop of Rome, although greatly respected, was not considered to possess authority over the bishops of these other ancient centers of Christianity. When "pope" Sylvester accepted an alliance between church and state, the so-called papacy made vast strides under the protective wings of the Emperor. Malachi Martin writes:

Constantine first established the bishop of Rome in full power in Western Europe. The popes received from him considerable real estate, extensive judicial authority, much liquid wealth, control over the armed forces, and political dominance. The Roman Church and Christianity thereby acquired inestimable status in the eyes of the public and very privileged access to the great emperor himself. In short, because of Constantine, the Bishop of Rome became a monarch and his church a monarchy. <36>

The Roman Church, of course, consented to Constantine's usurpation of Jesus' role as Messiah. Not only did the church consent to it but it promoted this view. Eusebius, bishop of Caesarea and a close associate of the Emperor, actually declares the Logos, in effect, to be incarnate in Constantine in a personal address to the Emperor. He states, "Most God-fearing sovereign, to whom alone of those who have yet been here since the start of time has the universal All-Ruling God Himself given power to purify human life." <37> Authors Baigent, Leigh and Lincoln quote Alistair Kee on the implications of Eusebius' address as follows:

Since the beginning of the world it is to Constantine alone that the power of salvation has been given. Christ is set aside, Christ is excluded and now Christ is formally denied....Constantine now stands alone as the saviour of the world. The scene is the fourth century not the first. The world, spiritual and material, was not saved until Constantine. <38>

Where are Ignatius, Irenaeus, Tertullian now that we need them? Where is some good old orthodox "only Jesus is the Logos" rhetoric? It didn't apply to Constantine apparently. It was from this point of view that Eusebius wrote his *Ecclesiastical History* in which he traced the development of the primitive church up to and including the reign of Constantine. Eusebius' history, although valuable in many respects, is based upon the premise that the orthodox Christianity of the fourth century which triumphed with Constantine's accession was, in fact, the authentic Christianity of the first century. Eusebius portrays the innumerable early sects of Christianity as heretical and blasphemous and as a deviation from true Christianity. He condemns the ancient Ebionites, the Valentinians and others. Fortunately, he has nothing but praise for Origen, but fails to elucidate Origen's doctrine which, as we know, was actually antithetical to Constantinian Christianity. We find no real history of Christianity for the first crucial 150 years of the Christian era in Eusebius' text. Eusebius, like Irenaeus, assumes an unbroken chain of pure orthodox teaching from the earliest years of apostolic preaching. Nothing, of course, could be farther from the truth, as we have sought to prove. The fourth century Christianity of Eusebius was not the first century Christianity of apostolic times. Much of Eusebius' history appears as whitewash and partly fabricated, which is understandable considering that the book was written as a front for Constantine and from the viewpoint that Christianity itself had been finally vindicated by Constantine and not by Jesus. In effect, the Second Coming of Christ had occurred through Constantine—the world had become Christian—and heaven had descended to earth—that is, the orthodox earth. Heaven was going to be no fun for anyone else.

Constantine continued his revolutionizing of Christianity by ordering new copies of the scriptures to be printed in A.D. 331. It is especially significant that no complete copies of the Bible exist prior to the fourth century. The books comprising our present-day Bible are essentially the books chosen during the reign of Constantine. Since we have no complete record of the proceedings of the Council of Nicea, we may assume that numerous scriptures dealing with the life and teaching of Jesus, some of which we have examined in this book, were consigned to the flames to support the increasingly rigid orthodoxy of Constantine. From the time of Constantine, all scriptures not approved by the church/emperor were either destroyed or secretly hidden. Such is the case with the carefully hidden texts discovered at Nag Hammadi.

During his reign, Constantine sought out the sacred places where Jesus lived, worked, died and rose again. He constructed monumental basilicas over the alleged sites of Golgotha and Jesus' tomb in place of previously constructed Roman temples of the second century. Basilicas to Christ rose up as did the temples to the Roman deities. There was no god but Jesus, and Constantine was his Messiah.

In honor of his new god Jesus Christ, Constantine, during the last years of his reign, commanded so-called pagan temples and images to be destroyed.<39> Heresies were cursed and heretics were deprived of their right to hold meetings; Constantine as the new Messiah had his likeness represented on golden coins, eyes uplifted in the attitude of prayer. <40> In place of the Sabbath, the Emperor commanded the Lord's day should hereafter be celebrated on Sunday, that is Dies Solis, the Day of the Sun, a day of observance in honor of Sol Invictus, the Son-God.<41> The imperial religion of Rome had finally merged with the new-fangled Christianity to become the Roman Catholic Church.

Constantine continued to build churches and compose religious discourses up to his last days. After a 31-year reign, on May 22, 337, Constantine died at age 63. On his deathbed, he finally received baptism, although he ruled the church unbaptized as Sovereign Pontiff for most of his reign. He was buried in the Church of the Apostle at Constantinople, the city which he had dedicated to himself as the Nova Roma, the New Rome, the city he set aside as the model for his imperial, totalitarian Christianity. W.H.C. Frend reflects on the Constantinian revolution as follows:

Without his (Constantine's) restless energy and sense of purpose, the Council of Nicea, which established the Christian episcopate as a force on a world scale, could not have taken place. Henceforth bishops became men of power and influence in political as well as religious life, advisors to the emperor like Eusebius of Casearea and Eusebius of Nicomedia, or prestigious representatives of their people such as Athanasius. The "Age of the Fathers" could have been impossible without Constantine's conversion. The church's councils under the emperor's guidance became assemblies where the new binding relationship with the Christian God, on which the safety of the empire depended, was established.

As such, these gatherings, in which rival theologies and individuals wrestled for supremacy, had political, as well as religious importance. There could only be one orthodoxy. The ministers of the Supreme God would speak with one voice only.

This was the other side of the coin. In practice, the ancient world had exchanged the guardianship of one set of divine masters, capricious but generally benevolent, for another that would brook no opposition. There were already signs that the church which had suffered persecution for so long would soon be persecuting its opponents. The movement of protest could not be tamed overnight—to the victor belonged the spoils. Ecclesiastical decisions were to be enforced by the secular power. Within a few years of the Edict of Milan, heretics were being denounced in unequalled terms and denied the right of assembly. The dynamic of change that had favored the triumph of Christianity did not favor its unity. The arrival of a Christian emperor of Constantine's dedication and political stature fanned the flames of division. <42>

Christological controversies raged throughout the fourth century and into the fifth. Whereas Constantine succeeded in merging state and church, he failed to unify the Arian and orthodox factions. The orthodox church chose to reject the ancient Christian sects and their teaching. It had denied and condemned Origen, the orthodox church's first theologian, and, almost as a recompense, it fell prey to controversy and disunity.

Aftermath of the Arian Controversy

After the Council of Nicea, discontent erupted among the warring factions of bishops, eventually spreading to Alexandria where the controversy had first taken hold. Constantine's efforts to check contentions within the church were proving fruitless. With the death of Bishop Alexander, Arius was recalled from banishment by the Emperor in an attempt to unify the two factions. Athanasius, now the bishop of Alexandria, refused to admit Arius as a presbyter or even allow him to enter Alexandria. Constantine then had Athanasius deposed and banished, and ordered Arius to present himself to Alexander, bishop of Constantinople, for recognition as a presbyter. The bishop likewise refused. Constantine then fixed a day when Arius should be recognized, by command of the Emperor. Bishop Alexander is said to have prayed publicly in the church that God would interpose in his favor. That same evening Arius died. His enemies, of course, never tired of relating that Alexander got what he prayed for. It was the opinion of Arius' friends, however, that Arius had been killed by sorcery, i.e., witchcraft or a form of "psychic murder" via mass hatred directed against Arius by his enemies, the good bishops Alexander and Athanasius and their allies. Ironically, the doctrines of Arius spread more rapidly after his death than before, and the Christological controversies continued unabated. <43>

According to Martin Larson, after Nicea efforts were made to revise the creed, first by the Arians, then by Semi-Arians who also taught that the Son of God was not identical to the Father but was like the Father. <44> The orthodox party, eventually headed by Athanasius and known as Homoousians, taught that the Son/Word/Christ was of identical substance with the Father. Whereas Arius differentiated between the man Jesus, the Word and the Son, the orthodox made no differentiation. Therefore, the views of the Arian party appeared to be blasphemous to the orthodox, who were not subtle enough to understand the differences in emanation from the Supreme

Godhead. The concept of Homoousia (the Son as identical to the Father), according to Larson:

...let loose a fury among mankind that has rarely been paralleled. Millions suffered violence or death in the pursuant wars and persecutions. Hundreds of bishops were exiled or murdered at the command of other bishops who when the tide turned, visited the same treatment upon their rivals. The great Athanasius was driven from his see five times, and on, at least, two occasions barely escaped with his life. His Arian enemies, seated in his place of power, were not so fortunate: two of them were lynched, and the other was barely saved from the bloodthirsty mobs by the police. Arians and Athanasians alike sought to use the secular arm to terrify and assassinate their opponents, and to seize their congregations, churches, and revenues by force. <45>

Between 325 and 367, says Larsen, twenty-eight synods were held of which four were orthodox. <46> A number of creeds were adopted at these synods.

The orthodox party consolidated its position in 379 when Theodosius became emperor of the West. In 381 the Second Ecumenical Council was convened in Constantinople and reaffirmed the Nicene Creed while condemning the Eunomians, yet another sect of the Arians. In this landmark council, it was finally established that "the Son and the Word were not merely identical but also co-equal, co-eternal and consubtantial (of the same substance) with the Father; and exactly the same status was accorded the Holy Spirit."<47>

The man Jesus, the teacher and Guru, was not only proclaimed as identical with the Supreme Deity, but it was now taught that Jesus had never been created since he was the Absolute Deity Himself! Thus it was that the Council of Ephesus in 431 A.D. proclaimed Mary, the mother of Jesus, "Theotokos," i.e., Mother of God, much to the chagrin of one Nestorius, a "heretic" with decidedly Arian sympathies, who proclaimed Mary only as Mother of Christ. If Jesus was God, Mary of course had to be God's mother. This new dogma was not taught with the understanding that Mary nurtured the indwelling "God" or Divinity within Jesus, and thus became the mother of the "God" in Jesus, but was meant to remove Mary as an exemplar of spiritual and material motherhood and to reconstruct her as a remote goddess, one who actually gave birth to the Supreme Deity. The cult of Mary within orthodox Christianity was stolen from the cults and rites of the innumerable feminine deities of the mystery religions such as Isis, Vesta, Venus, Demeter, Diana/Artemis and others, some of whom gave birth to saviour gods, while others were virgin deities. The ancient doctrine of primordial matter as the mother-womb of the universe (the Son) was debased into a literal dogma of a woman giving birth to the Creator of the universe! Such was the legacy of the Nicene Council.

The dogma of the Deity of Jesus, as we have said, not only contradicted the far more ancient doctrines of Paul, Peter, the Christian-Gnostics and Origen, but also contradicted the New Testament itself. With the establishment of this doctrine, it finally remained for Augustine to plunge Christian doctrine into further bondage.

Chapter XIII

The Bondage of Orthodoxy

Augustine

The sublime theology of the Christian-Gnostics and Origen was finally buried and its headstone chiseled with the theology of orthodoxy during the fourth and fifth centuries. The dogmas of Augustine (354-430) more than any other Church Father, literally defined Christianity for centuries, well into the Middle Ages and beyond. It is also quite arguable that the "Dark Ages" were precipitated, to some degree, by the philosophy of Augustine and other theologians who promoted his theology throughout the Christian world. Christianity is essentially what it is today because of Augustine.

Born in North Africa, Augustine was raised a Christian due to the determination of his mother, Monica, since Augustine's father was a "pagan." He received a classical education, and his father inspired him with an ambition for a public career. Augustine was to grow up wanting to succeed at whatever he undertook. <1> This characteristic was to come to the fore most strongly in his future theological debates; Augustine's theology had to triumph whatever the cost or the sacrifice of truth. In 371, Augustine continued his studies at Carthage. Two important episodes marked his life there: his decision to pursue wisdom through philosophy and his "conversion" to the religion of Mani.

During his youth in Carthage, Augustine led a somewhat dissolute life; he had love affairs, took a mistress and eventually had a son. He was also stimulated by a lively intellectual society versed in Aristotelian logic and rhetoric. Augustine became a "hearer" in the Manichaean faith in 373.

Part of the reason for his interest in Manichaeism was his obsession with the problem of evil and his own sexual guilt. Augustine remained a "hearer" for nine years, but failed to "advance" in the Manichaean faith to the degree of the "elect." This was due to his retaining a mistress, his ambition for a career, and his continual pursuit of that ambition during his association with the Manichaean church. Augustine later claimed that his discussion with Faustus, the leading Manichaean in North Africa, was a disappointment. More than likely, Augustine's ambition was thwarted. Seeing he could not rise to the place of honor he desired, he gradually became disillusioned with the faith, which he later claimed did not provide him with the "answers" to the perplexing questions of good and evil. It is doubtful, however, that this was his true motive for leaving. Augustine deserted the Manichaean fold and ever after sustained a deep hatred for Mani, his religion and his disciples.

Previously, Augustine had despised the Christian faith, at least the prevailing version of orthodox Christianity familiar to him in North Africa, and he considered Christianity a superstition. This state of affairs was to change rapidly when Augustine encountered Ambrose, the bishop of Milan. By this time, Augustine had maneuvered himself into a career as professor of rhetoric and public orator at the court of the Emperor Valentinian II. He had listened enraptured to the sermons of Ambrose, who sought to harmonize so-called Platonic logic and reason with an allegorical interpretation of Scripture, ultimately derived from Origen. For Ambrose, there was no Christianity unless it could be proved both logical and reasonable in an Aristotelian sense. This was one of the early roots of what was later termed "Scholasticism" in the thirteenth century—the attempt to "prove" the truth of Christianity by logic and dialectic, as opposed to insight, revelation or spiritual intuition. Ambrose's Christianity was of the narrow orthodox kind and was based on the following doctrines:

1) All truth rests on biblical authorities (not on individual

perception, insight or spiritual experience).

2) Authoritatively transmitted truth can be rationally explained.

3) Sin and guilt in the human race were transmitted from Adam and Eve through physical propagation.

4) The believer is justified by faith alone. <2>

These are the four pillars on which Augustine based his theology—a theology that had been slowly developing since Justin's and Irenaeus' time, devised exclusively to counter and exterminate Christian Gnosis.

In 386, Augustine "converted" to this brand of Christianity, which doubtless was appealing to him, based as it was on the church hierarchy as the ultimate dispenser of truth. In the church, Augustine could rise on the ladder of success without spiritual attainment commensurate with his office, as was necessary, for instance, in the Manichaean church. Another reason for Augustine's alleged "conversion" to Christianity was his desire to rid himself of guilt and the fear of lust which plagued him all his life. Augustine, therefore, was baptized by Ambrose in 387 at Milan; prior to his baptism, he deserted his mistress and child and vowed to live a life of continence and asceticism. In his *Soliloquies* and *Confessions*, Augustine attempts to present his search for truth as a spiritual journey and as a desire to know God. In our opinion, Augustine, in the *Confessions*, seems to be couching his spiritual ambitions in the language of a mystic, a language frequently overwhelmed by emotionalism and guilt feelings. As we shall see, Augustine's theology and his actions as a bishop belie his words.

Augustine was ordained a presbyter and eventually realized his ambition to become a bishop in 396. He was now ready to combat all those who disagreed with him—which it seems was everyone. Firmly ensconced in his office as bishop, Augustine first turned his attention to the Manichaeans, his former friends—with a vengeance!

Augustine Attacks the Manichaeans

And so I fell among men who were arrogant in their madness, exceedingly carnal and loquacious; on whose lips were the snares of the Devil which were smeared with a birdlime compounded out of a mixture of the syllables of your name and of the Lord Jesus Christ and of the Holy Spirit our Paraclete and Comforter. These names were forever on their lips, in as much as they were the rattling noise of the tongue as their hearts were devoid of any truth whatsoever....Truth was never in them but falsehood which they uttered not only about you...but also about the elements of this world which was your creation. <3>

Such is the manner in which the good bishop acquaints the reader with the Manichaeans in his book *Confessions*. These are the same people whom Augustine considered his friends—fellow devotees of Christ—and who, no doubt, were on the same spiritual journey as he claimed to be. In his ivory battle tower as bishop, Augustine may have felt that he could judge all and be judged by no one, all in the name of truth. Nevertheless, it is a common psychological truism that the motives one imputes to others are, in fact, one's own hidden motives. We leave it to the reader to evaluate Augustine on the basis of his own words.

The Manichaean scriptures, prayers and psalms we have previously reviewed contradict Augustine's assessment of the Manichaeans. We could conclude that Augustine must have felt resentful toward the Manichaean church and its hierarchy for their failure to recognize his capacities for spiritual leadership. But the motive spring of an Augustine is surely deeper. What we see here and shall see unfold in his theology—for this man's ultimately insane theology is only understood as a mirror of his psychology—is a deep desire to avoid, to escape in any way, responsibility for his actions.

Whether this held purely for this life, or for past lives, we do not know. But already we see the attempt, before God, to blame the Manichaeans, not himself, for the actions of his youth, not only his beliefs, but likely for his lusts. This root motif is augmented here by an obsessive desire born of some deep fear to cleanse himself in the eyes of God of any taint or stain of all former participation in "heresy"—as if to God salvation is all a matter of dogma, of "right thinking," yes, of orthodoxy, and not a matter of the heart and the desires of the soul. This has always been the profound error of the orthodox frame of mind. We cannot otherwise explain his sudden turn-around and his prolonged anti-Manichaean stance.

The publication and dissemination of Augustine's *Confessions* in 398 was, indeed, as scholar Samuel Lieu asserts, "a major media setback for the [Manichaean] sect." <4> Then, as now, the media can make you or break you. It is not what you truly believe and the true nature of your being, but what, in ignorance or from motives such as Augustine's, they say you believe and what they say you are. From the Christian-Gnostic sects, to the Arians, to the Manichaeans, a media disinformation campaign was in full sway, and Augustine contributed mightily to the campaign. He was followed in this campaign by countless others in Church and State—all, like him, attempting to establish a monopoly on the truth.

Prior to the publication of *Confessions*, Augustine debated with the local Manichaean presbyter, Fortunatus. The debate lasted for two days, the 28th and 29th of August, 392. According to the record, Fortunatus affirmed the incorruptibility of God as an opening to the debate which was, ostensibly, concerning the origin of evil and the cause of sin. Lieu states that Fortunatus "completely underestimated his opposition" in Augustine who kept repeating the same question to Fortunatus: "Why did God have to send forth his soul if he was incorruptible?" <5> To this question Fortunatus could find no answer that satisfied Augustine and avowed that he would refer this argument to his superiors. Augustine, of course, determined to debase the Manichaean concept of the "Father of

Greatness" by attempting to prove that the Manichaeans taught a God that was corruptible or that could suffer harm. We recall that God, according to the Manichaeans, sent a portion of himself as Soul, the Primal Man, into the Darkness to combat the evil archons, thus weakening them as they were infused with the light elements. Augustine took this to mean that the God of the Manichaeans was subject to corruption, and so he convinced the audience that this was true. By presenting God as absolutely incorruptible, Fortunatus was attempting to show that no evil exists in God and that the source of evil is a principle distinct from God. The debate, as manipulated by Augustine, had shown, on the contrary, that the Manichaean God was neither incorruptible nor omnipotent. Fortunatus then quietly left town and was heard of no more. Some may attribute Augustine's winning of the debate to his skillfulness. Augustine was, indeed, brilliant in his intellectual capacity and in his skill at clever manipulative argumentation. But more likely it was the lack of skill in Fortunatus. If we attempt to probe the Manichaean doctrine, we find that they taught the concept of the "lamb slain from the foundation of the world" (cosmos)—a doctrine, by the way, that Augustine himself adhered to and which had always been a part of Catholic Christianity. This doctrine asserts that the Lamb (Soul/Primal Man) allows itself to be "slain" as a sacrifice for the redemption of the cosmos. God, in his essence, is not corrupted but permits a portion of himself to be "slain" or corrupted, (misqualified) so that the Light now infiltrating the Darkness can triumph over Darkness. The God of Mani is a God whose very essence permeates the universe—he is a God of self-sacrifice and love. As we have said, Augustine himself believed in a distorted form of this doctrine: the Nicean Christ, as God from all eternity, gives up his omnipotence, is born on earth and is "slain" by the forces of evil. This is essentially the identical teaching of Mani. Augustine's God is a Trinity—the Second Person (still essentially God) descends to the corruption of earth, takes sin into himself and dies for it, shedding every drop of blood as the ultimate sacrifice. We see, then, that the

God Augustine was preaching performed the same act as the God of the Manichaeans! This is illustrative of a repetitive pattern in Augustine's theology: he absorbs his enemies' doctrines, transforms them into his own personal theology (now distorted) and then turns his enemies' own doctrines against them. We would suggest that Augustine hated the Manichaeans because he inwardly feared (or secretly admired) their doctrine, which in their fearless exposure of evil threatened to expose his own less than Christ-like motives.

Twelve years later, Augustine again successfully debated with the Manichaean Felix, the successor to Fortunatus. <6> As in his previous debate, Augustine won by manipulation, but this time he resorted to intimidation. Augustine set up the debate in the cathedral at Hippo (where he reigned as bishop) before a small and select audience. He had prepared questions beforehand to trip up his opponent and conducted himself as an inquisitor on behalf of the civil authorities of Hippo, who placed the Manichaean books under the public seal. From the beginning, Felix felt uneasy and did not consider the debate impartial. Augustine was again determined to demonstrate that Felix believed in a God that was corruptible and not omnipotent. As Lieu states: "Augustine was able to maneuver Felix into a position in which not to anathematize Mani would mean giving consent to a worse error of Christian doctrine." <7> That "worse error," of course, was to deny the incorruptibility of God. Augustine again won the debate, and Felix surrendered completely. He was at the mercy of Augustine, who immediately forced Felix to curse (anathematize) Mani and to sign a "formula of abjuration." <8> Augustine then successfully "deprogrammed" Felix, who later converted to Catholicism.

Admirers of Augustine will undoubtedly affirm that Augustine won the debate because he was a superior debater or that his brand of Christianity was superior to Manichaean Christianity. Augustine may have possessed superior debating skills, but we would suggest that at the time of the Augustinian debates, Manichaean doctrine may have been slowly undergoing a transformation and may have been absorbing orthodox concepts of Deity which affirm a transcendent God, separate from creation, and not a God immanent in the universe, which had been Mani's original teaching. Mani also taught that God suffers in and with his creation. By the process of "erosion" and, no doubt, through pressure from the orthodox, Manicheaism had become infiltrated with the notion that an omnipotent God could not or would not experience the "pain" of creation. Thus we find a certain vulnerability in the Manichaean teachers, subject as they were to the "mass consciousness" of orthodoxy—an orthodoxy which refused to accept the ancient Christian doctrine of the dual aspects of Deity: the eternal unmanifest God and the manifested creative God who involves Himself in creation.

As a result of his debates with the Manichaeans, Augustine promoted the theology that evil is an absence of good, a state of nonbeing; he denied that evil is an active power having an existence apart from God, i.e. an energy veil or misuse of God's pure original energy. Augustine therefore condemned the doctrine of the fall of the Watchers to earth and the concept of embodied evil; the Book of Enoch (which New Testament author Jude quotes), with theological self-confidence approaching the proportions of King Kong, placing himself on his doctrinal skyscraper far above Enoch or the author of the book, he rejected as heretical, apocryphal and not genuine. Commenting on the Enochian scripture of the physical mating of the fallen sons of God with women, he writes, "...I could by no means believe that God's holy angels could at that time have so fallen." <9> Thus Augustine, by refusing to consider the physical fall of the angels, forever silenced further discussion on the problem of evil or "theodicy," as it is termed. The doctrine concerning the archons found in St. Paul and the Christian-Gnostics, the fall of angels into bodies as taught by Origen, and the Manichaean exposé of a cosmic conspiracy of Darkness were judged blasphemous and heretical. Augustine drew the veil over the "mystery" of evil, a "mystery" which persists to this day on planet Earth and which the Christian church has failed to grapple with effectively.

The Theology of Augustine—The Theory of Original Sin

We cannot understand Augustine's theology and his theories on sin, sex and free will without some understanding of his personal and psychological attitudes on these subjects. Augustine fought nearly a lifelong battle against concupiscence—the desire for sexual activity. This desire and its attendant guilt dominated and undergirded his psychology. Augustine may have sustained this guilt, to a certain extent, as the result of his association with Manichaeism, which taught that concupiscence had been injected into the body through the sexual activity of the evil archons (demons) who gave birth to Adam and Eve. Yet, we see that Augustine possessed sexual guilt feelings before his becoming a "hearer" in the Manichaean church. The problem, as he describes it, arises in the will:

Because of a perverse will, desire was made; and when I was enslaved to desire it became habit; and habit not restrained became necessity. By which links...a very hard bondage had me enthralled. <10>

The word "desire" must be understood as the libido or sexual drive. In his *Confessions*, Augustine makes the reader aware that he suffered these temptations of the flesh against his own will and did not possess the resolve to overcome the desire. The cause of this conflict within was "sin," not his own but the voluntary "sin" of Adam, which Augustine was convinced he had inherited "because I was the son of Adam." <11>

Augustine may have been a "physical" son of Adam, but in examining his writings, we find that he apparently lost sight of or chose to ignore the ancient Christian teaching (now considered heretical in the fourth century) that the soul originally preexisted the body and, in essence, was derived from

Spirit. So taught the Christian-Gnostics, Mani and Origen before him. Augustine never made the leap in envisioning himself as a "son of God" or a "joint-heir with Christ." His sense of worthlessness not only infected himself, but in time infected all those who read his works who, likewise, may have been struggling on the spiritual path.

Augustine appears to have developed his doctrine of original sin, to a certain extent, as a result of these conflicts, although, as we have seen, the doctrine received its earliest formulation with Irenaeus and Tertullian. Augustine went back to St. Paul (Rom. 5:12) for his concept of the propagation of original sin from Adam to the human race. The Pauline verse reads:

Through one man sin entered the world, and through sin, death; and thus death came upon all men, in that all sinned.

As Elaine Pagels shows in *Adam, Eve, and the Serpent*, the above passage in Greek usually meant that Adam's sin brought death into the world, and death came upon all because all sinned (not just Adam). <12> She explains:

*But Augustine read the passage in Latin, and so either ignored or was unaware of the connotations of the Greek original; thus he misread the last phrase as referring to Adam. Augustine insisted that it meant that "death came upon **all men**, in whom all sinned"—that the sin of that "one man," Adam brought upon humanity not only universal death, but also universal and inevitable sin. Augustine uses the passage to deny that human beings have free moral choice, which Jews and Christians had traditionally regarded as the birthright of humanity made "in God's image." Augustine declares, on the contrary, that the whole human race inherited from Adam a nature irreversibly damaged by sin. "For we all were in that one man, since all of us were that one man who fell into sin through the woman who was made from him." <13>*

Pagels then questions the meaning of Augustine's assertion that we were all "in Adam." We also ask, "Is Augustine teaching a doctrine of preexistence?" Not quite. As Augustine explains and as Pagels points out, quoting Augustine, what already existed is "the nature of the semen from which we were to be propagated." <14> All souls, therefore, "preexisted" in the semen of Adam—which semen is "shackled by the bond of death." We have come a long way from the soul's existence in the Pleroma. The logical deduction, of course, is that all those conceived through semen are "contaminated with sin." <15> Pagels continues:

Through this astonishing argument, Augustine intends to prove that every human being is in bondage not only from birth but indeed from the moment of conception. And since he takes Adam as a corporate personality, Augustine applies his account of Adam's experience, disrupted by the first sin, to every one of his offspring (except, of course, to Christ, conceived, Augustine ingeniously argued, without semen). <16>

We have previously shown that the earliest doctrine, that of the Nazorean-Jewish Christians, concerning the conception of Christ was that he was conceived with semen, born in the normal manner and was the true son of Joseph and Mary. We recall that St. Paul makes no mention of the virginal conception or virgin birth and neither does John or Mark. In the chapter on Nazorean-Jewish Christianity, it was shown that the literal virginal conception/birth was no part of the earliest Christianity and is to be understood symbolically, allegorically and astrologically. We earlier concluded that Jesus was born in the same manner as all souls were born—yet he was the Son of God and Saviour of the world. We noted that the Gospel of the Holy Twelve shows that Joseph, likewise, received Gabriel's annunciation with the words, "Blessed be the fruit of thy loins. Joseph then went in unto Mary and she conceived." The "fruit" of Joseph's loins (his semen) was none other than Jesus. No wonder this gospel was banned. It challenged the doctrine of the virginal conception, effectively nullifying Augustine's theory that Christ was born without the agency of semen. Even considering for a moment Augustine's propagation theory, he appears to ignore the fact that spiritual gifts and graces may also be transmitted from parents to children as was undoubtedly the case with Jesus. In his obsession with sexual sin, Augustine ignored the possibility that virtue may also be propagated genetically through intercourse. Could not the transmission of virtue counteract the "sin" of Adam?

Augustine found himself in a dilemma as the result of his theology of original sin. He was, therefore, forced to conclude that mankind is a "mass of sin waited on by death, and incapable of raising itself to the good," as Harnack explains. <17> In other words, mankind have utterly lost the power to do good, through no fault of their own, and all because of Adam's disobedience. Only the grace of God dispensed by Christ through the orthodox church is capable of restoring man to the place where he can begin to make a freewill choice for the good. Without this grace, mankind have no free-will-to-good and are subject to eternal damnation. Baptism alone, as exclusively dispensed by the orthodox church, can remove the guilt or original sin, but not the effect of Adam's sin in the will. Man still has the propensity to sin, which can only be removed through the Holy Spirit's infusion. This act Augustine called "justification by faith," which produced a new frame of mind and capacity.<18> But Augustine is careful to explain that justification is a process never fully completed in this life. That is, absolute assurance of salvation is impossible. The experience of the "bridal-chamber" as the Valentinian Christian demonstrated—the mystical union of the soul with Christ—is not possible of achievement in this life, if we read Augustine correctly. Man can never be wholly transformed until he reaches the heavenly state. This concept is contrary to Origen's previous theology that man is capable of such sanctification that he becomes as God is.

What proof does Augustine present that original sin is present in the body of man? His "proof" lies in the fact that the male sexual organ cannot be controlled by the will and acts independent of the will. <19> This supposed "fact" demonstrates to Augustine that original sin is a "state of being" <20> in which humanity finds itself and that this sin "propagates itself with our nature." <21> Inherited sin, therefore, is the basis of all wickedness on earth and not actual sins.<22> Augustine teaches that all sexual intercourse, even in marriage, is lustful and hence all procreation is lustful. In other words, it is impossible to procreate without lust. The love of husband and wife for one another cannot and does not nullify the sin of lust. Augustine is saying, in effect, that there is no virtue within the hearts and souls of men and women that could counteract this dreadful sin. This present state of affairs, of course, was permitted by God, who all along knew that Adam and Eve would disobey him in the Garden of Eden. We can only conclude that the "God" of Augustine is a tyrant deity like the "God" of Irenaeus, Tertullian and Ambrose. He allows humanity, through no fault of their own, to inherit original sin—for thousands upon thousands of years. Man's only recourse is through the church and its sacraments—since there is nothing divine left in man worth saving! Only Christ, now a full-fledged "God," can save mankind—hopelessly lost and subject to damnation. Humanity can offer God no merits, no treasures in heaven to expiate this state of being, except belief in Christ and his "Church"—an orthodox church promulgating orthodox doctrine dispensed by none other than Augustine himself.

Augustine Denies Preexistence and the Law of Cause and Effect

Augustine paid dearly for formulating and promulgating this doctrine on original sin. We see him continually troubled about and questioning how a just God (which he claims he firmly believes in) could allow for sin and suffering on earth.

Yet he rejects the sane, logical answers to the questions he asks, those which were answered by Origen nearly two centuries earlier: the doctrine of the soul's preexistence and its freewill choice to move away from or towards God. Writing to Julian, his enemy and an exponent of free will, Augustine asks painfully:

> *...You must explain why such great innocence [of the new born] is sometimes born blind or deaf. If nothing deserving punishment passes from parents to infants, who could bear to see the image of God sometimes born retarded, since this afflicts the soul itself? (Brackets added) <23>*

The answer, of course, is to be found in the ancient doctrine of preexistence and reincarnation—taught in the ancient sects and churches and widely disseminated by the greatest of all Christian theologians, Origen of Alexandria. As noted earlier, Origen taught that the sufferings and diseases of this present life are the consequences or effects (i.e., karma) of sins committed in previous lives or in some other preexistent state. Preexistent spirits chose to move away from God by free will. As an ultimate consequence, they were forced to inhabit bodies to accommodate their state of separation from God— freely chosen. In Origen's view, then, all souls who find themselves suffering are themselves to blame, for they are experiencing the effects of their own choice to sin or not to sin. The soul's incarnations are for the purpose of expiating sins through bodily suffering and simultaneously for the edification of the soul. The sin or "karma" once expiated, the soul can ascend to God. Through reincarnation, as an opportunity to expiate sin, can be seen the mercy of God, who is absolutely just, as Origen teaches. The nature that man inherits, his body, his mental and emotional faculties, his capacities and his state in life, are the result of his past actions—his personal merits and demerits; they are not derived from original sin inherited from Adam.

What is Augustine's attitude toward this altogether just

and lucid doctrine of Origen's? He writes in *The City of God*:

> *But they say that souls, though not, indeed, parts of God, but created by Him, sinned by abandoning God; that, in proportion to their various sins, they merited different degrees of debasement from heaven to earth, and diverse bodies as prison-houses; and that this is the world, and this the cause of its creation, not the production of good things, but the retraining of evil....Origen is justly blamed for holding this opinion. For in the books which he entitles... **Of Origins**, this is his sentiment, this his utterance. And I cannot sufficiently express my astonishment, that a man so erudite and well versed in ecclesiastical literature, should not have observed...how opposed this is to the meaning of this authoritative scripture, which, in recounting all the works of God, regularly adds, "And God saw that it was good." <24>*

We also cannot sufficiently express our astonishment that Augustine had not the capacity to discriminate between the just doctrine of self-chosen merits and demerits and the doctrine of a tyrannical God who leaves the entire human race subject to damnation through no fault of their own. Contrary to Augustine's opinion, Origen did indeed consider that the earth and matter were good. God created matter, says Origen, to accommodate the fallen souls in order that, through the body and through creation, they might attain their freedom from embodiment through the resurrection. Matter is good, therefore, because it serves a good purpose. Augustine, again, has distorted and misrepresented this ancient doctrine of Christianity.

The Doctrine of Infant Damnation and the Eternality of Hell

Although Augustine was disturbed by the sufferings of infants, he was even more disturbed by the logical conclusion his theology led him to: the damnation of unbaptized infants tainted with original sin. He writes:

> *For before Thee none is free from sin, not even the infant which has lived but a day upon the earth. <25>*
> *...it is not lawful for us to deny that nothing else than perdition is the doom of the [infant] souls, even of little children, which have departed from the body without the sacrament of Christ.... <26>*
> *Unless infant children receive baptism they cannot be made alive in Christ. Those not made alive in Christ must remain under the condemnation. <27>*
> *...It is necessary still to investigate and to make known the reason why, if souls are created new for every individual at his birth, those who die in infancy without the sacrament of Christ are doomed to perdition; for that they are doomed to this if they do depart from the body is testified by Holy Scripture and by Holy Church. <28>*

We seek in vain for the teaching of infant damnation both in the scriptures and in the earliest sects and schools of Christianity. Yet Augustine firmly adheres to it as a corollary to his doctrine of the eternality of hell. The "God" of Augustine not only condemns unbaptized infants to hell, but as a consequence, they must suffer in hell eternally. For what possible benefit do infants suffer and die? Augustine answers: so that their parents may turn toward a better life. So goes the justice of Augustine's "God":

> *...for as his [the sinner's] wish was to have an eternal enjoyment of sin, so the reward which he finds is an eternal endurance of suffering. <29>*
> *...Every soul, moreover, which may at any age whatsoever depart from this life without the grace of the Mediator and the sacrament of this grace, departs to future punishment, and shall receive again its own body at the last judgment as a partner in punishment. <30>*

In *The City of God*, Book 21, Augustine attempts to prove that bodies are able to last forever in burning fire according to the orthodox doctrine of the resurrection of the body (which states that the resuscitated body will join the soul in hell at the final judgment). We can contemplate no more horrendous fate than to be damned to burning fire eternally. And to make matters worse, Augustine teaches that God foreknows whom he shall save (those who accept his grace) and those whom he will damn. For only a certain select number of souls are predestined to salvation; the rest are damned to perdition. This is a corollary doctrine to Augustine's denial of free will—grace is not bestowed by God through human merit. It is given indiscriminately by God. This doctrine was later developed by John Calvin and became the classic dogma of predestination during the Reformation. We see in this a perversion of St. Paul's doctrine that the souls who are called and who "elect" to do God's will are predestined to eternal felicity —that is their "blueprint" or "divine plan" should they choose to accept it. This is a far cry from Augustine's merciless and tyrannical doctrine of indiscriminate salvation and damnation.

The Christian-Gnostics, Mani and Origen, of course, did not accept the concept of an eternal hell, as we have seen. That hell or chaos existed in ancient Christian doctrine is well attested. In Christian-Gnosticism, Origenism and in Manichaeism, hell is eventually dissolved along with its inhabitants. Some rebellious spirits are subject to reincarnation, while others experience what is termed in the first century Book of Revelation the "second death," a final judgment or dissolution of the soul, not its eternal burning (along with its body) in hell. The "Lake of Fire" of Rev. 20:10, 14-15 is described as a place of purification and transmutation. The Devil and his angels, the Beast and the False Prophet, etc., and *Death and Hell itself are cast into the Lake of Fire*. How then, we may ask, could hell be eternal if it is dissolved in the Lake of Fire? Augustine—and others before and after him—mistook the perpetual burning of the Lake of Fire for the perpetual burning of hell and the devil in hell. All are mercifully dissolved, at the close of certain

Cosmic Cycles.

The ancient Judaic and early Christian conception of the final judgment was, originally, reserved for the fallen angels and the Watchers, and not for the children of God. The Watchers were either doomed to reincarnate until the end of the age or they were held in chains under the earth, presumably in one of the levels of hell, awaiting judgment. The fiery judgments pronounced by Enoch the Prophet, John the Baptist and Jesus upon the "wicked," the "godless" and the "vipers" referred exclusively to the fallen race of reprobate angels on earth. The evil archons of the various Christian-Gnostic sects and in Manichaeism were doomed to dissolution in the "Lake of Fire", their identities dissolved and their energy repolarized. They do not burn forever in hell. In Mani's system, as we have seen, the mass of Darkness, finally separated from the Light (the bolos), is rendered inactive and removed forever. Nowhere in ancient Christianity of the first three centuries do we find a concept of an eternal hell—except, of course, in the minds of the orthodox of the school of Irenaeus and Augustine.

True to his pattern, Augustine distorted and then reversed the doctrine of the final judgment away from the fallen angels and onto the children of God—the ordinary Christian believer (and the mass of non-Christians) who was supposed to have inherited "original sin." For this and this alone was he damned. Augustine blames the entire fall on Adam, not on Lucifer, Satan, the Prince of Darkness, the Watchers, archons and Nephilim who had corrupted the earth and mankind, as the earliest Christians taught. We observe that there is little or no mention of the fallen angels by Augustine or of the "Dragon" who appeared in heaven in Revelation 12, as the cause of the fall, as taught in ancient Christian doctrine. And what of the chief Archon, in the Apocryphon of John, who seduced Eve and taught Adam lustful sexual intercourse? No mention is made of this by Augustine (the book, naturally, had long since been suppressed). In the teaching of Mani, the body of Adam is produced through the intercourse of two archons or demons who are solely responsible for injecting concupiscence into humanity. Concupiscence did not originate through the fault of Adam, much less through the fault of his innocent posterity, as Augustine would have us believe. Concupiscence, lust, pride, rebellion, the capturing of the light in physical bodies—all of this was accomplished through the machinations of the powers of evil. Yet Augustine denounces a guiltless mankind to perdition for simply being the passive receivers of Adam's alleged lust, or so he believes. We should seriously question Augustine's propensity to shift the blame for the fallen angels' original rebellion against God onto humanity.

Augustine's Doctrine of the Soul

Augustine, of course, was accused by his fellow bishops, including Pelagius, with whom he engaged in controversy, of teaching Manichaeism. This was due to the fact that the Manichaeans, as we have said, believed that lustful sexual intercourse originated with the archons and was not native to the realm of Light, nor was lust native to the pure souls created by the Father, who later embodied on earth. Augustine's view on sexuality seems to be a twisted interpretation of Manichaeism. Mani, unlike Augustine, taught that the soul has the capacity to overcome lust or passion because it originated from the Light-Realm and its original nature was of the Light. We refer the reader to those excerpts quoted earlier from the Manichaean scriptures. The Manichaean Christian believed that his sole purpose on earth was to distill the Light from the darkness. His life is imbued with a sense of mission. He possesses the Light-Mind; he knows he is saved by Jesus, and he does not look forward to or fear eternal damnation. Moreover, in Manichaeism, the soul preexists not only the body but the physical cosmos itself. The soul, as the element of light, is indeed shackled by the body; but the body is meant for dissolution, and the soul looks forward to its absorption into God. Not so with Augustinian Christianity: there is no preexistence, and what's more, the soul is not intrinsically divine.

Augustine writes:

The soul is not a part of God. For if it were, it would be absolutely immutable and incorruptible, in which case it would neither go downward to be worse, nor go onward to be better....That which is liable to be changed in any manner, by any cause, or in any part whatever, is therefore not by nature immutable; but it were impiety to think of God as otherwise than truly and supremely immutable: Therefore the soul is not a part of God. <31>

Compare this to Manichaean Scripture, quoted in Chapter 11:

Now the Soul in men is part of the Light....You shall see the Great of Glories [the Father] from whom every Soul has come forth in the beginning, and they shall also return to the Light and ascend to it in the end....

In Augustine's convoluted logic, because the soul is subject to change through free-will choice, it cannot be a part of God. We ask, cannot the essence of the soul be composed of the "stuff" of God, i.e., of Light, and still possess free will and be subject to change? In the Manichaean universe, all is composed of Light elements, albeit mingled with Darkness. In Origen's doctrine, the soul has the capacity to be like God, therefore, it must be of God. And yet Origen teaches that the soul can change and move away from or toward God; nevertheless, this movement does not change the soul's essential nature. Again Augustine's doctrine irrevocably severs the tie between man and God—the one hope man has—by categorically denying man's intrinsic relationship with God. We cannot do otherwise than to draw the conclusion that the concept of God dwelling in man is alien to Augustine—yet this is the very root of Christian mysticism.

Augustine is furious with the Manichaeans for daring to teach the audacious doctrine that the soul is of the same substance as God—a doctrine absolutely fundamental to ancient Christianity:

> But they [the Manichaeans] desiring to be light, not "in the Lord," but in themselves, conceiving the nature of the soul to be the same as that which God is, are made more gross darkness; for that through a shocking arrogancy they went farther from Thee.... (Brackets added) <32>

It is well known that Augustine taught the doctrine of creationism, which holds that a new soul is created by God at the moment of conception and has never before existed. We hope it has been shown that this doctrine was fabricated out of whole cloth and was no part of ancient Christianity nor was it believed in the ancient world before Christ. In Augustine's doctrine, the new soul, once created, is immediately tainted with original sin by virtue of its simultaneous infusion in a body produced in lust. Augustine asserts that the new soul is simply a multiplication of the man God created on the sixth day—God multiplies what already existed. Yet the soul he refers to is not a soul in an individualized sense prior to the creation of the body, an autonomous being in God, having free will. Augustine is horrified that some believed that souls are responsible for their own sins by their own past choices in previous existences. He prefers, rather, to blame it all on Adam and, completing the shift of responsibility, indirectly, on God.

> But that souls sin in another life, and that for their sins in that state of being they are cast down into bodies as prisons, I do not believe. I reject and protest against such an opinion. <33>

Writing of the reembodiment of the soul, Augustine avers: "I do not know that anything more horrible could be conceived." Augustine apparently misunderstands the ancient doctrine that reincarnation is the very means, allowed for by God, by which the soul might expiate its past sins. The doctrine teaches that man by his unwise sowings in the past was the cause of reincarnation—not God. Had the pre-existent soul by free will not moved away from God, it would not have had to undergo reincarnation, unless, of course, as Mani taught, the soul had descended into "darkness" by free will on a mission of redemption for the judgment of the archons.

To rescue man from his deplorable state, Augustine invented the doctrine of grace. This grace could not be accessed by any other means except through Augustine's church. Augustine believed that man is basically evil; Origen believed that man is basically good, and taught that the general trend for rational creatures is to ascend to God. Joseph Trigg writes:

The classical formulation of that doctrine [of grace] did not occur until the early fifth century when Augustine of Hippo dealt with it. Only then did the church as a whole reject the notion that human beings had a natural capacity to do God's will. <34>

Free Will versus Human Bondage—The Donatist and Pelagian Controversies

When a British monk, Pelagius, read *The Confessions*, he criticized Augustine for "popularizing a kind of pious self-indulgence," as Pagels phrases it. <35> He also objected to Augustine's outright denial of free will and concluded that, in effect, Augustine had betrayed the ancient tradition of the church. Many Christians likewise found Augustine's doctrine "pernicious" and that Augustine's theory of original sin, as Pagels reports, "repudiated the twin foundations of the Christian faith: the goodness of God's creation; and the freedom of the human will." <36>

Shortly after the year 400, Pelagius arrived in Rome and began to disseminate his views upholding man's free will. <37> By the fifth century, we must remember, Christian Gnosis, "Origenism" and Manichaean Christianity had long been considered serious heresies; as a consequence, we do not find Pelagius supporting the idea of preexistence, the law of cause and effect or reincarnation. Nevertheless, he and his followers did uphold the doctrines of free will and the basic goodness of man—key doctrines of Origen and several orthodox Church Fathers before him, such as Justin and Clement of Alexandria.

Ironically, Pelagius had been a supporter of Augustine when, as a young man, the latter had written his treatise *On Free Will* praising human freedom. But during the ensuing years, Augustine had hardened as a result of his ongoing controversies with the Manichaeans and the schismatic Donatists. The Donatists believed that the efficacy of baptism and all sacraments depend on the purity of the priest administering them. Augustine, as a supporter of the institutionalized Roman Church:

> *...persuaded the western Emperor Honorius to issue the most drastic rescripts against his opponents [the Donatists], calling for the seizure of all their churches, the confiscation of their private property, and the exile or death of their leaders....* <38>

Martin Larson explains that, during the Donatist controversy, Augustine formulated his "administrative and political theories" of the Catholic Church.<39> He lists them as follows:

1) The Unity and Universality of the Church (religious truth could not reside in any man who has broken with the Catholic Church; heretics and schismatics have no right to own property).

2) The chaff must not be separated from the wheat (murderers, antichrists, infidels, the sacrilegious and servants of the devil must be admitted into the Church as long as they profess to know God, accept the creed and submit to the Church hierarchy).

3) Baptism and the Sacraments of the Church (these are valid whether or not the ministrant is a sinner, heretic or infidel).

4) Church coercion and persecution (it is necessary for the Church to utilize these tactics to compel conformity and obedience to the Church).

5) The function of the secular arm (the state should implement the decision of the ecceliastical authority in the Church). <40>

The Donatists sought to purify the church and to preserve it as a "communion of saints." As St. Paul advocated the expulsion of murderers, idolaters, fornicators, etc. from his churches, so did the Donatists. The Donatist concept of the church, however, would have made it impossible for the church to become a worldwide institution backed and supported by the state as it had been since Constantine. The church would then have had to relinquish its power and its totalitarian tactics. This could never be. Augustine, therefore, determined to win the controversy over the Donatists to preserve the authority of the church, and naturally, his own position as bishop. His underlying motive had always been to preserve unity and mass conformity within the church. When, in 411, the Council of Carthage failed to establish peace and unity between the Donatists and the Catholics, Augustine, who engineered the council, then persuaded the Emperor to issue rescripts against the Donatists. At this point, the controversy for all practical purposes was at an end.

In the midst of Augustine's battle for absolute authority in the church, Pelagius popularized and promulgated the following theses, as here listed by Martin Larson, to counteract Augustine's theory of original sin:

1) Each individual soul is a new creation endowed with pristine purity; we derive only our bodies from Adam.

2) Infants who die are without sin and will therefore attain paradise without baptism.

3) Human nature as the creation of God is basically good.

4) The will of man possesses an inalienable freedom which cannot by destroyed even by force of habit.

5) The grace of Christ is universal.

6) Jesus was a teacher and exemplar not a sacrifice or an atonement for sin.

7) Man can attain perfection through the practice of the Gospel ethics as well as through faith.

8) Salvation is within the power of the human will and can be attained by practical works. <41>

Pelagius also denied that God had predestined each person to either heaven or hell. The grace of God is an aid to righteousness and not the sole source of righteousness. <42> Pelagius taught that sexual activity within marriage is not, in and of itself, sinful or lustful; celibacy and virginity are not preferable to marriage, nor is an individual holier or purer if he espouses the married state. Both states, he taught, are blessed by God. Pelagius and his first convert, a Roman advocate named Coelestius, made the unfortunate mistake of travelling to Africa where Augustine was firmly ensconced as bishop. As fate would have it, the two aroused "the implacable enmity of Augustine." <43> Pelagius departed to Palestine, but Coelestius made another mistake in applying for ordination as a presbyter at Carthage. <44> He was accused by a deacon (possibly a front for Augustine) of seven heresies, among them, that Adam's sin injured only himself; that newborn infants are in the same condition as Adam was at creation; and that unbaptized infants have eternal salvation. <45>

Augustine himself then charged Coelestius with further heresies along the same lines, such as the idea that God's grace is bestowed according to merits, and that the "soul has the power of being sinless" since men are "partakers of the divine nature." <46> Coelestius neither recanted nor denied the charges, so he was excommunicated and driven from Africa.

Meanwhile, back in Palestine, Pelagius was living a quiet life, or so he thought, when a young man arrived, as Larson tells the story, with a message from Augustine to Jerome regarding the alleged heresy of Pelagius and Coelestius. <47> Pelagius was called before a local synod of fourteen bishops, who found him innocent when Pelagius "evaded the charges and minimized his heresies." <48>

Pelagius then published a document called *In Defense of Free Will,* which, naturally, reached Augustine, who, true to form, reacted with a vengeance. Larson states that Pelagius and his doctrine were condemned by two synods of African bishops at Carthage in 416. Pelagius and Coelestius appealed to Pope Zosimus who "went over to their side on condition that they might abide by any decision he might render." <49> The Pope then wrote letters to the African bishops with orders that they appear at Rome to either drop or substantiate their charges. At the same time he wrote an encyclical, decreeing that the doctrines of Pelagius and Coelestius were orthodox. This, of course, infuriated Augustine, who was not to be outdone or contradicted by even the bishop of Rome. Augustine acted quickly. He assembled 200 bishops at Carthage and a second time anathematized Pelagius. Pope Zosimus, intimidated by Augustine and the council, pompously declared, writes Larson, that he would further investigate the charges to prepare for his final judgment. But Augustine, determined to outmaneuver the Roman Pontiff, prevailed upon the Emperor Honorius to issue a "rescript from Ravenna," ordering Pelagius, Coelestius and their followers banished from Rome. <50> As Larson adds, "From this there was no appeal"; thus Pelagius became an outlaw without a hearing.

The weak and vacillating Zosimus then made a quick reversal, no doubt to save face. He excommunicated Pelagius and Coelestius and issued a rigid "Test Act" upholding the African anathemas which all bishops were coerced into signing on pain of excommunication. Larson tells us that eighteen Italian bishops refused to subscribe, including Julian of Eclanum, who thereafter became the spokesman for the Pelagians. Larson summarizes the events as follows: The Test Act was imposed on Africa in 419; exiled bishops were driven from Constantinople in 424; these formed a coalition with the heretical Nestorians in 429, and both were condemned at the Council of Ephesus in 431. <51>

Soon after his exile, Pelagius died. His follower, Julian of Eclanum, challenged Augustine; the debate between Julian and Augustine continued throughout the last twelve years of Augustine's life. It was during this period that Augustine, driven to the wall by Julian, developed his rigid doctrine denying man's free will, which we have previously examined, as well as his doctrines of original sin, infant damnation, pre-destination and prevenient grace. In the last year of his life, Augustine attacked one Vitalis, who actually had been brought to trial for saying that "the capacity for faith is universally innate."<52> As a consequence of his last and latest vendetta, Augustine developed his final doctrine of prevenient grace, which Larson explains:

There are two kinds of sinners who hear the voice of the preacher: those who are moved to believe, and those who are not so moved. In the former, the Father speaks from within, and incites them with a prevenient grace; those whom the Father does not so actuate, remain cold, and never respond to the call since they are not of the Elect.

That this congenital impulse is also irresistible is developed in detail. Each saint chosen from the foundation, and no one else, possesses this grace, "which is the effect of that predestination." <53>

In a final treatise, Augustine wrote that no one—saint or sinner turned saint—can be sure of possessing final perseverance so long as he is alive on this earth. God's grace may be withdrawn at any moment. In one instant a saint may find himself damned to perdition; and a sinner may find himself saved.

In the course of the Pelagian controversy, Augustine developed his doctrines on sex and marriage. He declared that all sexual intercourse in marriage, unless it is for the purpose of begetting children, makes of the wife a harlot and of the husband an adulterer. <54> The sacramental bond of matrimony can never be abrogated even by adultery, impotence, childlessness, separation, etc. <55> This had remained the doctrine of the Roman Church for centuries.

In 539, the Council of Orange made the doctrines of Augustine (except the doctrine of prevenient grace) a dogma of the Roman Catholic Church, binding on all Catholics. Thus Augustinianism won the day and remained the epitome of the Roman Catholic faith throughout the ensuing centuries. Larson concludes:

The Pelagian heresy was a brave, though futile, struggle for freedom. We believe that had either this or Arianism prevailed, there would have been no Dark Ages, for then there would have been no priest-state, no renunciation, no destruction of learning and philosophy, no persecution for differing convictions concerning speculative doctrines. <56>

The Legacy of Augustine

When the church hierarchy ratified and pronounced as dogma Augustine's doctrines and theories, especially that of original sin, they set the course of western civilization for centuries. It is a truism that man can rise no higher than his religious principles. It is also true that man defines his self-image in and through his concept of God and his relationship to God. Augustine's theology, now official church dogma in the sixth century, had an incalculable effect on the psyche of man. Man, according to this dogma, was born tainted with original sin through no fault of his own; this doctrine translates to the psyche immediately as a sense of worthlessness and sinfulness. The logical deduction to be made from this doctrine is that God is unjust and is, in point of fact, a tyrant. The male semen is tainted with sin and lust; woman becomes an object of scorn and hatred as she represents temptation, par excellence, and is to be avoided at all costs. Thus, thousands of Christian men took to the monasteries to avoid the so-called temptations of the flesh and the alleged sinfulness of their own bodies. The straight and narrow path to heaven was through celibacy and virginity. The figure of woman was debased in the church, as it was believed that she represented Eve, who caused Adam to sin through sexual lust. Sexual desire was either inordinately suppressed or unleashed, both producing serious psychological repercussions. Thus from the fifth century to the Renaissance and beyond, men and women defined their self-images through these doctrines—doctrines that were alien to original Christianity.

Augustine's theology finally replaced the theology of Origen to the utter detriment of the race. Augustine's victory can certainly be attributed in part to his tenacity, his sheer will power and his ability to maneuver and manipulate emperors and popes alike in order to achieve his ends. We would tend to conclude that Augustine was so successful in promoting his doctrine primarily because he had the backing of the State. Logically, if men are inherently sinful and have not the innate ability to make a moral choice for the good, they need external government and must be controlled from without—just as the Brahmins argued with Issa. Elaine Pagels contends that Augustine's theory of original sin "proved politically expedient," as it supported the necessity for a "Christian state and an imperially supported church." <57> Thus the totalitarian rule of Church and State working hand in hand is the primary legacy of Augustine and the foundation of the Church of the Middle Ages—a dictatorship over the faithful, who, now stripped of their self-worth, were powerless to challenge the hierarchy in both Church and State. They had naught to do but capitulate or else be threatened by eternal hell.

Martin Larson comments further on the legacy of Augustine with regard to his doctrine of original sin:

It is impossible to overestimate the practical effect of the doctrine of original sin. No speculative opinion has ever made one portion of humanity so cold, so cruel, so merciless in its treatment of the rest. Once the Church attained unchallenged power, it was only necessary to say of any person who did not conform that he was possessed by Satan and acted in accordance with his congenital, Adamic nature. The property of this "criminal" could then be confiscated, and he could be tortured, imprisoned, exiled, burned, or whatever else the ecclesiastical judges might determine; and the sentence when executed by the "secular arm," was received with complete public approbation....And, since no one could escape the damnation consequent upon original sin outside the Catholic communion, this made moral lepers of all others, who must always be feared and hated and with whom there must never be the slightest communication. The segregation of Catholics from non-catholics must be absolute. <58>

Of men, the Christ said, "By their fruits, ye shall know them." And the same is true of dogmas. The ugly fruits of Augustinian orthodoxy ultimately blossomed for all history to see. The quality of truth in the tree which bore them should also be apparent.

Manly P. Hall, writing about Augustine as the "apostle of infallibles," states:

In the case of Augustine it is impossible to understand his philosophy without understanding the man. To the modern psychologist he is a case in point for nearly all complexes, fixations, neuroses, inhibitions and introversions. He carried in his consciousness such a burden of unfinished business that *there appears to be no period in his life in which he was not recovering from one fallacy or falling into another. <59>*

Unfortunately, Augustine's "fallacy" of original sin, although untrue, was believed in by countless millions down through the centuries and infected the psychology of Western and Eastern Christendom alike. Yet this is the man whom orthodox Christians regard as the greatest theologian in the church. One can only attribute this adulation of Augustine to his success in promoting the orthodox church as an all-powerful institution at any and all costs.

Hall quotes Rev. Frederic Farrar on Augustine as follows:

In the course of year-long discussions be became a dogmatist, and his final victory was sometimes won at the cost of love and tolerance. His personality becomes less attractive as his episcopacy becomes more triumphant, until at last the man who sighed so ardently for Christian charity, and was so much opposed to sacerdotal tyranny, uses expressions and arguments which become the boasted watchwords of the most ruthless inquisitors, and are quoted to sanction deeds so un-Christian and so infamous as the brutalities of Alva and the massacre of St. Bartholomew. <60>

In the St. Bartholomew's Day massacre, over 70,000 "protestant" men, women and children in Paris and the towns of France were systematically dragged from their homes and slaughtered over a period of two months alone. In Rome, the church bells were rung in celebration and thanksgiving, and a medal was struck in commemoration of the event. Hall continues:

Augustine attacked the Tertullianists, Priscillianists, the Abelonians, Marchonites, Origenists, and Arians. With all of these he differed, and his differences created wounds that the centuries have not been able to heal. In these arguments *and debates, Christian charity was sacrificed to dogma, with the result that a very curious attitude developed in the Augustinian faction. Charity gained a new definition. It became synonymous with the complete destruction of the opposition. It became an act of divine kindness to destroy your adversary if you could not convert him. <61>*

All of this amounts to saying that, through his ideas and concepts on God, man and the church, Augustine influenced and indirectly promoted that most heinous of institutions, the Inquisition—the terror of Christendom for centuries. Augustine won the day, not through the sublime logic of his theology, but through force, coercion and manipulation. Augustine's Christianity made him the fulcrum of a movement marked by suppression, intolerance and control—a movement whose activities in the realm of theology we have been tracing through this book. These forces culminated and triumphed in Augustine, and through Augustine, Christian Gnosis was eradicated from the orthodox church for centuries, only to come to light at the close of the Middle Ages, as we shall see. The legacy of Augustine to Christendom was, therefore, twofold:

1) The debasement of man (from a creation in God's image bearing a divine spark and preexisting the body to a creature tainted with original sin and doomed to perdition).

2) A totalitarian form of Christianity supported by the State.

We continue to the conclusion of our survey.

Chapter XIV

The Legacy of the Orthodox Conspiracy

The Triumph of Institutionalized Christianity

In 383 Gregory Nazianzen, one of the Church Fathers, formulated the "Theory of Suppression," as Martin Larson phrases it, by use of secular force against all those who disagreed with the orthodox creed. Writing against Apollinaris, another "heretic," he states:

Any permission of assembly granted to them is nothing less than a declaration that their view is more true than ours. For if they are permitted to teach...it is manifest that the doctrine of the church has been condemned. <1>

On such convoluted logic, the Church Fathers promoted persecution, hatred and bigotry all in the name of Christ, his "church" and his so-called creed, which, as we have shown, had itself become blasphemous.

Pope Leo the Great, writing in 450, proclaimed that the Roman Empire was established by God's providence so that:

*· The preaching of the word might quickly reach all people...the most blessed Peter, chief of the Apostolic band, was appointed to the citadel of the Roman Empire.... **Here the tenets of philosophy must be crushed**, here the follies of earthly wisdom must be dispelled, here the cult of demons must be refuted, here the blasphemy of all idolatries must be rooted out. (Emphasis added)* <2>

Peter then, according to his alleged successor Leo, sat as the head of the Roman Empire just so freedom of religion could be crushed. This was the legacy of orthodox Christianity and its leadership—legacy which lasted for over a thousand years more—a legacy of intolerance and persecution unequalled in the history of the ancient world.

Larson adds:

In short, it was the peculiar mission of the Petrine succession to assume the throne of the Caesars and use its power to extirpate all philosophy, all learning, all secular science, and all competing religions...from the face of the earth. Leo regarded the heretic in exactly the same light as we would the poisoner of our water supply. <3>

Leo continues:

There is no doubt that our enemy, Satan...is aroused...that under a false profession of the Christian name he may corrupt those whom he is no longer allowed to attack with open and bloody persecution, and for this work he has heretics in his service whom he has led astray from the Catholic Faith. <4>

Heretics, of course, are all those who disagree with Leo—the "lineal descendant" of the throne of Diocletian from whom issued the first major Christian persecution. History repeats itself—Caesars become Popes and Popes become Caesars. Whatever the enemy Satan is supposed to have represented in the mind of Leo, we can think of no more worthy successor to Satan than Leo himself, the archenemy of Christian tolerance and compassion, the suppressor of the mind of man, the exterminator of free will. This, we believe, is typical of anti-Christ.

Pope Leo the Great represents the epitome of totalitarian Christianity in the fifth century, the destroyer of ancient

Christianity and the gospel ethic—the love of one's fellow man. Leo and Augustine were two pillars of intolerance in the fifth century—one working in the realm of politics and power, the other in the realm of theology. Leo believed that the so-called Christian empire inherited the power of the Roman Empire. The Christian Empire, however, with Leo at its head, was thought to be a reflection of the supernatural world which offered men salvation through Leo's earthly Church. When Leo addressed the Roman people three years after he convinced Attila not to invade Rome, he designated the Roman Christians as "a priestly and royal nation" because "thanks to the Presence of the Holy See of Blessed Peter, you have become lords of the world and by holy religion you are able to extend your dominion further than by earthly might." <5> Leo is using religion to extend his power and influence, the earmark of totalitarian Christianity, and he is the first to so exert his authority. Leo indeed brought the papacy to new heights of power and dignity. Durant records that when Hilary, Bishop of Potiers, refused to accept Leo's decision in a dispute with another Gallic bishop, Leo sent him "peremptory orders." These orders were seconded by Emperor Valentinian III with an edict that Will Durant calls "epoch making." The Emperor confirmed the authority of the Roman bishop over all Christian churches for the first time in history. <6>

In his famous Tome in 449 A.D. Leo set forth the basic beliefs of orthodox Christianity in order to assert his authority over the Eastern bishops and specifically over the Patriarch of Constantinople. Although the Patriarch wrote back to Leo that he accepted the tenets of Leo's Tome, he was accepting what the Eastern bishops had always taught. <7> Leo did not lose a step in his bid for power over the Patriarch, however. When the famous Council of Calcedon (451) reaffirmed the Patriarch of Constantinople as second in honor to the pope of Rome, Leo replied, writes Malachi Martin, that "the bishop of Rome was not merely first in honor but first in authority and orthodoxy. Every bishop and patriarch was second to the bishop of Rome, said Leo." <8> The fifth century was one of rivalry for power between Eastern and Western bishops, the Patriarch of Constantinople and the Pope of Rome and the Christologies of rival theologians. But Leo went one step further, as Martin writes:

> *But more than that, he has declared the authority of the Roman bishop over all temporal rulers as well. And that is staking out a huge new claim. Leo has asserted that Christian faith and practice mean not merely a hope of immortality, but order and wisdom in this life.*
> *Eventually Leo's claim will become so central to papal policy, that to most mortal eyes the temporal concern will almost eclipse the spiritual. <9>*

The result is the "legacy of Leo" succinctly stated by Malachi Martin: "a Christian church indistinguishable from the Roman Empire, or a Christian church that was, for good or for evil, the Roman Empire." <10>

Martin explains that the church and its pope took over the idea of a landed political empire from old Rome, that is, the imperial idea or imperium. <11> The attributes of classical Rome had now become the attributes of Roman Christianity. <12> Leo I assumed the old Roman title Pontifex Maximus and thus became the effective ruler over Rome and other numerous territories. <13>

Martin describes the totalitarian Christian state as follows:

> *Within three centuries, the Roman church had transformed the administrative organization of the Roman Empire into an ecclesiastical system of bishoprics, dioceses, monasteries, colonies, garrisons, schools, libraries, administrative centers, envoys, representatives, courts of justice and a criminal system of intricate laws all under the direct control of the pope. His Roman palace, the Lateran, became the new Senate. The new senators were the cardinals. The bishop who lived in Rome and the priests and deacons helped the pope*

administer this new imperium. This bureaucracy elected the head of the imperium, and they carried on the tradition from pope to pope. <14>

We are a long way from the Jesus of the gospels, the spiritual adept of the first century who proclaimed, "What doth it profit a man if he gain the whole world, yet suffer the loss of his soul?" We are a long way from the original Christian sects who offered a path of transcendence over the material world. And we are a long way from the apostle John, who wrote:

You must not love this passing world or anything that is in the world. The love of the Father cannot be in any man who loves the world, because nothing the world has to offer—the sensual body, the lustful eye, pride in possessions—could ever come from the Father but only from the world...but anyone who does the will of God remains forever. (1 John 2:15-17, Jerusalem Bible)

And of his disciples Jesus said, "They do not belong to the world any more than I belong to the world." (John 17:16, Jerusalem Bible) The church of the fifth century, if it can be called a church, had moved from a series of initiatic schools, sects and assemblies in the first century to a worldwide political machine in the fifth century. We have seen the beginnings of this transformation, with the establishment of the so-called monarchial episcopate, in the writings of Clement of Rome and Ignatius of Antioch, through whose vaulting ambition, the power of the bishops made tremendous headway. The Christian church of Leo in the fourth century and of Gregory the Great in the sixth century had become inseparable from what has been termed the "Cain civilization"—a civilization of materialism headed by prelates equal in ambition to the builders of the legendary tower of Babel who desired to usurp the position of God himself.

Malachi Martin further elaborates on this "Holy Roman Empire" as follows:

Every pope called the Roman state the "patrimony of Peter," and the "Holy Roman Empire." Before the end of the 700's, the Roman ecclesiastical state was considerable: cities and towns conceded by emperors to the pope; church estates and colonies annexed or bought by popes; other portions of territories and cities donated by local princes to the pope. Faithfully, all these were said to be added to what was called the "Roman army" or the "Holy Roman republic." Around the pope in Rome there grew an entire bureaucracy of clerics, bishops, priests, deacons, laymen, to administer papal towns, papal armies, papal fleets, papal treasuries, papal caravans, papal tax collectors, papal justices of the peace, papal police, papal envoys and missions, applying papal laws—civil and ecclesiastical.... <15>

By the end of the eighth century, the pope was, in fact and practice, a temporal ruler of gigantic proportions. The papal states had been established. As time went on, in addition to the papal states which were ruled directly by the popes as their own possessions, the Roman pope gained feudal power over other states: they were obligated to pay yearly tribute and to contribute to the defensive and offensive policies of the popes. The Roman pontiffs also required political control in still other lands: the rulers were appointed with papal approval, and they were bound by offensive-defensive alliances with the papacy. <16>

Hand in hand with the transformation of the church into the Roman Imperial bureaucracy there emerged what Malachi Martin calls "The New Anthropology" and a new "geography of the spirit." <17> Essentially this "anthropology" elaborated on man's relationship to God, Church and Pope, heaven and hell. All was fixed, dogmatic and predetermined. There was no room to pursue one's personal path to God. The theology developed after the Nicean Council through and beyond the reign of Pope Gregory the Great (d. 604) applied in many respects to the lowest common denominator in the Christian faithful. The theology espoused by Pope Gregory was far removed from the Christian theology of the second and third centuries as evolved by the Christian-Gnostics and by Origen. Will Durant elaborates on the theology of Gregory the Great— a theology of hellfire and damnation:

> *The tragedy of man is that by original sin, his nature is corrupt and inclines him to wickedness; and this basic spiritual malformation is transmitted from parent to child through sexual procreation. Left to himself, man would heap sin upon sin, and richly deserve everlasting damnation. Hell is no mere phase; it is a dark and bottomless subterranean abyss, created from the beginning of the world; it is an inextinguishable fire, corporeal and yet able to sear souls as well as flesh; it is eternal, and yet it never destroys the damned, or lessens their sensitivity to pain. And to each moment of pain is added the terror of expected pain, the horror of witnessing the tortures of loved ones also damned, the despair of ever being released, or allowed the blessing of annihilation. <18>*

Needless to say, Pope Gregory I was a follower of Augustine. He accepted Augustine's theology and elaborated on it still further, especially with regard to the delicious subject of the eternality of hell. The average Christian believer was no doubt terrified by the prospect of eternal damnation, as this one weapon alone was instrumental in coercing submission from the populace. We would suggest that the doctrines of Augustine, reaffirmed by Gregory, were born within the minds of Lucifer, Satan, Ildabaoth, the Nephilim, and the Watchers who, throughout their incarnations on earth, bore a revengeful rage against the children of God on earth (since they could no longer wreak vengeance against God and the spiritual Hierarchy for having cast them out of the heaven-world). The once lofty and mystical teaching of Jesus was slowly degraded into a series of pious superstitions, all to keep the populace in ignorance, and more importantly, to keep them under control. The teachings we have previously examined regarding the soul's preexistence, the divine spark within man—sign of man's intrinsic divinity—the nature of evil, man as a spiritual being before his descent to earth, man as co-redeemer of the cosmos and joint heir with Christ, were ignored or suppressed. In place of these teachings there developed a dogmatic, simplistic "anthropology" of God in Heaven and the Devil in Hell under the earth; the disobedience of Adam and Eve; man as a creature of body and soul (as opposed to the original doctrine of body, soul and Spirit or Divine Nature) and the inheritor of original sin; the death of Christ as an atoning sacrifice to an otherwise unappeasable Father; eternal life in either heaven or hell, and the last judgment. To Gregory the Great belongs the honor of officially proclaiming the dogma of purgatory (604) as a place for purification for those not good enough for heaven or evil enough for hell. <19> This idea of purgatory, it can be suggested, was likely cleverly used by the Church Fathers from the third century on as a replacement for the universal doctrine of reincarnation. Man, now essentially degraded, had no recourse but to turn to the church for salvation and the sacraments it dispensed. To be cut off from the church meant certain damnation.

From the fourth to the eighth centuries, this totalitarian theology was developed by the first "media men" in history, as Malachi Martin calls them—the Fathers of the Church, who codified, explained, elaborated and defined the "New Anthropology." <20> "No matter," writes Martin, "that to us their language seems abstruse, their thinking convoluted, their tomes inaccessible to all but a few. They worked in a society of severely restricted literacy." <21>

What had emerged in the Dark Ages in Europe, now under the control of the church, was a one-world order designed to restrict individual thinking and enterprise, scientific pursuit; and more significantly, it was designed to submerge forever the "Lost Christianity" of the original Christian sects, the esoteric teaching of Jesus. The Pope, thought to be the vicar of Christ, was the final word on matters of religion and theology.

The argument has been made that the scriptural prophecies of Daniel 7 and Revelation 13 are corollary statements, both applying to the Roman church, the "fourth kingdom, different from all other kingdoms." <22> When viewing the origin and history of this "Church," this hypothesis is worth considering:

> *Then I wished to know the truth about the fourth beast, which was different from all the others, exceedingly dreadful, with its teeth of iron and its nails of bronze, which devoured, broke in pieces, and trampled the residue with its feet;*
>
> *And about the ten horns that were on its head, about the other horn which came up, before which the three fell, namely, that horn which had eyes and a mouth which spoke pompous words, whose appearance was greater than its fellows.*
>
> *I was watching; and the same horn was making war against the saints, and prevailing against them, until the Ancient of Days came and a judgment was made in favor of the saints of the Most High, and the time came for the saints to possess the kingdom.*
>
> *Thus he [Gabriel] said: 'The fourth beast shall be a fourth kingdom on earth, which shall be different from all other kingdoms, and shall devour the whole earth, trample it and break it in pieces.*
>
> *'The ten horns are ten kings who shall arise from this kingdom. And another shall rise after them; he shall be different from the first ones; and shall subdue three kings.*
>
> *'He shall speak pompous words against the Most High, shall persecute the saints of the Most High, and shall intend to change times and laws. Then the saints shall be given into his hand for a time and times and half a time.' (Daniel 7: 15- 25)*
>
> *Then I stood on the sand of the sea. And I saw a beast rising up out of the sea, having seven heads and ten horns, and on his horns ten crowns....*
>
> *...And he [the beast] was given a mouth speaking great things and blasphemies, and he was given authority to continue*

for forty and two months.

Then he opened his mouth in blasphemy against God, to blaspheme His name, His tabernacle, and those who dwell in heaven.

And it was granted to him to make war with the saints and overcome them. And authority was given him over every tribe, tongue, and nation. (Revelation 13: 1, 5-8)

The interpretation is as follows: from three great empires, Babylon, Medo-Persia and Greece, rose a fourth, Rome. The ten kingdoms arising from it constitute the nations later to conquer by (roughly) the fall of Rome in 476—the Vandals, Visigoths, Franks, etc. The little horn (power) rising in turn having the "eyes of a man" and "different from the first"—the Roman Church, being not only a political, but a religio-political power, with its leader, in posture and appearance "greater than its fellows," speaking "pompous words" and persecuting the saints—denying freedom of religion and perpetrating torture and death upon them; changing times—arbitrarily overthrowing the sabbath to establish the Roman Sun-day as the day of worship; changing laws—among these the denial of the law of karma. And the duration given this power to hold power: The biblical key is that a "day" is equivalent to a year—"I have appointed thee each day for a year." (Ezekiel, 4:6) In Revelation 11:2, the Holy City—the true church of Christ—is tread underfoot also for forty and two months as in Rev. 13 above. This is (42 x 30 days) = 1260 "days," i.e., 1260 years. A similar duration is given by the "time, times and half of a time" of Daniel. A "time" is a (biblical) year or 360 days. A "time, times (2) and half a time" is 360+(360+360)+180, and totals 1260 days, i.e., 1260 years. Thus the duration of this "fourth kingdom," as forty and two months or "a time, times and half a time," is 1260 years. It is possible to accept a date of 538 A.D. when the Papacy can be said to begin officially with a decree of the Emperor Justinian taking effect which finally and definitively assigned complete preeminence to the bishop of Rome. Its power was broken definitively, never to be the same, in 1798 when Napoleon's armies under General Berthier entered Rome, made the pope a prisoner (who later died in exile) and decreed no pope should ever again reign—a period of 1260 years.

It is clear that the "beast" is a vast conglomerate of evil forces, of which the Church and Papacy are but one aspect—simply one "horn" as symbolized. If this work has shown anything, it would be that it is not simply the Papacy, but that which the Papacy symbolizes, i.e., the entire orthodox state of consciousness, that forms a "beast" causative of the effects this prophecy would seem to envisage. The interpretation described above has also concentrated thus far on the "Protestants" as those persecuted by this beast. <23> Yet it is clear that despite the degree of persecution, mainline Protestantism was yet but a minor recipient of this intense persecution of the saints. In reality it was those whom the normal Protestant would scarcely consider a member of this holy company—the heretics, the Christian-Gnostics, the Manichaen-Christians, the Cathars and Albigenses (as we shall discuss), the Valentinians and Marcionties, the Hypatias and the Origens—who bore the greatest burden of this persecution—and yet do. For the power of this "kingdom" cannot completely be dissolved until the truth is understood by all—in fact, according to scripture, the wound given the beast, and realized in the fall of Papacy in 1798, is "healed" (Rev. 13:3), and the papacy and what it symbolizes retains yet a certain degree of allegiance. We leave it to the reader to evaluate the validity of this interpretation in the light of the historical facts presented.

We turn our attention further, then, to the papacy in an attempt to analyze its origins.

The Keys of the Kingdom and the Supremacy of Peter

The rationalization for the existence of the papacy lies in the theory that the popes are successors of St. Peter, whom Jesus is alleged to have ordained head of his church, presumably bearing the authority of Christ himself, and that this power was passed on to successive Roman bishops.

The claims for Peter's ultimate authority derive from Jesus' declaration to Peter as recorded by Matthew, 16:17-19, following Peter's confession that Jesus is "the Christ, the Son of the living God." Jesus says:

Blessed art thou Simon Bar-Jona; for flesh and blood hath not revealed it unto thee, but my Father who is in heaven.

And I say also unto thee, that thou art Peter, and upon this rock I will build my church and the gates of hades shall not prevail against it.

And I will give unto thee the keys of the kingdom of heaven; and whatsoever thou shalt bind on earth shall be bound in heaven; and whatsoever thou shalt loose on earth shall be loosed in heaven.

The first thing that strikes us about this passage is that Peter's confession of Jesus as Messiah is a revelation to him from the Father, as Jesus states, not a product of Peter's own reasoning or human perception. The second most significant thing in this passage is the play on words, as Scofield points out in his footnote on verse 18: He states: "In the Greek there is a play upon words in this statement: 'Thou are Peter (petros, stone), and upon this rock (petra, a massive rock) I will build my church.' It is upon Christ Himself that the church is built." <24>

The massive rock then is Christ or as we would suggest that portion of the mind of Christ that Peter was able to perceive or focus within himself. Jesus at first admits that Simon is a stone (of stumbling?), no doubt in his limited mortal awareness, but this assessment is shortly followed by Jesus' designating Peter as the Rock—that is, having the mind of Christ, as demonstrated by Peter's confession. This is similar to St. Paul's exhortation to the faithful: "Let that mind be in you which was also in Christ Jesus." The Petra or massive rock is, in fact, the mind of Christ or the portion thereof that resides within the faithful who gather in the ekklesia (assembly), a gathering of people who are called out. Ekklesia is usually translated as "church" in English. The church, therefore, is built on the Rock (Mind of Christ) in all its members. Verse 19 obviously relates to certain powers given to Peter by Jesus. The keys to the kingdom of heaven, we suggest, may refer to the powers of the spiritual world—those powers possessed by Jesus but meant for all those who would follow him in the regeneration. They could have included the power to give initiations into higher states of consciousness—this being the meaning of the "kingdom of heaven", and perhaps even to re-ignite the Divine Spark in the Heart Chakra. The "binding and loosing" in all likelihood refers to the power to either release another from certain karmas, as in a healing of a disease or forgiveness of past acts, or, to bind one to that karma, and require its descent—a judgment. These powers are within the range of the spiritual attainment of a Master, but they are not mechanically passed on by pure succession. The powers given in this vein to Peter were demonstrated by him in his healings as recorded in Acts. However, there is no further description of the "binding and loosing" power in the New Testament. Nor is there any historical record of Peter's having passed this power or powers on to another pupil, student, bishop or teacher. There is nothing in St. Paul's epistles to warrant the belief that Peter was, at that time, believed to be the "pope" or "prince of apostles" or was considered such by the early Christians. The apostles John, Thomas, James and others, including Mary Magdalene, at one time or another possessed certain spiritual gifts and graces bestowed on them by Jesus, according to various texts discovered at Nag Hammadi. If Peter truly possessed the power to "bind and loose" as Matthew records, how long did he possess this power and was it, in fact, transmitted to another?

There is no mention in the New Testament or in the Nag Hammadi texts of Peter holding the office of "bishop of Rome." Again, St. Paul makes no mention of it, nor does he mention the concept of "apostolic succession." According to

Dr. William Stuart McBirnie, the tradition that Peter founded the church at Rome is "unverifiable." <25> St. Paul's epistle to the Romans contains no statement relating to Peter's founding the church at Rome. St. Paul mentioned twenty-nine individuals by name in his epistle to the Romans, and Peter is not one of them. This omission is astonishing if Peter was the bishop of Rome. <26> In Peter's own presumed letter in the New Testament, he states simply that he is an apostle of Jesus Christ, one of the elders and a witness to the sufferings of Christ (1 Peter: 1, 5:1), and nothing more. He writes with no more authority than St. Paul, his fellow apostle.

In A.D. 300, Eusebius, the church historian, wrote: "Peter is reported to have preached to the Jews throughout Pontus, Galatia, Bithynia, Cappadocia and about the end of his days, tarrying in Rome, was crucified." <27> Had Peter been bishop of Rome, bearing a greater authority than all other apostles, surely Eusebius would have mentioned it as part of his "official" history.

Author Peter De Rosa states that in the earliest lists of bishops of Rome (which as we have seen were partially concocted) Peter's name never appears. <28> Further, as De Rosa shows, Irenaeus enumerated all the Roman bishops up to the twelfth, Eleutherius. According to Irenaeus, the first bishop of Rome was not Peter or Paul but Linus. <29> In 270 A.D. the Apostolic Constitutions name Linus first bishop of Rome appointed by St. Paul! Peter chose the second bishop of Rome, Clement. <30>

Returning to the statement in Matthew, "And I will give thee the keys to the Kingdom of Heaven," De Rosa writes that the Fathers of the Church saw no connection between this statement and the "pope." Not one of the Fathers applies this statement to anyone but Peter, nor do these Fathers (Cyprian, Origen, Cyril, Hilary, Jerome, Ambrose, Augustine) call the bishop of Rome a "rock" <31> or apply to him specifically the promise of the "keys":

It never occurred to the eighteen or so Fathers who

commented on this text [Jesus' bestowal of the Keys to Peter] *that there is a promise in it to 'Peter's successors.' Peter as an individual had no successors.... (Brackets added) <32>*

...So the early church did not look on Peter as Bishop of Rome, nor, therefore, did it think that each Bishop of Rome succeeded Peter.... <33>

The Bishop of Rome became increasingly important, especially when the Imperial Court was transferred to Constantinople in the fourth century. That left an enormous political, administrative and emotional gap. The Bishops of Rome were on hand, so to speak, to fill it. From this time on, the Bishops of Rome started to separate Peter from Paul, and applied to themselves the promises made in the gospel to Peter. Such was the prestige of the Bishop of Rome that scholars searched the scriptures for texts that would underpin his role as civil leader and patriarch of the West. What could be neater than to apply texts which in the gospels refer only to Peter, to the bishop who rules in the city where Peter died? The gospels did not create the papacy; the papacy, once in being, leaned for support on the gospels. This support did not come easily.... <34>

So much, then, for the authenticity of the papacy. We have already shown that the succession lists of bishops of Rome and other churches were partially concocted to compete with the succession lists of teachers preserved by the Christian-Gnostics. Ironically, several texts in the Nag Hammadi library claim that Peter himself was the recipient of a secret, gnostic doctrine. However, as we have said, several other apostles had also received secret teaching from Jesus. But what of the so-called "keys to the Kingdom of Heaven," bestowed upon Peter by Jesus? That Peter had received "keys" or powers from Jesus cannot be denied. We ask again, were they capable of being transmitted? Did Peter alone possess these powers? According to the several apocryphal Acts still extant, many apostles, including John, Andrew, Thomas, etc., possessed the power to work miracles. Although the miracle stories related in the apocryphal Acts are at times grossly exaggerated, they are, no doubt, based on true events.

The "keys to the Kingdom of Heaven" and the power to "bind and loose" bestowed upon Peter may refer to the lost mystery teachings of Jesus and the powers they imparted. According to H.P. Blavatsky, who designates Peter as a "Jewish Kabbalist," the term Peter, or Patar, and the hieroglyph PTR refer to one who is the interpreter of the mysteries. She also states that the term Petroma referred to a pair of stone tablets used by the hierophants at the initiation during the final mystery. The Petroma (the Rock) contained the final revelation which, of course, remained secret. <35> What Jesus had actually told Peter was: "Thou art Peter, my interpreter, and upon this Petroma (stone tablet containing the Divine Mystery) I will build my assembly of initiates, and the gates of Hades shall not prevail against it." Peter, therefore, must have received a secret doctrine along with certain powers or siddhis which he may or may not have passed on to another. It is doubtful that this doctrine was transmitted to the bishops of Rome, as the successive Roman bishops persecuted those who possessed this doctrine, namely the Christian-Gnostic sects. It becomes questionable whether Peter himself retained the powers once given to him, in the light of his denial of Jesus. We also sense a rivalry between Peter and John in the last enigmatic chapter of John's gospel where Peter seems overly concerned as to what will be the fate of John. Jesus predicts that John, not Peter, will remain till Jesus comes again (no doubt to reveal the Apocalypse to John). It is likewise significant that James, Jesus' brother, a strict Nazorean, became head of the "church" at Jerusalem and not Peter. Peter and Paul are obvious rivals as depicted in Acts and in Paul's letters. It is certainly possible that the "keys" may have been bestowed on either John or Paul or both during the lifetime of Peter. If Peter retained throughout his lifetime the full power of the "keys," why did Jesus find it necessary to initiate Paul as an apostle, seemingly in place of Peter?

In whichever way we approach the question, it cannot

be proven that the power of the "keys" was automatically passed on to a succession of exclusively Roman bishops. As earlier suggested, the "keys" must have referred to a spiritual science used to unlock the powers of the Divine Nature in man which could only be "unloosed" by a hierophant such as Jesus or one appointed as hierophant by Jesus. Such powers are won and received from another only by spiritual attainment, not by the simple fact of succession. The simple succession model is again the "flesh and blood" consciousness of the orthodox. One of the effects of these "keys" was, as we have stated, the working of miracles. These keys were part and parcel of the Secret Doctrine retained by Christian-Gnostic teachers, but lost to the bishops of orthodox churches. Certain Christian-Gnostics of the second century apparently possessed the esoteric doctrine and were, as a result, capable of receiving revelations from the spiritual world. Clement of Alexandria and Origen, as we have seen, were both witnesses to an esoteric teaching handed down from the apostles, not just from Peter alone. Neither Clement nor Origen mentioned Peter as "Prince of the Apostles." Unfortunately, the office of bishop in Rome and in other churches soon became merely administrative and had nought to do with the transmission of Jesus' original Secret Doctrine. We, therefore, cannot authenticate the claims of the Roman Papacy, which, in light of the above, remain doubtful. We would aver, however, that the science of the Secret Doctrine had always been passed on, sometimes in secret, and that there continued both within and without the established church the passing of the "keys" to those who were appointed "vicars of Christ." Certain popes who achieved sanctity down through the centuries would certainly have received the mantle of "Vicar of Christ" from Jesus. Other saints who bore that mantle were not the bishops of Rome. These saints and mystics bore the sins (karma) of the world and of the church. The "keys" therefore were not automatically transmitted.

The Destruction of the Mysteries—The Martyrdom of Hypatia

With the accession of the "Christian" emperor Theodosius in A.D. 379, every vestige of religious toleration ceased. The orthodox bishops, backed by the emperor, initiated a campaign of suppression against the ancient temples of the deities in Rome and throughout the various provinces. The bishops were aided by fanatical monks who gleefully tore down temple after temple to the dismay of the devotees of the Gods. The Serapeum in Alexandria, which housed the magnificent statue of Serapis, was destroyed and the statues toppled and dismembered. The Serapeum was the greatest and most magnificent temple in the city and was the center for the practice of the mysteries of Serapis. Theophilus, bishop of Alexandria, whom Gibbon designates "the perpetual enemy of peace and virtue," <36> masterminded this sacrilege motivated, no doubt, by jealously, for the devotees of Serapis in the city were great indeed. Even more tragic was the burning of the great library at Alexandria by order of Theodosius in 389 A.D., the greatest repository of ancient learning in the East. This precious library housed the "secrets" of knowledge and science. It contained innumerable scrolls and books pertaining to prophecies, mystery teachings, works of philosophy, ancient occult (hidden) wisdom and, we suspect, much that would have illumined the origins of the true doctrines of Christianity and their unity with the doctrines of ancient philosophy and the mystery religions.

The mere destruction of physical temples, however, was not as significant as the destruction of the doctrines of the mysteries hand in hand with the persecution of the Christian-Gnostics. As we have shown, the doctrines of the Mysteries were concerned with the release of the Divine Nature within man through following the initiatic path prescribed by one of the allegorical mystery Gods of antiquity. The doctrines of the mystery religions dedicated to Osiris, Mithras, Serapis, etc. were identical to the ancient Christian mysteries, and ancient

Christianity itself was, in fact, a mystery religion. Once orthodox Christianity became the state religion, the mysteries had to be destroyed lest they unveil the roots and origins of the newfangled Christian-Orthodox dogmas. Every self-respecting Church Father secretly knew that their doctrines were distorted copies of the teachings of Pythagoras, Plato, the mystery religions and the Gnostics. Whoever unveiled the mysterious "Isis" suffered the unrelenting hatred of the Christians.

Such was the fate of the unfortunate Hypatia, who taught the sublime doctrines of Pythagoras, Plato and Aristotle at Alexandria at the close of the fourth century. Hypatia, as the head of the Neo-Platonic school, was a disciple of Plutarch and the daughter of the great mathematician Theon. She was not only beautiful but learned and, worst of all, she was not a Christian. However, as M.P. Hall writes:

A number of writers have credited the teaching of Hypatia with being Christian in spirit; in fact, she removed the veil of mystery in which the new cult had enshrouded itself, discoursing with such clarity upon its most involved principles that many newly converted to the Christian faith deserted it to become her disciples. Hypatia not only proved conclusively the pagan origin of the Christian faith but also exposed the purported miracles then advanced by the Christians as tokens of divine preference by demonstrating the natural laws controlling the phenomena. <37>

Hypatia's exposure of the true origins of Christianity and her overwhelming popularity aroused the implacable hatred of "Saint" Cyril, bishop of Alexandria. Cyril unquestionably communicated his hatred to a group of fanatical monks from the Nitrian desert. Hypatia must not be allowed to continue to teach, for, as Cyril attested, the magistrate of the city of Alexandria was her disciple and the learned of several nations flocked to the academy where she lectured. The doctrines taught by Hypatia were more clear, more lucid and more scientific than the orthodox dogmas of Cyril's Christianity. What is worse, Hypatia popularized the Platonic and Gnostic doctrine of preexistence, reincarnation, and taught the existence of the "Gods," understood as a spiritual hierarchy who themselves emanated from the Ultimate, Absolute Source. Man, in Hypatia's Platonic viewpoint, was essentially divine. There was no room in Hypatia's philosophy for a deity named Jesus Christ considered by the orthodox to be the only "God" in the universe, who created a humanity stained with original sin. Hypatia, like others before her, revered Jesus as a teacher and expositor of the mysteries. Hypatia's exposès of Christian pseudo-theology threatened to undo all that the Church Fathers had attempted for four centuries—to exterminate the Gnosis from the earth. Cyril considered it his "Christian" duty to denounce Hypatia as a sorceress in league with the devil. The fanatical monks, of course, were ready to believe anything Cyril told them. One day, as Hypatia was traveling home from the academy where she lectured, she was attacked by the fanatical monks led by a savage and illiterate man called Peter the Reader. Hypatia was torn from her chariot, her body dragged through the streets to the Caesaren Church. Ripping away her garments, the monks pounded her to death with clubs, then carried away the remains and burned them to ashes. With her death in 415 A.D. the Neo-Platonic school of Alexandria collapsed; thus began the Dark Ages wherein the light of Gnosis was all but extinguished.

The Debasement of Woman—Adam and Eve—The Celibate Movement

We refer the reader to Jesus' sublime teaching on woman as preserved in the Tibetan text translated by Notovitch wherein Jesus equated woman with the Divine Mother, the Mother of the Universe. In this text Jesus bids his listeners to respect woman for "all the truth of divine creation lies in her. "Woman", teaches Jesus, "is the basis of all that is good and beautiful," and "the wife and mother are inappreciable treasures given unto you by God." Woman "possesses the divine faculty of separating in man good intentions from evil thoughts." From woman are born "all the inhabitants of the world," and "after God your best thoughts should belong to the women and the wives, woman being for you the temple wherein you will obtain the most easily perfect happiness." In short, Jesus equated woman with the creative and nurturing aspect of God, i.e., God as Mother. Woman also becomes the paragon of truth and wisdom. Jesus warns that whatever is done unto woman is done unto God. As we shall shortly discuss, the feminine aspect of man represents the soul; the masculine aspect the Spirit. If the woman "fell" in Eden, it is symbolical of the fall of the feminine nature in man, i.e., the fall of the soul. The highest duty of the masculine aspect or Spirit then becomes to exalt the feminine. To exalt the feminine is to exalt or raise one's very soul. This becomes an ascending spiral as the feminine in turn exalts the masculine, each moving the other to ever greater spiritual heights. This then is the significance of Jesus' exaltation of woman. Jesus, in his relation to Magdalene, for example, becomes the supreme symbol of the Christ-Spirit exalting and raising the soul—the most noble aspect of the masculine nature of man—while Magdalene in turn, in her worship and her love, exalts the Christ. Conversely, the debasement of woman can be seen as a consciousness of enormous and tragic consequence, for it is then the undermining of all possibility of spiritual evolution.

The rationalization for the eventual debasement of woman in and among the orthodox Fathers goes back to an interpretation of Genesis 2-3 wherein woman is taken out of man (which was erroneously interpreted to express her inferiority) and eventually succumbs to the temptations, sexual or otherwise, of the serpent. Genesis I, apparently overlooked by these reinterpreters, reveals that God (Elohim in Hebrew) created mankind (Adam) male and female in his own image. The crucial passage reads thus:

And Elohim said: Let us make man (mankind), in our image after our likeness....So Elohim created man in his own image, in the image of Elohim he created him; male and female he created them. (Gen. 1:26-27.)

We recall that the Hebrew Elohim is a plural noun meaning "Gods" (but usually translated "God"), but in this passage it apparently refers to "God" as male-female since "God" addresses himself-herself in the plural. If humanity, male and female, were created in Elohim's image, then Elohim must, of necessity, also be male and female. In Genesis I, woman or the female remains on an equal footing with man and is, like the man, a reflection of the male-female polarity of Elohim. The passage continues with Elohim blessing man and woman and bidding them be fruitful and multiply and to replenish the earth. There is no fall, no sin and no degradation. Procreation is considered natural and a blessing to the earth. Genesis I, therefore, reflects the period known in esoteric tradition as the "first three root races" wherein man and woman experience three successive "golden ages" before the invasion and incarnation of the fallen angels.

Genesis 2-3, however, which bears close affinities with the Sumerian creation accounts which stress man's role as subservient to the gods, does not follow logically from Genesis I. The two are obviously separate accounts and were written at separate times. Genesis 2-3 strikes the reader as an allegory. Being an allegory the text would be subject to varying interpretations. Even from a cursory reading of Genesis 2-3, it appears that some cosmic event must have occurred between Genesis 1 and Genesis 2. In Genesis 1 mankind, blessed by Elohim and made in his image, is commanded to replenish the earth. In Genesis 2, suddenly the "Lord God" forms man from the dust of the ground and breathes unto him the breath of life and man then becomes a living being. If man was created in Chapter 1, why the second creation from dust in Chapter 2? We have previously reviewed the texts that treat of the Fall of the Angels or the serpent/vipers who were responsible for infecting humanity. We would suggest that the Fall of the Nephilim/ Watchers/angels, etc. and the eventual descent of spiritual man (male-female) into duality and separation necessitated the creation of a dense material body of the earth, earthy. The whys and wherefores of this fall were elaborated in innumerable apocryphal texts, some of which we have reviewed, and other passages relating to the same are included in the Old and New Testaments.

The writer of Genesis 2-3 was clearly influenced, as we have stated, by the Sumerian concept of the creation wherein the gods created man as a tiller of the soil. Along with this conception comes the familiar story of Eve's being tempted by the serpent, eating of the forbidden fruit and giving it to Adam. In this account, Eve is "created" by being taken out of Adam's side, thus suggesting to the reader that the woman is somehow inferior to man. We would propose that these passages, interpreted literally over the centuries, have influenced our conceptions of woman, especially in theological circles. The esoteric or allegorical interpretations, however, have been numerous from the standpoint of ancient Judaism and ancient Christianity, and these alternate interpretations have been virtually ignored.

It is clear, then, that in Chapter 1 of Genesis, as God (Elohim) is male-female, so is humanity male-female. The ancient esoteric doctrine of Jesus on this subject of Adam and Eve was, as we have shown, preserved by the Christian-Gnostics. We recall to the reader certain passages in the Valentinian text, The Gospel of Philip, whereby it was stated that the original "creation" of humanity was androgynous, that each part of the Divine Whole contained in itself both male and female principles. The "Fall" was the separation of these principles within humanity: the female representing the soul and the male, the spirit. These two aspects, furthermore, are not to be interpreted as superior or inferior elements, per se, but as polar parts of the Divine Whole. The female aspect of both man and woman is the soul or portion that has descended from Spirit into matter. The soul archetypically is always feminine. Hence Sophia-Achamoth in the Christian-Gnostic texts falls through presumption and misplaced desire. The soul must be united to Spirit; then and only then is the androgynous polarity of male-female restored.

The so-called creation of Eve out of Adam's side, interpreted allegorically, (which may have been the original intent of the writer) was to demonstrate the androgyneity of the divine couples. Added to this was the gradual descent of the earth from an archetypal paradise to a denser globe as a result of the intrusion of the fallen ones, archons, etc., and their attempt to recreate the universe of archetypes on a lower level of dense matter. Esoterically, "Eve" is the soul or feminine aspect gone astray in all humanity. The Church Fathers perverted this universal conception of esoteric Judaism and Christianity into the idea that woman and woman alone is responsible for the fall because of her weakness in submitting to the serpent. Thus all women, as the so-called descendants of Eve, would share in the guilt of the fall. Even though Adam likewise ate of the forbidden fruit, (i.e., the consciousness of duality and separation) the blame was put upon Eve for instigating him. Some interpreters gave the "sin" of Eve a sexual connotation and taught that the sin of Adam and Eve was their discovery of the act of sex. Yet, in the first chapter of Genesis, Elohim strictly commands the couple to "multiply." How else were they going to accomplish this? There is nothing in the text to lead one to believe that procreation was sinful in and of itself. Once the "sin" of Adam and Eve was interpreted as a sexual sin alone and not as a disobedience to "the Lord," sex and its chief symbol, woman, began to be debased.

Some Christian-Gnostics, however, saw it differently, as we have seen. For them the feminine was also the Wisdom aspect of Deity, and in certain texts Adam is saved by a feminine being of light. In other texts, the "god" who created the first couple from dust was a malevolent creator, and the serpent was the symbol of the Saviour-Redeemer, the Revealer of Gnosis. The Christian-Gnostics saw the woman as embodying the original matrix from which the universe was evolved. They also saw the feminine aspect as the matter or "mother" side of creation. To the Christian-Gnostics God was

Father-Mother.

The esoteric teaching of the Christian-Gnostics and that of Mani concerned the creation of dense bodies by evil archons and their originating of lustful sexual intercourse to keep the soul chained to those bodies through procreation. It was a misuse and abuse of this doctrine that caused the Church Fathers to so detest sex and woman, whom they considered a lure for man. They neglected to teach the laity that the establishment of lustful sexual intercourse in lower bodies through genetic manipulation was the work not of woman but of archons/fallen ones and that there existed a form of procreation in the archetypal universe and on the "etheric" earth (paradise) which man once inhabited quite different from the present method as we now know it. The other aspect of this teaching they suppressed was the doctrine that when man and woman come together in love and not in lust (which was the trademark of the Watchers and archons) and when "God hath joined them together" (i.e., when their union is infused with the spiritual element) they can bring forth sons and daughters of God into incarnation. We see this illustrated in the Apocryphon of John where Adam and Eve through sexual intercourse bring forth Seth, the Son of God, whom some sects believed to be a prior incarnation of Jesus. Furthermore, as we have seen, the earliest Christians, the Nazorean-Ebionites, believed Jesus, the Son of God, to have been fathered by Joseph and to have been born in a natural manner, i.e., through sexual intercourse. This doctrine had to be declared heretical and replaced by the virginal conception and birth of Jesus, as the Church Fathers were constructing the dogma of the deity of Jesus over against the innate deity or divinity of all humanity! Therefore the esoteric teaching ignored and/or suppressed by the Church Fathers was that the fruit of the union of man and woman can potentially be the Son of God! The Light i.e. the Christ Mind, in man and woman can nullify the machinations of the fallen ones. To counteract this doctrine, the dogma of original sin was evolved as well as the attendant dogmas of the evil of woman and sex or procreation even within marriage as lustful and responsible for transmitting original sin.

However, the tale of the Garden of Eden may not be solely allegorical as H.P. Blavatsky states in *Isis Unveiled:*

...The garden of Eden as a locality is no myth at all; it belongs to those landmarks of history which occasionally disclose to the student that the Bible is not all mere allegory. "Eden or the Hebrew...Gan-Eden, meaning the park or the garden of Eden, is an archaic name of the country watered by the Euphrates and its many branches, from Asia to the Erythraian Sea," (quote from A. Wilder) ...In the Assyrian Tablets, it is rendered gan-dunyas. "Behold," say the Elohim...of Genesis, "The man is become as one of us." The Elohim may be accepted in one sense for gods or powers, and taken in another one, for the Aleim, or priests; the hierophants initiated into the good or evil of this world; for there was a college of priests called the Aleim, while the head of their caste, or the chief of the hierophants, was known as Java Aleim . Instead of becoming a neophyte, and gradually obtaining his esoteric knowledge through a regular initiation, an Adam, or man, uses his intuitional faculties and prompted by the Serpent...tastes of the tree of Knowledge—the esoteric or secret doctrine—unlawfully. The priests of Hercules...the "Lord" of the Eden, all wore "coats of skin." <38>

And here we have the historical kernel of the Adam-Eve story in Genesis 2-3. The "Lord-God" of Genesis 2-3 would then have been a hierophant of the mystery school, a Guru or God-man, an embodiment of Divinity, in the same sense that Jesus was designated by the circle of initiates surrounding him. Adam and Eve, then, as symbolical of all initiates in the mystery schools and colleges, chose to partake of the secret doctrine unlawfully rather than go through the gradual initiation by the Guru or Lord. The failure to obey the Guru at the prompting of the "serpent" or fallen angel caused the two initiates, Adam and Eve, to be driven away from the sacred school. Thus they are forced to experience all the exigencies of their "karma" as compensation for their desertion of the teacher. It was, we propose, in this sense that Jesus uttered the words to his disciples, "No man (initiate) cometh unto (can gain access to) the Father (Man's Divine Nature symbolized by the Tree of Life) except through me (the Guru Initiator/Teacher/Hierophant who progressively leads the initiate to an awareness of his or her own Divine Self)." Adam and Eve, code names for initiates, are representative of numerous initiates through the millennia who, rather than subject themselves to the arduous training required by the Guru, use their own faculties to attempt to wrest secrets of the "Kingdom of Heaven" and take it by force, thus bypassing the Guru and becoming a law unto themselves. The compensation, according to Genesis, is to experience life on earth without the spiritual faculties awakened and without the knowledge or Gnosis of the Divine Self. According to Blavatsky, there were numerous schools and colleges of this sort, some of which were in the East. The names "Adam and Eve," then, would refer to any and all initiates who in past ages likewise transgressed, disobeyed the Guru and thus lost the tie to their Divine Self. The real mission of Jesus, then, would have been to restore and re-ignite the Divine Spark in the initiates who lost it in past epochs of history. To do this they would have to accept Jesus as Guru, hierophant and "Lord," compensate for their past disobedience, and begin again to walk the path of initiation, the end result of which would be the awakening of "the fruit of the Tree of Life," or the Divine powers in man, not the lower "psychic" faculties.

Seen from this viewpoint, the Adam-Eve story has little to do with the debasement of woman. For according to the doctrine of reincarnation, any and all individuals could have at one time disobeyed the Teacher or several Teachers in past lives. By "Teacher" we refer to one who is a divine incarnation, thus the appellation in Genesis "Lord God."

We can see from the above that the varying interpretations and misinterpretations of the Garden of Eden story must have produced ongoing controversies in the early centuries of Christianity. By the third century, most of the Church Fathers arrived at the conclusion that the real lesson in the Adam-Eve story was that woman (Eve) had allowed herself to become a "tool of Satan," therefore was responsible for the Fall, and that the Fall was sexual intercourse and not disobedience to God. This interpretation was strictly adhered to in order to counteract the doctrine of Origen that all souls who find themselves in the matter universe fell of their own free will from various paradisiacal heavenly states. For the Church Fathers to have accepted this doctrine they would have had to admit that all souls preexist the body, are individually responsible for their state on earth and that the "sin" of Adam and Eve was not transmitted via sexual intercourse. This they were not prepared to do. One of the earliest interpretations of the Adam-Eve story was that of moral freedom or freedom of choice. Adam and Eve were given a command, and they had the free-will choice to accept or reject it. The lesson is clearly that all mankind have free will bestowed upon them by God. The freedom to choose, known as free will, was, unfortunately, done away with as the dogma of original sin gained ascendancy from the period of Irenaeus to Augustine (second to fifth centuries). If man is tainted by sin from birth, he obviously had no free-will choice to sin or not to sin, since according to the orthodox dogma, there is no pre-existent state prior to birth.

The Christian-Gnostics, who interpreted the Adam and Eve story in various ways, gave preeminence to woman in their churches. Kurt Rudolph writes of the position of women in Christian-Gnostic communities:

The percentage of women was evidently very high and reveals that Gnosis held out prospects otherwise barred to them, especially in the official church. They frequently occupied leading positions either as teachers, prophetesses, missionaries or played a leading role in cultic ceremonies (baptism, eucharist) and magical practices (exorcisms). <39>

Rudolph cites the example of Marcellina, who taught

the doctrines of the Christian-Gnostic Carpocrates circa 150 A.D. <40> Ptolemy, a disciple of Valentinus, wrote a detailed letter to one he addresses as "sister Flora" regarding the Christian-Gnostic interpretation of the Mosaic code. <41>

In the third century text Pistis Sophia, a Christian-Gnostic gospel, Jesus' female disciples play prominent roles, such as Mary his mother, Mary Magdalene, Salome and Martha. The Gospel of Mary (Magdalene) discovered at Nag Hammadi portrays Mary as receiving personal visions and revelations of the resurrected Jesus which Peter hotly disputes and refuses to believe. He states that Jesus would not have given these revelatory teachings to "a woman." Peter, no doubt, is representative of the "patriarchal society" prevalent in exoteric Judaism which was nurtured on the concept that Eve was a "fallen woman" as were her descendants. Esoteric, Kabbalistic Judaism, however, taught otherwise, and Jewish-Gnostic texts display feminine imagery.

In the Gospel of Philip, Jesus himself is portrayed as having a close relationship to female disciples. To quote:

There were three who always walked with the Lord; Mary his mother and her sister and Magdalene, the one who was called his companion. <42>

The same gospel also asserts that Jesus loved his "companion" Mary Magdalene "more than all the disciples" and "used to kiss her often...." The disciples also question Jesus as to why he loves Mary more than them. What relationship Jesus had to Mary Magdalene other than Master/disciple, we have yet to discover, but it is evident that Jesus held her in high esteem. Some writers have suggested that Jesus was married to Mary Magdalene, who bore him children, as the authors of *Holy Blood, Holy Grail* have attempted to prove, as well as Dan Brown the author of the popular novel *The DaVinci Code*.

We see nothing unusual in Jesus' marrying and fathering children; he would have done so to demonstrate for all time the sanctity of fatherhood and the sanctity of the family. If

Jesus did, indeed, marry, he most likely would have done so after his post-resurrection arrival in Kashmir, India. In fact, the son of the caretaker of Jesus' tomb in Kashmir, Sahibzada Basharat Salim, claims descent from Jesus, whom he calls Yuzu Asaph. He has stated that Jesus married a Kashmiri shepherdess variously named Mirah or Marjam, and that, by descent, he is a "Palestinian." (See *A Search for the Historical Jesus* by Fida M. Hassnain: Gateway Books, Bath, England, 1994 pp 198, 205-6 n. 1 and 2.)

The divine feminine principle is the saviouress of Adam and his posterity according to the Apocryphon of John. The text explains that the beneficent "Mother-Father" sent luminous Epinoia (Divine Intelligence), a feminine spiritual being, to Adam and his seed. She restores Adam to his fullness and awakens his thinking and is "hidden from Adam." She also assists the whole creation about the "way of ascent."

In the suppressed Gospel of the Hebrews, Jesus addresses the Holy Spirit as "My Mother, the Spirit." <43> In Pistis Sophia, when Mary Magdalene complains to Jesus that Peter "hates the female race," Jesus replies that "whoever the Spirit inspires is divinely ordained to speak, whether male or female." <44>

The above texts and numerous others like it, were, of course, banned by certain Church Fathers and subsequent church councils. But the more enlightened Church Fathers thought otherwise. To quote Clement of Alexandria:

Men and women share equally in perfection, are to receive the same instruction and the same discipline. For the name "humanity" is common to both men and women; and for us "in Christ there is neither male or female." <45>

We have seen that women held positions of leadership in Christian-Gnostic schools, communities and churches as teachers, priestesses and prophetesses—a fact which outraged orthodox Church Father Tertullian:

These heretical women—how audacious they are! They have no modesty; they are bold enough to teach, to engage in argument, to enact exorcisms, to undertake cures, and it may be, even to baptize! <46>

Tertullian, writes Elaine Pagels, was scandalized when Marcion, whose teachings we have reviewed, appointed women as priests and bishops on an equal basis with men. He writes:

It is not permitted for a woman to speak in church, nor is it permitted for her to teach, nor to baptize, nor to offer (the eucharist), nor to claim for herself a share in any masculine function—not to mention any priestly office. <47>

As the Christian-Gnostics fell into disfavor among the orthodox as a result of the writings of Irenaeus, Tertullian, Justin, Hippolytus and others, and as the theology of Clement of Alexandria and Origen began to be replaced by the orthodox pseudo-theologies, women began to lose favor in the churches. By the fourth century, the debasement of women took the form of a rigid celibacy which was then being promoted by the Church Fathers as the surest way to salvation. The celibate movement eventually came to be a cancerous growth in the body of the orthodox church. It started as a movement within Christianity at large, promoted by those who preferred ascetic Christianity, a renunciation of the world, marriage and responsibility to devote themselves to the spiritual life, pure and simple. Strains of ascetic teaching can be found in the gospels, the letters of St. Paul and the Christian-Gnostic texts. But as women lost their position in the churches and their respect, the Church Fathers began preaching against women and marriage. All of this, of course, was linked to the Adam and Eve story in Genesis 2-3. Elaine Pagels explains:

Ascetically inclined Christians even projected their idealized celibacy back into Paradise, and turned the story of *the first marriage into a story of two virgins whose sin and consequent sexual awakening ended in their expulsion from the "Paradise of Virginity" into marriage and its attendant sufferings, from labor pains to social domination and death. <48>*

Thus, sex and marriage, along with the image of woman, began to be debased. Gregory of Nyssa, toward the close of the fourth century, could write:

Marriage, then, is the last stage of our separation from the life that was led in Paradise; marriage therefore...is the first thing to be left behind; it is the first station, for our departure from Christ. <49>

We are a long way from the early Christians who penned the Gospel of Philip:

...How much more is the undefiled marriage a true mystery! It is not fleshly but pure. It belongs not to desire but to the will. It belongs not to the darkness or the night but to the day and the light. <50>

We recall that the Valentinians partook of a sacrament known as the "bridal chamber," which memorialized the union of the soul (feminine) with the Spirit (masculine). Marriage was seen to be an emblem and sign of this Divine Mystery. Although there was an ascetic, celibate strain in Christian-Gnostic teaching, the celibate life was never forced on an individual from without.

By the fourth century, as the so-called desert Fathers such as Anthony praised the celibate path and forsook all sexual intercourse, thousands of would-be monks followed them into the "Paradise of Virginity," as Pagels phrases it. Unfortunately, the celibate movement more often than not masked a subconscious and, at times, conscious hatred and revulsion for woman due to the misinterpretation of the Adam and Eve story, the degradation of the feminine principle, and by the misuse of the term "virgin," which in its spiritual sense related to the purity of the soul and consciousness of the Christian, not necessarily to the body. Before the celibate movement, sexual intercourse in marriage was a sacred honor and privilege and, as St. Paul wrote, "The marriage bed is undefiled." During the first and second centuries of the Christian era "ministerial celibacy was neither required nor recommended." <51> The married state was considered no less holy than the celibate state. By 300, however, Methodius, bishop of Tyre, wrote of virginity in a way that demonstrates to us that celibacy had become an obsession to the Church Fathers instead of an adjunct to spiritual attainment. Instead of Christ, virginity had become the god of the Church Fathers. Methodius writes:

Virginity is something supernaturally great, wonderful and glorious....This best and noblest manner of life is the root of immortality. <52>

Jerome, whose hatred of woman is scarcely veiled, followed suit:

Christ Himself is a virgin; and His mother is also a virgin; Yea, though she is His mother, she is a virgin still....The apostles have either been virgins, or...have lived celibate lives...bishops, priests, and deacons are vowed to perpetual chastity. <53>

Nothing, of course, could be farther from the truth. There is no absolute proof that Jesus was never married, especially in consideration of the vast period of time that ensued between Jesus' resurrection and his final passing, some fifty years later. It should be stressed again that the earliest Christians believed Jesus to have been born in a natural manner. It was well known that he had several brothers and sisters, according to the gospel accounts. Jerome, in his unnatural revulsion towards sex and marriage, decided to fabricate his own Christianity and remake Jesus, Mary and Joseph (whom he also claimed was a perpetual virgin) in his own image. Unfortunately, this image, perpetuated and fostered by the powerful Augustine, is the one that remained in the Western and Eastern orthodox churches for centuries to come.

Jerome retired to the desert for a portion of his early life, became a strict ascetic renouncing all comforts of the flesh, especially marriage and women. He later was ordained priest, and we find him in Rome as secretary to Pope Damasus. <54> Wearing the brown robe and tunic of an anchorite, Jerome lived amidst the luxuries of the papal court. Forthwith, he began to denounce not only Roman society but priests and bishops who were leading loose moral lives—those who were either married or had concubines. Jerome, during this time, appointed himself a "spiritual" advisor to a circle of aristocratic Roman Christian ladies whom he attempted to force into the celibate life. He advised his lady friends, married or not, to live as virgins in their homes! Durant writes that Jerome comes close to rating marriage a sin. <55> He quotes Jerome as saying, "I praise marriage, but because it produces me virgins." Jerome proposes to "cut down by the ax of virginity, the wood of marriage." <56> Jerome admonishes a young virgin, Eustochium, to "learn from me a holy arrogance: know that you are better than they are [married women]." <57> Jerome wrote a letter in 384 to this same young girl praising the glories of virginity; he bid her to fast, water her couch with tears, seclude herself in her own chamber and "let the Bridegroom (Christ) sport with you within." <58> He continues:

When sleep falls upon you He [Christ] will come behind the wall, and will put His hand through the door and will touch your belly. And you will wake and rise up and cry, "I am sick with love." And you will hear Him answer; "A garden enclosed is my sister, my spouse; a spring shut up, a fountain sealed." (Brackets added) <59>

The sexual allusions in this letter are obvious. It demonstrates clearly that Jerome was far from extricating himself from repressed sexual desire. Some months after writing this letter, Jerome counselled a twenty year-old-widow, Blaesilla, to subject herself to severe austerities and to remain a virgin. Two months later, wasted away, she died. Critics of Jerome blamed him for causing the death of the young girl. Jerome's reputation suffered as a result of this incident, and he fled to Palestine. <60>

Several years later, Jerome found himself in a severe controversy with Jovinian, a celibate monk, who wrote a document arguing that celibacy is no holier than marriage. He accused fanatical Christians of inventing the dogma of celibacy, which, he claimed, was "against nature." He wrote:

Virgins, widows and married women, who have gone through Christian baptism, if they are equal in other respects, are of equal merit. <61>

As Pagels describes it, these proposals and others concerning fasting and abstinence "brought down upon their author a storm of abuse." <62> Pope Siricius, led by the three pillars of totalitarian orthodoxy—Jerome, Ambrose and Augustine—excommunicated Jovinian. Although Jovinian protested and wrote commentaries on scripture attempting to prove his doctrine from the words of Jesus and St. Paul, Jerome also used the same scriptures to prove that celibacy is superior to marriage. Jerome's book *Against Jovinian* when published set off a storm of controversy, as many readers were chagrined by Jerome's hatred and vehemence toward Jovinian. Despite protestations, Jovinian remained condemned, and celibacy won the day.

Needless to say, it is the indefatigable Augustine who influenced the final decision concerning celibacy and marriage. Martin Larson summarizes:

It is in the African Code, adopted by the Council of Carthage in 419 under the influence of Augustine, that we find *for the first time an expression of the drastic celibate views which permeated the Western Church in the fifth century. Those who pray must abstain from their wives, as must all communicants during periods when the eucharist is to be received. Every bishop, presbyter or deacon must renounce his wife or his office. <63>*

This decree of the council translates to the psyche that sexual intercourse even in marriage is sinful, that the body is defiled and that the normal, natural acts of procreation among humanity are debased. We suggest that enforced celibacy and the celibate movement itself was an aberration within Christianity as it was presented and taught by the Church Fathers. Again, the psychological repercussions down through the centuries as a result of the church's debasement of woman and of the handing down of these traditions are incalculable. The repercussions, we suggest, would include homosexuality, a karmic consequence of violent sexual suppression in past lives with its attendant hatred of women, which, in fact, is hatred of God as Mother.

It should be added, however, that voluntary celibacy, according to Eastern adepts, for the purpose of raising what in the East is known as the "kundalini" or serpent-energy of the Divine Mother at the base of spine upwards to the crown or highest spiritual center, as a spiritual exercise and yogic science, can lead to a raised consciousness. The practitioner, however, must have the attainment whereby he is able to sublimate the sexual energy and not suppress it. The science of the transmutation of the sexual energy through either meditation or mantra was, no doubt, taught by the original mystical Christian schools who preserved the secret doctrine of Jesus on these subjects. It was in this sense, or with this purpose in mind, that Jesus, St. Paul or other gnostic teachers may have advocated celibacy at times. However, it was always voluntary and never enforced. The Church Fathers, as we have seen, made it their practice to steal the doctrines of the Christian-Gnostics and pervert and distort them and, what is worse, to force those doctrines and practices such as celibacy upon the unsuspecting faithful. The motive for choosing a celibate way of life in the original mystery teaching of Christianity was not out of detestation toward woman, sex or the body, but in order to transcend the mortal consciousness by the upward channeling of the "mother light" or sexual energy.

We move to our next subject—the emergence of the theory of the Vicarious Atonement.

The Emergence of the Vicarious Atonement Theory

We have previously elaborated on St. Paul's teaching regarding Jesus' atoning sacrifice. To briefly recapitulate: by Jesus' life, resurrection and sacrifice on the cross, Jesus set aside the planetary debt (karma) of many previous ages due to mankind's collective transgressions for a prescribed period of time, i.e. a 2000 year cycle. That sin or karma would be returned to mankind for redemption at the close of the age. Jesus therefore bore the sin/karma of the world to give opportunity to the faithful who accepted him as saviour to walk the path of their own personal crucifixion and resurrection—that resurrection that would spell an end to reincarnation. Jesus' prophecy of the end of the age (Matthew 24, Mark 13, Luke 21) clearly demonstrates that the collective karma/sin of ages would come due for redemption at the close of the age and would be causative of cataclysms, wars, earthquakes, etc. The "blood" of Jesus, which, it was taught, was the propitiation for sin, was viewed by the early Christians, apostles and initiates as the agency of transmutation. It was understood that Jesus, as Master, adept, and Divine Incarnation had so purified his consciousness and body that the blood which flowed in his veins and was shed on the cross had become an energizing fire to transmute that sin. For the early Christian sects and schools, whether or not they accepted Jesus' literal death on the cross, the blood of Jesus was synonymous with the "life" of Jesus and with the "Light" flowing in his body; some Christian-Gnostics even claimed that Jesus' whole body was composed of Light.

The crucifixion and "death" of Jesus, as understood by St. Paul, did not replace the necessity for each individual to redeem his own personal sins in present or future incarnations; as St. Paul himself declares, "Work out your own salvation with fear and trembling." By allowing the fallen ones (fallen angels, archons, etc.) to execute him, Jesus sealed their judgment, for by the very act of slaying the Messiah/Avatar, the judgment of the fallen powers was pronounced; as Jesus himself stated, "For judgment I am come into this world." In this manner, so taught St. Paul, Jesus "disarmed" the evil powers and triumphed over them through the resurrection. Moreover, the judgment of the fallen angels remains with them throughout all of their incarnations on earth until the close of their cycle, at which time they go through the "second death", the dissolving of the id or psyche by the sacred fire.

According to Adolph Harnack, the oldest doctrine concerning Jesus' sacrificial atonement on the cross, taught by Irenaeus and then Origen, was that Jesus delivered humanity from the power of the devil by allowing the fallen powers to vent their wrath upon him rather than upon humanity at large. This was based upon Jesus' utterance in the Matthew and Mark gospels (Mt. 20:28; Mk. 10:45) that the Son of Man came to give himself as a ransom for many. Harnack discusses Origen's doctrine as follows:

Origen, however, was the first to explain the passion and death of Christ with logical precision under the points of view of ransom and sacrifice. With regard to the former, he was the first to set up the theory that the devil had acquired a legal claim on men, and therefore to regard the death of Christ (or his soul) as a ransom paid to the devil....With reference to the sacrifice of Christ, Origen was of epochmaking importance....He was strongly influenced by the Graeco-oriental expiatory mysteries, and was the first to introduce into the Church, following the precedent set by the Gnostics, a theology of sacrifice or propitiation based on the death of Christ....He

*taught that all sins required a holy and pure sacrifice in order
to be atoned for, in other words, to be forgiven by God; this
sacrifice was the body of Christ presented to the Father. <64>*

We also find Origen teaching the very significant doctrine that *"all sins require expiation, and conversely, that **all innocent blood has a greater or less importance according to the value of him who gives up his life.** "*
(Emphasis added) <65>

The first or "ransom" idea, Harnack states, was derived from the doctrine of Valentinus and Basilides prevalent in the early mid-second century. The foremost purpose of Jesus' crucifixion was to disarm and thus triumph over the evil archons. The second or corollary concept was the idea of a pure sacrifice as an expiation for sin or karmic debt. Planetary karma was thus set aside (forgiven) by Jesus' sacrifice. Yet Origen also taught that all innocent blood was effective to a greater or lesser degree for the expiation of sin. We repeat that the term "blood" is synonymous with "life" and "light" or "lifeblood," and the esoteric teaching embedded here is that as one becomes purer and holier, he or she can become the vehicle for the transmutation of sin/karma on a personal level, as on a planetary level, by virtue of the sacred "lifeblood" coursing through the body, understood both physically and spiritually. Jesus was the supreme example of one whose body and blood was thus made sacred and holy, therefore he could become the vehicle of redemption for many.

The doctrine of Origen that all sins require a holy and pure sacrifice to be atoned for obviously implies that to atone for one's personal sins or personal karma, one must make a "holy and pure sacrifice" of the self to God, the indwelling Divinity. A life of holy and pure sacrifice entails the doing of corporal and spiritual works as a "penance" or satisfaction for one's karmic debt. Through the first two centuries of Christianity, the idea that one could satisfy or compensate for one's past transgressions without "good works," prayer, fastings, and practice of virtue, and without walking the path to one's own spiritual crucifixion and resurrection, was unknown. This, in fact, was the teaching of St. Paul and of Origen. This doctrine was the root of the slowly developing sacrament of penance, whereby the "clergy" meted out corporal works, prayers, pilgrimages and fasting to be accomplished by the penitent in satisfaction for past sins. Note that the term "past sins" as understood during the first two centuries of the Christian era included the "sins" or karmic debt of all past lives, which were to be expiated. We have seen that through the writings of certain Fathers such as Justin, Irenaeus, Tertullian, Ambrose, Augustine and Epiphanius, the universal doctrine of pre-existence and reincarnation slowly came into disfavor and eventually was eliminated from the official dogma of the church by the fifth century. Although it was believed that the crucifixion and "death" of Jesus was an atonement for world sin, we find it nowhere taught that works of "penance" were unnecessary to expiate sin or that some form of physical sat-isfaction was unnecessary to atone for the sins of past lives.

The doctrine, however, of the so-called vicarious atonement of sin by Jesus' death on the cross emerged hand in hand with the gradual submergence or suppression of the doc-trine of preexistence and reincarnation. As this doctrine was at first ignored, then condemned, Jesus' death was made the sole substitute for the satisfaction of sin, rather than the process of reincarnation itself as the method of expiation. Instead of teaching, as St. Paul did, that Jesus' crucifixion and resur-rection bought time and opportunity for the faithful to follow him in the regeneration, it was taught that Jesus' death wiped away all personal debt due to sin once and for all and that "penance" in its strictest sense was unnecessary. Since there were no past lives nor reincarnation (e.g., in the theology of Augustine) the only way for humanity to be forgiven was by Jesus' vicarious sacrifice. The changes in the doctrine relating to the forgiveness of sins were subtle and devious. For cen-turies penance was administered rigorously by prelates for the sins of only one lifetime, as they later came to accept it. For by the fifth century, reincarnation was anathema; and by the sixth century, it was condemned outright. Humanity, it was believed, had no responsibility to expiate its own accumulated personal sins (karma) since their sins had been laid upon Christ. Yet contradictory as it may sound, the "Church" continued to preach the vicarious atonement of sin by Christ along with the idea of penance. But we can ask, if Jesus' death wiped away all sin and guilt from the human race, why the need for expiatory penance? This question was never fully answered satisfactorily by any of the Church Fathers after Origen.

From the third century onwards, the orthodox Christian religion, such as it was, continued to draw in masses of people from all walks of life and from divergent backgrounds. The immense popularity of "mass Christianity" especially among the so-called lower classes can be explained by the developing "vicarious atonement" doctrine. Popular orthodox Christianity was offering a quick and easy way out of sin: belief in and acceptance of Jesus' death as the sole atonement for sin. The rigors of the mystical path to Oneness with Christ taught by the Christian Gnostics, Mani and Origen entailing progressive, initiatic degrees of advancement in Gnosis, were all but forgotten. The rituals of the ancient mystery schools, including the Christian mysteries, were now superfluous. There was no need to experience one's own crucifixion and resurrection, or to compensate for one's sins by "fear and trembling." Jesus had done it all. He had wiped away all sins. Why not enter the Christian fold? Why be concerned about the "sins" of past lives when there were no past lives? Once orthodox Christianity had aligned itself with the Roman imperial system, its popularity knew no bounds: one life to live, belief in Christ's death and an eternal heaven for the "good" orthodox Christian, and an eternal hell for the non-Christian. Nothing could be simpler. And thus, in the minds of the populace at large who received its orders from the church hierarchy, salvation was reduced to a simple formula and, with little variation, remained so for centuries.

The vicarious atonement theory received its greatest

exposition from the pen of Anselm of Canterbury (1033-1109). Previous to this, no detailed theory or doctrine had been propounded relating to the vicarious atonement. And yet this doctrine is considered the cornerstone of Christianity. In *Cur Deus Homo*, Anselm argued that the death of Christ, whom he called the "God-Man," must be understood as a reparation or satisfaction paid to God for the sins of mankind by which his honor is offended. This violation, being infinite in character, demands a retribution infinite in value. In Jesus, wrote Anselm, God became man in order to make this payment possible in his voluntary death on the cross, which, infinite in character, constitutes a superabundant satisfaction for human sin. <66>

The theory of Anselm, of course, would not have become tenable without (1) the Council of Nicea, which proclaimed Jesus as the eternal God, and (2) the elimination of the doctrine of reincarnation, which formerly was the means and opportunity for the expiation of sin. Since humanity cannot make satisfaction for its own sins, according to this theory, the God Jesus was brought in to perform the act of compensation by his death. Thus the predominating theme of Christianity of the Middle Ages was the Death of Christ rather than his Resurrection. Another corollary to this theory was that mankind was the sole cause of Christ's sufferings and death, a burden which to this day has not been erased from the collective psyche of the Christian. Whereas formerly the "ransom" doctrine stated that Jesus delivered himself up to the wrath of the Devil and his angels who through their pawns were solely responsible for his execution and "death," the vicarious atonement theory elaborated to the nth degree by the Scholastics and later by the Protestant Reformers such as Luther and Calvin promoted the doctrine of an angry, wrathful God and a guilt-ridden humanity whose terrible sins caused the "death" of Christ. Such was the legacy of the orthodox movement.

The Hidden Gnostic Legacy

With the establishment of a totalitarian Christian state by Constantine, the secret doctrines of Jesus slowly went underground and were preserved in various forms throughout the coming centuries. Manichaen Christianity, so terribly persecuted, continued until the eighth century. After that time, it becomes very difficult to trace it in its original form. A sect termed the Paulicans emerged in Armenia from the seventh to the twelfth centuries and promulgated gnostic and Manichaen doctrines. Another sect, known as the Bogomiles (the friends of God), thrived from the tenth to eleventh centuries in Thrace and elsewhere. The doctrines of these various sects were similar to the teachings of Mani, and, like Manichaen Christianity, they taught the existence on earth and in other spheres of fallen angels, archons, etc., which had penetrated to the highest levels of Church and State. They taught the doctrines of reincarnation and rejected the resurrection of the physical body at the end of the world. They were usually ascetic and some were celibate. Various sects calling themselves the Cathari or the Pure Ones penetrated into Bulgaria, Germany, Italy, and gained a stronghold in Southern France in the area known as the Languedoc. In essence, these sects were Christian-Gnostic, Manichaean and Origenist, but differing from one another on various points of doctrine. They were all united, however, in their detestation of the Roman Catholic Church, which, they taught, was under the dominion of Satan. The Cathari were most widespread in the area around the town of Albi in Southern France and were known as Albigensians. By 1150 the sect was dominant throughout the whole of Southern France. Like the Christian-Gnostics of the first and second centuries, they became a threat to the Roman Church. The Cathar-Albigensians, however, did not choose to remain a sect, but became a fully-established Church in their own right, and, what is worse, they claimed that they preached original Christianity as it was taught by Christ and his apostles. They rejected the Roman Church's doctrines on the Eucharist, the vicarious atonement and the resurrection of the body. The Cathari taught the preexistence of the soul and its subsequent reincarnation as a form of expiation of sin. They possessed their own clergy (the Perfecti or Perfect) and partook of their own sacraments. By the twelfth century, the Catholic Church had grown indescribably corrupt, and in comparison with the worldliness of its bishops and priests, the Albigensian Cathars appeared as veritable saints. By 1180 a preaching "crusade" was dispatched by the Pope to convert the Albigensians to the Catholic Faith. Various church councils in the mid-twelfth century had condemned the Cathars, but the sects grew stronger as a result of persecution. Finally in 1207 Pope Innocent III launched a military crusade against the Albigensians, partly because of their doctrines and partly because the powerful Counts of Toulouse were their protectors and rivaled the power of the Pope. Southern France had reached a pinnacle of civilization during the time of the Cathars. Troubadours spread throughout Europe ostensibly singing of Love, but in reality veiling the Cathar doctrines in song and rhyme. The Cathars of whatever sects may have had a connection with the Grail Romances being popularized at the time. (An entire volume could be written on the elucidation and interpretation of the Grail stories.) As a result of the "Albigensian Crusade," thousands of "heretics" were murdered by the Pope's armies. In the town of Bezier, 20,000 were massacred. When the city of Carcassone was taken, 400 Albigensians were burned alive and fifty hanged. At Minerve, 137 were burned alive as martyrs, and at Casser, all sixty taken were burned at the stake. This genocide was accomplished under the auspices of the Pope, who had previously established the Inquisition under "Saint" Dominic to convert and/or destroy every member of the sect. The kingdom of the Cathars finally fell on March 16, 1244, when their last stronghold, the castle at Montsegur, was taken and hundreds of Cathars were burned. By the close of the thirteenth century, Catharism was in its last gasp, and outwardly at least, the sects appeared to have been totally obliterated.

It would take a volume to trace the history and doctrines

of the various Cathar sects from the eleventh to the thirteenth centuries. It will suffice to say that the gnostic secret doctrines of Jesus continued to exist side by side with the orthodox church and continue to exist to this day. Various mystics in and outside of the Catholic Church preserved the teaching in part, such as St. Francis of Assisi, St. Bonaventure, Meister Eckart, Jacob Boehme, St. Catherine of Siena, St. Catherine of Genoa, St. John of the Cross, St. Teresa of Avila and others. All of the above taught the intrinsic Divinity of Man and demonstrated a path to Absolute Oneness with God through initiatic degrees. In addition to these, the Masonic and Rosicrucian Fraternities in the sixteenth and seventeenth centuries preserved the esoteric doctrines of Jesus, although these societies became corrupted in whole or in part in subsequent centuries.

The existence of the esoteric gnostic doctrines of Jesus and their oneness with the teachings of the major world religions was revealed to the world with the founding of the Theosophical Society in 1875 through H.P. Blavatsky, who published *Isis Unveiled* the following year. In the last sixty years, various movements, sects and organizations have arisen revealing esoteric and/or Gnostic doctrines similar, if not identical, to those of the first and second centuries. <67> These movements, such as The Summit Lighthouse, sponsored by the Masters of Wisdom, also known as the Ascended Masters, like the Christian-Gnostics and the mystical Christians of ancient times, affirm progressive revelation and continue to receive the "testimony of Jesus Christ." <68> Thus, as the winds of the New Age blow, the Gnostic Christians of today continue to seek Self-Knowledge as knowledge of God, making use of spiritual techniques such as the science of the spoken Word (mantra yoga, agni yoga) and the use of the violet flame (the fire of the Holy Spirit/Shiva) for the transmutation of personal and planetary karma and for the mitigation of cataclysm, pro-phesied for the end of the age, i.e., through the year 2002, and into the decades of the twenty-first century.

Thus, initiates of the New Age (Christian and non-Christian alike) are preparing for their personal resurrection, ascension and ultimately their Nirvana through meditation and invocation of the sacred fire. (See *The Science of the Spoken Word* by Mark and Elizabeth Prophet as an example.)

Conclusion

In conclusion, it should be said that the ill effects of the suppression of "Lost Christianity" remain with the Christian Church today. The average Christian believer has abdicated his right to be the arbiter of his destiny, yet through prayer and invocation of the sacred fire the "records" in the psyche (sub-conscious) of each and every Christian concerning the betrayal of the original Christian message by those who styled themselves "Church Fathers" can indeed be transmuted and erased, making way for individual and collective illumination. We would make a plea that the reader of this book make an unbiased assessment of what we have termed the original or oldest doctrines of Christianity. There are many books that are definitely worth reading: the Christian-Gnostic texts that have been judged heretical, such as those in the *Nag Hammadi Library*; the Tibetan text of Jesus' journey to the East between the ages of 13 and 30; <69> the Book of Enoch and the Dead Sea Scrolls; the documents concerning Jesus' travels after the resurrection; the works of Origen of Alexandria, especially *On First Principles*; The *Pistis Sophia* translated by G.R.S. Mead; *The Gnostic Gospels* by Elaine Pagels; *Jesus Lived in India* by Holger Kersten; *The Lost Years of Jesus* by Elizabeth Clare Prophet; *The Lost Teachings of Jesus* by Mark and Elizabeth Prophet; the volumes of the *Climb the Highest Mountain* series, especially *The Path of The Universal Christ*, by Mark and Elizabeth Prophet which brilliantly illumines the entire mission and message of Jesus, and other texts mentioned in the course of this work. Only in this way can a fair assessment be made of what, in fact, constituted the teaching of the original Christianity of the first two centuries.

We would ask the reader, therefore, to "sit under his own vine and fig tree," his own higher Self and Divine Nature and with an intuitive heart resting on the breast of Jesus, as did John the Beloved at the Last Supper, glean the truth from Jesus' own Heart. The reader will discern that his or her heart is one with Jesus' Heart, that, in Reality, there is no separation; that the Christ of Jesus is the same as the Christ in himself—that we all originated aeons ago from the One Source and to it we shall one day return; that Jesus is the Way-shower, our Elder Brother, whom we ought to follow but not worship as a "god" external to ourselves. The winds of the New Age are indeed blowing, and it is up to each individual to reassess his place in the universe and the purpose of life on earth. We would ask that every Christian become a seeker after Jesus' true doctrine, to become a Gnostic or Knower rather than a believer—to ask the eternal questions about life and death, but to be aware that the answers are deep within the heart. The question of evil should be faced squarely, grappled with, both evil within and the evil without. Only thus can there be a resurgence of true Christianity which is "Christ in you, the hope of glory," and only then can we look forward to a "new heaven and a new earth" when "the tabernacle of God is with men," as it is written in Revelation. We affirm that the dwelling place, the tabernacle of God, is, in fact, within the hearts of humanity and thus it has ever been. Let us then conclude with this statement of Jesus:

Wherefore I say unto you, sully not your hearts,
for the Supreme Being dwells therein eternally.

Epilogue

What Is Christianity and Who Is Jesus?

We have traveled through a perhaps bewildering mass of doctrines once known as "Christianity." At this juncture the reader may well ask, "What is Christianity?" and "Who is Jesus?" The average Christian will reply that all one needs to know about Christianity is in the New Testament. In answer, we remind the reader that the texts which compose the New Testament itself were arbitrarily decided upon by bishops, Church Fathers and church councils from the close of the first century on to the fifth. Before the Nicene Council the writings of certain Church Fathers were extremely influential in determining which books should be admitted into the canon— men, as we have seen, with questionable understanding or spiritual enlightenment and therefore trustworthiness in such a decision. Thus the New Testament contains only a small portion of the teachings and doctrines that once comprised "Christianity." Excluded were sayings, texts and an oral teaching that conveyed the goal of Christianity in mystical union with God, the initiatic steps along this path, the description of the forces arrayed against the aspirant and the techniques for the battle.

We again suggest that Christianity was meant to be a universal religion of Truth. Although Jesus was born in Palestine, his mission extended to the East where, as depicted in the Tibetan texts, he attempted to reform certain abuses of the priestcraft in the religions of India and Persia. This reformation was evidently meant for Judaism also. Jesus identified himself with the Messiah or anointed one (Greek: Christos) expected by the Hebrew prophets as well as with the saviour/redeemer prefigured in the mystery religions of antiquity and in

Zoroastrian texts. Jesus was also seen by the Buddhist of the first century (according to Notovitch) as another Buddha who preached the message of Gautama and by the Hindu as yet another incarnation of Vishnu. This points to the fact that Jesus was a universal avatar with a universal message and that, in fact, Christianity was meant to be a synthesis, distillation and reform of the major religions with the added understanding that the soul's mystical union with God through love was the real purpose of religion. Thus Christianity offered the hope of freedom from sin, ignorance, karma and reincarnation through the soul's resurrection and absorption into God. The "resurrection" and "ascension" were physically and allegorically demonstrated by Jesus, who was seen as the Wayshower and Exemplar of men's ultimate destiny. Thus the message of Christianity was "Christ in you, the hope of glory," and this "Christ" referred to the Divine Spark resident in humanity, which, if it had been snuffed out through neglect, could be restored by Jesus. The Divine Spark was the instrument whereby the soul attained union with God, its own Divine Nature. Understood in this context, the "resurrection" had naught to do with bodies resuscitating from the graves. The resurrection initiation related to the expansion of this Divine Spark. When the initiate, through service, devotion, invocation, meditation and the passing of tests, is able to then expand this Divine Spark, the flame itself eventually encompasses the body and forcefield. The initiate then walks the earth as a "resurrected" being, and ultimately, through the ascension process, the soul of the initiate returns to the Divine Source, his or her own God-Self or God-Consciousness. He or she is then designated a Master of Wisdom or an Ascended Master. Such was the case with Jesus.

The banned texts of Christianity, later termed "gnostic," portray a familiarity with preexistence and reincarnation (as do also the prevailing Jewish beliefs) as well as an explication of the causes of evil, which we have discussed at length. Thus the Christian was made aware of a "conspiracy of darkness," of principalities and powers within embodiment and out of embodiment, and was given the tools and techniques to combat these.

However, it becomes quite clear that Jesus was not looked upon by the original church as a mere teacher of ethics but as a Saviour. For Christianity, the Person of Jesus was just as significant, if not more significant, than his teaching. Jesus held out the hope that each disciple could follow him in the regeneration, but only after he had accepted Jesus as Lord and Saviour. As aeons ago humanity fell from their true estate by rejection of God and his representatives, so also must humanity accept Jesus as the representative or embodiment of God in order to find forgiveness of past karma or sin and walk again on the path to ultimate reunion. While Jesus held back planetary karma or sin, every man, woman and child could walk the "path of initiation," experiencing his or her own spiritual birth, baptism, transfiguration, crucifixion, resurrection and ascension. Thus, as humanity rejected the Guru/Father in "Eden," they must accept the Guru/Son in the person of Jesus, who became one with the Father and thus was the Father in the flesh (I and my Father are One). By accepting the Son, the disciple gains access to the Father (the Divine Self) and the Son (the inner Divine Spark). The soul, then, finally absorbed into the Father and the Son, becomes the manifestation of the Trinity and men become wholly Divine.

Finally, it must be understood that the only difference between Jesus and other "Sons" of God is in the realization of the inner Divine Nature. As many souls chose to fall in past aeons, thus forgetting their divine origin, in past epochs and past lives the soul of Jesus chose to cling tenaciously to God, his Divine Self, and thus became Divinity in the flesh, able to lead others back to the Source. According to esoteric tradition, Jesus, eons ago, volunteered to take incarnation on earth and has lived many lifetimes including embodiments on the now lost continents of Mu and Atlantis. According to The Summit Lighthouse, Jesus was previously incarnated as Abel, Seth, Joseph, son of Jacob, Joshua, King David, and the prophet Elisha, disciple of Elijah. In his final incarnation, Jesus truly was the fullness of the Godhead in manifestation. It is in this sense that Jesus can be called "God," in that he became the embodiment of his Divine Self, I AM, as he expressed it, thus enabling him to lead others to that realization and that attainment. This, we believe, is the ultimate goal of true Christianity and the essence of the original Christian teaching.

Reference Notes

Chapter I

The Lost and Hidden Years

1. Charles B. Waite, *History of the Christian Religion,* (Chicago: C. V. Waite and Co., 1881), pp. 84-89.

2. Elizabeth Clare Prophet, *The Lost Years of Jesus,* (Summit University Press, 1984), pp. 17-18.

3. Ibid., p 95.

4. Ibid., p. 195: Chap. IV, vs. 3-4, *Unknown Life of Jesus Christ,* N. Notovitch.

5. Ibid., p 199: Chap. V, vs. 18.

6. Ibid., vs. 21.

7. Ibid., vs. 23.

8. Ibid., p. 204: Chap. VII, vs. 18.

9. Ibid., p. 206: Chap. VIII, vs. 18-22.

10. Ibid., p. 208: Chap. VIII, vs. 12-15.

11. Ibid., p. 215: Chap. XII, vs. 10-21.

12. Ibid., p. 234: Chap. IV, vs. 1-3, Jesus Christ, the Leader of Men, S. Abhedananda.

13. Ibid., p. 237.

14. Ibid., p. 277.

15. Ibid. Chapter I The Lost and Hidden Years, p. 90

16. James M. Robinson, ed., *The Nag Hammadi Library in English,* (New York: Harper and Row, 1988, rev. ed.), "The Apocryphon of James," pp. 29-37.

17. G. R. S. Mead, trans., *Pistis Sophia,* rev. ed., (London: John M. Watkins, 1921), p. 1.

18. Irenaeus, Against Heresies 2,22,5, in Alexander Roberts and James Donaldson, eds., *The Ante-Nicene Fathers,*

American reprint of the Edinburgh ed., 9 vols. (Grand Rapids, Michigan: Wm. B. Eerdmans Co., 1981), Vol. 1, The Apostolic Fathers with Justin Martyr and Irenaeus, pp. 391-92.

19. Ignatius' Letter to the Smyrneans, in *The Lost Books of the Bible and the Forgotten Books of Eden*, (Collins and World Publishing Co., 1977), p. 186.

20. Holger Kersten, *Jesus Lived in India*, (Longmead, Shaftsbury, Dorset: Element Books Ltd., 1986), pp. 124-175.

21. Virgilius Ferm, ed., *An Encyclopedia of Religion*, (New York: The Philosophical Library, 1945), see "Atonement in Christianity. "

22. Charles H. Vail, *The World's Saviours*, (London: N. L. Fowler and Co.), p. 82.

23. Ibid., pp. 83-84.

24. Ibid., p. 85.

25. M. J. Vermassen, *Mithras, The Secret God*, (London, 1963), P. 104.

26. M. Baigent, R. Leigh, and H. Lincoln. *The Messianic Legacy*, (New York: Dell, 1989), p. 79.

27. Vail, pp. 90-92, 106-107.

28. M. P. Hall, *The Secret Teachings of All Ages*, (Los Angeles: The Philosophical Research Society, 1975), p. CLXXXIII.

29. See, Kersey Greaves, *The World's Sixteen Crucified Saviours* ; M. P. Hall, *The Secret Teachings of All Ages*; and Samuel Angus, *The Mystery Religions and Christianity.*

30. Hall, pp. xxi-xxix, "The Ancient Mysteries and Secret Societies. "

31. Annie Besant, *Esoteric Christianity*, (Adyar: The Theosophical Publishing House, 1966), pp. 169-170.

32. Mead, pp. 3-4.

33. Ibid., pp. 5-8 ff.

34. Donald Walters, *The Path*, (Nevada City, California: Ananda Publications, 1977), p. 427.

35. Lama Anagarika Govinda, *Foundations of Tibetan Buddhism*, (New York: Samuel Weiser, 1975), pp. 213-214.

36. Kersten, pp. 177-178.

37. Ibid., p. 179.

38. Ibid., pp. 179-189.

39. Montague R. James, ed., *The Apocryphal New Testament*, (Oxford University Press, 1924, 1983), "The Acts of Peter," p 333.

40. Kersten, pp. 183-4.

41. Michael Burke, *Among the Dervishes*, (London: Octagon Press, 1973), pp. 107-108.

42. Ibid., p. 108.

43. Ibid., pp. 108-109.

44. M. Yasin, *The Mysteries of Kashmir*, (Kesar Srinagar, 1972), p. 13.

45. Ibid., p. 14.

46. Aziz Kashmiri, *Christ in Kashmir*, p. 45.

47. Kersten, p. 195.

48. Ibid.

49. Ibid., p. 196.

50. Ibid., p. 200.

51. Ibid., p. 209.

52. Ibid., pp. 205-6. Chapter I The Lost and Hidden Years 92

53. Walters, pp. 538-539.

54. Swami Nikhilananda, *Vivekananda: A Biography,* (New York: Ramakrishna-Vivekananda Center, 1953), P. 178.

Chapter II

The Oldest Christian Sects, Communities, and their Teachings—Part I

1. Charles Ponce, *Kabbalah*, (Wheaton, Illinois: Theosophical Publishing House, 1983), pp. 134-142.

2. The Book of Enoch, 46:2; 48:3-6 in Elizabeth C. Prophet, *Forbidden Mysteries of Enoch*, (Los Angeles: Summit University Press, 1983), pp. 128-130.

3. Hugh J. Schonfield, *Those Incredible Christians*, (New York: Bantam, 1969), pp. 245-245.

4. Ibid., p. 246.

5. Ibid., pp. 246,247.

6. Ibid., pp. 248-249.

7. Ibid., p. 249.

8. Ibid., p. 250.

9. Ibid., p. 251.

10. John Rossner, *In Search of the Primordial Tradition and the Cosmic Christ*, (St. Paul: Llewellyn Publications, 1989), p. 189.

11. John Hicks, ed., *The Myth of God Incarnate*, (Phil.: Westminister Press, 1977), "A Cloud of Witnesses" by Frances Young, p. 21.

12. A. Powell Davies, *The First Christian: A Study of St. Paul and Christian Origins*, (New York: Mentor, the New American Library, 1957), see Chapter Two, "Paul and the Pagan Redeemers," pp. 108-129; Kurt Rudolph, *Gnosis*, (New York: Chapter II The Gnostic Theology of Paul 139 Harper and Row, 1987), pp. 301-2; Elaine Pagels, *The Gnostic Paul*, (Philadelphia: Fortress Press, 1975), see Intro., A. Besant, *Esoteric Christianity*, pp. 36-46; W. H. C. Frend,

The Rise of Christianity, (Philadelphia: Fortress Press, 1984), p. 104.

13. In our elucidation of Paul's theology we are equating the word "sin" with the Eastern concept of "karma," i.e., accumulation of effects resulting from prior causes—the thoughts, words and deeds of past lives—considered from this viewpoint as negative effects or negative karma, hence "sin," lodged in the subconscious.

14. Schonfield, p. 242.

15. Pagels, *The Gnostic Paul*, p. 119.

16. James J. Hurtak, *Gnosticism: Mystery of Mysteries*, (Los Gatos, California: Academy For Future Science, 1980), p. 89.

17. Pagels, *The Gnostic Paul*, p. 119.

18. Ibid.

19. Ibid., p. 58.

20. Adolph Harnack, *History of Dogma*, Vol I., (Gloucester, Mass.: Peter Smith, 1894, 1976), pp. 191-2.

21. Ibid. p. 93.

Chapter III

The Oldest Christian Sects, Communities, and their Teachings—Part II

1. Helmut Koester, *History and Literature of Early Christianity*, Vol. 2, (Philadelphia: Fortress Press, 1982), pp. 86-7.

2. Schonfield, *Those Incredible Christians*, p. 85.

3. Kersten, *Jesus Lived in India*, p. 94.

4. Hugh J. Schonfield, *The Passover Plot*, (New York: Bantam Books, 1967, 1971), p. 199.

5. Kersten, *Jesus Lived in India*, pp. 94-5.

6. A Hierophant is the expositor of the sacred mysteries. The chief priest of the Greek Eleusinian Mysteries was designated a hierophant.

7. Morton Smith, *The Secret Gospel: The Discovery and Interpretation of the Secret Gospel According to Mark,* (Clearlake, California: Dawn Horse Press, 1982), p. 17.

8. H. P. Blavatsky, *Isis Unveiled,* Vol. II, (Pasadena, California: Theosophical University Press, 1976), pp. 131, 132, 137.

9. Ibid., p. 132.

10. Ibid., p. 137.

11. Ibid., p. 138.

12. Ibid., p. 151.

13. Ibid., p. 154.

14. Ibid.

15. Ibid., p 294-5.

16. Schonfield, *The Passover Plot,* p. 204.

17. Ibid., p. 203-4.

18. Kersten, *Jesus Lived in India,* pp. 177-8.

19. Schonfield, *The Passover Plot,* pp. 202-3.

20. Harnack, *History of Dogma,* Vol. I., p. 299 n. 2.

21. Ibid., p. 295 n. 2.

22. Ibid., p. 301.

23. Jack Finegan, *Hidden Records of the Life of Jesus,* (Philadelphia: Pilgrim Press, 1969), p. 47, quoting Eusebius, Clement of Alexandria and Hegesippus.

24. Ibid., p. 165, 171, 1 73, quoting Irenaeus and Epiphanius.

25. Ibid., p. 172.

26. Ibid., p. 171, quoting Epiphanius' translation (Pan. haer XXX, 13, 7-8 GCS 25, 350-51)

27. Harnack, *History of Dogma,* Vol. 1, p. 192 n. 3.

28. Ibid., p. 191 n. 3.

29. Martin Larsen, *The Religion of the Occident*, (New York: Philosophical Library, 1959), p. 514, quoting Hippolytus: "Refutation of All Heresies" VII, xxii.

30. Ibid., pp. 468, 469, 470. Emil G. Kraeling, *The Clarified New Testament*, Vol. I, (New York: McGraw-Hill Co., 1962), p. 121.

31. Kraeling, p. 120.

32. Prophet, *The Lost Years of Jesus*, p. 376 n. 2., quoting Raymond Brown, *The Birth of the Messiah*, pp. 143-53.

33. Kraeling, p. 121.

34. Kersten, *Jesus Lived in India*, p. 121.

35. Kraeling, p 197.

36. Archibald Robertson, *The Origins of Christianity*, (New York: International Publishers, 1962), pp. 166-67.

37. Prophet, *The Lost Years of Jesus*, p. 379 n. 2, quoting William E. Phipps, *Was Jesus Married?* (New York: Harper and Row, 1970), pp. 39-40.

38. Ibid., 379-80, quoting Phipps.

39. *The Humane Gospel of Jesus*, "The Gospel of the Holy Twelve," (Imlaystown, New Jersey: The Edenite Society, 1979), p. 14.

40. Besant, *Esoteric Christianity*, p. 106.

41. Ibid., p. 107.

42. Ibid., pp. 107-108 ff.

43. William Whiston, trans., Josephus: *Complete Works*, (Grand Rapids, Michigan: Kregel Publications, 1960, 1986), "Wars of the Jews," Book II, Ch. 8, p. 478.

44 Ibid.

45. Ibid.

46. Prophet, *Forbidden Mysteries of Enoch*, pp.16-17, " The Untold Story of Men and Angels. "

47. Joseph Head, S. L. Cranston, eds., *Reincarnation*, (New York: Causeway Books, 1967), p. 89, quoting Philo, De Somniis, 1:22.

48. Ibid., p. 90, quoting Philo, De Gigantes, 2 et seq.

49. Theodore H. Gaster, ed., *The Dead Sea Scriptures,* (Garden City, N. Y.: Anchor Books, 1956, 1976), pp. 14-16.

50. Ibid., p. 17.

51. Prophet, *Forbidden Mysteries of Enoch*, p. 5.

52. Ibid., p. 10.

53. Ibid., p. 105, Enoch 15:8.

54. Ibid., p. 71.

55. Ibid., pp. 63-67, discussing Hebrew scholar Julian Morgenstern's exegesis (Hebrew Union College, 1939) regarding the concept of two separate "falls" in the Bible.

56. Ibid., pp. 50-51.

57. Willis Barnstone, ed., *The Other Bible*, (New York: Harper and Row, 1984), "The Gospel of Bartholomew," p. 357.

Chapter IV

Brief Scenario of Early Christian History

1. Paul Johnson, *A History of Christianity*, (New York: Atheneum,1977), p. 35.

2. Ibid.

3. Ibid., p. 37.

4. Ibid., p. 44.

5. Ibid.

6. Ibid.

7. Ibid., p. 52.

8. Rossner, *In Search of the Primordial Tradition and the Cosmic Christ.*, p. 83, quoting Benz' article, "Christianity" in

the 1974 ed. of Encyclopedia Brittanica, Vol. IV, Macropedia, pp. 530 ff.

9. Koester, *History and Literature of Early Christianity*, Vol. II, pp. 178-181, 196-198. See "The Dialogue of the Saviour" and "Acts of John".

10. Bently Layton, ed., *The Gnostic Scriptures*, (Garden City, New York, 1987), Part IV, "The School of St. Thomas, pp. 359-409.

11. Ibid., Gen. Intro., pp. xvii-xviii.

12. Ibid., p. xviii.

13. Ibid.

14. Ibid.

Chapter V

The Lost Christianity of the Original Sects

1. G. R. S. Mead, *Fragments of a Faith Forgotten*, (London; Benares: Theosophical Publishing Society, 1906), p. 162.

2. Ibid.

3. Jean Doresse, *The Secret Books of the Egyptian Gnostics*, (Rochester, Vermont: Inner Traditions Int'l Ltd., 1986), p. 189 n. 74.

4. Stephan A. Hoeller, *Jung and The Lost Gospels*, (Wheaton, Illinois: Theosophical Publishing House, 1989), p. 65.

5. *Nag Hammadi Library*, "The Three Steles of Seth," p.396 ff.

6. Ibid., pp. 396-7.

7. Hoeller, *Jung and the Lost Gospels*, p. 226.

8. Layton, *The Gnostic Scriptures*, pp. 187, 189, quoting Epiphanius, Against Heresies, chap. 39.

9. W. Morgan, *St. Paul in Britain or the Origin of British*

Christianity,(Thousand Oaks, Ca.: Artisan Sales, 1984),
pp. 12-13.

10. E. Raymond Capt, *The Traditions of Glastonbury*,
(Thousand Oaks, Ca.: Artisan Sales, 1983), 37-48 ff. ;
George F. Jowett, *The Drama of the Lost Disciples*,
(London: Covenant Publishing Co., 1961), 58-88; Morgan,
St. Paul in Britain, p. 62 ff.

11. Rudolph, *Gnosis*, pp. 297-98.

12. Hoeller, *Jung and the Lost Gospels*, pp. 72-3.

13. Blavatsky, *Isis Unveiled*, Vol. II, p. 91, see footnote.

14. Rudolph, *Gnosis,* p. 294.

15. Mead, *Fragments of a Faith Forgotten*, p. 170.

16. Ibid., p. 167.

17. Ibid., p. 173.

18. Ibid., p. 169, quoting Irenaeus' outline of Simon's
system.

19. Hoeller, *Jung and the Lost Gospels*, pp. 71-72.

20. Ibid., p. 71.

21. Mead, *Fragments of a Faith Forgotten*, pp. 167-8.

22. Elaine Pagels, *The Gnostic Gospels*, (New York: Vintage
Books, 1979), p. 162, quoting Hippolytus, Refutation of All
Heresies, 6. 9.

23. Mead, *Fragments of a Faith Forgotten*, p. 175.

24. Ibid.

25. Ibid., p. 176.

26. Ibid.

27. *The Nag Hammadi Library*, "The Gospel of Thomas,"
p. 137; "The Gospel of Philip," p. 147.

28. Mead, *Fragments of a Faith Forgotten*, p. 177.

29. Rudolph, *Gnosis*, p. 298.

30. Mead, *Fragments of a Faith Forgotten*, p. 179.

31. Ibid., p. 178.

32. Rudolph, *Gnosis,* p. 185.

33. See *The Nag Hammadi Library*, "The Apocryphon of John," "The Hypostasis of the Archons," "On the Origin of the World," "The Apocalypse of Adam. "

34. See *The Twelfth Planet* and *Genesis Revisited* by Zechariah Sitchin.

35. Hoeller, *Jung and the Lost Gospels*, pp. 78-9.

36. Ibid., p. 137. Thus, according to these Christian sects, the "original sin" was an original fall or rebellion of angels, archons or other divine powers. Adam and Eve were seduced by these fallen powers but did not originate evil.

37. Rudolph, *Gnosis*, pp. 172-3, quoting Origen, Contra Celsum, vii, 40.

38. Mead, *Fragments of Faith Forgotten*, p. 181-197. C. W. King, *The Gnostics and Their Remains*, (San Diego: Wizards Bookshelf), pp. 82-103.

39. See, for example, The Martyrdom and Ascension of Isaiah a possible pre-Christian work with Christian interpolations.

40. R. M. Grant, *Gnosticism and Early Christianity*, 2nd edition,(New York: Columbia University Press, 1966), pp. 48-9.

41. Layton, *The Gnostic Scriptures*, pp. 74-5, "The Reality of the Rulers," n. 95 b. c., Rudolph, *Gnosis*, p. 73.

42. Hans Jonas, *The Gnostic Religion*, (Boston: Beacon Press, 1958, 1963), pp. 296-7.

43. *The Nag Hammadi Library*, "The Apocryphon of John," pp. 110-111.

44. Ibid., pp. 112-113.

45. We define myth as a narrative in story form, which presents archetypal spiritual-psychological (inner or soul) experiences under the forms of allegory, symbol and metaphor. A myth may partially veil esoteric truths yet simultaneously provide keys to their interpretation.

46. Hoeller, *Jung and the Lost Gospels*, pp. 148-9.

47. *The Nag Hammadi Library*, "The Apocryphon of John," p. 113.

48. Ibid., "On the Origin of the World," p. 175.

49. Ibid., "The Apocryphon of John," p. 113.

50. Ibid., p. 119.

51. Ibid., p. 121.

52. Ibid., p. 122.

53. Robert Monroe, *Journeys Out of the Body*, (Garden City, New York: Doubleday, 1977), p. 261.

54. Hans Jonas, *The Gnostic Religion*, (Boston: Beacon Press, 1963), p. 169.

55. *The Nag Hammadi Library*, "On the Origin of the World," pp. 187, 188.

56. Mead, *Fragments of a Faith Forgotten*, pp. 198-99.

57. Ibid., p. 199.

58. Ibid., p. 203.

59. Pagels, *The Gnostic Gospels*, Chap. 3, especially p. 68.

60. Doresse, *The Secret Books of the Egyptian Gnostics*, facing p. viii, quoting Hippolytus, "Philosophumena", v. 10, 2.

61. Mead, *Fragments of a Faith Forgotten*, p. 203.

62. Mead, trans., *Pistis Sophia*, pp. 207-9.

63. Ibid., pp. 218-19.

64. Ibid., p. 236.

65. Ibid., p. 249.

66. Ibid., p. 240, 239.

67. Ibid., p. 312.

68. Mead, *Fragments of a Faith Forgotten*, p. 217, see generally pp. 217-221 for a discussion of the Docetae.

69. *The Nag Hammadi Library*, "The Second Treatise of the Great Seth," p. 365.

70. Ibid., "Apocalypse of Peter," p. 377.

71. *The Other Bible*, "Acts of John," pp. 418-20.

72. Duncan Greenlees, ed., *The Gospel of the Gnostics*, (Adyar, Madras: The Theosophical Publishing House, 1958), pp. 102, 112.

73. Kersten, *Jesus Lived in India*, pp. 158, 169.

74. Ibid., p. 153.

75. Ibid., p. 152.

76. Ibid., p. 154.

77. Ibid., pp. 171-172.

78. Ibid., p. 172.

79. Ibid., pp. 172-174.

80. Mead, *Fragments of a Faith Forgotten*, p. 238.

81. Waite, *History of the Christian Religion*, p. 63, quoting Jerome, "Commentary on Matthew", 12. 13.

82. Blavatsky, *Isis Unveiled*, Vol II, pp. 181-183.

83. Mead, *Fragments of a Faith Forgotten*, pp. 229-233.

84. Morton Smith, *The Secret Gospel: The Discovery and Interpretation of the Secret Gospel According to Mark*, (Clearlake, Ca.: The Dawn Horse Press, 1982, 1984), p. 15.

85. Ibid., p. 137.

86. Ibid., p. 142.

87. Ibid.

88. Ibid., p. 17.

89. Ibid., p. 134-5.

90. Paramahansa Yogananda, *Autobiography of a Yogi*, (Los Angeles, California: Self-Realization Fellowship, 1946), pp. 166-67.

Chapter VI

The Emergence of Orthodoxy

1. Koester, *History and Literature of Early Christianity*, vol II, pp. 297-305.

2. *The Lost Books of the Bible and the Forgotten Books of Eden*, "Lost Books," I Clement 2:3-5, pp. 113-4.

3. Ibid., I Clem. 17:25, 27-28, p. 129.

4. Ibid., I Clem. 18:2,4,6,7,p. 130.

5. Ibid., I Clem. 18:15, 16, 18-21, p. 131.

6. Pagels, *The Gnostic Gospels*, pp. 41-2.

7. *The Lost Books of the Bible and the Forgotten Books of Eden*, I Clem. 23:15-16, p. 138.

8. Ibid., Ignatius to Ephesians. 1:8-9, p. 167.

9. Ibid., Eph. 1:12-13, p. 167.

10. Ibid., Eph. 2:3,4, p. 168.

11. Ibid., Eph. 4:9, p. 171,

12. Ibid., Eph. 4:10, p. 171.

13. Ibid., Eph. 4:13, P. 171.

14. Ibid., Magnesians. 2:4-5, 9, p. 173.

15. Ibid., Ignatius to Trallians 1:8-9, p. 176.

16. Ibid., Trall. 2:2, p. 177.

17. Prophet, *The Lost Years of Jesus*, pp. 205-6.

18. *The Lost Books of the Bible and the Forgotten Books of Eden*, Trall. 2:4-5, p. 177.

19. Frend, *The Rise of Christianity*, p. 139.

20. Ibid., pp. 127, 139.

21. Ibid., p. 120.

22. Ibid., p. 138.

23. Elaine Pagels, *Adam, Eve, and the Serpent*, (New York: Random House, 1988), pp. 57-8.

24. *The Lost Books of the Bible and the Forgotten Books of Eden,* Trall. 2:10-12, p. 177.

25. Ibid., Trall. 2:13-14, p. 177-8.

26. Pagels, *The Gnostic Gospels*, pp. 114-15

27. *The Lost Books of the Bible and the Forgotten Books of Eden,* Ignatius to Smyrneans, 3:4,7, p. 188.

28. Koester, *History and Literature of Early Christianity,* Vol. II, pp. 284-5.

29. Ibid., p. 286.

30. *The Lost Books of the Bible and the Forgotten Books of Eden,* Bar. 5:9, p. 150.

31. Ibid., Bar. 7:4, p. 153.

32. Ibid., Bar. 6:6-13, p. 152.

33. Vail, *The World's Saviours*, pp. 17-31 (Messianic Prophecies); Graves, *The World's Sixteen Crucified Saviours* pp. 34-42.

34. Waite, pp. 265-6.

35. Harnack, Vol. I, p. 269.

36. Blavatsky, Vol. II, p. 163.

37. *The Nag Hammadi Library*, "Apocalypse of Adam," p. 279.

38. Hoeller, pp. 152-3.

39. Walter Nigg, *The Heretics*, (New York: Alfred A. Knopf, 1962), p. 64.

40. Larson, p. 526.

41. Johnson, pp. 47-8.

42. Larson, p. 531.

Chapter VII

The Great Schools of Christian Gnosis

1. Mead, p. 254.
2. Ibid., p. 273.
3. Rudolph, p. 312.
4. Mead, p. 278.
5. Ibid., p. 272.
6. King, p. 261, quoting Irenaeus.
7. Ibid.
8. Layton, ed., p. 436.
9. Ibid., p. 440. Mead, p. 275.
10. Mead, pp. 276-77, quoting Clement of Alexandria.
11. Ibid., p. 277.
12. Ibid., p. 278.
13. Layton, p. 217.
14. Ibid.
15. Pagels, *The Gnostic Paul*, pp. 4-5.
16. Layton, p. 220.
17. Ibid.
18. Ibid., pp. 220-21.
19. Ibid., pp. 221.
20. Mead, p. 303, Clement of Alexandria quoting Valentinus.
21. Ibid., pp. 300-301, Clement of Alexandria quoting Valentinus.
22. Ponce, pp. 136-7.
23. Mead, p. 305, Clement of Alexandria quoting Valentinus.
24. Ibid.
25. Ibid., p 303.
26. Grant, p. 8-9.
27. Ibid., p. 9.

28. *Ante-Nicene Fathers*, Vol. I, Irenaeus, "Against Heresies," Ch. 21, p. 346.

29. Greenlees, pp. 47-8.

30. Hurtak, p. 89.

31. Greenlees, pp. 48-9.

32. Ibid., p. 49.

33. Ibid., p. 54.

34. Ibid., p. 50, n. 2.

35. Ibid., p. 56.

36. Ibid., p. 58-9.

37. Ibid., p. 60.

38. Ibid.

39. Ibid., p. 61.

40. Ibid., pp. 60-61, n. 2.

41. Ibid., pp. 63-64.

42. Ibid., p. 64.

43. Hoeller, p. 113.

44. Ibid., p. 148.

45. Greenlees, pp. 66-7, Irenaeus quoting Ptolemy, "Against Heresies. "

46. Ibid., p. 68, Greenlees' commentary.

47. Ibid.

48. Ibid.

49. Elaine Pagels, *The Johannine Gospel in Gnostic Exegesis: Heracleon's Commentary on John,* (Nashville, New York: Abingdon Press, 1973), pp. 109, 121.

50. Ibid., pp. 95, 98, ff.

51. Ibid., pp. 102-104.

52. Layton, p. 267, "The School of Valentinus. "

53. Ibid.

54. Ibid., p. 268.

55. Ibid.
56. Ibid., p. 267.
57. Ibid., p. 272.
58. Ibid., p. 271.
59. Ibid., p. 251.
60. Ibid., p. 250.
61. *Nag Hammadi Library*, "The Gospel of Truth," p. 46.
62. Ibid., p. 42.
63. Ibid., p. 47.
64. Ibid., p. 51.
65. Mead, p. 307, Hippolytus quoting Valentinus.
66. Hoeller, p. 204.
67. Ibid., p. 204, quoting "The Gospel of Philip."
68. Ibid., p. 204.
69. Ibid., p. 205.
70. Ibid.
71. Ibid.
72. Ibid.
73. *The Nag Hammadi Library*, "The Gospel of Philip,"
p. 154.
74. Hoeller, p. 206.
75. Ibid.
76. Ibid.
77. Ibid.
78. Ibid., p. 207.
79. Ibid.
80. Ibid., p. 208.
81. *The Nag Hammadi Library*, "The Gospel of Philip,"
pp. 151, 149.
82. Ibid., p. 160.
83. Layton, pp. 316-17.

84. *The Nag Hammadi Library*, "Treatise on the Resurrection," pp. 54-5.

85. Ibid., p. 56.

Chapter VIII

The Orthodox Movement Formulates "Anti-Christian-Gnostic" Theology

1. Layton, p. 271.

2. Frend, p. 232.

3. Harnack, Vol. 2, p. 21.

4. Ibid., p. 24.

5. Ibid., p. 27.

6. Ibid., p. 33.

7. Ibid., P. 40.

8. Ibid,, p. 41.

9. Ibid., p. 203.

10. Frend, p. 239.

11. Harnack, Vol. 2, p. 182.

12. Anthony Flew, ed., *A Dictionary of Philosophy*, (New York: St. Martins Press, 1984), pp. 215, 339-40.

13. Prophet, 1984, p. 394 n. 1, quoting Sir John Woodroofe in *The Garland of Letters*, 7th ed., (Pondicherry: Ganesh & Co., 1979), p. 4.

14. Albert Pike, *Morals and Dogma of Freemasonry*, (Richmond, Va.: L. H. Jenkins, Inc., 1871, 1946), p. 603, quoting the *Bhagavad Gita*.

15. Prophet, 1984, pp. 137-8.

16. Ibid., p. 184.

17. Ibid., p. 185.

18. Ibid., p. 195-6.

19. Ibid, p. 234.

20. G. de Purucker, *Occult Glossary*, (Pasadema, Ca.: Theosophical University Press, 1933, 1972), p. 15-16; G. de Purucker, *Fountain-Source of Occultism*, (Pasadena, Ca.: Theosophical University Press, 1974), p. 484.

21, Prophet, 1984, p. 137.

22. Purucker, *Fountain-Source of Occultism*, p. 496.

23. Nikhilananda, p. 14.

24. Purucker, *Fountain-Source of Occultism*, p. 496.

25. Ante Nicene Fathers, Vol. I, "Dialogue with Trypho," pp. 196-7.

26. Frend, p. 239.

27. Enoch 50:1,2,5

28. Enoch, 61:18.

Chapter IX

Irenaeus and the Formulation of Orthodox Pseudo-Theology

1. Layton, p. 270.

2. Ibid.

3. Ibid.

4. Ibid., p. 271.

5. Pagels, *Adam, Eve and the Serpent*, 1988, p. 152.

6. Pagels, *The Gnostic Gospels*, 1975, Intro, p. xxxix.

7. Pagels, *Adam, Eve and the Serpent*, 1988, pp. 59-60.

8. Harnack, vol. 2, p. 231, n. 1.

9. Ibid., Vol. 1, p. 228.

10. Ibid., p. 255, n. 1.

11. Louis Ginzberg, *Legends of the Bible*, (Phila.: Jewish Publication Society, 1909, 1956), see, for example, the

appearance of the angel Michael to Moses in the burning bush, and appearances of the angel Gabriel to patriarchs and judges. The legends are drawn, in the main, from Old Testament apocrypha.

12. Enoch, 18:12-16; 21:1-6; Testament of Ruben,2:2; 3:2 6.

13. Harnack, Vol. 2, p. 237.

14. Ibid., p. 247-48.

15. Ibid., p. 248.

16. Ibid., p. 263.

17. Ibid., p. 276.

18. Ibid., pp. 267-8.

19. Ibid., p. 268.

20. Ibid.

21. Ibid., p. 271.

22. Ibid.

23. Ibid.

24. Ibid.

25. Ibid.

26. Ibid., p. 283.

27. Irenaeus, *Against Heresies*, Bk. 3., 3. 2.

28. Pheme Perkins, *The Gnostic Dialogue: The Early Church and the Crisis of Gnosticism,* (New York: Paulist Press, 1980), pp. 196-7.

29. Ibid., p. 199.

30. Koester, Vol II., p. 10.

31. Perkins, pp. 201-2.

32. Ibid., p. 200.

33. Ibid., p. 200-201.

34. Johnson, p. 23, quoting Papias.

35. Waite, p. 236.

36. Ibid., quoting Eusebius, *Ecclesiastical History*.

37. Ibid., p. 237, quoting Eusebius.

38. Ibid., quoting Eusebi us.

39. Johnson, p. 23.

40. Ibid.

41. Ibid., p. 22.

42. Ibid.

43. Ibid.

44. Ibid., p. 24.

45. Ibid., p. 32.

46. Koester, Vol. II., p. 15.

47. Ibid., p. 16.

48. Ibid., pp. 48-9.

49. Johnson, p. 23.

50. Ibid., p. 52.

51. Ibid., pp. 52-3.

52. Archibald Robertson, p. 194.

53. Ibid., p. 198.

54. Ibid., p. 200.

55. Ibid.

56. Ibid.

57. Johnson, *A History of Christianity*, p. 53.

58. Ibid.

59. William Stuart McBirnie, *The Search for the Twelve Apostles,* (Wheaton, Ill.: Living Books, Tyndale House Publishers, Inc., 1973), pp. 140, 179-80, 208.

60. Hoeller, *Jung and the Lost Gospels*, p. 224.

61. Johnson, *A History of Christianity*, p. 54.

62. Blavatsky, *Isis Unveiled*, Vol. II, p. 198.

63. *The Lost Books of the Bible and the Forgotten Books of Eden,* "Lost Books", pp. 282-83.

64. Koester, Vol II, p. 163.

65. Ibid.

66. Martin Larson, *The Essene Heritage or the Teacher of the Scrolls and the Gospel of Christ,* (New York: Philosophical Library, 1967), 179.

67. Johnson, *A History of Christianity*, p. 54.

68. Ibid., p 53.

69. Harnack, *History of Dogma*, Vol. II, p. 70, n. 1.

70. Pagels, *The Gnostic Gospels*, p. 30.

71. Ibid., p. 124.

72. Ibid., p. 126.

73. *The Nag Hammadi Library*, "Apocalypse of Peter," p. 376.

74. Pagels, p. 5, quoting Tertullian, *De Carne Christi*, 5.

75. Ibid.

76. Ibid.

77. Head and Cranston, *Reincarnation,* p. 99.

78. Virgilius Ferm, *An Encyclopedia of Religion*, "Creationism. "

79. Larson, *The Religion of the Occident*, p. 507.

80. Ibid., pp. 507-8, quoting Tertullian, *"Prescription against Heretics",* xv, xix, xxxvii.

81. Ibid., p. 508, xxi.

82. Ibid., pp. 504-5.

83. Ibid., p. 508, quoting Cyprian, Epistles LIV 5; xxvi 1.

84. Ibid., quoting Cyprian, *"On the Unity of the Catholic Church",* 6.

85. Ibid., quoting Cyprian, Epistle LI 24.

86. Ibid., p. 508.

87. Frend, *The Rise of Christianity,* p. 352, quoting Cyprian, On the Unity of the Catholic Church, iv and v.

88. Ibid., p. 351.

Chapter X

Origen of Alexandria and the Golden Age of Christian Theology

1. McBirnie, *The Search for the Twelve Apostles*, p. 255.
2. Manly P. Hall, *Journey in Truth*, (Los Angeles: Philosophical Research Society, 1945), p. 177.
3. Ibid.
4. Frend, *Rise of Christianity*, p. 195.
5. Ibid., p. 211.
6. Ibid., pp. 242-3.
7. McBirnie, *The Search for the Twelve Apostles*, p. 177.
8. Frend, *Rise of Christianity*, p. 369.
9. Besant, *Esoteric Christianity*, p. 50, quoting Clement, Miscellanies, Bk. 1.
10. Ibid., p. 51.
11. Ibid., p. 53.
12. Ibid., p. 56, quoting Bk VI, ch. vii.
13. Ibid., p. 58, quoting Bk I, ch. xiii.
14. Frend, *Rise of Christianity*, p. 371.
15. Ibid., pp. 369, 371-2, (on Clement's teaching)
16. G. W. Butterworth, ed., Origen: *On First Principles*, (Gloucester, Mass.: Peter Smith, 1973), Intro., p. xxiii.
17. Ibid., p. xxiii.
18. Ibid., p. xxiv.
19. Ibid.
20. Ibid.
21. Ibid.
22. Ibid., p. xxvii.
23. Ibid., Bk. II, Chap. VI, p. 112.
24. Ibid., p. 110.

25. Ibid.

26. Ibid. pp. 111-12.

27. Ibid., p. 112.

28. Ibid., pp. 129-30.

29. Ibid., p. 130.

30. Ibid., p. 124.

31. Ibid., p. 125.

32. Ibid., p. 40-41.

33. Ibid., p. 67.

34. Ibid.

35. Ibid., pp. 47-49.

36. Ibid., pp. 50-51.

37. Ibid., p. 53 n. 3.

38. Ibid., p. 56 n. 4.

39. Ibid.

40. Ibid., p. 38.

41. Ibid., p. 39.

42. Ibid., Intro., p. lvi.

43. Ibid., p. 245-6.

44. Ibid., p. 145, see also n. 5.

45. Ibid., pp. 72-3, see n. 8, p. 72, n. 1, p. 73.

46. Ibid., p. 135.

47. Geddes McGregor, *Reincarnation in Christianity*, (Wheaton, Ill: The Theosophical Publishing House, 1978), p. 58;

48. *On First Principles*, pp. 250-51.

49. Harnack, *History of Dogma*, Vol. II, p. 373.

50. Ibid., p. 369.

51. *On First Principles*, Intro., p. xxxii.

52. Ibid.

53. Ibid.

54. Ibid., p. xxxiii.

55. Ibid.

56. Ibid., p. xiv.

57. Ibid.

58. Ibid., p. xlvi.

59. Ibid., quoting Apology, 111. 9.

60. McGregor, *Reincarnation in Christianity*, p. 55.

61. Ibid., p. 56.

62. Ibid.

63. Ibid., p. 57.

64. Ibid.

65. Ibid.

66. Prophet, *The Forbidden Mysteries of Enoch*, p. 318, "The Origen Conspiracy. "

67. Ibid. See also Elizabeth Clare Prophet, *Reincarnation: The Missing Link in Christianity,* (Corwin Springs MT. Summit University Press, 1997)

Chapter XI

The Manichaean-Christian Revolution

1. This narrative on the life and teaching of Mani is taken variously from the following sources: *Mani and Manichaeism* by George Widengren; *Gnosis,* by Kurt Rudolph; and *The Gospel of the Prophet Mani,* by Duncan Greenlees.

2. George Widengren, *Mani and Manichaeism*, (New York: Holt, Rinehart and Winston, 1965), p. 26.

3. Ibid., pp. 26-27.

4. Ibid., p. 27.

5. Duncan Greenlees, *The Gospel of the Prophet Mani,* (Adyar, Madras, India: The Theosophical Publishing House, 1956), p. xxvii.

6. Widengren, p. 28.

7. Ibid.

8. Ibid., pp. 29-3 0.

9. Ibid., p. 30.

10. Ibid.

11. Ibid., p. 31.

12. Ibid.

13. Ibid.

14. Ibid., p. 34.

15. Ibid., p. 38.

16. Greenlees, Preface, pp. ix-lxi.

17. Widengren, p. 45.

18. Greenlees, pp. 2-3.

19. Ibid., pp. 51-83.

20. Ibid., p. 7.

21. Ibid., p. 164.

22. Ibid., p. 214. All references from the "Gospel of Mani" are derived from the Manichaean scriptures as quoted by Greenlees and are drawn from compilations of thirty extant works in Coptic, Chinese, Syrian, Arabic, Iranian, Turkish, Greek and Latin.

23. Samuel N. C. Lieu, *Manichaeism*, (Oxford: Manchester University Press, 1985), p. 10.

24. Greenlees, pp. 4-6.

25. Ibid., p. 7.

26. Ibid., pp. 7-8.

27. Ibid., pp. 8-9.

28. Ibid., p. 8 n. 4

29. Ibid., p. 9.

30. Ibid., pp. 9-11.

31. Ibid., p. 11.

32. Ibid., pp. 156-58.

33. Ibid., pp. 12-15.

34. Widengren, pp. 54-5.

35. Greenlees, p. 16.

36. Ibid., p. 20, commentary.

37. Ibid., p. 23, commentary.

38. Ibid., pp. 24-5.

39. Jonas, *The Gnostic Religion*, Chap. 9, pp. 225-6.

40. Greenlees, p. 31.

41. Ibid.

42. Ibid., p. 32 n. 1.

43. Ibid., p. 32.

44. Ibid., p. 33.

45. Ibid., p. 34.

46. Ibid., p. 35, 37.

47. Widengren, p. 67.

48. Lieu, p. 21.

49. Widengren, pp. 67-8.

50. Greenlees, p. 237.

51. Ibid., p. 252-53.

52. See Greenlees, preface, pp. clvii-clxvi and Widengren, pp. 76-94.

53. Widengren, p. 139.

54. Ibid., p. 140.

55. Ibid., pp. 140-41.

56. Ibid., pp. 142-43.

57. Ibid., pp. 107-108.

58. Ibid., p. 144.

59. Greenlees, p. cii.

60. Larson, *Religion of the Occident*, pp. 555-6, quoting Augustine, Reply to Faustus, xviii 3.

61. Ibid., p. 5 56, xxix, 1.

62. Ibid., p. 559.

63. Ibid., p. 464, Reply to Faustus, xxiii, 2, 3, 4.

64. Greenlees, p. 225, 227.

65. Ibid., p. 193.

66. That is, either without a dense physical body or "body" of sin/karma, or with a body of a higher grade of matter, as the Valentinians taught. This statement also refers to the fact that the "Jesus of Light" or "Light- Mind" has no permanent "body" or focus subject to the limitations of time and space.

67. Ibid., pp. 101-102.

68. Ibid., pp. 105-106.

69. Ibid., p. 106 n. 2.

70. Ibid., p. 105 n. 1, quoting Faustus.

71. Lieu, p. 127.

72. Ibid.

73. Widengren, p. 66.

74. Lieu, p. 127.

75. Ibid.

76. Ibid., p. 164-65.

77. Ibid., pp. 165-66.

78. Ibid., p. 167.

79. Ibid.

80. Ibid., p. 170.

81. Ibid., p. 175.

82. Ibid.

83. Greenlees, p. 212.

84. Ibid., p. 214-15.

85. Ibid., p. 216.

86. Ibid., p. 221.

87. Ibid., pp. 222-23.

88. Ibid., p. 242.

89. Ibid., pp. 288-290.

90. Ibid., title page.

Chapter XII

The Arian Controversy and the Council of Nicea

1. Larson, *Religion of the Occident,* p. 543.

2. Ibid.

3. Ibid., p. 544.

4. Dean Dudley, *History of the First Council of Nice*, (New York: Peter Eckler Publishing Co., 1925), pp. 34-5.

5. Ibid., pp. 37-38, Letter of Alexander of Alexandria.

6. Ibid., pp. 39-40.

7. Ibid., p. 86.

8. Ibid., pp. 51-52.

9. Ibid., p. 60.

10. Ibid.

11. Ibid., p. 67.

12. Ibid., p. 69.

13. Ibid., see footnote.

14. Ian Wilson, *Jesus the Evidence*, (New York: Harper and Row, 1984), p. 168.

15. Dudley, p. 80-81.

16. *The Song of God: Bhagavad-Gita*, (New York: New American Library—Mentor Books, 1951)

17. Ibid.

18. E. Raymond Capt, *The Traditions of Glastonbury*, (Thousand Oaks, Ca: Artisan Sales, 1983), pp. 9-10.

19. Ibid., p. 9.

20. Iman Wilkens, *Where Troy Once Stood: The Mystery of*

Homer's Iliad and Odyssey Revealed, (New York: Saint Martin's Press, 1990).

21. Capt, *The Traditions of Glastonbury*, pp. 28-29.

22. For example, E. Raymond Capt, W. Morgan, George F. Jowett.

23. W. Morgan, *St. Paul in Britain or the Origin of British Christianity,*(Thousand Oaks, Ca: Artisan Sales, 1860, 1984), pp. 14-15.

24. Joseph Campbell, *The Masks of God: Occidental Mythology* (New York: Viking Penguin, 1964, 1976), pp. 305-6.

25. Dudley, *History of the First Council of Nice*, Forward, by Hilton Hotema, p. 1.

26. Ibid., pp. 2-3, Hotema's Forward.

27. Ibid., p. 2.

28. Wilson, *Jesus the Evidence*, p. 160.

29. Ibid.

30. Ibid.

31. Ibid.

32. Ibid., p. 162.

33. Ibid., p. 172.

34. Ibid.

35. Michael Baigent, Richard Leigh, Henry Lincoln, *The Messianic Legacy,* (New York: Dell Publishing, 1986), p. 38.

36. Malachi Martin, *The Decline and Fall of the Roman Church,* (New York: G. P. Putnam's Sons, 1981), p. 53.

37. Baigent, Leigh, Lincoln, p. 45.

38. Ibid., p. 45, quoting Alistair Kee, Constantine Versus Christ, pp. 41-42.

39. Dudley, p. 19.

40. Ibid.

41. Ibid., p. 21.

42. Frend, *Rise of Christianity*, p. 505.
43. Dudley, pp. 116-17, see n. p. 117.
44. Larson, p. 572.
45. Ibid.
46. Ibid., p. 574.
47. Ibid., p. 578.

Chapter XIII

The Bondage of Orthodoxy

1. Frend, p. 659.
2. Ferm, *Encyclopedia of Religion*, see "Ambrose of Milan. "
3. Lieu, *Manichaeism*, quoting Confessions, p. 117.
4. Ibid., p. 132.
8. Ibid., p. 160.
9. Marcus Dods, ed. and trans., Augustine, *The City of God* (New York: Hafner, 1948), 2:92-93, quoted in Prophet, *Forbidden Mysteries of Enoch*, p. 56.
10. St. Augustine, *Confessions,* (Cambridge: Harvard University Press, 1977), p. 69.
11. Ibid., p. 40.
12. Pagels, *Adam, Eve, and the Serpent*, p. 109.
13. Ibid.
14. Ibid., quoting Augustine, *De Civitate Dei*, 13, 14.
15. Ibid., quoting Augustine.
16. Ibid.
17. Harnack, Vol. 5, p. 204.
18. Ibid., pp. 207-8.
19. Ibid., p. 211.
20. Ibid., p. 210.
21. Ibid., p. 211, n. 5.

22. Ibid.

23. Pagels, *Adam, Eve and the Serpent*, p. 135, quoting Contra Julianum 3, 3-5.

24. *Nicene and Post-Nicene Fathers*, Vol. II, "The City of God," Chap. 23, pp. 217-218.

25. Ibid., Vol. I., *Confessions*, Bk. 1., Chap. VII, p. 48.

26. Ibid., "Letter to Jerome," CLXVI, Chap. IV-8, p. 256.

27. Ibid., Chap. VII-21, p. 530.

28. Ibid., p. 531.

29. Ibid., Letter of Augustine, CII, p. 422.

30. Ibid., Letter to Jerome, CLXVI, p. 524-5.

31. Ibid., Letter to Jerome, CLXVI, p. 523-4.

32. Ibid., Confessions, Bk. VIII, p. 125.

33. Ibid., Letter to Jerome, CLXVI, p. 532.

34. Joseph Trigg, *Origen,* (Atlanta: John Knox Press, 1973), p. 16.

35. Pagels, *Adam, Eve and the Serpent*, p. 117.

36. Ibid., p. 131.

37. Larson, *Religion of the Occident*, p. 610.

38. Ibid., p. 622.

39. Ibid.

40. Ibid., 622-628.

41. Ibid., p. 610. We have enumerated these for easy reading. Larson includes Pelagius' theses in one paragraph.

42. Ibid.

43. Ibid.

44. Ibid.

45. Ibid.

46. Ibid., p. 611.

47. Ibid.

48. Ibid.

49. Ibid.

50. Ibid., p. 612.

51. Ibid.

52. Ibid., p. 617.

53. Ibid., paraphrasing Augustine's Predestination of the Saints, 7.

54. Ibid., p. 618-19.

55. Ibid., p. 618.

56. Ibid., p. 619.

57. Pagels, *Adam, Eve and the Serpent*, p. xxvi.

58. Larson, p. 618.

59. Hall, *Journey in Truth*, p. 206.

60. Ibid., p. 220-21.

61. Ibid., p. 221.

Chapter XIV

The Legacy of the Orthodox Conspiracy

1. Larson, p. 601, quoting letter to Nectarius.

2. Ibid., quoting Sermons, LXXXII, ii-iii.

3. Ibid.

4. Ibid., quoting Sermons, XVI, iii.

5. Malachi Martin, *The Decline and Fall of the Roman Church* p. 71, quoting Leo.

6. Will Durant, *The Age of Faith,* (New York: Simon and Schuster, 1950), p. 50.

7. Martin, p. 72.

8. Ibid.

9. Ibid., p. 64.

10. Ibid., p. 72.

11. Ibid., p. 104.

12. Ibid.

13. Ibid., p. 105.

14. Ibid.

15. Ibid., p. 106-7.

16. Ibid., p. 107.

17. Ibid., pp. 63-116, 108.

18. Durant, *Age of Faith*, p. 523, quoting F. H. Dudden, Gregory the Great, Vol. II, p. 434 ff.

19. Larson, p. 629.

20. Martin, p. 111.

21. Ibid.

22. Joseph Crews, *The Beast, the Dragon, and the Woman*, (Frederick, Maryland: Amazing Facts, Inc., 1967). The development of the interpretation of the prophecy in Daniel is taken from this remarkable little work.

23. Ibid.

24. *The New Scofield Reference Bible*, ed., C. I. Scofield, (New York: Oxford University Press, 1967), p. 1021 n. 1.

25. McBirnie, *The Search for the Twelve Apostles*, p. 62.

26. Peter De Rosa, *Vicars of Christ*,(New York: Crown Publishers, Inc., 1988), p. 14.

27. Ibid., quoting Eusebius, *Ecclesiastical History*.

28. Ibid.

29. Ibid.

30. Ibid.

31. Ibid., p. 24.

32. Ibid.

33. Ibid., p. 25.

34. Ibid.

35. H. P. Blavatsky, *The Esoteric Writings of H. P. Blavatsky*, (Wheaton, Illinois: The Theosophical Publishing House, 1980) p. 120-121, "Section16"

36. Edward Gibbon, *The Decline and Fall of the Roman Empire,* Abridgement by D. M. Low,(New York: Harcourt, Brace ad Co., 1960), p. 416.

37. M. P Hall, *The Secret Teachings of All Ages*, p. cxcviii.

38. H. P. Blavatsky, *Isis Unveiled*, Vol. I, p. 575

39. Rudolph, *Gnosis,* p. 211

40. Ibid.

41. Ibid., p. 211-12.

42. *The Nag Hammadi Library*, "Gospel of Philip," p. 149.

43. Pagels, *The Gnostic Gospels*, p. 62, quoting "Gospel to the Hebrews".

44. Ibid., p. 78, quoting *Pistis Sophia.*

45. Ibid., p. 81-2 quoting Clement.

46. Ibid., p. 72, quoting Tertullian.

47. Ibid.

48. Pagels, *Adam, Eve and the Serpent*, p. 79.

49. Ibid., p. 80, quoting Gregory of Nyssa.

50. *The Nag Hammadi Library*, "Gospel of Philip," p. 149.

51. Larson, p. 634.

52. Ibid., quoting Methodius.

53. Ibid., quoting Jerome.

54. Durant, *Age of Faith*, p. 52.

55. Ibid., p. 53.

56. Ibid., quoting Jerome, epistle xxiii.

57. Pagels, *Adam, Eve and the Serpent*, p. 90. quoting Jerome's letter to Eustochium.

58. Durant, p. 53, quoting Jerome's letter xxii to Eustochium.

59. Ibid.

60. Pagles, *Adam, Eve and the Serpent*, p. 91.

61. Ibid., p. 91, quoting Adversus Jovinianum, 1,3.

62. Ibid., p. 92.

63. Larson, p. 635, Council of Carthage, canon IV, XXV and LXX.

64. Harnack, Vol. 3, p. 308.

65. Ibid., Vol. 2, p. 367 n. 1.

66. *Encyclopedia of Religion*, see "Atonement in Christianity"

67. For example, the I AM Movement, founded in 1930 by Guy and Edna Ballard; The Summit Lighthouse, founded in 1958 by Mark L. Prophet and Elizabeth Clare Prophet.

68. See Mark L. and Elizabeth Clare Prophet, *Climb the Highest Mountain*, (Summit University Press, 1973,1986); Mark and Elizabeth Prophet, *The Lost Teachings of Jesus*, Vol. I and II, (Summit University Press, 1986) For further information write Summit University Press, 63 Summit Way, Gardiner, MT 59030-9314.

(Web site www.SummitUniversityPress.com)

69. See *The Lost Years of Jesus* by Elizabeth Clare Prophet, as noted in Chapter I.